Cases in

Leadership, Ethics, and Organizational Integrity

A Strategic Perspective

Cases in

Leadership, Ethics, and Organizational Integrity

A Strategic Perspective

Lynn Sharp Paine
Harvard Business School

Boston, Massachusetts   Burr Ridge, Illinois   Dubuque, Iowa
Madison, Wisconsin   New York, New York   San Francisco, California   St. Louis, Missouri

Irwin/McGraw-Hill

A Division of The **McGraw·Hill** *Companies*

Irwin Book Team

Publisher: *Rob Zwettler*
Executive editor: *Craig S. Beytien*
Editorial assistant: *Kimberly Kanakes*
Marketing manager: *Michael Campbell*
Project supervisor: *Karen J. Nelson*
Production supervisor: *Pat Frederickson*
Designer: *Crispin Prebys*
Director, Prepress Purchasing: *Kimberly Meriwether David*
Compositor: *Quebecor Printing/Dubuque*
Typeface: *10/12 Palatino*

Library of Congress Cataloging-in-Publication Data

Paine, Lynn Sharp.
   Cases in leadership, ethics, and organizational integrity: a
strategic perspective / Lynn Sharp Paine.
      p. cm.
   ISBN 0-256-19790-3
   1. Leadership—Case studies. 2. Business ethics—Case studies.
3. Integrity—Case studies. I. Title.
HD57.7.P345 1996
   658.4'092—dc20   96–6377

Printed in the United States of America
4 5 6 7 8 9 10   FGRFGR   9 9 8

C O N T E N T S

CONCLUSION

LEADING FOR INTEGRITY: *CORPORATE PURPOSE AND RESPONSIBILITY*

This book is intended for those who lead or aspire to lead business organizations. It is about the challenges of building and maintaining organizational integrity in the business environment of the 1990s—an environment that is dynamic, competitive, culturally diverse, and information-intensive.

I hope that anyone who studies the materials in this book will be rewarded with a rich understanding of organizational integrity in both concept and practice. But it is important to note at the beginning that the term *integrity* is not being used in its narrow sense as a synonym for honesty, but in its broad sense to refer to the qualities of self-governance, responsibility, moral soundness, adherence to principle, and constancy of purpose. The general concern of the book is how leaders build and maintain organizations with such qualities—in short, how they build self-governing organizations guided by a sense of purpose, responsibility, and ideals.

More specifically, the cases, introductory essays, and readings in the book aim to shed light on three main topics:

- Why organizational integrity is important.
- What strategies managers can use to build organizational integrity.
- What knowledge, skills, and concepts managers need to lead high-integrity companies.

Two facets of the leader's role are emphasized: the leader as decision maker and the leader as organization builder.

Although integrity is typically regarded as an attribute of individuals, the materials in the book show why it is important to think about integrity in organizational as well as personal terms. As the cases illustrate, there are essential links between organizational integrity and the personal integrity of an organization's members. High-integrity organizations cannot exist without high-integrity individuals, but at the same time individual integrity is rarely self-sustaining. Without organizational support systems and ethical boundaries, good people can lose their bearings when faced with pressures, temptations, and heightened performance expectations. Organizational integrity, moreover, goes beyond personal integrity. It rests on a concept of purpose, responsibility, and ideals for an organization as a whole. Part of the leader's role in building organizational integrity is to develop this ethical framework and the organizational capabilities needed to make it operational.

In an important sense, this is a book about ethics. But in another sense, the ethics label is misleading. The book, more fundamentally, is about management and organizational leadership. The basic thesis of these materials is that ethical thinking is an important leadership skill and a source of organizational strength. It is a building block for organizational integrity, which is a valuable corporate asset. But building and maintaining organizational integrity require more than ethical thinking alone. As the cases show, technical competence, appropriate organizational structures, and excellent communications skills are among the other capabilities required.

This strategic perspective on ethics sets this book apart from many texts on business ethics. Indeed, some may reject the approach taken here on the grounds that it is dangerous or inappropriate to think strategically about ethics. Ethics, we are told, must be valued for its own sake. While there is an important kernel of truth behind this warning, it is equally important for organizational leaders to understand that ethics is intensely practical. Ethical norms and ideals serve an important purpose in facilitating cooperation, providing direction, and setting limits—all of which can enhance organizational effectiveness. In my view, the real danger lies in losing sight of this purpose and relegating ethics to the domain of superstition or irrationality.

Of course, every organizational leader must consider what ethical norms and ideals should be embraced. What framework of responsibilities should be adopted? The cases and readings collected here allow students to consider these issues in concrete circumstances where the stakes are substantial. Although the text includes conceptual and background essays, as well as excerpted readings, central emphasis is placed on the cases to bring this material alive.

One of the primary benefits of learning through cases is the opportunity to explore ideas in action. Readers unfamiliar with the case method will want to make a special effort to put themselves in the shoes of the case protagonists. They should try to approach the issues as decision makers and actors rather than passive observers. Although much can be learned from simply reading the cases, even more value can be derived from imaginative participation in the situations presented. The cases, moreover, provide a laboratory for examining the concepts and frameworks outlined in the text, while giving readers the chance to hone their analytical and decision making skills.

The cases in the book have been selected to allow discussion of a wide range of ethical issues. Among these are the perennials of honesty, fair-dealing, product safety, and adherence to law, as well as newer and emerging issues such as information privacy, human rights, environmental protection, and conflicting standards of responsible behavior around the world. These issues are explored through situations set in a variety of industries and companies, large and small. Financial services, health care, global retailing, aerospace, hospitality, and electrical power production are among the industries covered. Several cases are set in an international context, allowing readers to compare and contrast differing national environments for corporate ethics.

While offering important opportunities to learn about topical issues of ethics, the cases have also been selected to promote learning at a deeper level. The most fundamental learning concerns the processes and criteria managers use to make decisions and lead their organizations. In-depth study of the Lotus MarketPlace:Households case, for example, should give readers not only a better understanding of data privacy issues but also a better understanding of sound approaches to making business decisions. By comparing the E. F. Hutton case with the Salomon Brothers series, readers will see dramatically different approaches to leading an organization through a crisis triggered by misconduct. One approach led to the demise of a once-successful corporation, while the other led to an organizational rejuvenation. The cases offer many opportunities for such comparisons.

This collection of materials throws a spotlight on ethics, but it makes no attempt to separate questions of ethics and corporate responsibility from the other issues organizational leaders must deal with. In fact, the opposite is true. In each case, the ethical issues are closely intertwined with strategic, organizational, financial, and legal issues.

Readers accustomed to a neat separation between ethical issues and management issues may be puzzled by the wide-angle approach reflected in this book. They may question whether some of the cases are *really* about ethics at all. However, the cases have been selected to reveal the ethical underpinnings of what might otherwise be seen as straightforward management issues having nothing to do with ethics. As managers grapple with choices about organizational structure, compensation practices, new product development, or worldwide sourcing, they are also dealing with issues of organizational values and responsibilities. Both ethical and economic understanding must be brought to bear on these choices. Moreover, as the introductory case suggests, getting the management enterprise off the ground at all can be a formidable challenge in the absence of a basic ethical framework to guide the organization's development.

The cases reflect the inconvenient reality that ethical issues typically arise in situations that are complex and highly charged. The true ethical challenge is to chart a responsible course of action in the face of multiple, and often competing, considerations. Framing the issue and identifying the relevant considerations are often the most important steps in working toward a responsible solution. For this reason, the cases are rich with information. Although ethics, like many subjects, may and indeed should be studied as a discrete field of inquiry, this book assumes that in the final analysis, ethics cannot be treated as something separate from management decision making and organizational leadership. Business leaders must be sensitive to ethics and skilled in ethical thinking, but they must also have a practical approach to integrating ethics into their decision processes and into the fabric of their organizations.

The structure of the book is straightforward. It has three main parts, each consisting of an introduction followed by a series of cases, and a brief concluding section. The introductory segment of each main part provides the conceptual background needed to understand the cases and a framework for analyzing them. The concluding section includes explanatory background and a series of readings on corporate purpose and responsibility.

Part I introduces the concept of organizational integrity and explores the reasons executives have turned their attention to ethics in recent years. Four problem-centered cases give students an opportunity to examine the different ways sound ethics contributes to organizational effectiveness. In each case, senior managers must diagnose the problem presented and decide on a plan of action for going forward.

Part II concerns strategies for building organizational integrity. Two of the four cases illustrate strategies focused on preventing misconduct. The other two present strategies based on positive concepts of ethical excellence. Through this series of cases students examine the leader's role in building integrity, consider the various levers executives can use in this endeavor, and assess the merits of alternative approaches.

Part III focuses on responsible decision making, the ultimate expression of organizational integrity. The module presents several high-stakes decisions involving difficult ethical issues for senior management. Each involves at least one of the classic challenges of responsible decision making: (1) interpreting ethical principles in light of social and technological change; (2) applying ethical principles in the face of factual uncertainty; (3) making trade-offs when stakeholder interests compete; and (4) dealing with conflicts among ethical standards in different regions of the world.

The cases give students an opportunity to apply the decision framework outlined in the introduction to Part III and to explore the corporation's responsibilities to its different stakeholders. The emphasis is not on right versus wrong, but on developing a decision process that will help managers make responsible, ethically informed choices.

The conclusion focuses on corporate purpose and responsibility, the central element of a company's ethical framework. This section contains a series of short readings illustrating different conceptions of corporate purpose and responsibility. Readers are encouraged to examine these conceptions critically and to reflect on their own views as they prepare to build, lead, or maintain high-integrity organizations.

My hope is that readers find this book compelling as an argument and useful as a guide. The materials presented here underscore the central importance of ethics and organizational integrity in today's dynamic marketplace. Perhaps more important, the materials provide concepts and frameworks that can be put to practical use. I hope these ideas will prove valuable to executives and managers who every day strive to make sound decisions and build more effective organizations.

Lynn Sharp Paine
Boston, Massachusetts

A C K N O W L E D G M E N T S

This book is based on a five-year research and course development project sponsored by the Harvard Business School's Division of Research. This project, which resulted in a second-year MBA elective course called "Managing for Organizational Integrity," involved extensive field work and the development of 30 new cases set in 20 corporations. The materials included in this collection reflect the central concepts and cases taught in the course and in an elective seminar offered in the school's Advanced Management Program: International Senior Managers Program since 1993.

This project involved contributions and support from many individuals and institutions in the business and academic communities. I am deeply grateful to the Harvard Business School's Division of Research and in particular to Dean John H. McArthur and senior associate deans Thomas R. Piper and F. Warren McFarlan, without whose generous support the project would not have been possible. Besides providing the essential resources and time needed for the project, they also extended their personal support for the intellectual themes I was exploring. I am particularly indebted to Tom Piper, who proved an indefatigable sounding board and critical reader of cases, articles, and teaching materials. I have benefited enormously from his perspectives as a teacher and management educator, as a professor of finance, and as a concerned citizen.

A special debt of thanks is due to my colleagues Joseph L. Badaracco and J. Gregory Dees, co-venturers in developing courses on management ethics, with whom I talked almost daily about some aspect of the project. I want to thank them and the many other colleagues who read and commented on materials produced at various stages of the project: Kenneth R. Andrews, James E. Austin, Raymond E. Corey, Dwight B. Crane, William E. Fruhan, Mary C. Gentile, Joseph Hinsey, George C. Lodge,

Scotty McLennan, Sharon Daloz Parks, Henry B. Reiling, Richard S. Ted-low, and Richard E. Walton. In addition, Richard Tedlow provided valuable support throughout the project in his capacity as my research director. I am doubly grateful to Joe Badaracco and Dwight Crane for, in addition, allowing me to include their cases in this collection: to Joe for "AT&T Consumer Products," and to Dwight for "Salomon and the Treasury Securities Auction." A special thanks is due also to N. Craig Smith, professor at Georgetown University Business School, for giving me permission to include his case "Dow Corning: Product Stewardship."

My understanding of the issues covered in this book has been immeasurably enhanced by what I have learned from my colleagues in teaching. I am particularly indebted to those with whom I have taught the first-year MBA module "Decision Making and Ethical Values." In addition to those mentioned earlier, I also want to acknowledge other members of this group who contributed, often unknowingly, to my project: Michael Beer, Robert H. Hayes, Cynthia A. Montgomery, Walter J. Salmon, Malcolm S. Salter, W. Earl Sasser, Debora Spar, Howard H. Stevenson, and Shoshana Zuboff. Among other Harvard Business School faculty who offered challenges, insights, and advice, I also want to thank Lynda M. Applegate, Samuel L. Hayes, and John A. Quelch. Among those with whom I formerly taught at Georgetown University Business School, I am especially indebted to Norman E. Bowie (now at the University of Minnesota), Mary J. Culnan, Thomas Donaldson, Karen L. Newman, Dennis P. Quinn, and Pietra Rivoli.

I must also express my gratitude to members of the business community, especially to the executives and managers who cooperated in the development of case studies for the project. Without exception, these individuals gave generously of their time and shared valuable insights. At talks, seminars, and workshops related to the project, countless executives and managers raised questions and offered perspectives that helped shape my thinking. Thanks are also due the alumni and other contributors whose donations help fund the Harvard Business School's Division of Research.

In developing the ideas reflected in this book, I have benefited from the work of many business ethicists and philosophers in the fields of professional and practical ethics. Many of their names can be found in the footnotes to the text, but I would like to acknowledge a special debt to two individuals. The first is philosopher Richard M. Hare, under whose supervision I wrote my doctoral thesis on utilitarian ethics at Oxford. Dick's vision of a rigorous but practical moral philosophy has served as a continuing source of inspiration for much of my work. The second is Dennis Thompson, director of Harvard University's Program in Ethics and the Professions. To Dennis, I owe thanks for his superb leadership of this program which has stimulated work on professional ethics across the university. My involvement in the Program—as a Fellow in 1990–1992 and as a Faculty Associate since that time—has been an important stimulus for my thinking about ethics in business.

The final manuscript was much improved as a result of suggestions offered by reviewers selected by Irwin. I deeply appreciate the time and attention devoted by reviewers Larry Alan Bear, New York University's Stern School; Norman E. Bowie, University of Minnesota's Carlson School; Prompilai Khunaphante, Chulalongkorn University; Patrick E. Murphy, University of Notre Dame; and Patricia H. Werhane, University of Virginia's Darden School.

In working on this project, I was assisted by a number of outstanding research associates and doctoral candidates. Charles A. Nichols, III, has been an invaluable associate, contributing to all phases of the project. Jane Palley Katz and Michael A. Santoro also deserve special mention for the scope and duration of their involvement. Others who made valuable contributions to particular cases or aspects of the project include Lexanne J. Abbott, Marc W. Boatwright, Sarah B. Gant, Bronwyn Halliday, Joshua Margolis, Sarah C. Mavrinac, and Andrea L. Strimling.

Superb administrative support was provided by Eugenie T. Moriconi, my assistant for nearly five years, and by Yvonne A. Green, who joined me in the concluding phases of the project. Both managed the seemingly endless drafts and redrafts of materials conscientiously and cheerfully. Credit also goes to the staff of the Harvard Business School Word Processing Center for turning the drafts around under tight deadlines without sacrificing attention to quality and detail.

Finally, I am indebted to my husband, Tom Paine, and to members of my family for the many ways in which they have supported and contributed to my work.

L.S.P.

I   UNDERSTANDING ORGANIZATIONAL INTEGRITY

The Role of Ethics

Once considered a frill or even a costly diversion, attention to ethics is increasingly seen as a fundamental aspect of organizational leadership. In recent years, many executives have launched corporate ethics or values initiatives. Some have created corporate ethics offices, board-level ethics and corporate responsibility committees, or task forces to deal with difficult ethical issues. Others have introduced training programs to heighten awareness of ethical issues or to help managers integrate ethical considerations into their decision processes.[1]

An observer of these developments might well ask, "Why all the attention to ethics?" The cases in Part I of this book suggest a range of answers to this question. As the cases illustrate, there are several quite distinctive reasons that business leaders have added ethics to their agendas. However, the simple overarching explanation is that many have come to regard a value system based on sound ethical principles as a foundation of organizational excellence. They seek to develop their company's capacity for ethical self-governance because they see organizational integrity as a corporate asset. Although organizational integrity depends on far more than ethics alone, it starts with an ethical framework grounded in a company's purpose and responsibilities.

According to the *Economist*, these executives are on the right track. A 1995 editorial declared, "[T]omorrow's successful company can no longer afford to be a faceless institution that does nothing more than sell the right product at the right price. It will have to present itself more as if

---

[1] For information on the numbers of companies undertaking such initiatives, see Ronald E. Berenbeim, *Corporate Ethics Practices* (New York: The Conference Board, Report No. 986, 1992); Ethics Resource Center, Inc., *Ethics Policies and Programs in American Business* (Washington, D.C., 1990); Ethics Resource Center, Inc., *Ethics in American Business: Policies, Programs and Perceptions* (Washington D.C., 1994).

it were . . . an intelligent actor, of upright character, that brings explicit moral judgments to bear on its dealings with its own employees and with the wider world."[2]

Before turning to the cases in Part I, it is worth reviewing the reasons behind today's increased attention to ethics as well as some common arguments for skepticism.

Ethics and Organizational Effectiveness

Although many executives regard sound ethics as a cornerstone of organizational effectiveness, some people find this idea counterintuitive. Caught in a belief system that equates ethics with self-sacrifice, they cannot reconcile attention to ethics with organizational strength. But if we understand what ethics is all about, the linkage between ethics and organizational effectiveness will hardly seem surprising.

Although ethics has historically been defined in many different ways, a central focus of ethical thought has been the principles and standards that should govern human interaction. Ethical ideals such as honesty, trustworthiness, or fairness are not just personal ideals. They are standards for how people should behave toward one another. Ethical concepts such as rights, duties, and responsibilities map the infrastructure of social relationships. They define the scope of individual authority and specify what individuals, whether persons or organizations, owe to one another and to their communities. While ethics is also concerned with the nature and sources of value in life—often referred to as "the good"—issues of right and responsibility are at the center of what most people today think of as ethics.

Broadly speaking, the aim of ethics is to enhance human development.[3] A framework of rights, responsibilities, and ideals helps people achieve their fullest potential as human beings—both individually and collectively. For individuals, such a framework serves the vital purposes of guiding action and establishing expectations. For groups and communities, it facilitates cooperation and mutual trust. In general, life tends to go better when people can count on one another at least for justice and mutual respect, if not for mutual assistance. Although ethics does not require self-sacrifice, it does require an ability to understand the needs and interests of others and to conduct oneself in a manner that, at a minimum, acknowledges their legitimate claims. Ethics may be thought of as an invisible infrastructure of norms and precepts that ideally supports positive human interaction.

---

[2] "Saints and Sinners," *The Economist,* June 24, 1995, p. 16.
[3] An excellent discussion of the purpose of morality is found in G. J. Warnock, *The Object of Morality* (London: Methuen & Co. Ltd., 1971).

Given the functions of the executive, the path to ethics is straightforward. An ethical outlook is essential to engaging the support and positive involvement of all the constituencies essential to a company's success: its employees, customers, shareholders, creditors, and suppliers, as well as the public by whose license it operates. Unless these constituencies enjoy a high level of confidence in the company, feel they are treated fairly by it, and benefit by their involvement, they are unlikely to contribute with any great enthusiasm. They may withdraw their support altogether, especially if more attractive options are available.

Effective managers realize that outstanding organizational performance requires the ongoing confidence and cooperation of all the organization's constituencies, but especially of the employees and others who do its day-to-day work. In today's knowledge-based economy, attracting creative and energetic employees and nurturing their talents has become a high priority. Without imaginative and industrious employees, companies cannot hope to maintain the levels of innovation needed to remain competitive in a rapidly changing environment. Managers are becoming increasingly aware that many people do their best, most creative work in an environment of trust, responsibility, and high aspirations. Such an environment can only be built on values such as honesty, reliability, fairness, and respect.

An organizational value system grounded in sound ethical principles is an asset that pays multiple dividends. The benefits can be seen most clearly in three areas: organizational functioning, market relationships, and social standing. A closer look at each of these areas will show why more executives are coming to regard ethics as a help rather than a hindrance in building and maintaining effective organizations.

Organizational Functioning

Studies of organizational excellence consistently show the importance of a well-defined value system for achieving and maintaining outstanding performance.[4] A compelling purpose and a set of deeply held values provide a focus for organizational effort. They are a source of organizational identity that can generate pride and commitment while helping companies weather the adaptations necessary to survive and thrive over time. In periods of adversity, a sound value system is a buffer against temptations to generate short-term results in ways that will impair long-term

---

[4] See, e.g., Donald K. Clifford, Jr., and Richard E. Cavanagh, *The Winning Performance* (New York: Bantam Books, 1985); James C. Collins and Jerry I. Porras, *Built to Last* (New York: HarperCollins Publishers, 1994); John P. Kotter and James L. Heskett, *Corporate Culture and Performance* (New York: The Free Press, 1992).

performance. These are the lessons learned from large successful companies that have stood the test of time,[5] as well as high-growth midsized companies that have outpaced their competitors in more recent history.[6]

The case for a well-defined value system is particularly compelling in today's dynamic environment where the advantage often goes to companies that can identify and adapt to change at an increasingly rapid rate. The traditional hierarchical organization with decision rights centralized at the top of a multilayered bureaucracy has become too slow and too cumbersome for today's conditions. Within such structures, employees' knowledge and energies are often underutilized. At the same time, decentralizing decision-making authority and empowering the organization can be a risky proposition without some means of guiding and limiting employee discretion.[7] A well-defined value system serves just this purpose. As one executive explained, "In a more volatile and dynamic business environment, the controls have to be conceptual. They can't be human anymore . . . It's the ideas of a business that are controlling, not some manager with authority."[8]

With a clear set of guiding ideals and behavioral boundaries, executives can feel confident in putting decision rights in the hands of those employees with the knowledge needed to exercise them quickly and effectively. They can reduce layers of management supervision without losing control and organizational focus. By the same token, a clear value system gives employees a frame of reference for decision making. They can feel more confident in making decisions without seeking approval from higher-ups or home office managers who are likely to be less informed about local circumstances.

While every organization has distinctive purposes and values, not just any set of values will do. Researchers have found, for example, that decisions are more likely to enjoy employee support when they are perceived as "procedurally just."[9] Correspondingly, decisions are more likely to be subverted if they benefit particular groups at the expense of the organization. Another line of research indicates that employees are more likely to engage in discretionary behavior to benefit the organization if they trust their supervisors to treat them fairly.[10]

---

[5] Collins and Porras, *Built to Last.*

[6] Clifford and Cavanagh, *The Winning Performance.*

[7] On this subject, see Robert Simons, "Control in an Age of Empowerment," *Harvard Business Review,* March–April 1995, pp. 81–88.

[8] Robert Howard, "Values Make the Company," *Harvard Business Review,* September–October 1990, p. 134.

[9] W. Chan Kim and Renee A. Mauborgne, "Making Global Strategies Work," *Sloan Management Review,* Spring 1993, pp. 11–27.

[10] R. H. Moorman, "Relationship Between Organizational Justice and Organizational Citizenship Behaviors: Do Fairness Perceptions Influence Employee Citizenship?" *Journal of Applied Psychology* 76, 1991, pp. 845–855.

How do employees gauge the trustworthiness of their supervisors? According to a survey of 1,500 U.S. managers, they judge by behavior that demonstrates honesty, forthrightness, and principled conviction.[11] The same survey found integrity to be the quality employees most admire in their superiors. Other researchers have found that employees are more likely to take pride and feel ownership in their organization when top management is perceived to have high credibility and a coherent set of values.[12]

As these and other studies indicate, executives wishing to build an environment of trust, responsibility, and high aspirations must work to cultivate an organizational value system based on sound ethical principles. While no single set of values is right for every company, the values commonly associated with integrity—such as honesty, fairness, and reliability—will play an essential role in any effective framework.

Market Relationships

Besides helping to mobilize and steer the organization, an ethical outlook can distinguish a company in the marketplace and contribute to strong relationships with its primary stakeholders. According to *Fortune* magazine, which periodically lists America's most admired corporations, the integrity factor can boost or depress a company's reputation beyond what strict financial measures would suggest. The most admired companies, says *Fortune*, are "good guys."[13]

A good reputation can help a company attract customers and investors as well as potential employees and business partners. Today, many consumers and investors look for high standards in the companies they deal with. An increasing number of consumers are interested not only in the products and services they buy, but also in the behavior of the companies that produce them.[14] The growth of ethical investing over the past decade suggests that investors, too, are increasingly likely to

---

[11] James M. Kouzes and Barry Z. Posner, *The Leadership Challenge* (San Francisco, CA: Jossey-Bass, 1987), p. 16.

[12] The research of Charles O'Reilly as cited in Kouzes and Posner, *The Leadership Challenge*, p. 16.

[13] Jennifer Reese, "America's Most Admired Corporations," *Fortune*, February 8, 1993, p. 44 ff.

[14] Some evidence of consumer attitudes is reflected in recent surveys. See, e.g., Nicole Dickenson, "Consumers Get Ethical With Choices," *South China Morning Post*, May 29, 1993, supplement; "Study Shows 67% of Adult Consumers Consider a Company's Ethics When Purchasing Products or Services," *Business Wire*, November 15, 1993; "Consumers Put a 'Surprisingly High' Priority on Clean Conduct: Public Demands Better Ethics, Says Survey," *South China Morning Post*, May 9, 1994.

consider a company's reputation and ethical performance in deciding to invest.[15]

While the relative number of investors and consumers actively seeking out exemplary companies is small, those shunning firms involved in fraud or other misconduct is far greater. Misbehavior affecting customers can have a dramatic and difficult-to-reverse impact on market share. As many companies have learned the hard way, once shaken consumers' trust is difficult to regain. Unlike today's financial losses that can be offset by tomorrow's gains, lost trust can be restored only with consistent effort over time. Companies involved in misconduct often see a direct impact on their share price. Although the amount of lost equity value varies widely, the loss can be severe, particularly if high-level officials are implicated or misbehavior appears to be pervasive in a company.[16]

By adhering to sound ethical principles and focusing on the needs of their constituencies, companies can limit such losses and build strong relationships with their core stakeholders. While good relationships are of intrinsic value, they are also sources of organizational advantage. Companies that gain the trust of their customers, employees, and suppliers also gain revenues, efficiency, and flexibility. At the same time, they reduce monitoring and transaction costs. Highly detailed contracting over future contingencies becomes unnecessary when parties have confidence that they will be treated fairly in the future. Detailed rules and regulations can be minimized when employees operate within a common value system.

Of course, fraud, broken promises, underperforming products, inadequate disclosures, and abuses of position are possible in many circumstances. In fact, unethical behavior can be quite profitable when its victims are powerless or ignorant and when no third party is willing and able to address the wrongs done. But the critical question for company leaders is not whether such behaviors are possible or even whether they are profitable in particular cases. The question is whether they are the basis of outstanding organizational performance over time.

Seen from this perspective, the issues are somewhat different. For one thing, questionable behaviors typically involve high levels of reputational, market, legal, and political risk. Business strategies that depend

---

[15] Studies on the growth of ethical investing are cited in "Morals Maketh Money," *The Economist*, September 3, 1994, pp. 74–75; Scheherazade Daneshkhu, "The Ethics of Being an Ethical Investor," *The Financial Times*, August 27–28, 1994.

[16] One study of firms convicted of misconduct found that legal penalties including criminal fines, civil penalties, and restitution amounted to only 5 percent of the drop in share value. J. Karpoff and J. Lott, "The Reputational Penalties Firms Bear from Committing Criminal Fraud," The Wharton School, University of Pennsylvania Working Paper, 1991, p. 25, cited in Mark A. Cohen, "Corporate Crime and Punishment: An Update on Sentencing Practice in the Federal Courts, 1988–1990," *Boston University Law Review* 71, 1991, pp. 266–267, 279.

on them are difficult to sustain in free enterprise economies where information is free flowing, business transactions are voluntary, economic power is continually shifting, and law is enforced. Few people voluntarily choose to be taken advantage of, and when given the choice, most prefer to do business with companies that treat them honestly, fairly, and with respect for their rights and interests.

More fundamentally, such behaviors reflect a value system increasingly seen to be at odds with enduring organizational success. As recent research indicates, companies that remain focused on the needs of their core constituencies are more adaptive and tend to turn in superior economic performance over the long term.[17] To excel in today's environment, organizations and their leaders must understand the needs and interests of their stakeholders. They must be oriented toward strategies that create value and generate mutual benefits rather than strategies that capture value by taking advantage of others. They must focus on beneficial relationships rather than beneficial transactions. In short, they must bring an ethical point of view to bear on their dealings in the marketplace.

Social Standing

The benefits of an ethical orientation are also apparent in a third area: a company's non market relationships especially with constituencies representing the broader social community. Business plays a vital role in society, and the information revolution has brought new levels of transparency to that role. Today, executives around the world find that they and their companies are under intensified scrutiny by the media, by governments, and by nongovernmental watchdogs of the public interest. High-integrity companies that operate responsibly enjoy the pride of good corporate citizenship and generally find themselves in better standing with these various constituencies. They also reduce their exposure to lawsuits, damaging legal sanctions, and overly restrictive government regulations. In some cases, active involvement with external stakeholders, such as environmental groups, has helped companies develop creative solutions to business problems.

The value of positive relationships with such "public" stakeholders should not be underestimated. In some industries, public officials play a critical role in shaping competition through their power over product approvals, licensing, or other requirements of doing business. Companies with a history of good faith cooperation often find they can negotiate such hurdles more easily and more quickly, sometimes gaining competi-

---

[17] Kotter and Heskett, *Corporate Culture and Performance*. See also James L. Haskett, W. Earl Sasser, Jr., and Christopher W. L. Hart, *Service Breakthroughs Challenging the Rules of the Game* (New York: The Free Press, 1990).

tive advantage in this way. Companies involved in wrongful or socially harmful behavior may find themselves targeted in a variety of forums from the press to the courtroom. In the United States, aggrieved parties often look to the courts, to lawmakers, or to government regulators to enforce existing laws or to create new ones in response to perceived wrongs.[18]

Getting on the wrong side of the law, moreover, can be quite costly for companies and their executives. In addition to the management time lost to investigations, negotiations, and litigation, legal expenses and damage awards can be severe. Penalties for criminal misconduct can reach into the hundreds of millions of dollars, not to mention the possibility of imprisonment for offending individuals. Settling private claims can be even more expensive. One financial services company, for instance, is expected to pay an estimated $1.1 billion to settle customer claims that it used misleading sales practices.[19] A few companies have been forced into bankruptcy by product liability claims.

The legal argument for ethics is particularly compelling in the United States given the potential for class-action litigation and large punitive damage awards. The recent proliferation of criminal penalties, particularly for offenses once regarded as only regulatory violations, adds further weight.[20] Yet another incentive for good conduct is found in recent U.S. laws that increase the penalties for misconduct while offering reduced fines to companies with effective legal compliance programs. The federal guidelines for sentencing convicted organizations explicitly reward effective efforts to prevent unlawful behavior. They also penalize companies whose executives fail to demonstrate their company's acceptance of responsibility for its misdeeds.[21]

Legal considerations are becoming increasingly important in other countries as well. In Europe and Japan, for example, new laws have stepped up requirements in areas such as environmental protection,

---

[18] For discussion of the relationship between law and ethics, see Lynn Sharp Paine, "Law, Ethics, and Managerial Judgment," *The Journal of Legal Studies Education*, vol. 12, no. 2 (Summer/Fall 1994), pp. 153–169.

[19] Phillip L. Zweig, "Prudential: Making It Rock-Solid Again," *Business Week*, October 31, 1994, p. 96.

[20] For discussion of these trends, see Kathleen F. Brickey, "Criminal Liability of Corporate Officers for Strict Liability Offenses—Another View," 35 *Vanderbilt Law Review* 1337 (November 1982); John C. Coffee, Jr., "Does 'Unlawful' Mean 'Criminal'? Reflections on the Disappearing Tort/Crime Distinction in American Law," 71 *Boston University Law Review* 193 (March 1991); Leonard Orland, "The Proliferation of Corporate Crime Legislation," *Corporate Criminal Liability Reporter*, vol. 1, no. 2 (Spring 1987).

[21] See Part II, below, for discussion of the Federal Sentencing Guidelines. For a detailed description of the fine reductions available for organizations with effective compliance programs, see *Note on the Federal Sentencing Guidelines for Organizations*, Harvard Business School Note No. 393–060 (1992).

product safety, employment opportunity, and securities trading.[22] Law enforcement authorities in several European countries have recently intensified their efforts to enforce existing laws against bribery and improper payments. In 1994, the 25 industrialized nations of the Organization for Economic Cooperation and Development (OECD) agreed to develop anticorruption laws similar to the U.S. Foreign Corrupt Practices Act, which prohibits bribery of foreign officials by companies issuing shares under U.S. securities laws.[23] Officials in many emerging economies are working to upgrade their legal systems and build respect for law.

At the same time, international legal and regulatory regimes are beginning to take shape in a number of areas. Transnational standards of good corporate citizenship are being developed through regional trade agreements, global institutions such as the World Trade Organization and the World Bank, as well as international efforts targeted to specific issues such as environmental protection, business practices, and employee rights.[24] Although many of these emerging standards of business conduct are not legally enforceable, they nevertheless function as public norms of corporate responsibility with implications for the social standing of companies worldwide.[25]

Ethics and Free Enterprise

Companies that operate responsibly in accordance with sound ethical principles contribute to public confidence in business and to the vitality of the free enterprise system. As historian James Willard Hurst has shown, the legitimacy of corporations in the United States has rested on twin foundations: social utility and social responsibility.[26] History indicates that public challenges to corporate authority have arisen whenever corporations have failed to produce goods and services in a manner that society deems to be both efficient and responsible.

↳ *producing goods/services needed by the community*

---

[22] Discussed in David Vogel, "The Globalization of Business Ethics: Why America Remains Distinctive," *California Management Review*, Fall 1992, pp. 30–49. See also Jathon Sapsford, "Japanese Firms Brace for First Laws on Consumer Rights, and Insurers Gain," *The Wall Street Journal*, March 8, 1994, p. A13.

[23] Michael Elliott, "Corruption: How Bribes, Payoffs and Crooked Officials Are Blocking Economic Growth," *Newsweek*, November 14, 1994, pp. 40–42.

[24] For an overview and analysis of the many emerging policy regimes, see Lee E. Preston and Duane Windsor, *The Rules of the Game in the Global Economy: Policy Regimes for International Business* (Boston: Kluwer Academic Publishers, 1992).

[25] For coverage of emerging transcultural norms, see William C. Frederick, "The Moral Authority of Transnational Corporate Codes," *Journal of Business Ethics* 10, 1991, pp. 165–177.

[26] James Willard Hurst, *The Legitimacy of the Business Corporation in the Law of the United States 1780–1970* (Charlottesville: The University Press of Virginia, 1970).

Typically, such failures have been met with new laws, regulations, and public policies to reduce the scope of managerial discretion. In the late 19th and early 20th centuries, for example, many new laws were enacted to deal with the undesirable social impacts of increasingly large and powerful corporations. This period saw the creation of numerous statutes and regulatory agencies to protect investors, workers, and consumers. Among the agencies created were the Federal Trade Commission, the Interstate Commerce Commission, and the Securities and Exchange Commission.

While government regulations are certainly valid and indeed necessary in many situations, they sometimes have unanticipated and socially adverse consequences, particularly when enacted as a form of corporate punishment by politicians and lawmakers who view business as society's adversary. When companies ignore the social harms caused by their behavior or when they disregard legitimate ethical standards, however, they only increase the public's mistrust and its willingness to support additional limitations on business. Moreover, since power implies responsibility, companies with greater economic power are often held to a higher standard of social responsibility.

The linkage between corporate responsibility and public attitudes toward business also can be seen in more recent history. In the 1970s, a period marked by widespread corporate misconduct, business lost an estimated 80 percent of its public goodwill.[27] Confidence was shaken by incidents such as the Equity Funding scandal, which involved the fabrication of phony insurance policies worth $2 billion, and Allied Chemical's dumping of Kepone, a highly toxic pesticide that threatened worker health and the environment. Hundreds of firms admitted making illegal campaign contributions in the United States and bribing government officials overseas.[28]

Such incidents raised questions about management's commitment to basic ethical standards and about the corporation's role in society. As the U.S. Securities and Exchange Commission noted at the time, the public regards a company's reputation for ethical conduct not as one asset among many, but as the basis on which the entire business system rests.

In the 1990s, free enterprise is being tried and tested in many countries around the world. In Asia, Eastern Europe, and South America, new types of market economies are springing up. While these systems are in many cases creating vast amounts of wealth, they are also in some countries generating ethical questions about the business methods being used

---

[27] Fred D. Baldwin, *Conflicting Interests* (Lexington, MA: D.C. Heath and Company, 1984), p. 85.
[28] For discussion of these and other incidents, see Baldwin, *Conflicting Interests*, pp. 75–87.

by economic actors and about the resulting distribution of wealth and opportunity. If history is a guide, the long-term prospects for these systems will depend on their ability to satisfy both the economic and ethical needs of society. Business leaders who wish to uphold confidence in free enterprise worldwide should not forget the historic importance of both efficiency and responsibility in maintaining the legitimacy of corporations and the economic system of which they are part.[29]

Reasons for Skepticism

Although the case for attention to ethics is compelling, it is far from universally accepted. In fact, it runs counter to some deeply held beliefs about personal development, about individual behavior, and about the marketplace. But how sound are these beliefs? A close examination suggests that some of the most common reasons for skepticism toward ethics are themselves open to question. Consider the following:

Belief: Ethics is learned in childhood. It's too late for managers to have any influence.

Some managers believe it is futile to concern themselves with ethics. Ethics, they say, is learned in early childhood—often at the proverbial "mother's knee." After that, it's just too late.

While the powerful impact of childhood experiences on ethical development can hardly be denied, research and experience show that ethical growth can and typically does continue throughout life. Experiences of success and failure, exposure to novel environments, new knowledge, changes in the world—all these can have a profound effect on the value system that informs a person's behavior. Beliefs about right and wrong, good and bad, the elements of a worthwhile life may become more secure—or less secure—as they are tested and refined through experience and reflection.

The popular conviction that ethical growth stops somewhere between ages six and eight does not square with existing research on individual development.[30] Studies consistently indicate that adults show more change than younger participants in moral education programs, and that moral development continues with age.[31] Psychoanalyst and develop-

---

[29] For discussion of legitimacy issues for multinational corporations, see Eric W. Orts, "The Legitimacy of Multinational Corporations " in *Corporate Law: Issues for a New Century*, edited by Lawrence E. Mitchell (Boulder, CO: Westview Press, 1995), pp. 247–279.

[30] Sharon Daloz Parks, "Is It Too Late? Young Adults and the Formation of Professional Ethics," in Thomas R. Piper, Mary C. Gentile, Sharon Daloz Parks, *Can Ethics Be Taught?* (Boston: Harvard Business School Press), 1993, pp. 13–72.

[31] For studies of the impact of moral education programs, see James R. Rest, *Moral Development* (New York: Praeger Publishers, 1986), p. 177. On moral development, see Lawrence Kohlberg, *Essays on Moral Development. Volume II. The Psychology of Moral Development* (New York: Harper & Row, 1984), pp. 429–431, 459–460.

mental psychologist Erik Erikson found that individuals achieve integrity, which he defined as a state of ethical and psychological wholeness, only in the final stage of life.[32] Erikson's finding echoes a theme found in the writings of Confucius, the ancient Chinese philosopher, who believed that people develop the capacity to do the right thing gradually over their lifetimes. Only when fully mature, in the last stage of life, do people do what is right naturally.[33]

A 1994 survey of 4,000 U.S. workers supports the developmental theory of ethics. The survey found that nearly half (49 percent) believed their business ethics had improved over the course of their careers.[34] Notably, the belief was strongest in companies with comprehensive corporate ethics programs. Moreover, nearly 20 percent of the survey respondents reported that their personal ethics had improved because of their ethics at work.

It is important to observe that even if fundamental attitudes toward responsibility, right, and wrong were fixed in childhood, it would not follow that attention to corporate ethics comes too late. Though children learn important values at their parents' knees, few learn about the specific responsibilities of business executives or the specific responsibilities of securities companies, health care companies, or manufacturing companies. Ethical people will not only want to learn about the responsibilities of the roles they occupy, but they will want to improve their effectiveness in fulfilling these responsibilities over time. In this sense, ethical education is a life-long endeavor.

Belief: Ethics is personal. It has nothing to do with management.

Another belief behind the hands-off approach to ethics is rooted in strong individualism. For many people, ethics is a purely personal matter between an individual and his or her conscience, having nothing to do with management or the environment in which people work.

At a deep level, this view expresses a profound truth. Ultimately, individuals must exercise their own judgment and take personal responsibility for their choices. Maintaining a belief in one's own independence and autonomy is critical.

At the same time, contextual factors clearly exert a strong influence on behavior. The famous Milgram experiments, for example, showed how readily people adapt to the expectations of authority figures. Professor Milgram found that his research subjects, volunteers for his "study of

---

[32] Erik H. Erikson, *Childhood and Society* (New York: W. W. Norton & Company, 1950).

[33] Confucius, *Confucian Analects*, Book II, Chapter IV, Dr. Legge's Version edited with notes by Yoshio Ogaeri (Tokyo: Bunki Shoten, 1950), pp. 7–8. Original edition: James Legge, *The Chinese Classics*, 7 vols. (Hong Kong and London: 1861–1872).

[34] Ethics Resource Center, Inc. *Ethics in American Business: Policies, Programs, and Perceptions* (Washington, D.C., 1994), pp. 14, 31–32.

memory and learning," were willing to administer painful electrical shocks to anonymous "learners" on the instructions of the experimenter.[35] When asked after the experiment why they administered the shocks, many explained, "I wouldn't have done it by myself. I was just doing what I was told."[36]

Many executives are quick to take credit for creating cultures that motivate employees to improve sales or productivity and equally quick to deny responsibility for cultures that encourage misconduct or ethical laxness. Ethical lapses are typically seen as individual rather than organizational failures. Yet, countless examples of corporate misconduct can be traced to organizational factors such as unrealistic performance pressures, perverse incentive systems, poor controls, careless hiring practices, inadequate training, and lack of ethical leadership. Organizational culture has been found to be a major contributor to corporate crime.[37]

The influence of organizational context on behavior is seen most readily in cases of misconduct. But it is no less important in cases of good conduct. The well-known Tylenol incident at Johnson & Johnson illustrates the power of an organizational ethos to shape decision making and action in a positive direction.[38] In that situation, company executives decided to do a nationwide recall of Tylenol capsules after six people died from product tampering. Without a framework of guiding principles for addressing the situation, it is unlikely that the company would have responded as coherently, effectively, and responsibly as it did.

The power of organizational context is felt by employees every day. It is especially apparent to individuals who join organizations built on strong ethical commitments after working in companies where ethics is not a priority. One recruit to a company with a strong culture of honesty described her experience of adjustment, after working in a firm where lying to suppliers was the norm. At first, she was skeptical that honesty was even possible. But over time, through a process she described as "osmosis," she came to believe that honesty was not only possible but that it made sound business sense.[39]

In the face of such evidence, it is hard to maintain that ethics has nothing to do with management. Managers shape the organizational context through their behavior, their design of the organization and its systems,

---

[35] Stanley Milgram, *Obedience to Authority* (New York: Harper & Row, 1974).

[36] The account of the Milgram experiments is taken from Ruth R. Faden and Tom L. Beauchamp, *A History and Theory of Informed Consent* (New York: Oxford University Press, 1986), pp. 174–175.

[37] Marshall B. Clinard and Peter C. Yeager, *Corporate Crime* (New York: The Free Press, 1980), pp. 58–60.

[38] *Jame Burke: A Career in American Business (A), (B),* Harvard Business School Case No. 9–389–177, 9–390–030 (1989).

[39] See *Wetherill Associates, Inc.,* Harvard Business School Case No. 9–394–113 (1993), in Part II below.

and their leadership in developing the ethical framework that guides decision making. To the extent that organizational factors such as these influence individual values and behavior, ethics has everything to do with management.

Belief: We're all decent people. We don't need to worry about ethics.

A third reason some managers choose to do nothing about ethics starts with belief in the fundamental decency of human beings. This belief is not only noble, it is essential to effective leadership. Without it, mistrust would only breed mistrust. However, the assumption that all decent people naturally share an ethical framework that steers them automatically in the right direction flies in the face of reality.

Research indicates that individuals relying on conscience alone can make very different ethical judgments about business situations. In one company, for example, employees in the competitor information group were asked individually whether it would be all right to have a copy of a competitor's proposal in a competitive bidding situation. The answers ranged from "It seems fine to me—what's the issue" to "It would be highly unethical." Between these extremes were responses such as "It would be okay so long as the proposal was freely offered" and "It might be a problem if the proposal contained proprietary information."

Although complete uniformity of ethical judgment is neither attainable nor desirable, managers should not assume that even the basic requirements of lawful behavior are widely understood. Increasingly, companies are made up of individuals from diverse cultures and ethical traditions who inevitably bring to their jobs different assumptions about ethics in business and different frameworks for ethical thinking. Even among capitalist countries, the differences can be striking.[40]

Executives aspiring to lead high-integrity organizations must start with the assumption of basic human decency, but they cannot stop there. Shared organizational aims and values must be developed. A common framework for judgment and a process for addressing ethical conflict are essential for any company wishing to present a coherent, responsible face to its members and to the world.

Clarity about organizational ethics is more, not less, important for people who consider themselves to be decent, law-abiding citizens making a contribution to their families, companies, and communities. It is all too easy to get drawn into situations that prove to be embarrassing or questionable, if not unethical or illegal, when operating in a culture of ethical indifference where there are only shades of gray. Humans, even decent, well-intentioned ones, are fallible.[41] Few people are

---

[40] For a study of different ways of thinking, see Charles Hampden-Turner and Alfons Trompenaars, *The Seven Cultures of Capitalism* (New York: Doubleday, 1993).

[41] For some examples of common ethical failings, see Solomon Schimmel, *The Seven Deadly Sins* (New York: The Free Press, 1992); Judith N. Shklar, *Ordinary Vices* (Cambridge, MA: Harvard University Press, 1984).

knowledgeable about ethical traditions other than their own. In an increasingly dynamic and diverse business environment, responsible business leaders, more than others, should understand the value of an ethical compass to chart the way.

Belief: Business is an ethics-free zone. Companies that take ethics seriously won't survive.

Some managers dismiss ethics, not because they think it a matter best left to individual conscience, but because they believe it to be out of place in a commercial context. Within a familiar model, market transactions are viewed as exchanges between rational, autonomous actors each trying to maximize his or her self-interest. Although most proponents of this model stipulate that the parties must refrain from force and fraud, this ethical constraint is sometimes overlooked in practice. Some have even argued that certain types of misrepresentation are required to play the "business game" successfully.[42]

According to this model, successful businesspeople and companies should seek to maximize their own self-interest in each transaction without regard to the interests of the other party. Rather than displaying self-restraint and a sense of fairness, successful players should aggressively pursue their personal aims until checked by the opposing party. Following this model, the motto of sellers should be "Buyer Beware." The most successful businesspeople should be those who follow the so-called "Iron Rule" of "Do unto others before they do unto you."

But is "Buyer Beware" the motto of successful companies? Common sense suggests that a business based on repeated transactions would operate more effectively with a mutual gains strategy based on a sense of fairness. Most people prefer to do business with someone who is not only trustworthy and honest, but also demonstrates respect for their needs and interests. As noted earlier, few people knowingly elect to be taken advantage of unless they have no other choice. Certainly those who are taken advantage of are a poor source of repeat business and positive word-of-mouth advertising. A commitment to ethical behavior would seem to be a more promising starting point than the "first strike" mentality of the "Iron Rule".

Studies of successful service companies lend support to the common-sense view.[43] In today's environment, the watchword of high-performance companies is customer focus. Such companies try to stay close to their customers, seeking to understand and better meet their needs. They are on the lookout not for opportunities to benefit at the customer's expense but for opportunities to create value for customers and to build

---

[42] Albert Z. Carr, "Is Business Bluffing Ethical?" *Harvard Business Review* 46, no. 1 (January–February 1968), pp. 143ff.

[43] James L. Heskett, W. Earl Sasser, Jr., and Christopher W. L. Hart, *Service Breakthroughs Changing the Rules of the Game* (New York: The Free Press, 1990).

customer loyalty. Rather than have their buyers beware, these companies want them to have trust. Like Armstrong World Industries, a company that in the 1860s took as its motto "Let the buyer have faith," they realize that caveat emptor is a doctrine for the courtroom, not for the market-place.[44]

Support for the view that success is built on ethical attitudes and mutual gains thinking also can be found in recent game theory research. According to this research, cooperative behavior leads, in general, to better outcomes than behavior that follows the standard model of market transactions.[45] Although some economists treat this result as an anomaly because it defies the conventional model, others see it as quite understandable.[46] People who adopt a norm of cooperation do well because they are able to elicit cooperation from others and attract interactions with other cooperators.[47] One economist has argued that adherents of the conventional model consistently generate suboptimal outcomes for all involved.[48] He cautions that the *purely* "economic man" of the standard model is "close to being a social moron."

If the behavioral precepts implied by the economic model are an incomplete guide to success in the marketplace, they appear even more problematic as guiding principles inside the organization. Outstanding companies are built on extraordinary levels of effort and commitment. To become outstanding rather than merely acceptable or even good, companies depend on employees who are willing and able to do more than is required by their contract, their boss, or their job description. Employees must regularly engage in what has been called "discretionary citizenship behavior." Such behavior serves the organization's purposes, but it is not obligatory. In fact, its content cannot even be specified in advance.

While a tight job market is undoubtedly conducive to such behavior, the internal environment of the company is also important. As noted earlier, employees are more likely to engage in discretionary citizenship behavior when they trust their supervisor to treat them fairly and when they perceive the organization to operate fairly, especially in a procedural justice sense.[49] Another important factor is employees' view of

---

[44] Information about Armstrong World Industries is taken from Francis J. Aguilar, *Managing Corporate Ethics* (New York: Oxford University Press, 1994), p. 73.

[45] Robert Axelrod, *The Evolution of Cooperation* (New York: Basic Books, 1984).

[46] Robyn M. Dawes and Richard H. Thaler, "Anomalies Cooperation," *Journal of Economic Perspectives* 2, no. 3, (Summer 1988), pp. 187–197.

[47] Robert Frank, "If *Homo Economicus* Could Choose His Own Utility Function, Would He Want One with a Conscience?" *American Economic Review* 77, September 1987, pp. 593–605.

[48] Amartya K. Sen, "Rational Fools: A Critique of the Behavioral Foundations of Economic Theory," *Journal of Philosophy and Public Affairs* 6, 1977, pp. 317–344.

[49] R. H. Moorman, "Relationship Between Organizational Justice and Organizational Citizenship Behaviors: Do Fairness Perceptions Influence Employee Citizenship?" *Journal of Applied Psychology* 76, 1991, pp. 845–855.

their relationship with the organization. Research suggests that extra effort is more likely when employees see the relationship broadly as a social exchange rather than just an economic *quid pro quo* of formal rewards for specific behaviors.[50] Economic incentives and rewards are clearly a vital component of this relationship, but they are not the whole of it. Moreover, if perceived as inequitable, they may have an inhibiting effect on performance.

Ethics and Financial Performance

Today's emphasis on ethics and value systems reflects a recognition that management by financial objectives alone is generally a poor approach to bringing out the best in people. In some cases, it can even bring out the worst. Too many examples show that exclusive focus on financial targets can lead otherwise decent people to cut ethical corners leading to a range of problems from financial misreporting to defective products to disregard for the environment. In some settings, overemphasis on financial performance can lead to imprudent judgment, if not gross recklessness. In other situations, the impact may be just the opposite. Overemphasis on financial results may simply fail to energize and engage.

Of course, outstanding managers are keenly attuned to the fundamental economics of their businesses. They know that losing money is not an option and that profit is an imperative. Without attractive profits, a company cannot survive, let alone raise capital to create jobs, develop new products, and generate wealth. Failure to earn returns adequate to compensate suppliers of capital leaves companies vulnerable to being taken over and run by more efficient managers. But good managers also realize that in the final analysis, financial performance is best understood as an outcome—a result of the individual and collective behavior of all those contributing to the organization. The art of management lies in understanding and encouraging the behaviors necessary to achieve the desired outcome.

Moreover, financial performance is just one of several outcomes that matter to the people essential for organizational success. Employees who invest in developing firm-specific skills are certainly concerned about their company's financial health and about their own compensation. But for many inside the company, personal development, mastering new skills, maintaining their health and well-being, contributing to a worthwhile objective, and interacting with others are equally important, if not more so.

---

[50] For discussion of the differences between social and economic exchange, see D. W. Organ, "The Motivational Basis of Organizational Citizenship Behaviors," in B. M. Stow and L. L. Cummings (eds.), *Research in Organizational Behavior*, vol. 12 (Greenwich, CT: JAI Press, 1990), pp. 43–72.

For other constituencies, too, financial considerations figure among a variety of important factors. Customers with high switching costs want to deal with companies that are financially sound, and they want attractive prices. But they also want to deal with trustworthy companies whose products satisfy their expectations for quality, suitability, safety, and effectiveness. Suppliers want to be well compensated, and before making firm-specific investments, they look for assurances about the financial well-being of their prospective customers. But quality suppliers are also apt to favor customers that treat them fairly, pay on time, and offer opportunities for learning and development. Communities, too, want businesses to create economic value and spread prosperity. At the same time, they want enterprises to obey the law, uphold and strengthen the social fabric, and respect the natural environment.

The primary job of company leaders is to engage and coordinate the efforts of these and other contributors in a direction that yields the financial and other outcomes that enhance individual, organizational, and social well-being. While engaging the best efforts of the organization's people and partners requires a wide range of skills and capabilities, managers increasingly understand that developing and maintaining a corporate value system grounded in sound ethics is one of the most fundamental.

Overview of Cases in Part I

Responsibility for defining and maintaining an organization's ethical framework rests with company leadership. The cases in Part I illustrate vividly some potential perils of neglecting this important task. Each case provides a different window for understanding how shared values grounded in sound ethical principles contribute to organizational effectiveness. Each case also provides a window for understanding the range of problems that can arise when managers seek to manage by financial results alone. Collectively, the cases underscore the role of an ethical framework for motivating, harmonizing, and channeling behavior in positive directions.

The first case, "Problems at InSpeech," concerns a rapidly growing health care company that was faltering badly in the summer of 1988. Originally a regional speech therapy company, InSpeech had been acquired by a venture capital firm in 1985. Through a series of aggressive acquisitions it had become by 1988 the largest provider of speech, occupational, and physical therapy to nursing homes and hospitals in the United States. Although revenues had increased sevenfold since 1985 and prospects for the rehabilitation services business were bright, the company's problems cast a pall over its future. Employee turnover had reached 50 percent per year, customers were defecting, and the company's share price had fallen to $7.00 from a high of $27.00 the year before. Top management must diagnose the company's problems and develop a plan to address them. A critical issue is developing a value system for the organization.

"Sears Auto Centers (A)" presents the situation at retailing giant Sears, Roebuck & Co. in June 1992 when the company's auto centers were being accused of misleading customers and selling them unnecessary auto repairs. In the wake of charges by consumer affairs officials in California, Florida, and New Jersey, Sears's stock price has dropped some 9 percent, and auto centers' revenues have fallen by 15 percent nationwide. California's Department of Consumer Affairs is seeking to revoke the licenses of the company's 72 auto repair centers in the state for violating California's Auto Repair Act. The CEO must assess the charges and decide how to respond.

The third case is about New York–based brokerage firm E.F. Hutton & Company. "Hutton Branch Manager (A)" centers on the manager of one of Hutton's Washington, D.C., branch offices. The case involves a situation that arose in 1982 when Hutton's local bank balked at the company's aggressive cash management practices and threatened to drop Hutton as the broker for its trust department. The Hutton branch manager must decide how to respond to the bank's challenge and how to deal with a colleague whose overdrafting of Hutton's bank accounts has precipitated the current problem. An important issue is the legitimacy of Hutton's approach to cash management.

In "Salomon and the Treasury Securities Auction," a top executive at Salomon Brothers must decide what to do in June 1991 after learning that a managing director on the government trading desk has submitted an unauthorized bid in a United States Treasury auction. He has raised the matter with the company's two top executives and general counsel, but no one has taken any action. As the vice chairman in charge of trading in U.S. securities, the executive is responsible for the activities of Salomon's government traders. He must decide whether the trader's conduct merits further action.

Study Questions for Cases

The analysis of each case in Part I should include an evaluation of the problems presented, a diagnosis of their origins, and a plan of action for addressing them. Special attention should be paid to the critical relationships involved in each situation. The following study questions provide a guide to preparing each case.

CASE 1: *Problems at InSpeech*

1. What's your appraisal of the situation at InSpeech in 1988?
2. What are the origins of InSpeech's problems?
3. What would you advise InSpeech management to do to turn the company around and get it back on track?
4. How would you develop an ethical framework to guide the company forward?

CASE 2: *Sears Auto Centers (A)*

1. As Brennan, what would be your principal concerns on June 19, 1992?
2. What's your assessment of the allegations against Sears? Which of the alleged practices do you find problematic? Why?
3. What are the origins of Sears's problems? Who is responsible?
4. How well has Sears handled the matter to date? What should Brennan do now?

CASE 3: *Hutton Branch Manager (A)*

1. What's your appraisal of Howe's technique for boosting his branch's interest income?
2. What about the other cash management techniques used by Hutton? How strongly should management encourage (1) overdrafting, (2) chaining, and (3) remote disbursement?
3. What are the origins of Pedersen's problem? What accounts for Howe's overdrafting practices?
4. How would you advise Pedersen to handle the problem with Howe? Be specific.

CASE 4: *Salomon and the Treasury Securities Auction*

1. As Meriwether, what would be your principal concerns in June 1991?
2. What's your appraisal of Mozer's conduct?
3. What are the origins of Meriwether's problem?
4. What options should Meriwether consider? What course of action would you advise him to take?

CASE 1
PROBLEMS AT INSPEECH

In the summer of 1988, InSpeech, Inc., was faltering badly. Since its acquisition by Foster Management Company in 1985, InSpeech had become the United States's largest provider of speech, occupational, and physical therapists to nursing homes and hospitals.[1] Anticipating the growing market for rehabilitation services, InSpeech revenues had increased more than seven times and the number of patients served had risen from 700 to more than 4,000 through a series of aggressive acquisitions. Yet, the company was in trouble, and senior managers were concerned for its future. James Killough, a consultant and investor in InSpeech, recalled: "It became apparent that however wonderful this opportunity [InSpeech] was, it could be dead in the water. . . . The viability of the company and its management was at stake."

The company's inability to integrate the administrative systems of acquired companies contributed to rising support and administrative expenses and declining margins. Operations, too, were increasingly problematic: InSpeech was having trouble retaining frontline employees—the therapists and clinicians who provided its services. Turnover climbed to more than 50% per annum, and the number of billable hours per therapist declined sharply, contributing further to falling margins. A speech therapist who joined the company in 1986 recalled:

> In two years . . . I had three different supervisors. I had seen almost all of my friends leave. Only two people remained constant through the two years. There was no leadership. The turmoil was very apparent. . . . I got the feeling that InSpeech might not make it.

Keeping its customers also proved to be a problem. According to Timothy E. Foster, then a director and senior vice president of operations, "We would acquire a business and lose half of it [employees and customers] within one year, and we were losing our base, as well."

The deterioration of the company and its reputation became evident inside and outside the organization. Universities would not allow students to fulfill their required clinical internships at InSpeech. The company was having difficulty paying people on time. Tim Foster remembered,

---

[1] **Rehabilitation therapy** is the use of medical, social, and educational means for training people disabled by disease, trauma, or injury. Individuals helped by rehabilitation therapy may be those suffering from ailments common to the elderly, those suffering from chronic illness, or those recovering from injury, surgery, or removal of a cast. **Speech therapy** focuses on improving speech, language, swallowing, and hearing capability. **Physical therapy** uses heat, cold, water, electricity, massage, or exercise to relieve pain and improve muscular and neural responses with the aim of increasing physical strength and range of motion. **Occupational therapy** improves muscular neural responses with the aim of enhancing the patient's ability to perform the activities of daily life, including eating, dressing, and grooming.

This case was prepared by Jane Palley Katz under the supervision of Lynn Sharp Paine.
Copyright © 1994 by the President and Fellows of Harvard College. Harvard Business School case 394–109.

In January 1988, it was clear we were hitting the wall in operations . . . by the summer of 1988, it was clear that our financial systems were a mess . . . Accounts were misstated; general ledgers didn't balance . . . We were not going to be able to complete the SEC filings due at the end of September.

InSpeech's problems did not go unnoticed on Wall Street. Its stock price, as high as $27 on September 30, 1987, fell to $6.88 on December 4. In January 1988, InSpeech stopped its program of acquisitions to consider what to do about the "meltdown." By late summer of 1988, the stock price was still languishing at between $7.00 and $8.00 a share. Top managers were searching for an approach to turning the company around.

The Origins of InSpeech, Inc.

InSpeech originated as a regional speech therapy business in Valley Forge, Pennsylvania. In May 1985, Foster Management Company (FMC), led by John H. Foster, acquired the 10-year-old practice—believed to be the nation's largest at the time. Foster, a graduate of Williams College and the Tuck School at Dartmouth, worked for five years in the investment and venture capital operations of J.P. Morgan before starting FMC at age 29. InSpeech was only one of the many companies Foster had launched or financed under the umbrella of FMC, a private investment firm that funded various venture capital opportunities. Among the enterprises that Foster had taken public were

- The Aviation Group, which provided air cargo services and was later acquired by Primark in December 1985 at $23 a share, well above the $8.67 paid by investors for the initial public offering four years earlier.
- Foster Medical, a medical supply distribution business, later bought by Avon in May 1984 at $17 a share, a 150% increase over the $6.88 paid by investors for the initial public offering in August 1982. After seven months as an Avon executive, Foster resigned, returning to venture capital. In January 1988, Avon sold Foster Medical, taking large write-offs in the transaction.
- Chartwell Group Ltd., which manufactured and marketed interior furnishing accessories to interior designers and retail furniture outlets. The company went public in April 1986 at $14 a share. By summer 1988, its stock price was at $7.

Described by an associate as "the most performance oriented person I've ever met," John Foster had developed an excellent reputation in the financial community. One analyst wrote, "Foster Management . . . at least with companies that have come into public view, has clearly been extraordinarily successful."[2]

In acquiring and managing InSpeech, John Foster worked closely with Tim Foster (no relation), a young associate in venture capital activities at FMC with prior experience in General Electric's fast-track financial organization. Tim Foster became InSpeech's senior vice president of operations and served on its board of directors. Jeffrey W. Rose, a veteran of Foster Medical, was appointed president

---

[2] S. L. Handley, "Chartwell Group, Ltd.—Company Report," Smith Barney, Harris Upham & Co., December 3, 1986.

and chief operating officer. Rose, who also sat on the board, had a background in information systems and prior experience as a consultant in an accounting firm.

John Foster served as InSpeech's chairman and chief executive officer from his New York office, where he continued to oversee his venture capital business. Other Foster associates invested in InSpeech and sat on its board. James Killough, a friend of John Foster's and an investor at the time of the initial public offering, served as a consultant and advisor. A member of the Harvard Business School MBA class of 1959, Killough brought experience in general management and marketing with Procter & Gamble and Johnson & Johnson to the company.

Once established, InSpeech quickly bought additional therapy practices in several areas across the country, including California-based Irwin Lehrhoff & Associates, Inc., the nation's second largest. Lehrhoff was "considered by many to be the father of speech-language pathology in the private-practice format, and his affiliation with InSpeech has clearly enhanced the credibility and reputation of the company within the industry."[3] Several of InSpeech's acquisitions included physical therapy and occupational therapy practices, although the greater part of its business continued to be speech therapy. See **Exhibit 1** for information on InSpeech's acquisitions. Most of its services were provided under contract to nursing homes and to some hospitals.

John Foster's Strategy

In December 1986, John Foster took InSpeech public, at an initial price of $17 a share. The company's business strategy was

> to capitalize upon (1) the highly fragmented nature of competition in the speech therapy industry; (2) the presently underserved demand for speech therapy services; (3) the growing demand for speech therapy due in part to an aging population; and (4) the lack of professional management, information systems and access to capital which characterizes most speech therapy practices. . . . As part of its strategy, the Company is seeking to increase the revenue and operating margins of its current business through programs designed to increase the productivity of its speech therapists, the number of nursing homes under contract and the number of patients served in each facility. Over time, the Company intends to leverage its customer base and marketing and management systems by diversifying into other rehabilitative therapies including physical and occupational therapy and into healthcare settings other than nursing homes.[4]

At the time of the offering, InSpeech—though the largest speech therapy firm in the country—still accounted for less than 5% of all therapists in the industry. Foster believed that by consolidating and expanding the provision of therapy services through acquisition and disciplined internal growth, InSpeech could become "the leading factor in the industry."

---

[3] J. France, "InSpeech, Inc.—Company Report," Smith Barney, Upham & Co., March 18, 1987, p. 4.

[4] InSpeech, Inc., *Prospectus*, November 5, 1986, p. 12.

Exhibit 1 InSpeech, Inc., Acquisitions, 1985–1988

Date Acquired	Name	Location	Type of Practice	Estimated Revenues (at date of purchase)
May 1985	InSpeech, Inc.	Valley Forge, PA	speech	$6.0 million
January 1986	Center for Communication Disorders	Raleigh, NC	speech	0.1 million
September 1986	Irwin Lehrhoff & Associates, Inc.	Los Angeles, CA	speech, physical, occupational	4.8 million
September 1986	SHC, Inc.	Oak Park, IL	speech	0.9 million
September 1986	Speech-Language Rehabilitation Center, Inc.	Chicago, IL	speech	not available
December 1986	Florida East Coast Rehabilitation Center, Inc. and Affiliates	Ormond Beach, FL	physical, occupational	4.2 million
February 1987	Northwest Rehabilitation, Inc., and Northside Physical Therapy Services, Inc.	Minneapolis, MN	physical	6.0 million
February 1987	Len M. House and Associates and United Rehabilitation, Inc.	Minneapolis, MN	speech	0.4 million
March 1987	Norma Bork Associates, Inc., and Norma Bork Medical Services, Inc.	Napa, CA	speech, physical, occupational	1.0 million
April 1987	Marina Professional Services, Inc.	Los Angeles, CA	speech, physical, occupational	3.0 million
May 1987	Whitley & Associates, Inc., and Whitley Rehabilitative Services, Inc.	Hudson, FL	speech, physical, occupational	1.0 million
June 1987	Marilyn Hawker, Inc.	Phoenix, AZ	speech	not available
June 1987	David Rafkin, P.C.	Los Angeles, CA	speech	not available
July 1987	Craig and Ford Rehabilitation Services, Inc.	Los Angeles, CA	speech, physical, occupational	1.0 million
July 1987	First Rehab, Inc., and Affiliates	Commerce, GA	speech, physical	6.0 million
September 1987	Suburban Rehabilitation Associates, Inc.	Pittsburgh, PA	physical, occupational	1.6 million
September 1987	Mitchell-Zoltowicz-Hotz and Associates, Inc.	Cleveland, OH	speech, physical	1.0 million
October 1987	Rehab Therapy, Inc.	Denver, CO	physical	1.0 million
November 1987	Rehabilitation Systems of Illinois, Ltd. and RSI, Ltd.	Oak Park, IL	physical	3.0 million
January 1988	Virginia Speech & Language Associates, Inc.	Virginia Beach, VA	speech	0.3 million

Source: Compiled from *Moody's Industrial Manual,* analysts' reports, and news wires.

In InSpeech's first annual report as a public company, John Foster addressed the stockholders:

> InSpeech is strategy driven. Effective strategy depends upon day to day execution. Successful execution in a national service organization requires management systems with concomitant monitoring and training. We have pioneered a system solution for the delivery of rehabilitative therapies on a contract basis to healthcare institutions that enhances quality of care and clinician productivity. At the core of the nation's healthcare cost explosion is inefficient delivery of services. The "value added" by In-speech to the healthcare community is an efficient delivery system.[5]

With superior management and access to capital, InSpeech anticipated benefits all around. Soon-to-be-developed systems for finance and claims processing, marketing, clinical and productivity management, and personnel training were expected to free therapists from many of the administrative and marketing tasks involved in running their own practice and allow them to concentrate on identifying and treating patients. Therapists would be able to treat a large and diverse group of patients and gain opportunities for further training or a career path into management. Nursing homes and hospitals would benefit by securing well-supervised, high-quality care from the best clinicians available. They would receive help with the paperwork and accurate documentation of patient care, both necessary when seeking reimbursement. InSpeech also expected to expand the scope of rehabilitation services offered in the nursing homes by training its staff to recognize all patients who might benefit from therapy and by offering to cosponsor seminars and other joint marketing programs with the facility administrators.

After the initial offering, InSpeech continued to grow rapidly, with investors reacting favorably. Its stock price increased to $45 in June 1987, then split two-for-one, and rose again to $27 in September 1987. One industry observer explained investors' confidence: "John Foster has twice gobbled up local operations in fragmented fields (home medical care and air freight), amalgamated them and sold them to big corporations for stratospheric prices."[6]

The Rehabilitative Therapy Industry

InSpeech's early success was sustained by a large and growing market for rehabilitation services. The burgeoning demand for rehabilitative services reflected a number of factors—the aging of the U.S. population, the increased recognition that rehabilitative therapy could improve patient functioning, and greater acceptance of rehabilitation as a cost-effective addition or alternative to surgery, medication, extended convalescence, or doing nothing. Company studies suggested that just one out of three nursing home patients needing rehabilitative services was receiving them. Tim Foster noted that in the nursing home rehabilitation industry, "If you are not growing 50% a year, you are losing market share."

In 1988, InSpeech estimated that the total market for rehabilitative therapy was $3.4 billion and was expected to grow at an annual rate of 10% for the next five years.[7] Of the total, about three-quarters of the market was for physical

---

[5] InSpeech, Inc., *Annual Report*, 1987, p. 1.

[6] David Henry, "Goodwill, Bad News," *Forbes*, July 13, 1987, p. 481.

[7] InSpeech, Inc., *Annual Report*, 1988, p. 3. This growth rate proved to have been a gross underestimate.

therapy, with the rest split between speech therapy and occupational therapy. The industry was highly fragmented, consisting of more than 1,000 small competitors, mostly local firms, and a few larger regional practices, generally with revenues of well under $10 million. One industry analyst calculated that the six largest firms in speech and physical therapy accounted for no more than 15% of the total market.[8]

The services of rehabilitation therapists were used by university and acute-care hospitals, rehabilitation hospitals, nursing homes, private offices, clinics, and in the home. Nursing homes—InSpeech's target market—did not uniformly provide speech, occupational, or physical therapy to their residents. Most nursing home space and effort were devoted to providing room and board, not health care. Rehabilitation generated a very small portion of nursing home revenues, mostly through Medicare or other reimbursement. Nursing home administrators were not always well informed about the profitability and procedures of Medicare reimbursement, nor were they always aware of the potential benefits that therapy offered geriatric patients. One government survey found that 65% of nursing home residents received no therapy of any type during the survey month. Of the 35% who did, 20% received recreational therapy, 17% counseling, and 7% reality orientation. Only 14% received physical therapy and 6% occupational therapy, despite other evidence suggesting that 47% needed physical therapy and 35% needed occupational therapy. Less than 1% received speech or hearing therapy, even though 19% of the residents had partially or severely impaired speech and 26% had partially or severely impaired hearing.[9]

Nursing homes and hospitals that did provide speech therapy hired therapists on a contract basis, because the patient caseload at a single facility was usually too small to justify hiring a full-time clinician. Physical and occupational therapists were more likely to be hired as full-time staff members, though an industry analyst estimated that more than one-third of total institutional physical therapy revenues were generated by contract services.[10]

The most serious constraint on industry revenue growth was the problem of recruiting and retaining licensed or registered clinicians. During the 1980s, increasing demand for therapy services far surpassed the increase in licensed therapists. The resulting chronic shortage of therapists nationwide contributed to rising salaries (8% to 10% per year, according to industry analysts)[11] and average attrition rates of about 25% throughout the industry.

InSpeech in 1988

By 1988, InSpeech operated in 29 states and served over 1,400 nursing homes and hospitals. Of its 1,000 employees, about 80% were therapists. Net revenues had increased sevenfold since 1986, with much of the growth a result of acquisitions.

---

[8] J. France, p. 3.

[9] E. Hing, "Characteristics of Nursing Home Residents, Health Status, and Care Received: National Nursing Home Survey, United States, May-December 1977," *Vital and Health Statistics,* Series 13, Data from the National Health Survey, no. 51, p. 24.

[10] J. France, p. 13.

[11] Dorothy E. Ryan and Cheryl L. Alexander, "NovaCare, Inc.," Robertson Stephens & Company, August 3, 1990, p. 5.

Approximately half of InSpeech's revenue was attributable to speech therapy patients, down sharply from 1986 and expected to fall further as the bulk of newer acquisitions was for physical therapy practices.[12] Nursing home contracts were the largest source of InSpeech's revenues; about 40% of its business came from the country's 25 largest nursing home chains.[13] See **Exhibit 2** for a summary of financial results and company data. See **Exhibit 3** for the history of InSpeech's stock price.

Reimbursement

InSpeech usually collected payment for its services from the nursing home, which then sought reimbursement from one of four sources: Medicare, a federally funded health insurance program for certain disabled persons and those over the age of 65; Medicaid, a program funded by the federal and state governments to provide health insurance for financially or medically needy persons, regardless of age; private insurance; or the patient. In instances when the nursing home was denied reimbursement, InSpeech helped prepare and present an appeal. InSpeech usually indemnified its customers against final reimbursement denials.[14] An estimated 85% of the company's net revenue was attributable directly or indirectly to Medicare.

Speech therapy and occupational therapy were reimbursable under Medicare on a per treatment basis at the prevailing market rate. In 1988, the rate stood at $18 to $20 per "unit," or 15-minute treatment.[15] Nursing homes charged Medicare for the direct costs of contract therapy (as charged by the contractor) plus an allocation for overhead, thus making these services profitable for nursing homes as well as for InSpeech. More than 90% of the company's speech therapy services was covered under Medicare.[16]

About half of InSpeech's physical therapy revenues came from Medicare. Almost a third were covered by private insurance or the patient's pocket, and 15% to 20%, by workmen's compensation insurance. Medicare reimbursement for physical therapy services was on a salary equivalency basis: repayment was linked to the theoretical cost of having a full-time physical therapist on staff at the nursing home. These theoretical costs were escalated annually on an index substantially below the actual market inflation of physical therapy salaries. As a result, salary equivalency resulted in lower profitability for InSpeech. In fact, margins in physical therapy were so low that it was used as a loss leader, but the company easily compensated with profits from speech and occupational therapy.

There was some concern in the industry that the federal government might move to salary equivalency for all three types of rehabilitative therapy, but most industry analysts tended to discount the possibilities at least for the time being, especially because speech and physical therapy were believed to represent less than 10% of Medicare's total nursing home expenses.[17] Moreover, speech and ocupational therapy caseloads were typically still too small to warrant hiring full-time therapists.

---

[12] "NovaCare, Inc.," Robert W. Baird & Co. Incorporated, December 31, 1991, p. 5.

[13] M. A. Martorelli, "NovaCare, Inc.—Company Report," Janney Montgomery Scott, Inc., November 17, 1987, p. 2.

[14] James Brian Quinn, "NovaCare, Inc." The Amos Tuck School of Business Administration, Dartmouth College, 1992, p. 12.

[15] J. France, p. 11.

[16] J. France, p. 11.

[17] J. France, p. 2.

Exhibit 2 InSpeech, Inc. and Subsidiaries—Financial Summary, 1986–1988 ($ in thousands except for share-related data)

	Year Ended June 30		
	1988	*1987*	*1986*
Statement of Operations Data[a]			
Net revenues	$57,796	$26,996	$8,211
Expenses:			
Operating	35,941	15,364	5,361
Selling, general and administrative	18,693	6,772	2,670
Income (loss) from operations	$ 3,162	$ 4,860	$ 180
Loss on marketable securities	(2,468)	(710)	—
Interest expense	(1,516)	(696)	(758)
Dividend and interest income	1,416	1,357	—
Amortization of excess cost of net assets acquired	(887)	(341)	(144)
Income (loss) before income taxes and extraordinary item	$ (293)	$ 4,470	$ (722)
Income taxes (benefit)	752	2,157	—
Income (loss) before extraordinary item	$(1,045)	$ 2,313	$ (722)
Extraordinary item:			
Tax benefit from utilization of net operating loss carryforward	—	566	—
Net income (loss)	$(1,045)	$ 2,879	$ (722)
Per Share Data			
Income (loss) before extraordinary item	$ (0.08)	$ 0.20	$(0.09)
Benefit from extraordinary item	—	0.05	—
Net income (loss)	$ (0.08)	$ 0.25	$(0.09)
Weighted average shares outstanding[b]	13,277,225	11,648,992	7,695,582

	June 30		
	1988	*1987*	*1986*
Balance Sheet Data			
Working capital (deficiency)	$31,515	$4,280	$(6,260)
Total assets	72,386	58,105	13,083
Long-term obligations, excluding current installments	17,459	8,337	3,894
Total indebtedness	18,915	9,516	11,577
Stockholders' equity (deficit)	44,605	43,013	(706)

[a] Includes the results of operations of businesses acquired from the effective dates of each acquisition.
[b] The share-related data for 1986 are based upon the number of shares of common stock outstanding as of September 30, 1986 (effected for the June 1987 2-for-1 stock split), since all shares issued prior to that date were issued at prices significantly below the initial public offering price. The per share data for the 1987 period gives effect to the above-mentioned stock split.

Source: InSpeech, Inc., Annual Report, 1988.

EXHIBIT 3

InSpeech, Inc. Stock Price, December 1986 to September 1988 (adjusted for stock splits)

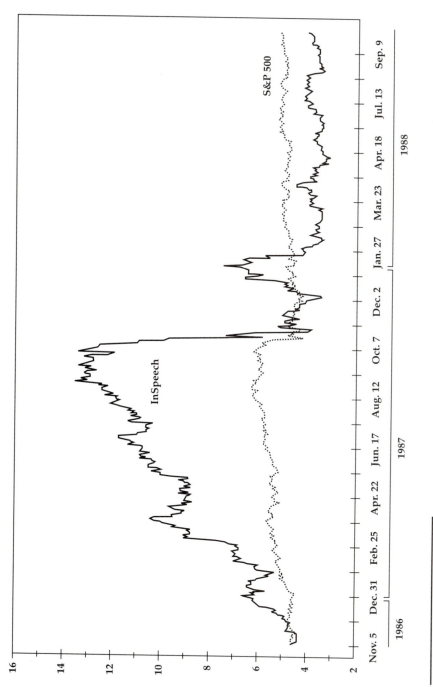

Source: Interactive Data Corp.

Corporate Management and Organizational Structure

InSpeech was tightly managed by a relatively small corporate staff, located at the firm's headquarters in Valley Forge. Finance, human resources and recruiting, marketing, and the other functions were centralized at corporate headquarters where most business decisions were made by the senior management. During 1987 and early 1988, InSpeech misfired in the hiring of several senior executives whose appointments were soon terminated. Tim Foster noted:

> Senior management turnover was related to the maturity of our management team. We had not yet learned that you have to hire far in advance of your needs. And . . . to be unafraid of hiring people in excess of your own capabilities. I had held positions in almost all functions because I was the most qualified guy, and that [situation] was ridiculous.

Operations were divided into two separate businesses: speech therapy and occupational and physical therapy, called rehab care. Each business negotiated its own contracts and supervised its own therapists. Tim Foster managed the speech therapy business and Dennis G. Sherman, the vice president of rehab care, handled the occupational and physical therapy business. Both reported to Jeffrey Rose. The sharp division between speech and the other therapy services was reflected not only in the organization's structure, but also in its terminology: Speech pathologists were called "clinicians," whereas occupational and physical specialists were termed "therapists."[18] Integration of the three therapy services had been suggested and rejected, in part because both clinicians and therapists resisted being supervised by anyone outside their specialty.

Field Organization

InSpeech's field organization consisted of the clinicians and field managers who were directly responsible for providing care in the local market. About 90% of the field staff were women, and about 10% to 15% worked part-time. To facilitate the delivery of its services, the field operation was divided into 10 areas nationwide, each with $5 million to $15 million in revenues.

Therapists and Clinicians   InSpeech's clinical staff was a highly educated group. Medicare required that therapists be licensed in the states in which they practiced. State licensing authorities typically required occupational and physical therapists to hold at least a four-year bachelor's degree, have four months of clinical training, and pass a national licensing examination. Speech pathologists were required to hold master's degrees and complete a nine-month internship as well. InSpeech clinicians were characterized both by strong professional identification and diverse objectives, as illustrated in the comments of three care givers:

- I got into therapy because I wanted to help people . . . In college, I took a psychology course and got curious. Then, I took a sign language course, and the teacher was deaf. I became very interested in why she could not talk—in the scientific part of it . . . I joined InSpeech after receiving my master's degree. One of the things that attracted me to InSpeech was the security. The for-profit nature of the company was also attractive to me. I

---

[18] This case uses the terms "clinician" and "therapist" interchangeably.

thought I could learn other skills, such as marketing and program development. . . . Some clinicians are interested in how the company's profits are calculated, and some are not. I don't see an essential conflict between patient care and profitability. In the not-for-profits, they don't talk about it so much, but they are still measuring. It's the same thing.

- I had been in private practice, specializing in pediatrics for a number of years. In 1988, due to the economics of a divorce, I needed the benefits and security that InSpeech provided. I needed the opportunity to grow professionally, and I wanted to learn about geriatrics. I needed to be able to work part-time, and I needed some flexibility to arrange my work schedule around my children. InSpeech was really helpful there . . . I think anyone in rehab is idealistic. Most of us as clinicians don't have a for-profit orientation. I understand that we have to meet salaries and so on, but the average clinician doesn't worry about profit. The majority of clinicians are very focused on patients.

- I started at InSpeech in 1987 straight out of college. . . . I was interested in geriatrics. I liked adult rehab. . . . For me, [the for-profit nature of the company] meant it would be on the cutting edge of therapy and new techniques . . . I get satisfaction from demonstrating the best possible skill level and providing the best treatment available.

InSpeech therapists had a wider range of duties than clinicians who worked in nonprofit hospitals and universities. These responsibilities included:

- Identifying every nursing home patient who could benefit from rehabilitation.
- Diagnosing their condition and developing a plan of treatment.
- Meeting with the family and physicians to discuss the patient's care.
- Working with nursing home facility personnel to make sure that the rest of the patient's care supported the rehabilitation program.
- Educating nursing home staff, physicians, and hospital discharge planners about available rehabilitation services.
- Providing the documentation that the nursing home needed for state certification and Medicare requirements.

On a typical day, an InSpeech therapist would see patients in one facility in the morning, and drive 15 to 45 minutes to reach another building for work in the afternoon. Some were responsible for servicing as many as three or four buildings. At the end of the day, the therapist would complete the documentation on each patient's diagnosis, treatment, and discharge to support the nursing home's reimbursement application. It was extremely important for clinicians to keep accurate records to meet Medicare requirements and to minimize denial of reimbursement claims.

InSpeech's clinicians were expected to treat patients and do other reimbursable work for 100 "units"—or 25 hours—per week, where a unit was a 15-minute treatment period.[19] Senior managers arrived at this weekly yardstick

---

[19] Preparation, meetings, and paperwork directly connected with patient care were included in the time counted toward billable units.

in 1984 by surveying therapists outside InSpeech and finding that they typically administered to patients about 30 to 33 hours in a week. Because InSpeech therapists traveled more than their counterparts working elsewhere, the company settled on the 100-unit gauge. The remainder of their work week was devoted to building a practice (identifying patients, marketing), travel, paperwork, and meetings with families, physicians, and nursing home staff.

Therapists were paid a base salary, competitive with the average market salary for that therapy discipline in the relevant geographic market, and offered a bonus for every treatment unit above 100. In theory, this formula meant that InSpeech's compensation package for therapists was better than the industry average. It presupposed, however, that each clinician was able to identify and treat more patients than were actually being served at the time. In fact, actual compensation, which averaged $25,000 for full-time clinicians in 1988, was not appreciably higher than could be received outside the company. With the additional paperwork and travel time between nursing homes, the compensation was sometimes perceived as lower. Several therapists reported that competing companies offered higher compensation, but required more hours of clinical treatment per week.

Reflecting the company's pay for performance philosophy, therapists received a yearly performance evaluation assessing the quality of their clinical care, their professional growth, and their communication skills. These evaluations were used to set yearly raises in base pay and to aid the clinician in career development.

Field Managers   Clinicians and therapists reported directly to their **clinical supervisor,** a clinician in their therapy discipline who was generally still engaged in direct patient care. Clinical supervisors were charged with providing direction and aid to therapists in clinical matters, such as diagnoses and treatment protocol. They also oversaw therapist productivity—the weekly number of units performed by each therapist—but had little other business responsibility. Most clinical supervisors held monthly meetings, frequently in their homes, during which they honored the most productive therapists and introduced any new procedures or corporate initiatives. In contrast to the clinicians, turnover among clinical supervisors remained relatively low.

Clinical supervisors reported to their **area manager,** also operating out of his or her home. Area managers on the speech therapy side of the business reported to either the eastern or western **division manager.** Area managers in occupational and physical therapy reported directly to senior executives in Valley Forge, known collectively to clinicians as "the suits." See **Exhibit 4** for InSpeech's organization chart. Tim Foster noted that InSpeech was the "ultimate in vertical organization—one over one over one . . . "

Clinical supervisors and area managers were paid a base salary, competitive in the local market for that position, and could receive bonuses based on billable treatment units per full-time therapist, the total number of units, and the retention rate of therapists. Like the therapists' evaluations, managers' performance evaluations were used to set yearly raises in base pay and for career development.

The field managers' primary management tool was the number of treatment units delivered by each therapist—clinical supervisors and area managers typi-

Exhibit 4

InSpeech, Inc. Organization Chart, Clinical Supervisor Model

	John H. Foster **Chairman** **Chief Executive Officer** **(New York, NY)**	
	Jeffrey W. Rose **President** **Chief Operating Officer** **(Valley Forge, PA)**	
Coporate Vice Presidents **-Regulatory Affairs** **-Marketing and Sales** **-Human Resources** **-Finance** **-Corporate Development** **(Valley Forge, PA)**	**Timothy E. Foster** **Senior Vice President-** **Operations** **Speech Therapy** **(Valley Forge, PA)**	**Dennis G. Sherman** **Vice President-** **Operations** **Rehab Care Division** **Occupational and** **Physical Therapy** **(Valley Forge, PA)**
Vice President- **Operations** **Eastern Division**	**Vice President-** **Operations** **Eastern Division**	
Area Manager **(5 areas)**	**Area Manager** **(2 areas)**	**Area Manager** **(3 areas)**
Clinical Supervisor	**Clinical Supervisor**	**Clinical Supervisor**
Clinician **(Speech)**	**Clinician** **(Speech)**	**Therapist** **(Occupational** **and Physical)**

cally did not have access to profit and loss information. Once a week, all therapists telephoned their clinical supervisor to report their units. Clinical supervisors relayed the figures to the area managers, and so on, up the reporting line. One clinician described the company's information flow: "It was entirely a one-way reporting system; there was nothing coming down in terms of information. All the management wanted to know was the units."

Some field managers felt hampered by their lack of management tools and decision-making authority. Valley Forge set the productivity standard, secured contracts, and handled hiring and firing. Field managers had neither training nor authority to handle relations with the nursing homes, nor to mediate problems between clinicians and the nursing home staff. One area manager, a former clinician, recalled:

> There were utterly no financial management data for area managers. Senior management was stunned when I asked for a P&L. They had the philosophy that therapists didn't want to know these things. There was a complete lack of management empowerment. All decisions were managed tightly, and all were made at Valley Forge. It was management by procedure. Senior management created very specific procedures as to what we should do. The procedures took the form of a big "to-do" list, which re-

stricted and limited any creativity that we could show. Also, the procedures began to take on a life of their own. Everyone began to be more concerned with getting these procedures done than with ensuring that good care was provided.

Senior Management Assesses InSpeech's Problems

After plummeting in October 1987, InSpeech's stock price continued in a slump into the summer of 1988. While the initial slide reflected the company's losses on junk bond investments, along with the market crash of late October, the stock's failure to recover related to the company's operating problems. When buy-side analysts learned that the attrition rate for therapists had risen above 50%, they were totally turned off. According to Jim Killough who did a study to evaluate the company's image with its various constituencies in the summer of 1988, "Analysts perceived the attrition rate as a sure sign that top managers were still stock jockeys at heart, interested in selling to a third party at a high multiple, rather than . . . building an enduring franchise."

Tim Foster attributed many of the company's problems to its growth through acquisition, a process he called "distracting and exhausting." A field manager explained:

> This was a tightly centralized company that grew very fast. With all of the acquisitions, we had no human resource function or payroll systems to integrate the company. There was no infrastructure, no system to support the integration so management continued to operate as before.

The new acquisitions brought cultural and operating problems that required costly fire-fighting efforts. Tim Foster put it this way:

> We had acquired 20 clinical practices in less than three years. . . . The InSpeech name was still around, even though physical and occupational therapy were now becoming a big part of our business. . . . We were bringing together several previously competing practices in the same geographic area. They didn't trust one another at all. Since we gave the owners earnouts, we pitted them against one another.[20] They accused one another of being unethical and giving bad care. They couldn't work together . . . I was seeing incredible conflict. All these people seemed to be really good people. I couldn't figure out what was wrong . . . In one area, there were three or four groups who really disliked one another. The only thing they had in common was their hatred of Valley Forge.

Another senior manager remarked: "Many of the small owners did not want to be a part of us. We made them rich when we bought their businesses, but then they were irritated by us."

Tim Foster believed that the nature of the industry contributed to the difficulties:

> Before we entered, this was a very "Mom and Pop" industry. The companies in the industry were not businesses, but cultures dominated by the personalities of the founders. The organizations were successful if the personality was successful. We came and

---

[20] An earnout was the part of the acquisition price that depended on the acquired practices' financial performance over several years into the future.

destroyed the personality cults that formed the basis of the businesses we had acquired—we emasculated them—and did not replace them with anything. With every new acquisition, we were trying to integrate 20 cultures into a thing that had no culture.

Foster also pointed to what he called a "huge disconnect" between the clinicians and financial managers:

Clinical professionals don't come here to make money. They are very altruistic. They want to help patients, develop themselves, and feel good about themselves and their colleagues. It is a feeling group of people. My background is in financial services, which is an unfeeling group. . . . My language is financial and analytical. Financial success. Long-term strategic success.

In addition, the company's financial organization was "an absolute mess." According to Tim Foster, "No one had confidence in the CFO's ability to communicate and integrate finance into the whole of the company—because finance didn't understand the clinical side of the business."

Customer Relations

Although the number of contracts and facilities had increased with each purchase of a new practice, InSpeech was having trouble retaining customers. In one instance, InSpeech bought a local practice with more than $4 million in revenues; three months later, revenues were less than $1.3 million, and two-thirds of the therapists had quit. A senior manager recalled:

We bought one contract three times over. We purchased a practice, and the nursing home canceled the contract and switched to another provider. We bought that practice, and they canceled and switched again. Eventually, we bought a third practice and finally got them to stay.

Typically, nursing homes were looking for a number of features in addition to adequate care giving and consistent staffing: patient identification, appropriate referrals, usable documentation and reports, expertise in reimbursement, and user-friendly communication from management. Relations with major customers were handled at Valley Forge. When contracts were canceled, rumors circulated that senior management arrogance was causing trouble. But, there were other problems as well.

One of the most frequent sources of complaints was that InSpeech did not act as one company. Larger customers, such as nursing-home chains, were frustrated by their inability to do business with InSpeech as one integrated, nationwide practice. Individual facility administrators often had to make arrangements with three supervisors—one for each clinical specialty. One manager declared, "Customers did not have a clue as to how to deal with us." Field management was not able to help. According to one clinician, "The clinical supervisors had no support and were not trained in how to handle customer expectations and conflicts." Most important, problems with recruiting and retaining therapists meant that InSpeech was "dramatically overpromising our customers, and we could not deliver." Tim Foster summed it up: "Customers didn't value us highly. We couldn't meet their basic needs. We didn't have the staff."

Moreover, in concentrating on nursing homes, InSpeech was dealing with an inexperienced customer, doubtful of the profitability in rehabilitation services. A speech therapist in New England recalled:

> Speech therapy was not well received in many nursing homes. They didn't exactly know what we were and how to make use of us. The nursing home staff perceived us as disruptive. We were dumped in a facility that didn't know what to do with us . . . We made work for them.

A speech pathologist and clinical coordinator elaborated.

> In the long run, we make life easier for the nursing facility, because our goal is to have the patients do as much for themselves as possible. But that means that sometimes, in the beginning, things take longer. The nursing staff needs to take the extra time to allow the patients to dress or eat for themselves, rather than doing it for them . . . Also, sometimes the staff at the nursing facilities didn't understand that geriatric patients can make gains. The older nurses believed that the patients were there to die. They didn't believe that they could be helped.

Clinical Staff

The recruiting and retention of therapists was seen as InSpeech's single biggest challenge. "In any local market," noted the head of human resources, "the company can go south very quickly when the direct care providers start leaving. The word gets out. Leaving therapists complain to their friends that the supervisor is bad. the facility is bad. You might as well close down the facility until you make some changes. "

The company faced the same clinician shortage that hindered the rest of the industry. In summer 1988, InSpeech had 383 open positions to fill, for which staffing, managers estimated, would increase revenues by more than $28 million. However, InSpeech's reputation among hospitals, nursing professionals, and clinicians outside the company was very poor, according to several InSpeech clinicians. The company had become known for being unit-driven and not caring about the quality of patient care. One therapist remembered: "When I talked with other clinicians at professional meetings, they would exclaim, 'You're working with InSpeech!? How could you do that?'" Furthermore, the caseload—consisting almost entirely of geriatric patients—was more frustrating and less diverse than caseloads in other settings and contributed significantly to clinician burnout. As a board member noted, "Clinicians can easily go elsewhere. There are lots of places for these people to work."

In previous attempts to address staffing problems, senior management had upgraded InSpeech's benefits and increased its salary and bonus plans in fiscal year 1987. They also expected that the establishment of a career ladder and opportunities for further training, along with the variety and practice size that InSpeech's resources permitted, would give the company a competitive advantage in the recruitment and retention of the best professionals available. Despite these efforts, turnover among the direct care providers climbed to more than 57% in 1988, and the company had trouble hiring even 25 people a month.

Some managers believed that clinicians were leaving InSpeech because of the productivity requirements. Accustomed to a traditional hospital or school environment where their caseload was assigned, many were uncomfortable marketing their services and expanding and managing their own practices. At the same time, some senior managers felt that the productivity standard of 100 units per week was too low. They criticized clinicians for not taking more initiative to build their own practices and for treating only the most obvious disorders.

Working Conditions   Interviews with departing clinicians pointed to several concerns. Although contracts with hospitals and nursing homes sometimes included provisions for equipment, therapists often worked without proper office space or even access to a telephone. "The facilities were less than prestige settings," observed Gerry Johnson Geckle, director of corporate staffing and employee relations, and nursing home personnel sometimes took out their frustrations with InSpeech on individual therapists and clinicians. Geckle explained, "We were working with national chains that became our customers through our acquisitions, and we couldn't always deliver what we had committed. The nursing home administrators sometimes pounded on the clinicians for it."

In addition, many therapists felt lonely and isolated working in buildings owned by the nursing home, where they might see no colleagues from InSpeech. Because contracts for the three therapeutic services were negotiated separately, the other therapists working in the facility might be freelancers or from another company. A speech therapist who left InSpeech in 1988 recalled the isolation of working "one-on-one, all day, with people who can't communicate. One of the reasons I left was that I wanted to have lunch with other clinicians to discuss clinical issues. I had patients with neurological problems that I didn't know anything about . . . I wanted to be part of a medical team."

Supervision   Therapists overwhelmingly ranked the quality of supervision as their number one reason for leaving InSpeech in 1988. They reported that their supervisors—while often trying their best—were overworked, hard to get in touch with, and lacking in both clinical and communication skills.[21] Human resource managers related that some of the supervision problems were a result of the acquisitions and diversification into physical and occupational therapy, alien fields to speech therapists.

> We didn't know how to manage them . . . Every person worked for an immediate boss. That was the company. We had no culture, no common thread to bring us together, not even a common [job] name for clinicians. The physical therapists and the occupational therapists resented working for a speech company. They wanted to report to someone in their specialty.

A speech therapist described her experience:

> I wanted to have a clinical supervisor with experience in the clinical problems that I faced. But there was turnover in every position. It was a revolving door . . . Supervisors didn't know enough to coach us. Some of them had just a year or two of experience as a clinician . . . To a human services provider, a unit of time is not a very relevant measure. I would call in every week and report units to my clinical supervisor, who would yell and scream at me if I hadn't maintained my units—regardless of the circumstances, such as whether a patient had died or been discharged . . . If you

---

[21] Alan Chuang, Tamara Kushwaha, Gary Lessing, Mark Moseley, Brent Rice, Robin Sullivan, and Vicki Whiting, "The Role of the District Manager in the Retention of Therapists at NovaCare, Inc.," December 3, 1990, provided by the company.

> needed a funeral leave because someone in your family died, you would get "Who is going to do your units?"—not "I'm sorry. How can we help?" . . . In the end, I left because I was a clinician who went above and beyond, and I didn't get recognition for it.

Another clinician agreed:

> When I came to InSpeech, my previous experience had been in pediatrics . . . I was placed in a facility that hadn't had a speech therapist for three years. I was given a box of materials on the kinds of speech problems common in a geriatric environment. My supervisor said: "Make your units. Good-bye."

One area manager concurred, adding: "There was lots of emphasis on getting patients, often without any guidance as to where, how, and what patients would be appropriate. Management did not know how to translate number objectives into activity. It was simply, go do it or die."

But Arthur T. (Bud) Locilento, the new vice president of human resources, was the senior manager who faced the turnover problem most directly:

> My immediate challenge was to significantly increase our recruiting capacity. Corporate management would say, "Just go hire people." I started challenging the notion that there was an unlimited supply of people out there who were as excited about the fast-growing, high-flying business as they were. And frankly, I think the clinicians were offended by their attitude.

InSpeech Management Considers Its Options

Senior management considered what InSpeech should do to turn itself around. Some thought the problems would work themselves out as the organization "digested" its many acquisitions and integrated its payroll, accounting, and other systems. Others suggested devoting more resources to the field staff and using sales contests and other financial incentives to induce clinicians to serve more patients and remain at the company.

Bud Locilento thought that the company needed more than an "HR fix." He felt that "Turnover wasn't the problem; it was the symptom. It was not just a question of pay and benefits. It was much more fundamental and systemic." Jim Killough remained cautiously optimistic.

> I thought InSpeech could be the Johnson & Johnson of rehab care. But, I suggested that there was no point in going forward unless people agreed to change their behavior. . . . Management would have to demonstrate that it was committed to the virtues of care giving.

But others did not see what the virtues of care giving had to do with getting the stock price climbing again.

Case 2
Sears Auto Centers (A)

On Friday, June 19, 1992, CEO Edward Brennan and other top executives of Sears, Roebuck & Co. were considering how to respond to allegations that the company's auto centers had been misleading consumers and charging them for unnecessary repairs for a period of more than three years.

A week earlier, on June 11, California's Department of Consumer Affairs had filed an administrative action to revoke the auto repair licenses of all 72 auto centers in California for violations of the state's Auto Repair Act. On the day of the announcement, the company's stock price fell 62.5¢ (**Exhibit 1**). Since that time, Sears had experienced a 15% drop in its auto center revenues nationwide and a 20% drop in California. Charges by New Jersey consumer affairs officials and Florida's attorney general had followed within a few days of the California action, though New York's Department of Motor Vehicles had gone on record as saying it did not believe there was a serious problem in that state.

Company Background

Chicago-based Sears, Roebuck & Co. traced its history to 1886 when Richard W. Sears, a Minnesota railway agent, founded a company to sell watches. In 1888, Sears published its first general catalog of mail-order consumer goods. The company offered low prices and money-back guarantees to the farmers who were its principal customers. Anticipating changes the automobile would bring to rural life, Sears opened its first retail store in 1924, serving farmers who could drive to town to buy merchandise. The next year, the company brought out a line of tires under the name Allstate. In 1931, the Allstate division expanded into auto insurance and, in 1957, into life insurance.

In 1981, Sears acquired the real estate broker and developer Coldwell Banker and the stock brokerage firm of Dean Witter Reynolds. Under the Dean Witter umbrella, Sears launched the Discover credit card in 1985. In 1992, Sears was organized into four divisions: (1) the Merchandising group, which included the retail stores, appliance business, and auto centers; (2) Allstate; (3) Coldwell Banker; and (4) Dean Witter.

In 1992, the Merchandising group operated 868 department stores and 875 auto centers, nearly all of which were connected with a Sears department store. Through most of the 20th century, by virtue of its penetration into the U.S. market, the Sears Merchandising group was the undisputed global leader in retailing. Its strategy was based upon selling high-quality Sears-label brands.

But in the 1980s, the Merchandising group's lead began to narrow. Attempting to reverse declining market share, Sears in 1988 restructured its retail division and acquired the 405-store Western Auto Supply Co. The company introduced an "everyday low pricing" policy and added non-Sears name brands in

This case was prepared by Michael A. Santoro from public sources, under the supervision of Lynn 47 Sharp Paine.

EXHIBIT 1   **Daily Closing Stock Price, Sears, Roebuck & Co. Common Stock, June 1–19, 1992 (344,924,000 shares outstanding)**

June	1	43-2/8
	2	42-6/8
	3	42-4/8
	4	42-4/8
	5	42-4/8
June	8	42-1/8
	9	41-6/8
	10	42
	11	41-3/8
	12	40-4/8
June	15	40-7/8
	16	40-3/8
	17	38-4/8
	18	38-6/8
	19	38-1/8

Source: Standard & Poor's *Daily Stock Price Record: New York Stock Exchange,* April, May, June 1992, p. 434.

early 1989. Despite these measures, Sears suffered a 40% drop in earnings in 1990; earnings for the Merchandise group dropped 60%. The group slipped to the number three spot among retailers, after discounters Wal-Mart and Kmart.[1] (See **Exhibit 2** for financials.) Edward Brennan, chairman of the company since 1985, instituted numerous cost-cutting measures, including a plan to eliminate 48,000 jobs by the close of 1992.

In the effort to spur performance, Sears introduced a productivity incentive for its auto mechanics in 1991. Of Sears's 13,500 mechanics, 9,000 had earned more than 17,000 certificates of Automotive Service Excellence, a nationally recognized standard for auto technicians. Many received training at one of Sears's four training centers. The new productivity incentive was comparable to a "piece rate" paid to a factory worker. Mechanics completing a job, such as installation of shock absorbers, within a specified period were paid a fixed dollar amount in addition to their base salary. A Sears mechanic described the change:

> On January 1, 1991 the mechanics, installers, and tire changers had their hourly wages cut to what Sears termed a fixed dollar amount, or FDA per hour which varied depending on the classification. At present, the mechanic's FDA amount is $3.25 which, based on current Sears minimum production quotas, is 17% of my earnings. What this means is that for every hour of work, as defined by Sears, that I complete, I receive $3.25 plus my hourly base pay. If I do two hours worth of work in one hour I receive an additional $3.25 therefore increasing my earnings. . . . Prior to this commission program when the mechanics were paid only an hourly wage, our production quotas were $35.00 per hour with the shop flat rate being $55.00 per hour. As of January 1,

---

[1] Stanley Ziemba, "Sears Slips to No. 3 in the Retail Kingdom," *Chicago Tribune,* February 21, 1991, Business Section, p. 1.

EXHIBIT 2   **Financial Highlights (millions, except per common share data)**

	1991	1990	1989	1988	1987
Sears, Roebuck and Co.					
Revenues	$57,242	$55,972	$53,794	$50,251	$45,904
Net income	1,279	902	1,509	1,454	1,633
Common share dividends	608	686	702	758	756
Per common share:					
Net income	3.71	2.63	4.30	3.84	4.30
Dividends	2.00	2.00	2.00	2.00	2.00
Investments	46,567	38,675	33,705	29,136	25,210
Total assets	106,435	96,253	86,972	77,952	75,014
Shareholder's equity	14,188	12,824	13,622	14,055	13,541
The Merchandising Group					
Revenues (millions)					
Total Merchandising group	31,433	31,986	31,599	30,256	28,085
Merchandising (excluding credit and international)	24,757	25,093	25,002	24,252	22,894
Net Income					
Total Merchandising group	486	257	647	524	787
Merchandising (excluding credit and international)	90	37	292	240	503

Source: Sears, Roebuck and Co., 1991 Annual Report.

1991 our quotas were changed to, and judged on, an FDA rate of $3.25 per hour. Since the FDA rate of $3.25 per hour is equal to one hour of shop flat rate work, the mechanic's quota was therefore increased $20.00 per hour.[2]

In the same year, Sears began the process of harmonizing the compensation of its California service advisors with that prevailing in the rest of the country. The company's 3,500 service advisors, who were responsible for processing repair orders, consulting with mechanics on a vehicle's condition, and advising customers on potential repairs and parts, were generally compensated by a base salary plus commission. Commissions had been introduced as part of the company's effort to improve sales in 1990.[3] Service advisors also had to meet certain product-specific sales quotas, such as a certain number of alignments per shift, and dollar volume quotas based on the value of goods and services sold per hour. Until 1991, California service advisors had been paid a straight salary.[4]

[2]Letter from Chuck Fabbri, a Sears auto mechanic, Hearing Before the Subcommittee on Consumer [sic] of the Senate Committee on Commerce, Science, and Transportation, 102d Congress, 2d Sess., July 21, 1992 (S. Hrg. 102–972), p. 83. (Hereafter, "Hearing.")

[3] Gregory A. Patterson, "Sears's Brennan Accepts Blame for Auto Flap," *The Wall Street Journal,* June 23, 1992, p. B1.

[4] Richard J. Barnett, senior regulatory counsel, Sears, attachment to letter to case author, June 9, 1993.

The Merchandising group continued to flounder in the early 1990s (**Exhibit 3**). Although its 1991 revenues of $31.4 billion were more than half of the company's $57.2 billion total, the Merchandising group contributed just $486 million ($393 million from credit operations) to Sears's $1.27 billion in profits. Sears auto centers serviced 20 million vehicles in 1991, employed some 34,000 people, and accounted for 9%, or $2.8 billion, of Sears's 1991 retailing revenues. Automotive was the least profitable of Merchandising's three units, contributing some 5% of the division's profits.[5]

In February 1992, in the hopes of achieving efficiencies, Sears consolidated management responsibility for its Western Auto Supply subsidiary with its Sears auto centers. Western Auto's chairman and chief executive officer, John T. Lundegard, was put in charge of the newly consolidated nationwide automotive centers group. In addition to the 875 Sears automotive centers, the consolidated operations included 548 Western Auto Supply stores, of which 175 sold only tires. Lundegard reported to Forrest R. Hasselton, who had recently been promoted to president of Sears retail from vice president of Sears automotive.[6]

The Auto Repair Industry

Sears auto repair centers, the largest company-owned automotive service organization in the United States, focused on what were known as "undercar services"—mainly brake repair and replacing mufflers, shock absorbers, and struts. The undercar business absorbed about $26 billion of the $100 billion spent annually on auto parts and services by owners of the 187 million registered vehicles in the United States.[7] The auto repair industry consisted of four types of shops: dealerships, specialty shops, independents, and mass marketers like Sears.

Relative to services, such as engine tune-ups and transmission overhauls, that might take longer to perform—and that could be difficult to estimate—undercar services had volume profit potential because they could be performed reliably on a routine basis. Technicians, also known as mechanics, could deliver these services with little training and low levels of service equipment. Even so, some repair shop owners found it increasingly difficult to find good, trained technicians knowledgeable about increasingly complex auto systems.[8] A few mechanics were beginning to consider licensing schemes to raise competency levels and improve the industry's reputation.[9]

During the late 1980s and early 1990s, the auto repair industry was generally in a slump. During this period, competition in the undercar business intensified. Car dealerships were increasingly looking to the repair market for profits.

---

[5] Richard Ringer, "A President for Sears Automotive," *The New York Times*, April 13, 1993, p. D5.

[6] "Sears Restructures Its Automotive Subsidiary," *Discount Store News*, February 17, 1992, vol. 31, no. 4, p. 4.

[7] Adam Bryan, "All About Dealer Repairs," *The New York Times*, January 26, 1992, Section 3, p. 10.

[8] Edward L. Kaufman, "Competition Hotter Among Service Retailers for Undercar Business," *Automotive Marketing*, June 1991, vol. 20, no. 6, p. 15.

[9] John R. White, "A Proposal to License Mechanics," *The Boston Globe*, November 30, 1991, p. 53.

EXHIBIT 3

Sears Merchandising Quarterly Net Income (Excluding Credit Operations) ($ Millions)

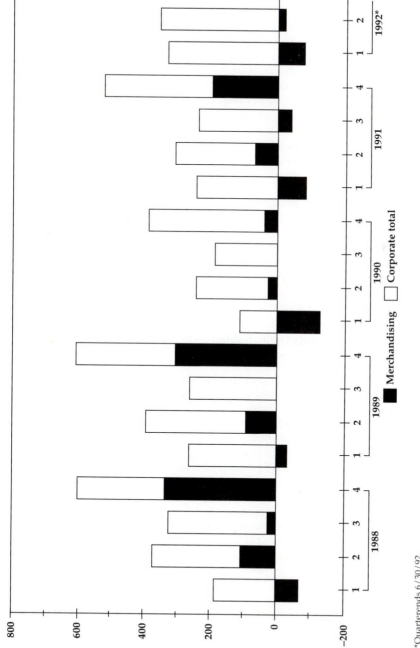

*Quarterends 6/30/92.

Source: Paine Webber Report (9/11/92).

Among dealers, profits from car repairs grew from 11% to 86% of total profits between 1983 and 1990. The brake repair market became especially competitive as the dealers and muffler specialists turned to brake repairs to cope with the lengthening useful life of tires and exhaust systems. During this time, the market for brake parts increased about 3% to 4% a year. Profit margins among those offering brake jobs were under increasing pressures.[10]

In 1991, the "magic number" for a brake job was $59.95 per axle. For that price, repair shops would change pads, inspect and fill the hydraulic system, resurface rotors or drums, and inspect calipers. Some in the industry questioned whether brake jobs could be conscientiously provided at this price. One car repair shop owner declared: "$59.95 is just a low-ball price. When the customer comes in, the shop tries to step him up to a higher-priced job. In fact, the job may wind up costing much more because the crew is told to find work: replace calipers, whether worn or not, sell a brake job for the second axle, and so on." Paul Corkins, vice president of marketing for Allied Signal Inc.'s Brake Division, commented: "A realistic price on a two-axle brake job is $175–$200. A price of $59.95 for a front-axle job is realistic if only the pads have to be replaced, and that's rare."[11]

Historically, a substantial percentage of brake jobs performed by Sears were the basic one-axle brake job. Commonly referred to as a "hang and turn" job, Sears's basic brake service included replacing pads, turning the rotors or drums, and repacking wheel bearings. Also, calipers and other brake parts were inspected at the time of service. Sears took special care in its advertising to put consumers on notice that brake jobs could sometimes be more complex and expensive than one might anticipate. This advice was reflected in the disclosure appearing in its advertisements (**Exhibit 4**).[12]

The California Investigation

The California Department of Consumer Affairs (DCA) action against the Sears auto centers resulted from a year-long investigation of the Sears shops by the DCA's Bureau of Automotive Repair (BAR). The investigation was part of a broader campaign against fraudulent repair shops, which, according to BAR, cost California motorists $2.2 billion each year. The BAR also pointed to a recent consumer survey: more than half of the respondents believed that repair shops were dishonest and did unnecessary repairs. Fraud-related complaints lodged with the BAR against the 40,000 registered repair dealers in California had increased 14% each year since 1985.[13] The BAR sought to target high-volume shops that had been the subject of complaints and to save California's 20 million motorists some $200 million a year in repair costs.

Citing a pattern of complaints against Sears, the BAR decided to investigate. According to a Sears official, however, the number of complaints against the

---

[10] Id.

[11] Id.

[12] Material in this paragraph was provided by Richard J. Barnett, senior regulatory counsel, Sears, attachment to letter to case author, June 9, 1993.

[13] Department of Consumer Affairs/Bureau of Automotive Repair, Consumer Protection Initiative Fact Sheet, 1992.

EXHIBIT 4

The Hook—Sample Sears and Roebuck Print Advertisement

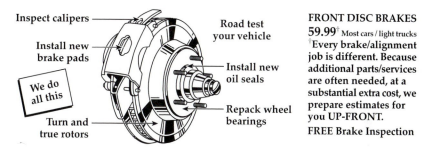

Source: California Department of Consumer Affairs, Bureau of Automotive Repair.

company had increased only from 137 per year to 223 per year during the three-year period beginning in 1989, a small fraction of the 18,000 complaints received annually.[14]

Between December 1990 and December 1991, BAR conducted 38 undercover "runs" at Sears shops throughout California (**Exhibit 5**). According to the BAR, Sears employees recommended and performed unnecessary service or repairs in 34 of these runs. The overcharges averaged $223 and, in certain instances, amounted to as much as $550. According to the BAR, some cars left Sears in worse condition than when they had entered, and one left without any brakes[15] (**Exhibit 6**).

The BAR investigation focused on braking system repairs, a widely advertised service offered by the centers. Print ads offered a $48 (or, in some instances, $58) brake job (**Exhibit 4**). According to the BAR, when undercover operators brought vehicles requiring a simple brake job, they were often told that calipers, shock absorbers, coil springs, idler arms, or master cylinders needed to be repaired or replaced, even though those parts were in good working order, usually with less than 20 miles of use. Jim Schoning, chief of the BAR, alleged that some Sears employees resorted to scare tactics to sell repairs. He commented that "one of our undercover operators was told that the front calipers on his car were so badly frozen that the car would fishtail if the brakes were applied quickly."[16]

To conduct the investigation, the BAR used vehicles needing minor brake repairs. Before taking a vehicle to Sears for repair, BAR employees disassembled the brakes and suspension and inspected, marked, and photographed the parts. A transport then moved the automobiles to a location near the shop, where they were dropped off to be driven by an undercover operator to the shop being investigated. Most shops displayed the Sears auto center slogan, "We Install Confidence." After arriving at Sears, the undercover investigator requested a brake inspection. In 34 of 38 instances, the investigator was told that additional, more

---

[14] Richard J. Barnett, senior regulatory counsel, Sears, attachment to letter to case author, June 9, 1993.

[15] State of California, Department of Consumer Affairs, News Release, June 11, 1992.

[16] Id.

Exhibit 5

Cities where BAR conducted undercover operations at Sears, Roebuck

Source: California Department of Consumer Affairs, Bureau of Automotive Repair.

expensive repairs were necessary. The undercover investigator authorized the repair and paid the amount due, after which the vehicle was transported back to a BAR facility for examination.[17]

    The BAR investigation and results recalled a similar study done 50 years earlier by the *Reader's Digest*. In 1941, investigators for the *Digest* found that 75% of the garages asked to make repairs on cars with a defect created for the experiment misrepresented the defect and the work that was done. For a defect that should have cost 25¢ to repair, the average charge was $4, and some charged as

---

[17] Id.

Exhibit 6　Sears, Roebuck Case Summary—Initial Investigation and Random Runs

Location	Date of Run(s)	Estimated Oversell	Items Oversold
Los Angeles Metropolitan Area			
Brea (100 Brea Mall)	7-10-91	$350	front brake overhaul including calipers, struts and shocks
Canoga Park (6433 Falbrook Ave.)	6-12-91	130	front brake pads, turned rotors, rebuilt calipers
Covina (1414 N. Azusa Ave.)	3-30-91	136	adjust rear brakes, calipers
	4-07-91	307	front brakes, idler arms
	8-08-91	305	front brakes, rotors, calipers, shocks, idler arm
Hemet (25201 San Jacinto St.)	8-28-91	126	calipers
L.A. (2711 E. Olympic Blvd.)	7-11-91	170	rear springs, alignment, front calipers
Northridge (100 Northridge Fashion Ctr.)	7-10-91	480	coil springs, shocks, new calipers
City of Industry (100 Puente Hills Mall)	6-13-91	290	front/rear coil springs, repaired calipers
San Bernardino (100 Inland Center)	4-09-91	180	coil springs, calipers
	7-18-91	535	coil springs, calipers, four shocks
Santa Monica (302 Colorado Ave.)	8-29-91	230	caliper repairs, one rotor, four shocks
Fresno			
Fresno (3636 N. Blackstone Ave.)	7-08-91	328	head lamps charged for/not installed, front brakes, idler arms, new tires
Chico			
Chico (1982 East 20th St.)	10-30-91	275	calipers, master cylinder, front brake service
Redding			
Redding (1403 Hilltop Dr.)	7-25-91	229	replaced calipers, master cylinder, alignment
Visalia			
Visalia (3501 S. Mooney Blvd.)	8-08-91	106	calipers
San Francisco Bay Area			
Antioch (2600 County E. Mall)	3-13-91	158	oversold front pads, turned rotors
	4-04-91	126	idler arm
	6-19-91	275	shocks, struts
Concord (1001 Willow Pass Rd.)	1-31-91	100	front-wheel bearings, front calipers
	2-06-91	585	front brake pads, front and rear springs, control arm bushings
	2-13-91	185	master cylinder, charged for cylinder kits not installed
Fairfield (1549 Gateway Dr.)	7-31-91	74	calipers
Hayward (660 W. Weston Ave.)	4-23-91	110	calipers
	6-13-91	306	front brakes, coil springs, radiator hoses, adjust steering box, tires, calipers
Mountain View (455 San Antonio Rd.)	4-23-91	265	calipers, rear springs
San Jose (2180 Tully Rd.)	8-22-91	430	calipers, shocks, coil springs
San Rafael (9000 Northgate)	6-13-91	340	calipers, wheel cylinders, rotors, wheel bearings
Santa Rosa (100 Santa Rosa Mall)	6-17-91	314	2 idler arms, 4 shocks

much as $25.[18] Auto repair fraud had long been a main source of consumer complaints in many jurisdictions.[19]

---

[18] Roger W. Riis and John Patric, *The Repairman Will Get You If You Don't Look Out* (Garden City, NY: Doubleday, 1942).
[19] Hearing.

EXHIBIT 6   **Continued**

Location	Date of Run(s)	Estimated Oversell	Items Oversold
Monterey County Area			
Salinas (1100 Northridge Mall)	8-07-91	$115	repaired left caliper, charged for right caliper and did not do, front seals, front brake pads
Sacramento			
Arden (1601 Arden Way)	4-23-91	376	calipers, rear drums, linings
Citrus Heights (5900 Sunrise Mall)	12-04-90	138	master cylinder, rear wheel cylinder
	12-19-90	85	rear brake repair
	2-02-91	187	calipers, spark plugs, bleeding of rear brakes

Source: California Department of Consumer Affairs, Bureau of Automotive Repair.

Summary of Investigations and Total Amounts Oversold

	Date(s) of Investigation	Total Oversold
Bay Area	March 1991–August 1991	$3,268
Chico	October 1991	275
Fresno	July 1991	328
Los Angeles	July 1991–August 1991	3,229
Redding	July 1991	229
Sacramento	December 1990–January 1992	786
Visalia	August 1992	106
Total amount oversold to BAR statewide:		$8,221

Source: California Department of Consumer Affairs, Bureau of Automotive Repair.

In December 1991, before publicizing the results of its investigation, California Senior Assistant Attorney General Herschel T. Elkins wrote a letter that was hand-delivered to Sears CEO Brennan. Accompanying the letter were copies of the BAR investigation. Elkins informed Brennan that the investigation revealed "substantial problems" at Sears auto centers, which "went deep" into the management structure.[20] The BAR and the attorney general's office discussed the results of the investigation with the Sears national service manager, national sales manager, senior counsel, and auto training manager.

Sears Challenges the Investigation[21]

Immediately after receiving the letter, Sears asked to meet with state officials in California and requested information about the investigation. The state provided

---

[20] Telephone interview with California Senior Assistant Attorney General Herschel T. Elkins, January 12, 1993.

[21] Material in this section provided by Richard J. Barnett, senior regulatory counsel, Sears, attachment to letter to case author, June 9, 1993.

two or three "examples" of runs conducted during its investigation. When the parties met later in December, the state was represented by the BAR, the district attorney from the County of Contra Costa, and the attorney general. The Contra Costa district attorney took the lead role at that time and throughout the negotiation period. At the meeting, Sears presented evidence that suggested there were significant problems with the way the BAR had prepared its vehicles for the runs and that these problems could have led mechanics to make good faith misdiagnoses. The Contra Costa district attorney and the attorney general's office suggested that the parties review their respective information. Sears asked for one month to conduct an internal investigation and report its findings. The request was granted.

Sears had several concerns about the BAR's investigatory methods. First, BAR took the position that no system or part should be repaired or replaced unless it had failed. Thus, it considered recommendations based on preventive maintenance inappropriate. Second, most of the vehicles the agency used were high-mileage, older models (1978–1986) with significant repair problems. BAR first repaired the vehicles by replacing failed parts with new parts, and then disguising the deed by "aging" the new parts so that they appeared to be original to the vehicle. Symptoms of the original repair problem(s) were, however, left on the vehicles. For example, BAR used a 1984 Chevrolet station wagon equipped with a trailer hitch on a number of runs. The vehicle exhibited symptoms of weak or inadequate rear springs, including: (a) undercarriage damage to the rear bumpers and exhaust system; and (b) clear evidence that the strike-out bumpers (rubber bumpers that protect the rear axle from damaging itself or the vehicle's frame when its springs are weak or inadequate) were hitting the vehicle's frame. Examples like these prompted Sears service advisors to recommend repairs based on the symptoms appearing on the vehicles.

Moreover, virtually all of BAR's runs involved brake jobs and raised the controversial question of whether brake calipers should be reconditioned at the time brake pads were replaced, especially if the pads showed highly significant wear, as did those in BAR-prepared vehicles. Some industry members, including Sears, thought that caliper reconditioning or replacement should be completed as a matter of course when brake pads were replaced in order to bring the entire system up to original standard. Others, including BAR, believed that only brake parts that had failed should be replaced.

BAR regulations recognized accepted trade standards as determinative of appropriate conduct under the law. Sears believed the caliper reconditioning issue should have been treated as a controversy over what constitutes "accepted trade standards," rather than as the basis for allegations of fraudulent overselling. During the negotiations, Sears took this position and suggested that BAR undertake an administrative rule-making to determine what should be classified as the accepted trade standard in this area. BAR had previously adopted rules dealing with ball joints in this manner.

A month after discussing its findings with Sears managers, BAR investigated 10 additional shops, where investigators found that Sears was no longer overselling springs, shocks, and front-end parts, but was continuing to oversell calipers[22](**Exhibit 7**).

---

[22] Gregory A. Patterson, "Sears Gets a Harsh Lesson from States in Handling of Auto-Repair Inquiries," *The Wall Street Journal,* October 2, 1992, p. B4A.

EXHIBIT 7   Sears, Roebuck Case Summary—Follow-up Runs

Location	Date of Run(s)	Estimated Oversell	Items Oversold
Costa Mesa (3333 Bristol St.)	1-18-92	$150	calipers replaced, rear brake service unnecessary
El Cajon (575 Fletcher Pkwy., #1)	2-05-92	129	calipers replaced
Glendale (236 N. Central Ave.)	1-17-92	130	calipers replaced, rear brake adjustment not needed
Hayward (660 W. Winston Ave.)	1-30-92	0	no unnecessary repairs
Oakland (2633 Telegraph Ave.)	2-03-92	22	lube charged for not provided, front rotors turned out of specification
Palmdale (1345 W. Ave.)	2-05-92	160	calipers, rear brake clean/adjust, rear brake bleed charged/not done
Sacramento (1601 Arden Way)	1-02-92	50	caliper seals and dustboots replaced unnecessarily
Salinas (110 Northridge Mall)	2-06-92	135	calipers replaced
San Luis Obispo (273 Madonna Rd.)	2-04-92	170	four shock absorbers, caliper seals and dustboots replaced unnecessarily
Visalia (3501 S. Mooney)	1-21-92	0	no repairs performed

Source: California Department of Consumer Affairs, Bureau of Automotive Repair.

Negotiations

The parties spent several months meeting to see if a reasonable resolution to the controversy could be worked out. Again, the Contra Costa district attorney and the attorney general took the lead. Sears entrusted the handling of its negotiations to a San Francisco law firm known for its trial work.[23] After many meetings during several months of difficult negotiating, the parties agreed on a consent decree dealing with how business would be conducted. The decree was acceptable to all, including the Contra Costa district attorney, the California attorney general, BAR, and Sears. Negotiations then turned to reaching a financial settlement, but the parties could not reach agreement. BAR left the negotiating table just after a newspaper article entitled "Consumer Affairs Is Target of Budget Ax" appeared in the June 7 edition of the *Los Angeles Times*.[24]

Legal Actions

The administrative action filed by the DCA on June 11 sought to revoke the license of all 72 Sears auto centers in California for violating the state's Auto Repair Act. The complaint charged Sears with making false or misleading statements, fraud, false advertising, failure to state clearly parts and labor charges on invoices, and willful departure from accepted trade standards (**Exhibit 8**).

The case was due to be heard by an administrative law judge in Sacramento. At the hearing, both sides could call witnesses and provide evidence. Although the judge had the power to recommend a permanent or temporary revocation of Sears's auto repair licenses or to dismiss the charges, the DCA had the authority to make the final decision. If the DCA ruled against Sears, the company could file an appeal with the California Superior Court.

[23] Patterson, "Sears Gets Harsh Lesson."

[24] Unless otherwise indicated, material in this paragraph is from Richard J. Barnett, senior regulatory counsel, Sears, attachment to letter to case author, June 9, 1993.

EXHIBIT 8 Sears Roebuck Case—Business and Professions Codes Relating to Accusations

Business and Professions Codes	*Related Accusation Examples*
9884.7(1)(a) **False or misleading statements**	• Took vehicle with worn tires. No cord showing. Requested alignment advertised for $24.99 and a lube and oil change. Given estimate for $70. Told operator tires worn down to cords, required replacement. False statement—tires not worn to cord, in fact had usable tread left. (Citrus Heights)
	• Operator asked for brake inspection. Respondent was advised that brakes were not releasing, which would cause the vehicle to fishtail. Advised the operator the vehicle needed front and rear brakes, that the rear drums were damaged and need replacement. Invoiced new calipers when in fact they were remanufactured. (Arden)
	• Went to purchase four new tires. Told that she needed shocks and struts. Both were "blown out and leaking." Estimate $419.95. Second dealer said no sign of leakage, returned and discussed with manager who, with mechanic, reinspected and said nothing wrong. (Stockton)
	• Vehicle taken to shop with worn pads. Advised vehicle needed front brakes, front struts, and rear shocks. Only brake pads needed repair. (Antioch)
	• Recommended front brakes, right idler arms, and front and rear shocks. (Santa Rosa)
	• In addition to front brakes, coil springs, and alignment, operator was told two new tires were needed because "they pull to the right or left." (Mountain View)
	• New springs because riding low and shocks because these parts are rusty. (San Bernardino)
	• Needed alignment "the front end that controls steering keeps pulling to the right." "The rear of the car is low and prevents alignment being properly set." Springs $79.99 a pair and $30 for labor. (Los Angeles)
	• Needed shocks because they were old, cracked, leaking and the rubber was falling out. Had to turn rotors by California law. (Northridge)
9884.7(1)(d) **Fraud**	• Charged $34.95 for time saver oil change agreement without her knowledge or consent. Charged $54.99 for Road Handler. (Citrus Heights)
	• Sold alignment, new cargo springs, and complete front brake job at a cost of $333, when all parts except brake pads were in good condition and vehicle did not need alignment. (Los Angeles)
	• Sold repair and replacement of front brakes, calipers, rotors turned, shock absorbers and idle arm, and an alignment, when all but worn brake pads were in good condition and did not require repair, adjustment or replacement. (Covina)
	• Sold replacement idler arms and an alignment, when all parts except for brake pads and rotors were in good condition. Charged $22.50 to unnecessarily "clean and adjust rear brakes" without her consent. Charged $60 for a front brake kit, including brake caliper hardware—the only hardware installed were two mounting springs. (Covina)
9884.8 **Failure to clearly state parts and labor on invoice**	• Incidence widespread.

Source: California Department of Consumer Affairs, Bureau of Automotive Repair.

Exhibit 8   Continued

Business and Professions Codes	*Related Accusation Examples*
9884.10 **Failure to return parts**	• Failed to return old parts as requested. When asked, mechanic said they could not find them and asked what he could do to make it right. (Santa Rosa)

California Code of Regulations	*Related Accusation Examples*
3372.1 **False advertising**	• Advertised that a customer could "save 10%–15%" on the purchase of tires. Advised operator that the Road Handler Response tires she requested were on sale for $54.99 each, but the tire was not in stock and that respondent would provide an upgrade for the same price, but charged $67.99 for each upgraded tire. (Citrus Heights)

Shortly after the filing of the revocation proceedings by the DCA, the California attorney general's office and the district attorney for the County of Contra Costa announced that they, too, were considering legal action. Unlike the DCA action, which could result only in a revocation of Sears's licenses, a civil lawsuit by the attorney general could lead to fines and other monetary damages against Sears.

Employee Perspectives

The BAR attributed the overselling at Sears auto repair centers to the employee compensation and monitoring systems. Current and former Sears employees told BAR investigators that they were instructed to sell a certain number of alignments, springs, and brake jobs during every eight-hour work shift. They were also pressured to sell a specified number of shock absorbers or struts per hour. At one store, employees were told to sell five front-end alignments, eight sets of springs, eight sets of shock absorbers, and two tires each day. These employees also told BAR that if they did not meet these goals, they often were cut back in their work hours or transferred to another Sears department.[25]

One mechanic, Jerry C. Waddy, who had worked in Sears's San Bruno, California, store, filed suit against Sears, claiming that he was fired for failing to meet his quota of 16 oil changes a day. Waddy, who sought $1 million from Sears in a wrongful discharge suit, claimed that his manager even advised him in the last week to cheat in order to save his job. Waddy reported that before being fired, "we talked about the pressure, pressure, pressure to get the dollars."[26] Another mechanic, who asked to remain anonymous, commented: "I'm torn between moral integrity, losing my job, and trying to figure out how to work all this out."[27] A service advisor at a Sears in Orange County said he had requested a

---

[25] State of California, Department of Consumer Affairs, News Release, June 11, 1992.
[26] Julia Flynn, Christina Del Valle, and Russell Mitchell, "Did Sears Take Other Customers for a Ride?" *Business Week*, August 3, 1992, p. 25.
[27] T. Christian Miller, "Sears Admits 'Mistakes' at Auto Service Centers," *The San Francisco Chronicle*, June 23, 1992, p. A1.

transfer to another job because he "couldn't stomach the pressure to sell. It wasn't right. You sold things to people to meet your quota for that day, but you didn't feel right about doing it."[28]

Regulators' Perspectives

Some government investigators and law enforcement officials regarded Sears's compensation policy as a willful, systemic fraud upon consumers. "There was a deliberate decision by Sears management to set up a structure that made it totally inevitable that the consumer would be oversold," stated Roy Liebmen, a California deputy attorney general.[29] DCA director Jim Conran accused Sears of a "systematic effort to bilk and rip off consumers on auto repair sales and parts."[30] Compensation specialists noted that it was fairly common for automotive service employees to receive commissions, though it was less usual for service employees to have specific sales quotas. Nevertheless, similar quotas were reportedly used at Firestone, a Sears competitor.[31]

The auto centers were not the only Sears units to have experience with quotas. Although the Allstate insurance subsidiary had eliminated sales quotas several years earlier, one former employee who claimed he was fired for not meeting a $600 monthly quota for life insurance premiums, filed a complaint with Maryland regulators charging that his manager had pressured him to ignore underwriting guidelines to close a sale.[32]

State regulators were concerned also about the sale of maintenance agreements on expensive appliances. Such agreements generated up to 50% of a store's annual earnings and could cost more than 35% of an appliance's price. In March 1992, Sears changed its pay structure for its appliance salespeople, cutting base salaries and emphasizing commissions. One 30-year Sears salesman, who retired in Sacramento in 1992, reported that he had received a dozen letters in two years from his manager stating that he would be fired if he did not sell more maintenance agreements. The salesman declared, "An unhappy salesman who figures he's been shafted is going to shaft someone else." A saleswoman in Sears's Vernon Hills, Illinois, store commented that "the pressure is much greater today than it used to be."[33]

California's Department of Consumer Affairs

The Sears investigation helped to save the DCA from being closed because of the state's budget crisis. At a press conference that achieved wide coverage in June 1992, DCA Director Jim Conran announced the results of its 18-month under-

---

[28] Denise Gellene, "New State Probe of Sears Could Lead to Suit," *Los Angeles Times,* June 12, 1992, Part D, p. 1.

[29] *Business Week,* op. cit., August 3, 1992.

[30] Michael Miller, "California Seeks to Shut Down Sears Auto Shops," Reuters, Los Angeles, June 11, 1992.

[31] Letter from Mark Lewis, Hearing, pp. 86–87.

[32] *Business Week,* op. cit., August 3, 1992.

[33] Id.

cover investigation. The announcement came just weeks after legislators had targeted the department for elimination as part of an effort to close an $11 billion shortfall in the state budget.[34]

The investigation was estimated to have cost between $300,000 and $500,000, including the purchase of 18 late-model cars used in the probe.[35] Shortly after the press conference, a *Los Angeles Times* editorial, citing the Sears investigation, noted that closing the department "would produce a direct savings of only about $2 million since most of the agency's budget comes from fees collected from the dozens of professions and trades it regulates. But the cost to Californians of this move—in dollars and consumer confidence—could be unacceptably high."[36]

Less than a week after the investigation was made public, the California legislators who sought to eliminate the DCA announced that they had dropped their proposal.[37]

Sears Responds

In the first two days after the administrative action was filed, the responses of Sears management were varied. One unidentified spokesman denied the allegations and said that Sears would defend itself vigorously against them. He stated: "Our policy, in California and nationwide, has always been to put the safety of our customers first when recommending repairs to their vehicles." Another spokesman, Greg Rossiter, called the investigation "seriously flawed." He continued: "Our technicians are not paid at all in any way related to what is sold."[38]

Dirk Schenkkin, a San Francisco lawyer representing Sears, said: "I think it's disgraceful that [the state] is trying to portray this as a fraud. . . . There may have been some honest mistakes. But there was no fraud." The lawyer alleged that the BAR used older cars with signs of wear that tricked Sears's employees into thinking certain repairs were necessary. He denied that employees were driven to sell by quotas, conceding only that the company had established "modest" and "easy-to-attain" goals. He said that employees who were not meeting the goals were probably not providing enough "preventive maintenance" on the cars.[39]

---

[34] Denise Gellene, "State Spares Consumer Department," *The Los Angeles Times*, June 17, 1992, Part D, p. 1.

[35] Denise Gellene, "State to Seek to Lift Auto Repair License of Sears," *The Los Angeles Times*, June 11, 1992, Part A, p. 1.

[36] Editorial, "A Case of Consumer Confidence; Sears Investigation, While Unresolved, Proves the Value of a State Agency," *The Los Angeles Times*, June 13, 1992, Part B, p. 7.

[37] Denise Gellene, "State Spares Consumer Department," *The Los Angeles Times*, op. cit., June 17, 1992, Part D, p. 1.

[38] T. Christian Miller, "Nine Bay Area Sears' Included in Overcharging Probe," *The San Francisco Chronicle*, June 12, 1992, p. A23.

[39] Denise Gellene, "New State Probe of Sears Could Lead to Suit," *The Los Angeles Times*, June 12, 1992, Part D, p. 1.

Forrest R. "Woody" Hasselton, Sears's president of retail, commented that "for 105 years Sears has promised Americans "Satisfaction Guaranteed" when it comes to products and services. While we disagree with the allegations made about us in California, we will correct any mistakes that may have been made and will work in the coming months to resolve these issues. We immediately want to reassure our customers that this commitment to satisfaction continues unabated."[40]

DCA director Conran did not back down from his allegations in the face of Sears's denials: "They can say what they want. You can see the places where they screwed the public."[41]

On June 16, Sears published in major California newspapers an "open letter" from CEO Brennan. Brennan wrote: "With over two million automotive customers serviced last year in California alone, mistakes may have occurred. However, Sears wants you to know that we would never intentionally violate the trust consumers have shown in our company for 105 years." Brennan questioned the California investigation because it challenged the industry practice of replacing worn parts before they fail. He continued, "You rely on us to recommend preventive maintenance measures to help insure your safety, and to avoid more costly future repairs. This includes recommending replacement of worn parts, when appropriate, before they fail. This accepted industry practice is being challenged by the Bureau." Brennan also accused the Department of Consumer Affairs of trying to save itself from being eliminated by its high-profile attack upon Sears.[42]

The Probe Spreads to Other States

On June 15, the day before Brennan's open letter appeared in California newspapers, the New Jersey Division of Consumer Affairs charged Sears with systematically giving motorists inflated estimates for unnecessary repairs. The New Jersey investigation, which had been in progress for four months, covered Sears and non-Sears shops. Undercover investigators twice brought a late-model car with a disconnected alternator wire to 38 auto repair shops. Instead of simply reconnecting the wire, 23 shops at least once either incorrectly diagnosed the problem or recommended unnecessary repairs. Eleven shops did so both times. And all six Sears shops misdiagnosed the problem both times and gave some of the most expensive prescriptions, such as replacing the battery and the alternator at a cost of up to $406.[43]

---

[40] "State Attorney General Probing Sears Auto Centers," UPI, Los Angeles, June 12, 1992.

[41] Id.

[42] "Sears Hits Back at California Probe," UPI, Los Angeles, June 16, 1992.

[43] "Sears Charges More for Auto Work, New Jersey Consumer Watchdog Says," UPI, Newark, New Jersey, June 16, 1992.

A Sears spokesman said that the firm had requested further information about the allegations. He stated: "The charges made are of extreme concern to us. We are beginning an internal review as to what happened in each case and will work closely with New Jersey officials to resolve this situation as quickly as possible."[44]

A Sears official later elaborated on the New Jersey investigation. He explained that service advisors' preliminary assessment—alternator failure—resulted from the use of computerized machines for evaluating the vehicles' electrical systems. The computerized diagnostic systems, used by Sears as well as other large auto repair facilities, correctly reported that no electrical current was passing through the alternator. However, the machines could not detect the reason for the failure: the detachment by New Jersey officials of the incoming alternator lead, a wire located at the rear of the alternator and not readily visible. Because New Jersey officials refused to authorize work on vehicles brought in for repair, Sears mechanics had no opportunity to discover the detached leads and reconnect them. Citing General Motors, the Sears official noted that the likelihood of such a detachment was less than one-half of 1%. He also noted that, contrary to the state's allegations, Sears had in fact detected and reconnected the lead in one instance.[45]

On Thursday, June 18, two days after the New Jersey probe was announced, the Florida attorney general's office announced that it would be launching an investigation into Sears auto centers because of the large number of complaints. However, in New York, the Department of Motor Vehicles announced that it had found overcharging in only one of eight Sears shops investigated and that the department did not believe that there was a serious problem in New York.[46]

The Investigation and Publicity Continue
In the week following the filing of the administrative action, the California Consumer Affairs Department received more than 800 complaints about Sears auto centers.[47] Approximately two dozen Sears employees not involved in the original investigation came forward and provided statements to the department. Said one: "Employees at Sears auto centers deserve better treatment and the customers deserve better treatment than they've been getting." That same employee, a store manager, reported that the district manager ordered that customers be charged $5.99 for inspections of electrical systems during a battery installation,

---

[44] Thomas Witom, "Sears Promises Quick Action on Auto Repair Flap," Reuters, Chicago, June 16, 1992.
[45] Richard J. Barnett, senior regulatory counsel, Sears, attachment to letter to case author, June 9, 1993.
[46] Denise Gellene and George White, "Florida Probes Sears' Car Repair Centers," *The Los Angeles Times*, June 19, 1992, Part D, p. 2.
[47] Id.

regardless of whether such an inspection was requested.[48] The California attorney general was reviewing the new charges coming forward and considering filing a separate civil lawsuit against Sears.

Publicity about the allegations spread throughout the nation. One analyst commented: "Sears is almost built on its guarantee of satisfaction. Anything that undermines that trust is very serious."[49] David Letterman, the late-night television talk show host, turned Sears's problem into a national television joke with a list of "Top 10 repair jobs recommended by the Sears Automotive Department." Number 10 was "grease the ashtrays"; Number 1, "add a redwood deck."[50]

The Decision

As Brennan met with other Sears executives on June 19, he considered what the company's next step would be.

---

[48] Id.

[49] Denise Gellene, "New State Probe of Sears Could Lead to Suit," *The Los Angeles Times*, June 12, 1992, Part D, p. 1.

[50] *Newsday*, June 28, 1992, op. cit.

CASE 3
HUTTON BRANCH MANAGER (A)

In the early spring of 1982, Mark Pedersen, a Washington, D.C., branch manager for retail broker E. F. Hutton & Company, received word that one of his branch's customers, the trust department of First American Bank, was taking its securities business elsewhere. According to officials of First American, which was Hutton's D.C.-area bank as well as a Hutton customer, Hutton's practice of overdrafting its accounts had resulted in large losses for the bank. Pedersen also learned that other area banks were holding Hutton's checks, having been alerted by First American about these practices.

Pedersen was at first surprised since Hutton had always enjoyed a very good business relationship with First American, but he quickly realized that much of the problem lay with Hutton's Alexandria branch, also in the D.C. area. The Alexandria branch, managed by Rod Howe, had established an account at First American in June of 1981. The account carried constant debit balances throughout the year, including debits exceeding $2 million in each of the last four months of 1981, compared to average balances of $25,000 in the accounts of the three other local Hutton branches. Although the problem did not relate directly to Pedersen's office, First American regarded Hutton's D.C.-area branches as a single entity and Pedersen as the point person for Hutton. Pedersen had to figure out what to do about the First American situation.

Company Background

E. F. Hutton originated in 1904 as a partnership between Edward Hutton and bond dealer George Ellis, after Hutton had the idea of establishing a New York Stock Exchange (NYSE) firm capable of serving investors both in New York and California. Early on, through an arrangement with Western Union, Hutton became the first company with a private transcontinental telephone wire, which allowed it to execute customer orders in minutes, as opposed to an hour or more for other brokers. The company quickly became very successful, building a "network of retail brokerage offices that would become the envy of Wall Street."[1]

In 1972, when Hutton went public, it ranked eighth in commissions among the NYSE's 593 members, fifth in the number of branch offices, sixth in registered representatives, and eighth in gross income. Three years later, through an aggressive strategy of internal growth and outside acquisitions, the company had become the number two retail firm, "sprinting past a string of top contenders into a comfortable niche right behind Merrill Lynch, the biggest U.S. broker of them

---

[1] Mark Stevens, *Sudden Death: The Rise and Fall of E. F. Hutton* (New York: New American Library, 1989), p. 18.

This case was prepared by Jane Palley Katz from public sources, under the supervision of Lynn Sharp Paine. Research Associates Bronwyn Halliday and Charles A. Nichols, III, also contributed. Copyright © 1995 by the President and Fellows of Harvard College. Harvard Business School case 396–044.

all."[2] In 1980, Hutton achieved annual revenues of $1.1 billion, second to Merrill Lynch at $3 billion, and a net return on equity of 38.2%, trailing only Shearson Loeb Rhoades. Its 1980 annual report trumpeted 77 years of uninterrupted profit "unmatched in the securities industry."[3] See **Exhibit 1** for a selected summary of Hutton's financial results from 1977 through 1982.

As in its early days, Hutton's biggest strength continued to be its retail outlets and distribution network. By 1981, the company had 4,532 account executives working in 318 sales offices.[4] Sales of stocks, bonds, commodities, and other products through its retail network remained Hutton's single largest revenue source. Long known for catering to wealthy individuals, Hutton was able to hold on to their business by creating Wall Street's first tax shelter department and a personal financial planning service. At the same time, it was also making itself a broker for the masses. The company aired a successful string of memorable television commercials with the slogan "When E. F. Hutton talks, people listen."

Most industry observers noted that Hutton lagged behind other Wall Street firms in areas such as basic research, institutional brokerage, corporate finance, and trading and positioning.[5] While remaining more closely tied to traditional brokerage than Merrill Lynch, Hutton did make efforts to diversify. An aggressive attempt to increase its presence in investment banking for both corporate and municipal clients boosted its share of the total underwriting market from 4.7% in 1977 to 10.2% in 1981; in 1980, it either managed or co-managed almost 10% of all corporate finance offerings.[6] In 1973, Hutton began selling life insurance, and, in 1981, the parent company, E. F. Hutton Group Inc., had an insurance subsidiary, Hutton Life Insurance.[7]

The Financial Services Industry

Market pressures in the financial services industry in the early 1980s were strong and intensifying. Since the 1960s Wall Street had been undergoing a long-term consolidation, with a greater concentration of securities revenues among the top firms as well as mergers and consolidations among many of the top Wall Street firms and other financial services providers. Increasingly sophisticated telecommunications technology allowed information and transactions to be processed faster and at a lower cost, while increasingly sophisticated consumers of financial services were attracted by new products which blurred the boundaries between traditional products and providers. The deregulation of brokerage commissions in 1975 led to the rise of discount brokerage houses and put downward pressure on the commissions charged by the full-service firms. Finally, additional competition was provided by securities brokers, insurers, travel-service companies, commercial banks, and retailers, all of whom began to look to financial services for diversification opportunities.

---

[2] Nancy Belliveau, "How Tough Is E. F. Hutton?" *Institutional Investor*, December 1975, p. 33.

[3] E. F. Hutton, *Annual Report 1980*, p. 3.

[4] E. F. Hutton, *Annual Report 1981*, p. 1.

[5] For example, see "A Hard-Sell Strategy at Hutton," *Business Week*, January 19, 1981, p. 109. Similar assessments can be found in Nigel Adam, "The Productivity Game at E. F. Hutton," *Euromoney*, December 1981, p. 75, and Gregory Miller, "Bob Fomon: Is Being Tough Still Enough? "*Institutional Investor*, April 1985, pp. 59–60.

[6] "A Hard-Sell Strategy at Hutton," pp. 109–110.

[7] Adam, p. 76.

EXHIBIT 1   The E. F. Hutton Group Inc. and Subsidiaries—Selected Financial Data (in thousands)

	1982	1981	1980	1979	1978	1977
Operating Results						
Revenues:						
Commissions	$ 416,945	$ 378,763	$ 421,316	$ 287,669	$ 256,741	$ 176,335
Interest	489,702	580,411	379,651	235,383	100,685	56,461
Investment banking	201,541	154,586	117,114	72,036	59,307	56,312
Insurance	192,398	151,978	75,245	60,768	47,571	7,759
Principal transactions	170,140	100,730	78,722	63,246	40,495	33,506
Investment income of insurance subsidiaries	29,851	23,726	20,393	16,205	11,211	
Other	95,910	53,814	32,830	14,960	5,632	4,056
Total revenues	$1,596,487	$1,444,008	$1,125,271	$ 750,267	$ 521,642	$ 334,429
Expenses:						
Employee compensation and benefits	$ 580,635	$ 471,375	$ 393,248	$ 271,607	$ 223,137	$ 163,177
Interest	396,362	462,457	283,828	185,327	63,108	29,953
Communications	81,068	65,214	49,173	39,848	35,311	28,656
Occupancy and equipment	76,881	56,896	41,957	36,996	27,901	22,928
Brokerage, clearing and exchange fees	31,209	27,186	29,175	20,757	19,652	14,544
Advertising and sales promotion	46,367	25,345	18,049	16,036	7,679	8,574
Policyholder benefits	111,495	95,588	56,411	51,359	40,770	
Other	46,764	115,652	97,581	59,760	48,402	33,072
Total expenses	$1,470,781	$1,319,713	$ 969,422	$ 681,690	$ 465,960	$ 300,904
Income before taxes	$ 125,706	$ 124,295	$ 155,849	$ 68,577	$ 55,682	$ 33,525
Income tax expenses	44,624	45,483	73,219	31,302	27,440	17,415
Net income	$ 81,082	$ 78,812	$ 82,630	$ 37,275	$ 28,242	$ 16,110
Financial Condition						
Total assets	$7,364,740	$5,637,885	$4,706,635	$3,315,842	$1,875,006	$1,593,795
Stockholders' equity	$ 414,703	$ 335,159	$ 259,208	$ 173,934	$ 146,462	$ 123,152
Sinking and fund debentures	30,000	30,000	30,000	—	—	—
Convertible subordinated debentures	59,910	59,991	60,000	—	—	—
Subordinated liabilities of subsidiaries	103,448	109,342	98,829	64,020	64,414	51,124
Capital funds	$ 608,061	$ 534,492	$ 448,037	$ 237,954	$ 210,876	$ 174,276
Per Share Data[a]						
Average common and common equivalent shares outstanding	19,364,000	18,950,000	16,815,000	16,031,000	16,792,000	14,432,000
Earnings per share:						
Per common and common equivalent share	$ 4.33	$ 4.31	$ 4.93	$ 2.33	$ 1.68	$ 1.12
Assuming full dilution	$ 4.33	$ 4.31	$ 4.92	$ 2.32	$ 1.67	$ 1.12
Dividends per common share	$ .80	$ .76	$ .49	$ .31	$ .28	$ .26
Book value per common share	$ 23.35	$ 19.40	$ 15.52	$ 11.05	$ 9.03	$ 7.82

Source: The E. F. Hutton Group Inc., 10-K, 1981 and 1982.
[a]Gives effect to the five-for-four stock splits paid June 30, 1981, and November 24, August 13, and January 29, 1980.

Top Management

Robert Fomon, Hutton's president and CEO since 1970, joined the company in 1951 as a sales trainee in California. But his real interest was in corporate finance, and he eventually became head of the West Coast corporate finance department and chief assistant to the head of all West Coast operations. In 1969, in a surprising and controversial move, he was offered the top position as the board's compromise candidate when the company became engulfed in a bitter battle between the two senior officers in line for the post. Fomon's time as CEO was characterized by substantial growth. He was instrumental in Hutton's move public in 1972, which strengthened its capital position, and he pursued an aggressive strategy of expansion through the acquisition of local and regional brokerages.

On Wall Street, Fomon had a larger-than-life image as an intensely private and eccentric man who could display great charm with important clients. A lover of gourmet food and fine wine, he had been married three times, once to a former Miss America. Stories in the press often characterized him as

> a mercurial pragmatist. . . . a street fighter. . . who doesn't always have respect for the traditional rules by which the Street game is played . . . a man who thinks, breathes, and talks nothing but business . . . [who] gradually put his stamp on the entire firm.[8]

Fomon remained aloof from day-to-day management of Hutton, although he paid close attention to business deals and had been known to veto any he disliked or believed unsuitable for the company, even after the directors had voted spending the necessary funds.[9]

Day-to-day management was handled by George Ball, president and head of retail operations, who had joined Hutton in 1962 as an account executive trainee. Appointed president in 1977, he was highly regarded and considered a complement to Bob Fomon:

> Ball, his ambition outweighed only by his capacity for hard work, kept his finger on retail, taking on new duties without ever relinquishing the old. Chairman Fomon oversaw corporate finance, the institutional businesses and Hutton's diversification, and let President Ball assume many of the powers—but never the title—of CEO. Ball was the gregarious executive, the restless, creative mind and the cheerleader who energized the system. He was the perfect surrogate for the reclusive Fomon, who had neither the desire nor ability to do the same.[10]

Other commentators made similar observations about Fomon's and Ball's teamwork:

> In demeanor they contrast sharply with each other. Ball is at ease and eloquent in discussion; Fomon is restless, preferring to move around the room, even leaving it altogether at times . . . . Ball is the image of the Hutton retail broker who's constantly in the public eye . . . He has the key responsibility of supervising Hutton's branch network and cajoling the sales force into higher productivity . . . Fomon is the backroom dealmaker.[11]

---

[8] Belliveau, pp. 33–35.

[9] Adam, p. 80.

[10] Miller, p. 60.

[11] Adam, p. 76.

Hutton's board of directors consisted of 22 insiders until 1974, when they were joined by a business school professor. Two additional outside directors were added by 1982.[12] But Fomon did not allow the board to constrain his management style. In May 1984, for example, he hired a new executive vice president at an unusually high salary, without first seeking the required approval of the board. Fomon explained, "You do many things in business assuming that the board is going to act as you recommend."[13]

The Organization

Fomon ran Hutton in a loose manner, even after the company went public. He disliked tight organizational structures and was proud of the firm's decentralized arrangement. One press account noted that "no fewer than 25 different executives (from sales to financing) report[ed] directly to him."[14] Remarked a senior manager, "Even as a vice president in a regional office, I could call Bob Fomon whenever I wanted."[15] In fact, by design, Hutton had no formal organization chart showing who reported to whom.

Hutton was headquartered in New York, where, along with Fomon and Ball, the principal operating officers during 1980 to 1982 were

- Thomas P. Lynch, executive vice president and managing director who served as de facto chief financial officer.[16]
- Paul G. Hines, head of corporate planning and control. The controller and accounting staff reported to him.
- Norman M. Epstein, head of operations.
- Thomas W. Rae, general counsel and head of legal affairs and compliance.

Other top officers included Controller Michael P. Castellano, First Vice Presidents Thomas E. Lillis (assistant controller) and Thomas P. Morley (money mobilizer), and Senior Vice Presidents Richard Genin (head of trading operations) and Robert Ross (cashier).

> Amongst this group, there was a great deal of overlapping of functions, with vague lines separating the division of responsibilities, some dual reporting, and generally a loose management structure. . . . Ball was a dominant figure in the company and one that the other senior officers responded to *ex officio* as support officers. [17]

Morley, the money mobilizer, was responsible for implementing and monitoring Hutton's cash management procedures. Because Hutton lacked a separate financial function, Morley reported to Epstein, Lynch, and Ross on an "as necessary" basis. Cash management practices were determined within the operations

---

[12] Hutton's board had a total of 29 members in 1981 and 22 in 1982.

[13] Miller, p. 63.

[14] Belliveau, p. 34.

[15] Sarah Bartlett, "The Fall of the House of Hutton," *Business Week*, December 21, 1987, p. 99.

[16] Hutton had no chief financial officer, but when it was required that certain documents be signed by a CFO, Lynch was the person who signed them. See Griffin B. Bell, *The Hutton Report* (Atlanta: King & Spalding Law Offices, 1985), p. 93.

[17] Bell, p. 79.

section that included Genin and Ross, although Castellano, as controller, was responsible for the company accounts. Epstein was responsible in 1979 for seeing that Hutton had the internal accounting controls required under the Foreign Corrupt Practices Act, although the "procedures enacted in response [to the Act] . . . did not extend to specific controls in the area of cash management."[18]

Hutton was divided into 10 geographic regions, 9 domestic and 1 international, each headed by a regional vice president in charge of staffing branch offices and creating new business. The regional vice presidents enjoyed considerable independence from New York, but had little input into the operations side of their regional office. In contrast, regional operations managers reported directly to New York operations. Compensation for regional operations managers, including discretionary bonuses, was determined in New York, and hiring decisions were often greatly influenced, if not made, in New York.

Under each region were the branches. Following the pattern established by the regions, the branch manager's primary responsibility was to supervise the sales force. In most instances, branch operations functions were supervised by the regional operations office.

Thus, there were only four layers of management: Account executives reported to their branch managers, branch managers reported to their regional vice presidents, and the regional vice presidents reported to Ball. Branch operations personnel reported to regional operations personnel, who reported through Genin (in charge of trading operations) to Epstein. Ball and Epstein, in turn, reported to Fomon. Hutton management had only two standing committees of any importance: a commodity credit committee, which evaluated the creditworthiness of customers, and an underwriting commitment committee.[19]

Corporate Culture

Hutton's success was predicated on a competitive environment in which bright, aggressive people could develop and sell its products. One commentator observed, "If Merrill Lynch is perceived as the thundering herd, Hutton has something of a cowboy image."[20] Another noted, "[Bob Fomon] describes his management role as that of a 'chief psychiatrist,' trying to run a company full of entrepreneurial types who tend to dash off in different directions."[21] Fomon explained that he "makes a bet on people—I let them go out and do it. And when I bet on the wrong person, I don't mind changing."[22]

Base salaries were low, but Hutton's average payout commission of 40% was comparable to the best private firms and better than most public firms. Moreover, Hutton would increase commissions to more than 50% for any products it decided to push. The company was generous with entertainment allowances, gifts, and free holidays for its big producers. As Ball noted, "A lot of creative energy has been spent making the account executive believe he matters."[23] And, as if in response, a Hutton salesman remarked, "At Hutton, the AE [account execu-

---

[18] Bell, p. 99.

[19] Adam, p. 79.

[20] Adam, p. 75.

[21] Miller, p. 19.

[22] Belliveau, p. 34.

[23] Belliveau, p. 36.

EXHIBIT 2   Selected U.S. Interest Rates, 1970–1985 (percentage per annum)

Year	U.S. Treasury Securities (3-month)	Corporate Bonds (Moodys, Aaa)	Prime Rate Charged by Banks
1970	6.458	8.04	7.91
1971	4.348	7.39	5.72
1972	4.071	7.21	5.25
1973	7.041	7.44	8.03
1974	7.886	8.57	10.81
1975	5.838	8.83	7.86
1976	4.989	8.43	6.84
1977	5.265	8.02	6.83
1978	7.221	8.73	9.06
1979	10.041	9.63	12.67
1980	11.506	11.94	15.27
1981	14.029	14.17	18.87
1982	10.686	13.79	14.86
1983	8.630	12.04	10.79
1984	9.580	12.71	12.04
1985	7.480	11.37	9.93

Source: Economic Report of the President, 1991.

tive] is king; there's no reason why anyone would want to leave."[24] Hutton estimated that in 1980, its average revenue per retail broker was $168,000, and claimed to be "number one in that category by a margin of at least 15%."[25]

Hutton was also well known within the industry for the extent and quality of its training programs. Brokers were trained in the technical aspects of the business, as well as in public speaking, and effective reading and writing. Unlike some firms that trained their brokers in only a narrow area, Hutton trained its people as generalists, who then were free to choose where they wanted to work. Hutton also pioneered training for seasoned brokers, concentrating on improving sales techniques rather than merely emphasizing product lines, laws, and regulations.

Fomon and Ball encouraged all employees, not just brokers, to be aggressive. Ball traveled to regional offices, delivering speeches to encourage staff to increase earnings. The bonuses of most branch managers were a percentage (usually 10%) of the branch's net profit, thus reflecting both sales revenues and other factors such as interest income. In the early 1980s, when interest rates were running at historically high levels, Ball set up a contest in which branches and regions were pitted against one another to increase interest income. (See **Exhibit 2** for data on selected interest rates in the United States, 1970–1985.) Winners received titles, such as "Office of the Month," and branches that were below average were criticized and exhorted to do better.

---

[24] Belliveau, p. 36.

[25] Adam, p. 75.

Cash Management at Hutton

Careful cash management was one way to boost branch earnings. Devised in 1978 by Thomas Morley's predecessor, Hutton's cash management system was designed to collect and obtain use of the funds received at Hutton's branch offices throughout the United States as quickly as possible. On a daily basis, each branch deposited the cash and checks received from its clients into its local bank. These deposits would be transferred that day to a regional bank and then into a central **concentration bank account,** where the funds could be invested in money markets or used to meet the firm's other obligations. Like many corporate customers, Hutton also had a **zero-balance account**—a special account for paying bills, often at the same bank as its concentration account, into which Hutton could instantly transfer only enough money to cover checks as they were presented for payment.

Bank Compensation

As was customary among corporate customers, Hutton ordinarily used **compensating balances** to pay its more than 400 branch and regional banks during 1980 to 1982. Although compensating balances were the most common form of bank payment, direct fees or a combination of fees and balances were also used. Under the compensating balances system, the bank customer would leave an agreed-upon (average) level of available funds on deposit in a noninterest-bearing account. The bank retained the interest on these funds to cover the cost of the services provided to the customer. Most arrangements of this kind between a bank and its corporate customers were not formalized or put in writing. At the end of some specified period, the bank would review the situation, and it could ask for direct fees or an increase in the target level of funds, if the average balance of available funds was found to be inadequate.

Banks generally did not expect customers to draw intentionally against unavailable funds without prior consent or agreement, although they realized that this would occur occasionally by accident or inadvertence.[26] However, banks varied greatly in their ability and diligence in monitoring a customer's available balances; they varied also in their policies and procedures for monitoring and handling overdrafts beyond an occasional small amount. The absence of uniform methods was due to the prevailing business climate, as well as to differences in geographic location and bank size, the purpose of the deposit, the identity of the customer, and the nature of the customer's business. In practice, matters of compensation and possible overdrafts were most commonly resolved through "informal dialogue" between the bank's account officers and the corporate customer. Customers generally expected a bank to communicate its policies and assumed that if a bank did not object to a customer's actions, it should not object or prevent similar actions in the future.[27]

Interest Income

Maximizing the interest earned on cash reserves was an important aspect of Hutton's cash management system at the national, regional, and branch levels. The

---

[26] Bell, p. 23.
[27] Bell, pp. 22–25.

high interest rates of the late 1970s and early 1980s increased the cost of ineffective cash management and prompted the use of ever-more sophisticated methods for reducing the amount of cash left in noninterest-bearing checking accounts and for squeezing the maximum interest earnings from the rest. Managers in a variety of firms and industries, aware that aggressive cash management practices could add millions of dollars to the bottom line, encouraged them, even to the point of setting up cash management departments as profit centers.[28]

Ball and Morley circulated many memos detailing opportunities to increase interest income. In one memo, Ball instructed, "Please be sure that each of your managers (and your regional staff) know and are adhering to the sound precepts of Tom Morley's Department. Interest is an excellent way to legitimately optimize a branch's or region's results."[29]

Regional vice presidents and regional operations managers encouraged attention also to even seemingly small details such as mailing confirmations early in the day and mailing drafts late in the day. Other suggestions included developing short sales and margin accounts (Hutton charged its customers a higher interest rate than it was charged), overdrafting the branch's bank account, avoiding prepaid commissions to account executives, delaying the payout of customer credit balances, charging account executives for waiving interest charges to customers, limiting the number of customers on automatic dividend, and discouraging account executives from mailing out small credit balances at the end of the month, unless the customer requested it.[30] The subject of interest income was frequently mentioned in memos and at meetings of branch managers and regional personnel. According to one memorandum:

> Net interest profits are a vital aspect of every branch's profitability. In leaner times, they sometimes represented the difference between a profit and a loss for a branch. Fortunately this is not true today, however net interest profits still account for approximately 50% of the average branch's profits. And by paying insufficient attention to net interest profits, a branch may be ignoring potential revenue that would be brought directly to the "bottom line."[31]

The memorandum also noted that 45% of net interest profits came from interest on general ledger balances, most of which was due to the float earned on checks and overdrafting.

There was regular and extensive praise for branches and regions that excelled in generating interest income. For example, in an October 1981 memorandum, George Ball noted that "without gigantic interest profits, the bottom line [in Sep-

---

[28] Suzanna Andrews, "Should Cash Management Be a Profit Center?" *Institutional Investor*, July 1985, pp. 203–204.

[29] Interoffice memorandum from George Ball to Regional Sales Managers (cc: R. Fomon), dated May 21, 1981, titled "Region of the Month—April," in Bell, Appendix.

[30] See, for example, Interoffice memorandum from Joe McAdams and Gene Cahalan to All Branch Managers, dated October 21, 1980, titled "Net Interest Profits," and Interoffice memorandum from Louis Milazzo, dated October 19, 1982, titled "How to Increase Interest Income," in Bell, Appendix.

[31] Interoffice memorandum from Joe McAdams and Gene Cahalan to All Branch Managers, dated October 21, 1980, titled "Net Interest Profits," in Bell, Appendix.

tember 1981] would have been a dismal one as I know you are aware."[32] In December 1981, Ball named the New England region "Region of the Month," noting that "We certainly had the luxury of high interest profits, profits which may be importantly lower in the year ahead. Our corporate goal is to earn in excess of $100,000,000."[33]

Each month, Hutton's directors received a "Statement of Results of Operations," which showed monthly interest profits as a percentage of total product revenues. The percentage shown for the Alexandria, Virginia branch for the month of November 1981 was 117.8%, with 76.7%, 109.7%, 13.0%, 167.4%, and 25.8% reported for other months in late 1981 and early 1982.[34] At year-end 1981, Hutton reported that its revenues had risen 28%, to $1.4 billion, and that "Interest income was the largest contributor to this gain, reflecting high rates and increased client borrowings."[35]

Hutton's Cash Management System and Float

Hutton's cash management system was designed to maximize interest earnings by (1) transferring funds from local banks to the central concentration banks as quickly as possible and (2) deliberately overdrafting accounts to recapture lost interest income.

In order to achieve the first objective, Hutton tried to maintain its concentration accounts at banks that gave one-day availability so that it could transfer available funds from the local to the national level on the same day. However, cash deposits not made immediately available, delays in the transfer or check-clearing process, or other holdups in gaining access to its funds meant that Hutton lost the use of these funds for a day or more.

> From Hutton's perspective, someone other than Hutton has use of Hutton's funds during the period between the time Hutton deposits checks into its local bank accounts and the time the funds represented by those checks are made available to Hutton. For some or all of this period those checks are in the process of collection. Because of delays inherent in the collection process, during this period the funds represented by those checks are of benefit not to Hutton, but to banks and other participants in the check clearing process. Hutton, not unlike other corporate depositors, believes that it is entitled to share in the value of those funds while they remain in the process of collection in the payments system. Those funds are commonly referred to as **float,** or more accurately, collection float.[36]

Hutton's overdraft system was designed so that Hutton could recapture interest lost through collection float and other inefficiencies in the payments process. See **Exhibit 3** for an illustration of Hutton's overdraft system. Overdrafts were

---

[32] Interoffice memorandum from George Ball, dated October 20, 1981, titled "September Performance," in Bell, Appendix.

[33] Interoffice memorandum from George Ball to Regional Vice Presidents and Regional Sales Managers (cc: R. Fomon), dated December 18, 1981, titled "Region of the Month," in Bell, Appendix.

[34] Bell, p. 170.

[35] E. F. Hutton, *Annual Report 1981*, p. 2.

[36] Bell, p. 21.

EXHIBIT 3   Illustration of E. F. Hutton & Company's Overdraft System to Recapture Lost Interest

	Day 1	*Day 2*	*Day 3*
HUTTON ACTIONS	• Branch office deposits day's receipts in noninterest-bearing account in local bank; Assume $10,000 cash and $5,000 checks		• Branch office makes deposit to cover $10,000 overdraft of local bank account
	• Regional office writes check for $25,000 on local bank and deposits it in regional bank		
BANK ACCOUNTS	• Headquarters writes check for $25,000 on regional bank and deposits it into central interest-bearing account.	• All checks clear • Local bank earns interest on $10,000 cash deposited on Day 1)	• Local bank loses interest on ($10,000) Day 2 balance • Hutton earns interest on $25,000 Day 2 available balance in central account
	Account Balances:	*Account Balances:*	*Account Balances:*
	Local bank: $10,000 available 5,000 uncollected	Local bank: $(10,000)[a]	Local bank: $ 0
	Regional bank: $25,000 uncollected	Regional bank: $ 0	Regional bank: $ 0
	Central bank: $25,000 uncollected	Central bank: $25,000 available	Central bank: $25,000 available

[a]In actuality, Hutton's new deposits of customer receipts on Day 2 will offset the negative balance created by the overdraft. Assuming adequate deposits, the local bank account will generally show a positive ledger balance.

Source: Prepared by casewriter.

used to "ensure that banks were not overcompensated if, for whatever reason, available balances were left in the account above the level required for adequate bank compensation."[37] Hutton developed drawdown formulas and worksheets to help branches determine how much they should overdraft their accounts. The formulas were complex, taking into account the type of items deposited (e.g., wire transfer, check drawn on the local bank, check drawn on another bank) and whether it was a weekend or holiday.

The procedure was premised on Hutton's ability to draw against unavailable funds. To cover these overdrafts and insure adequate ledger balances in its bank accounts, Hutton's national cash managers furnished branches and regions with **branch reimbursement checks** (BRCs)—presigned checks made payable to Hutton and drawn on one of its three zero-balance accounts at its national banks.

---

[37] Bell, p. 26.

Similar overdraft systems were used by many U.S. managers, as part of a widely used approach to cash management, **target balancing,** which involved a drawdown formula designed to keep compensating balances at the minimum target level. Hutton managers were encouraged to use the target balancing and drawdown formulas to increase their net interest earnings and branch profits.[38] Overdrafting of branch bank accounts was the single most important source of interest profits. Various operations personnel were taught through seminars how to use the drawdown formula; a memo written after one such seminar reminded Atlantic Region cashiers, "Drawdown as discussed. You may drawdown more than formula but not less! This will depend on individual Branch/Bank circumstances."[39]

However, some employees did not have the proper training and used the formulas incorrectly. Others withdrew their accounts without regard to the drawdown formula, overdrafting amounts unrelated to either customer receipts or recapture of collection float. In one instance, Hutton's Alexandria, Virginia, office wrote a check for almost $10 million on an account backed by less than $71,000 in customer funds. That same day, a $925,000 check was drawn on the account of the firm's Williamsport, Pennsylvania, office based on $92,500 of business.

In such cases, Hutton's branch manager would cover the overdraft with a branch reimbursement check on Hutton's zero-balance disbursement account. Hutton received one-day availability on the branch reimbursement checks used for the drawdowns, though it often took two days for them to clear. Only when they cleared would funds actually be transferred from the concentration account to the zero-balance account. Meanwhile, Hutton earned interest on the overdraft, in effect getting an interest-free loan from its banks. On some days, Hutton was able to borrow as much as $250 million through liberal use of the drawdown formula.[40] One company memo noted, "A good branch cashier is worth as much as an AE [account executive]."[41]

At short-term rates of 18% to 20%, the interest earned on these overdrafts could constitute a substantial portion of Hutton's profits. For example, during March 1980, two branches, Casper, Wyoming, and Washington, D.C., earned more than $30,000 and $82,000 in net interest income, respectively. The bulk of this income resulted from "general ledger interest," due almost entirely to drafts outstanding and overdrafting. A memo reporting these results to George Ball stated that "Both offices have one thing in common; they overdraft substantially. . . At 20% interest, it is a very profitable product for the

---

[38] Interest income reflects interest generated both by overdrafting and by other activities.

[39] Interoffice memorandum from James Kelly to Atlantic Region Cashiers, dated June 2, 1981, titled "Reminders From Seminar," in Bell, Appendix.

[40] Barbara Donnelly, "Cash Management: Where Do You Draw the Line," *Institutional Investor,* September 1985, p. 72.

[41] Interoffice memorandum from Tom Lillis to Tom Morley (cc: M. Castellano, P. Hines), dated May 12, 1981, titled "Interest," in Bell, Appendix.

branches."[42] In another instance, proposed plans for operations in Canada were rejected, in part because "The system of overdrafting is not available in the Canadian Markets necessitating much higher outside sources of capital, or increased debt."[43]

In another cash management technique, regional operations personnel sometimes routed Hutton's deposits outside the prescribed path from branch to region to concentration account. Instead, they constructed elaborate **chains** of successive deposits and transfers from branch to branch or branch to atypical region. For example, in one chain, deposits from two Hutton branches in New York City and one in White Plains, New York, were routed through a bank in Wilkes-Barre, Pennsylvania, which was drawn down through a bank in Batavia, New York, before finally ending up back in a New York City account. In some cases, the chains were intended to improve the availability of funds or for convenience.[44] However, they were also used to generate interest income by creating clearing delays. Chains were generally created and implemented by the region,[45] and some branch managers were unaware that they were being drawn down by another branch.[46]

Check-crossing was another method used to manage the company's flow of funds. By simultaneously issuing checks in identical amounts on two different banks and cross-depositing each check into the other bank, Hutton added to its next-day opening balances and insured sufficient funds to cover its early morning requirements. Developed by the Cash Desk in New York, this method of funding permitted Hutton to avoid borrowing to insure a sufficient opening ledger balance.[47]

The disbursement side of Hutton's cash management system offered other opportunities to boost interest earnings by creating or extending float. **Remote disbursement**—paying customers or suppliers with checks written on distant, slow, or out-of-the-way banks—delayed disbursements by adding travel and processing time. Hutton also benefited from slow-downs in the check-clearing process created, for example, when Hutton's poor quality check printing caused problems with the banks' microencoders, necessitating manual rather than automated processing. One bank complained that almost 50% of Hutton's checks were being rejected, compared with a normal proportion of 1%.[48]

Many companies used remote disbursement techniques, though often employing them selectively to avoid offending major suppliers. One cash manager noted, "The trade-off in remote disbursing is the corporate image. . . . I will use

---

[42] Interoffice memorandum from Tom Lillis to George Ball (cc: M. Castellano), dated April 23, 1980, titled "Interest Income," in Bell, Appendix.

[43] Interoffice memorandum from Norman Epstein to George Ball, dated March 19, 1980, in *Hearings Before the Subcommittee on Crime of the Committee on the Judiciary, House of Representatives, Ninety-ninth Congress, First Session* (Washington: U.S. Government Printing Office, 1986), Part 2, p. 1572.

[44] Bell, p. 55.

[45] Bell, p. 52.

[46] Bell, p. 54.

[47] Bell, pp. 100–115.

[48] Donnelly, p. 76.

it to pay a tax check but not if I'm paying a major vendor."[49] Companies sometimes used bank-devised products called "disbursement networks," which paid suppliers from the slowest clearing point in the network; located company disbursement points in areas of the country far from creditors' banks; and covered zero-balance disbursement checks with other checks, rather than with cash wired from a concentration account. Some believed that much of the cost of float was borne by the Federal Reserve Bank, not creditors. The Fed claimed that of the $40 billion worth of checks in process of collection at any one time in 1976, only $19 billion was handled by the Fed, and, of that $19 billion, less than $2 billion resulted in Federal Reserve float.[50] But by 1979, Fed float had reached $6.7 billion.[51]

Hutton regional offices and national headquarters received monthly statements of account, account analyses, details of customer deposits, and daily statements of bank account balances. Its accounting department under Paul Hines and Michael Castellano assembled numerous reports reflecting interest earnings, many showing irregularities that existed because of overdrafting.[52] Profit-and-loss statements that reflected interest income were sent monthly to the directors as well as vice presidents. However, many of these statements were difficult to interpret,[53] and Hutton had not yet installed automated systems for cash management control[54] and for reporting interest profits.[55]

Legal and Regulatory Standards

In 1980, as part of a study and evaluation of internal accounting controls, Arthur Andersen & Co. (Arthur Andersen), Hutton's auditors, requested that Thomas Rae, Hutton's general counsel, render a written legal opinion affirming the legality of Hutton's cash management system, particularly "the company procedure of writing checks even though the balance per books is zero or negative." However, Rae

> declined to render such an opinion, stating that the banks are fully cognizant of Hutton's procedures, that this is an accepted banking practice and there is no question as to the propriety of such transactions, again making reference to the "means of payment" principles [intent and ability to cover the check].[56]

---

[49] "Treasurers Try to Fine Tune the Float," *Business Week,* May 17, 1976, p. 124.

[50] Federal Reserve float occurred when the Fed paid the commerical bank that received the check before it delivered the check to the issuer's bank. According the the Fed, bad weather, computer errors, and mechanical breakdowns were the main source of this $2 billion cost. See "Treasurers Try to Fine Tune the Float," p. 130.

[51] William Ford, "Interest Sparked in Cash Management; Float, Inflation, Competition Spurs Growth of Field," *American Banker,* April 27, 1982, p. 16 ff.

[52] Bell, p. 90.

[53] Bell, p. 90.

[54] Morley made two requests for an automated system that he claimed would have placed controls on cash management. A system was finally installed in 1985. (Bell, p. 82.)

[55] Thomas Lillis said that "it took five years to get the type of automated system that he requested to report interest profits." (Bell, p. 92.)

[56] Interoffice communication from Louis T. Lynn and John Tesoro, dated March 7, 1980, titled "E. F. Hutton Money Management Procedures," in Bell, Appendix.

After Rae declined to issue a legal opinion, Bill Sullivan, Morley's predecessor as the money mobilizer, justified overdrafting based on "collectability." He saw no problem since there was never any question that Hutton would be able to settle the uncollected balances and, if necessary, borrow against customers' margin accounts to raise funds quickly.[57] In most states, writing checks backed by insufficient funds could be prosecuted as larceny or theft if criminal intent could be proven. In general, an intent permanently to deprive the bank of funds was required. Since Hutton managers fully intended to cover and, in fact, did cover every check written, it could be argued that traditional state laws against bad checks did not apply.

Rae was further convinced that Hutton's practices raised no legal problem by a 1981 U.S. Supreme Court decision which ruled 5–4 that writing bad checks was not a crime under a federal law prohibiting false statements to federally insured banks.[58] The Court reasoned that a check is not a "statement" but a "promise to pay," obligating the person drawing the check to pay if the check is dishonored. Justice Blackmun argued that otherwise, "any check, knowingly supported by insufficient funds, deposited in a federally insured bank could give rise to criminal liability, whether or not the drawer had an intent to defraud." Justice Marshall's dissent criticized the "overly technical" definition of a check, noting that it "will come as quite a surprise to banks and businesses that accept checks in exchange for goods, services, or cash on the representation that the drawer has sufficient funds to cover the check."[59]

Pedersen's Decision

Pedersen was not happy about First American's decision to take its business elsewhere or about Howe's behavior. Several weeks earlier, Pedersen had mentioned his concerns about excessive overdrafting to Howe, but obviously Howe had ignored them. After calling Tom Morley, Hutton's money mobilizer, to get help on restoring Hutton's credibility with First American, Pedersen's thoughts turned to what he should do about Howe.

---

[57] Richard Gotcher, "House Probe Shows Hutton Officials Knew of System of Bank Overdrafts," *The Bond Buyer*, August 2, 1985, p. 4 ff.

[58] *Williams v. United States*, 458 U.S. 279 (1982).

[59] See "Check Overdraft Not Criminal Act, Supreme Court Rules in Check-Kiting Case," *Daily Report for Executives*, July 8, 1982, p. A16; and "Justices Overturn Check-Kiting Case," *The New York Times*, June 30, 1982, p. A21.

CASE 4
SALOMON AND THE TREASURY SECURITIES AUCTION

In early June 1991, Salomon Vice Chairman John Meriwether had a problem. The U.S. Treasury was inquiring about the possibility that Salomon had engineered a "squeeze" in the market for $12 billion in new Treasury notes auctioned on May 22, 1991. Ordinarily, the Treasury's concern over the possibility of a squeeze was not particularly problematic. Squeezes—that is, an unpredicted shortness of supply or high demand for a security—were not uncommon and developed for a variety of reasons. Unfortunately, Meriwether had reason to believe that one of Salomon's bond traders had recently violated the Treasury's auction rules. Paul Mozer, the managing director under Meriwether overseeing Salomon's trading in U.S. Treasury securities, had disclosed to Meriwether in late April that he had broken the Treasury's limit on the size of a dealer's bid in Treasury auctions. Mozer had admitted that he submitted a bid in a February auction using the name of a customer without authorization and had managed to buy more bonds than the Treasury guidelines allowed.

The problem struck close to the heart of Salomon's business. Although Salomon was among the leaders in the traditional investment banking activity of debt and equity underwriting—acting as the intermediary between issuers of new securities (corporations and governments) and the investors who bought them—its trading in securities markets drove the firm's profitability and was a key part of its heritage. Profits from "principal transactions," largely the buying and selling of securities for Salomon's own account, generally provided 20% of Salomon's revenues, considerably more than the 10% to 12% found at most investment banks (**Exhibit 1**). In addition, Salomon's corporate culture revolved around trading. The CEO's desk was located on the firm's trading floor and seven of Salomon Brothers's nine vice chairmen had come up through the trading side of the business. John Gutfreund (pronounced goodfriend), Salomon's chairman and CEO, had also worked his way up to the top of the firm as a successful trader.

Salomon and the Investment Banking Community

The primacy of bond trading at Salomon Brothers dated to the firm's founding in 1910, when the social dynamics of investment banking limited the firm's opportunities. At the time of Salomon's founding, an aristocracy of established firms such as Morgan Stanley, Kidder Peabody, and Kuhn Loeb controlled the traditional investment banking activity of securities underwriting. As underwriters, these banks worked closely with the finance departments of large corporations to help them raise capital by selling new equity securities (stocks) and debt instruments (notes and bonds) through each bank's sales force. In exchange for a guarantee to buy any new securities that outside investors were unwilling to buy, the

EXHIBIT 1   Selected Financials, Salomon Inc, 1986 to 1990

Year Ending December 31	*1986*	*1987*	*1988*	*1989*	*1990*
(all figures in millions)					
Revenues					
Interest and dividends	$4,932	$4,161	$3,360	$5,758	$5,920
Principal transactions	1,064	1,154	1,711	2,513	2,389
Investment banking	577	403	564	470	416
Commissions	208	266	206	226	207
Other	8	19	35	32	14
Total	6,789	6,003	6,146	8,999	8,946
Interest expense	(4,484)	(3,973)	(3,541)	(6,093)	(5,959)
Noninterest expense	(1,512)	(1,805)	(1,852)	(2,166)	(2,481)
Income before taxes	793	225	753	740	506
Net income	516	142	280	470	303
Total assets	78,164	74,747	85,256	118,250	109,877
Stockholders' equity	3,454	3,481	3,459	3,565	3,523

Source: Annual Reports, Salomon Inc

investment banks received an underwriting fee. At the time of Salomon's founding, only the reigning investment banks had the connections and reputations necessary to approach potential investors and assure them of the quality of the new securities. With this distribution capability, the established investment banks could assure their corporate customers that they would be able to find enough investors for the new securities.

In contrast, the original three Salomon brothers, Arthur, Percy, and Herbert, were recent entrants to both the country and the investment banking industry and had little access to the wealthy investors who controlled much of the country's capital before the Second World War. As a result, Salomon was less able to approach the large corporations as an underwriter because it lacked adequate placement power (the ability to find investors for new securities). Instead, the firm focused on U.S. government debt where the Treasury selected underwriters on the basis of competitive bids[1] and Salomon could place the new securities with insurance and trust companies rather than individuals.[2] Unlike corporations that hired underwriters for new securities, the U.S. government did not pay underwriting fees. Instead, Salomon and other government debt underwriters made their money by buying the securities in a government-run auction, then reselling them to investors at a slightly higher price.

---

[1] Robert Sobel, *Salomon Brothers 1910–1985: Advancing to Leadership* (New York: Salomon Brothers, (1986), p. 17.

[2] Ibid., pp. 33, 66.

To carve a place for itself in U.S. government debt underwriting, Salomon worked hard to build its reputation for customer service. A key element of this service was the firm's commitment to trading and making a market in the securities it sold. When it placed new U.S. government securities with a customer, the firm stood ready to buy them back at the prevailing market price if the customer needed to sell the bonds. If another customer for the bonds could not be found immediately, Salomon carried the bonds in its inventory.[3] This willingness to trade earned Salomon the loyalty of many of its customers.

Carrying bonds in inventory entailed considerable risk, but the trading skills that this risk forced Salomon to develop ultimately proved quite lucrative. While the bonds were held in inventory, a fall in prices could cost the firm dearly. As a result, Salomon had to hone its trading skills so that it did not get caught by changing market conditions. Conversely, an upward movement in the price of bonds held in inventory could generate substantial profits. As Salomon's knowledge of the bond markets grew, the firm expanded its trading activities beyond that which was necessary to meet the needs of its customers and began seeking trading opportunities that generated profits for the firm.

In contrast to Salomon's emphasis on trading, the more traditional firms continued to focus on corporate securities underwriting. Although these banks had to engage in some trading as a service to their customers, these activities were secondary to the underwriting and advisory services they provided to their corporate customers. The bulk of their income resulted from the fees they received for underwriting new securities. Several of these banks extended their traditional underwriting relationships with large corporations into the area of investment advice on mergers and acquisitions. For a fee, these firms would help their clients evaluate potential acquisitions or respond to merger proposals. (In the merger boom of the 1980s, this line of business proved exceptionally lucrative.)

Salomon eventually built a successful corporate underwriting business, ranking fourth among its United States–based competitors in 1990. However, its core competence remained in the buying and selling of securities for its own account. The firm's $52 billion inventory of securities dwarfed that of Merrill Lynch, the leading corporate underwriter on Wall Street, due largely to the enormous trading positions that Salomon was willing to take. Consistent with this large inventory, Salomon had a $3.5 billion capital base that was easily the largest among investment banks.

Salomon's trading orientation and culture made it possible for "star" performers to shine. Successful traders were highly compensated and favored with managerial responsibilities. For example, Lewis Ranieri rose from the trading desk to vice chairman of Salomon because of his success in developing mortgage backed securities.[4] Beginning in 1979, Ranieri created the market for these newly developed securities, and then built a team of traders, analysts, and salespeople who dominated the product into the mid-1980s. In its heyday, the mortgage backed securities trading desk reportedly accounted for 50% of Salomon's net earnings, generating an estimated $225 million in 1985.[5]

---

[3] Ibid, pp. 23–24.

[4] A mortgage backed security was an interest-paying ownership share in a pool of mortgages.

[5] John F. Berry, "Under Siege," *Business Month*, June 1988, p. 67.

In the late 1980s, the bond arbitrage group and its traders rose to prominence within the firm. In its simplest form, arbitrage involved buying securities at a low price in one market then selling them in another market at a slightly higher price, or trading to take advantage of price discrepancies between two securities. Although price discrepancies were often small and transient, firms that were willing to commit large amounts of capital could generate substantial returns from these small opportunities.

Salomon's John Meriwether, who headed the firm's arbitrage unit until the late 1980s when he was picked to head all of Salomon's fixed income securities activities,[6] was one of the first people on Wall Street to spot the opportunities presented by sophisticated arbitrage trading. Under his direction, the arbitrage unit became an acknowledged star in the Salomon organization. In 1990, the group produced an estimated $400 million in profits for Salomon, roughly 80% of the firm's pretax earnings.[7]

In spite of its contribution to Salomon's bottom line, the bond arbitrage unit had raised a considerable amount of rancor within the firm in 1990 because of a controversial compensation system it negotiated with Chairman John Gutfreund and Salomon President Thomas Strauss. Under the compensation arrangement, the 12 members of the arbitrage unit shared a bonus pool equal to 15% of the profits that the unit earned. In 1990, the group's bonus pool was reported to total $60 million. The five most senior managers of the unit shared 90% of the bonus pool, with Lawrence Hillibrand, the unit's head, receiving an estimated $23 million bonus.[8] The size of the bonuses angered many managers within other areas of Salomon, whose compensation continued to be based on more subjective evaluations of how their units performed and the overall performance of the firm. Notwithstanding these managers' complaints, total compensation at the firm had risen by 22% since 1988, while Salomon's profits had fallen by 19%. By 1990, 106 people earned more than $1 million per year.[9]

Salomon's Government Bond Trading

Among participants in the market for U.S. government securities, Salomon had the reputation as the biggest and most active trader. Approximately $20 billion in Treasury bills, notes, and bonds (short-, medium-, and long-term securities) moved through its trading operation each day.[10] The firm bid aggressively for new securities in the Treasury auctions and held large inventories of those securities it believed would rise in value. In addition, Salomon often acted as the buyer of last resort when its customers needed to sell securities in weak markets. Customers might not like the price Salomon offered, but they knew the firm would submit a bid.

Salomon's large share of the Government bond trading activity allowed the firm to make money on trades where other dealers could not. Unlike equity secu-

---

[6] Fixed income securities consist of debt securities issued by governments and corporations.

[7] *The Wall Street Journal,* January 7, 1991, p. C1.

[8] Ibid.

[9] *The New York Times,* October 29, 1991, p. D14.

[10] Bernice Kanner, "Saving Salomon," *New York,* December 9, 1991, p. 43.

rities, Treasury securities were not traded on an exchange where all participants in the market could easily see the going price for a given security. Government securities were traded over the telephone and often, only the two parties involved in the trade knew the price and volume of the transaction. Therefore, the largest firms that handled the most transactions had the best information about which investors were seeking to buy or sell U.S. government securities.[11] This knowledge of "who holds the bonds" allowed Salomon to see and act on opportunities before its competitors.

For example, two days before the May 22, 1991, auction for $12 billion in two-year notes, Steinhardt Partners, a large New York money manager, approached Salomon with a request to finance a $6 billion position in the forthcoming notes. Essentially, Steinhardt had committed to buy $6 billion worth of notes and needed to borrow the money to pay for them when it took delivery after the auction (a common practice on Wall Street). This request signaled to Salomon that demand for the notes in the auction would be brisk. As a result, Salomon bid aggressively in the auction on the assumption that the notes would rise in value because the high demand would lead to an escalation in the price of the securities.[12]

Since 1988, Paul Mozer had directed Salomon's Treasury bond trading activities with the assistance of another managing director, Thomas Murphy. The two oversaw six traders arranged in a cluster of desks on the bond trading floor and assigned to securities of varying maturities. The close physical proximity of the bond group meant that each trader could overhear the activities of the other members of the group, and therefore, incorporate the changes in securities of one maturity quickly into trading decisions for another. Both Mozer and Murphy reported to John Meriwether, whose desk on the trading floor allowed him to observe, hear, and manage the sea of fixed income securities traders spread out over the entire 41st floor of Seven World Trade Center in lower Manhattan. Meriwether, in turn, reported to both Thomas Strauss and John Gutfreund.

Mozer had joined Salomon Brothers as a corporate bond salesman in 1979 after completing a master's degree in management at Northwestern University and a bachelor's degree in economics from Whitman College in Walla Walla, Washington. After switching to U.S. Treasury securities in 1980, Paul Mozer steadily worked his way up the Salomon hierarchy until he was named a managing director in 1985, working for John Meriwether's bond arbitrage group. After only a year and one-half as a managing director, senior managers asked Mozer to head Salomon's Treasury securities trading activities.[13]

As the head of U.S. government bond trading activities, Paul Mozer's energy, intelligence, and fairness earned him the respect of his colleagues at Salomon. Confident yet soft-spoken and composed under pressure, Mozer was a hard-working trader who kept in constant touch with the bond markets. He also maintained close relationships with Salomon's clients. Mozer often talked to the firm's largest customers and took their orders directly rather than communicating via

---

[11] Lynn Feldman and Jack Stephenson, "Stay Small or Get Huge—Lessons from Securities Trading," *Harvard Business Review* (May–June 1988): 117–118.

[12] *The Wall Street Journal*, September 17, 1991, p. C21.

[13] *The New York Times*, August 25, 1991, Sec. 3, pp. 1 and 10.

Salomon's bond sales force.[14] His trading instinct, hard work, and close relationships with the firm's customers made him an unqualified success at Salomon and earned him a reported $10 million in bonuses between 1988 and 1990.[15]

The Treasury Securities Market

At $2.4 trillion, the public market for U.S. government debt was the largest securities market in the world. On average, $110 billion in securities traded hands every day, making the Treasury securities market the most liquid as well. This liquidity—the ability to immediately find a buyer or seller for virtually any volume of securities—made Treasury securities particularly attractive to many investors and reduced the government's borrowing costs. Each week the U.S. Treasury sold approximately $30 billion in new Treasury securities of selected maturities, ranging from 90 days to 30 years. In a typical year, the Treasury conducted over 150 separate auctions. The new securities sold in these auctions replaced maturing government debt and funded the ongoing deficits of the U.S. government. Once issued, Treasury securities quickly changed hands and moved throughout the globe in an active "secondary" market. In this market, the investors, brokers, and dealers holding U.S. government debt could sell the securities to others seeking investments that were free of credit risk.

The Market for Government Securities

There were vast numbers of investors, brokers, and dealers in the market for U.S. government securities. Investors typically bought the securities and held them to maturity or until they found more profitable investments in which to invest. The brokers generally acted as intermediaries between investors, buying from one and quickly reselling to another. Brokers invested very little of their own money in Treasury securities and held only enough securities in inventory to serve the needs of customers who wished to buy U.S. government debt. Their earnings were based on the narrow spread that they maintained between the price at which they purchased the securities (the bid price) and the price at which they sold them (the asked price). The dealers, in contrast, actively invested their own capital in principal transactions and attempted to make money from the changes in the price of securities over time.

The large number of players in the U.S. government bond market forced profits down to an absolute minimum. Therefore, successful bond trading required a willingness to exploit any opportunity that presented itself. Since information was key to the market, traders ruthlessly turned any confusion or misjudgment on the part of their fellow traders into a profit for their firm's account. In the words of Salomon Chairman and erstwhile trader John Gutfreund: "It's a harsh world, where mistakes are not charitably dealt with."[16]

In the January 1990 auction of 40-year bonds, for example, several dealers were duped into buying the new issue when one of the large dealers started a rumor that a major pension fund would place a substantial bid for the bonds. At the time, many dealers were uncertain about the demand for an issue with a ma-

---

[14] Ibid.

[15] *The New York Times*, September 11, 1991, p. D1.

[16] *The New York Times*, August 17, 1991, p. 44.

turity considerably longer than the Treasury's benchmark 30-year bonds. The rumor that a major investor would bid on the bonds eased the concerns of many dealers and encouraged them to bid aggressively at the auction. After the auction, bond prices fell when the rumor proved to be false and customer demand for the bonds failed to materialize. Dealers who sat out the auction then earned hefty profits by buying the notes cheaply from dealers who had believed the rumor and gotten stuck with the notes.[17]

Primary Dealers

Salomon Brothers was the largest and most active of a group of Treasury market participants designated as primary dealers by the Federal Reserve Bank. The term *primary dealer* referred to the fact that the Federal Reserve Bank bought and sold securities only from these dealers when it implemented money supply policy through its open market committee.[18] The Fed also permitted primary dealers to submit bids on behalf of other investors in the Treasury's weekly auctions of new securities.[19] As of August 1990, the Fed had 39 primary dealers with which it maintained this special relationship. In exchange for the special treatment provided to primary dealers, the Fed required these dealers to bid at every Treasury auction and to actively make a market in Treasury securities of all maturities.

From a securities dealer's perspective, the primary dealer designation provided several benefits but not necessarily higher profits. First, the title provided a measure of self-assurance because it was limited to only those firms that the Fed recognized as leaders in the U.S. government securities market. Second, the Fed allowed primary dealers to submit bids without a deposit. Most other bidders had to deposit the full amount of their bid at the Fed or present a guarantee from a commercial bank or primary dealer. Third, the ability to bid for other buyers provided primary dealers with additional market information with which to improve the accuracy of their bidding efforts. Finally, the information about market conditions gathered in the Treasury auctions could be leveraged in the markets for many other securities that were either linked or strongly influenced by the market for U.S. government debt. Unfortunately, these benefits did not translate into consistently higher profits from Treasury securities. As recently as 1989, primary dealers as a group lost $10 million on their U.S. government securities business. As a result a number of securities firms had withdrawn as primary dealers since the group peaked at 46 in 1988.

The Treasury Securities Auctions

At regularly scheduled weekly intervals, the Federal Reserve Bank, acting as the Treasury's fiscal agent, conducted the Treasury securities auctions by accepting competitive bids from interested bond buyers. In the auction, potential buyers submitted bids to the Fed that stated the amount of securities they were willing to purchase and the yield that they required on the securities. For example, a

---

[17] *The Wall Street Journal,* August 19, 1991, p. A1.

[18] The Fed open market committee bought securities from primary dealers when it wished to increase the money supply and sold securities to primary dealers when it wished to decrease the money supply.

[19] The Fed also permitted commercial banks and other depository institutions to submit bids on behalf of other customers.

dealer might submit a bid for $100 million in two-year notes at a yield of 6.5 %.[20] The yield a bidder requested was the effective interest rate at which the buyer was willing to loan money to the U.S. government.

After receiving tenders from all interested buyers, the Fed awarded the securities to the bidders in order of lowest yield to highest. That is, the Fed first filled the bid of the buyer requesting the lowest interest rate. Next, it filled the bid of the buyer requesting the next lowest interest rate, and so forth until the entire issue had been awarded. In virtually every auction, the Fed reached a point where the bids at a given yield exceeded the number of securities still to be awarded. At this point, known as the "stop-out yield," the Fed allocated the remaining securities among all the bidders who submitted bids at the stop-out yield. These bidders received a prorated share of the remainder based on the size of their bid relative to all bids received at the stop-out yield. For example, in the February 21, 1991, auction of five-year notes, the notes available at the stop-out yield amounted to only 54% of the amount desired at that yield. Therefore, bidders at the stop-out yield received only 54% of their bids (**Exhibit 2**). Because of the efficiency of this market, the interest rate spread between the lowest bidder and the highest bidder receiving securities generally ranged from .02 to .03 percentage points (2 to 3 basis points).

In spite of its size and importance, the Treasury auction was probably the least automated securities market in the United States. Bond dealers bought and sold huge volumes of securities through verbal agreements made over the telephone. These transactions were largely governed by the unwritten code of ethics among traders, "my word is my bond," a code so strong it was given the weight of a legal contract. The legality of these verbal agreements was clearly illustrated by a court case involving a savings and loan that reneged on a telephone commitment to buy mortgage backed securities from Salomon Brothers. In its case, the thrift argued that the transaction was a real estate deal and in real estate, an oral agreement was not binding. In the end, the court ruled in Salomon's favor, deciding that the deal was a bond transaction and therefore, that oral commitments were binding.[21]

In bidding at Treasury auctions, the dealers frantically took orders from their customers over the telephone as the auction approached. Just before the 1:00 P.M. deadline for bids, the dealers called their runners in the lobby of the Federal Reserve Bank of New York with instructions for bidding. The runners filled out paper copies of the dealers' orders and literally stuffed them into a box at the Fed. Two hours later the Fed announced the winners of the auction.

The bidding among dealers in the auction was extremely competitive and very sophisticated. Bidders in the Treasury securities auctions always tried to bid a yield just low enough to get their orders filled. If they bid a yield too high, dealers ran the risk of not receiving any securities or only a portion of their bids, in which case they might not have enough securities in inventory to sell to their customers. Conversely, if they bid a yield too low, the dealers would fill their or-

---

[20] The yield quoted was the total yield to maturity and represented the internal rate of return generated by the future interest payments (coupons) and repayment of principal at maturity.

[21] Michael Lewis, *Liar's Poker* (New York: Norton, 1989), p. 101.

EXHIBIT 2   **Example of Treasury Auction Bids and Awards**

February 21, 1991 Auction of 5-Year Notes	*(millions)*
Notes Available	$9,040
Bids at 7.50% (lowest yield)	3,914
Bids at 7.51% (stop-out yield)	9,492
Bids above 7.51%	15,780
Notes available	9,040
less notes awarded at lowest yield (7.50%)	−3,914
Notes available at stop-out yield (7.51%)	5,126
Bid proration at stop-out yield:	
Notes available at stop-out yield	5,126
Bids at stop-out yield	+9,492
Proration percentage	54%

Source: Casewriter's estimates.

ders but at a yield that might be below the average interest rate and leave them with bonds that would have to be sold at a loss. In the days and hours leading up to the auction, dealers and investors discussed their likely orders in an elaborate ritual of bluffing and betting. Each player tried to sway the others' perception of the market in a manner that would create a profitable opportunity in the auction or later secondary market. David Mullins, vice chairman of the Federal Reserve Bank, once quipped that the U.S. government securities market was full of "dealers who'd turn in their grandmothers for a quarter of a point."[22]

Given the often conflicting information prior to an auction, market share was critical to successful bidding. Those firms with the largest share in U.S. government securities markets had the best feel for the likely yield on a new issue. This superior information, in turn, attracted more customers and extended the firm's reach into the market, enhancing further its information and position. Therefore, the major dealers sought to capture a significant share of each auction at the highest yield in order to maintain their position.

The competition for market share between the major dealers in the securities market spilled over into the markets for securities issued by quasi-government agencies like Fannie Mae and Freddie Mac.[23] In the auctions for the securities issued by these agencies, dealers routinely bluffed each other and the agencies by

---

[22] Mike McNamee, "David Mullins' Brisk Stride at the Fed," *Business Week*, December 6, 1991, p. 86.

[23] Fannie Mae, the Federal National Mortgage Association, was created in the 1960s to insure home mortgages. It was subsequently sold to the public in the 1970s. Freddie Mac, the Federal Home Loan Mortgage Corporation, was created by the Federal Home Loan Bank (the central bank for the savings and loan system) to insure mortgages issued by S&Ls. These agencies buy mortgages, package them into securities and then resell them via securities dealers.

overstating their customers' interest in the new issues. As Fannie Mae Chairman James Johnson once conceded, dealers' orders always contained "a certain amount of puffery, hype, and uncertainty."[24]

Regulation[25]

The Treasury securities auction and secondary market were governed principally by the actions of the Department of the Treasury. These actions were both informal and evolutionary, driven by the Treasury's perception of the changing dynamics of the market. In general, the Treasury would reject any bid it deemed disruptive to the auction. On August 27, 1962, for example, the Treasury rejected a bid that would have given a dealer an exceptionally high portion of an auction for three-month Treasury bills. The next day, the Treasury announced that it would limit auction winners to a maximum award of not more than 25% of any new issue of three- or six-month Treasury bills. No limits were placed on the size of bids, but a bid in excess of 25% of the auction would not be filled above the 25% award limit. Subsequently, it became generally understood that the 25% rule applied to Treasury securities of all maturities, although the Treasury never announced formally any additional rule changes. After some minor modifications in the intervening years, the Treasury announced via a press release in 1981 that it would raise the award limit to 35%.[26]

The market for Treasury securities was also governed to a limited extent by the Securities and Exchange Commission (SEC), which implemented regulations set forth in the Securities Exchange Act of 1934 (often referred to as the Exchange Act). Section 10 of the Exchange Act gave the SEC the authority to protect investors from "any manipulative or deceptive device" in the sale of securities (**Exhibit 3**). Under Section 10, the SEC could issue rules banning specific activities as per se manipulative. In addition, the SEC could bring a court action against brokers and dealers that had acted in a way that the SEC believed violated Section 10, even if the dealer or broker had not broken a specific rule. The Exchange Act also gave the SEC authority to issue rules governing record keeping (Section 17) and officer liability (Section 20). However, the SEC believed that its authority in the government securities markets was extremely limited and had historically deferred to the Treasury with respect to the regulation of Treasury securities.[27] Thus, there were no specific SEC rules explicitly governing the auction and sale of Treasury securities.

Although Congress modified the Exchange Act in 1986 to give the Treasury (but not the SEC) formal rule-making authority over the market for government debt, the Treasury chose not to issue formal, codified rules in the belief that new

---

[24] *The Wall Street Journal*, October 2, 1991, p. C1.

[25] Michael A. Santoro assisted in the preparation of this section under the supervision of Lynn Sharp Paine.

[26] Statement of the Honorable Jerome H. Powell, assistant secretary of the treasury for domestic finance, before the Subcommittee on Telecommunications and Finance, United States House of Representatives, September 4, 1991, p. 8.

[27] Testimony of Richard C. Breeden, Chairman of the Securities and Exchange Commission before the House Subcommittee on Telecommunications and Finance, September 4, 1991.

EXHIBIT 3   **Selected Sections of the Exchange Act and SEC Rules**

Sec. 10(b) [It shall be unlawful] to use or employ, in connection with the purchase or sale of any security . . . any manipulative or deceptive device or contrivance in contravention of such rules and regulations as the [S.E.C.] may prescribe.

Sec. 17 Every . . . broker or dealer who transacts business in securities . . . shall make and keep for prescribed periods such records . . . as the [S.E.C.] prescribes.

S.E.C. Reg. §240.17a-3. (a) . . . every broker or dealer registered pursuant to Section 15 of the Securities Exchange Act of 1934, as amended, shall make and keep current the following books and records relating to his business:

(1) Blotter (or other records of original entry) containing an itemized daily record of all purchases and sales of securities, all receipts and deliveries of securities, all receipts and disbursements of cash, and all other debits and credits.

(3) Ledger accounts itemizing separately as to each cash and margin account of every customer and of such member, broker or dealer, and partners thereof, all purchases, sales receipts, and deliveries of securities and commodities for such account.

(6) A memorandum of each brokerage order, and of any other instruction, given or received for the purchase or sale of securities, whether executed or unexecuted.

(7) A memorandum of each purchase and sale for the account of such member, broker, or dealer showing the price and, to the extent feasible, the time of execution; and, in addition, where such purchase or sale is with a customer other than a broker or dealer, a memorandum of each order received, showing the time of receipt, the terms and conditions of the order, and the account in which it was entered.

(8) Copies of confirmations of all purchases and sales of securities, including all repurchase and reverse repurchase agreements, and copies of notices of all other debits and credits for securities, cash, and other items for the account of customers and partners of such member, broker, or dealer.

Sec. 20(a) Every person who, directly or indirectly, controls any person liable under any provision of this title or any rule or regulation thereunder shall also be liable jointly and severally with and to the same extent as such controlled person . . . unless the controlling person acted in good faith and did not directly or indirectly induce the act or acts constituting the violation.

Source: Commerce Clearing House, Federal Securities Law Reports.

---

rules would create unnecessary costs, reduce the efficiency of the government debt market, and ultimately increase the borrowing costs of the United States government. Instead, the Treasury continued to rely upon informal rule announcements via press releases. These rule changes were based in part upon feedback the Treasury received during quarterly meetings with representatives of several large U.S. government securities dealers. At these informal meetings, the Treasury suggested possible changes and asked the representatives of the dealers to comment.

The New Bidding Regulations

The Treasury's 35% limit on awards remained the only significant limit on the auction until the summer of 1990, when the regulators began to worry about the inflation in bids at the stop-out yield by the large bidders. Because the Fed awarded a prorated share of the issue to all bidders at the stop-out yield, Salomon and other large bidders used a bidding strategy that entailed submitting very large orders at the estimated stop-out yield in order to increase their prorated share. Salomon also used a similar approach in submitting bids for its customers. The strategy generally resulted in Salomon and its customers receiving the largest shares, often up to the 35% maximum, among all bidders at the stop-out yield. In 30 out of the 230 auctions of notes and bonds held between 1986 and 1990, Salomon and its customers acquired in aggregate over 50% of the securities in the auction.[28] (Neither Salomon nor any of its customers received more than the 35% maximum award in any of these auctions.)

Salomon's aggressive strategy raised concerns among Treasury officials who worried that the firm's bidding might undermine the integrity of the auctions. On June 27, 1990, Salomon submitted a bid that exceeded the total value of the issue. Michael Basham, the deputy assistant secretary of the Treasury for federal finance, promptly warned Salomon about submitting excessively large bids. The conflict came to a head two weeks later when Salomon submitted a massive bid of $30 billion for $10 billion in 30-year notes.[29] The size of the bid, three times the total size of the auction, embarrassed the Treasury and prompted an immediate response from Michael Basham. He announced that, henceforth, the Treasury would not accept any bid, either for a dealer's own account or on behalf of its customers, in excess of 35% of the total auction. At the time, Michael Basham commented: "We want to maintain the competitive nature of the auction process for the taxpayers as well as the investment community."[30]

In response, Paul Mozer blasted the Treasury for its attempts to curtail Salomon's bidding activities: "The Treasury made a rash decision without consulting the dealer community about this change. . . . Potentially, this ties the hands of the larger dealers, who, time in and time out, buy the bulk of the debt."[31] He went on to note that curbing the big dealers' ability to take large positions in the auction could undermine their ability to provide the liquidity that was an essential component of the Treasury securities markets. Mozer's outburst rankled Basham and led to chilly relations between Mozer and the Treasury (the new rule became known on Wall Street as the Mozer/Basham rule). As a result of the bitterness, Mozer's assistant, Thomas Murphy, took over the responsibility of interacting with the Treasury.

---

[28] *The New York Times,* September 22, 1991, Sec . 6, p. 1.

[29] *The New York Times,* August 25, 1991, Sec. 3, p. 10.

[30] *The Wall Street Journal,* July 13, 1990, p. C1.

[31] Ibid. p. C23.

The conflict between Salomon and the Treasury highlighted an inherent ambiguity in the Treasury's role. On the one hand, the Treasury needed to find a market for the $30 billion in new government debt that was auctioned each week. To this end, the Treasury wanted to ensure that bidders in the auction made enough profit to compensate them for assuming the risk inherent in underwriting new government debt. Since the large dealers like Salomon took the bulk of each auction, the Treasury had an undeniable interest in seeing that Salomon and the other large dealers earned a profit on their government debt underwriting activities. On the other hand, the Treasury had responsibility for regulating the auctions and ensuring their fairness. If the market perceived that Salomon and other large dealers had too large an advantage in the auction, smaller dealers might choose not to participate, thus reducing competition and ultimately raising the government's borrowing costs.

Mozer's Treasury Auction Activities[32]

When Paul Mozer came to John Meriwether on April 27, 1991, he disclosed that he had used a customer's name without authorization. Mozer admitted that on February 21, 1991, he submitted an unauthorized bid for 35% of the $9 billion five-year note auction in the name of Warburg, a Salomon customer, in addition to a bid for 35% in Salomon's name. Salomon's two bids turned out to be at the stop-out yield and the Fed awarded $1.7 billion in notes each to Salomon and Warburg. After the auction, Mozer instructed the trading desk to transfer the notes awarded to Warburg to Salomon's account and to suppress the written customer confirmation of the activity. In the end, Salomon ended up with 38% of the auction, only slightly more than the 35% limit because the unauthorized Warburg bid crowded out Salomon's own bid and lowered the proration percentage to 54%.

What brought Mozer to Meriwether's desk was the fact that the Federal Reserve had noticed that Warburg had submitted two different bids in the auction, one for its own account of $100 million and another via Salomon Brothers for $1.7 billion. When the Fed contacted Salomon to ask about the Warburg bid, Mozer instructed Thomas Murphy to tell the Fed that the bid should have been in the name of Mercury Asset Management, an operationally separate affiliate of S.G. Warburg, another primary dealer.

When the Fed forwarded the correction received from Salomon to the Treasury, the Treasury decided that the relationship between S.G. Warburg and Mercury Asset Management was close enough to limit the combined bids of both entities to 35% of the auction. In a letter dated April 17, 1991, sent to the head of Mercury, the Treasury reviewed the two bids by Warburg and noted that the legal relationship between the two required that they limit their combined bids to 35% of an auction. The Treasury sent a copy of the letter to Paul Mozer, S.G. Warburg, and S.G. Warburg, plc, the parent of Mercury and S.G. Warburg.

---

[32] This section draws heavily on the written statement of Salomon Inc submitted in conjunction with the testimony of Warren Buffett before the House Subcommittee on Telecommunications and Finance on September 3, 1991.

In an effort to stem any further investigation by the Treasury, Paul Mozer contacted Mercury and requested that the firm not respond to the Treasury's letter.[33] Mozer explained the problem as a mistake and asked that Mercury not embarrass Salomon by volunteering information about the mistake to the Treasury. Thomas Murphy also tried unsuccessfully to set up a meeting between Paul Mozer and an acquaintance of his at S.G. Warburg, who happened to be the managing director who had received the Treasury's letter. When Murphy failed to arrange a meeting, Mozer notified Meriwether on April 27, 1991, of the Treasury's letter. In the meeting, Meriwether warned Mozer "that the matter was very serious and represented career-threatening conduct."[34] When Meriwether pressed Mozer on the extent of his unauthorized use of customers' names, Mozer had assured him that there had been only one such incident.

Over Mozer's objections, Meriwether immediately notified Tom Strauss and informed him of Mozer's disclosures. The following morning, April 28, 1991, Meriwether, Strauss, and Donald Feuerstein, Salomon's chief legal counsel, met to discuss Mozer's admissions. All three agreed that John Gutfreund, who was traveling on business at the time, needed to be informed of the violations. When the group informed Gutfreund the next day, April 29, 1991, all four agreed that they had to report Mozer's offense to the regulators supervising the sale of Treasury securities. The group discussed how best to report the matter, but did not reach a decision on how to approach the government with the disclosures. Mozer remained the head of the Treasury securities trading activities.

The May Squeeze

Meriwether's attention was drawn again to Mozer's Treasury securities trading activities shortly after the May 22, 1991 auction of $12 billion in two-year notes. In that auction, Paul Mozer submitted a $4.2 billion bid in Salomon's name (34% of the auction), a $2 billion bid for Tiger Investments (17% of the auction), and a $4.3 billion bid for Quantum Fund (35% of the auction). All three bids were at the aggressive yield of 6.81%, two basis points below most dealers' expectations for the auction. As a result, Salomon's and its customers' bids offered the government the best rate in the auction and the Treasury awarded Salomon, Tiger, and Quantum the full amount of their bids without proration.

Salomon and its customers now controlled $10.6 billion of the new notes awarded to bidders at the May 22 auction. One week after the auction, Tiger sold its entire position to Salomon, which in turn sold $600 million in notes to Quantum. These two transactions occurred at market prices that were higher than the auction price and generated a profit for Tiger. Salomon and Quantum continued to control the majority of the notes issued in the auction.

After the auction, the two-year notes rose in price as dealers scrambled to buy notes with which to meet their commitments to provide new notes to their customers and other dealers. Because so few notes were available for sale after the auction, many dealers had to borrow them from Salomon and Quantum under "repurchase agreements," a standard arrangement under which the notes would

---

[33] The letter did not request a response.
[34] *New York Times*, September 5, 1991, p. D23.

go back to Salomon after a specific period of time. Because of the short supply, Salomon and Quantum were able to charge a higher than normal interest rate for the temporary use of the new notes.

For example, Michael Irelan, a trader for St. Louis–based Boatmen's Bank had made preauction commitments to deliver $120 million in notes to other dealers after the auction. In making these commitments, Irelan had ignored the advice of his friend, Thomas Murphy at Salomon, who had suggested that demand for the notes would be high after the auction and that they would be hard to find. After the auction, no notes were available and Irelan was forced to borrow them from Salomon, costing Boatmen's Bank a net loss of $8,000 per day.[35]

Irelan was not alone in getting caught in the May squeeze. Many speculators had expected lackluster demand for the notes and declining prices after the auction. Together with Irelan, they complained bitterly to the Fed about Salomon's position. In response to these complaints, the Fed contacted Salomon and asked that it sell or loan its two-year notes to alleviate the squeeze. Paul Mozer told the Fed that he would do what he could to make sure that the notes were available to short sellers at a rate that allowed them to meet their commitments.

Tight markets like the May squeeze were not uncommon in Treasury trading. Just one month prior, Salomon itself had been caught short of two-year notes in a squeeze that developed when two large investors, Caxton Corp. and Steinhardt Partners, each bought $8 billion of April two-year notes. The squeeze developed when the two investors sold the securities to foreign banks that would not lend them to dealers on Wall Street. As late as June, many of the biggest dealers continued to lose money in the squeeze.[36]

Although the Treasury was upset about Salomon's possible involvement in the May squeeze, the U.S. government and American taxpayers probably benefited from Salomon's aggressiveness. Salomon's bid of 6.81% saved the government almost $5 million in interest. Furthermore, most of the large and small investors in the U.S. government securities market were not hurt. The state governments, pension funds, and government bond mutual funds that held most of the government debt did not make preauction commitments like the ones arranged by Michael Irelan. If these investors bought the notes at the May auction, they benefited from the tight conditions that developed.

Meriwether's Concerns

By early June, 1991, Salomon had still not disclosed Mozer's unauthorized bid in the February auction and the Treasury was now upset about the firm's possible role in the May squeeze. As the vice chairman with responsibility for U.S. Treasury securities trading activities, Meriwether was ultimately responsible for the actions of Mozer and the other traders in his department.

---

[35] *The Wall Street Journal*, October 31, 1991, p. A1.
[36] *The Wall Street Journal*, October 7, 1991, p. A1.

II   BUILDING ORGANIZATIONAL INTEGRITY

Creating Context

Executives today increasingly recognize that corporate ethics should not be left to chance. As the CEO of a major international securities firm underscored in a 1993 speech, one of the key tasks of a chief executive is "establishing, maintaining, and communicating the company's ethical standards."[1] The cases presented in Part I illustrate vividly some of the potential perils of neglecting this task. Part II explores the strategies company leaders have followed in carrying it out.

The idea that corporate leaders are responsible for organizational ethics is not a new one. In 1938, management theorist Chester I. Barnard described the executive's role in "creating morals for others" in his book *The Functions of the Executive*.[2] According to Barnard, the function of developing organizational morals is a distinguishing characteristic of executive work going far beyond the moral challenges faced by individuals generally. Besides superior technical skills, a high capacity for responsibility, and a complex personal morality, this task requires moral creativity in defining an organization's code of ethics and instilling the fundamental attitudes that support it.

Although few executives today would describe themselves as "creating morals for others," many would acknowledge their role in shaping corporate ethics. A growing body of research indicates that organizational factors play a critical role in fostering—or in discouraging—

---

[1]Robert E. Denham, "Remarks Before the 20th Annual Securities Regulation Institute," Coronado, CA, January 21, 1993 (unpublished manuscript).
[2]Chester I. Barnard, *The Functions of the Executive* (Cambridge, MA: Harvard University Press, 1938), p. 272 ff.

responsible behavior on the job.[3] Individual characteristics such as personal values, stage of moral development, knowledge, and skills are critically important. But behavior and values also are shaped by organizational factors such as opportunities, incentives, information, and the example set by others. Whether explicitly or implicitly, executives influence company value systems through their choices both as decision makers and as designers of their organizations.[4]

A survey of corporate ethics initiatives would show that executives have conceived of ethics and ethics leadership in many different ways. Some regard ethics as a floor—a set of minimum standards of behavior. For this group, questions of ethics typically revolve around the level at which the floor is set. The characteristic ethical dilemma is whether to commit an unethical act to achieve a desired outcome. Others view ethics as a set of guiding ideals or aspirations that can never be fully realized. Executives with this conception are more likely to be concerned with their company's core values. For these executives, the characteristic ethical dilemma involves a conflict between competing values or responsibilities.

Ideally, an ethical framework should include both minimum and aspirational standards of behavior, along with a conception of the organization's purpose and the parties to whom it is accountable. Taken together, these dimensions anchor a company's value system firmly in its core responsibilities. Recent research suggests that some executives are coming to think of ethics in this more comprehensive way, as encompassing both principles and prohibitions.[5] This approach lines up with research on corporate control systems which underscores the importance of both belief systems and boundary systems in guiding employee behavior.[6]

While there are many approaches to building a corporate value system based on sound ethical principles, all require the active involvement of company leaders. Four aspects of the leader's role in developing and managing organizational ethics deserve special attention:

- Developing the ethical framework.
- Aligning the organization.

---

[3]See, e.g., Linda Klebe Trevino and Stuart A. Youngblood, "Bad Apples in Bad Barrels: A Causal Analysis of Ethical Decision-Making Behavior," *Journal of Applied Psychology* 75, no. 4 (1990), pp. 378–385. See also Karen N. Gaertner, "The Effects of Ethical Climate on Managers' Decisions," in *Morality, Rationality, and Efficiency: New Perspectives in Socioeconomics*, Richard M. Coughlin, ed. (New York: M. E. Sharpe 1991), pp. 211–223.

[4]To see how executive philosophies implicitly shape company value systems, see Joseph L. Badaracco, Jr., and Richard R. Ellsworth, *Leadership and the Quest for Integrity* (Boston, MA: Harvard Business School Press, 1989).

[5]A 1992 survey of large U.S.-based corporations found that 49 of the 235 companies responding had developed three different types of ethics documents: a values statement, a credo identifying the company's stakeholders, and a code of conduct. Patrick E. Murphy, "Corporate Ethics Statements: Current Status and Future Prospects," *Journal of Business Ethics* 14, 1995, p. 732.

[6]Robert Simons, "Control in an Age of Empowerment," *Harvard Business Review*, March-April 1995, pp. 81–88.

- Leading by example.
- Addressing external challenges.

Attention to these four leadership tasks is important whether an organization is a large global corporation, a subunit within a company, or a small group working as a project team. Before examining these four tasks in more detail, a preliminary issue for discussion is the choice of a basic ethics strategy.

Corporate Ethics Strategies

Executives who take their responsibility for corporate ethics seriously must address two fundamental issues. First, what ethical standards and values should guide the organization? Second, how should the standards be instilled and maintained over time? Although companies have given a variety of answers to these questions, corporate efforts to define and maintain ethical standards tend to fall into one of two general categories.

Compliance-Oriented Strategies

One group regards ethics as essentially a matter of legal compliance. Following the dictum "if it's legal, it's ethical," these companies look primarily to the law to define their standard of behavior. Ethics is conceived as a constraint or a set of boundaries defining an area of permissible, but otherwise ethically neutral conduct. Compliance-oriented approaches tend to emphasize the avoidance of unlawful conduct and typically rely on rules, controls, and strict discipline to maintain standards. Responsibility for corporate ethics is often vested in the company's chief legal officer.

The compliance-based approach to ethics has gained popularity in the United States since the Federal Sentencing Guidelines for Organizations took effect in 1991. Under these guidelines, companies can earn substantial reductions in potential fines for criminal misconduct by implementing programs to detect and prevent violations of law. (See **Box 1**.) Seven "hallmarks" are considered indicative of an effective program:[7]

- A set of compliance standards and procedures.
- The appointment of high-level personnel to oversee compliance with the standards.
- Assurances that discretionary authority will not be delegated to anyone who is likely to act illegally.
- The adoption of systems for communicating the standards and procedures.
- The adoption of systems for monitoring, auditing, and reporting criminal misconduct.

---

[7]United States Sentencing Commission, *Guidelines Manual*, §§8A1.2 and 8C2.5 (November 1992), pp. 362, 374–378.

BOX 1

Corporate Fines Under the Federal Sentencing Guidelines

What size fine is a corporation likely to pay if convicted of a crime? It depends on a number of factors, some of which are beyond a CEO's control, such as the existence of a prior record of similar misconduct. But it also depends on more controllable factors. The most important of these are reporting and accepting responsibility for the crime, cooperating with authorities, and having an effective program in place to prevent and detect unlawful behavior.

The following example, based on a case studied by the United States Sentencing Commission, shows how the 1991 Federal Sentencing Guidelines have affected overall fine levels and how managers' actions influence organizational fines.

Acme Corporation was charged and convicted of mail fraud. The company systematically charged customers who damaged rented automobiles more than the actual cost of repairs. Acme also billed some customers for the cost of repairs to vehicles for which they were not responsible. Prior to the criminal adjudication, Acme paid $13.7 million in restitution to the customers who had been overcharged.

Deciding before the enactment of the sentencing guidelines, the judge in the criminal case imposed a fine of $6.85 million, roughly half the pecuniary loss suffered by Acme's customers. Under the sentencing guidelines, however, the results could have been dramatically different. Acme could have been fined anywhere from 5 percent to 200 percent of the loss suffered by customers, depending on whether or not it had an effective program to prevent and detect violations of law and on whether or not it reported the crime, cooperated with authorities, and accepted responsibility for the unlawful conduct. If a high ranking official at Acme were found to have been involved, the maximum fine could have been as large as $54,800,000 or four times the loss to Acme customers. The following chart shows a possible range of fines for each situation:

What Fine Can Acme Expect?

	Maximum	Minimum
Program, reporting, cooperation, responsibility	$2,740,000	$685,000
Program only	10,960,000	5,480,000
No program, no reporting, no cooperation, no responsibility	27,400,000	13,700,000
No program, no reporting, no cooperation, no responsibility, involvement of high-level personnel	54,800,000	27,400,000

Based on Case No.: 88–266, United States Sentencing Commission, *Supplementary Report on Sentencing Guidelines for Organizations.*

Source: Lynn Sharp Paine, "Managing for Organizational Integrity," *Harvard Business Review*, March–April 1994, p. 110. © 1994 by the President and Fellows of Harvard College.

- Consistent enforcement of the standards through discipline.
- A history of appropriate responses to identified offenses, including preventive action as needed.

Using these seven hallmarks as a template, many companies have put in place ethics programs based on the legal compliance model.

Integrity-Oriented Strategies

A second group of companies has taken a broader approach, one focusing on self-governance according to guiding principles. In these companies, ethics is conceived more robustly as a set of values to guide rather than just constrain behavior. While adherence to law is typically embraced as an important principle, it is not regarded as the whole of ethics. Nor is it a matter of external compulsion. Such companies may have well-defined rules and controls to ensure legal compliance, especially if they are large companies operating in a regulated industry, but for them adherence to law is primarily a matter of "who we are" or "what we stand for."

This second approach, which may be called integrity-based, rests on a conception of organizational identity that includes not only commercial objectives, but a set of organizational ideals and responsibilities as well. Merck, one of the world's most admired pharmaceutical companies, provides an example. Known for its outstanding financial performance as well as its good deeds, Merck has long thought of itself as first and foremost a provider of medicine to patients, with responsibilities to this and other groups.[8] In integrity-based companies, primary emphasis is placed not on preventing wrongdoing but on supporting responsible behavior. Ethical standards are instilled and maintained through the organization's central management systems: its leadership, governance structures, operating systems, and decision processes. Detecting and punishing misconduct are regarded not as the goal of an ethics system but as at best an unpleasant necessity.

Comparing the Two Strategies

These two generic ethics strategies provide an instructive contrast. (See **Box 2**.) But it would be a mistake to regard them as totally unrelated. In practice, companies sometimes evolve from a compliance orientation toward an integrity orientation. Moreover, certain elements may be found in companies adopting either approach: training in law, systems for investigating misconduct, controls to ensure compliance, for example.

Nevertheless, an integrity orientation is both broader and deeper than a compliance orientation. It encompasses adherence to law as a first-order responsibility, but it goes beyond compliance in several important ways. First, it regards the law as only a partial catalogue of ethical standards—one that is silent on important responsibilities and ideals that should inform decision making and behavior in the organization. Second, it takes a systemic approach to maintaining standards, relying in the first instance on the organization's driving systems and only secon-

---

[8]For discussion of Merck's philosophy, see James C. Collins and Jerry I. Porras, *Built to Last* (New York: HarperCollins Publishers, 1994), p. 48.

Box 2

Strategies for Ethics Management

Characteristics of Compliance Strategy		*Characteristics of Integrity Strategy*	
Ethos	Conformity with externally imposed standards	Ethos	Self-governance according to chosen standards
Objective	Prevent unlawful conduct	Objective	Enable responsible conduct
Leadership	Lawyer driven	Leadership	Management driven with aid of lawyers, human resources, others
Methods	Education, reduced discretion, auditing and controls, penalties	Methods	Education, leadership, accountability, organizational systems and decision processes, auditing and controls, penalties
Behavioral Assumptions	Autonomous beings guided by material self-interest	Behavioral Assumptions	Social beings guided by material self-interest, values, ideals, peers
Implementation of Compliance Strategy		*Implementation of Compliance Strategy*	
Standards	Criminal and regulatory law	Standards	Company values and aspirations, social obligations, including law
Staffing	Lawyers	Staffing	Executives and managers with lawyers, others
Activities	Develop compliance standards, train and communicate, handle reports of misconduct, conduct investigations, oversee compliance audits, enforce standards	Activities	Lead development of company values and standards, train and communicate, integrate into company systems, provide guidance and consultation, assess values performance, identify and resolve problems, oversee compliance activities
Education	Compliance standards and system	Education	Decision making and values, compliance standards and system

Source: Lynn Sharp Paine, "Managing for Organizational Integrity," *Harvard Business Review,* March–April 1994, p. 113. © 1994 by the President and Fellows of Harvard College.

darily on after-the-fact controls. The primary emphasis is channeling behavior through processes rather than output controls. Above all, an integrity-based approach regards ethics as a function of management, not of the legal department. Company lawyers may play a role in defining and maintaining company standards, but managers at all levels recognize that how they lead and manage is the critical factor in shaping corporate ethics.

Beyond Legal Compliance?

There is no question that today's company needs a sound approach to legal compliance. Through the legal process, society defines a base-level of responsibilities for which companies and their agents and employees may be held accountable. Companies operating in countries with legitimate systems of government have a presumptive duty to obey the law. Given the complexity of law today, few companies operating in the major markets of the industrialized world can effectively fulfill their legal responsibilities without specific compliance mechanisms. A purely aspirational approach to corporate ethics leaves them excessively vulnerable to legal failure.

Moreover, as seen in Part I, legal failures can have serious consequences for managers and their companies. Besides costly legal and market penalties, legal problems can undermine confidence in a company or its management and generate organizational crises of major proportions. Without an effective compliance system, companies and their executives increase the risk of substantial fines if they are found guilty of a criminal offense. In the worst case, legal breakdowns can lead to the demise of a company, the end of a career, or even to imprisonment for corporate executives.

The case for compliance is compelling, but is there any reason to go further? The argument for a broader, more systemic approach rests on the limitations of standard compliance efforts as well as on the positive aspects of an integrity-driven approach. Some considerations bearing on the design of a basic ethics strategy include the following.

Limitations of a Legal Standard

Although compliance with law is a must, the law is quite limited as a guide to responsible behavior, and it is no guide at all to the exemplary behavior sought by leadership companies. For one thing, the law is backward looking. Geared to the circumstances and technologies of the past, it is typically a lagging indicator of social expectations. Companies on the cutting edge of technology and those looking for the best practices of the future will find little guidance in the law. For another thing, the law must apply to everyone.[9] Therefore, it can demand only what can reasonably be expected of the average company. Companies aspiring to more must look elsewhere for benchmarks.

As for companies seeking refuge for questionable behavior in the letter of existing law, they are well advised to remember that the law is not static. It evolves over time in response to social, political, and economic forces. Unless managers wish to make their company the "test case" or the trigger for new legislation, they will be as concerned with the underlying ethical principles that shape people's sense of justice as with the current state of the law.

---

[9]This point is discussed in Frederic G. Corneel, "The Role of Law: Musings on Solzhenitsyn," *Boston Bar Journal*, June 1983, p. 9.

A law-based approach to ethics presupposes well-developed legal and regulatory systems. Yet, national legal systems around the world are in various stages of development. In many countries, the legal system is in its infancy, and resources for developing and enforcing laws are scarce. Companies doing business in these countries have no choice but to set their own standards if they are to have companywide standards at all. In the absence of a legal infrastructure, it is meaningless to speak of legal compliance as the measure of responsible behavior.

The limits of law as a guide to responsible conduct are reflected in the experiences of companies with formal ethics programs. Many have found that the majority of concerns raised by employees have little to do with law. While allegations and concerns about possible illegality are indeed raised, employees more often call to discuss matters of fairness, supervisory style, treatment of people, competing responsibilities, corporate policy, and decisions in grey areas. The experiences of these companies suggest that a law-based approach to ethics will be found wanting by many employees.

Limits of the Compliance Ethos

In today's business environment, the prevailing watchwords are *empowerment* and *accountability*. In an increasingly dynamic and knowledge-driven economy, companies are ever more dependent on the creativity and initiative of people at all levels of their organizations. Employees, especially those on the front lines, must be able to act quickly and decisively in response to changing conditions and customer needs. In this context, a work environment characterized by trust, responsibility, and high aspirations is not a luxury. It is a competitive necessity. In practical terms, this means entrusting people with greater discretion, authority, and resources to make decisions and do their jobs, while at the same time expecting high levels of personal accountability and responsibility.

With its emphasis on reduced discretion, increased oversight, and tighter penalties for rule violations, a compliance-driven approach to ethics can run directly counter to the spirit of empowerment. This is not to deny the importance of clear ethical boundaries and penalties for violating legitimate organizational norms. Indeed, most employees regard appropriate discipline as an important aspect of organizational justice.[10] But an overemphasis on internal whistleblowing and potential sanctions can be counterproductive. Rather than building trust, this approach may, in fact, diminish it. One company that introduced a compliance-based ethics program and an empowerment initiative within a period of several months found the net result to be cynicism about both.

---

[10]For supporting research, see Linda Klebe Trevino, "The Social Effects of Punishment in Organizations: A Justice Perspective," *Academy of Management Review* 17, no. 4 (1992), pp. 647–676.

In principle, empowerment and adherence to law are fully compatible. Certainly, empowerment should presuppose legal compliance. But, in practice, compliance-driven ethics initiatives sometimes have a heavy-handed, top-down feel about them, especially when reporting illegality is presented not as one important aspect of ethics but as the whole of it. Although empowerment implies high aspirations, the message implicit in some compliance-based ethics programs is quite different. Former SEC Chairman Richard Breeden made the point effectively when he quipped, "Aspiring to get through the day without being indicted is not an adequate ethical standard."[11]

The Effectiveness of Compliance Programs

The limited reach of the typical compliance program is yet another reason for something more. Such programs generally aim to prevent unlawful conduct through education about the law, oversight, and control systems. But the root causes of unlawful corporate conduct typically lie in the decision processes, behavioral norms, culture, and reward systems of organizations.[12] Compliance programs rarely address these fundamental behavioral influences and the management systems behind them.

While compliance systems are necessary to facilitate legal compliance, their effectiveness is likely to be limited unless respect for law is part of the corporate value system. If the value system favors financial results at any cost, corporate leaders should not be surprised if enterprising individuals seek to bypass even sophisticated compliance and control mechanisms. Experience indicates that compliance efforts are most effective when embedded in a belief system that values obedience to law. Even if the primary goal of an ethics initiative is preventing unlawful behavior, the place to begin is the company's basic framework of values.

Toward Organizational Integrity

For these and other reasons discussed in Part I, some companies have chosen to approach ethics holistically as a matter of organizational

---

[11]Quoted in Kevin V. Salwen, "SEC Chief's Criticisms of Ex-Managers of Salomon Suggests Civil Action Likely," *The Wall Street Journal*, November 20, 1991, p. A10.
[12]For research supporting this account of unlawful corporate conduct, see the following sources: Marshall B. Clinard, *Corporate Ethics and Crime* (Beverly Hills, CA: Sage Publications, 1983); Marshall B. Clinard and Peter C. Yeager, *Corporate Crime* (New York The Free Press, 1980); John C. Coffee, Jr., "Beyond the Shut-Eyed Sentry: Toward a Theoretical View of Corporate Misconduct and an Effective Legal Response," *Virginia Law Review* 63, November 1977, pp. 1,099–1,278; Jeffrey Sonnenfeld and Paul R. Lawrence, "Why Do Companies Succumb to Price Fixing?" *Harvard Business Review*, July–August 1978, pp. 145–157; Christopher D. Stone, *Where the Law Ends: The Social Control of Corporate Behavior* (New York: Harper, 1975).

integrity. The term *integrity* is rich in meaning and history. Derived from the Latin word *integritas* meaning wholeness or purity, integrity is often identified with the qualities of honesty, reliability, and fair dealing. But it also implies a general sense of responsibility, a set of commitments, and a capacity for self-governance. In its broad sense, integrity suggests a coherent integration of identity and responsibility. As with many qualities, integrity comes in degrees. The highest levels are associated with principled behavior in the face of adversity or temptation.

Companies taking an integrity-oriented approach to corporate ethics follow many different paths, depending on their business, their history, their leaders. There is no single approach that is right for every company. As illustrated in the cases in this segment, some focus on fulfilling basic obligations and avoiding misconduct, going only slightly beyond legal compliance. Often found in highly regulated industries, these companies place strong emphasis on adherence to law and on the core values of integrity: accountability, honesty, reliability, and fair play. They may use detailed codes of conduct to communicate essential standards of behavior. While legal compliance is critical in such companies, it is embraced as a matter of corporate citizenship.

Other companies place great emphasis on their distinctive purpose and values, often focusing on guiding ideals. For these companies, integrity is rooted as much in their distinctive organizational identity as in their socially defined responsibilities. Instead of relying exclusively on codes of conduct with specific behavioral requirements and prohibitions, they look in addition to attitudes, decision processes, and ways of thinking to channel behavior in responsible directions.

Like quality or competitiveness, integrity is an abstract concept. But it is grounded in everyday behavior that is consistent with the organization's responsibilities and with its distinctive purposes and ideals. Though ethical frameworks and implementation methods may differ, high-integrity organizations typically exhibit the following characteristics:

- Members take ownership of their conduct. They do not pass the buck or try to deflect accountability for their choices.

- Members are trustworthy and conscientious. They can be relied on to be truthful, to be fair, to stand by their promises, and to carry out their responsibilities in a competent manner.

- Members have a strong sense of organizational identity. They are committed to the organization's purposes and ideals, and strive to achieve them in a responsible manner.

- The organization, as a collective, consistently fulfills its responsibilities to its various stakeholders and acts as a good corporate citizen. The organization relies on a variety of self-governance mechanisms to achieve this aim.

- There is a high degree of coherence between the principles and values espoused by corporate leadership and the day-to-day practices of the organization. The coherence is never perfect since ethical ideals are by their nature aspirational, but the divergence between practice and principle is not so great that it impugns the credibility of the organization and its leadership.

Building Organizational Integrity

Building and maintaining organizational integrity around a sense of purpose, responsibility, and shared ideals is a far greater challenge than setting up a legal compliance program. Integrity does not happen automatically. The proverbial "tone at the top" is critical, but anyone aspiring to lead a high-integrity organization must be concerned with several important leadership tasks requiring attention, effort, and resources.

Task One: Developing the Ethical Framework

Integrity presupposes a substantive set of responsibilities and ideals. Any effort to achieve integrity must be based on an ethical framework defining these fundamentals. Such a framework serves as an ethical compass to guide planning, decision making, and the assessment of performance. Moreover, it notifies prospective investors, members, and business partners of an organization's ethical stance.

The elements of a framework can be sketched by considering three important dimensions of responsibility and posing the questions suggested by each:

- **Purpose:** *What is the organization's ultimate mission? What are its goals in furtherance of this mission?* These questions probe the organization's reason for being and the ways it seeks to create value.
- **Principle:** *What are the organization's obligations? What is the scope of its legitimate authority? What ideals does it seek to uphold?* These questions seek to identify the organization's duties, rights, and values.
- **People:** *What are the organization's key constituencies? What are their rights, claims, and legitimate interests?* These questions aim to define the social interests served by the organization.

The answers to these questions establish the defining elements of the corporate value system. They help map the field of responsible action and set up directional guides for decision making and corporate action.

Some companies have a clear, concise ethical framework. It may be expressed in a written code of conduct, in a vision statement, or in some other type of document.[13] Or it may exist only through the words and deeds of the organization's members. Whether it is written like the U.S. Constitution or unwritten like the British Constitution matters far less than whether it is understood and lived. To be sure, the process of developing a written document is a useful way to enhance understanding and commitment. Writing encourages clarity and facilitates later communication. Still, elaborate documentation of an ethical framework is neither a necessary nor a sufficient condition for achieving integrity.

The process for developing the framework and periodically redefining it deserves careful consideration. An interactive process encompassing a variety of perspectives is preferable by far to a corner-office effort. Ethical guidelines delivered from on high may presume too much—or too little—about the organizational capabilities of subunits and the social and economic context in which they must operate. Moreover, such guidelines may be perceived as a public image program of little internal importance. While the involvement of those expected to use the framework is crucial, management cannot shy away from leadership in developing standards and making tough calls when important values are at stake.

Task Two: Aligning the Organization

It is not unusual for companies to devote substantial effort to developing an ethical framework only to discover that actual practice falls far short of the ideal. Up to a point, such divergence is to be expected. After all, people are fallible, and the framework is intended to express a set of aspirations that, by definition, go beyond actual behavior. But in many cases the "ethics gap" is symptomatic of a serious misalignment between the articulated ethical framework and the systems and processes that drive the organization. A common culprit is the one-dimensional reward system, which focuses exclusively on "making the numbers." When short-term performance is all that counts, the risk of misconduct is intensified. In high-pressure situations, without countervailing incentives, such systems can lead employees to ignore other dimensions of their conduct and even to infringe basic legal obligations.

Similarly, the diffusion of information and responsibility associated with traditional large-company hierarchies can result in serious accountability gaps. For example, sales personnel may unwittingly make deliv-

---

[13]Recent research on ethics documents can be found in Ronald E. Berenbeim, *Corporate Ethics Practices* (New York: The Conference Board, Report No. 986, 1992); Ethics Resource Center, Inc., *Ethics Policies and Programs in American Business* (Washington, D.C., 1990); Ethics Resource Center, Inc., *Ethics in American Business: Policies, Programs, and Perceptions* (Washington, D.C., 1994); Patrick E. Murphy, "Corporate Ethics Statements: Current Status and Future Prospects," *Journal of Business Ethics* 14, 1995, pp. 727–740; D. C. Robertson and B. B. Schlegelmilch, "Corporate Institutionalization of Ethics in the United States and Great Britain," *Journal of Business Ethics* 12, 1993, pp. 301–312.

ery promises the company cannot keep because they lack up-to-date information about production schedules and capabilities. Or, to take another example, product safety problems may be hidden from view if customer complaint information is scattered across the company or if knowledgeable employees have no authority to take corrective action.

Careful attention to the design of organizational structures and systems is essential to building and maintaining integrity. When these are out of sync with the governing framework, members receive mixed messages and may lack adequate support for responsible action. Conversely, executives can build favorable conditions for ethical conduct into the fabric of the organization by insuring that members have adequate opportunities, abilities, and incentives to act responsibly. Particular attention should be paid to the following systems:

- Leadership and supervision.
- Hiring and promotion.
- Performance evaluation and rewards.
- Employee development and education.
- Planning and goal setting.
- Budgeting and resource allocation.
- Information and communications.
- Audit and control.

In recent years, some companies have built additional support for corporate integrity by adding ethics, corporate responsibility, or integrity committees to their boards of directors. Some have also created corporate ethics offices, or business practices committees to perform functions such as fielding employees' questions, conducting training, solving problems, dealing with allegations of misconduct, or evaluating ethical performance on an ongoing basis. The value of adding such infrastructure depends very much on the particulars of the organization. In companies with a strong ethical culture where such activities are performed within existing functions, an ethics function might be superfluous. But it could be quite valuable for a company seeking to change its culture, to enhance support for ethical conduct, or to satisfy the Federal Sentencing Guidelines. While no single approach is right for all companies, alignment between an organization's management processes and its ethical framework is essential.

Task Three: Leading by Example

Perhaps the most important factor in building and maintaining integrity is the example set by the organization's leaders. Employees typically look first to the example set by their immediate supervisor for indications of their organization's ethical standards. But a company's ethical stance is most powerfully defined through the behavior of individuals invested with greatest authority. Their behavior sends a message far clearer than any in a corporate ethics statement.

Obvious inconsistencies with espoused standards, even when unintentional, inevitably lead to cynicism and erosion of the standards. Well-meaning talk about respecting the law, for example, is quickly undermined by a manager's thoughtless tolerance of unlawful software use. Thousands of dollars on quality training are wasted if managers turn a blind eye when conscientious employees raise quality concerns.

By the same token, leadership that clearly and forcefully exemplifies espoused values reinforces commitment and respect. A particularly powerful statement is made when adherence to principle involves risk and uncertainty. The Johnson & Johnson Tylenol recall discussed in Part I is a case in point.[14] As noted earlier, Johnson & Johnson did a nationwide recall of Tylenol, its highly successful pain reliever, after six people died from product tampering in 1982. Although the recall decision ultimately redounded to the benefit of the company, it was at the time extremely costly and fraught with uncertainty. Marketing experts were predicting the demise of the brand. But Johnson & Johnson's response validated the customers-first commitment espoused in its credo, cementing customer confidence and casting a positive image over the company and all its products. Tylenol subsequently regained its position of market leadership.

Leading by example is perhaps even more important in ordinary day-to-day situations that are invisible to the public. As one successful entrepreneur noted, managers establish ethical standards simply in how they deal with the routine pressures of business life:

> How much do you embellish your financial condition, the resources behind you, the success of your customers? . . . To get the sale, do you promise things you know you can't deliver? Do you make promises to your employees you know you can't keep? . . . You have to realize that as a CEO, you're a role model and an example. People learn from your actions more than you ever believe. . . .[15]

Satisfying the full array of important responsibilities and values can be difficult if not impossible in some cases. Leaders, even outstanding ones, do not always "get it right." What matters from an integrity perspective, however, is how such conflicts and tradeoffs are handled, and whether the company's diverse responsibilities are fulfilled over time.

---

[14]*James Burke: A Career in American Business (A), (B),* Harvard Business School Case No. 389–177, 390–030 (1989).
[15]"The Ethics of Bootstrapping," *Inc.,* September 1992, pp. 87, 95.

Task Four: Addressing External Challenges

In some situations, the main impediments to organizational integrity lie outside the organization. When their competitors use bribes or kickbacks to secure business, or when they endanger worker safety to control costs, responsible companies may find themselves at a disadvantage. In regions lacking the social and legal infrastructures needed to support responsible business practices, companies aspiring to higher ideals may find they are pressured to compromise even basic standards to remain competitive.

In such situations, changes in external conditions may be necessary to enable high-integrity companies to compete successfully. As leaders in many industries have found, it may be necessary to work toward changes in laws, regulations, or industry practices. Collaboration with government, industry groups, community representatives, or nongovernmental organizations may be called for.

Initiatives to address external challenges to corporate integrity can be found in a variety of industries.[16] Two well-known examples are the U.S. Defense Industry Initiative on Business Ethics, launched in 1986, and the chemical industry's "Responsible Care" program also launched in the mid-1980s.[17] Worldwide efforts have been undertaken by the agricultural chemicals and infant formula industries, among others.[18] Unless companies take steps like these to address the external conditions that depress ethical standards, they may face the unhappy choice of either compromising their core values or forgoing otherwise desirable opportunities.

Leaders of responsible companies will want to be aware of the integrity challenges inherent in industries and environments in which they operate. Although it is not always feasible to change problematic conditions, it is important to recognize the pressures they create and to consider carefully the organization's stance. As managers develop business strategies, they should understand the ethical as well as the economic characteristics of possible moves, and plan accordingly.

---

[16]For examples of industry self-regulation, see *Note on Industry Self-Regulation and U.S. Antitrust Laws*, Harvard Business School Case No. 395–214 (1995). See also David A. Garvin, "Can Industry Self-Regulation Work?" *California Management Review* 25, no. 4 (Summer 1983), pp. 37–52; Thomas A. Hemphill, "Self-Regulating Industry Behavior: Antitrust Limitations and Trade Association Codes of Conduct," *Journal of Business Ethics* 11, 1992, pp. 915–920.

[17]See *Responsible Care*, Harvard Business School Case No. 391–135 (1991). For a description of the Defense Industry Initiative on Business Ethics, see *Martin Marietta: Managing Corporate Ethics*, Harvard Business School Case No. 393–016 (1992), pp. 5–6.

[18]For discussion of industry and government efforts to address the ethical issues involved in the global agricultural chemicals industry, see Lynn Sharp Paine, "Regulating the International Trade in Hazardous Pesticides: Closing the Accountability Gap," in *Ethical Theory and Business*, 4th ed., Tom L. Beauchamp and Norman E. Bowie, editors (Englewood Cliffs, NJ: Prentice-Hall, 1993), pp. 547–556.

A somewhat different challenge is posed by the diversity of ethical ideals in different cultures. Today, international managers are likely to face conflicting norms of right behavior, reflecting the distinctive ethical traditions, laws, customs, and economic and social conditions of different regions of the world. Among the most common are different norms concerning:

- Gift-giving.
- Gender and race relations.
- Environmental responsibility.
- Employment and workplace practices.
- Human health and safety standards.
- Worker and consumer privacy.
- Intellectual property rights.
- Competitive fairness.
- Whistleblowing (reporting on misconduct).

Such differences present managers with difficult ethical choices. They also present opportunities to draw on the world's varied traditions to work toward an organizational value system that is viable and ethically sound on a worldwide basis. Although it is unlikely that a single global standard of responsible business practice will emerge any time soon, the minimum requirements of such a standard can be discerned in the concept of free, informed, mutually beneficial exchange, and in the basic needs and interests of human beings everywhere.[19]

In recent years, business leaders, management thinkers, and philosophers have begun to address the challenge of articulating the elements of a global business ethic.[20] In 1994, for example, the Caux Roundtable of business leaders from Japan, Europe, and the United States issued a proposed set of ethical principles for global business.[21] In the same year, a

---

[19]For an argument that the outlines of a global business standard can be found in a variety of multilateral compacts adopted by governments since the end of World War II, see William C. Frederick, "The Moral Authority of Transnational Corporate Codes," *Journal of Business Ethics* 10, 1991, pp. 165–177. For skepticism about a global ethic, see David Vogel, "The Globalization of Business Ethics: Why America Remains Distinctive," *California Management Review* 35, Fall 1992, pp. 30–49. General skepticism toward a global ethic is expressed in Samuel P. Huntington, "The Clash of Civilizations?" *Foreign Affairs* 72, no. 3 (1993), pp. 22–49. See also Georges Enderle, "A Comparison of Business Ethics in North America and Continental Europe," *Business Ethics: A European Review* 5, no. 1 (January 1996), pp. 33–46.

[20]See, for example, Richard T. De George, *Competing with Integrity in International Business* (New York: Oxford University Press, 1993); Thomas Donaldson, *The Ethics of International Business* (New York: Oxford University Press, 1989).

[21]Caux Roundtable, *Principles for Business* (Minneapolis, MN: Minnesota Center for Corporate Responsibility, 1994).

group of business leaders representing the Christian, Muslim, and Jewish traditions issued an interfaith code of ethics for international business.[22] Numerous individual companies have sought to develop a value system to guide their businesses worldwide.[23] Today, managers everywhere have the opportunity to build on these foundations to help shape a global business system that will promote human development and efficient use of the world's resources in the 21st century.

The Limits of Corporate Ethics Management

Some managers have erred by taking too little responsibility for corporate ethics. Believing ethics to be a purely personal matter between individuals and their consciences, they have taken a hands-off approach. As managers recognize their role in leading and maintaining corporate ethics, it is important not to err in the other direction by assuming complete control. Even if managers take all the steps outlined above, they cannot rule out the possibility of ethical failure and even gross misconduct in their companies.

Leadership, systems, structures, culture—these can influence individual behavior, but they do not determine it. They can support individuals who *choose* to act responsibly, but they cannot determine what is responsible in a given situation or force people to act responsibly against their will. Nor can they eliminate human fallibility. As managers work to build and maintain high-integrity organizations, it is essential to remember that integrity starts with an acceptance of accountability and a desire to do what is right. But success depends ultimately on knowledge, skills, and continuous effort.

It is also worth noting that ethical failures are often symptomatic of management shortcomings. Behind irresponsible conduct frequently lurks poor strategic planning, inadequate job training, a shortage of resources, or faulty communications. The focus on organizational value systems should not obscure the central importance of basic managerial competence in achieving integrity.

Overview of Cases in Part II

The cases in Part II illustrate a variety of strategies for building organizational integrity. The companies presented range in size from 300 to 60,000 people. They represent industries that are highly regulated, some-

---

[22]*An Interfaith Declaration: A Code of Ethics on International Business for Christians, Muslims, and Jews* (London: British-North American Research Association, 1994).
[23]For an early example, see *Dow Corning Corporation: Business Conduct and Global Values (A)*, Harvard Business School Case No. 385–018 (1984). In this collection, see particularly *Levi Strauss & Co.: Global Sourcing (A)*, Harvard Business School Case No. 395–127 (1994).

what regulated, and only lightly regulated. The collection includes old companies seeking to change and young ones seeking to break new ground. All but one are publicly held. In every case, however, company leaders have taken steps to develop their organization's capacity for ethical self-governance. As the cases show, the challenges and the results are sometimes surprising.

All the companies examined in these cases have gone beyond legal compliance—to a greater or lesser extent—either in the ethical standards espoused or in the methods used to instill and maintain them. As noted above, managers have a wide range of methods for influencing behavior and shaping organizational values. While every case involves a variety of levers, each illustrates one or two that are particularly important.

Leadership and Compliance Systems   The first case, "Forging the New Salomon," highlights the role of company leadership and effective compliance systems. In August 1991, Salomon Brothers, the New York–based international securities firm, was thrown into a tailspin after publicly disclosing "irregularities and rule violations" in bidding for U.S. government securities. A funding crisis ensued when creditors learned that Salomon's four top executives had known about the misconduct for four months but had failed to do anything about it. Top management was forced to resign. Under the leadership of outside director and shareholder Warren Buffett, Salomon's new management moved swiftly to contain the crisis and restore confidence in the firm. The case provides an opportunity to evaluate the origins of Salomon's problems and the effectiveness of its crisis management effort, as well as the company's approach to maintaining integrity into the future.

Corporate Ethics Programs   The second case centers on the role of the corporate ethics program. In "Martin Marietta: Managing Corporate Ethics," top executives are searching for ways to assess the effectiveness of Martin Marietta's seven-year-old ethics program. In 1985, when the company was being investigated for possible wrongdoing, senior executives of the U.S. defense and aerospace firm decided to set up a corporate ethics office that would report to an executive-level Ethics Steering Committee. Clear ethical standards were established, and a system for reporting suspected misconduct was put in place. Ethics was made a factor in performance evaluations and a condition of incentive compensation for executives. As executives review the program in 1992, they are also concerned about employee fears of retribution for reporting suspected misconduct to the ethics office.

Performance Evaluation and Compensation Systems   A very different approach to ethics is seen in the third case, "Wetherill Associates, Inc.," which focuses on the role of performance evaluation and compensation systems. WAI, a supplier of electrical parts for the automotive aftermarket, grew from a small upstart to a major industry player by following its "right-action ethic" and eschewing the bribes and kickbacks common in its markets. Concerned that commissions might tempt employees away from "right action," company managers opted to compensate the sales force with competitive salaries rather than with commissions as was common in the industry. In 1993 top management is reviewing the sales force compensation issue again at the request of some recently hired members of the sales force. Company leaders must decide whether to modify WAI's sales force compensation policies.

Organizational Structure   The fourth case, "AES Honeycomb," centers on the role of organizational structure in supporting company values. When the founders of AES Corporation, a U.S.-based independent power producer, took their company public in 1991, the prospectus declared that AES aimed to be socially responsible as well as profitable. The company would conduct its affairs according to four values: integrity, fairness, fun, and social responsibility. Over time AES developed a "honeycomb" structure, based on 15-person "families," as an expression of these values. But in 1992, the company's values and the honeycomb structure came under attack after an incident of employee fraud at one plant and a community relations problem at another. AES executives must decide whether to modify the company's values and structure in response to critics and disgruntled shareholders.

Study Questions for Cases

In preparing the cases in Part II, special attention should be paid to three issues: (1) how the company's leaders define ethical behavior; (2) how the company's ethical standards are maintained; and (3) how the emphasis on ethics has affected the organization and its members. The following questions may be used to prepare each case:

CASE 1: *Forging the New Salomon*

1. Why did the August disclosures trigger a crisis? How big a deal were the Treasury auction irregularities?
2. How effectively did management handle the crisis? As Maughan, what would have been your primary concerns on assuming leadership responsibility?

3. When was the Treasury auction matter over? What were its major consequences? Should Salomon have pleaded guilty to a minor criminal charge in order to conclude the Treasury auction matter in November 1991?

4. What's your appraisal of the new management's ethics strategy? To what extent is it anything more than a legal compliance strategy?

CASE 2: Martin Marietta: Managing Corporate Ethics (A)

1. What's your appraisal of Martin Marietta's ethics program? What have been its costs and benefits? To what extent has it served its purpose?

2. How would you advise the Ethics Steering Committee to assess the ethics program's effectiveness? (Be specific.)

3. How concerned would you be about employees' fear of retribution? How would you advise the Steering Committee to deal with it?

4. What are the main features of Martin Marietta's ethics strategy? To what extent is it transferable to other companies, industries, regions of the world?

CASE 3: Wetherill Associates, Inc.

1. Should Wetherill Associates, Inc. (WAI) modify its compensation system? Would you advise management to introduce individual sales commissions for the sales force?

2. How does WAI's approach to ethics compare with others you have studied? What are the main features of WAI's approach?

3. How important is the right-action ethic for WAI's effectiveness as an organization and its performance in the marketplace? In what ways does this ethic affect performance?

4. WAI managers say their approach is "very different from the conventional attitudes thought to beget success." What is your assessment of this claim?

5. Is the right-action ethic sustainable? What challenges do you anticipate as the company grows? How would you advise management to address them?

CASE 4: AES Honeycomb

1. Why is Sant feeling pressure in the summer of 1992? As Sant, what would be your concerns?

2. What are the origins of Sant's problems? What's your diagnosis of the Cedar Bay and Shady Point episodes?

3. What changes, if any, would you advise Sant to endorse? Be sure to consider whether Sant should:
    a. Reorganize the company.
    b. Hire the recommended staff specialists.
    c. Revamp and strengthen internal controls.
    d. Drop the emphasis on values.
4. The founders of AES thought they were creating a new form of business enterprise. In your opinion, is there anything new or distinctive in the AES approach?
5. What should Sant say to shareholders about AES's values?

CASE 1
FORGING THE NEW SALOMON

> Our goal is going to be that stated many decades ago by J. P. Morgan, who wished to see his bank transact "first-class business . . . in a first-class way." We will judge ourselves in fact not only by the business we do, but also by the business we decline to do. As is the case at all large organizations, there will be mistakes at Salomon and even failures, but to the best of our ability we will acknowledge our errors quickly and correct them with equal promptness.

> —Warren E. Buffett
> *October 1991*

Introduction

It was Sunday afternoon, August 18, 1991, at the World Trade Center offices of Salomon Brothers, the New York–based international securities firm. Nearly all of Salomon's New York employees were at home coping with spoiled weekend plans and the aftermath of Hurricane Bob, which had hit the New York area that weekend. Deryck C. Maughan, co-head of Investment Banking, and John G. Macfarlane, III, the treasurer, however, were on Salomon's trading floor, awaiting the Monday morning opening of the Tokyo market and working on an emergency financial plan for the firm. Salomon's board of directors was meeting upstairs to decide on new leadership for the firm. Normally abuzz with the animated conversation of hundreds of trading employees, the floor was eerily quiet. Maughan commented to Macfarlane, "When your home government throws you out of the home market for government securities, you know you're in trouble."

Auction Irregularities Unfold

Events had unraveled quickly in the previous 10 days. On Friday, August 9, Salomon Brothers publicly disclosed that it had uncovered "irregularities and rule violations" in connection with the firm's bids in three U.S. Treasury security auctions. In auctions held in December 1990 and February 1991, Salomon's government trading desk, staffed with two managing directors, six traders, and twelve support personnel, had submitted unauthorized bids in customers' names. In a May 1991 auction, "due to an apparent oversight," Salomon failed to disclose a "long when-issued position" (i.e., commitment to buy Treasury securities after they were issued). In each instance, Salomon's wrongdoing enabled it to circumvent Treasury Department rules limiting each firm's bid and award to no more

This case was prepared by Lynn Sharp Paine and Michael A. Santoro.
Copyright © 1994 by the President and Fellows of Harvard College. Harvard Business School case 395–046.

than 35% of the total issue.[1] The press release reported that the firm had suspended the two managing directors in charge of the government trading desk, later identified as Paul Mozer and Thomas Murphy, as well as two other employees, and that John Meriwether, a vice chairman, was assuming responsibility for the government bond department. It also noted that the firm's internal review had uncovered unspecified "irregularities in addition to those described."

On Wednesday, August 14, at the insistence of Maughan and managing director William A. McIntosh, among other senior Salomon executives, the company issued a second press release reporting additional details and other Treasury auction improprieties. By this time the company was under increasing pressure from irate government officials. The second announcement also made a revelation that would send shockwaves throughout the worldwide financial community: Salomon's top executives had all been aware since April of the unauthorized February bid, but had failed to report the violation to government authorities. The executives were identified as the chairman and CEO, John H. Gutfreund; the president, Thomas W. Strauss; and the vice chairman in charge of the government trading desk, John W. Meriwether.

On Thursday, the day after disclosing senior management's knowledge of the Treasury violations, Salomon Brothers was on the front page of virtually every major newspaper in the world. In London, the tight-knit financial community was shocked to learn that Salomon had submitted an unauthorized bid in the name of Warburg, one of the city's most respected financial institutions. Creditors were balking at rolling over Salomon's commercial paper and threatening to cut its credit lines. The share price of the publicly traded parent company Salomon Inc was tumbling (**Exhibit 1**). The company was bombarded with calls from clients, creditors, employees, shareholders, and government officials seeking an explanation of the disclosure.

After the announcement, the Federal Reserve Bank of New York notified Gutfreund that Salomon's status as a primary dealer was in jeopardy because of management's delay in reporting the fraudulent bids. "Primary dealers" were designated firms with which the Federal Reserve conducted all its market transactions. As one of 39 primary dealers, Salomon had the privilege of bidding for customers as well as for its own account in auctions conducted by the Federal Reserve Bank as the Treasury's fiscal agent and was permitted to submit bids without putting up a deposit.

On Friday, August 16, CEO John Gutfreund and President Thomas Strauss announced their resignations—under pressure from Salomon senior managers and from government officials. By Friday morning, it had become clear to all of Salomon's remaining executives that Gutfreund and Strauss had lost the ability to lead. Gutfreund would later observe that he knew his days as chairman of Salomon were numbered when at his doorstep on August 15 he saw his picture on

---

[1] The Treasury instituted the 35% bidding limitation in July 1990, in response to concerns about the size of Salomon's bids. On Wall Street, the rule was known as the Mozer-Basham rule, a reference to Michael Basham, a Treasury official, and to Mozer, head of Salomon's government trading desk.

Exhibit 1

Salomon Inc Stock Price, 1991–1992

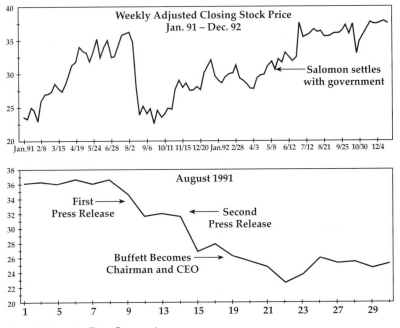

Source: Interactive Data Corporation.

the front page of the *New York Times.* "No apologies to anyone for anything," Gutfreund was quoted as telling a group of managing directors. "Apologies are bull—."[2]

Outside director and shareholder Warren E. Buffett arrived on Friday afternoon to take over from Gutfreund. A board meeting was scheduled for Sunday to name Buffett interim chairman and to designate the firm's new leadership. On Saturday, Buffett conferred individually with Salomon's remaining top executives before deciding on Gutfreund's successor.

The fate of John Meriwether, Mozer's immediate supervisor and a major contributor to the firm, was also an issue. Opinion at Salomon Brothers was divided since Meriwether's highly successful bond arbitrage group had generated $400 million in profit for Salomon in 1990. Still, some called for his resignation. Meriwether's supporters argued that his behavior had been entirely correct: after learning of Mozer's misconduct, he had immediately reported it to Gutfreund, Strauss, and Donald M. Feuerstein, the company's chief legal officer. Others thought Meriwether should have disciplined Mozer and could not understand why he hadn't. Buffett did not ask Meriwether for his resignation, but in the end, Meriwether offered it. On Sunday the board accepted Meriwether's resignation along with Gutfreund's and Strauss's.

---

[2]Linda Grant, "Taming the Bond Buccaneers at Salomon Brothers," *Los Angeles Times Magazine,* February 16, 1992, p. 22.

Sunday's Events

While the board of directors met in a special session on Sunday afternoon, Maughan and Macfarlane were on the phone to Tokyo, anticipating the market's Monday morning opening. Salomon's debt was widely held and traded over-the-counter by Tokyo institutions. Maughan and Macfarlane anxiously looked upon the Tokyo market, which had not yet adjusted to the most recent developments in the Treasury scandal, as a bellwether for other markets. They wanted to make sure Tokyo-based employees understood what was going on in New York and to get a sense of how Japanese creditors were responding to changes in the firm's leadership and to the quick-breaking developments regarding Salomon's primary dealer status.

For Maughan, it had been a demanding week. Unbeknownst to the financial press, he had played an important behind-the-scenes role.[3] Maughan and 30-year Salomon veteran McIntosh had led the call for a second press release after discovering that Salomon's top executives were trying to conceal their long-standing knowledge of the Treasury auction violations. In fact, McIntosh had been calling for a second press release even before discovering the new information. "The first press release," said McIntosh, then head of fixed income sales, "was lousy. It sounded like a lawyer's document. It was designed to protect Gutfreund, not to protect the company." Maughan had also pressed Gutfreund to convene Salomon's board. Without swift action to get the matter out and dealt with, Maughan feared the firm would be without effective decision making.

Maughan was called from the trading floor. As he approached the elevator bank on the 43rd floor, the elevator doors opened to reveal Warren Buffett who spoke directly to Maughan: "You're tapped." Together they rode down to the auditorium where reporters were gathered for a press conference. Buffett introduced Maughan to 500 people as the new chief operating officer of Salomon Brothers. At the time, Maughan did not know that 10 of Salomon's 12 most senior managing directors had recommended him to succeed Gutfreund. The press quoted Maughan as being "astonished" at his appointment.[4]

Others at the firm were not surprised at Maughan's rise, though it proved swifter than expected. Maughan had only just returned from Japan, where he had built Salomon's Asian business into a major force, to assume the position of co-head of investment banking. Along with Meriwether, Maughan had been considered a contender for the firm's future leadership.

Facing the Uncertain Future

As Buffett and Maughan faced the press during a break in the August 18 board meeting, Salomon's future was far from secure. No one knew the full extent of the firm's misconduct. Creditors, customers, employees, Salomon's insurers, and the markets were all waiting to see what management would say and do. Authorities were moving forward to investigate fully. Of great concern was whether Salomon would face a criminal indictment. Recalling the demise of E.F. Hutton and Drexel, Burnham, many feared that Salomon could not survive a criminal

---

[3]See "Leadership Problems at Salomon," HBS case No. 395–044.
[4]Lawrence Malkin, "5 Top Officers Leave Salomon as Buffett Takes Control of Firm," *International Herald Tribune,* August 19, 1991.

conviction. Buffett explained his role to the assembled group: "My job is to clean up the sins of the past and to capitalize on the enormous attributes that this firm has."[5] "Salomon," he said, "has to earn back its integrity." [6]

Buffett's posture was one of complete candor. Vowing to stay until the last question, he told the audience he would provide answers to the best of his ability. Buffett opened Salomon's doors to government regulators and promised to waive the attorney-client privilege and turn over all reports and notes prepared by the firm's lawyers investigating the government trading desk's transgressions. "Warren set the tone from the beginning," said Maughan. "Our working philosophy was that we had better just follow the facts wherever they led and get them out. We didn't know where that would lead."

Immediately after the press conference, Buffett convened an executive committee meeting where he made it clear that Maughan was in charge. Buffett sought to draw the curtain on Salomon's past and to lay the groundwork for a fresh start on Monday. Henceforth, noted one executive, Salomon's history would have two parts—BC "before crisis," and AD "after Deryck."

New Leadership

Buffett enjoyed an enviable personal reputation in the United States, though in London and Europe he was called the "mystery man from Omaha." As one securities industry analyst observed, "He is such a highly credible personality, that his taking over should reassure everyone that the place is going to be well run."[7] But a few observers spoke disdainfully of his "Jimmy Stewart" uprightness and criticized his lack of compassion along with his "pandering to the regulators."[8] Buffett's $4 billion personal fortune was routinely mentioned in U.S. news accounts about "the Sage of Omaha," "the folksy Midwesterner," the "Reluctant Billionaire," and the man in the "rumpled old tweed suit."

Within the firm, Buffett's appointment was widely endorsed. "We were so lucky to have him on our side," commented Denise Cumbey, government products manager in the area where the violations occurred. "He lifted everyone's confidence." A senior executive noted, "We were tremendously relieved that someone with a good reputation was taking over." Some, however, were less enthusiastic, and only reluctantly went along with the new regime.

Even before he was elected, Buffett's reputation for integrity began to work to Salomon's advantage. As the board was meeting on Sunday, the Treasury Department announced that Salomon would be suspended from participating in Treasury auctions. Upon learning of this development, Buffett excused himself from the meeting to phone the Treasury. He persuaded Treasury Secretary Nicholas Brady to allow Salomon to participate in Treasury auctions for its own account. In announcing his change of mind, Secretary Brady said that he "looked forward to a constructive working relationship with the new chairman."[9]

[5]Michael Siconolfi and Laurie P. Cohen, "How Solomon's Hubris and a U.S. Trap Led to Leaders' Downfall," *The Wall Street Journal*, August 19, 1991, p. A1.
[6]Malkin, "5 Top Officers Leave Salomon . . ."
[7]Christina Toh-Pantin, "Salomon Says Gutfreund, Strauss 'Proposed' to Resign," *Reuters*, New York, August 16, 1991.
[8]Grant, "Taming the Bond Buccaneers . . ."
[9]Patrick Harverson and George Graham, "Tough Curbs Imposed on Salomon Bond Deals," *Financial Times*, August 19, 1991, p. 1.

Maughan's appointment also reassured Salomon's internal and external constituents. Dubbed "Mr. Integrity" in the press, Maughan had served for 10 years in the Treasury Department of the United Kingdom and had worked for four years in the London office of Goldman Sachs. Maughan held an MS from Stanford Business School and an undergraduate degree from King's College at the University of London. In testimony before the U.S. Congress, Salomon highlighted Maughan's "strong understanding of the proper relationship between financial institutions and government authorities."

Maughan, the 44-year-old son of a British coal miner, was described by a Salomon associate as a "cultured, reasoned person who never raises his voice, more reflective of the traditional Salomon than the tough arrogant Gutfreund" who had run Salomon behind closed doors as his personal fiefdom. Maughan was perceived as both a strong intellect and a highly competent, communicative manager. On assuming his new position, Maughan pledged "an absolute insistence on the correct moral as well as legal behavior," though he added, "I don't think we want to remove all the elements of our success."[10]

Personnel Actions

Upon taking control, Buffett severed all relations with Mozer and Murphy, terminated their employment, and declined to pay their legal expenses. Maughan named Eric R. Rosenfeld, previously co-head of U.S. fixed income arbitrage, and a former assistant professor at Harvard Business School, interim head of the government trading desk, an area in which he had no previous experience.[11]

Later on that week, Donald M. Feuerstein, the general counsel, resigned.[12] The law firm of Wachtell, Lipton, Rosen and Katz, which had conducted an internal investigation of Salomon in July, also stepped aside. Martin Lipton, a partner at the firm and a close friend of John Gutfreund, had helped craft the August 9 and August 14 news releases.[13] Robert E. Denham, a long-time associate of Buffett, replaced Feuerstein as general counsel. Denham had been the managing partner of Munger, Tolles & Olson, the Los Angeles law firm which had long represented Buffett's business interests.[14]

Two weeks later, the Salomon board met and announced that it would not pay compensation and future legal or other expenses of Gutfreund, Strauss, Meriwether, or Feuerstein, except to the extent that the firm was legally obligated to do so under pre-existing agreements.

---

[10]William Power and Michael Siconolfi, "Mr. Integrity is Promoted to a Top Post," *The Wall Street Journal,* August 19, 1991, p. A5.

[11]"Statement of Salomon Inc submitted in conjunction with the testimony of Warren E. Buffett," House Subcommittee on Telecommunications and Finance, September 3, 1991, p. 42.

[12]Kurt Eichenwald, "Chief Legal Counsel Quits Salomon Under Pressure," *The New York Times,* August 24, 1991, p. D1.

[13]Jonathan Feurbinger, "Salomon's Law Firm Resigns," *The New York Times,* August 31, 1991, p. 33.

[14]Eben Shapiro, "Buffett Picks Top Lawyer for Salomon," *The New York Times,* August 26, 1991, p. D1.

Initial Evaluations

Throughout the firm, the week's revelations engendered much speculation and soul searching. Ironically, when news of the rule violations reached Stephen J.D. Posford, co-head of Salomon's 900-person London office, he was on his way to the opera with the head of the Bank of England, the official responsible for Treasury auctions in the United Kingdom. Posford's initial reaction of disbelief turned to "outrage" when he realized the "full horror" of what had occurred. To Posford, putting bids in customers' names without authorization was "appalling behavior which flouts the whole integrity of your relationship with clients."

Another senior executive described Gutfreund's actions as "against the standards of our business and against the standards Gutfreund himself preached." Comparing Gutfreund's actions to those of a trader attempting to hide a bad trade, the executive observed, "John put the ticket in the drawer." Noted another, "John could be brutal to people, but he was very sensitive to ethical issues."

By and large, Salomon managers saw both the government trading desk misconduct and management's inaction as inexplicable aberrations, isolated and uncharacteristic incidents. However, primed by the unflattering account of Salomon's culture described in the best-selling book *Liar's Poker*,[15] the press and outsiders tended to see them as symptomatic of a flawed organization and a culture of irresponsibility. One managing director recalled, "People here were shocked at the public uproar . . . people had a lot of trouble understanding why such a big deal was being made of this."

Company Background

Founded in 1910 by the sons of an immigrant, Salomon Brothers was primarily a bond-trading firm which had prospered mainly by buying and selling large positions for its own account. The firm entered the equities business in the 1960s, and investment banking in the 1970s. Until 1981, Salomon operated as a partnership. In 1981, Gutfreund engineered the sale of the firm to Phibro Corp., a publicly held dealer of commodities, particularly oil and metals. Three years later, Gutfreund became the chairman of the merged entity, which was renamed Salomon Inc.

The 1980s were a decade of expansion at Salomon Brothers (Salomon). From 1981 to 1987, the firm grew from 2,300 employees to 6,800. In 1985, it earned a record $557 million. These profits were achieved mostly through bond trading during a period of explosive growth in corporate and government debt and through Salomon's pioneering development of the mortgage-backed securities business. The firm invested millions of dollars in developing separate research, equity, and investment banking operations in Frankfurt, London, and Tokyo. It became one of the world's preeminent financial institutions, with expertise in underwriting, distributing, and trading U.S. government securities, corporate bonds and equities, and mortgage-backed securities. From 1985 through 1987, Salomon was market share leader in U.S. corporate underwriting. But in 1987, Salomon's expenses began to overwhelm its revenues. Adversely affected by the bond market decline in the second quarter, and then by the October stock market crash, Salomon earned only $142 million in 1987, returning 3.7% on equity.

---

[15]Michael Lewis, *Liar's Poker* (New York: W.W. Norton & Company, 1989).

The firm's weakened financial position in 1987 led to a hostile takeover bid by corporate raider Ronald O. Perelman, who was operating with the financial backing of Drexel, Burnham, Lambert, Inc. Acting as a "white squire," Berkshire Hathaway, Inc., the $10 billion Omaha holding company of which Warren Buffett was chairman and CEO, invested $700 million in Salomon Inc. The infusion of cash from Berkshire Hathaway enabled Salomon to purchase the shares Perelman had targeted and allowed Gutfreund to retain control of the company. Berkshire Hathaway's investment consisted of preferred stock yielding 9% interest, redeemable for cash in five installments starting in 1995, and convertible at any time before redemption into shares which would constitute 14% of the common stock of Salomon Inc at a price of $38 per share. As a result of the investment Buffett also secured a position on the board of Salomon Inc.

In 1991 Salomon Brothers served some 2,200 clients. Among its 6,600 employees, about a quarter of whom were employed abroad, were 158 managing directors. Salomon's businesses were dynamic. Its products and processes changed constantly. The organization was relatively nonbureaucratic and teams formed and disbanded to take advantage of market opportunities. Beginning in 1989, management had initiated a five-year program to develop an appropriate structure and business process for the firm as it faced the 1990s.[16] The Office of the Chairman began to require each of the then 22 business units to submit budgets, reports, and business plans as part of an effort to push accountability downward (**Exhibit 2**). Work began on better systems for evaluating the performance and contributions of individuals and the business units. However, many were concerned that the use of management tools and controls to facilitate resource allocation, planning, and accountability would undermine the firm's entrepreneurial culture. At the time of the Treasury auction crisis, many of the proposed management processes were still under development or not yet implemented.

Managing through the Crisis

As Buffett and Maughan assumed leadership of the firm, three issues had to be resolved immediately: who would run the main businesses; what clients had to be contacted; and how the firm was going to fund itself. There were governments, as well as regulators and the media, to be dealt with. Employee concerns were also pressing. "Nothing could go 'on hold,' " recalled Maughan. "With one engine on fire we had to keep in forward motion to avoid going down." Initially, the Executive Committee acted as a *de facto* crisis committee with daily update and coordination meetings. But over time, as areas of responsibility became better defined, meetings became sporadic and problem-focused.

Early in the week, Buffett sent the firm's senior managers a letter informing them that they were "each expected to report, instantaneously and directly to me, any legal violation or moral failure on behalf of any employee of Salomon." He exempted "only minor . . . failures (such as parking tickets or nonmaterial expense account abuses by low-level employees) not involving a significant breach of law by our firm or harm to third parties." Buffett gave his private office telephone number, which could be used to reach him at his Omaha home.

---

[16]"Salomon Brothers: Managing the Firm," Harvard Business School Case No. 490–011.

Exhibit 2　**Salomon's Business Units—July 1989**

Number	*Business Unit*
Product Emphasis	
1	Domestic Equities
	Domestic fixed income:
2	Domestic Corporate Debt
3	Government Trading
4	Mortgage Trading
5	New York Arbitrage
6	Firm Finance
7	Foreign Exchange
8	High Yield
9	Merchant Banking
10	Real Estate
11	Asset Management
Product and Function Emphasis	
12	Investment Banking
Function Emphasis	
13	Fixed Income Sales
14	Research
	Support:
15	Business Technology Organization
16	Operations
17	Facilities Management
18	Government Services
19	Human Resources
20	Financial
Location Emphasis	
21	London/Europe
22	Tokyo/Asia

Source: Adapted from Salomon Brothers: "Managing the Firm," Harvard Business School case No. 490–011, **Exhibit 4**, p. 16.

In follow-up meetings with the investment banking, sales, and trading operations, Buffett advised employees: "Lose money for the firm, I will be very understanding; lose a shred of reputation for the firm, I will be ruthless."[17] As Buffett looked to the future, he encouraged employees (utilizing a tennis metaphor) to "play in the center of the court. . . . Close-to-the-line acrobatics are not necessary to make money."

Funding Problems

The most immediate problem facing Salomon on August 19 was the funding situation. Like most large trading firms, Salomon was highly leveraged, including some $18.4 billion in short-term unsecured borrowing. (See **Exhibits 3** and **4** for selected financial data.) The second press release had dramatically escalated the funding problems set in motion by the initial disclosure of auction improprieties. The firm was unable to roll more than 10% of its $8.4 billion in commercial paper

---

[17]"SEC Probes Collusion by Traders," *Wall Street Journal*, August 27, 1991, p. C1, Col. 6.

EXHIBIT 3 Salomon Inc—Five-year Summary of Selected Financial Information (dollars in millions, except per share amounts for the year)

	1992	1991	1990	1989	1988
Revenues:					
Principal transactions, including net interest and dividends	$3,201	$2,793	$2,350	$2,178	$1,800
Investment banking	450	496	416	470	564
Commissions and other	221	248	221	258	241
Revenues, net of interest expense	$3,872	$3,537	$2,987	$2,906	$2,605
Noninterest expenses:					
Compensation and employee-related expenses	$1,638	$1,375	$1,393	$1,369	$1,164
Other noninterest expenses	993	1,043	933	797	688
Philipp Brothers downsizing charge	—	—	155	—	—
Charges relating to U.S. Treasury auction matters	185	200	—	—	—
Total noninterest expenses	$2,816	$2,618	$2,481	$2,166	$1,852
Income before taxes	$1,056	$919	$506	$740	$753
Income taxes	506	412	203	270	473
Net income	$ 550	$ 507	$ 303	$ 470	$ 280
Return on average common stockholders' equity:					
Primary	13.6%	13.9%	8.3%	14.6%	7.6%
Fully diluted	12.9	12.9	8.3	13.4	7.6
Income (loss) before taxes by segment:					
Salomon Brothers	$1,390	$1,036	$ 416	$ 534	$ 513
Phibro Energy Division	(194)	47	361	202	73
Phibro USA	(47)	(80)	146	173	154
Philipp Brothers	—	—	(323)	(116)	48
Corporate and other	(93)	(84)	(94)	(53)	(35)
Income before taxes	$1,056	$ 919	$ 506	$ 740	$ 753
At year-end:					
Total assets	$159,459	$97,402	$109,877	$118,250	$85,256
Short-term borrowings	88,417	40,393	42,888	62,716	31,829
Term debt	8,533	7,082	4,976	2,911	1,586
Redeemable preferred stock	700	700	700	700	700
Stockholders' equity	3,608	3,315	2,823	2,865	2,759
Common shares outstanding (in millions)	109.8	113.2	109.9	119.0	126.4
Per common share:					
Primary earnings	$4.18	$3.90	$2.08	$3.26	$1.65
Fully diluted earnings	4.05	3.79	2.05	3.20	1.63
Cash dividends	0.64	0.64	0.64	0.64	0.64
High market price	39	37	27	29 3/8	28 3/8
Low market price	26 5/8	20 3/4	20	20 1/2	19 3/8
Ending market price	38 1/8	30 5/8	24 3/8	23 3/8	24 1/8
Book value at year-end	32.06	28.77	25.73	24.08	21.82

Salomon Brothers' 1992 results include a $185 million pretax charge related to the U.S. Treasury auction and related matters.
Salomon Brothers' 1991 results include a $200 million pretax charge related to the U.S. Treasury auction and related matters.
Philipp Brothers' 1990 results include a $155 million pretax charge in connection with the downsizing of the segment.
Results for 1988 include a special $180 million income tax provision resulting from the remittance of certain non-U.S. earnings to the United States and a decision to provide taxes on certain non-U.S. earnings that were no longer deemed to be indefinitely invested outside the United States.

Source: Salomon Inc 1992 Annual Report.

EXHIBIT 4   Salomon Inc and Subsidiaries Selected Financial Information and Statistics (dollars in millions)

December 31,	1992	1991	1990	1989	1988
Short-term borrowings:					
Securities sold under agreements to repurchase	$81,032	$34,776	$28,690	$40,242	$17,971
Bank borrowings	2,080	1,649	4,528	11,304	4,749
Deposit liabilities	1,599	1,287	170	227	137
Securities loaned	1,402	1,324	1,700	1,845	2,853
Commercial paper	1,143	546	6,697	7,207	5,439
Other	1,161	811	1,103	1,891	680
Total short-term borrowings	$88,417	$40,393	$42,888	$62,716	$31,829
Long-term capital:					
Term debt	$ 8,533	$ 7,082	$ 4,976	$ 2,911	$ 1,586
Redeemable preferred stock	700	700	700	700	700
Stockholders' equity	3,608	3,315	2,823	2,865	2,759
Total long-term capital	$ 12,841	$11,097	$ 8,499	$ 6,476	$ 5,045
Total assets	$159,459	$97,402	$109,877	$118,250	$85,256
Leverage ratios:					
Total assets divided by total equity (including redeemable preferred stock)	37X	24X	31X	33X	25X
Total assets divided by long-term capital	12.4X	8.8X	12.9X	18.3X	16.9X

Source: Salomon Inc 1992 Annual Report.

outstanding, banks were threatening to cut credit lines, and creditors were asking Salomon to buy back outstanding unsecured debt. Both Moody's and Standard and Poor's downgraded Salomon's credit ratings, further impairing its ability to borrow.[18]

"With $11 billion in core capital and a highly liquid balance sheet, it was clear we had financial strength," explained John Macfarlane, Salomon's treasurer, "but creditors and clients were refusing to do business with us because they lacked confidence in the firm's leadership and management. We were put in 'the penalty box' by public institutions that felt they needed to make a statement."

Responsibility for averting a liquidity crisis fell to Macfarlane, working with Maughan and with chief financial officer, Donald S. Howard. Macfarlane, a tall, soft-spoken Virginian, had been with Salomon since receiving an MBA from the Darden School in 1979. Having begun his career as a trader, Macfarlane still spent almost half his working day on the trading floor. As treasurer, he was also responsible for Salomon's global liquidity management, including "matchbook" operations, i.e., collateralized lending and borrowing.

"The pressure after August 14 was enormous and it became apparent that we would have to shift into our contingency funding plan," explained Macfarlane. The contingency plan had been put in place after the 1987 stock market crash to protect the firm's funding base should market conditions make it difficult to roll

---

[18] Moody's Investor Service, Inc., downgraded Salomon's senior debt from single-A2 to single-A3 and its unsecured commercial paper from Prime-1 to Prime-2. Craig Torres, "How Salomon Slashed Its Balance Sheet," *The Wall Street Journal,* October 24, 1991, p. C1.

EXHIBIT 5

Short-term Unsecured Funding Balances

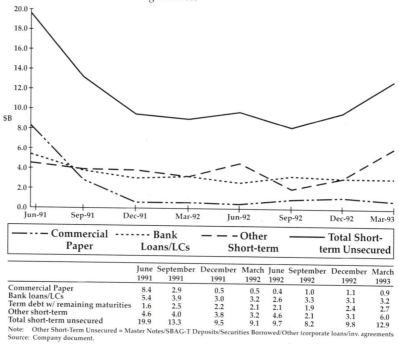

	June 1991	September 1991	December 1991	March 1992	June 1992	September 1992	December 1992	March 1993
Commercial Paper	8.4	2.9	0.5	0.5	0.4	1.0	1.1	0.9
Bank loans/LCs	5.4	3.9	3.0	3.2	2.6	3.3	3.1	3.2
Term debt w/ remaining maturities	1.6	2.5	2.2	2.1	2.1	1.9	2.4	2.7
Other short-term	4.6	4.0	3.8	3.2	4.6	2.1	3.1	6.0
Total short-term unsecured	19.9	13.3	9.5	9.1	9.7	8.2	9.8	12.9

Note: Other Short-Term Unsecured = Master Notes/SBAG-T Deposits/Securities Borrowed/Other (corporate loans/inv. agreements

Source: Company document.

Note: Other Short-Term Unsecured = Master Notes/SBAG-T Deposits/Securities Borrowed/Other (corporate loans/inv. agreements)

Source: Company document.

unsecured liabilities. In the event of a "great depression," Don Howard had anticipated the unwinding of leverage. At considerable cost, Salomon had restructured and extended the maturities of its debt, and stockpiled unencumbered securities which could be quickly liquidated or used to collateralize repurchase agreements. The plan was based on the assumption that secured borrowing would remain intact, but allowed for an orderly reduction in assets if necessary.

When unsecured creditors balked after the August disclosures, Salomon began to use its unencumbered high grade government securities to collateralize repurchase agreements.[19] Proceeds from these short-term borrowings were used to pay off holders of commercial paper (**Exhibit 5**).

No one had anticipated using the contingency funding plan in quite these circumstances, but the plan proved indispensable. Said Macfarlane, "It was all I could do to keep up with the brush fires and answer the telephone calls. . . . I didn't go home for five weeks." Throughout the crisis, Macfarlane was attentive to creditor relations, attempting to avoid surprises, and supplying as much information as possible through fax and personal communications.

---

[19]In a repurchase agreement, one party "sells" securities, usually Treasury securities, to the other and simultaneously promises to repurchase the securities at an agreed-upon price at a later date. A repo is a borrowing collateralized by securities of the "seller."

By August 23, however, it became clear that the funding problem could not be completely solved by shifting to repurchase agreements. Salomon's liquidity was in doubt and borrowing costs were escalating. A few potential creditors were unwilling even to do repos with Salomon. The decision was made to sell off assets and reduce the balance sheet. "The critical element in accomplishing this was time to sell off our positions in an orderly way according to the plan," explained Macfarlane.

To effect the sell-off in assets, Macfarlane decided that the fairest, easiest, and most efficient way was to raise the internal interest rate charged to Salomon traders for the use of firm capital. Macfarlane's Asset Liability Management Committee announced the hike with a half-page memo to Salomon's 15 trading department heads around the world. As a result of the increase, including an extra 4% surcharge effective at the end of the quarter, many of the firm's trading positions became unprofitable. Others became much less attractive. As heavy users of capital, equity traders were affected most by Macfarlane's memo. The amount of firm capital required for an equity position, 50% of its value, was substantially greater than for a position in government securities.

Despite the memo, many traders were unwilling to give up potentially profitable positions. To encourage further sell-offs, Maughan organized weekly meetings of traders to review all the positions being held. "Stanley Shopkorn [head equity trader] had a lot to say about my positions and I had a lot to say about his," one trader commented. "Everybody saw everybody else's numbers."[20]

Overall, Salomon reduced its balance sheet from $150 billion in mid-August to $97 billion at September 30, 1991. The firm's widely respected trading skills helped it to minimize losses and retain its highest producing assets while making these sales. As the head equity trader commented: "Our expertise is in the distribution of securities. We made a switch. We distributed our own."[21]

Salomon's ability to liquify assets and exploit alternative funding sources saved it from the credit crunch which forced Drexel, Burnham to close its doors after pleading guilty to securities fraud in February 1990. Unlike Drexel, whose assets had consisted primarily of relatively illiquid junk bonds, Salomon's assets were mainly safe, relatively liquid government bonds.

As of September, both Moody's and Standard and Poor's put Salomon on "credit watch" status for possible further downgrade. In an effort to avert further cuts in bank credit lines, Buffett met with bankers for a question and answer session on the firm's liquidity on September 13.

Client Relations

Except in the government trading area, Salomon managers were on the phone attempting to reassure clients as soon as news of the auction improprieties began to break. Nevertheless, matters deteriorated quickly, aided by factual inaccuracies appearing in some news reports. In the United States and the United Kingdom, and to a lesser extent in Europe, some clients felt they had to sever ties to punish what they regarded as a serious violation of trust and a threat to the public system of government funding. Even if they were sympathetic, large institutions with their own reputations to protect felt that they could not afford to do

---

[20]Torres.

[21]Id.

business with Salomon so long as it was under a cloud. And many government and quasi-government clients operated under statutes which limited their authority to do business with a company involved in wrongdoing.[22]

Maughan's chief of staff, William J. Jennings II, saw Salomon's former reputation for arrogance, abrasiveness, and brashness as coming home to roost. According to Jennings, some clients took the opportunity to get even for past slights, as "the time a trader slammed the phone down in my ear."

Almost immediately after the disclosures of misconduct, Salomon lost several major clients. The California Public Employees Retirement System (CALPERS), the largest private pension fund in the world (with $63 billion in assets), announced that it would suspend trading government securities with the firm.[23] The Pacific Investment Management Company (a fixed income investment manager with $32 billion in assets), in whose name a Salomon employee had submitted an unauthorized bid as a "practical joke," and Mercury Asset Management, in whose name Salomon had entered a fraudulent bid, also stopped doing business with Salomon. Regarding the loss of Mercury as a client, Salomon announced that "we deeply regret this clear violation of a valued customer relationship."

One highly publicized client loss was the World Bank. In announcing the World Bank's decision to suspend business, Salomon apologized to the Bank and its member governments "for any embarrassment caused by our actions," and stated the firm's intention to implement corrective measures and to "work closely with the World Bank to secure a resumption of our business dealings as soon as possible."

Government sales managers and traders waited several weeks before approaching customers they felt they could get back. According to a manager in the area, the group decided to focus more on research in order "to offer customers something others didn't have," and to "sharpen their pencils" in executing trades to give customers better pricing.

Maintaining client relationships severely tested the mettle of managers throughout the firm. Denise Cumbey, a manager responsible for sales of government securities products, explained, "Customers transpose the violations of others onto you personally. You try to defend the firm. But there is always doubt in the customer's mind." Stephen Posford spent many hours on the phone with clients in London, making sure they were fully informed. Noted Posford, "They were as embarrassed as I was about having to have the conversations we had. I knew them personally. I had a reputation from having worked in London for 22 years. I played my integrity card pretty hard."

---

[22]The Resolution Trust Corporation (RST), for example, operated under a statute which required it to discontinue business with a firm causing a loss to the government. Paulette Thomas, "Salomon's Other U.S. Ties May Have Been Salvaged," *Wall Street Journal*, August 19, 1991, p. A4.

[23]The Wisconsin Investment Board (with $26 billion in assets), the Massachusetts State Teachers Employees Pension (with $5.3 billion in assets), and the Colorado Public Employees Retirement Association (with $10.6 billion in assets) also suspended trading with Salomon.

Richard J. Barrett, then head of New York financial institutions in Salomon's 1,000-member investment banking unit, described his calls to the chief executive officers of the bank's corporate clients after learning of Mozer's transgressions on August 8. "These were very emotional calls for me. . . . You know you are going to get sermonized. It was especially upsetting because the scandal occurred just as we were gaining a lot of momentum in the investment bank. . . . The first press release knocked the wind out of us."

The second press release was devastating. "I had to call people back eating crow [admitting he was wrong] twice within a week," said Barrett. "This was very, very bad. . . . It was demoralizing that a problem on the trading floor, something we had nothing to do with, affected the [investment] bank in the most profound and direct way. We are telling clients how to handle their affairs. But our credibility is suspect when we are unable to manage our own affairs properly."

According to Barrett, clients would "start separating people from the firm. This is difficult for you as an individual. You have your Salomon jersey [team uniform] on, trying to defend the firm. But CEOs would say 'we know that you personally are ethical, but I can't go to the board and recommend Salomon. You understand that.' You say you understand, but of course you don't really understand. This is the sort of embarrassment and torture you go through after you've worked so hard over many years to build a business."

In September, the British Treasury dropped Salomon as an underwriter of an $8.5 billion public offering of British Telecommunications, P.L.C. Other clients reduced Salomon's role in projected transactions. "That," said Barrett, "is insulting to your professional pride. You have contracts, but you can't hold customers to them. Are you going to litigate? In this situation you really have to go along."

Barrett felt the problem of maintaining and restoring relationships was particularly difficult in the investment banking areas. "In trading there are many opportunities for customers to give you a little bit of business. Investment banking is much lumpier. There are fewer, bigger deals. And the perceived risk of selecting Salomon is high."

Despite the difficulties, Barrett and others got out and spoke personally with the bank's core, best relationships in the first couple of weeks. "If we lost these clients we felt we might never get them back. . . . I can't overemphasize how emotional that was. You were so mad. You couldn't talk very long without getting upset." Buffett's openness proved to be an important point in dealing with clients. According to Barrett, "We said to clients, 'this is unprecedented. We have said look at all our books. We are not Drexel!' " Barrett summarized, "You play the hand you have. We had a very bad hand, but Buffett gave us a card."

On September 4, Buffett sent letters of apology to the firm's major customers, promising to do business in the future with honesty and candor.

Employee Concerns

As events unfolded, many employees considered leaving the firm. Denise Cumbey recalled: "Basically our lives fell apart. We were wondering if the firm was going to survive. I was thinking about all these people and their jobs and families. Everybody was thinking about leaving. Headhunters were calling everybody." Cumbey, herself, resisted overtures. "A lot of people were depending on me," she commented, "but the firm had treated me fairly in the past. So I was not going to leave when the going got tough."

Thomas W. Brock, head of operations, noted that prior to the crisis, Salomon had not been the "most communicative organization in the world. [As the crisis developed] it was critical to figure out the right way to communicate with employees, in part to avoid panic. People were concerned about getting paid and getting fired."

Following Buffett's model, individual managers met with their supervisees. The communications department began distributing press releases throughout the firm and introduced a daily fact sheet detailing developments in the government investigation and in firm business. "The information flow was very open," said one employee. "On Wednesday afternoons we would meet and Deryck would answer everyone's questions. Even though they were under a lot of pressure from outside the firm, top management was making a real effort to keep all employees in the loop."

Employees were invited to submit anonymous written questions to be answered in large group sessions. But the information sessions were not enough to address employees' individual concerns. Supervisors in all parts of the company spent much of their time reassuring employees or trying to talk them out of leaving. In the government trading area, said one manager, "We were just trying to hold the department together." Trading area employees also spent a lot of time collecting data for the various investigations being initiated.

The crisis put a great deal of pressure on operations employees to perform at a zero-defects level. Failure to settle trades on time could provoke doubt, or even panic, among customers. The crisis couldn't have come at a worse time for operations, which was in the process of moving to Tampa, Florida. Nevertheless, even workers scheduled to be laid off turned in peak performances.

Government and Regulatory Investigation

As market developments were sending Salomon into a tailspin, government investigators were swooping in to determine the extent of wrongdoing. The Securities and Exchange Commission (SEC), the Treasury Department, the Justice Department, the Federal Reserve Board, the Federal Bureau of Investigation (FBI), and the Manhattan District Attorney were all looking into potential rule violations by Salomon. The Antitrust Division of the Justice Department was investigating whether Salomon had colluded with others to rig the bidding at auctions and subsequently to manipulate the secondary market in Treasury securities.[24] Congressional committees were gearing up for hearings, and new legislation was being considered.

Salomon was also being investigated by the New York Stock Exchange (NYSE),[25] which considered inaccurate documentation and concealment of unauthorized customer bids as serious violations of Exchange rules which undermined NYSE examiners' ability to review transactions.[26]

---

[24]Gary Weiss, et al., "Clearing the Wreckage," *Business Week,* September 2, 1991, p. 67.
[25]The New York Stock Exchange was a self-regulatory organization (SRO) whose oversight and self-regulatory authorities were backed by the SEC.
[26]"SEC is Probing Possible Violations by Firms in Government Securities Offerings," *BNA Banking Daily,* September 17, 1991. In 1991, Salomon paid a record $1.3 million fine to the Exchange for allegedly shortchanging customers involved in computerized trading.

Depending on the results of the investigations, Salomon faced a variety of potential sanctions in addition to criminal fines and civil damages: censure, suspension, or debarment from acting as a broker/dealer and as a primary dealer in government securities; administrative probation; modification of its operations; required appointment of board members or managers acceptable to the SEC. Jennings recalled that some were putting the chance of a criminal indictment as high as 80% in the early days of the crisis.

Dealing with government officials and the media fell primarily to Buffett, Maughan, and Robert Denham, the new general counsel. Despite the many uncertainties facing the firm, Salomon cooperated fully with the authorities. "We were taking the approach that we had to develop the case for the government," commented Denham. "We felt that the firm had done something wrong, had lost the confidence of the government, and that we had an obligation to the government to explain what had happened. That meant cooperating—not being dragged kicking and screaming."

Denham saw his job as achieving a resolution as quickly as possible. This meant addressing two additional issues that had come to light with Buffett's invitation to bring forward ethical issues. The first was the practice of overstating customer orders for the debt securities of certain government-sponsored enterprises (GSEs), such as "Fannie Mae," the Federal National Mortgage Association. The second was Salomon's practice of purchasing medium-term notes from corporate issuers as principal while representing that the notes were being purchased as an agent for a customer. Both practices were common on Wall Street.

Unlike Drexel, Salomon did not hire a public relations firm to generate favorable stories in an attempt to influence the government investigation. Said Maughan, "We felt we would be judged by the way we conducted ourselves. We had no PR campaign. We played it very straight. We would just take the heat." As Denham noted, the objective of getting information out quickly had to be tempered with concern for accuracy in order to avoid a mistake, which could be worse than saying nothing at all. Salomon suspended all the activities of its Washington, D.C. office, believing that it would not be appropriate to seek to influence government regulation in the wake of the scandal.

Maughan stressed the global nature of Salomon's governmental problems, "It's important to bear in mind that there were 14 governments involved, not just one. . . . In Germany, the United Kingdom, and Japan, we also operated as primary dealers. . . . I visited these capitals, talked with those governments. I was frank about the risk of financial difficulty for the firm."

Private Lawsuits

Salomon's legal trouble did not stop with governmental investigations. The firm also faced the potential of lawsuits from customers, shareholders, and other private parties allegedly injured by its actions.[27] One group of actions claimed that Salomon violated federal securities law by knowingly or recklessly not disclosing the Treasury improprieties. These actions sought compensation for the reduction in stock value following public disclosure of the improprieties. Another group of class action lawsuits were instituted by purchasers of Treasury securities. These suits claimed that the firm violated provisions of the federal securities laws,

---

[27]Salomon Inc 1991 Annual Report, p. 64.

antitrust laws, and Racketeer Influenced and Corrupt Organization Act by re-
peatedly purchasing quantities of Treasury securities in excess of federal regulatory limits and by manipulating the primary and secondary markets for Treasury
securities. Yet another group of actions was derivative suits brought on behalf of
the firm by shareholders seeking to require individual defendants, including
Gutfreund and Strauss, to repay the firm for damages they caused and to return
compensation received by them.

Buffett Reports to Congress

On September 4, 1991, Buffett answered questions before a Congressional committee investigating Salomon and the Treasury securities market. Buffett characterized Mozer's improprieties as "almost like a self-destruct mechanism . . . not
the act of a rational man at all."[28] Buffett also said that the former management's
delay in coming forward was one of the most troubling aspects of the situation,
raising questions "whether there was a climate within Salomon that appeared to
tolerate or even encourage wrongdoing."[29]

Buffett, whose father had been a Nebraska congressman, spoke persuasively.
Said one former Congressional staffer, "Buffett respects Congress; he doesn't
think, like most Wall Streeters, that we have no right to ask questions. He has a
respect for the process, and when he testified it showed."[30]

At the hearing, Buffett unveiled changes in Salomon's compliance system intended to "make Salomon a leader in setting new standards in regulatory behavior in the financial services industry." The old system had failed to detect
Mozer's unauthorized bids in part because the trade tickets had been coded "do
not bill or confirm." In the normal situation, traders would send confirmation of
a trade to the client with a copy to the salesperson in charge of the account. However, confirmations were sometimes held back to accommodate last-minute
changes from clients and for other legitimate reasons. In 1989, Salomon had eliminated a daily report by the compliance department on all "do not bill or confirm" orders from the previous day.[31]

The new compliance system announced by Buffett included a new Treasury
bidding control system covering three main areas: reporting net long positions
on Treasury auction tender forms; documentation of customer bids; and issuance
of customer confirmations. Under the new system, "do not confirm" orders on
customer confirmations of Treasury securities transactions required prior written
authorization of the customer and the prior review and approval of the Compliance Department. The firm also developed a "Treasury Auction Failsafe Form."
All correspondence from and to the Treasury and the Federal Reserve was required to be submitted to the legal department.[32]

---

[28]Peter G. Gosselin, "Buffett Endorses Tougher Regulation," *The Boston Globe*,
September 5, 1991, pp. 51–52.

[29]Kevin Salwen, "Buffett Gives Details to Inquiry by House," *Wall Street Journal*,
September 5, 1991, p. C1.

[30]Grant, "Taming the Bond Buccaneers . . ."

[31]Peter Grant and Marcia Parker, "Hurtling Toward Scandal," *Crain's New York Business*,
June 1, 1992.

[32]Id.

All relevant personnel received written materials describing Salomon's new compliance program, along with examples of new documentation forms to be used throughout the firm. Staff members from the Compliance and Internal Audit departments held training sessions for employees and were stationed by the government trading desk during auctions to monitor compliance and answer questions. Departing from traditional Wall Street practice, the firm moved compliance officers physically onto the trading floor to make compliance more of an ongoing part of the business. In London, Posford took steps to integrate the legal side with the compliance side. Despite the increased presence of compliance officers, Buffett stressed that each person had to be "his or her own compliance officer."

At the hearing Buffett also described Salomon's new board-level compliance committee, to be chaired by Lord Young, a British executive who had previously served in the Thatcher cabinet. "The committee will have responsibility for ensuring that all regulatory procedures will be followed to the letter—both in the United States and wherever else we may do business throughout the world. Compliance officers throughout the firm will have the right to report directly to the compliance committee, and will have the *obligation* to do so in circumstances where they are not fully satisfied with existing or any future practices."

Shortly after the formation of the compliance committee, Buffett held a firmwide meeting outlining the firm's high expectations for ethics and compliance. Salomon also hired the accounting firm of Coopers & Lybrand to review internal controls and compliance procedures for all of Salomon's U.S. securities trading operations. The London office, too, undertook a thorough review of its compliance procedures.

Organizational Culture

In addition to modifying compliance procedures, the new leadership turned its attention to Salomon's culture. Although confident that the firm was not "endemically corrupt" as charged by some outsiders, Maughan believed that "certain aspects of the culture needed to be modified." Maughan continued, "Mozer's behavior was out of the ordinary, but still we had to reassert the traditional values of the firm. In some way, in some fashion, we had lost our way. A certain permissiveness had entered the air. A bravado was attached to the taking of risk and the making of money. As a result, we were inattentive to shareholders and external constituencies, and not as customer-oriented as we should be."

Maughan pointed to control and compliance as functions needing additional support. "This has nothing to do with the individuals involved, but with the culture and the system," he said. Accordingly, he took steps to reassert the significance and independence of the general counsel and chief financial officer.

Maughan's view of managing ethics was a mixture of discipline and leadership. "I lead by example. But when things go wrong, you can't turn a blind eye. Leadership must enforce values through punishment. If they don't exercise that power, then the values can't be upheld. People begin to believe the behavior is okay. I don't think anyone doubts that current management would act forcefully if someone does something wrong. And I don't just mean compliance with the law. I also mean issues of diversity, the treatment of women, putting customer interests first, not cutting corners. These things are communicated to employees in the speeches we make and in our daily routine. And the vast majority of employees are glad to hear it because they want to work in a quality place."

Nevertheless, noted Maughan, "The money culture is out there. Some people join the firm for a few years to make a lot of money. The person who earns $10 million for the firm is more valued than the person who makes $1 million. The person who earns $100 million is a god. The industry has a certain inexorable logic to it." Maughan continued, "If you pay someone $10 millon for three years in a row, what leverage do you have over that person? Moral suasion doesn't work."

Bill McIntosh stressed the importance of personal character. Said McIntosh, "Management procedures can help, but if someone wants to get you, they will—these are very bright people. Wall Street creates some massive egos. Anytime you have big money, you attract people who want to get it."

End of Third Quarter, 1991

On September 25, as the third quarter was coming to an end, Buffett, Maughan, and other top executives met with over 300 customers in New York and via satellite worldwide. Buffett attempted to assure clients that the worst was behind Salomon. He suggested that the government would not file criminal charges against Salomon because, unlike Drexel, Burnham, Lambert or E.F. Hutton, Salomon had not "circled the wagons and stonewalled." During the meeting, Maughan compared the former managers of Salomon to drunk drivers whose reckless driving had resulted in "a dent" which the current "sober" driver had "pulled out." Buffett told the audience the firm would be taking an unspecified charge in the third quarter to cover legal expenses and potential damages, but that he did not anticipate any operating losses.[33]

The next day Maughan spoke to a congressional committee about the many changes at Salomon, including steps taken to strengthen the role of the board of directors and to improve the board's access to information. In late September, Coopers & Lybrand issued a brief formal opinion stating that Salomon's newly adopted trading procedures were sufficient to meet the Treasury's guidelines. Less than a week later, Salomon announced completion of its internal examination of government trading desk activities in 68 auctions between January 1, 1990 and August 8, 1991. The internal examination revealed unauthorized bids in a total of seven, and possibly eight, auctions, though none prior to July 1990 when the Treasury instituted its 35% bidding limitation.

The thorough internal review of compliance proved critical for assuring clients that Salomon's problem was not systemic. Stephen Posford commented, "By October we were able to say to our clients 'you know that this firm is whiter than white because we have been gone through with a fine-tooth comb and no additional problems were discovered.' This went down very well."

By the end of the third quarter, Salomon had reduced its assets to $97 billion from $150 billion just prior to the scandal, demonstrating both its flexibility and liquidity to the financial community. "I think that the financial community was shocked that we were able to accomplish this," said treasurer John Macfarlane. "From a liquidity standpoint, we were out of the woods with the release of third

---

[33]Jolie Solomon, "Salomon Working Out the 'Dents'; Firm Tells Customers It Will Survive Trading Scandal," *The Boston Globe,* September 24, 1991, p. 49.

EXHIBIT 6   **Salomon Inc: Selected Quarterly Financial Data (unaudited) (dollars in millions, except per share amounts)**

	Three Months Ended			
	December 31	*September 30*	*June 30*	*March 31*
1992				
Total revenues	$2,142	$1,747	$2,366	$1,941
Revenues, net of interest expense	1,009	636	1,312	915
Income before taxes	248	11	466	331
Net income	143	6	211	190
Earnings (loss) per share:				
Primary	$ 1.10	$(0.09)	$1.68	$1.51
Fully diluted	1.06	(0.09)	1.56	1.41
1991				
Total revenues	$1,554	$2,423	$2,508	$2,690
Revenues, net of interest expense	522	880	952	1,183
Income (loss) before income taxes	(51)	186	297	487
Net income (loss)	(29)	85	178	273
Earnings (loss) per share:				
Primary	$(0.41)	$ 0.60	$ 1.43	$ 2.30
Fully diluted	(0.41)	0.59	1.33	2.06
1990				
Total revenues	$1,927	$2,573	$2,093	$2,353
Revenues, net of interest expense	434	1,109	754	690
Income (loss) before income taxes	(27)	134	198	201
Net income (loss)	(15)	79	120	119
Earnings (loss) per share:				
Primary	$(0.28)	$ 0.55	$ 0.89	$ 0.88
Fully diluted	(0.28)	0.54	0.87	0.86

The 1992 second quarter results include a $185 million pretax charge related to the U.S. Treasury auction and related matters.

The 1991 third quarter results include a $200 million pretax charge related to the U.S. Treasury auction and related matters.

Earnings (loss) per share for quarterly periods are based on average common shares outstanding in individual quarters; thus, the sum of earnings per share for each quarter may not equal the full year.

Source: Salomon Inc 1992 Annual Report.

quarter earnings in late October." Despite a $200 million charge to cover expected fines and legal fees, net income for the third quarter of 1991 was $85 million compared with $79 million for the third quarter of 1990. (See **Exhibit 6** for selected quarterly data.)

By October, the firm was beginning to win back some of its government securities clients and to recover much of its international business. On October 24, Salomon announced that overall profits generated from its improper bids—then believed to be eight in number—were in the range of $3.3 to $4.6 million. The profit study, the effort of 20 people working a month, helped put Salomon's problem in perspective, though, as Denham noted, the magnitude of Salomon's gain was not the only issue raised by the improprieties.

Buffett Speaks to Shareholders

In late October, Buffett spent $600,000 publicizing his third-quarter letter to the shareholders. On October 31, two-page ads displaying the letter appeared in *The Wall Street Journal, The New York Times, The Washington Post,* and *The Financial Times.* Buffett trumpeted the firm's new compliance procedures, noting his directive that Salomon's 9,000 employees "be guided by a test that goes beyond rules: contemplating any business act, an employee should ask himself whether he would be willing to see it immediately described by an informed and critical reporter on the front page of his local paper, there to be read by his spouse, children and friends. At Salomon we simply want no part of any activities that pass legal tests but that we, as citizens, would find offensive."

Buffett expressed his belief that the misconduct was limited to a few individuals who behaved egregiously. Wrote Buffett: "I believe that we had an extremely serious problem but not a pervasive one." Buffett promised to make amends to those damaged by Salomon's past misconduct, but warned that "we will be no one's patsy."

Buffett also applauded the firm's asset reduction: "I am no fan of huge leverage in general, and in Salomon's case, I believe that the swelling of the balance sheet that took place in the past was often done for the sake of all-too-marginal returns. Larger totals can actually lead to smaller profits: undisciplined decision making is a frequent consequence of ultra-easy access to funding, as both commercial and investment banks have learned in recent years." Buffett concluded by stating again that Salomon could earn superior returns "without resorting to close-to-the-line acrobatics. Good profits simply are not inconsistent with good behavior."

The "Second Curve"

Both Buffett and Maughan saw the Treasury auction crisis as an opportunity to address underlying management issues predating the Treasury irregularities. To the surprise of some managing directors, Maughan chose to work on these issues "as soon as possible rather than wait until after the Treasury securities matter was resolved." Although pleading guilty to a minor criminal offense might have achieved a quick resolution of the government's legal charges, Salomon's management was unwilling to consider this possibility. With the legal situation still unsettled, Maughan turned to what he called the "Second Curve" to focus on compensation reform, management reorganization, and improved management systems. "What we're trying to get," said Maughan, "is a system where we have alignment between the management, its business definition, its P&L and its pay system, and where these things are all coherent."[34]

To correct what Buffett termed "irrationalities" in the compensation system, overall compensation was reduced and departmental compensation was linked more closely to department performance. Although Salomon earned approximately 10% on equity in 1990, which Buffett characterized as "far under the average earned by American business," 106 individuals earned over $1 million. As a result of a special arrangement, Lawrence E. Hilibrand, the 31-year-old head of

---

[34]"Taking Arms Against a Sea of Troubles," *Euromoney,* March 1992, p. 42.

the bond arbitrage group, which made $400 million in profits, took home $23 million.[35] Moreover, although operating profits remained relatively flat from 1989 to 1990, compensation increased by $120 million. To address this "irrationality," Buffett cut bonuses and reduced the firm's compensation expense by $110 million for the third quarter.

Buffett criticized the prevailing "egalitarian, share of the wealth" method of compensation as more suitable for a private partnership than for a public company dependent on shareholder capital. He wrote, "employees who produce exceptional results for the firm, while operating both honorably and without excessive risk, should expect to receive first-class compensation. On the other hand, employees producing mediocre returns for owners should expect their pay to reflect this shortfall." Buffett thought that recent losses in the equities area, for example, should be reflected in compensation.

Buffett applauded previous management's decision to award in 1991 an increased amount of compensation in the form of restricted stock which could not be sold for five years. Such compensation, Buffett thought, would align the interests of employees with those of shareholders and serve to emphasize the long-term risks and rewards associated with employees' decisions. Wrote Buffett: "We wish to see . . . managers become wealthy *through* ownership, not simply free-riding on the ownership of others."

Inside Salomon, some saw Buffett's compensation reforms as a gesture of appeasement toward regulators who believed that Wall Streeters made too much money. They warned that the changes could drive away some of the firm's best people. Others saw Buffet's aim as shifting some of the financial impact of the scandal from shareholders to employees.

In his letter to shareholders, Buffett addressed the possibility that some employees would leave the firm because of the announced changes. However, he indicated that the changes were just as likely to induce top performers to stay. He went on, "[W]ere an abnormal number of people to leave the firm, the results would not necessarily be bad. Other men and women who share our thinking and values would then be given added responsibilities and opportunities. In the end we must have people to match our principles, not the reverse."

Management Reorganization

In early November, Salomon put in place a new Executive Committee to replace the old Office of the Chairman and the internal board of directors. Under Gutfreund, power had been concentrated in the hands of a few traders. The new nine-person Executive Committee, led by Maughan, included executives from virtually all of the firm's businesses.[36] Two members of the old Office of the Chairman were absent from the new committee: Stanley B. Shopkorn and Jay F. Higgins.

---

[35]Bernice Kanner, "Saving Salomon," *New York Magazine*, December 9, 1991, p. 43.

[36]The other members of the nine-person committee were Thomas W. Brock, head of operations; Bruce C. Hackett, equities; Leo I. Higdon, Jr., investment banking; Lawrence E. Hilibrand, arbitrage; Martin L. Leibowitz, research; James L. Massey, international; William A. McIntosh, fixed income sales; and Eric R. Rosenfeld, fixed income trading.

Initial Impact of Reforms

Almost immediately after the management changes were initiated, it was announced that Stanley B. Shopkorn, the head of the equities division, would leave at the end of the year after collecting a $3 million bonus that would become payable to him.[37] In December, the firm announced that Jay F. Higgins, founder of the firm's mergers and acquisitions department and former head of investment banking, would also leave at the end of the year. Other employees followed Shopkorn and Higgins.

Particularly hard hit was the equities area, which lost some 35 people in November, including research staff as well as sales and trading personnel. According to one managing director, no one anticipated the impact of the compensation changes on the equities research area. "People did not realize how underpaying [in equities research] exposed us. This area was literally bought away from us." Those departing cited two reasons—the new compensation system and fear that the firm would neglect other areas in favor of the two most profitable departments, bond sales and trading.[38] The scandal had also stopped the pipeline of banking deals which fueled the equities department's distribution activities, the high-margin segment of its business.

The loss of equities sales and research personnel further impaired the investment bank's ability to offer full services to clients. Investment banker Richard Barrett commented: "In the greatest equity market of all time, the head of equities [Stanley Shopkorn] and one-third of the research division left. . . . We had no capability to sell, no people to sell. Deals for new issues we were competing on were taken away. It was like getting to the Super Bowl[39] and not being able to play because of a sprained ankle." For October, the firm's share of domestic new issues, excluding mortgage-backed securities, dropped to 2.6%.[40]

Maughan described the fourth quarter as a "once-in-a-decade opportunity to underwrite stocks—$18.5 billion issued in the market versus two and change the year before."[41] By the end of 1991, Salomon's share of the underwriting market stood at 5.7%, down from 9.9% for the first half of 1991 (**Exhibit 7**). Moreover, as the rest of Wall Street earned record profits in the fourth quarter of 1991, Salomon's investment banking unit posted a loss.[42]

Developments after the scandal highlighted the interdependence between equities and the investment bank, areas that had previously been run as independent operations. Maughan installed new heads of each and called for cooperation and alignment of their goals, with research an integral component of both.

---

[37]"Chief Stock Trader Leaves Salomon Brothers," *UPI*, New York, November 6, 1991.
[38]Patrick Harverson, "Salomon resignations continue as top analysts quit for First Boston," *The Financial Times*, January 17, 1992, p. 25.
[39]The "Super Bowl," held in January, is the championship match of the NFL (the U.S.'s National Football League).
[40]Tom Pratt, "Salomon's Market Share Slips as Clients Play It Safe," *Investment Dealers' Digest*, November 4, 1991, p. 9.
[41]"Taking Arms . . . ," *Euromoney*, March 1992.
[42]Leah Nathans Spiro, "Rescuing Salomon Was One Thing, But Running It . . . ," *Business Week*, February 17, 1992, p. 120.

EXHIBIT 7   Salomon Brothers Underwriting Proceeds and Market Share, 1985–1992 (semiannually)

Year	Proceeds (millions)	Rank	Market Share
Domestic Issues			
85:1	$12,366.3	1	21.5%
85:2	18,233.1	1	22.6
86:1	28,689.3	1	19.8
86:2	22,517.7	2	15.6
87:1	23,589.8	1	14.8
87:2	16,549.7	1	14.1
88:1	20,213.7	2	13.9
88:2	13,875.2	5	10.5
89:1	15,325.1	4	10.6
89:2	16,805.2	5	10.1
90:1	16,343.6	5	10.0
90:2	16,430.4	3	11.0
91:1	27,118.7	3	9.9
91:2	16,210.6	8	5.7
92:1	39,451.2	6	8.9
92:2	34,513.8	5	8.4
Domestic Equities			
85:1	2,344.6	1	16.5
85:2	2,289.8	3	12.0
86:1	4,704.0	1	15.7
86:2	1,836.3	6	6.8
87:1	1,387.8	10	4.2
87:2	1,630.9	5	8.1
88:1	1,041.5	8	5.3
88:2	647.1	9	3.6
89:1	288.7	11	2.6
89:2	732.6	9	3.7
90:1	1,415.0	5	9.0
90:2	620.5	5	7.7
91:1	2,753.1	5	8.6
91:2	1,092.8	7	2.7
92:1	1,036.0	10	1.8
92:2	1,032.0	11	2.3
Domestic Debt			
85:1	10,021.7	1	23.1
85:2	15,943.3	1	25.9
86:1	23,985.3	1	20.9
86:2	20,681.5	2	17.7
87:1	22,202.0	1	17.6
87:2	14,918.8	1	15.3
88:1	19,172.1	1	15.2
88:2	13,228.1	4	11.6
89:1	15,036.4	4	11.3
89:2	16,072.6	5	11.0
90:1	14,928.7	5	10.1
90:2	15,809.9	4	11.2
91:1	24,365.6	3	10.1
91:2	15,117.8	8	6.2
92:1	38,415.2	6	9.9
92:2	33,481.8	6	9.1

Equities Reforms

After sending the European and Asian equities books back to their home countries to be managed, Maughan asked Bruce C. Hackett to head U.S. equities and develop a business plan to prepare for the opportunities of the 1990s. Having been in Salomon's equities department for 25 years, Hackett knew the business well. According to Hackett, the equities area was already in trouble at the time of the scandal, lacking in the systems, culture, discipline, and skill sets needed for success. Company business was in conflict with customer business, risk management was nonexistent, the area was rife with politics. "Equity traders," he said, "had never understood that they were custodians of firm revenues. There was no accountability."

While the departure of so many equity employees left the area understaffed, it presented Hackett with the opportunity to strip out the culture and rebuild the business. The firm ceased proprietary trading in equities, a volatile business which generated a $170 million loss in the final quarter of 1991, and began to concentrate on customer businesses including the distribution of investment bank underwritings and the purchase and resale of customer positions.

Buffett emphasized that the decision to drop proprietary trading in equities did not imply "diminished willingness to make large commitments that involve arbitrage-like activity." Buffett also affirmed that Salomon would continue to engage in pure risk arbitrage in announced stock deals, and that the firm had "no diminished interest in buying very large amounts of bonds, mortgages or equities that we expect to resell in a short period."[43] "It's unthinkable that we would stop trading for our own account, since we are extremely good at it," said Maughan. "All we have to do is analyze it and do better."[44]

Risk Management System

At the suggestion of Coopers & Lybrand, Salomon introduced more formalized risk management processes in late 1991. Historically, risk had been managed informally and personally by Gutfreund and the equities and bond trading heads. In the new environment, a more formal and a more collegial system was thought desirable. The new risk management system addressed not only market risks, but also "regulatory risks," "credit risks," "operational risk," and "environmental risk." The system was designed to provide senior management with a companywide perspective on exposure.

Salomon invested heavily in developing appropriate communications and information systems. At the beginning of 1992, Buffett observed: "We do not have adequate information now to use a return-on-equity benchmark for each unit." Buffett found it "rather strange . . . having a business that employs close to $4 billion of equity capital and not knowing exactly who is using what in measuring manager performance, but we don't have that now. We will get that over time . . . and people's compensation may be affected based on how those determinations come out."[45]

---

[43]Id.

[44]"Taking Arms . . . ," *Euromoney*, March 1992.

[45]Id.

Responding to criticism that Salomon had become too risk-averse under the new management team, Maughan commented, "I don't want to stifle those things that made Salomon great. I just want to guide and measure and control it. I don't want to turn it into a business where rewards go to those who write nice papers and go to a lot of meetings."[46] Denise Cumbey agreed, "I don't think the management systems being implemented will impede risk taking. Now, however, management can measure and evaluate risk."

Governance and Financing

In the annual report to shareholders for 1991, Buffett announced a change in the relationship between Salomon Inc, the parent company, and Salomon Brothers, the securities subsidiary. Rather than existing primarily to serve Salomon Brothers, the parent would instead become an "intelligent and involved" owner of "two large and important businesses, Salomon Brothers and Phibro Energy, that enjoy equal standing and that are independent of each other."

The annual report also announced a change in funding procedures. Under previous management, the parent had supplemented its equity capital with substantial debt used to fund the equity requirements of Salomon Brothers and Phibro Energy. Observing that this "double leverage" strategy was common among other financial institutions, Buffett noted that it "leaves us uneasy." Buffett's objective was to move the parent company into a position where its equity capital exceeded the combined equity capital of the subsidiaries. To accomplish this goal, the Salomon Brothers subsidiary paid a $1 billion dividend, over 75% of which was derived from non-U.S. subsidiaries to the parent.[47]

Year End

As 1991 came to a close, some U.S.-based customers, such as the World Bank, were returning. In early 1992, the state of California resumed all dealings with Salomon. Despite fourth-quarter losses of $29 million, the firm earned $919 million before taxes for the year, compared with $506 million in 1990. Maughan noted in the annual report that "the disparity between those figures illustrates clearly that our earnings are volatile. We mark to market daily and we make no attempt to smooth out the volatility by other operational or accounting methods."

According to Macfarlane, the financial crisis was 90% gone by year end. Repurchase agreements stood at 86% of Salomon's short-term financing compared to 67% a year earlier. By late January, Salomon was beginning again to issue unsecured commercial paper and medium-term notes, though in small quantities. In the government securities area, managers were making plans for a comprehensive effort to rebuild the business.

Nevertheless, the firm faced many uncertainties with the government investigation still incomplete. In late November, Securities and Exchange Commission Chairman Richard Breeden had publicly taken Gutfreund and Salomon's former management to task for their "long and thunderous silence" which, he said, raised questions about whether management "appear to tolerate or even to en-

---

[46]Grant and Parker, "Hurtling Toward Scandal."
[47]Salomon Inc 1991 Annual Report.

courage wrongdoing." Breeden continued, "We're not talking about the failure to cross a 'T' or to dot an 'I' in this kind of case. It is not an adequate ethical standard to aspire to get through the day without being indicted."[48] Federal Reserve Chairman Alan Greenspan also saw Salomon's violations as "extremely serious" and potentially increasing the government's cost of raising money.[49]

More Employees Leave

After the payment of 1991 bonuses at the beginning of 1992, Salomon experienced a second wave of employee departures. Equities, investment banking, and international operations, an area which accounted for about one-third of the firm's profits, were the areas of greatest turnover. Stephen Posford reported that in London Salomon lost 75% of its equity group, most of its salespeople, and all but two analysts, as well as a few good people in fixed income who were being paid "ridiculous amounts of money." Posford, who was on the job from 6:30 AM until 10:30 PM trying to dissuade people from leaving, learned that London headhunters had two piles of resumes—one for Salomon and one for the rest of the firms in London. The head of the Paris office also departed about the same time.[50] Estimates varied, but one managing director put the firmwide loss of professionals at 200, about three times the normal turnover.

The continuing departures of U.S. equities employees, both voluntary and involuntary, advanced Hackett's ultimate objective of restaffing the area, but at the same time made it extremely difficult to begin hiring new people. Equities lost nearly half of its 250 professionals within a six-month period. Continuing publicity about the departures and rumors that Salomon was "losing its whole equity department" fueled doubts about the future of the equities and investment banking areas. Competitors took full advantage of the turmoil to look for employees and sign on customers. But Hackett pursued his search for talent and persuaded some 30 new people to join the equities department.

The blows to the investment bank were serious as the loss of confidence spread and employees questioned Salomon's commitment to the bank. According to Richard Barrett, "When you lose people, you lose relationships. Even a good person hired from the outside cannot restore those relationships." Barrett spent many hours helping people work through their situations and trying to persuade them to stay. But many perceived the risk as too great. "It was like being a shrink [psychiatrist]. People have their whole net worth tied up in the firm. They come into my office, sit down, and explain that they have to think about their family," said Barrett.

To stem the tide of defections and demonstrate Salomon's commitment to the bank, the firm revised the compensation system announced in October and guaranteed a bonus pool for the investment banking unit and equities researchers. Though individuals were not given personal assurances, the guarantee worked as intended. The investment bank succeeded in meeting its business plan, and

---

[48]Kevin V. Salwen, "SEC Chief's Criticism of Ex-Managers of Salomon Suggests Civil Action Likely," *The Wall Street Journal*, November 20, 1991, p. A10.

[49]Roger Fillion, "Greenspan Says Market Violations Very Serious," *The Reuter Business Report*, November 6, 1991.

[50]Sara Webb and Patrick Harverson, "Salomon Suffers a Wave of Staff Departures," *The Financial Times*, January 13, 1992, p. 15.

compensation based on actual earnings exceeded the guaranteed pool. However, reflected Barrett, "The guarantee cost the investment bank in terms of internal relations. It was a macho thing—a perceived loss of nerve. Other departments did not have to guarantee their bonus pool to hang on to their people, so why should the investment bank?"

While investment bank revenues increased 9% to $108 million, the bank was unable to participate in the continuing prosperity which other investment banks enjoyed in the quarter. According to Buffett, the firm "did not participate on the investment banking side to the extent we would have expected [before the scandal] . . . and that hurt us."[51] Maughan observed that "there is significant opportunity cost from our present situation. But boards of directors do feel reluctant to award this firm the lead management while it's under investigation."[52]

Funding Situation

By February, the funding situation had stabilized further, though at a slightly more expensive level than before this crisis. Noted Maughan, "Our uncommitted bank lines have stabilized. In fact, we've won back some lines that were impaired. We have restored significant repo and securities borrowing lines. We have resumed the issuance of commercial paper as well as medium-term notes, and we continue to monitor very carefully the quality and liquidity of the asset side of the balance sheet."[53] Nevertheless, creditors continued to demand a premium given the lingering uncertainty over the government investigation.

Management Changes

Also in February, Maughan restructured the management of international operations, replacing James L. Massey as head with co-chief executives for both the European and Asian divisions. Shigeru Myojin, known as a savvy trader, and Toshihara Kojima were named co-heads of the Asian operations. Stephen Posford and Dennis J. Keegan, both important proprietary traders, were appointed to a newly formed European Management Committee. Posford and Myojin also joined the Executive Committee. According to Maughan, the changes were intended "to give the London and Tokyo regions, which are very important to us, direct representation in the management of the firm. It's of great benefit to have senior management in both centers regarded as well-connected to the markets and the community."[54]

Internal Review Completed

In March, Coopers & Lybrand (Coopers) reported the results of its audit of Salomon's U.S. securities trading operations to the board's Compliance Committee. The result of 20,000 professional hours by 66 full-time Coopers' employees at a cost of $4 million, the audit resulted in 270 recommendations, including internal control recommendations for each trading desk.

---

[51]Michael Siconolfi, "As Rivals Prosper, Salomon Profit Keeps Withering Due to Scandal," *The Wall Street Journal*, May 7, 1992, p. C1.

[52]"Taking Arms . . . ," *Euromoney*, March 1992.

[53]Id.

[54]Michael Siconolfi, "Salomon Brothers Realigns Divisions in Europe, Asia, With Co-Chiefs at Helm," *The Wall Street Journal*, February 11, 1992.

The trading desk suggestions focused on five areas: authorization of transactions; segregation of duties to reduce opportunities for one person to both perpetuate and conceal irregularities; monitoring and recording of transactions and events; access and security safeguards; and independent checks. Coopers also recommended improvements to Salomon's information technology to better manage the control and compliance function.

To implement Coopers' proposals, Maughan established an internal control and compliance task force under the chairmanship of James L. Massey, former head of international operations and a member of the executive committee and the Salomon Inc board. In addition, Salomon initiated a similar internal review of control procedures in parts of the firm not covered by the original Coopers review, including asset management, investment banking, research, and all non-U.S. businesses.

Salomon Pushes to Settle Claims

By spring 1992, Salomon was eager to resolve the situation with the government. Maughan was very conscious of the loss of personnel and the opportunity cost of a protracted negotiation. Though the SEC's investigation was largely finished by late February, the Antitrust Division of the Justice Department had not decided what to do with the antitrust counts, and the U.S. Attorney had not decided whether to bring criminal charges against the firm for the false bids. Salomon's lawyers increased their efforts to convince the government that delay was imposing costs on the firm that were unfair given its exemplary cooperation and reform.

The Settlement

On May 20, 1992, the U.S. Justice Department announced that it would not be bringing criminal charges against Salomon. As part of a negotiated settlement approved by the Treasury Department, the Justice Department, the Federal Reserve Board and the SEC, Salomon agreed to pay a total of $290 million, including $100 million to a fund to satisfy private damage claims.[55] Though the Federal Reserve permitted Salomon to continue as a primary dealer, the firm was to be suspended from trading activity with the Federal Reserve Bank for two months beginning June 1, 1992. Salomon agreed to be censured, to maintain procedures designed to prevent a recurrence of similar misconduct, and to cooperate for three years in the government's ongoing investigation of the government securities market. The settlement, which covered antitrust charges related to the May 1991 auction as well as securities law charges related to the submission of false bids, represented the government's second largest settlement with a financial firm, trailing only the $600 million assessed against Drexel, Burnham.[56] (**Exhibit 8** details charges brought against Salomon.)

---

[55]Of the $290 million, $122 million went to the U.S. Treasury as civil fines under the securities laws, and $68 million represented fines and forfeitures to settle Department of Justice claims.

[56]Mike McNamee, et al., "The Judgment of Salomon: An Anticlimax," *Business Week,* June 1, 1992, p. 106.

EXHIBIT 8   **Settlement of Charges in Administrative and Court Proceedings**

SEC Charges in Administrative Proceeding[a]

- Failure reasonably to supervise the head of the government trading desk to prevent violations of federal securities laws.
- Failure reasonably to supervise through implementation of procedures to prevent and detect violations of federal securities laws by the head of the government trading desk.

Government Charges in Court Proceeding[b]

Violations of antifraud and record-keeping provisions of the Securities Act of 1933 and the Exchange Act, including

- Submission of nine false bids and one nominee bid in nine separate auctions for U.S. Treasury securities between August of 1989 and May of 1991 resulting in the illegal acquisition of $9.548 billion of U.S. Treasury securities.
- Creation of false books and records in connection with the submission of the false and nominee bids and the handling of securities obtained pursuant to the bids.
- Failure to disclose in July 1991 registration statement material facts discovered in firm's internal investigation of illegal activities in the government securities market.
- Issuance of a press release on August 9, 1991 which failed to state material facts, including the fact that senior management had known of one false bid as early as April 1991.
- Use in 1986 of pre-arranged trades in U.S. Treasury securities to create the false appearance of $168 million in trading losses for income tax purposes.
- Prior to August 1991, engaged in a practice of overstating the amount of customer orders for debt securities of certain government-sponsored enterprises (GSEs) in discussions with representatives of the GSEs, and created records falsely stating the size of customer orders.
- Prior to August 1991, engaged in a practice of purchasing medium-term notes from corporate issuers as principal while representing to issuers that the notes had been purchased as agent for a customer, provided issuers with confirmations that falsely stated the purchases were made by a customer, and creation and use of a fictitious omnibus customer account.

---

[a]In the matter of *Salomon Brothers Inc*, SEC, Release No. 30721 (May 20, 1992).
[b]*SEC v. Salomon Inc* and *Salomon Brothers Inc.*, SEC, Litigation Release No. 13246 (May 20, 1992).

Despite the large fines, the settlement was widely hailed as a victory for Buffett and Salomon. The government probe uncovered little more than Buffett publicly admitted in the fall of 1991, when he had been at Salomon for only a few days and Salomon's internal investigation was still incomplete.[57] And, unlike in the cases of E.F. Hutton and Drexel, Burnham, no criminal charges were brought.

In announcing the settlement, Richard Breeden, Chairman of the SEC, said that while Salomon had engaged in "serious wrongdoing," its misconduct had been confined to a "fairly limited part of the firm." When asked to comment on the government's different treatment of Salomon and Drexel, Burnham, Chairman Breeden noted that "there are a great many differences, both in the scope of the behavior that occurred and in the response to it by the firm as that conduct was discovered. So we regard those as two very, very different cases. . . ."[58] The U.S. Attorney for the Southern District of New York noted that Salomon's cooperation in the investigation was "virtually unprecedented." The head of the Federal Reserve Bank of New York also pointed to the extensive management and operational changes undertaken to strengthen the integrity of the firm and to prevent future misconduct. Buffett commented on the settlement that, "All's well that ends."[59] Maughan was equally succinct, "No Warren, no firm."[60]

For many inside Salomon, the settlement marked a turning point. "We were not out of the woods until it was clear we wouldn't face criminal charges," said Bill Jennings. On the day the settlement was disclosed, Buffett announced that the firm would be taking a $185 million pretax charge-off which was added to the $200 million previously set aside.[61] The same day, Salomon's stock rose $2.875 to $33.50 in heavy trading on the New York Stock Exchange (**Exhibit 1**). A week after the settlement, Standard & Poor's removed Salomon Inc from its Credit Watch list. S&P commented that the settlement "resolves the major uncertainties that have been plaguing Salomon." S&P did not, however, raise Salomon's credit ratings from their September 1991 levels.[62]

Buffett Hands Over the Reins

Shortly after the settlement, Buffett relinquished his executive position, retaining only his role as chairman of Salomon Inc's executive committee. Maughan was elected chairman and CEO of Salomon Brothers. In a press release, Buffett pointed to Maughan's "ability—and every bit as important, his character" as ideally suiting him for the post of chief executive officer. Denham was named chairman and CEO of Salomon Inc. Denham's election made Salomon the only Wall Street holding company with a chief executive independent from its business units. The choice of a lawyer for the role was also somewhat unusual. Denham saw his job as guiding and overseeing strategy, governance, capital allocation and risk, as well as the firm's ethical standards.

---

[57]Id.

[58]"Securities and Exchange Commission Press Conference," *Federal News Service,* May 20, 1992.

[59]Robert J. McCartney, et al., "Salomon Settles Bond Case," The Washington Post, May 21, 1992, p. A1.

[60]Seth Faison, Jr., "Salomon's Renovation Enters New Phase," *The New York Times,* February 11, 1992, p. D1.

[61]Mike McNamee, et al., "The Judgment of Salomon . . ."

Despite the charge of $185 million in connection with the settlement, the firm's posted aftertax profits for the first half of 1992 were $401 million. Pretax earnings were $1.02 billion, the most ever reported by a publicly held U.S. securities firm.[63] Denham commented, "With these earnings it should be clear that Salomon Brothers' core businesses remain intact." While Salomon's performance exceeded the expectations of security industry analysts, some outside observers thought it was still too soon to tell if Salomon was "out of the woods."[64]

Back to Business

On August 3, pursuant to the May settlement, Salomon was cleared to resume bidding for customers at Treasury auctions and to undertake full trading activities with the Federal Reserve Bank of New York. With the government investigation resolved, both New York and London were able to step up hiring in equities. The investment bank, too, was bringing new people on board. The government securities area was well on its way to complete recovery.

In September, Salomon hired a new general counsel, Robert Mundheim, who had served at the SEC and the Treasury Department, and as former dean of the University of Pennsylvania's law school where he established a center on legal ethics. Mundheim, who prior to joining Salomon had been a partner at a large New York law firm, emphasized the importance of a strong, independent counsel who could back up the compliance people in the event of "pressure to bend to the business view." He oversaw some 10–15 lawyers and 35 compliance officers, including the recently hired head of fixed income compliance whose desk was right on the trading floor—not upstairs as was typical for compliance executives.[65]

Continuing Challenges

During the fall of 1992, Salomon continued the struggle to establish strong investment banking and U.S. equities businesses. At the end of the first half of 1992, the firm stood in sixth place with 8.9% of the market for all domestic securities issues. In equities underwriting, Salomon ranked tenth, with 1.8% compared to fifth with 8.6% for the first half of 1991 (**Exhibit 7**). Indeed, in the second half of 1992, the future of investment banking at Salomon was cloudy. As Buffett commented: "If, five years from now, investment banking kept losing money, it would raise the question of whether we ought to be in the business."[66]

Richard Barrett, investment banking head, gave the unit a "B+" for hanging in there and keeping business. In October Salomon's share of equities underwriting

---

[63]"Salomon Second Quarter Results," *Extel Examiner*, July 23, 1992.

[64]Christina Toh-Pantin, "Salomon Inc Q2 Results," *Reuters*, New York, July 23, 1992.

[65]Michael Siconolfi, "Salomon Names Charles Williams a Compliance Chief," *The Wall Street Journal*, June 16, 1992, p. B12.

[66]Kurt Eichenwald, "Salomon Still Struggling to Diversify Its Business," *The New York Times*, September 8, 1992, p. D1.

appeared to be picking up.[67] The tide of employee departures had been stemmed and Barrett was anticipating the challenge of upgrading the unit's new work force.

Equities was facing a similar challenge. Bruce Hackett, however, was optimistic about the new talent brought in over the year and about the new equities management committee he had formed. Since August 1991, 150 out of 250 equities professionals had left the firm, some 30–40 involuntarily. But Hackett had hired about 180 new people. In the summer, Rodney Berens, a highly respected professional, formerly with Morgan Stanley, joined Hackett as co-head of equities. Though equities revenues were still lagging, trading volume was up.

By the end of 1992, the government securities area was again thriving, with a market share position ahead of prescandal levels.

Continuing Government Activities

In the fall of 1992, the government was continuing to address issues raised by Salomon's Treasury auction activities. The Justice Department continued to investigate whether unnamed "co-conspirators" had conspired with Salomon in the Treasury's April or May 1991 auctions for two-year notes. The U.S. Treasury Department, after a review of the Treasury auction process prompted by the Salomon irregularities, decided in September 1992 to test a new *single-price* "Dutch auction" system for two- and five-year note auctions to try to encourage more aggressive bidding. The Treasury was also, for the first time, assembling a compendium of rules governing the bidding process.[68]

Opening up the primary dealer system was also being discussed. Former Fed Chairman Paul Volcker explained that the primary dealer system was intended to enable the Fed and the Treasury to ensure they were dealing with institutions of "unquestioned probity and financial strength." But he acknowledged that after the Salomon affair, the primary dealers' probity was no longer so clear.[69] Congress was considering new regulations for the massive government securities market.[70]

SEC Settles with Individual Defendants

In early December, the SEC settled charges against Salomon's four senior executives. The SEC found that their failure "to take action to discipline Mozer or to limit his activities constituted a serious breach of their supervisory obligation." John H. Gutfreund was banned for life from being a chairman or CEO of a securities firm and fined $100,000. Thomas W. Strauss was suspended from the securities business for six months and fined $75,000. John W. Meriwether was suspended from the securities business for three months and fined $50,000.

---

[67]"Salomon Gaining Lost Ground in Equity Underwriting," *Corporate Financing Week,* October 26, 1992, p. 9.

[68]"Treasury Issues Circular on Securities Auctions," *The Wall Street Journal,* January 6, 1993, p. C10.

[69]"Salomon Scandal Calls for Auction Overhaul," *The Wall Street Journal,* August 28, 1991, p. A1, Col. 5.

[70]John Connor, "Senate Panel Clears Bill on Marketing of U.S. Securities," *The Wall Street Journal,* May 28, 1993, p. A5A.

Although the SEC did not discipline former General Counsel Donald M. Feuerstein,[71] he was sharply criticized for "failure to discharge his supervisory responsibilities over Mozer which he acquired by virtue of the circumstances of a particular situation."[72] The government was continuing its criminal investigation of the activities of Mozer and Murphy.

Shortly after the SEC settlements with Salomon's former management, the firm reached a settlement of employment compensation claims with Strauss, Meriwether, and Feuerstein, though not with Gutfreund. All three collected amounts to which they were entitled under agreements existing when they left the firm, as directed by the Salomon board in 1991. Meriwether was paid an additional $8 million in compensation for 1991, an amount which was, according to Denham, well below what he would have received in the absence of the Treasury auction matter.

At the end of 1992, Salomon had yet to settle or go to trial on any of the 50 some lawsuits filed by its customers, shareholders, and other private parties allegedly injured by the Treasury auction improprieties. No payments had yet been made out of the $100 million restitution fund set up as part of Salomon's settlement with the government.

Rethinking the Business

As the year was coming to a close, Salomon managers were beginning to think of the firm's businesses in two main categories—client-driven businesses and proprietary businesses—rather than as a collection of discrete products and functions. Traditionally, risky and volatile proprietary trading, particularly in bonds, accounted for a very large percentage of the firm's profits. In 1992, for example, the firm had $276 million in business unit contributions from customer businesses and $1.4 billion in proprietary trading.[73]

Said Maughan, "I think of the firm as employing both hunters and farmers. The hunters, i.e., the traders, deal with proprietary businesses. The farmers deal with customer businesses." To differentiate the areas and address the conflicts between them, Maughan was beginning to separate the management and profit and loss accounting systems for proprietary and customer businesses. Sometimes, however, the neat separation of hunters and farmers was not possible as in the government securities area where proprietary traders executed trades on behalf of customers serviced by a sales staff. Maughan noted,

> There are inherent conflicts in both investing capital for shareholders and trading for clients. Who are you representing? The buyer or the seller? Salomon owns and trades a lot of bonds. Clients know this and come to us because they need liquidity. The only way to manage this ethically is to make sure that the client is fully informed. We also need to have high quality salesmen and controls on trading. You have to have the long-term in mind. Customers represent a stream of income. You will lose that stream of income if you treat them unfairly.

---

[71]Considerable controversy had been engendered by the SEC's potential censure of Feuerstein. Lawyers' groups, in particular, were concerned about imposing managerial responsibility upon an attorney working in the employ of a firm.

[72]In the matter of John H. Gutfreund, et al., Admin. Proc. File No. 3–7930, SEC 34 Act Release No. 31554, 1992 SEC LEXIS 2969 (December 3, 1992).

[73]Kurt Eichenwald, "As Firms Shift Strategies, the Old Order Moves On," *The New York Times*, July 23, 1993, p. D2.

To insure that the traders had proper incentive to execute customer transactions, trader compensation in the government securities area had been changed to make customer sales volume a component of the trader's compensation formula. Previously, traders were compensated solely on the basis of the profits and losses on their trades.

Despite poor third-quarter results, Salomon posted record pretax earnings for 1992. As the year ended, the firm was developing a number of ancillary systems and structures, such as the Risk Management Committee and the Business Practices Committee, to help guide the business. New projects, such as the recently established unit to trade interest rate swaps and other derivative products, were underway.

It was clear, however, that what Maughan called the "billion-dollar error of judgment" had severely tested the firm and propelled a new generation of managers into leadership positions. Salomon had lost 800 to 900 employees in the year after disclosing the Treasury auction improprieties, including 40 to 45 managing directors. Observing that Salomon's new leaders were still working toward a "common vision of who we are," one managing director looked ahead: "The question for 1993 is whether we will repeat the old model or invent a new one."

Case 2
Martin Marietta: Managing Corporate Ethics (A)

Martin Marietta had earned a reputation for having one of the best ethics programs in the defense industry, and its top managers were committed to keeping it that way. Established in September 1985, the program had become an integral part of the corporation's comprehensive approach to self-governance. In 1992, Martin Marietta's chairman and CEO, Norman Augustine, reflected on the impact of the program.

> Ten years ago, people would have said there were no ethical issues in the business. Today, that is different. Today's employees think their number one objective is to be thought of as decent people doing quality work. We all have a much greater consciousness of ethical issues. With the program, you are less likely to get into trouble, and you feel better about yourself. The program has also helped us compete. We have been afforded opportunities because we were trusted.

Augustine brought a broad perspective to his job as CEO. Before joining Martin Marietta, in 1977, as a vice president of Aerospace Technical Operations, he had held a variety of private sector and Defense Department positions, including several at the level of assistant secretary and undersecretary of the Army. He once quipped that he had started at the top—putting tar on roofs with a roofing gang in Denver for $1.69 an hour. A graduate of Princeton University, Augustine was a prolific writer and author of two books, *Augustine's Laws* (1983) and *The Defense Revolution* (1990).

As CEO, Augustine saw himself as having multiple commitments: to shareholders, customers, employees, and the community. "The toughest decisions," he explained, "are those involving conflicts among these groups. You have to decide what's fair in these situations and constantly work to fulfill and balance these commitments." He went on, "Sometimes, you have to go against conventional business logic." Augustine advised anyone aspiring to high levels of management to "have a good boss. Get in a company that will permit you to raise ethical questions." He noted, "Most people get into trouble for doing what is the norm for the small group they operate in, but not for the larger society."

Senior managers on the Ethics Steering Committee kept a close watch over Martin Marietta's ethics program. Chaired by Corporate President Tom Young, the committee included:

- Senior Vice President and CFO—Marc Bennett
- Vice President and General Counsel—Frank Menaker
- Vice President, Audit—Dave Clous
- Vice President, Human Resources—Bobby Leonard
- Vice President, Public Affairs—Phil Giaramita

This case was prepared by Lynn Sharp Paine with the assistance of Albert Choy and Michael Santoro. Copyright © 1992 by the President and Fellows of Harvard College. Harvard Business School case 393–016.

Every three months, the committee met with George Sammet, a retired general who had served as vice president and ethics program head since 1988, to consider issues and developments.

In early 1992, Sammet and members of the Ethics Steering Committee were wrestling with two persistent issues. The first was employees' fear of retribution, real or imagined, for raising concerns with the corporation's ethics offices. So long as employees feared retaliation, they would hesitate to use the ethics offices, thus increasing the likelihood that serious wrongdoing could go unnoticed until too late. The second was how to assess the effectiveness of the ethics program. Although committee members all believed the program was a good one, they were searching for ways to evaluate it more objectively. It was easy to measure activity—much more difficult to measure effectiveness.

Company Background

Martin Marietta was known for the leading-edge aerospace and defense technologies it produced for the U.S. government. The corporation had led the construction of the Viking spacecraft that landed on Mars in 1976, and had built the Magellan spacecraft, which began orbiting Venus in 1990. A number of the corporation's missile and electronic systems were successfully proven in combat by U.S. forces in Operation Desert Storm. Martin Marietta's businesses also included information management technologies and systems, as well as energy and materials. Each of the corporation's four main operating units, known as "companies," was headed by a president. Most of the corporation's 60,000 employees worked at nine U.S. locations, including corporate headquarters in Bethesda, Maryland.

Martin Marietta's origins dated to 1905, when Glenn Martin started a small airplane factory while working as an automotive salesman and barnstormer in California. In World Wars I and II, Martin developed bombers for the War Department. With the support of Pan Am World Airways in 1932, he entered the commercial aircraft business with the "China Clipper," a 32-passenger plane capable of flying from San Francisco to Honolulu. But, after incurring substantial losses in the 1950s, the company left the aircraft business and concentrated on developing missiles, rockets, aeronautic equipment, and weapons systems. In 1961, Martin merged with the American-Marietta Corporation, a producer of chemicals and construction materials, to form Martin Marietta.

Many of the American-Marietta businesses were later sold to reduce the $1.3 billion debt incurred in fending off a hostile takeover attempt by the Bendix Corporation in 1982. By 1986, the company's debt had dropped to $220 million, yielding a more comfortable debt-to-total-capitalization ratio of 24%. At that time, nearly 75% of Martin Marietta's revenues were defense related, and the company embarked on a strategy to reduce its reliance on defense contracts in anticipation of cutbacks in federal defense spending. Two years later, in 1988, Norman Augustine was named CEO.

For 1990, Martin Marietta ranked fifth among defense contractors in the dollar value of government defense contract awards and fourth in total federal contract awards.[1] Defense contracts accounted for about 75% of its revenues of $6.1 billion

---

[1]Tom Shoop, "The Top 20 Government Contractors," *Government Executive,* August 1991.

EXHIBIT 1   **Martin Marietta Corporation, Five-Year Summary**

	1991	1990	1989	1988	1987
Operating Results					
Net sales	$6,075,415	$6,125,939	$5,796,182	$5,727,482	$5,172,954
Cost of sales, other costs, and expenses	5,537,926	5,683,462	5,331,544	5,330,762	4,766,510
Earnings from Operations	537,489	442,477	464,638	396,720	406,444
Other income and expenses, net	(58,980)	34,504	7,789	117,189	(1,472)
	478,509	476,981	472,427	513,909	404,972
Interest expense on debt	57,660	41,790	43,084	38,734	24,972
Earnings before taxes on income and extraordinary item	420,849	435,191	429,343	475,175	380,000
Taxes on income	107,700	107,600	122,400	155,400	149,350
Earnings before Extraordinary Item	313,149	327,591	306,943	319,775	230,650
Extraordinary item—utilization of tax capital loss carryforward	=	=	=	39,100	=
Net Earnings	$ 313,149	$ 327,591	$ 306,943	$ 358,875	$ 230,650
Per Common Share					
Net earnings:					
Before extraordinary item	$6.30	$6.52	$5.82	$6.02	$4.25
Extraordinary item	=	=	=	.73	=
	$6.30	$6.52	$5.82	$6.75	$4.25
Cash dividends	$1.50	$1.3875	$1.225	$1.10	$1.05
Condensed Balance Sheet Data					
Current assets	$1,616,490	$1,400,617	$1,440,605	$1,291,322	$1,130,688
Property, plant, and equipment, net	1,315,472	1,340,688	1,300,939	1,297,507	1,185,455
Investments and other assets	964,911	869,244	763,835	730,158	497,274
Total	$3,896,873	$3,610,529	$3,505,379	$3,318,987	$2,813,417
Current liabilities	$ 947,989	$ 993,647	$ 926,327	$ 908,587	$ 815,962
Long-term debt	595,942	463,288	477,504	483,784	294,586
Other noncurrent liabilities	301,581	355,033	232,033	253,275	254,398
Noncurrent deferred income taxes	247,458	257,558	514,555	472,729	540,739
Shareowners' equity	1,803,903	1,540,963	1,354,960	1,200,612	907,732
Total	$3,896,873	$3,610,529	$3,505,379	$3,318,987	$2,813,417

Source: Martin Marietta Corporation Annual Report, 1991.

in 1990, and other government contracts for another 15% (**Exhibits 1** and **2**). Management was careful not to let any single contract account for more than 20% of the company's total sales. The remaining 10% of revenues reflected commercial and foreign military sales. The company's contract-backlog-to-sales ratio was 2:1, the highest of any defense contractor.

One Wall Street defense analyst saw Martin Marietta as "one of, if not the best positioned company" in the industry. He noted that the company was one of the dominant space companies and was emerging as one of the dominant defense electronics companies.[2] Nevertheless, with the likelihood of continued declines in defense outlays, the company faced a challenging future (**Exhibit 3**).

Ethics Program Background

Martin Marietta's formal ethics program emerged in 1985 from the efforts and concerns of many individuals. The program was one facet of an effort to create

---

[2]Ibid.

Exhibit 2

Contributions of Major Business Segments — Martin Marietta Corporation

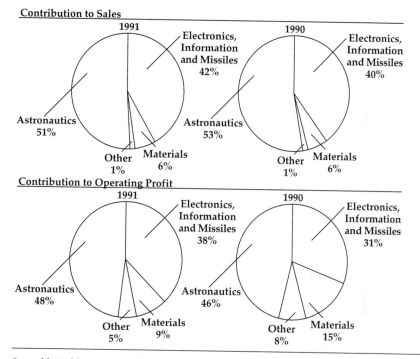

Contribution to Sales

1991
- Astronautics 51%
- Electronics, Information and Missiles 42%
- Other 1%
- Materials 6%

1990
- Astronautics 53%
- Electronics, Information and Missiles 40%
- Other 1%
- Materials 6%

Contribution to Operating Profit

1991
- Astronautics 48%
- Electronics, Information and Missiles 38%
- Other 5%
- Materials 9%

1990
- Astronautics 46%
- Electronics, Information and Missiles 31%
- Other 8%
- Materials 15%

Source: Martin Marietta Annual Report, 1991.

Exhibit 3   Federal National Defense Outlays in Current Dollars, 1984–1991

Year	(in $ billions)	Percentage Change from Previous Year
1984	227.4	8.3
1985	252.7	11.1
1986	273.4	8.2
1987	282.0	3.1
1988	290.4	3.0
1989	303.6	4.5
1990	299.3	−1.4
1991	273.3	−9.5

Source: U.S. Department of Commerce.

and maintain a "do-it-right" climate at a time when the defense industry was facing serious attacks from the government and the public for fraud and mismanagement. The immediate catalyst for the program was a failure to credit an overhead account on a government contract, but the idea had been "in the air" for some time.

Jacques Croom, associate general counsel, was one important contributor to the program. Croom first suggested a formal code of ethics in 1983, but long before then he had advocated a business approach based on integrity and fair play. With the federal government's campaign against defense industry fraud, waste, and abuse in the early 1980s, the company's campaign for integrity and fairness took on a new seriousness. By mid-1983, Croom's "Hellfire and Brimstone" speech, initially developed in the late 1970s, had become a standard opening to a variety of training programs. He told people:

> There are a lot of reasons to be good. And I'm sure you've all got your own. But I want to give you one more reason. If you fall off that path, you could go to jail. You'll be terminated from this company and you'll lose your security clearance. That means you won't be able to turn around and go over to a competitor. You may also be involved in a civil suit by the company. So don't claim you were helping us out of a difficult spot. You are not doing the company or yourself a favor by cutting corners. We'll stand behind you if you make an innocent mistake. But if you deliberately violate the law, you won't get support, and I, personally, will probably turn you in to the authorities.

Some managers thought Croom was taking the wrong approach. But Croom was convinced there were some things people should be afraid of—prosecutors, the FBI, and auditors, for example. And he thought people should know what could happen to them if they did something wrong. "The guy who does things ethically doesn't have to worry," he told his critics. "We want employees to know and practice a simple philosophy that 'there is no substitute for doing what is right.'" He reminded cynics and skeptics that "You may get away with dishonesty all your life, but all it takes is getting caught once."

In 1984, shortly after Croom suggested a code of ethics, an incident of mischarging occurred. The company was being investigated for improper travel billings in a small, wholly owned subsidiary. Evidence of wrongdoing could expose the company to suspension from defense contracting. A conviction could lead to debarment—a prohibition on doing business with the government for a specified period of time.

Martin Marietta's president decided the time had come to institute a companywide ethics program. About the same time, Frank Menaker, Martin Marietta's general counsel, decided the company should take an aggressive approach to compliance. He advocated an ethics office and code of conduct. He also launched an internal investigation of the alleged travel incident.

Croom was given the task of drafting a code. He worked on it over a period of four months, during which he reflected on his 17 years at Martin Marietta—on what the company stood for and how it felt about its people and the communities in which it was involved. He wanted a code employees could use both as a guide and as a protective shield. A draft was circulated among top management.

As the program began to take shape, a few managers were put off by what they saw as an implication that they were unethical and needed to be reformed. Objections were raised by marketers, who feared the code would limit their ability to get information and put them at a competitive disadvantage. Nevertheless, in September 1985, Martin Marietta's board of directors approved the proposed corporate Code of Ethics and Standards of Conduct and authorized the establishment of a Corporate Ethics Office. The Audit Committee of the board was

EXHIBIT 4

Organization Chart: Corporate Ethics Infrastructure, 1991

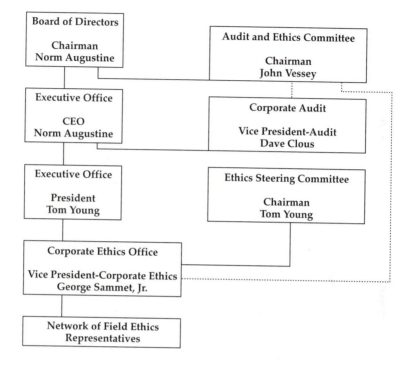

renamed the Audit and Ethics Committee, and the Ethics Steering Committee was appointed to implement and guide the ethics program. At about the same time, the head of corporate internal audit was directed to begin reporting to the chairman and CEO "to enhance senior management attention to key audit issues." With these changes, the company created the basic infrastructure for its ethics program (**Exhibit 4**).

The following month, a copy of the Code of Ethics and Standards of Conduct was sent to Martin Marietta's 60,000 employees at their homes. The Code, a 12-page pamphlet, laid out the company's guiding principles, key constituencies, and basic standards of conduct employees were expected to follow in bidding, negotiating, and performing contracts (**Exhibit 5**). It covered topics such as conflicts of interest, accurate books and records, gifts and entertainment, insider trading, antitrust law, and political contributions. It prohibited payments to secure business abroad. Each employee was required to return an acknowledgement card certifying receipt of the Code.

During the same period, ethics was made an explicit requirement of eligibility for awards under the Corporate Executive Incentive plan for company executives (**Exhibit 6**). The Code was later supplemented by a publication providing examples to help employees interpret the standards of conduct and make decisions in the "gray areas" (**Exhibit 7**).

EXHIBIT 5   **Excerpt from Code of Ethics and Standards of Conduct**

Martin Marietta Credo

Statement of Unifying Principles

In our daily activities we bear important obligations to our country, our customers, our owners, our communities, and to one another. We carry out these obligations guided by certain unifying principles:

- Our foundation is INTEGRITY. We conduct our business in an open and forthright manner in strict compliance with applicable laws, rules, and regulations so that we are correctly perceived to be an ethical organization of dedicated and competent individuals of high integrity and credibility producing quality products and services that contribute significantly to our communities and to our nation.
- Our strength is our PEOPLE. The collective talents of our employees comprise our most important asset. Therefore, we provide an organization and operating environment that attracts, nurtures, stimulates, and rewards employee professionalism and creativity, providing a safe workplace and an opportunity for hands-on accomplishment, a criterion highly regarded for promotion and growth.
- Our style is TEAMWORK. As pioneers and leaders in technology advancement, from design and systems development to manufacturing, testing, and operational integration, the corporation emphasizes teamwork, recognizing within that framework the critical contribution of the individual. Providing a workplace environment that effectively balances and stimulates the individual and the team is our hallmark.
- Our goal is EXCELLENCE. Excellence in the form of quality is a shared attribute of the customers and markets we serve and the products we build. Attention to detail and performance are stressed in every line and staff function from the factory floor through the highest levels of management, resulting in a total dedication to mission success.

Code of Ethics and Standards of Conduct

Martin Marietta Corporation believes in the highest ethical standards. We demonstrate these beliefs through our commitments—commitments we are dedicated to fulfill.

- To our EMPLOYEES we are committed to just management and equality for all, providing a safe and healthy workplace, and respecting the dignity and privacy due all human beings.
- To our CUSTOMERS we are committed to produce reliable products and services at a fair price that are delivered on time and within budget.
- To our COMMUNITIES in which we live we are committed to be responsible neighbors, reflecting all aspects of good citizenship.
- To our SHAREHOLDERS we are committed to pursuing sound growth and earnings objectives and to exercising prudence in the use of our assets and resources.
- To our SUPPLIERS we are committed to fair competition and the sense of responsibility required of a good customer.

To ensure continuing attention to matters of ethics and standards on the part of all Martin Marietta employees, the Corporation has established the Corporate Ethics Office. This office is charged with responsibility for monitoring performance under this Code of Ethics and for resolving concerns presented to the Ethics Office.

Martin Marietta calls on every employee to report any violation or apparent violation of the Code. The Corporation strongly encourages employees to work with their supervisors in making such reports and, in addition, provides to employees the right to report violations directly to the Corporate Ethics Office. Prompt reporting of violations is considered to be in the best interest of everyone.

Employee reports will be handled as confidentially as possible. No employee will suffer indignity or retaliation because of a report he or she makes.

The Corporate Ethics Office is a part of the executive office of the Corporation. Its toll-free number is 800–3–ETHICS (800–338–4427) and its MARCALL number is 356–9400. Employees may also write P.O. Box 16234, Orlando, FL 32861.

Source: Company document.

EXHIBIT 6 Excerpt from Martin Marietta—Corporate Executive Incentive Plan

---

II. STANDARD OF CONDUCT AND PERFORMANCE EXPECTATION

A. It is expected that the business and individual goals and objectives established for this Plan will be accomplished in accordance with the Corporation's policy on ethical conduct in business with the Government and all other customers. It is a prerequisite before any award can be considered that a participant will have acted in accordance with the Martin Marietta Corporation Code of Ethics and fostered an atmosphere to encourage all employees acting under the participant's supervision to perform their duties in accordance with the highest ethical standards. Ethical behavior is imperative. Thus, in achieving one's goals, the individual's commitment and adherence to the Corporation's ethical standard will be considered paramount in determining awards under this Plan.

B. Plan participants whose individual performance is determined to be less than acceptable are not eligible to receive incentive awards.

Source: Company document.

EXHIBIT 7 Excerpt from *Guidelines Martin Marietta Corporation Code of Ethics and Standards of Conduct*

False Claims or Statements

False claims against the government or false statements to the government can arise in many forms and through many actions which we take in the performance of our duties. The following examples are given to show how relatively simple these matters can be:

- It's near closing time on Friday afternoon. You are in the 99th hour of a 100-hour test of a component, as prescribed in contract specifications, before shipping it to another facility for assembly as part of a military system. You're already filling out the certification papers, preparatory to putting the component in its box for shipment when your carpool driver

---

Exhibit 7 Continued

- You are required to submit a report and discover that one of the requirements you are supposed to have completed has not been done. However, it can be completed in a few days. The report is due immediately. Should you, out of loyalty, keep the company from looking bad by falsifying the report, since you should have the task completed prior to anyone checking it? No. Martin Marietta sincerely expects that all employees be completely honest, irrespective of the consequences.

- Contract specifications for a component your department builds call for all welds to be made by a certified welder. One welder is on vacation, and the other calls in sick. But you have an apprentice, nearly ready for certification, who you think is at least as good as the two regulars, so you tell the apprentice to weld the component. He does so, and your X-ray inspection shows that he has made a perfect weld. You apply the inspection sticker, sign the paperwork, pack up the component and ship it, congratulating yourself on getting the job done in spite of obstacles. But even though the apprentice's weld was perfect, you have violated the terms of the contract, because the apprentice was not a certified welder. In applying the inspection sticker and signing the paperwork, you have attested falsely that the terms of the contract were met—another unethical procedure that also is a criminal violation.

Source: Company document.

calls to tell you that they are ready to leave. But the 100-hour test isn't completed, and your supervisor has told you the part has to be shipped. "What the heck," you tell yourself, "99-plus hours is just as good as 100, and besides, the 100-hour requirement is just an arbitrary number." So you sign the certification document, pack the component, and call for Shipping to pick up the package. The moment you sign that certification, you have made a false statement to the government—a federal crime. You have certified that the component meets a contract requirement—the completion of the 100-hour test—when in truth, the requirement has not been met. When the invoice for the component is mailed, it becomes mail fraud as well.

Defense Industry Initiative

Martin Marietta established its ethics program during a turbulent period for the U.S. defense industry. As the Reagan Administration increased defense spending in the early 1980s, allegations of contractor fraud made headlines. Journalists charged the industry with "a penchant for taking more than is rightfully theirs, and for delivering less than perfect products, overcharging, falsifying tests and on occasion bribing government officials."[3] One commentator traced the problems to the economics of the business.

> The defense industry is a one-customer market in which the customer spends money in chunks ranging from a few hundred dollars to tens of billions. . . . With only a single customer to focus on, relationships between buyer and seller have been very cozy, with

---

[3]Robert Wrubel, "Addicted to Fraud?" *Financial World,* June 27, 1989, p. 58.

people often switching roles through a well-oiled revolving door. . . . Winning a large contract often means the difference between feast and famine for the large prime contractor. For the second-tier supplier . . . getting hooked up with the right prime contractor can mean doubling sales or profits in a single year. The reward for marketing hard, bidding low and making unrealistic promises sometimes can be enormous.[4]

To address the industry's problems, David Packard, chairman of Hewlett-Packard and former deputy secretary of defense, was asked to chair a blue ribbon commission to study defense management, including the budget process, procurement, organization, operations, and legislative oversight, and to find ways of streamlining and improving defense contracting. Congress was threatening more legislation even though there already existed more than 30,000 pages of regulations and a Department of Defense (DoD) audit staff of 22,000 employees with a budget of close to $1 billion. The Packard Commission's recommendation of industry self-governance was embraced by the leading defense contractors as a way of addressing congressional concerns without additional legislation.

Led by General Electric, 18 defense contractors, including Martin Marietta, worked together in June of 1986 to create the Defense Industry Initiative on Business Ethics and Conduct (DII). By the fall, 32 leading defense contractors had signed on. Signatory corporations agreed to adopt and implement principles of business ethics based on their responsibilities under federal procurement laws and to the public. They also agreed to create an environment in which compliance with the laws and timely reporting of violations became the conscious responsibility of every employee in the industry. Specifically, they pledged to:

- Have a written code of conduct.
- Train their employees in the code's requirements.
- Encourage employees to report violations of the code without fear of retribution.
- Monitor compliance with the federal procurement laws and adopt procedures for voluntary disclosure of violations to the appropriate authorities.
- Participate annually in an industrywide Best Practices Forum in which ideas were freely exchanged.
- Provide for public accountability by outside review of company programs.[5]

Initially endorsed for a period of three years, the DII was carried forward for three more years in 1989 and would be up for review again in 1992. By 1990, 55 companies were part of the DII and it seemed likely the DII would continue. One Martin Marietta executive noted, "Ethics programs are here to stay. Corporate America is not going to operate without codes of conduct and strong ethics programs."

Martin Marietta's Menaker had helped shape the DII, and Martin Marietta was an original signatory. The company's self-governance program was further strengthened in 1986 by the promotion of the director of Corporate Audit to the position of vice president and by the creation of an assistant general counsel for compliance. The position, later upgraded to associate general counsel, included

---

[4]Ibid.

[5]*Control and Accountability,* a report by the President's Blue Ribbon Commission on Defense Management, June 1986.

EXHIBIT 8   **Ethics Component of Performance Appraisal Criteria**

Business Ethics and Conduct

During the preparation of this performance appraisal, the Business Ethics and Conduct of the employee, as outlined below, were carefully reviewed.

This manager accepts the commitment and responsibility to create an environment in which compliance with the company Code of Ethics and the federal procurement laws are achieved.

Evidence of Support:

- Demonstrates support for company Code of Ethics by personal business conduct.
- Assures the receipt of the company Code of Ethics by all current employees and secures the necessary training to assure complete understanding.
- Provides new employees with orientation to the company Code of Ethics.
- Monitors conduct of employees in their dealings with suppliers, consultants, and customers.
- Encourages reporting by employees of suspected violations.

Source: Company document.

acting as the liaison with government investigative and enforcement agencies such as the Inspector General and the FBI, and advising the Ethics Office. In addition, in 1986, performance review criteria for supervisory and management positions were amended to include each employee's commitment to the ethics effort (**Exhibit 8**).

Voluntary Disclosure

Some contractors balked at the requirements of the DII, particularly its provision on voluntary disclosure. Their reluctance may have arisen from failure to fully understand that DII did not mandate that a company voluntarily disclose every instance of employee misconduct. It merely required a company to have in place adequate procedures to effect disclosure.

Although the Defense Department set up a program to accept disclosures in July 1986 and the Justice Department, which was responsible for prosecuting and litigating claims against defense contractors, agreed to participate, the benefits of disclosure were not apparent to all. The government made it clear that voluntary disclosure would not lead to amnesty and made no commitment regarding ultimate resolution of matters voluntarily disclosed. Even with disclosure, contractors might still face suspension or debarment by the DoD and prosecution by the DoJ. However, the program did offer contractors accelerated consideration of their cases and the opportunity to do their own initial investigations, and the government indicated that disclosure and full cooperation would be viewed favorably.

When the DII was created, Martin Marietta was already under an obligation "voluntarily" to disclose employee misconduct under the terms of an administrative settlement with the government of the travel billings incident. However, top management decided to adhere to the voluntary disclosure commitment even after the expiration of the requirement. In fact, the company went beyond the DII requirements. Its policy on voluntary disclosure clearly advised employees that employee misconduct *would* be disclosed. Menaker, the general counsel, explained the company's philosophy of openness. "If we've got a problem, we should admit it and get it behind us. Our business is making goods and services for the federal government. To succeed, we need to focus on our core business, not on these kinds of problems."

Augustine observed, "The [voluntary disclosure] program does sometimes cause me to reflect on my priorities as CEO. I feel a conflict between my obligations to the shareholders and what is required under the program since disclosure could lead to convicting the corporation. But there is a pragmatic side to disclosure—it diffuses the impact of a scandal, which can have more damaging effects. The media often see the crime of covering-up as worse than the crime itself."

Procedures for identifying and assessing potential disclosures were put in place in August of 1987 (**Exhibit 9**). The head of the relevant operating unit was assigned responsibility for the decision to disclose, though company lawyers offered advice and implemented any disclosure. Careful thought had to be given to the decision to disclose information that might otherwise be legally protected by the attorney-client privilege or work product doctrine because disclosure might be deemed a waiver of these protections.[6] Some U.S. government attorneys were very demanding in the information they required: "If a company wants the benefit of not being prosecuted, then I want the results of the investigation and the underlying interviews."[7] Yet disclosure of this information could result in the company's being legally compelled to disclose the same or related information to adverse parties in other lawsuits against it.

Total Audit Program
The Ethics Program and the Voluntary Disclosure program were closely linked to the audit function, headed by corporate vice president and Ethics Steering Committee member Dave Clous. Between 1986 and 1991, the audit office tripled in size in furtherance of the Total Audit mission of strengthening the company's self-governance environment. Audit provided investigative services to the ethics program, and Clous, who met privately four times a year with the Audit and Ethics Committee of the board, worked closely with Sammet. Some 12%–13% of the 70-person audit staff's time was devoted to investigating ethics inquiries. Another 48% was spent on audits for government compliance.

As a defense contractor, Martin Marietta was under the constant scrutiny of government auditors. Nearly 100 full-time government auditors were assigned to the company. Clous aimed to improve internal oversight and accountability and to demonstrate to the government the reliability of the company's own audit sys-

---

[6]The attorney-client privilege permitted a corporation to protect confidential communications between its employees and its attorneys if the communications were for the purpose of providing or obtaining legal assistance to the corporation. The privilege did not apply if the corporate client was seeking to further or cover up criminal wrongdoing. The work product doctrine protected documents and materials prepared by a party or the party's representative in anticipation of litigation. The law was very unclear on the extent to which the corporation's or its counsels' rights might be waived by disclosures to the government in the context of the Voluntary Disclosure program.

[7]Fred Strasser, "Dicey Dilemmas: Corporate Probe Use Expanding," *The National Law Journal,* January 9, 1989, quoting U.S. Attorney Anthony Valukas of Chicago.

EXHIBIT 9   **Martin Marietta Corporate Operating Instructions on Voluntary Disclosure, 8/14/87**

Subject: Voluntary Disclosure

   I. SCOPE
       This operating instruction is applicable to all companies and operating elements of Martin Marietta Corporation.

  II. POLICY
       Martin Marietta is committed to conducting its business according to the highest standards of business ethics, to self-govern its business conduct, and to monitor compliance with Federal procurement laws. The Corporation will not condone conduct by any employee who intentionally violates the federal procurement laws. The Corporation, on a voluntary basis, will promptly and fully disclose to the responsible Federal authorities violations of federal procurement law and instances of significant employee misconduct affecting or influencing its government operations. . . .

  VI. DISCLOSURES

       A. Voluntary disclosures of violations and significant employee misconduct will be made as expeditiously as possible.

       B. The results (facts) of an internal investigation will be neutrally presented to company-level senior management by the company's counsel as soon as an internal investigation is completed. Company management will determine, based on the facts presented, whether there exists "reasonable grounds to believe that federal procurement laws may have been violated or that significant employee misconduct may have occurred." If company-level management concludes that reasonable grounds exist, the Assistant General Counsel for Compliance will be immediately informed and will be responsible for reporting the violation to the Department of Defense Inspector General within 15 days.

       C. In assessing whether an incident is significant for disclosure, the following factors should be considered:
           1. Dollar impact attributed to the alleged misconduct. Generally, the higher the dollar value, the greater the significance.
           2. Whether the alleged misconduct indicated a broader pattern or practice of wrongdoing. The more extensive the perceived misconduct, the greater the significance.
           3. The level of the employee involved in the alleged misconduct. The more senior the level of the employee, the greater the significance.
           4. Whether the individual employee or the corporation was the intended beneficiary of the alleged misconduct. If the employee engaged in misconduct solely for his own benefit, this, when considered with other factors, may diminish the significance.
           5. Whether the alleged misconduct illegally affected the integrity of the federal procurement process.
           6. Whether there had been any attempt to either conceal or mislead the Defense Contract Audit Agency or any investigative agency as to the true nature of the wrongdoing. Any such attempt will be viewed as significant.
           7. Whether the law was clear on the issue. Was the particular act in question clearly violative of the law, or is there ambiguity?
           8. Whether a wrongful intent or an intent to deceive or defraud was evident.

Norman R. Augustine
President

Source: Company document.

tems. He also hoped to reduce the amount of management time spent on auditing activity by eliminating duplicate government audits and improving existing internal systems.

Clous saw the biggest stumbling block as the mindset of the government auditors. "We are concerned about systems. They are concerned about finding mistakes and errors to prove they've done their job. They get credit by bringing errors to the attention of Congress. It's hard for them to think we can be independent and objective."

Two efforts had begun to improve relationships with the government. Since 1990, the company had been involved in both the Coordinated Audit Planning and the Contractor Risk Assessment Guide (CRAG) programs to reduce overlap and improve audits in certain high-risk areas such as labor charging, estimating systems, materials management, accounting systems, and purchasing. With coordinated audit planning, Martin Marietta auditors and government auditors together reviewed their various audit plans for the year and attempted to reduce overlap. "Before CRAG," explained Clous, "We never really knew what the government auditors' concerns were, nor did we much care. By opening new channels of communication, the program has helped build trust."

As a result of these efforts, the number of full-time government auditors at the company declined from 139 in 1989 to 96 in 1991. The change was most dramatic at the Orlando facility, where a pilot CRAG program had been introduced in 1989. Full-time government auditors were down from 45 to 26. The full impact of these programs could not yet be assessed since full company commitment to CRAG was only a year old.

Managing the Ethics Program

George Sammet, who managed the ethics program from the Corporate Ethics Office at the company's aerospace facility in Orlando, Florida, saw himself as a spokesperson for the employee. With the assistance of Bud Reid, his deputy, and an administrative assistant, Sammet tried to ensure that employee concerns, questions, and complaints were being heard and dealt with satisfactorily throughout the corporation. In practice, this involved overseeing the network of 26 part-time ethics representatives stationed at the company's major facilities (**Exhibit 10**), monitoring and dealing with cases brought to the field reps and the corporate Ethics Office, keeping abreast of employee attitudes, and working to maintain the visibility of the program. In addition, Sammet oversaw ethics training and the periodic updating of the Code. He reported regularly to Corporate President Tom Young, and, every three months, to the Ethics Steering Committee. He also reported twice a year to the Audit and Ethics Committee of the board.

Handling Employee Concerns

Dealing with employee questions, concerns, and complaints was a core activity of the ethics program. Although employees were encouraged to raise concerns about ethics with their supervisors or their designated personnel reps and could also consult corporate counsel, the ethics program provided several other channels for questions or allegations of wrongdoing. The local ethics representative was one source of assistance. Chosen for their "approachability," local field reps were often in the best position to deal quickly with problem situations.

EXHIBIT 10

Martin Marietta Network of Ethics Representatives

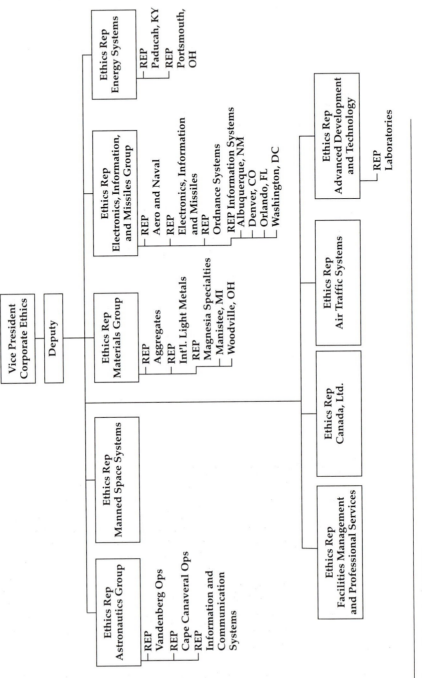

Vice President
Corporate Ethics

Deputy

**Ethics Rep
Astronautics Group**
- REP Vandenberg Ops
- REP Cape Canaveral Ops
- REP Information and Communication Systems

**Ethics Rep
Manned Space Systems**

**Ethics Rep
Materials Group**
- REP Aggregates
- REP Int'l. Light Metals
- REP Magnesia Specialties
  - Manistee, MI
  - Woodville, OH

**Ethics Rep
Electronics, Information,
and Missiles Group**
- REP Aero and Naval
- REP Electronics, Information and Missiles
- REP Ordnance Systems
- REP Information Systems
  - Albuquerque, NM
  - Denver, CO
  - Orlando, FL
  - Washington, DC

**Ethics Rep
Energy Systems**
- REP Paducah, KY
- REP Portsmouth, OH

**Ethics Rep
Facilities Management
and Professional Services**

**Ethics Rep
Canada, Ltd.**

**Ethics Rep
Air Traffic Systems**

**Ethics Rep
Advanced Development
and Technology**
- REP Laboratories

Source: Company document.

EXHIBIT 11   Martin Marietta Corporation—Ethics Cases

Year	Number of Cases
1991	572
1990	441
1989	573
1988	516
1987	293
1986	190
1985	25

Source: Company document.

However, employees concerned about confidentiality or those dissatisfied with the local reps' handling of cases could also call the corporate Ethics Office directly. All Martin Marietta employees had direct and immediate access to the corporate Ethics Office by means of a toll-free telephone line, a corporate hotline, and the Ethics Office's private post office box. In 1991, the Corporate Ethics Office had received some 9,625 calls. Many callers sought information or advice about difficult situations or asked questions about interpreting the Code. Others called to register their concerns or complaints about questionable behavior. Reports of questionable behavior that could not be dealt with quickly by telephone became "cases" to be looked into and resolved. They were entered into the Ethics Office computer, assigned a number, and tracked until closure.

The Ethics Office monitored the full range of cases brought to the network to ensure they were handled appropriately and in a timely way. In 1991, 572 cases of alleged questionable behavior were entered into the system (**Exhibit 11**). The office tried to see that cases were investigated and wrapped up within 60 days, although some took longer because of false starts, sick leave, or the involvement of outside investigators such as the FBI. Cases that were not closed within 90 days were reported to the local company president, the manager in charge of the relevant business unit. Any case extending longer than 120 days was brought to the attention of the Ethics Steering Committee.

Ethics officers were responsible for ensuring that complaints were fully investigated by the appropriate office, that the findings were supported by sufficient evidence, and that sanctions and corrective action were implemented as appropriate. Ethics officers informed complainants about the follow-up on their complaints and obtained feedback from them when the case was closed. In the early days of the program, division lawyers had sometimes functioned as ethics reps. It was later decided that lawyers should not be permitted to serve because of potential conflicts of interest between the corporation and employees. Many ethics reps also served as personnel reps for their area.

Handling cases required sensitivity and caution at every step—to protect the complaining party as well as the accused. Great care was taken to preserve the anonymity of complainants. Investigations were sometimes folded into routine audits to protect the identity of an accuser. Still, in a few instances, it was difficult to preserve absolute confidentiality. The nature of the questions asked could sometimes point directly or indirectly to the accuser. Sometimes, employees

EXHIBIT 12   **Sanctions**

	1985–1987[a]	1988	1989	1990
Terminations/resignations	12	9	29	10
Suspended without pay	7	10	8	5
Transferred	10	5	11	2
Written reprimand	22	21	37	11
Oral reprimand/counseled	23	54	116	41
Conditions corrected	b	b	b	35
Total	74	99	201	105

[a]Does not include energy systems.
[b]Not collected.

Source: Company document.

themselves told others about complaints they had lodged. Word sometimes spread informally as employees chatted during breaks or at the water fountain.

Typically, the person named in a complaint was not informed until investigation revealed facts supporting or verifying the allegation. The deputy for corporate ethics explained, "In many cases, the accused employee is in a position to drive evidence underground. This arrangement also minimizes possible retaliation against the employee making the complaint." Some people, however, felt that those accused of wrongdoing were entitled to know immediately and to be informed of their rights.

The company had maintained its policy of accepting anonymous complaints, even though the policy had been questioned from time to time. The substantiation rate for anonymous complaints was slightly higher than that for other complaints: 42% for anonymous complainants compared with 40% for known complainants for 1991. The most serious issues were often raised by anonymous parties.

Depending on the issues, ethics reps often called on audit, personnel, security, or legal staff to investigate complaints. Mischarging or defective pricing cases were usually investigated by audit. Potential procurement fraud or other cases possibly involving legal action or disclosure to the government were transferred to the office of corporate counsel so that information gathered during investigation would be protected by the attorney-client privilege. Investigators from Human Resources handled personnel-related complaints.

Cases that could not be substantiated were closed after investigation. The proportion of substantiated cases had ranged from 25% to 41% since the inception of the program in the fall of 1985. For the roughly 40% of cases that could be substantiated, closure required corrective action, discipline, or changes in corporate policy. Though the Ethics Office reviewed and sometimes questioned any sanctions or corrective action taken, the task of deciding on and administering sanctions was assigned to human resources professionals. Sanctions included counseling and oral reprimand, written reprimand, transfer, suspension without pay, and termination (**Exhibit 12**).

Fairness in administering sanctions raised difficult ethical issues. In a typical year, the company appeared before state labor boards to face two or three complaints about unfair sanctions. In 1991, a jury had found that a company sanction was too harsh. Complainants, however, sometimes felt that sanctions were too light. One victim of sexual harassment by a supervisor complained about the severance pay given the dismissed supervisor to induce him to seek professional help and never again to bother the victim. Assigning degrees of responsibility also was difficult. Generally, for instance, employees directed to mischarge by a supervisor would be sanctioned, whereas the supervisor would be terminated. The harder case was the employee who knew about mischarging but did nothing about it.

Complainants who wished to follow the progress of their case could call the ethics rep periodically for an update. Once a case was concluded, the ethics rep advised the complainant about its resolution and asked whether the complainant was satisfied or dissatisfied with how the case had been handled. Feedback from 154 complainants during the first three quarters of 1991 showed that 80% were pleased or satisfied with the results of the investigation.

Case records were kept on file for a year after closure. Sammet developed a system to categorize cases as serious, nonserious, and personnel. Serious allegations were those that might result in criminal charges, civil suits, voluntary disclosure to the government, or negative media coverage for the company. Some 48% of the allegations in the first three quarters of 1991 were considered serious, compared with 54% for 1990 and 46% for 1989. These cases typically involved:

- Inaccurate or false records.
- Poor management resulting in waste.
- Serious conflicts of interest.
- Drug use.
- Theft or security violations.
- Racial or gender discrimination or harassment.
- Serious safety problems.
- Defective quality.
- Other, such as procurement violations, retaliation, improper acquisition or use of proprietary information, and sabotage.

The largest category of serious cases concerned inaccurate or false records. About half of the 1991 cases and 43% of 1990 cases involved personnel-related issues such as salaries, promotions, assignments, nepotism, poor management, and supervisory style. Cases involved all levels of management, including the executive.

Sammet monitored the mix of cases and their variations in number, seriousness, and type reported at various company facilities. Sammet's data revealed potential problem areas and issues needing corporate attention. For example, the discovery that all the cases being filed at one location were anonymous prompted an investigation and removal of the field ethics rep. Too few cases, as well as too many, or a disproportionate number might prompt an inquiry.

Providing Ethics Education
Education was another key dimension of the ethics program. For Tom Young, corporate president and head of the Ethics Steering Committee, it was the most important part. "That's where you can reach the people who want to do the right thing, but who may not know what it is. It's also the way to combat any

excessive risk aversion people might feel as a result of not knowing what is acceptable."

Changing standards and laws, as well as employee turnover and promotion, necessitated constant attention to training. The late 1980s had seen changes in what was considered appropriate in entertaining customers, in negotiating strategy, and in competitor information gathering. As one executive explained, "What was once considered shrewd business in corporate America is no longer considered acceptable. In the old days, you'd put your best foot forward and try to negotiate the best deal. You'd put in contingencies that you could negotiate out. Today, that is defective pricing or false claims, and it's against the law."

Changing standards also meant that the Code of Ethics had to be periodically updated. Since its introduction, the Code had been modified twice. Changes proposed for 1992 would address environmental issues, the link between quality and ethics, and gift giving in international and nongovernment business.

Between 1986 and 1988, the company conducted an initial round of training for the entire work force. The objective was to communicate an understanding of the Code, heighten employee sensitivity to ethical problems, and demonstrate management commitment. By late 1989, the Ethics Training Subcommittee was recommending the second round, for which Young favored a change from open-ended discussions of problems and dilemmas to a format with greater closure. Augustine emphasized the importance of including hard cases in which the problem was not so much choosing right versus wrong, as it was choosing among or balancing conflicting responsibilities—to the customer, to employees, to the community, and to the shareholders.

The second round of training included a five-hour program for company presidents and their staffs to discuss the ethics program's results, the problem of conflict among ethical values, a case study involving company teaming, legal ramifications of unethical acts, the DII, and excerpts from the Public Broadcasting System presentation "Ethics in America." A shorter seminar was attended by program directors and staff with significant customer contact as well as all "new business" personnel, especially those in marketing, contracts, and finance. Employees who had significant contact with the customer or with competitors attended a two-hour session on ethics in marketing. A 50-minute session was presented for all remaining personnel. Attendance at the training programs was compulsory.

Ethics awareness training was complemented by specific training in compliance with the laws and regulations governing substantive areas such as cost and labor charging or cost accounting standards. Sammet was always seeking new approaches to ethics training and, for use in future sessions, was creating an ethics game to be called "Gray Matters."

Maintaining Program Visibility

Though training had heightened ethics awareness, Sammet and Reid maintained the visibility of the ethics program through their regular visits to Martin Marietta's domestic and overseas populations to give briefings. Those briefings were not limited to Martin Marietta employees. Suppliers and government officials were invited to attend. The Ethics Office even extended help to the company's suppliers in establishing their own ethics programs in hopes of helping prevent supplier misconduct for which Martin Marietta might be held accountable.

The Office of Public Affairs also promoted the ethics program's visibility internally through posters, articles in the corporate magazine, speeches by senior executives, a video program called "Insight," and company newspapers.

Integrating the Program into the Organization

The ethics program provided employees with a large umbrella of protection and an avenue of inquiry which they did not previously have. Issues raised with the Ethics Office went far beyond compliance with the law and the Code of Conduct. Employees raised questions about corporate decisions to lay people off and corporate policy on contributions to Political Action Committees. Employees unhappy with their supervisor's directives sometimes looked to the Ethics Office for support and relief.

Not everyone was comfortable with such a broad understanding of ethics or with the new channels of employee assistance. Some plant managers felt the program undermined their authority. A similar complaint was heard from first-line supervisors. Some human resources managers felt the ethics program should not handle personnel issues. Vice President for Human Resources and Steering Committee member Bobby Leonard noted, "It's hard to differentiate what is an ethics case and what is simply employee dissatisfaction. But if there is no wrongdoing such as discrimination or favoritism on the part of the supervisor, then it's purely a personnel issue, a judgment call. The case should not go into the ethics channels."

Sammet and other supporters of a more expansive definition of ethics thought the program should respond to whatever employees perceived as ethical concerns. And, indeed, many employees saw their complaints in terms of fairness. Young commented, "Since our standard says people will be treated fairly, we have to take these complaints seriously." Corporate counsel stressed the importance of answering people's questions—however categorized. "We don't want to turn anyone away, and besides, they have other avenues—the news media, the FBI, a federal grand jury."

Nevertheless, explained Reid, "The Ethics Office was not intended as a forum where regular supervisory directions were questioned." And he visited plants to talk to employees about the problem and to review the purpose of the Ethics Office.

The Ethics Office worked closely with the human resources function. In order to obtain the best expert judgment, most personnel cases received in the Ethics Office were routed back to Human Resources channels for investigation. Human Resources had responsibility for deciding on and implementing discipline and was responsible to the Ethics Office for delivering the company's ethics training. This procedure prompted Human Resources to take a close look at the company's disciplinary policies to ensure consistency in the penalties imposed for various kinds of misconduct.

The presence of the ethics program was felt in other areas, too. Phil Giaramita, vice president of Public Affairs and Ethics Steering Committee member, explained that the company's ethical values had to be reflected in all its activities, including dealing with the media. Giaramita made a point of being aggressive in getting to journalists, sometimes calling them with bad news. By getting the facts out early, he thought the company built credibility. "If you are going to stand for honesty, integrity, and candor, you can't be honest just when it suits you. These qualities have to be apparent to the average employee who often gets company news from the press. Failure to be honest, open, and candid would dramatically undermine the program."

Program Costs

The cost of the ethics program was hard to calculate. Sammet put the cost of training at $2.1 million a year, including lost production time and organizational costs. The salaries and travel expenses of the Ethics Office were about $360,000 a year. In addition, the salaries of the ethics representatives, time spent on investigations, and the expense of DII membership and annual audit had to be included.

Steering Committee Concerns

Employees' Fear of Retribution

Members of the Ethics Steering Committee were concerned about employees' fear of retribution for reporting questionable behavior. According to a 1987 corporate survey, 94% of the company's employees considered the ethics program effective, but 40% believed they would suffer retribution for calling the Ethics Office. A later, and more limited, sample survey had suggested the concern was even more prevalent. Six cases alleging retribution had been filed with the Ethics Office in the first three quarters of 1991, though only one had been substantiated. One committee member noted, "You know the fear is there when you go out and talk to people."

Committee members thought eliminating employee concerns about retaliation was important to the integrity of the ethics program. Without employee trust, the program was in jeopardy. Yet, it was very hard to figure out how much of the fear was justified, much less what to do about it. One member commented, "There have been instances where supervisors retaliated against employees for using the Ethics Office, but our investigations have also shown that employees have perceived behavior as retaliatory when it was not." Another member noted that weak employees would sometimes use the Ethics Office so that they could later claim retaliation. It was also observed that complaints about retaliation were more prevalent in locations undergoing downsizing.

Nevertheless, specific steps had been taken to try to address the problem. Young had written to all presidents, and reemphasis training of all employees had included specific modules and discussions on retribution. An article in the company magazine had also addressed the issue. Despite measures to combat fear of retribution, Young was concerned about employee distrust. He pointed to the percentage of anonymous reports: 38% for 1988; 33% for 1989; 44% for 1990; and 41% for the first three quarters of 1991.

Croom thought the fear of real or perceived retribution was a fact of life. "It's just human nature to want to get even. [We] have all been reared not to be a tattletale. We have to manage the fear by helping employees understand that the well-being of the company and employees themselves could be at stake if they do not report possible wrongdoing and by tracking down and dealing with anyone taking retaliatory action. We cannot have employees like the one who corralled his subordinates and refused to let them leave until he found out who turned him in. That is bad management."

The Ethics Office favored severe discipline in substantiated cases of retaliation. But substantiation required clear evidence, which was not always available. In flagrant cases, like the spray painting of "snitch" on the walls of an employee's office, the evidence was clear. In more subtle cases, such as downgrading someone's performance or not offering a promotion, the evidence was much more elusive.

In an effort to gauge the level of employee fear of retribution more precisely, the Steering Committee considered an employee survey. One possibility was to include in the upcoming corporatewide survey some questions about the Ethics Program. Conducted every three years, the survey was considered a fairly reliable barometer of employee opinion. Historically, the response rate had been about 90%. Responses to the questionnaire might provide some guidance on the problem of the perceived fear of retribution and on employees' perceptions of the program's effectiveness.

Program Effectiveness

Sammet and the Steering Committee were searching also for a way to assess the effectiveness of the ethics program. To date, the committee had relied on indicators such as compliance with the DII benchmarks (**Exhibit 13**), other outside studies (**Exhibit 14**), the perceptions and comments of government officials, case statistics, employee feedback, and their own feelings. Sammet cautioned about putting too much weight on the numbers, but nevertheless, they provided a natural focus for the discussion.

Typically, the committee looked at the trends in the number of reported cases, the number of serious substantiated cases, variations in the number of cases at various company locations, the number of anonymous cases, the proportion of calls received locally and centrally, and employee satisfaction with the disposition of cases. They also tried to compare data from other companies. But interpreting the data was difficult. "The decline in reported allegations could be due to a number of factors—better behavior, better subterfuge, ignorance, or fears of retaliation or retribution." said Sammet.

Young noted, "We still don't understand what the statistics tell us. But we look to see if there's an excessively low number of reported cases, or a high number of anonymous cases, or too many cases involving retaliation. We also invite regional ethics reps to the Steering Committee meetings and try to get to know what's going on." Young saw the percentage of anonymous cases as something to worry about, although he was not sure what it meant.

One proposal on the table was to arrange a peer review, based on the model of peer review by accounting firms. The committee thought it might be helpful to survey recently retired employees who had nothing to fear regarding employer or supervisor retribution and who were likely to be loyal and yet somewhat detached.

EXHIBIT 13   Defense Industry Initiative—Public Accountability Questionnaire

1. Does the company have a written code of business ethics and conduct?
2. Is the code distributed to all employees principally involved in defense work?
3. Are new employees provided any orientation to the code?
4. Does the code assign responsibility to operating management and others for compliance with the code?
5. Does the company conduct employee training programs regarding the code?
6. Does the code address standards that govern the conduct of employees in their dealings with suppliers, consultants, and customers?
7. Is there a corporate review board, ombudsman, corporate compliance, or ethics office or similar mechanism for employees to report suspected violations to someone other than their direct supervisor, if necessary?
8. Does the mechanism employed protect the confidentiality of employee reports?
9. Is there an appropriate mechanism to follow up on reports of suspected violations to determine what occurred, who was responsible, and recommend corrective and other actions?
10. Is there an appropriate mechanism for letting employees know the result of any follow-up into their reported charges?
11. Is there an ongoing program of communication to employees, spelling out and reemphasizing their obligations under the code of conduct?
12. What are the specifics of such a program?
13. Does the company have a procedure for voluntarily reporting violations of federal procurement laws to appropriate governmental agencies?
14. Is implementation of the code's provisions one of the standards by which all levels of supervision are expected to be measured in their performance?
15. Is there a program to monitor on a continuing basis adherence to the code of conduct and compliance with federal procurement laws?
16. Does the company participate in the industry's "Best Practices Forum"?
17. Are periodic reports on adherence to the principles made to the company's board of directors or to its audit or other appropriate committee?
18. Are the company's independent public accountants or a similar independent organization required to comment to the board of directors or a committee thereof on the efficacy of the company's internal procedures for implementing the company's code of conduct?
19. Does the company have a code-of-conduct provision or associated policy addressing marketing activities?
20. Does the company have a code-of-conduct provision or associated policy requiring that consultants are governed by, or oriented regarding, the company's code of conduct and relevant associated policies?

Source: DII, *1990 Annual Report to the Public and the Defense Industry,* February 1991.

Exhibit 14   Ethics Resource Center Study

Ethics Activity in Large U.S. Corporations
(50,000 or more employees)

95%	Written ethics guidelines
47%	Ethics training
28%	Hotline/reporting channel
23%	Board ethics committee
15%	Corporate ethics office

Source: Ethics Resource Center, Inc., "Ethics Policies and Programs in American Business," 1990.

As committee members searched for benchmarks to measure themselves against, they reflected on the program:

Marc Bennett, Senior Vice President and CFO, Finance:

The ethics program has not necessarily made Martin more ethical. It has made employees more aware of how their conduct might appear to others. The program has also made people more cautious. This is healthy, but it has also had a cost. "Ethics" sometimes stifles risk-taking and "open" communication. You can't speak bluntly or play the devil's advocate, because you might be misconstrued. Management has to be careful in articulating ideas. We've lost some of our entrepreneurial spirit.

One of the unanticipated benefits is that we learned about personnel practices that could be improved, and we are in better stead with our customers. I feel it's a lot less likely that we'll do something wrong, or create the appearance of doing something wrong. I have seen a decline in the number of problems that could cause us serious embarrassment. I attribute that to the program, but I can't prove it. Efficiency is also up, because we're not chasing a lot of problems. And there's a mind-set about ethics. It's closely related to the mind-set we're trying to create around quality. We think good quality the first time around is the best cost control. There's a link between quality and ethics.

Personally, my thought process has probably become a little more orderly. I'm more conscious of potential conflicts and careful in how I articulate things so I won't be misunderstood. For example, I give instructions differently, especially in a group. I won't say simply, "Make it happen."

Dave Clous, Vice President, Audit:

The program has given legitimacy to the concept of working with good ethical behavior. Employees have to have an avenue like the Ethics Office, and management needs to hear the good and the bad. An unanticipated benefit of the program has been the feeling of good citizenship created when people commend the program.

Phil Giaramita, Vice President, Public Affairs:

Without the program, I think we'd have more violations than we do. The program won't change the behavior of the person who will cut corners anyway, but it has had a positive impact in several areas. It helps inform people so they won't commit technical violations of rules they are not aware of. A lot more people are aware of potential ethical dilemmas and are very likely to consult with the Ethics Office before acting. The program has improved personnel management by sensitizing managers to explain their actions fairly and clearly. It demonstrates to customers and the public that we take these issues seriously, and this commitment makes the company a more appealing employer.

The program has also helped us compete for government contracts. Most people would agree that the government takes reputation into account and will lean toward quality and reliability of estimates. Integrity is an intangible asset, an asset the government views favorably when considering contractor bids. Martin's win ratio of bids averages 60%, compared with the industry average of 28%. The program has had an impact on how we bid. We have consciously not bid on certain programs and deliberately avoided bidding unrealistically low on others.

Bobby Leonard, Vice President, Human Resources:

Any company that doesn't have an ethics program is missing the boat. Formalizing it and putting it in writing has made us better than we were. Our communications surveys show us that employees have a good feeling about it. Morale has been bolstered by employees' knowledge that the company wants to do business the proper way.

I don't believe we are more ethical today, because we were never unethical before. But the program has done a lot for us in terms of how employees, customers, and the public view us. It has also increased the awareness of certain issues.

Frank Menaker, Vice President, General Counsel:

The situations handled through the ethics program arise in any company. If individuals have a place to go, the situations can be handled with a lot less pain. The program lets people know that management doesn't necessarily approve of everything that goes on. Without the program, many people would make that assumption. We're willing to take the program with all its warts.

Tom Young, President:

When we went into this program, we didn't anticipate the changes it would bring about. At the time, the industry was really being battered about. It was a matter of damage control. That was a good reason to do what we did, but not necessarily the right reason. Back then, people would have said, "Do you really need an ethics program to be ethical?" Ethics was something personal, and either you had it or you didn't. Now that's all changed. People recognize the value.

Though the program hasn't affected the company's business direction, I think it has probably affected our performance. Personally, it has enhanced my awareness in a lot of areas. Changes in industry standards have made employees feel more comfortable. There's a higher quality of work life. Ethics is something that cannot be left to chance. It's part of management's responsibility, and it should become part of the organizational structure.

CASE 3
WETHERILL ASSOCIATES, INC.

Think, say and do what is right to the exclusion of what is wrong. . . . Right behavior . . . is behavior that is simultaneously logically right, expediently right and morally right for all concerned.

—Statement of Right-Action Ethic™
WAI, Quality Assurance Manual

Wetherill Associates, Inc. (WAI), a supplier of electrical parts to automotive rebuilders and remanufacturers, stood out in an industry that had its start in the nation's junkyards. Marie Bothe, the company's 72-year-old president, stated it simply: "Our employees know that they will never be asked to do anything that is wrong or dishonest. We ask employees to do what reality calls for; to fill the needs of the situation in the highest possible manner—with absolute honesty and integrity." Treasurer Kevin Kraft underscored this policy. "We tell our employees, if you think something *might* be wrong, don't do it."

Since its beginnings, WAI, headquartered in Royersford, Pennsylvania, thirty miles outside Philadelphia, used this formula as the foundation for its expanding business. Teamwork and cooperation were emphasized throughout the company; rank and hierarchy were downplayed; everyone was on a first-name basis. Company estimates put the ratio of highest to lowest salary at four or five to one. During a month of record sales in the summer of 1993, people from all departments came to work at night and on weekends to help the warehouse staff pick, pack, and ship orders. Officers were "fully convinced that our success comes from right action." Bothe elaborated,

> A lot of companies go to great pains to weigh, decide and justify [a wrong action]. . . . We just don't do it. Decisions become easy. . . . This simplifies life rather than complicating it. Our policy, to do what is right, avoids the main thrust of activity for a lot of businesses—pleasing the boss. . . . It makes for an open corporation, with cooperation between departments. And it lessens personal conflict.

WAI's policy of right action was also reflected in its employee compensation system. Bothe stated, "We don't want money to be an issue. We want people to feel free to do the right thing." In an unusual arrangement for the industry, WAI paid all employees—including sales staff—with straight salary, supplemented with health and dental benefits, employees' retirement plan, 401K, and a year-end bonus based on the company's overall profitability. Overall, WAI's salaries were competitive in the local market and the company had no retention problems, but management was concerned that some employees were becoming distracted over the issue of how pay was determined. In the spirit of right action, top managers considered the matter in the fall of 1993.

This case was prepared by Jane Palley Katz and later updated by Charles A. Nichols, III, under the supervision of Lynn Sharp Paine. Copyright © 1993 by the President and Fellows of Harvard College. Harvard Business School case 394–113.

Company Background

Wetherill Associates, Incorporated (WAI) was founded in 1978 to demonstrate the management theories of writer and consultant Richard W. Wetherill and to provide financial support for 34 members of Wetherill's behavioral study group. Wetherill, author of many privately published papers and books,[1] had long insisted that enduring business success depended on a commitment to "right action" and principles of absolute honesty. Beginning in the 1930s, Wetherill attempted to refine and spread his ideas as a teacher, lecturer, and management consultant. In 1952, several of his adherents formed a behavioral study group— an informal, nonprofit organization devoted to helping Wetherill in his research and spreading his account of a behavioral law of nature. The group later called itself a "fellowship" and obtained tax-exempt status as a religious society.

Company Origins

When members of the group decided to start a business, naming it in honor of Richard Wetherill seemed appropriate. In 1978, Wetherill Associates, Inc., was incorporated in Delaware with two members of the study group as co-owners. E. Marie Bothe, business manager for Wetherill and his wife, and Edith M. Gripton, Richard Wetherill's secretary, each contributed capital of $1,250 for half the 200 shares issued. In 1993, Bothe and Gripton each continued to own 50% of the company's stock.

Bothe, a member of Wetherill's study group since 1958, became the company's president. According to Bothe, "We wanted to be successful in a financial sense, but mainly to show that the Right-Action Ethic is the wave of the future." Richard Wetherill served briefly as chairman of the board and was the company's consultant until his death in 1989 at age 82. Although WAI's founding members were all members of the fellowship, Bothe explained that the affairs of the fellowship and of the business were kept very separate, both financially and legally.

WAI first chose to broker ignition and transmission parts,[2] because "one member of the study group had a background in telemarketing and some knowledge of the automotive aftermarket." In the beginning, the cost of running the company was modest. Equipment consisted of telephones, the Yellow Pages, and selling sheets. As manufacturers' representatives involved in telemarketing, WAI was supplied with telephones, literature, and commissions on sales by the manufacturers they represented.

The company was financed in its early days by loans from Bothe and Gripton, and by employees, some of whom deferred payment of their full salary. WAI gave them demand notes for the deferred amounts at interest rates comparable to what they could earn on money market funds at the time. These loans peaked

---

[1]Among Wetherill's books were *Management Techniques for Foremen* (National Foremen's Institute, Inc., 1946), *The Dynamics of Human Relations* (Van Nostrand, 1949), and *Truth Is Power, A Preface to Humanetics* and *Tower of Babel, An Outline of Humanetics* (both privately printed, 1952). A recent summary of his ideas is found in *Right is Might* (privately printed by the Humanetics Fellowship, 1991).

[2]WAI's customers—automotive electrical rebuilders and remanufacturers— disassembled starters and alternators, tested the components, then cleaned, repaired and replaced any worn or faulty parts.

in 1987, amounting at year-end to $1,085,000. As the company became prosperous, all loans and back salaries were completely repaid over the course of the next four years.

When WAI decided to go into distribution, it sought outside financing for the first time. In 1987 the company obtained a loan of approximately $2.5 million secured with receivables. Bank financing peaked in 1989 at a little over $5 million at year-end, but declined to $558,000 by the close of 1992 and was continuing to decrease.

Sales for 1980, WAI's first year in the distribution business, were less than $1 million. Bothe noted,

> We had no formal sales training. We were "reality" taught. . . . We never tried to make money. We simply wanted to show that running a business that was right for the owners, officers, employees, customers, suppliers, and the community was not only possible, but desirable. We've had our lumps and bumps. In the end, we also made money.

Over the next decade, the privately owned company funneled all of its profits back into the business and gradually expanded, driven by its commitment to right action. When unreliable suppliers had made it difficult to keep promises to customers, WAI began to carry its own inventory and eventually established its own warehouses—first, in the Philadelphia area and, later, in four other locations across the country. Similarly, unable to provide the parts customers wanted, the company began to manufacture its own.

The Business in 1992

By 1992, WAI earned $6.9 million in pretax profits on revenues exceeding $81 million. Exports to customers in Mexico, Canada, Australia, Europe, Taiwan, and South America accounted for more than $7 million in sales. WAI's main warehousing operation, in Royersford, carried 6,000 parts. In addition, four regional distribution centers (RDCs) were located near Los Angeles, Atlanta, Chicago, and Dallas. The company developed a sophisticated engineering, research and development and quality control system, and modest, but growing, manufacturing capabilities which, by 1992, accounted for over 20% of total revenues. WAI succeeded in capturing 90% of the auto-electric rebuilding industry market in bearings by 1992. Kevin Kraft, WAI's treasurer, explained WAI's accomplishments, "During the period of our growth, the remanufacturing industry matured and, as a whole, was not growing. Much of our growth was based on winning business from other companies." See **Exhibit 1** for WAI's sales and **Exhibit 2** for additional data on its financial performance.

In 1992, WAI employed approximately 300 people, of whom about 250 worked in Royersford, with some 12 at each regional distribution center. Approximately half of all employees were women. The workers ranged widely in age, from teenagers on up, including two part-time employees in their nineties. About 70 participated in the Wetherill study group, which continued to operate despite Richard Wetherill's death. About 50 lived in Atrium House, a 36-unit apartment house located only a few miles from the WAI offices and built by the study group to demonstrate the Right-Action Ethic in a nonbusiness setting.

WAI's organizational structure reflected its Right-Action Ethic. Commenting on its configuration, Marie Bothe observed that "really, reality is in the center.

EXHIBIT **1**

Wetherill Associates, Inc., Sales Growth, 1980–1992 (amounts in millions of dollars)

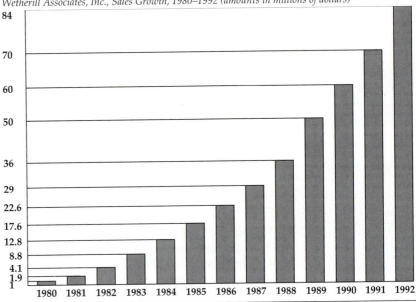

Source: Company document.

EXHIBIT **2** **Wetherill Associates, Inc.—Selected Financial Data, Years Ended December 31 (amounts in thousands)**

	1992	1991	1990	1989
Results of Operations				
Net sales	$81,037	$67,435	$57,656	$49,005
Cost of goods sold[1]	59,254	48,554	41,697	33,850
Gross profit[1]	$21,783	$18,881	$15,959	$15,155
Operating expenses	14,524	12,375	10,950	9,907
Operating income[1]	$ 7,259	$ 6,506	$ 5,009	$ 5,248
Other income (expenses)	(347)	(346)	(690)	(634)
Net income[1,2]	$ 6,912	$ 6,160	$ 4,319	$ 4,614
Financial Position				
Inventories[1]	$16,598	$17,644	$14,991	$11,016
Current assets[1]	30,448	29,399	24,722	20,030
Current liabilities	10,795	13,072	12,217	9,909
Working capital[1]	19,653	16,327	12,505	10,121
Total assets[1]	33,185	31,511	25,918	21,411
Current and long-term debt	558	4,311	4,411	6,116
Stockholders' equity[1,2]	22,185	17,881	13,199	10,196

[1]Amounts have been retroactively adjusted to present a change in accounting principle. Prior to 1991 the company capitalized certain overhead costs as part of inventory in accordance with federal income tax regulations.
[2]For federal income tax purposes WAI is a Subchapter S corporation and pays no federal income tax at the corporate level. All profits are retained within the company with the exception of distributions made to the owners for payment of federal income tax when due on their shares of the company's net income. These distributions amounted to $2,608, $1,478, $1,316, and $1,813 in 1992, 1991, 1990, and 1989, respectively.

Source: Audited company financial documents.

EXHIBIT 3

Wetherill Associates, Inc., Organizational Chart

Organizational Chart

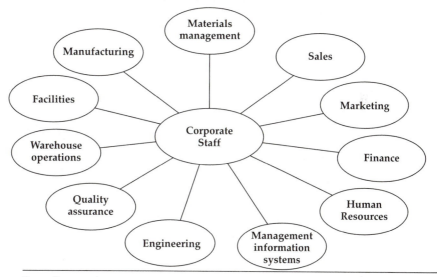

Source: Company document.

You have to let the needs of the situation determine the right action." In addition to Bothe and Kraft, the company's "top management"[3] consisted of Jeffery Sween, vice president, and Margo Callis, secretary. All four top managers had been with the company since its inception. See **Exhibit 3** for WAI's organization chart.

WAI's approximately 4,000 customers were rebuilders of starters and alternators for many types of engines—lawnmowers to locomotives. They ranged from individuals engaged in a one-person business in their basements to major companies that ordered in excess of $1 million worth of parts annually. However, managers estimated that 80% of the company's sales volume was in 20% of the parts.

By design, WAI's corporate strategy was to serve its customers to the best of its ability. From the beginning, the company sought to identify and serve unmet customer needs. They avoided areas that were already being well served. According to an industry observer,

> The rebuilders like dealing with WAI. They like the service they get. WAI's order-fill rate is excellent and that's the key for most rebuilders. As a result they don't run into too much price resistance. . . . They have done a nice job.[4]

Serving customers also meant staying abreast of current automobile designs so as to anticipate the need for parts as the vehicles aged, and developing a source of supply for those parts. Although the company developed sales projections, it did not set annual sales goals or targets. Managers expected to grow into other segments of the automobile aftermarket, into exports, and into industrial bearings,

---

[3]WAI, *Quality Assurance Manual*, p. 5.
[4]Telephone interview, September 1993.

but as Bothe explained, "We will not grow beyond what we can do consistent with the Right-Action Ethic." Noted another employee, "We are not 'in competition' with anybody. We just do what we have to do to serve the customer." Bothe preferred the term "co-suppliers" to "competitors."

WAI had an active list of 300 suppliers, around 100 of whom accounted for most of the company's sourcing needs. Most were relatively small, privately held companies with the exception of Ford, General Motors, and a few others. Early on, most suppliers had been located in the United States. According to Bothe, "We do as little ordering overseas as possible. We like to keep the business here, but there are some products that you can't always buy in the United States." By 1992, about one-third of WAI's purchases were offshore.

The Automobile Remanufacturing Industry

The automobile remanufacturing industry emerged in the early part of the twentieth century. It grew out of the junkyard business as a cheaper alternative to replacing worn out or broken automobile components, such as engines, brakes, water pumps, carburetors, clutches, and electrical components, with new ones. Automotive Parts Rebuilders Association (APRA), the industry trade association, put "the general price range for all its industry's offerings between 60% and 65% of an equivalent new product."[5] By the 1990s, even rebuilt electronic computer modules were coming to the market and some companies offered warranties on remanufactured parts that were three to four times longer than those offered on new parts.[6] APRA estimated that as many as 98% of alternators and starters sold were remanufactured.[7]

Reliable data on the industry were hard to come by. According to an APRA spokesman, "There are no statistics!" He estimated the entire rebuilding industry sales to be in the range of $15 billion. About $1 to $1.5 billion of that ("a real guesstimate") was to electrical rebuilders. This market was served by four companies—WAI, Ace Electric, International Products Manufacturers (IPM), and AMSCO/Valley Forge—that offered a full complement of products nationwide, each with revenues between $20 and $100 million per year. In addition, the industry included many smaller companies, with revenues from $1 to $5 million, serving local markets or offering niche products.

Overall, the automobile remanufacturing industry in the United States and Canada was considered a "mature industry," posting growth rates of only 3% to 6% a year, despite the fact that the average age of vehicles on U.S. roads rose to nearly 8 years in 1993, up from 4 to 4½ years in the early 1970s. The trade magazine, *Automotive Rebuilder,* surveyed various companies and found that sales for the engine remanufacturing business was "flat to declining" in 1991.[8] Industry observers attributed the slow growth to the rising prices of remanufactured parts, improved engineering of original parts, and slow growth in the auto industry. With 175 to 180 million vehicles in the United States, the total number of

---

[5]"Remanufactured Parts; Product Review," *Automotive Marketing,* June 1988, p. 133 ff.
[6]Bill Cannon, "Remanufactured Parts Better Than New," *Motor Age,* February 1992, p. 60 ff.
[7]Ibid.
[8]Quoted in Tom Incantalupo, "Rebuilt Engines Give Aging Cars New Lease on Life," *Orlando Sentinel Tribune,* May 30, 1991, p. G3 ff.

vehicles was rising only about 1 million per year. For all of these reasons, the entire U.S. automotive repair industry was in the midst of a several-year slump, despite the recession that began in July 1990—which had been expected to help the industry since traditionally people put off buying new cars and repaired them instead when the economy was stagnating or uncertain.

Industry observers agreed that the opportunities for dramatic growth were outside of the United States and Canada, particularly Mexico and other Latin American countries. As less developed countries became richer and acquired more vehicles, remanufactured parts were expected to be an appealing alternative to new parts, when the vehicles needed repair.

Management's Philosophy of Right Action

The first page of WAI's *Quality Assurance Manual,* its handbook of companywide policy and practices, sent to all employees, customers and suppliers, declared:

> This company adheres to a policy of honesty, integrity and quality. Whenever an action is known or felt to be right, the action is to be taken. Whenever action is known or suspected to be wrong, the action is not to be taken.[9]

WAI's management sought to use the Right-Action Ethic as the basis for decision making throughout the organization. WAI employees were instructed to be factual with customers and suppliers, not to promise what WAI could not deliver, and to "look to the needs of everybody" when making decisions. For WAI, the Right-Action Ethic was rooted in a deep belief in an objective reality, as well as a commitment to rationality and absolute honesty. According to Marie Bothe,

> Right action is a natural law, like a law of physics. . . . Nature planned for things to work together. . . . It is rational to be honest. It is irrational to be dishonest, because dishonest thoughts are out of touch with reality.

She added, "I have found absolutely no situation where it is not practical to tell the truth in the right way. And there could be a wrong way to tell the truth."[10] Furthermore, explained Bothe, a person who acts ethically raises the level of others' behavior and is rarely asked to do unethical things.

Believing that "self-motivation for profits, excellence and superiority contains a corrupting virus that, over a period of time, gets a wrong result," WAI favored the motivation of right action:

> At WAI, our training and experience clearly show that correct decisions are not "made" but are "found" in reality. WAI management takes no private credit for its growth. Rather success is thought solely to be the natural consequence of sticking to sound behavioral principles as opposed to private advantage. Any company so committed could achieve equivalent results.[11]

---

[9]WAI, *Quality Assurance Manual,* p. 1.
[10]Quoted in John Crudele, "We're Being Taxed More From All Directions," *The Morning Call* (Allentown, PA), October 6, 1991, p. D03 ff.
[11]WAI, *Quality Assurance Manual,* p. 4.

According to WAI, operating troubles such as poor-quality service and merchandise were caused primarily by "behavioral" problems and only secondarily by "technical" problems. Technical problems were solved through engineering and science. Behavioral problems were solved by using the principles of right behavior. Moreover, by reasoning in an impersonal way, from "the situation," and seeking "consensus with reality," emotions and interpersonal conflicts could be avoided:

> Wrong behavior results from emotional reactions to others and whatever is happening—which is reality. Emotional reactions ensure irrational decisions adversely affecting quality workmanship, quality products and quality service. Quality workmanship, products and service are natural by-products of reasoning from the need of the situation: reality. And so are quality relationships.[12]

For WAI, managerial excellence was

> found by conforming with [these] natural behavioral principles. . . . Management has learned to keep its options open when reality is unclear. We do not rely on personal opinion nor "coin tossing". . . . Simple motivation to take right action and fill the need of each situation, successfully generates profits, excellence and superiority as natural right results.[13]

The Right-Action Ethic taught that, "Right action gets right results. Wrong action gets wrong results." Accordingly, WAI employees were trained to take right action to the best of their ability, rather than to make profits or avoid losses. "Profits" according to WAI, "are a natural by-product of right action."[14] Thus, the "Wetherill formula for success":

> Let every decision be made by consensus among the persons involved in accord with the dictates of reality. Eliminate consideration of personal ambition and private profit for a few. Get thinking grooved into considerations of what is right for everyone—what will benefit the company and its customers and its suppliers and its employees and the community. Taken far enough these benefits would encircle the earth.[15]

WAI's management believed that its operating policies were very different from "the conventional attitude and motivations commonly thought to beget success."[16] Kevin Kraft explained that the big predicament in many companies was weighing the seeming advantage of a dishonest act with the advantages of honesty: "People are always trying to see which way the balance must fall. Here it is not a dilemma." According to Kraft, "Someone who thinks from the perspective of right action has his or her eyes on the foundations, the fundamentals, rather than on small, short-term advantages."

Early in its history, WAI's emphasis on the Right-Action Ethic distinguished it from many other companies. One Wetherill customer noted that automotive remanufacturing "may not be an industry with the highest ethical standards. But Wetherill stands out. We consider them very honorable, and we trust them."[17]

---

[12]Ibid., p. 1.

[13]Ibid., pp. 5–6.

[14]Ibid.,, p. 28.

[15]Ibid.,, p. 4.

[16]Ibid., p. 5.

[17]"Principles and Profits: WAI in the Automotive Aftermarket," *Ethikos,* March/April 1992, p. 6.

However, for WAI, establishing this reputation was not easy. Initially, the company was met with cynicism, and rumors circulated that the company was a cult or religious group. Bothe recalled, "People were a little suspicious of our talking about 'right action' and 'taking care of the customer.' Some made fun of us. . . . It's different now."[18]

Right Action in Practice

WAI employees credited the Wetherill Right-Action Ethic with fostering innovative policies and teamwork and with making the company a leader in the industry. Cross-functional communication and coordination were common. For example, the Credit Review Board, which met weekly to make decisions on how to handle outstanding accounts, included managers from both the credit and sales departments. This allowed managers to share information gathered across the organization and in the field, and, thereby, manage the whole relationship with the customer who, in some cases, was also a supplier. Similarly, the Material Review Board met every day to deal with products and materials WAI bought or sold that were not performing up to specifications. It comprised people from engineering, quality control, purchasing, sales, and manufacturing. The Inventory Control Team, with members from the warehouse, purchasing, and cost accounting, tracked down and resolved any discrepancies in product counts and inventory. One manager, with previous experience at another company in the industry, commented, "I have never seen such close cooperation among departments as at WAI."

Sales Practices

WAI developed a team approach to selling that was unique in the industry. Field salespeople, inside salespeople and the technical support people all worked as a unit. Steven Kurtzer, a field salesman in the northeast, explained:

> In my previous organization, I was it. Here, I'm the salesman in the field, but I'm not the only one to service the account. . . . There are a dozen different people backing me up inside. There are inside sales people. . . . If a customer calls with a research question, there are customer service people to back up inside sales. If there is a success, it affects the whole team; the whole team can bask in the glow.

Field sales employees communicated with Royersford via laptop computer, reporting both sales and other customer feedback. This allowed the internal sales staff to followup later by phone, and also allowed managers to monitor field sales effort. The entire sales staff received cross-functional training with the product research, engineering, purchasing, quality control and warehouse departments, enabling them to provide better information to their customers. Sales catalogs were produced in-house by the graphic arts department and designed to give the customer helpful information on specific applications and late-model products in the most useable format. Their catalogs set the technical standard for the industry, and were a significant improvement over old-style publications which, according to Kraft, reflected the attitude, "Here's what we have. Order it."

---

[18]Ibid., p. 7.

Also unusual for the industry, salespeople were coached not to pressure their customers, not to use negative selling tactics, and not to slam the competition. Kurtzer emphasized, "I describe the product and establish the customer's need. Sometimes, they don't know that they need the part, so you can tell them. . . . I *take* orders, but I don't necessarily ask for them." He continued,

> At [my previous company], if I went to see an account and didn't walk out with an order, it was treated as a failure. Here, if I talk to someone and they buy something later, it's a success. Here, we are looking for long-term business, not just the short-term. . . . We have a very good reputation for providing good information to our customers. If we are out of an item, we will tell them our competitor's part number. At my previous company, we weren't allowed to do this. We try to help our customers out whenever we can. . . . Nowhere can a customer get as complete information as with us.

In sales, as in other areas, honesty was a must. Kurtzer explained, "At WAI, we are not knowingly to lie." Moreover, special emphasis was placed on being specific and honest about quality or suitability features of the product that customers might be unaware of, or unable to detect. Whereas some companies took customers on trips or offered them skis or alcohol for placing an order, Wetherill offered customers a copy of its *Quality Assurance Manual* and technical seminars with information on new products, new technology, and current industry problems. At these seminars, the "strongest selling tactic was mentioning WAI's part number when that part was being discussed"; the only inducements were "donuts and sandwiches." WAI did invite its customers to buy *Leadership Into the 21st Century*, a book describing the Right-Action Ethic, edited by the Wetherill staff. Several hundred customers ordered the book and many contacted the company with favorable reactions. See **Exhibit 4** for the text of one customer's comments.

Customer Relationships

WAI's surveys found that customers consistently gave the company high marks for service. One rebuilder recounted an instance when he called for a part, and WAI only had a new one in stock:

> They [WAI] said, "If you buy the original from us, it will cost you $30. If you buy it in the aftermarket, from a competitor, it will cost you $14" They even told me the competitor's part number. . . . I *know* none of their competitors would do that.[19]

Stated another Wetherill customer of 10 years, "They are a sales-oriented company that doesn't sell. But they have the best sales department I've ever seen in my life."[20] One offshore customer even decided to simplify the payment process by setting up a joint bank account, with instructions for WAI to pay itself whenever parts were shipped.

Customers occasionally tried to take advantage of WAI by "using the company as a bank," or by returning material that was used, damaged, or not under warranty. Kevin Kraft explained,

> We don't let ourselves be taken advantage of. And we let people know it. . . . But if they try, we deal with it in a different way. If we can, we talk to them. If they are having troubles, we try to work something out. If necessary, we don't do business with them.. . . We *have* gotten burned every once in a while.

---

[19]Ibid., pp. 6–7.
[20]Ibid., p. 5.

EXHIBIT 4   **Wetherill Associates, Inc., Text of Electronic Mail Message to Company Headquarters from Employee at the Wetherill Regional Distribution Center, Georgia, March 12, 1993**

[CUSTOMER NAME] PHONED ME TODAY TO SAY THAT HE READ MR. WETHERILL'S BOOK "LEADERSHIP INTO THE 21ST CENTURY." HE SAID HE REALLY ENJOYED IT. HE SAID IF WE PRACTICE THE TRUTHS IN THE BOOK WE COULD GO NOWHERE BUT UP AND TOTALLY AGREED WITH THE TRUTHS. HE APOLOGIZED FOR THE WAY HE HAS BEEN SHORT WITH US IN THE PAST AND HE THINKS WE'RE DOING A GREAT JOB. HE IS PLEASED WITH EVERYTHING AT WAI. (HE DID SAY HE STILL HAS TO WATCH HIS MONEY AND PRICES), BUT THAT WAS JUST BUSINESS.

I THOUGHT THIS MAY BE [OF] INTEREST TO YOU. I THINK THIS PROVES THAT RIGHT DOES PREVAIL. HE DID TELL US THAT WE DON'T HAVE TO STOCK BOTH 68–9129 & 68–9130 BOSCH BRUSHES. HE SAID THERE IS A SLIGHT DIFFERENCE IN THE TWO BRUSHES, BUT ONCE INSTALLED AND USED IN FIVE DIFFERENT APPLICATIONS THAT HE CHECKED, THEY CAN BE USED ALONE.

I AM PASSING THE BRUSH INFO TO RESEARCH. HAVE A NICE WEEKEND.

In some instances, the right action was not immediately obvious. A salesperson described one situation involving a customer who had purchased one of WAI's more expensive units at $350. Thinking that there was something wrong with one component, the customer immediately took the starter apart and replaced the part, instead of calling WAI for help as required by the warranty. "In the meantime, he made a lot of other changes," recalled the salesperson. "When the unit still didn't work, he wanted us to take it back and give him full credit—but with the parts exchanged, it couldn't be resold. I proposed that I would take the part and test it. If it was defective. I would replace it." After testing the $70 part, WAI replaced it.

Purchasing Practices

Carol Sheehan, a purchasing manager who had previously worked for another supplier, compared WAI's purchasing practices to other companies in the industry:

> In my old job, the norm was management by intimidation. We were in constant fear of losing our jobs. We were always throwing darts at our competitors and looking over our shoulders at what the other guy was doing. [To get information on our competition, i.e. WAI,] We would call up suppliers and say we were WAI, and that we had changed our fax number—in order to find out what that they were charging WAI.
>
> In my interview here, I was told that I would get fired for yelling, screaming, lying, and backstabbing. I said, "Lying? I'm a buyer; I lie for a living!" They said, "No. You don't need to do that". . . . From the beginning, I knew they meant it, but I didn't think it could be done. Now, the salesman of one of the companies who supplies us with parts says, "You are the only customer we have who tells us when we over-ship."

Sheehan speculated, "Who will get the last bolt in stock—WAI or the company that complains only when the supplier has undershipped?"

Sheehan, one of 12 women in the 13-person purchasing department, said she could never go back to the ways at her previous company. "I used to tell suppliers that I could get certain items for $1, even though I couldn't. Now it's so simple . . . I just tell them why I need something at a certain price, at a certain date."

Relations with Bank and Auditors

Since its inception, WAI had maintained a relationship with the same bank for all of its cash management and external financing needs. A bank official spoke glowingly of WAI, noting that the favorable terms on which the company received credit reflected its financial strength. WAI stood out in the promptness and detail with which it provided financial information to the bank. The official remarked on the high degree of "computer literacy" and commitment to information technology among WAI employees. The official believed that in the area of employee empowerment WAI "practiced what a lot of companies preach," and that the resulting "employee buy-in" to company goals was an important contributor to WAI's success.

These perceptions were echoed at the firm of external auditors used by WAI since its formation. An auditor who participated in the WAI engagement asserted that WAI's internal control system for its accounts was "the best I had dealt with" and remarked on the "strong professionalism throughout the company." Company personnel stood out in their readiness to respond to every audit concern and in their commitment to improving their accounting practices wherever possible. According to the auditor, working with WAI was "an enjoyable audit experience."

Quality Assurance

WAI took to heart the right action emphasis on accuracy in details: "To make things really right, check every detail with reality."[21] In particular, WAI guaranteed the quality of its products and offered to repair or replace any defective parts. To facilitate this guarantee, WAI worked closely with suppliers. The engineering department used the best and latest equipment, software and machines to develop rigorous documentation for them. The quality control department employed advanced statistical methods to inspect suppliers' shipments. Through these efforts, WAI was able to obtain high-quality parts and was also able to notify its suppliers of any "risky trends in their products."[22] The company worked to help its "problem suppliers" but sometimes there was no satisfactory solution. Carol Sheehan recalled, "We had a loyal supplier, but his product kept getting rejected. We eventually had to get rid of him. We are here to serve the customer. It was very sad."

WAI sought to develop long-term relationships with its best, most cooperative suppliers. "We try to be their selling arm, and, in turn, they have to supply us with a quality product. Often it doesn't happen right away," noted Bothe. All suppliers received a copy of the *Quality Assurance Manual*. Sometimes, WAI would accommodate a supplier by taking extra production runs. In making long-range commitments to a smaller number of suppliers, WAI was able to better oversee and assure the quality of its purchases and to negotiate favorable prices.

---

[21]WAI, *Quality Assurance Manual*, p. 10.
[22]Ibid., p. 18.

It was also in a good position to woo offshore suppliers, who were cautious about entering the U.S. market, and were looking for trust and reliable access in their U.S. partners. One loyal overseas supplier, Kevin Chow, even tried to introduce the Right-Action Ethic into his trading company in Hong Kong. He explained,

> I was interested because I wanted to reduce the mistakes at my company. But, right action is easy to say and is not so easy to do. People in Hong Kong desire to show their ability and ambition and they want to work independently; they also are looking to increase their financial prospects. At WAI, money is not the most important thing. I am still trying to do it. I was thinking about trying to introduce it into my factory in China. But, since the doors opened to trade in 1978, even people there have changed. No matter what your philosophy, what matters is how you distribute the resources.[23]

Information Systems

To support the efforts of its sales, purchasing, and technical people, WAI had invested in the most advanced information systems in the industry. Everyone, both in the field and at Royersford, had access to a computerized list of WAI's inventory, including delivery dates for parts out of stock, the applications in which each part could be used, the numbers and published prices of its competitors' corresponding parts, and industry interchange information—the industry part number and the equivalent WAI part number. The computer database included the buying and price history of each customer, as well as "open issues"—anything that was discussed with the customer but left unresolved. It also contained a list of the customer's "prime products"—WAI's assessment of what the customer "should" be buying. Thus, all members of the staff could obtain the information necessary to settle customer problems or make a sale. They also had the authority to quote prices openly and steer customers to competitors' products, if WAI could not supply the needed item.

Work Environment

WAI sought to provide a fair and supportive work environment for all its employees. The primary responsibility for the "quality of corporate life"[24] fell to the personnel department, and company policy was quite explicit:

> Cooperation is emphasized. Bad behavior such as conflict, jealousy, empire-building, put-down humor is given the same careful attention as is given defective product. The corrective action is much the same as with defective customer service. The low quality behavior is treated as a mistake, requiring training and counseling to get changes in behavior.[25]

And, "Reality calls the shots, not human authorities ranked in a pecking order. Any person's job is given as much consideration as another person's, no matter what the scope of that job may be."[26] Bothe explained, "It is company policy to avoid all the nasty personality situations which tend to make people's working lives miserable."

---

[23]Keven Chow, telephone interview, November 22, 1993.
[24]WAI, *Quality Assurance Manual*, p. 31.
[25]Ibid., p. 31.
[26]Ibid., p. 32.

The resulting mood in the company offices was both serene and cheerful. The offices and warehouse were spotless, with the WAI parts displayed on the file cabinets like interesting small-scale industrial sculptures. No one shouted. Many people smiled as they worked. A few employees reported improvements in their health. According to Bothe, "We have demonstrated beyond a doubt, that when people function in an atmosphere of absolute honesty, they feel safe, they are happier, they suffer no stress. And as a result they are more productive and have a positive effect on everybody they deal with."[27]

Bothe knew many of the employees personally and she often exchanged greetings with them in the hallways. There were instances of family members who worked at WAI: Kevin Kraft's two younger brothers joined the company; Jeffery Sween's grandmother was also employed there. Carol Sheehan commented on the sense of calm she observed when she first joined WAI: "I wondered why people weren't yelling and screaming. I asked my supervisor if the phones were down." A customer was also struck by the atmosphere: "They've got 18-year-old people working with 80-year-olds. It's a happy work situation, and its reflected when you're on the phone with them."[28]

Both male and female managers praised the company for the absence of sexism. David Rowan, director of engineering, described the policies of that department:

> The director of engineering occupies a desk space equal to every other member . . . located in the middle of the seating area. The 70-year-old employee is given every opportunity to do any of the jobs every other department member is doing as long as he feels comfortable with it. This, despite the fact that he only works a 20-hour-week work schedule. Female employees (6 of 18) are given every opportunity to do any job any other member is doing, as long as she feels comfortable with it.

Added Diane LeBold, manager of the graphic arts department and a recent recruit to WAI, with experience as a consultant to many large companies: "People are not locked in here, but given an opportunity to grow, learn, and expand their capabilities." A number of WAI workers had been promoted to positions of considerable responsibility even though they had little prior formal training. Two conspicuous examples were top managers Kraft and Sween, who both began at the company shortly after high school with little previous business experience.

In some instances, WAI had used the Right-Action Ethic to counsel employees who were having personal problems or facing difficult situations in their own families. Managers were asked to be alert to employee difficulties and to help as appropriate. This might involve counseling or assistance with problems such as drug use by children, or financial difficulties at home. However, Bothe was quick to point out that while employees were expected to follow the Right-Action Ethic at work, they could do as they liked off the job: "We don't force it after hours."

Many companies within the industry credited WAI's principles and policies with helping to professionalize the entire industry. WAI employees recalled that in the early 1980s, the trade shows and conventions were attended by people in tee-shirts and jeans, and the tone was rather rowdy. "Now people come in business attire. The whole industry has changed." Reports of gifts to customers by

---

[27]John Crudele, p. D03 ff.
[28]"Principles and Profits: WAI in the Automotive Aftermarket," p. 8.

competitor's salespeople were much less common. A customer concurred, "People are learning to manage in a new way, mainly from their example. [At industry gatherings] they are the number one thing talked about these days."[29] Nonetheless, WAI employees still occasionally reported being offered kickbacks from some customers.

Perpetuating Wetherill's Vision

The job of imparting and perpetuating the Wetherill culture and vision began with the actions of those at the head of the organization. Noting that at WAI, "ethics is at the top," President Marie Bothe explained that, whereas other managers were responsible for technical and market knowledge, her job was "keeping behavior on the track of the Right-Action Ethic":

> I circulate, listen in, stay informed. When there is something that comes up. . . . I keep the company on the track of right action. . . . I'm there to help. . . . I also stay on the lookout for things we can do to benefit the community. For example, recently we've started to investigate opening a child care facility, and we had an unusually successful 1993 United Way campaign.

The conversations of all of WAI's top managers were frequently peppered with references to "Mr. Wetherill's behavioral principles," "the Right-Action Ethic," and "reasoning from reality." The experience of Diane LeBold was typical:

> Upper management sets the tone. . . . There is a built-in demand for mutual respect across the board. Everyone has respect from the 17-year-old to the 71-year-old. . . . I took a trip with Treasurer Kevin Kraft. We discussed a lot of things. I then took the information back to my boss. In a lot of companies, I would have been in trouble for discussing these issues out of the department, and over [my boss's] head. The free flow of communication that resulted would not have occurred in other companies.

LeBold also had an opportunity to see the benefits come back to her from the people she supervised:

> [As a new department head] I walked into a functioning department that had a system and a way of doing things. . . . I could have been undermined at every step: I had never worked on a MacIntosh [computer]; I didn't know how the department worked. There was a person who had been, de facto, running things. When I suddenly realized what I had gotten into, I really felt off balance. But, the two people necessary to get me rolling trained me. They put aside all their own emotions and ambitions, and never once did anything to undermine my actions.

Hiring

WAI introduced potential employees to the Right-Action Ethic early in the hiring process, usually in the initial interview. Thomas Burns, WAI's sales manager, recalled his initial experiences with the company, five years earlier. Burns, who had previously worked as a field representative for a competitor, decided to send WAI his resume after losing a long-time customer to WAI. The customer had told Burns that he'd rather deal with WAI even if it meant slightly higher prices.

---

[29]Ibid., p. 6.

The loyalty of WAI's customers told Burns that there was something very different about the company. So did his job interview with Kevin Kraft and Jeffery Sween.

> They immediately put me at ease, made me comfortable. The interview began at 11:30 AM and we didn't leave until 6:45 PM. It was very casual. They wanted to get to know me. They immediately presented me with the fact that honesty was the cornerstone of the company; that right action was the foundation of everything. . . . I was just amazed that two officers would spend seven hours with me. They made it very clear—although it was not directly verbalized—that it was not how much you do, but how you do it. They were trying to find out if I was the right sort of person for WAI.

Bothe emphasized the importance of the Right-Action Ethic in the hiring process. People who are hired, she noted, "must support our Right-Action Ethic and withhold support for wrongdoing. . . . We favor those who fit in rather than those with higher skills and more experience." Burns believed that it was usually possible to tell during an interview whether a person would fit in. "The sincerity of the person projects itself," he explained.

In fact, many people wanted to work at Wetherill because of its ethical policies. When she learned about WAI's policy of absolute honesty in her job interview, Pat Hahn, a project coordinator in the research and development department, found it "a welcome relief." Dave Rowan, who learned about WAI from a newspaper article, said that after working for 22 years at a major U.S. company founded on internal competition, WAI "was like walking into heaven." Rowan drove 60 miles each day to head up WAI's 18-person engineering effort. He praised the members of his department for their ability to handle the technically difficult work of designing "not-from-scratch," despite the absence of academic degrees and the usual technical credentials: "I'll take these people any day. They have the right attitude. . . . You can take people with the right attitude and teach them the technical stuff."

In several instances, employees turned down substantially higher wages elsewhere to come to or remain at WAI. After joining WAI, one salesman rebuffed his former employer's effort to hire him back at increased compensation: "No way would I go back, even at twice the salary."

Formal Orientation and Training

Once hired, employees had several formal opportunities to learn about WAI's behavioral principles and policies. Most employees took part in a 1992 orientation program designed and run by Margo Callis, the company's corporate secretary. The program, which consisted of a one-hour session every week for nine weeks, was based on Richard Wetherill's 1945 book, *Management Techniques for Foremen.* Newer employees and those in the regional distribution centers were not able to participate, so there were plans to create a videotaped version. In addition, employees received a copy of WAI's *Quality Assurance Manual,* which spelled out overall corporate policy and included a department-by-department rundown of the duties, training, policies, and future plans in each functional area.

Another formal mechanism was the Management Seminar, "a quality procedure for problem solving or for brainstorming innovative changes to upgrade quality, service, product or expansion."[30] The management seminar format, which involved no formal agenda, was used in all departments:

> A Chairperson asks for topics until he has five or six which may cover products or operations or any aspect of the business. The 12 to 15 participants vote for one topic although anyone may vote more than once. When the majority topic is decided, the person who suggested it is asked to state the topic again and then clarify it further. Next he is asked for his suggestions regarding it, and then the Chairperson takes priorities from those attending the seminar. Each person waves his hand and is called on in order of his priority so that no one is allowed to interrupt or take control of the proceedings. . . . When appropriate, sessions are abstracted to distill the essence of the subject matter. Abstracts are then distributed to the participants and also to top management for implementation at their discretion.[31]

Bothe elaborated: "If there is a question about what is the right action, break it down. Ask, 'What would the results be?' Don't look for agreement among people, but what is the right action to take in the situation. During a meeting, the right action usually stands out and people feel great."

Specific departments provided additional training and handouts to teach and facilitate the Right-Action Ethic and to promote interdepartmental cooperation. For example, the handout for new field salespeople stated clearly:

> In other companies, Sales was *Sales* and Operations was *Operations.* At WAI they go hand in hand. (a) Work closely with the RDC [Remote Distribution Center] as the salesperson is the eyes and ears for them. Provide insight on service levels and compliment when appropriate. (b) Work in consensus with the RDC manager on service levels expected. Be realistic. (c) Help the RDC manager with customers that need to change the normal routine, i.e. short notice on rush orders or pick-up times, etc. (d) Be willing to "pitch in" with operations, i.e. inventories, transfers. Help to "meet the needs."[32]

And

> With other companies, an employee occasionally has to distort the truth to get what you or the customer needs. Not so at WAI! Total and complete honesty is the tried and only method.[33]

Informal Training

Formalized training laid the foundation for the Right-Action Ethic, but it was perpetuated through day-to-day management and the behavioral patterns that defined WAI's way of doing business. One employee explained, "It's like osmosis. You absorb it. After a while you start acting that way." See **Exhibit 5** for excerpts from WAI's managerial performance appraisal form.

WAI treated mistakes as important learning experiences offering insight on how to root out errors and defects. Employees were encouraged to acknowledge

---

[30]WAI, *Quality Assurance Manual,* p. 6.
[31]Ibid.
[32]WAI, "Potential Hurdles for New Field Salespersons," company document.
[33]Ibid.

EXHIBIT 5   **Wetherill Associates, Inc., Performance Appraisal Form, Supervisory and Managerial, 1992**

[Description of criteria for receiving the highest ranking in each category. Categories are in alphabetical order.]

Achievement in Area of Responsibility. Consistently achieves outstanding levels of performance within the department.

Administration. Consistently follows all company policies and procedures and develops suggestions for new or improved processes.

Cooperation with Other Departments. Actively seeks and promotes cooperation with all other departmental managers and employees resulting in consistent good working relationships with them.

Communication—verbal and body language. Consistently uses understandable language that is relevant and meaningful; presents points with a flexible attitude and in an appropriate manner; listens exceptionally well.

Communication—written. Demonstrates superior skill in writing effective letters, memos, e-mail, faxes and/or reports.

Cost Management—within person's control. Effectively controls costs through economical utilization of personnel, materials and/or equipment; makes good suggestions for improving return on investment.

Delegating. Consistently effectively delegates while maintaining accountability and gives subordinates adequate authority to carry out delegated assignments; is developing a qualified backup.

Employee Evaluation Skills. Consistently devotes adequate time and attention to evaluations; accurately researches and assesses employees, objectives, and results; consistently handles evaluations in a timely manner.

Improvements. Often provides valuable insights and/or pinpoints areas in need of improvements; develops constructive courses of action; excels in promoting the flow of ideas from subordinates.

Leadership. Unusually effective in guiding and influencing others in a responsible, right manner; looks for implications (positive and negative) and takes appropriate steps.

Management Ability. Demonstrates superior abilities to manage; makes a proper behavioral example; effectively interacts with others.

Mistakes. Consistently handles mistakes as correctable misunderstandings; provides effective retraining and guidance.

Exhibit 5   Continued

Planning. Consistently and effectively plans and implements, allowing for changing reality; develops sound contingency plans.

Problem Solving—technical. Consistently makes sound decisions based on reality; appropriately involves others in consensus decisions when all the reality is not known.

Problem Solving—behavioral. Identifies and handles employee problems before they become critical, turning them into opportunities to provide effective counseling; knows when to involve management; consistently documents events in a timely manner.

Project Management. Demonstrates outstanding ability to carry out assignments in a systematic, organized manner; consistently inspires others to plan, organize and complete tasks in the shortest, most efficient manner.

Right-Action Work Ethic. Understands and actively supports and promotes right-action work ethic.

Time Management. Consistently on time for projects, reports, meetings.

Training. Consistently looks for opportunities to provide additional training and coaching to employees in the department; orients new employees exceptionally well to job function, policies, procedures and safety; effectively

Source: Company document.

errors and view them as opportunities rather than as causes for embarrassment. One employee recalled, "There were things that I did where I had to be corrected. I was pulled aside by my manager and told 'That's not how we do things here.'" This employee found that the WAI approach was comfortable, "a lot like how I function normally . . . I don't like to lie to people."

WAI also addressed the challenges of delivering unpleasant news—that a part was out of stock, or that a customer order had not been shipped as promised—and handling customer complaints or disputes. Bothe explained that WAI did not tolerate yelling or screaming.

> We consider it dishonest to fight or interrupt. . . . We train our salespeople to take that kind of call. We teach them just to listen. Let the customer spill. Remain calm, get his suggestions, and assure him you will look into the matter. Afterward, let the customer know what the problem was. . . . Work out the problem in a way that is right for the situation.

The WAI philosophy was to defuse the emotion that blocked a satisfying solution to the problem. "An angry person is someone who is afraid," said Bothe. "Sometimes it is tempting to respond to a [screaming] customer in kind," but WAI managers tried to help their people develop the skills to respond in a different way. One employee found this aspect of the Wetherill training to have been the most helpful aspect of the Right-Action Ethic.

Reeducating New Employees   People who came to Wetherill from other companies often needed to be "deprogrammed." Tom Burns commented that sales people from other companies "were order-driven. . . . Their orientation was 'YOU GET AN ORDER,' while ours is 'Take care of the customer and find the product he should be buying; set the scenario so that he will call when he needs something.'"

Changing the "order-taker" mentality could be difficult. Burns recounted his conversation with a new salesperson, who proudly reported getting an order. When Burns responded with, "We don't want you to feel pressured to take an order," the exasperated employee exploded: "What do you mean, 'Don't take an order!?'" Another salesperson described experiences at a previous company:

> We were trained to mislead customers. We had monthly quotas. We would keep running totals of how we were doing throughout the month. On the last day of the month, a customer might order 10 parts. We'd send 100 parts and hope he'd keep them. It was a "take-the-heat-the-next-month" approach. We were told to do this by our managers. . . . I tried to block this out of my mind. To tell you the truth, I don't like to be sold to that way.

Despite the low-pressure atmosphere, lack of effort was not a problem. Close working relationships among team members meant that shirking in the office could not occur without being immediately noticed. As for the field staff, sales managers could identify shirking when reviewing the computerized feedback reports. When a manager did notice inadequate effort, she would offer a helping hand and identify areas where training was needed. Usually, this approach cured any problems.

If an employee continued to have problems with the WAI approach and the training efforts failed, he or she would be fired. Bothe noted, "We don't reach everybody with talk of ethical behavior, and some people leave." However, this was a fairly rare event. WAI's employee turnover rate was low—9.2% in 1992. Still, as the company grew and expanded to new areas, special efforts would be required to insure that everyone fully understood the Right-Action Ethic and what it meant on a day-to-day basis.

Getting Right Results

WAI managers were openly enthusiastic about the results of the Right-Action Ethic. Carol Sheehan's comments were not unusual:

> At WAI, you can honestly sit down, roll up your sleeves and do your job. You never have to worry about your back. About being fired for a mistake. About being yelled at. About not knowing something and asking for help.

Dave Rowan agreed.

> In big corporations, there are three rules for success: protect your ass; serve your boss; and make the numbers come out. . . . Fifty% of the energy is wasted in politics. In that kind of environment it is difficult to survive *and* do the right thing. . . . WAI is

such a fertile ground. Here, 97% of the energy is put into making the business run . . . People are here to work.

Having previously worked in a multimillion dollar quality control program in a large, prestigious company, Rowan commented wryly, "Real quality comes from an environment where people have quality within." Diane Lebold elaborated:

> Wetherill training ultimately makes for the most pragmatic kind of environment to work in. What matters is getting the work done. . . . Right action works. People are more productive, live up to their potential. And what else is there?

She compared WAI's reality orientation with the "fantasy world" of former senior managers she had known: "If you think about profit, it is fantasy. You have to think about people, processes, and what it takes to get there." Noting that WAI was not perfect, she explained, "People get mad. They make mistakes. But, it's how the mistakes are dealt with, the process of working through them. . . . [At WAI,] You are not just asked to do something. You have an understanding of why it is required. . . . Everyone knows where the company is going, what we are trying to do. People rely on you, trust you, count on you."

New Challenges

In late 1993, WAI was continuing its plans for expansion. The company had hired a sales representative in Mexico, developed suppliers in the former Soviet Union, and was making preparations to expand into new lines of business. Noted Kraft, "We have discovered that opportunities exist in every field for our approach."

But growth brought many challenges—keeping systems in step with expansion, controlling costs, and perpetuating the Right-Action Ethic. The increased size and expanse of the organization meant trying to increase the contact between Royersford and, for example, the people at the regional distribution centers—who were not Wetherill trained. International expansion involved both meeting international standards and understanding the "needs" of other countries. Bothe elaborated, "We are not looking to be opportunistic . . . We want long-term growth, not fast business. We want people to learn about and apply the Right-Action Ethic." WAI had already walked away from overseas business that would have required the company to understate invoices so the customer could avoid paying duties.

Reducing expenses meant focusing on management's goal of zero errors for customers and negligible errors internally, to "get rid of variation and reduce the costs of 'unquality.'" In line with this effort, the company was looking for new ways to reorganize jobs and departments, make processes visible to employees at every level, and teach people how to resolve problems. In this way, senior managers planned to push power and right action decision making down the organization, reduce errors and defects, and, ultimately, "to compress time and costs." Additionally, a new cross-functional team was formed to overhaul the product development process so that each stage could occur concurrently. Members Kraft, Sween, and representatives from engineering, purchasing, marketing, and manufacturing expected to reduce the time to market while insuring that new products met customer needs.

Compensation

In the fall of 1993, WAI's top managers were thinking about whether to revamp the company's method of arriving at employee compensation, prompted, in part, by the fact that some employees were concerned about the issue. Early attention centered on whether to pay employees a premium, as Kevin Kraft put it, "for a premium environment," and whether to create a process for more frequent pay-out of profits. Management was particularly concerned to develop an appropriate compensation package for production workers and lower paid employees. Although no formal decision procedure had been set, the company formed a committee of Bothe, Callis, Kraft, and Sween, along with the controller and the sales manager, to consider the matter.

Kraft reported that WAI salaries had always been set with an eye to "market demand, what people in that job are making in the area. . . . We don't want money to be a motivating factor or a distraction." All employees were paid a straight salary, even the sales staff. This was unusual for the industry; compensation for salespeople in other companies ranged from straight commission to a base salary supplemented by a percentage of all sales exceeding a set target. In 1992, WAI employees also received a year-end bonus. A profit-sharing program funded the employee retirement plan. On occasion, WAI rewarded unusual efforts with an additional bonus. For example, WAI decided to give workers an additional week's pay in recognition of their extra efforts during the month of record-breaking sales in the summer of 1993. See **Exhibit 6** for details of WAI's expenses related to compensation.

The issue of whether to institute a commission system for salespeople had arisen a few times before. When WAI began, salespeople were given no territorial boundaries and were paid on commission because "we just fell in with common practice in the industry," noted Bothe. As the company grew and sales force earnings outstripped the salaries of other supporting employees, management decided to rationalize the sales effort on a geographic basis and to pay the sales force like everyone else in the company. The *Quality Assurance Manual* stated company policy, "There are no private sales secrets. There are no sales contests nor artificial incentives."[34]

Bothe recalled that the change in policy meant that, for some people, "Salaries were cut in half. But they understood. Those employees were all making the money they needed so money was not an issue. . . . I read that some CEO made $73 million dollars with stock options. Considering present economic conditions, that seems obscene!" According to Tom Burns, sales force salaries were still at the "upper end of the scale" at WAI. Salary increases and discretionary bonuses, determined at an annual review, were based not merely on sales, but also on such factors as team effort, and whether the salesperson had turned around an important account. "When Jeff [Sween] and I sit down to finalize bonuses, we don't have any territory sales figures in front of us," Tom Burns said.

More recently, sales and customer service employees hired from another company had suggested informally that a commission system be considered, but no

---

[34]WAI, *Quality Assurance Manual*, p. 8.

EXHIBIT 6 **Wetherill Associates, Inc.—Compensation Expenses (amounts in thousands except employee counts)**

	1992	1991	1990	1989
Salaries and wages	$7,685	$6,568	$5,680	$4,583
Fringe benefits				
Medical benefits	$ 740	$ 412	$ 351	$ 264
FICA taxes	565	489	434	348
Unemployment taxes	80	72	58	50
Workers' compensation	134	71	56	42
Life insurance	18	17	23	14
Retirement plan	294	200	124	1
Total fringe benefits	$1,831	$1,261	$1,047	$ 719
Total expenses	$9,516	$7,829	$6,727	$5,302
Employees				
Full-time	295	270	252	221
Half-time	13	13	8	11
Full-time equivalent	302	277	256	227
Expenses per employee				
Salaries and wages	$ 25	$ 24	$ 22	$ 20
Fringe benefits	6	5	4	3
Total	$ 32	$ 28	$ 26	$ 23

Note: Numbers may not add due to rounding.

Source: Company document.

such plan was ever implemented. Noting that some salespeople liked the idea of commissions, Bothe explained:

> Although, it has come up a few times for discussion, we couldn't find a way to justify it. . . . Is there a fair way to give incentives—to recognize and compensate everyone for his or her effort? Taking the order is the sales job, but getting it out the door is all part of a general effort on everybody's part. . . . It's not really fair to the organization to pay incentives to salespeople since meeting the customer's needs is the result of everybody's effort.

Tom Burns agreed, "If a salesperson has to choose between two calls, one for a $10,000 order or a second for $10,000 in problems, we don't want the person to ignore the problems, and we don't want to break down the team."

In the fall of 1993, senior managers began considering the compensation issue once again. Kraft explained:

> We have always asked ourselves, in setting pay scales, 'Are we paying a livable wage?' Maybe, this isn't rational. Maybe we should be paying a premium, in order to have a line out the door.

Bothe noted that compensation raised other thorny questions: "Is it ethical to pay people based on years of service even when they do the same job as newcomers?" With the Right-Action Ethic, she added, "we are not thinking of pay as an incentive, but as a benefit. We will continue to do additional pioneering in this area in the next year."

Case 4
AES Honeycomb (A)

Roger Sant, chairman and chief executive officer of the AES Corporation, was under intense pressure in July 1992. Earlier in the summer, AES had announced news of community relations problems in Florida and employee fraud at the company's Shady Point plant in Oklahoma. The share price of the independent power producer had fallen by half, and many of the firm's investment bankers, shareholders, and legal advisors were calling for explanations and change. (See **Exhibit 1** for illustration of AES's share price movements.) Some financial analysts had criticized the company's corporate culture and operating style, calling AES's managers "arrogant" and berating them for neglecting their responsibilities to shareholders and constituencies outside the organization.

Sant was troubled by the asperity of the criticisms. From a profit perspective, he believed the firm had performed well. Eleven years after its founding in 1981, AES was one of the largest publicly traded independent power producers in the world, generating over 1600 megawatts (MW) each year and employing an estimated 600 persons worldwide, including 500 in the United States.[1] AES operated five generating plants in the United States and would soon bring a new plant on-line in Hawaii. Several projects were under development in North America: two coal plants in Maryland, a natural gas plant in Ontario, a gas-fired facility in Wisconsin, and a pumped storage hydro facility in California. The company was also expanding actively overseas and had recently opened two new facilities in Northern Ireland and begun construction of a project in the United Kingdom. (See **Exhibit 2** for descriptions of AES plants.)

As a result of rapid and sustained growth, AES had achieved a market valuation of over $1.4 billion by early 1992. Year-end revenues for 1992 were expected to pass the $400 million mark, and 1992 earnings were expected to be $56 million, up 31% over 1991. (See **Exhibit 3** for corporate financial results.)

Sant knew that shareholders' concerns had less to do with profitability than with the company's espoused values and management style. Sant and Dennis Bakke, AES's chief operating officer, had founded AES in 1981 with the aim of fostering a new form of business enterprise—one which was socially responsible as well as profitable. Their mission was to provide electrical power in a way that was safe, clean, reliable, cost-efficient, and fun. In the prospectus accompanying AES's initial public offering in June 1991, Sant and Bakke had written:

> An important element of AES is its commitment to four major "shared" values: to act with integrity, to be fair, to have fun and to be socially responsible . . . AES believes

---

[1]The size of power producers was traditionally evaluated in terms of megawatts of power produced per annum. See **Exhibit 5** for more information on AES's and competitors' operating and financial performance.

This case was prepared by Sarah C. Mavrinac under the supervision of Lynn Sharp Paine, based on earlier work supervised by Robert G. Eccles. Charles A. Nichols, III, also provided assistance. Copyright © 1994 by the President and Fellows of Harvard College. Harvard Business School case 395–132.

EXHIBIT 1

AES Share Price Movement, June 1991–August 1992

AES Corp. Month-End Adjusted Stock Price.

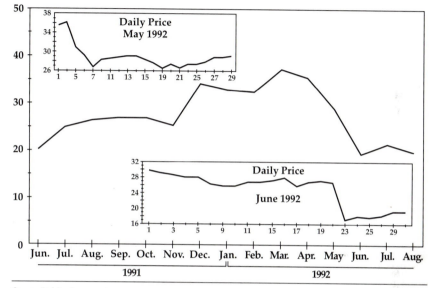

Source: Public document.

that earning a fair profit is an important result of providing a quality product to its customers. However, if the Company perceives a conflict between these values and profits, the Company will try to adhere to its values— even though doing so might result in diminished profits or foregone opportunities. Moreover, the Company seeks to adhere to these values not as a means to achieve economic success, but because adherence is a worthwhile goal in and of itself.[2]

In their effort to build a corporate culture compatible with these values, Sant and Bakke had maintained a loose management structure, keeping rules, staff, and hierarchy to a minimum. An unusual "honeycomb" system of employee management had evolved. Developed in 1988, the honeycomb system revolved around a web of worker families. According to Bakke, AES's honeycomb organization was a critical means through which the company's unique values and philosophies could be expressed and reinforced. The system encouraged shared responsibility, the reduction of hierarchy, and democratic control of the work environment.

Sant and Bakke believed deeply in the honeycomb approach, but in 1992, less than four years after its development, the approach was being challenged. Legal advisors and investors urged Sant to introduce more formal controls, to adopt the standard practices of large bureaucratic organizations, and to forget about the company's values.

---

[2]Although AES's board of directors actively supported the corporation's values, the Securities and Exchange Commission (SEC) had required that the statement quoted in the text be incorporated in the discussion of competitive and operating risk factors in the prospectus.

EXHIBIT 2   AES Facilities (as of August 31, 1992)

Name/Location	Primary Customer	Fuel	Contract Term (years)	Power (MW)	Construction Start Date	Date On-Line	Percent AES Ownership
Deepwater, Houston, TX[a]	Houston Lighting & Power/Lyondell Petrochemical	Petroleum Coke	N/A	140	December 1983	June 1986	0%
Beaver Valley, Monaco, PA	West Penn Power/ARCO Chemical	Coal	30	120	September 1985	July 1987	80
Placerita, Newhall, CA	Southern California Edison	Gas	25	100	July 1986	August 1988	98
Thames, Montville, CT	Conn. Light & Power/Stone Container	Coal	25	180	December 1986	March 1990	100
Shady Point, Poteau, OK	Oklahoma Gas & Electric/Tyson Foods	Coal	17	320	June 1986	January 1991	100
Barbers Point, Oahu, HI	Hawaiian Electric/Chevron Refinery	Coal	30	180	March 1990	September 1992	100
Medway, United Kingdom	Southern Electric/Seeboard plc.	Gas	N/A	660	April 1992	1995	25
Kilroot, North Ireland	NIE plc.	Coal and Gas	N/A	520		June 1992	50
Belfast West	NIE plc.	Coal	N/A	240		June 1992	50

[a]In 1983, AES created a wholly owned subsidiary, AES Deepwater, Inc., for the purpose of operating the AES Deepwater co-generation facility in Houston, TX. Company financial and operating data do not include AES Deepwater results.

Source: Adapted from company documents.

EXHIBIT 3 **AES Financial and Operating Performance: 1988–1992 (Expected); All Figures in Millions of Dollars Except per Share Data**

	1992(E)	1991	1990	1989	1988
Income and Operating Data:					
Revenues	$400.99	$333.51	$190.21	$ 99.22	$ 55.37
Operating costs	248.18	201.42	129.38	74.66	44.01
Operating income	152.82	132.09	60.83	24.56	11.36
Net income	55.81	42.63	15.53	4.19	1.63
Net income/share[a]	1.24	1.02	0.40	0.11	0.04
Dividends/share	0.60	0.31	0.00	0.01	0.02
Estimated sales backlog	$29,000.00	$34,000.00	$27,000.00	$27,000.00	$27,000.00
Net cash from operations	$77.72	$85.82	$30.47	$15.76	N/A
Net cash from financing	122.74	206.75	190.03	286.87	N/A
Net cash from investing	(186.90)	(249.80)	(217.32)	(296.36)	N/A
Balance Sheet Data:					
Current assets	$143.53	$101.16	$55.97	N/A	N/A
Net property, plant, and equipment	1,250.38	1,165.24	1,028.00	N/A	N/A
Total assets	1,551.77	1,366.47	1,127.81	860.70	569.84
Current liabilities	127.26	107.75	69.38	N/A	N/A
Revolving bank loan (current)	0.00	10.00	0.00	0.00	0.00
Project financing debt (long-term)[b]	1,146.42	1,093.29	995.96	781.00	517.06
Other notes payable	50.00	0.33	11.73	12.76	3.87
Total long-term liabilities	1,235.47	1,105.35	1,012.26	N/A	N/A
Stockholders' equity	177.22	140.86	34.42	17.36	7.54

[a]In 1991, AES had 43,017,676 common shares outstanding.
[b]Loans to AES subsidiaries that are substantially nonrecourse to the parent company.

Source: Company documents.

Sant leaned back in his chair and glanced through the open door into Bakke's adjoining office. When AES moved into its headquarters in Arlington, Virginia, he and Bakke had designed their offices to mimic those they had shared at the Mellon Institute years before.[3] Sitting behind their desks, they could talk easily across the hallway, keeping each other casually informed of their work, their ideas, and their moods. Sant knew that Bakke, the more vocal spokesperson for the company's values, would be disturbed by any change that threatened the current operating style and culture of the organization. For Bakke, any movement in the direction of greater hierarchy would threaten the environment of trust and individual responsibility he and Sant had worked so hard to develop.

Sant faced some difficult decisions. How should he respond to the criticisms and address the concerns of internal and external constituencies? How could AES prevent the recurrence of situations like Shady Point? As Sant prepared the agenda for the next day's special meeting of the company's officers, he anticipated a difficult and highly emotional discussion.

---

[3]The Mellon Institute was an energy "think tank" located in Washington, D.C.

Industry History: The Emergence of the Independent Power Producer

AES was founded at time when the U.S. electrical generation and transmission industry was undergoing major transformation. In 1978 U.S. President Carter signed the Public Utility Regulatory Policies Act (PURPA), allowing the creation of both new firms and new forms of competition in what traditionally had been a regulated oligopoly. In an attempt to decrease U.S. dependence on foreign oil and to spur efficiency in the utility industry, PURPA permitted the creation of two new types of privately held, nonutility facilities: qualifying facilities and co-generators, collectively known as independent power producers or IPPs. All IPPs were guaranteed the right to sell their electricity to electric utilities for "avoided cost."[4]

Qualifying facilities were typically small operators generating less than 80 megawatts of power from alternative energy sources such as waste coal, biomass, wood waste, or other renewable sources. Co-generators were operating plants which could produce two kinds of energy from a single fuel source. A typical co-generation plant might burn coal or natural gas for electricity while capturing the steam by-product for heating or industrial purposes. All AES plants were coal-burning, co-generation facilities. The Thames plant in Montville, Connecticut, for example, sold electricity to the local utility and steam to a neighboring recycled paperboard plant. AES's Shady Point plant recycled its processed steam to produce food grade liquid carbon dioxide for use in local food-processing plants. (See **Exhibit 4** for a description of the Shady Point co-generation process.)

By 1990, the generating capacity of the independent power producers had expanded to over 25,000 megawatts. IPP facilities had provided over 50% of all the new power generated in the United States since 1989 and were expected to provide almost as much as 12% of the country's required electricity by the end of the decade. In 1992, the combined value of IPP revenues was over $40 billion.

Market and Competitive Outlook

Demand The demand for electrical power in the United States was expected to increase rapidly over the remaining years of the century, despite the country's slow economic growth and increased investment in energy efficiency. To meet this demand, electric power supply was expected to increase by 20% by the year 2000. To cover replacement needs as well as required growth, facilities for the production of an additional 95,000 megawatts of power would be needed. As of 1992, industry expansion plans accounted for only one-half of this needed capacity.

Governmental Legislation One of the most important pieces of legislation affecting the new industry was the Clean Air Act Amendment signed into law by President Bush in November of 1990. This law was intended to reduce environmental pollution levels by reducing the electric industry's emissions of sulfur dioxide by an estimated 10 million tons per year. The industry's total production of sulfur dioxide was mandated to be less than 8.95 million tons annually by the year 2000,

---

[4]The "avoided cost" amount represented the utilities' best estimate of the incremental cost savings incurred as a result of purchasing rather than making electricity.

EXHIBIT 4

Illustration of Shady Point's Cogeneration Process

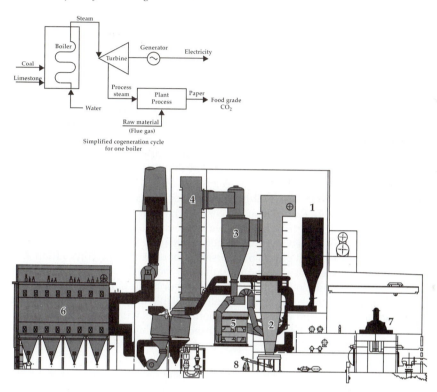

1. **COAL SILOS.** Oklahoma coal is crushed prior to being fed into the combustors. It is mixed with limestone in the combustion zone of the boiler.
2. **COMBUSTION ZONE.** A strong upward flow of air holds the fuel and limestone particles in suspension in the combustion zone. As the coal burns sulfur dioxide is absorbed by the limestone and the light particles move upward in the Combustion Chamber.
3. **HOT CYCLONE.** Ash and hot gases at 1,560 degrees fahrenheit flow out the top of the combustor to the hot cyclone. The gas exits the cyclone to the convective pass. Partially burned fuel and ash pass from the cycle back to the combustor for recombustion. Thus the combustor achieves a high degree of fuel efficiency.
4. **CONVECTIVE PASS.** Hot exhaust gas from combustor pass over the banks of water and steam piping, helping to produce the steam for the turbine.
5. **FLUID BED HEAT EXCHANGER.** Ash taken from the cyclones heats the final reheat and superheat steam then returns to the combustor. This is the steam that powers the turbine which spins the generator to produce electricity.
6. **FABRIC FILTERS.** After giving up most of its heat, the exhaust gas from the convective pass is routed through ducts to fabric filter baghouses. These act as huge vacuum cleaners and collect almost all the fine particulate for ash disposal.
7. **TURBINE GENERATOR.** A single shaft, 3600 rpm condensing turbine. Main steam to turbine is 1,135,000 lb./hr. at 1,890 psig, 1,005 degrees fahrenheit.
8. **ASH DISPOSAL.** Ash is collected in silos for environmentally sound disposal. Ash is trucked for disposal back at the coal mine.

Source: Adapted from company documents.

down from over 120 million tons in 1990. To comply with the law, utilities would have to invest substantial amounts of capital in scrubbers, allowances,[5] or plant conversions which would allow the plant to burn natural gas rather than high-sulfur coal, for example. Both co-generation and alternative energy suppliers were considered significantly more efficient and environmentally clean than traditional utilities.

Financing   IPPs were expected to bring between 47,000 and 57,000 megawatts of power on-line by the year 2000 at an estimated capital cost of approximately $98 billion.[6] Although the need for financing was clearly expanding, some analysts thought that IPP financing options were drying up. One report suggested that "(R)egulatory uncertainty, increased competition from other industries for a shrinking pot of available capital, and the memory of past NUG (nonutility generator) project failures" were limiting the availability of funds for all but the strongest IPPs.

Other analysts thought financing opportunities were not drying up; they were simply changing form. Rather than the commercial bank financing and joint-venture arrangements characteristic of the late 1980s, the public market had begun to accept more project-related debt which tied repayment to the cash generating capability of the project or power plant itself rather than to the corporation as a whole.[7] Most of this debt was "nonrecourse" to the corporation. In the event of default, creditors could look only to the cashflow or assets of the specific indebted project. Such nonrecourse debt was usually available only to the strongest firms for domestic projects and only to international projects with significant equity financing. Lenders in the 1990s shied away from the highly leveraged projects common in the 1980s, requiring greater sponsor equity and toughening terms.

Competitive Conditions   AES executives considered their operating environment extremely competitive. Despite the need for increased electrical generating capacity, demand for new plant construction in the United States was low, and coal projects were becoming difficult to site anywhere in the country. Natural gas, a substitute for coal, was becoming increasingly popular especially as pipeline transmission capabilities increased.

Virtually all of AES's major competitors, principally large corporations such as California Energy, Destec Energy, and Enron Corporation, had adopted an "environmentally friendly" operating policy, defining "clean operations" as a fundamental objective. (See **Exhibit 5** for data on competitors.) However, much of the continuing pressure for improvements in environmental performance

---

[5]Allowances were "rights" to emit predetermined amounts of sulfur dioxide which could be purchased from the federal government. This allowance scheme had been constructed as part of the Clean Air Act to create a "market" for emission controls. While the original price of these allowances was set at approximately $200/ton, prices had fallen substantially over the years as plants opted to invest in conversions or scrubbers to clean stacks.

[6]See RCC/Hager, Bailly, Inc., February 1991.

[7]See T. F. Berg, "IPPs, APPs, and the Credit Crunch," *Public Utilities Fortnightly*, vol. 12, no. 6, pp. 36–38.

EXHIBIT 5   **AES Competitors: Comparative Financial Information (fiscal year 1991)**

Item (dollar amounts in thousands)	AES	California Energy	Destec Energy	Enron Corp.	Enron Power[c]	Magma Power	Mission Energy[f]
INCOME STATEMENT							
Operating revenue[a]	$ 333,507	$106,184	$437,046	$5,562,67	76,577	$ 84,135	$ 154,239
Operating expense[a]	201,422	56,258	327,462	5,064,669	14,689	45,160	45,568
Net income	42,626	26,582	81,491	241,776	e	33,941	82,510
Net income per share	1.02	0.75	1.39	2.15[d]	e	1.44	f
BALANCE SHEET							
Property, plant, equipment[b]	1,165,242	378,266	162,055	6,574,415	5,560	118,541	2,202
Total assets	1,366,469	517,994	663,842	10,362,878	360,269	353,788	1,166,978
Long-term liabilities[c]	1,094,500	257,038	45,806	3,108,793	e	89,808	144,958
otal stockholders' equity	140,862	143,128	474,221	1,929,187	e	226,872	580,968
FINANCIAL RATIOS							
Return on assets (%)	3.1	5.1	12.3	2.3	e	9.6	7.1
Return on equity (%)	30.3	18.6	17.2	12.5	e	15.0	14.2
Return on revenues (%)	12.8	25.0	18.6	4.3	e	40.3	53.5
Long-term liabilities/equity	7.77	1.80	0.10	1.61	e	0.40	0.25
PRODUCTION MEASURES —MEGAWATTS[g]							
By plants under operation	710	250	1,006	—	1,255	148	2,845
By net project ownership	1,126	120	964	—	1,346	74	1,432

[a]Excluding interest and investment revenue and expense.
[b]Net of depreciation, except Enron Power.
[c]Excludes deferred income taxes.
[d]Primary net income per share is shown. Fully diluted is 2.04.
[e]Figures not available. Enron Power is a business segment of Enron Corporation.
[f]Mission is a wholly owned subsidiary and lacks publicly owned shares.
[g]Production estimates from *110 Independent Power Companies* by editors of *Independent Power Report, 1992*.

Source: Compiled by casewriter from public documents.

came from small firms and single-project facilities which were entering the secondary markets in increasing numbers, bringing with them a variety of innovative emission control solutions. Many IPPs, as spinoffs from large public utilities, had adopted traditional organizational structures and cultures.

Competitive pressures were also intensifying as public utilities modified their project bidding and negotiation processes. Utilities had traditionally purchased electricity on the basis of private negotiations with a single intended provider. Recently many had begun moving to competitive, sealed bidding from multiple providers, thus increasing the premium on competitive secrecy and cost efficiency.

With increased domestic competition, large firms like AES began looking more seriously at international opportunities. By the summer of 1992, AES had begun investigating development opportunities in Argentina, Puerto Rico, and China and was negotiating a power purchase agreement to deliver 420 megawatts of power to the state utility in Orissa, India. Despite the more complicated financing requirements, many of AES's major competitors were also active outside the United States. Enron, for example, had invested heavily in the development of its Teeside plant in the United Kingdom. Mission Energy, another major competitor, had invested in a co-generation plant in England and opened an office in Mexico City to oversee the construction of its 1400 megawatt coal-fired plant there. It was estimated that the international market for new projects and privatized ownership of existing facilities would approach 750,000 megawatts by the year 2002.

The Company's Beginnings

Sant and Bakke started AES with literally nothing more than an idea. Although they had investigated the possibilities for developing new slurried petroleum coke technologies, the two entrepreneurs quickly realized that new technology was not a prerequisite for start up. Speed in development, relationships in industry and government, and inexpensive financing would be their critical success factors. Because of their professional experience, Sant and Bakke believed they had enough of a reputation within the energy industry to leverage their ideas.

Sant and Bakke had met while working at the Federal Energy Administration (FEA) where Sant, a Harvard MBA, headed the Ford administration's energy conservation efforts. Bakke, another Harvard MBA, had served as his chief aide. In 1977, the pair moved over to the Mellon Institute's Energy Productivity Center where they spent four years conducting policy research on energy conservation and development techniques. Their work resulted in a series of consulting and advisory experiences, a number of articles, a book entitled *Creating Abundance—America's Least-Cost Strategy*, and the strategic plan for AES's development.

The Founders' Values   When the business plan for AES was finalized, it included more than a listing of strategic objectives and financial forecasts. The plan was an expression of the authors' philosophies on business, hierarchies, and the role of employment in people's lives.

Bakke's ideas of business were primarily the result of his upbringing and religious beliefs. Bakke held the classical Christian view that all things come from God and that individuals have a responsibility to minister to these things faithfully on His behalf. To describe his philosophy, Bakke often referred to a passage from Paul's letter to the Ephesians which endorses useful work so that a person "may have something to share with those in need."[8] The son of a laborer, Bakke had grown up on a farm in a small town 90 miles north of Seattle, Washington. By the time he was five, Bakke had already worked his first paying job picking strawberries. By the time he was 18, he had built up a profitable herd of 29 beef cattle. Business wasn't the only area in which Bakke's philosophies were revealed, however. As a good steward, Bakke believed he must make all his resources available to others during their times of need. His house and his cars, for example, were regularly made available for the use of others in the church which he and his wife, Eileen, had helped found in 1981. In 1983, Bakke and his wife had also established the Mustard Seed Foundation which provided small "seed-like" grants to Christians engaged in ministry. In 1991, the Foundation provided individuals and organizations with over $1.1 million of support.

---

[8]T. Eastland, "This Is Not Ours: Good Stewards Hold All Things Lightly," *The Washingtonian*, July 1991, pp. 31–33.

Sant had also grown up in a religious household where he was taught the value of sharing and building for the future. Following the Mormon tradition in which he was raised, Sant had attended Brigham Young University and spent two years working with Native Americans in Wisconsin as a missionary. Although he appreciated the values with which he was raised, Sant found himself feeling less and less comfortable with what he perceived as religious "dogma" as he grew older. He found the authoritarian, exclusionary attitudes of many organized religions inconsistent with their stated values. After years of examining his faith and his life critically, Sant came to believe that what is of fundamental value and what specifies the goodness of the individual or society transcends religious belief. According to Sant, respect, caring, and nonjudgmental acceptance could not be considered exclusively "Christian" values.

After leaving the Mormon church, Sant became active within the environmental movement, a cause in which he felt he could honestly express his concerns for individuals and the environments in which they lived. In 1992, Sant was vice chairman of the World Resources Institute, a member of the board of the World Wildlife Fund (U.S.), a director and former chairman of the Environmental and Energy Study Institute, and a member of the National Council of the Environmental Defense Fund. He and his wife had started two foundations to help support environmental and population causes. Before founding AES, Sant was chief financial officer of a major industrial corporation, a founder of several other businesses, and a lecturer at the Stanford University Graduate School of Business.

Creating AES was an opportunity for both men to test their values and attempt a change in business practice. Although they realized that developing environmentally friendly technologies and empowering individual workers might be good for business, they were committed to such policies not because they might be profitable but because they reflected their absolute beliefs. Sant and Bakke recognized the necessity and desirability of profits for a successful business, but neither regarded profit as the fundamental purpose of business. According to Bakke, "[T]he purpose of enterprise is . . . to steward resources to meet a need in society. . . . It's very important for AES that we start with that kind of premise because everything else follows."[9]

Sant and Bakke stated their values formally in the prospectus accompanying AES's initial public offering. They wrote:

> These values are goals and aspirations to guide the efforts of the people of AES as they carry out the business purposes of the company.
>
> - **Integrity.** AES has attempted to act with integrity, or "wholeness." The Company seeks to honor its commitments. The goal has been that the things AES people say and do in all parts of the Company should fit together with truth and consistency.
> - **Fairness.** The desire of AES has been to treat fairly its people, its customers, its suppliers, its stockholders, governments, and the communities in which it operates. Defining what is fair is often difficult, but the Company believes it is helpful to routinely question the relative fairness of alternative courses of action. AES has tried to practice its belief that it is not right to "get the most out of" each negotiation or transaction to the detriment of others.

---

[9]Dennis Bakke, "Values Don't Work in Business," speech given at Calvin College, 1991.

- **Fun.** AES desires that people employed by the Company and those people with whom the Company interacts have fun in their work. AES's goal has been to create and maintain an environment where each person can flourish in the use of his or her gifts and skills and thereby enjoy the time spent at AES.
- **Social responsibility.** The Company has acted on its belief that AES has a responsibility to be involved in projects that provide social benefits, such as lower costs to customers, a high degree of safety and reliability, increased employment and a cleaner environment.

This set of values was based on a very specific set of beliefs about individuals and their role in the workplace. Within the AES culture, individuals were recognized as: (1) thinking, creative, and capable of making hard decisions, (2) willing and able to assume accountability and responsibility, (3) unique and deserving of special treatment, (4) fallible, even intentionally at times, (5) positively disposed to work in groups, and (6) eager to make a contribution or to join a cause.

The impact of these values and beliefs could be felt throughout the organization. Reminders of AES values lined the headquarters in Arlington in the form of plaques and posters. They were discussed in company newsletters, in company operating meetings, and sessions of the boards of directors. They affected operating policies, the construction of plants, and hiring procedures. Each year's Letter to Shareholders reported on AES's performance in four areas—shared values, plant operations, assets, and sales backlogs. A Founder's Award was given annually to individuals who stood out as practitioners of AES values, as well as a President's Award for Technical Achievement.

Building Corporate Values

Organizational Design   AES brought its first plant on-line in June of 1986 after almost three years of planning and construction. Initially, the plant was run using the traditional organization structures and managerial routines found in most public utilities. According to Bakke, "The initial results were good. We began to understand, however, that doing what others had done for years would not allow us to close the gap between our experienced competitors and ourselves." Moreover, Bakke quickly came to believe that bureaucracy and hierarchy were incompatible with the values to which he and Sant aspired. As soon as the plant opened, they began discussing alternative systems of organization and structure. The first real inspiration for change came when Bakke sat in on a worker policy committee meeting while visiting the Deepwater plant during one of his annual "executive work weeks."[10] Bakke recalled the meeting:

> The group was trying to decide how much time should be given to employees who had a death in the family. They naturally began to get into all sorts of complications. What if the parent's funeral was overseas? What if the "parent" who died wasn't a natural parent but an uncle or an aunt or a foster parent?

---

[10]All senior executives were expected to spend at least one week each year working with technicians at one of the company's plants.

Feeling frustrated by the implications of so many policies and rules, Bakke started asking people what would happen if they got rid of the formal structures. He suggested that the group rethink the entire way they worked together and assured them that the group in Arlington would be willing to entertain any approach they came up with, even if it meant throwing out the personnel handbooks.

Six weeks later, the Deepwater plant people announced their restructuring. The approach, which was modeled on the ideas of Bill Arnold, the plant manager, had workers organized into "families," e.g., a turbine family, a coal-pile family, and a scrubber family. The purpose of these "honeycomb" families, each with 10 to 20 members and a leader, was to create self-sufficient communities which could police and organize themselves, deciding their own leave policy, for example. Eventually, all AES plants adopted the honeycomb system. Even the activities of the approximately 75 people at corporate headquarters in Arlington were honeycombed.

Employee Responsibility and Authority According to Bakke, one of the main advantages of the honeycomb structure was better alignment between responsibility and knowledge. Responsibility for personnel management, capital budgeting, and purchasing was returned to the plant floor where knowledge about needs and resources was greatest. Bakke suggested to all plant managers and workers when designing their organizational structures that, like headquarters, they have no central budgeting organization, no personnel department, and no safety, environmental, or engineering departments. According to Bakke, if an activity was important to the strategic or values orientation of the firm, there should be no separate organization to manage it.

In almost all cases, plant families *did* do all hiring, purchasing, maintenance and safety inspections themselves. A prerequisite for this form of operations was that all employees be willing to serve on special projects and task forces. At corporate headquarters, the honeycomb influence was reflected in the use of team-based project management techniques. All permitting, engineering, construction, public relations, and financing activities, for example, were managed as team projects. Membership on these teams changed periodically although an individual in charge of some strategic planning project might remain as team leader for several years.

Movement to the honeycomb structure eliminated a number of management levels. In 1993, there were no more than three layers of management between entry-level employees and the chief executive officer. In most plants there were only two. (See Thames's organization chart in **Exhibit 6.**) The company had also attempted to eliminate all separating distinctions such as hourly versus salary or maintenance versus operators.

The Thames Plant

One of the plants with the most developed honeycomb philosophy was the Thames plant in northern Connecticut. At Thames, members of families routinely

EXHIBIT 6
AES Thames Plant Organization Chart[a]

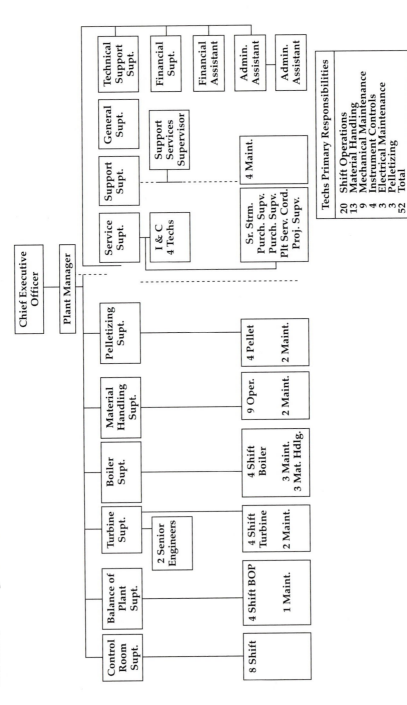

Source: Company documents.

[a]This chart was prepared by Thames workers for external and communications use only. Workers did not use the chart for management.

learned each others' jobs and occasionally switched off to keep themselves interested and challenged. Workers were also encouraged to switch across families to expand their range of skills. Bob Price, an AES Thames plant superintendent, summed up the organizational philosophy with these points:

- No employee handbooks, manuals, or rules (except safety).
- No operating, maintenance, or technical departments.
- No shift supervisors, or maintenance supervisors.
- No staff except for financial.
- No "turf."

According to Price, employee initiative was not just rewarded; it was expected. At the Thames plant, an employee needing a tool was expected to go to the local store and buy it using a corporate credit card. No permission was required. No spending limits were set. When a $30,000 hydraulic pump broke, the employee who discovered the problem called suppliers and authorized the repair. He notified his supervisor only after the fact. Employees also authorized their own overtime at Thames. Workers' authority extended even to the firing of subcontractors for safety violations. Visitors at the Thames plant were often told about the employee who found a subcontractor seriously violating safety precautions. The employee did not report the infractions to his supervisor or ask permission. He simply escorted the subcontractor to the plant gates and dismissed him. His manager bragged about the behavior.

The "We/They" Boundaries   Although most employees were sympathetic to the initial organizational change efforts, some doubted that the new culture was anything more than rhetoric. Building the new culture proved especially difficult in the company's retro-fitted Beaver Valley plant. When AES purchased the Beaver Valley plant in 1985, it inherited a unionized work force which was more than a little suspicious of AES's stated values. "AES values or not," they said, "as soon as profits go south, you'll treat us just as badly as every other executive has."[11] To convince the workers of their commitment, Bakke, Sant, and other executives began to spend more time working in the plant itself, improving their understanding of the people and actual operations. Often, if they asked why an operator performed a task in a particularly inefficient way, they would hear, "They make us." In his book, *Adhocracy: The Power to Change,* author Robert H. Waterman, one of AES's board members, described the "we/they" assault.

> A loose coalition . . . led by executive vice president Bob Hemphill moved fast to rout the spectral enemy. One day everyone in the company got a ceramic coffee cup in the mail with the words WHO IS THEY ANYWAY? baked into the glaze. They began a barrage of patches, lapel buttons, Post-it notes, and sheriff's badges. All had the word "they" covered by a circle with a line through it—the international don't-do-it symbol. . . . Shortly thereafter a difficult labor negotiation was disrupted by the sound of "gunfire." Four men—dressed in combat gear and carrying mock rifles—stormed the room with THEY patches sewn all over their fatigues. The guerrilla band, which called itself the Anti-They Liberation Front, turned out to be four of the company's senior officers (p. 77).

---

[11]Quoted in R.H. Waterman, *Adhocracy: The Power to Change* (New York: W.W. Norton, 1992).

Internal Measurement and Communications   AES executives believed strongly that if the decentralized structures were to be effective, people had to have access to information. A critical part of headquarters' job was to supply the information about environmental policies, laws, and innovation necessary to support the plant's honeycomb decision-making process. To facilitate still more communication, AES also invested heavily in the development of internal measurement and assessment systems. These systems focused on measuring the state of such operating conditions as environmental performance, safety, plant efficiency and daily levels of availability, sales backlogs, and generating cost/kilowatt hour. While the intent of these systems was to provide data useful for managing the plants, they also served as vehicles for enhancing communications within and across operating plants. To capture impressions of corporate values, AES conducted an annual survey of employees, customers, shareholders, and government and communications representatives. (See **Exhibit 7** for excerpts from the AES employee survey.) All these survey results and routine measurement data were made available to any employee on an "as wanted" basis. The company published its monthly financial reports in the corporate newsletter. From the perspective of the Securities and Exchange Commission (SEC), all employees were considered corporate "insiders."

The distribution of information was complemented by regular plant policy and planning sessions which—like the company's yearly strategic planning sessions—were open to all employees regardless of rank or tenure. In these meetings, workers from around the country discussed how priorities should be established, how tradeoffs between priorities should be evaluated, and how corporate values and profitability levels could both be strengthened. At AES's Thames plant, for example, workers met regularly to review their plant's performance along six critical dimensions: cost, safety, adherence to corporate values, housekeeping (cleanliness), environmental performance, and efficiency.

Values Training   During the "pre-startup" phase of every new plant, all people at all levels of the organization would participate in a three- or four-month training program. Two of the main subjects were company values and culture. Employees hired after the startup viewed videos of Sant and Bakke explaining the corporate philosophy and values within the first few weeks on the job. Within a year of joining the company, new employees and their spouses attended an orientation at corporate headquarters where again the corporate values, history, and philosophies were discussed with Sant, Bakke, and other corporate leaders.

Compensation and Hiring   To reinforce the corporate ideal that all workers were responsible decision makers, AES had adopted a compensation plan which salaried all employees to the extent permitted by law. Merit bonuses of up to $5,000 per person were allotted by a worker-led committee. (See **Exhibit 8** for Shady Point's bonus allocation criteria.) While plant performance dominated the bonus allocation process, individual performance evaluations were used to determine annual salary increases. All AES employees were also participants in the company's employee stock ownership or "wealth-sharing" program.

Exhibit 7 Excerpts From AES Employee Values Survey

9. Below is a list of words and phrases which people use to describe companies. For each word or phrase, please respond to how well it describes AES.

	Very Well	Pretty Well	Not Too Well	Not Well At All	Don't Know
Friendly	1	2	3	4	5
Arrogant	1	2	3	4	5
Shares my values	1	2	3	4	5
Environmentally minded	1	2	3	4	5
Is growing too fast	1	2	3	4	5
Compassionate	1	2	3	4	5
Honest	1	2	3	4	5
Makes significant contributions to the community	1	2	3	4	5
Cares less about promoting values than they used to	1	2	3	4	5
Is socially responsible	1	2	3	4	5
Makes people feel like they are part of a team	1	2	3	4	5
Has fostered a good relationship with its customers	1	2	3	4	5
Is only concerned with making a profit	1	2	3	4	5
Trustworthy	1	2	3	4	5
Fun	1	2	3	4	5
Is generous when it comes to salaries and benefits	1	2	3	4	5
Has integrity	1	2	3	4	5
Works hard to protect the environment	1	2	3	4	5
Is a company where people communicate well with each other	1	2	3	4	5
Has fostered a good relationship with its contractors	1	2	3	4	5
Has fostered a good relationship with environmental groups	1	2	3	4	5
Fair	1	2	3	4	5
Is taking on too much risk	1	2	3	4	5

10. Below is the stated AES value of fun. Please rate what kind of job AES is doing in supporting this value.

	Excellent	Good	Fair	Poor	Don't Know
We work because the work is fun, fulfilling and exciting and when it stops being that way we will change what or how we do things.	1	2	3	4	5
We want an environment where people can grow and develop by using their gifts and skills to the maximum extent possible.	1	2	3	4	5
We try to decentralize the authority and responsibility for getting a job done to the level of the person actually doing the work.	1	2	3	4	5

EXHIBIT 7   **Continued**

---

14. Below is the stated AES value of fairness. Please rate what kind of job AES is doing in supporting this value.

	Excellent	Good	Fair	Poor	Don't Know
We do not try to get the most out of a deal at the cost of being unfair to a customer, supplier, or related party.	1	2	3	4	5
We believe that a basic ability to put ourselves in the other person's position is essential.	1	2	3	4	5
We treat each other with respect and dignity and with sensitivity to each person's unique need and situation. We treat customers and other groups with which we interact as AES would want to be treated.	1	2	3	4	5
In dealing with others, either inside or outside the company, we try to ask, "Am I being fair on this issue?"	1	2	3	4	5

18. Below is the state AES value of integrity. Please rate what kind of job AES is doing in supporting this value.

	Excellent	Good	Fair	Poor	Don't Know
With AES people and non-AES people alike, we live with our agreements and statements written or orally communicated, even if it hurts the company economically.	1	2	3	4	5
Our organization and commitment are sufficiently strong that our people, our customers, and other business associates can rely on our performance.	1	2	3	4	5

22. Below is the stated AES value of social responsibility. Please rate what kind of job AES is doing in supporting this value.

	Excellent	Good	Fair	Poor	Don't Know
We feel we have a responsibility to be involved in projects that provide such social benefits as low costs to our customers, a high degree of safety and reliability, increased employment, the most appropriate environmental controls, and a nurturing environment.	1	2	3	4	5

Source: Adapted from company documents.

EXHIBIT 8

AES Shady Point Plant Bonus System

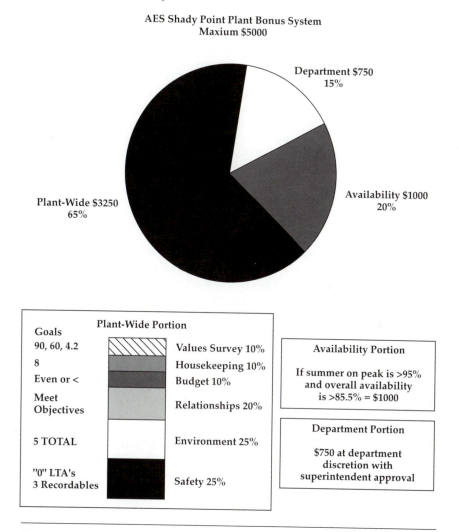

AES Shady Point Plant Bonus System
Maxium $5000

Department $750
15%

Availability $1000
20%

Plant-Wide $3250
65%

Plant-Wide Portion

Goals
90, 60, 4.2
8
Even or <
Meet
Objectives

5 TOTAL

"0" LTA's
3 Recordables

Values Survey 10%
Housekeeping 10%
Budget 10%
Relationships 20%
Environment 25%
Safety 25%

Availability Portion

If summer on peak is >95%
and overall availability
is >85.5% = $1000

Department Portion

$750 at department
discretion with
superintendent approval

Source: Company documents.

In most AES plants, hiring was a long, involved process. At Thames, it could often take up to six months. Emphasis was placed on finding a person who could support and "fit" the corporate culture. The field of applicants, sometimes as large as 400 people, was narrowed by a series of interviews conducted first over the phone, then with a family leader, then with the family hiring team. Interview sessions were organized around a series of questions designed to capture information on the applicant's communications skills, flexibility, willingness to work in teams and on administrative task forces, cultural attitudes, and attitudes towards work and self-improvement generally.

When the applicant set had been reduced to one or two individuals, Thames' plant manager would initiate a final interview. The point of the meeting was not to review the candidate's credentials but rather to "sell" the AES culture. AES executives believed firmly that all prospective AES people should have a clear and complete understanding of life at AES before joining the firm. Almost every AES person had to work his or her way up through the corporation. It was not uncommon for people with graduate degrees to start their AES careers shifting coal. People who resented this sort of work, who needed a structured, supervised environment, or who would not participate in team or task-force efforts would have difficulty surviving at AES.

Thames's hiring process resulted in the selection of large numbers of talented, achievement-oriented people. Plant workers recognized that part of their hiring success was due to the high educational standards in the Connecticut area and to the proximity of federal naval bases which served as an important source of experienced and highly skilled engineers. As a group, these individuals often had more than the average number of career opportunities. Consequently, the risk of people leaving AES for higher-paying or more prestigious jobs was high. However, when asked why he had turned down two offers of better-paying, more intellectually creative work to sweep floors at AES, one employee mentioned both the value of AES stock and the culture of individual responsibility. "You'll look over your shoulder to ask permission," he said, "and there's nobody there. And, I feel free to admit it honestly if I do screw up." He added, "You know what's really unusual about this place? Everybody shakes hands when they come to work in the morning."

Social Responsibility and Community Involvement

AES's corporate leaders actively encouraged workers and plant communities to adhere to the company's code of social responsibility, and as a whole, the corporation was active in developing technologies and operating methods that were cleaner than the traditional. The reliability and safety levels of AES's plants exceeded industry averages in every case. Emission levels of sulfur dioxides and nitrous oxides averaged 37% below the company's own permitted levels and 53% below the federal government's New Source Performance Standards. Plant availability, measured as the percentage of plant time available for generation, had increased from 88% in 1991 to 93% in 1992. In that same year, the Placerita, California, plant had operated at 100% availability during its peak periods, a feat the company had not expected nor promised to repeat. Because of increasing volume levels and enhanced cost controls, the company's cost effectiveness levels were also above industry standards. In 1992, average costs per kilowatt hour decreased 4% over the previous year, with one plant realizing a 10% decrease. (See **Exhibit 9** for the company's power availability levels and environmental and safety performance.)

When AES built its fourth plant, the Thames plant, in Montville, Connecticut, the company predicted that it would be the cleanest coal-burning facility in New England, with sulfur emissions 75% below EPA standards. Technology could not

EXHIBIT 9

AES Power Availability, Environmental, and Safety Performance

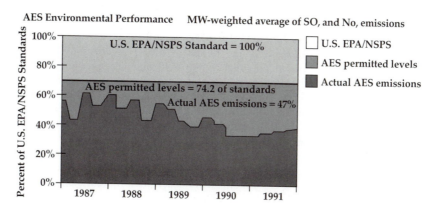

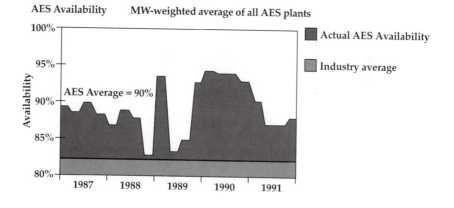

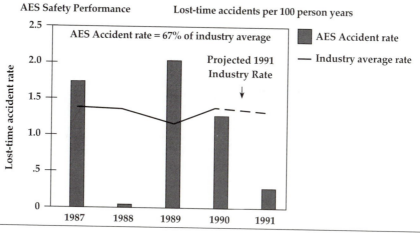

Source: Company documents.

take care of all the plant's emissions, however, so the company began to search for other unique solutions. In 1988, AES decided to implement its brainstorm: it would plant trees. With the assistance of the World Resources Institute (WRI), a Washington, D.C. research and policy group, AES calculated that it would take 52 million trees to absorb the 14 million tons of carbon dioxide gas the plant would generate during its 40 years in operation. With additional assistance from the Peace Corps, AES located an established reforestation project run by CARE in the village of Guachipilin, Guatemala. Planting began in 1989 and was coordinated by CARE with a $2 million grant from AES.

In 1991, AES initiated a similar program in Paraguay to offset the emissions of its plant in Oahu, Hawaii. In 1992, the company announced that it would donate $3 million to an Oxfam project to preserve the rain forests in the Northern Amazon region to offset the carbon dioxide emissions of its Shady Point plant. By 1992, carbon dioxide offsets were a standard aspect of AES power projects.

1992: A Year of Challenges

AES's 1992 letter to shareholders opened with the following words:

> Dear Fellow Shareholders:
>
> This was a year of testing for AES. We entered our second decade as a company with a year of outstanding performance in many arenas, but were challenged by other actions that fell well short of our standards for adherence to values and nurturing relationships. The words of a popular country song seem to fit our view of 1992: "Sometimes you're the windshield, sometimes you're the bug."

The company's troubles revolved around events in Jacksonville, Florida, where AES had been negotiating the development of the Cedar Bay plant with local and state officials, and at AES's Shady Point plant in Oklahoma.

Events at Cedar Bay   Since early 1991, AES had been involved in the development of the $485 million Cedar Bay plant. In May of 1992, construction was half completed when the project was abruptly threatened. Florida officials and local residents were protesting the company's state permit, complaining that AES had misrepresented the extent of its activities and led the public to believe, inaccurately, that it would use natural gas as an alternative to coal. Construction was halted while the Governor's Council on Power Plant Siting initiated permit review proceedings.

One of the community's chief concerns revolved around AES's ability to serve the energy requirements of a local company which had previously relied on five old, environmentally unfriendly boilers. A local environmental group claimed that AES's permit to build had been granted with the understanding that these boilers would be permanently closed. AES officials contested the group's claim, saying they had never planned to eliminate these boilers entirely. On the contrary, AES had intended to help the local company apply for a new permit and recondition the boilers to reduce emissions and alleviate their noxious odor.

The confusion and political debate drew national attention when local news stories were picked up by the news wire services. Although AES maintained the legality of its position and denied any attempts to consciously mislead the public, the company's share value fell from around $33 per share to $26 per share. The company's agent bank withdrew its financing when the political situation reached what it considered "untenable" levels. Finally, AES abandoned its efforts and sold the project to another developer.

The Shady Point Incident   As the Cedar Bay episode was coming to a head, AES officials publicly disclosed news of employee fraud at one of the company's newest and largest plants: AES Shady Point, located in Poteau, Oklahoma. On Thursday, June 18, 1992, AES officials filed notice with the Environmental Protection Agency (EPA) that a number of Shady Point employees in the plant's water treatment area, normally staffed by six or seven people, had been falsifying federally required reports on the quality of the facility's wastewater discharge for over a year. Rather than identifying and solving the cause of the water contamination, the group had simply diluted the discharge samples. It was estimated that the dilution had occurred on average two to four times each month and had involved nearly a dozen people over the course of the year due to turnover and promotions. The fraud was discovered in the summer of 1992 by Shady Point's assistant plant manager when one of the new water treaters forgot to cover up his dilutions.

Unsure of how best to communicate the news, senior executives decided not to issue a press release immediately and delayed communicating with other AES people until the following Sunday, June 21. Late Tuesday morning, encouraged by financial analysts who had heard rumors of the event, Sant and Bakke personally wrote a press release which was issued with copies of the internal letters distributed to AES people. (See **Exhibit 10** for a copy of the release.)

When asked about the event, Bill Arnold, who had moved from the Deepwater plant to become Shady Point's plant manager, suggested that the matter was partly the result of carrying the honeycomb idea too far. Although one of the inventors and proponents of the honeycomb system at the Texas plant, Arnold did not believe that such a loose organizational structure was appropriate for every organization. He noted that the workers employed at Shady Point tended to have very different professional and educational backgrounds than those at the Thames plant which he described as the "AES values showcase." Arnold also pointed out that Oklahoma was one of the highest welfare states in the country and that the Shady Point plant was located in one of the state's poorest counties.

Arnold believed that in this situation a more structured reporting situation could have provided the shareholder protection which was warranted. In fact, he argued that the Shady Point people might have developed a much more traditional and formal structure had they not already been compared unfavorably with the more "honeycombed" AES plants like Thames. After the EPA episode came to light, workers *did* revise the organizational structure creating specific human resource, technical, environmental, and operations functions, and adding a new layer of supervision. Those responsible for these functions reported directly to the plant manager.

EXHIBIT 10   AES Press Release—June 23, 1992

FOR IMMEDIATE RELEASE

For: The AES Corporation   Contact: Robert F. Hemphill, Jr.
        1001 N. 19th Street   (703) 522–1315
        Arlington, VA 22209

Arlington, VA, June 23, 1992   The AES Corporation (NASDAQ-AESC) today released the attached letter which had previously been sent to shareholders and people at AES. The Company does not believe that there will be any material/financial impact from this matter.

Sunday, June 21, 1992

Dear Shareholders and People of AES:

Some disappointing news has just come to our attention which, consistent with our values, we felt we should share with you at the earliest opportunity. On Thursday, June 18, we notified the Environmental Protection Administration [sic] (EPA) and the State of Oklahoma that we had discovered in an internal review that some water discharge reports have been falsified at the AES Shady Point Plant in Oklahoma. While our investigation is continuing, these are the facts as we understand them today.

From January 15, 1991 to the middle of April 1992, a portion of the AES people working in the water treatment family at Shady Point doctored a number of water discharge samples so that violations of the NPDES (National Pollution Discharge Elimination System) permit would not have to be reported. The primary exceedences were sulfates and acid concentrations. To our knowledge no damage resulted to the Poteau River and the local environment.

It appears that no one in the management structure outside of the water treatment area was aware of these violations. The people involved say that they falsified the samples because they feared for their jobs if they reported a violation. Yet no one at AES has ever lost his or her job for telling the truth, nor will they ever, as long as we have anything to say about it.

This answer is hard to understand because these were the sort of minor excursions to be expected during the first year of operation of a new plant. Since discovering violations, we have adjusted operating procedures and are adding new equipment so that it should be highly unlikely for such exceedences to occur in the future.

This is a very serious breach of the law and our own values. Nevertheless, we have provided job security to the technicians involved in order to ascertain the facts from those people as quickly as possible. We are not certain that this was the right thing to do and we are reviewing this policy in case a similar situation occurs in the future.

What disappoints us most is that no one mentions these violations in either of the two confidential and anonymous values surveys that were conducted at Shady Point during the time this was going on.

Clearly making false reports is a practice that cannot be tolerated. Accordingly, we have taken the following steps:

1. The technicians who are determined to have been involved in falsifying the samples will be subject to sanctions to include: being placed on probation; salary reduction of 50% for three months; and transfer out of the water treating section in to entry level positions elsewhere in the plant. They will also be required to complete a course on ethical behavior on their own time during the three month period.

2. An external Environmental Auditor will be selected and appointed to audit environmental compliance company wide. Each plant will be audited annually.

3. We have established an Environmental Audit Committee of the AES Board of Directors to provide oversight for all AES environmental reporting. They will also make suggestions as to any other steps we should take besides the ones we are reporting today. The Committee will be chaired by Russell Train, AES Board member and former Administrator of the EPA, and all of the outside directors will be members.

4. We already have in process a company-wide training program which includes a section on compliance with the law. This section of the training will be strengthened.

5. At a meeting we hope to have with the EPA this week, we will discuss the results of our investigation and findings to date. We will also inform the EPA of the other steps outlined above that we have taken.

This action raises serious questions in our minds about our performance relative to our values. One of the founding tenets of this Company is the shared values. We thought we had explained our values enough to everyone in AES that this sort of thing could never happen here. We are trying to treat people like adults, trusting in their honesty, judgment, maturity and professionalism—rather than relying on detailed procedures, manuals, and minute supervisory oversight. We cannot comprehend why anyone would trade our integrity to make our environmental performance look better. We hope that the steps we have taken today address the problem, but are embarrassed and disappointed and angry that this could have happened in AES.

This letter only describes our initial understanding of the situation and we will keep you informed as additional facts are learned or events occur.

Sincerely,

Roger W. Sant
Chairman and CEO

Dennis W. Bakke
President and COO

Describing the Shady Point version of honeycomb, Arnold said

> I suggested and argued for the honeycomb idea at the Deepwater plant because I know that families typically do a wonderful job of managing themselves. But of course not all families manage themselves in the same way. Here at Shady Point the families themselves decide how they want their organization to run. Not me and not corporate headquarters. They decided to have more layers of bureaucracy here than at Thames because nobody wants an ex-cashier or former video store clerk running the control room without someone to turn to when they need assistance or advice. You need a seasoned, experienced person in charge to protect the assets of the corporation. Shareholders pay for them. They should get what they contract for.

Honeycomb at Shady Point   In certain respects, operations of the Shady Point plant were markedly different from those at Thames. For example, the 120 workers at Shady Point had decided not to encourage rotations across families as they did at Thames, arguing that workers would feel more secure if they were allowed to remain in a single job and learn it well.

According to Bakke, the results of the values survey at Shady Point were also somewhat different than elsewhere. Compared to other plants, workers were more likely to cite good pay as their reason for liking their job. Many also seemed uncomfortable with the Shady Point "structure." (See **Exhibits 11** and **12** for Shady Point and company results of AES Values Survey.) Few Shady Point people had had experience working in a power plant. According to Bill Arnold, it was not surprising that they would have difficulty adjusting to the demanding technical tasks they faced in the plant. It was also true that many came from jobs in service or sales where wage rates were significantly lower. The average hourly wage of these workers had more than doubled from $6/hour to $13/hour.

Hiring at Shady Point was also much less elaborate than at Thames. Each family managed its own hiring practices. There was no formal plantwide hiring practice per se. According to Arnold, a family would typically announce its job opening within AES first. If there was no response, the announcement would be placed in local newspapers. Interviewing schedules varied within the families and rarely involved people outside of the area itself. Bill Arnold might not even meet the new hire until he or she had been on the job for several months.

Despite the differences in hiring and organizational practices, Shady Point was similar to all other AES plants in its devotion to community service and the corporate ethic of social responsibility. Shady Point workers, many of whom lived in or near the plant in Poteau, Oklahoma, were active in a variety of community activities and groups and had initiated such community projects as the renovation of a senior citizens center.

Social responsibility was practiced at the plantwide level as well. One of the larger plant projects involved the construction of an elementary school for the neighboring town of Panama. Early in 1992, Shady Point people learned that the second of two bond elections held to finance the construction of a new school had been defeated. In May of that year, Shady Point announced that it would pay the $1.5 million necessary for development. The workers' stated intent was to compensate the town for the traffic problems caused by the company's fleet of trucks, almost 200 of which passed through local neighborhoods each day. When asked to elaborate on the purpose of the donation at the ground-breaking ceremonies, Arnold replied simply, "We're trying to be a good neighbor."

EXHIBIT 11

AES Shady Point Values Survey: Results 1991

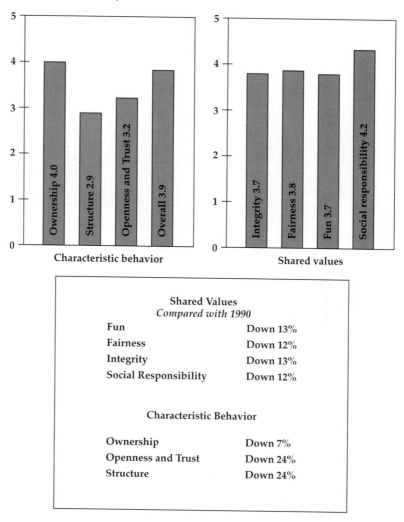

<table>
<tr><td colspan="2">Shared Values
Compared with 1990</td></tr>
<tr><td>Fun</td><td>Down 13%</td></tr>
<tr><td>Fairness</td><td>Down 12%</td></tr>
<tr><td>Integrity</td><td>Down 13%</td></tr>
<tr><td>Social Responsibility</td><td>Down 12%</td></tr>
<tr><td colspan="2">Characteristic Behavior</td></tr>
<tr><td>Ownership</td><td>Down 7%</td></tr>
<tr><td>Openness and Trust</td><td>Down 24%</td></tr>
<tr><td>Structure</td><td>Down 24%</td></tr>
</table>

Source: Company documents.

The Incident in Context Given his past experience with the industry and operating conditions, Arnold believed that the EPA incident itself was minor. The EPA fines had totaled only $125,000 and, in fact, there had been no contamination to the Poteau River. According to Arnold, most people in the firm were more concerned with AES's values and culture than with the EPA violation itself.

For some time, the Shady Point plant had been an item of concern for Bakke, who believed the honeycomb culture there was inadequately developed. Because of the complications and complexities of opening the plant, Shady Point leaders

EXHIBIT 12

AES Values Survey: Results 1991

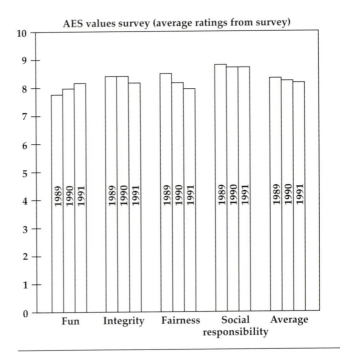

AES values survey (average ratings from survey)

Source: AES Corporation 1991 Annual Report.

had not invested heavily in AES values training nor had they worked actively to develop a "Thames" style of management, choosing instead to let the workers democratically decide their preferred methods of organization.

Months before the EPA violations were uncovered, Arnold had hired one of the Thames supervisors to be Assistant Plant Manager (APM) at Shady Point and to assist Arnold in both managing the plant and developing a stronger honeycomb ethic. Arnold was then preoccupied with development issues, public utility commission proceedings concerning the plant's electrical contract, and a ratepayers' lawsuit brought against AES Shady Point and OGE (Oklahoma Gas & Electric). As a result, he had had little opportunity to work directly with the Shady Point families. According to Arnold, the APM's efforts to "talk up AES values" and to encourage job and family rotations had met with a moderate level of worker resistance. When complaints were lodged with Arnold, he had asked the APM to "back off" the project. While Arnold believed strongly in the philosophy underlying honeycomb, he did not believe that the Thames interpretation of honeycomb was essential to the maintenance of AES's values. He said:

> We believe in the values of social responsibility and integrity here at Shady Point. That's obvious in the work we do here with the community. But I don't believe the

corporation should interpret these values and the form of an organization for their workers. When we talk about values here we talk about what it means to be socially responsible, what it means to contribute to the community, and what it means to be "a good person." I don't believe that the structure of the company has anything to do with whether or not workers respect these values. You get good and bad people in any corporation regardless of structure. We try to support people's best intentions here and we try to give them the resources to follow through on them. But that has nothing to do with how many organizational or reporting levels we have.

Shareholder Reactions   When news of the Shady Point incident was released, the capital markets reacted dramatically. Share values fell again, this time from $26.50 to $16.50. This one-day fall eliminated over $400 million worth of corporate market value. Financial analysts actively chided management both for failing to transmit news of the event sooner and for failing to provide fuller details on its long-term ramifications. One analyst remembered being shocked by the suddenness of the event and wondering whether the company had been "blowing smoke" about its values. "I remember wondering if this "problem" was limited to the employees in the water treatment area or if management were also involved," he said. "Obviously, I wasn't the only one with that concern. Some of the people who sold their stock after the news had been behind the company from the very start. They'd become fabulously rich off of their investment but they wanted out now."

When Sant and Bakke queried investors and analysts about the dramatic reaction, they discovered that their firm had developed a reputation both for arrogance and naiveté. On the advice of a conservative securities law firm, AES had maintained a certain aloofness from analysts and shareholders generally. One analyst, describing AES's attitudes as "holier than thou," said:

> They acted as if they didn't need us. They talked about corporate values and their responsibilities towards employees but what about their responsibilities towards shareholders? Most shareholders today are pensioners. The value of AES stock determines their income. Why should retired New York State police officers be second to employees? We put a lot of faith in the firm despite its attitudes and bid up the price of the stock probably higher than we should. This seemed like a slap in the face. We felt fooled.

AES's outside legal counsel and investment bankers also reacted vigorously to the news, advising Bakke and Sant to reorganize the corporation and revamp internal controls. They recommended that the company hire an environmental control specialist and a corporate general counsel who could implement a legal compliance program. Analysts urged Sant and Bakke to drop the values emphasis unless they were willing to show how the values helped the bottom line.

A Mandate for Change

Several weeks after the public disclosure, Roger Sant decided to call a special session of the company's officers. He hoped that together the officers could develop a plan to prevent any future threat to the stability of the company's assets and reputation. Sant knew, however, that Bakke would oppose any dramatic change in the company's organizational structure and culture.

Bakke, the leading candidate to succeed Sant as CEO, saw the company's structure as inextricably linked to its values. Any move toward centralized staff control was for him a move away from personal accountability on the front lines of the organization. He was convinced that broad discretion and autonomy were critical to employees' well-being and their ability to have fun on the job. Bakke was already disturbed by Shady Point's move to greater hierarchy, and he was adamantly opposed to the compliance programs which many competitors were adopting in response to new laws on organizational sentencing. "I'll go to jail," he said, "rather than do something so inconsistent with everything we believe in."

In earlier consultations with the officers, Sant and Bob Hemphill, a senior vice president, had identified five options for the group to consider. They were:

1. To hire a senior level officer to direct and control the various operating plants.
2. To split plant operations into two groups, one of which would be directed by Bill Arnold, the other by Dave McMillan, plant manager at AES Thames. (As officers of the corporation, both would attend this special session.)
3. To divide all of the company into separate divisions, each of which would be run by a division manager responsible both for operations and development and reporting to the office of the CEO. Shady Point and Thames, the company's largest plants, would be stand-alone operations.
4. To divisionalize all of the company plants, including Shady Point and Thames. Under this scenario, the division managers would be installed as presidents of these largely independent companies.
5. To maintain the status quo.

Also on the agenda was the question of whether to establish and fill positions for a corporate general counsel and for staff specialists in environmental compliance, safety, human resources, public relations, and shareholder relations.

The action items on the agenda reflected a deeper issue troubling some AES senior managers: Should AES rethink its values and operating style or perhaps abandon them altogether for a more traditional approach to business and organizational management? A vote to add a new layer of management and to hire corporate staff to introduce traditional control systems seemed to some a vote against everything AES stood for.

III MAINTAINING ORGANIZATIONAL INTEGRITY
Critical Decisions

The effort to build and maintain organizational integrity must be an on-going and integral part of the management process. Leadership, an ethical framework, and appropriate organizational systems are essential. As seen in Part II, these set direction and establish the necessary background conditions. But in the final analysis, organizational integrity depends on the decisions made by individuals and groups throughout a company. Unless these decision makers have the attitudes, skills, and knowledge needed to make decisions that are ethically sound, organizational integrity will be a haphazard achievement at best.

Part III focuses on the reasoning processes and perspectives associated with responsible decision making. Each case in this segment presents a high-stakes decision involving complex ethical issues interwoven with important strategic, organizational, and financial issues. In these situations, managers must make tough, politically-sensitive choices—often under intense time pressure. In the face of disputed facts, ill-defined standards, conflicting responsibilities, or ambiguous authority, they must take decisive action. In these cases, integrity is less a matter of choosing right over wrong and more a matter of charting a responsible course through a thicket of conflict and ambiguity. What decision makers need in such situations is a reliable process for identifying, analyzing, and integrating relevant considerations into a sound decision.

The framework sketched below outlines such a process. Based on three traditional modes of practical reasoning, the framework provides a set of lenses for viewing complex choices such as those presented in the cases in this segment. These lenses throw into sharp relief three critical dimensions of responsible decisions: their contribution to *purpose*, their consistency with *principle*, and their impact on *people*. Each lens highlights certain facts, norms, and decision criteria.

This framework is intended to integrate and supplement rather than replace the many specialized frameworks used in business decision making. It serves to illuminate the ethical blind spots inherent in many commonly used frameworks, but it presupposes mastery of essential analytical tools such as those used in finance, marketing, and strategic planning. Managers need frameworks that facilitate both economic and ethical understanding. In many situations, it is impossible to identify, let alone analyze, the ethical dimensions of a decision without a thorough understanding of its economics. Similarly, the economic outcome of a decision often reflects assessments of its ethical qualities.

Of course, decision making is not only an analytical exercise. Deciding is essentially a creative act, ideally reflecting both analysis and imagination. The framework presented below is intended as a stimulus for both. As background for considering the framework in more detail, a brief look at some common blind spots will illustrate the value of having a decision process infused with the ethical point of view.

Ethical Blind Spots

Many commonly used decision frameworks fail to capture important ethical and social dimensions of managerial problems and consequently lead to less than optimal choices. Often the problem lies less in the logic of the decision model than in its practical application. Consider, for example, cost-benefit analysis, a method often used in business decision making to evaluate the advantages and disadvantages of alternative options for action. In theory, cost-benefit analysis can capture the full range of potential consequences for all affected parties, including both monetary and nonmonetary impacts. In practice, however, the method is often used with a focus only on the costs and benefits for the actor, with greater attention to factors that can be readily priced and with more emphasis on immediate rather than remote, but important, consequences.

Harms and Wrongs

Decisions based on this method are particularly vulnerable to ethical challenge since the method does not readily distinguish between harms caused by legitimate activities and those resulting from infringements of ethical principle. Yet, there is an important difference between, for example, harming a competitor by introducing a superior product and harming a competitor by making false claims of superiority—even if the dollar impact is the same in both cases. The latter case, but not the former, involves a violation of a basic ethical obligation to avoid intentional deceit. In many jurisdictions, it is unlawful as well.

The rationale for the distinction between these behaviors lies in their social value and consequences. Introducing a superior product creates value for customers, for the product's producers, and for society. Beating out a competitor through false claims of superiority cheats customers, diminishes trust in commercial communications, and leads to a misallocation of society's resources.

When using frameworks that focus exclusively on the cash value of alternatives, decision makers are vulnerable to underestimating or even overlooking altogether the ethical principles implicit in their behavior. This failure often has consequences. As former U.S. Supreme Court Justice Oliver Wendell Holmes, Jr., once pointed out, even a dog knows the difference between being kicked and being tripped over. This difference can have a dramatic impact on the dog's reaction. Yet, it will not be apparent to someone who takes the veterinarian's bill as the sole measure of the dog's injuries. While quite important, the financial information contained in the bill contributes little to our understanding of how the situation arose or how it might be avoided in the future.

Thinkers with mathematical inclinations have long sought a method for quantifying, if not monetizing, the harm involved in wrongdoing such as fraud and other breaches of duty. Jeremy Bentham, the 19th-century British philosopher and advocate of a utilitarian approach to ethics, hoped for a fully rational calculus of pleasure and pain that would allow actions to be evaluated according to a single unified scale.

Whatever the ultimate feasibility or desirability of such a project, a ready methodology for quantifying or pricing the damage resulting from wrongful behavior is yet to be devised. But there is no doubt that such damage is real, leading to undesirable consequences not only for victims but in some cases for wrongdoers as well. Ironically, the consequences can even be costly in monetary terms. In many instances, such behavior also undermines social trust, an essential resource needed for effective collaboration in every sphere of human endeavor.[1] Quantifying the positive value of ethically conscientious behavior is equally problematic, though such value is widely acknowledged. Presumably, this value explains why the behavior has come to be regarded as "good."

The dangers of overlooking considerations of principle can be seen in the case of the food company executive who allowed his company to continue selling bottled fruit juice labeled "100 percent pure" and marketed as "all natural" after discovering the juice was being made from phony ingredients fraudulently supplied by a vendor. From company documents and testimony presented later at trial, it appears that the

---

[1]The role of social trust in creating economic prosperity is discussed in Francis Fukuyama, *Trust* (New York: The Free Press, 1995).

decision was based primarily on short-term cost considerations. According to an internal memo, the company's objectives were "To minimize . . . potential economic loss . . . conservatively estimated at $3.5 million (the cost of destroying unused inventory); and to minimize any damage to the company's reputation."[2]

Considerations of principle apparently played no part in the decision process. There was no evidence that decision makers considered their obligations to consumers and the public, the dishonesty involved in selling the juice as "100 percent pure," the possible harm to purchasers or users (such as diabetic babies), or the relevant laws prohibiting sales of adulterated and mislabeled products. The decision to continue sales ultimately led to criminal and civil suits against the company and its executives, resulting in financial costs of some $25 million, unquantified reputational costs, and serious personal cost to everyone involved. Five years after the incident became public, the company was still trying to restore consumers' trust and regain market share.

To insure that issues of ethical principle are included in their decision process, managers are well advised to focus on these issues explicitly. While making every appropriate use of quantitative and other analytical techniques, managers should not assume that such techniques alone will tell them all they need to know to make sound decisions. Directly considering whether a proposed action is honest, fair, lawful, and consistent with past promises is perhaps the simplest and most accurate way to insure that fundamental ethical principles are not overlooked.

Neglected Stakeholders

Besides their insensitivity to ethical principle, cost-benefit analysis and other familiar frameworks sometimes neglect the social consequences of business decisions. Whole classes of people affected by a decision may go unnoticed or their perspectives may be given insufficient attention because they are not easily accommodated within the analytical framework guiding a decision. Failure to recognize the full range of affected parties, sometimes called *stakeholders*, can result in costly problems.[3]

---

[2]*United States v. Beech-Nut Nutrition Corporation*, 871 F.2d 1181 (2nd Cir. 1989) at 1186–1187.
[3]The literature on stakeholder management is vast. For an introduction, see Thomas Donaldson and Lee E. Preston, "The Stakeholder Theory of the Corporation: Concepts, Evidence, and Implications," *Academy of Management Review* 20, no. 1 (1995), pp. 65–91; Kenneth E. Goodpaster, "Business Ethics and Stakeholder Analysis," *Business Ethics Quarterly* 1, no. 1 (January 1991), pp. 53–73; R. Edward Freeman, *Strategic Management: A Stakeholder Approach* (Boston: Pitman, 1984).

Consider the information services company that launched a business to collect, analyze, and repackage data about consumer grocery purchases.[4] The company enlisted several supermarkets through which to gather consumer shopping data and lined up packaged goods manufacturers interested in buying the data for marketing purposes. The concept made sound business sense when viewed through a standard competitive analysis framework. However, it proved problematic from quite another angle. The business plan failed to anticipate and address the concerns of an important stakeholder group—the shoppers whose purchase data were being tracked. Eventually, after investing millions of dollars, the company abandoned the business, unable to address shoppers' privacy concerns in a responsive and cost-effective manner.

The well-known Ford Pinto case provides another instructive example that is still relevant today.[5] The case, which arose in the mid-1970s, concerned a public controversy over the safety of the Pinto, a subcompact automobile introduced to the U.S. market in 1970 by the Ford Motor Company.

Under criticism for the Pinto's allegedly fire-prone gas tank, Ford management nevertheless fought proposed government regulations aimed at reducing the incidence of fuel-fed auto fires. According to the company's cost-benefit analysis, compliance with the regulations would have cost about $137 million, while achieving benefits worth only $49.2 million—the estimated value of saving 180 lives, avoiding 180 serious burns, and preventing the loss of 2,100 vehicles. Ford did nothing about the Pinto problems, citing evidence that the Pinto was no more hazardous than other subcompacts.

The decision not to address the Pinto safety concerns proved to be a mistake. For a period of some five years, Ford was embroiled in controversy. Class action suits by Pinto owners in two states, a spate of wrongful death and personal injury claims, negative publicity, and government findings of fuel system defects eventually led Ford to recall and modify the fuel tanks of some 1.5 million Pintos. Though the total costs of Ford's initial decision not to address the Pinto concerns are unknown, they far exceeded $49.2 million, the anticipated cost of the injuries, deaths, and

---

[4]This example is taken from "Avalon Information Services, Inc.," Harvard Business School case No. 395–036 (1995).
[5]This discussion is based on the facts as recounted in "Managing Product Safety: The Ford Pinto," Harvard Business School case No. 383–129 (1984).

property damage expected to result in the absense of the government's proposed safety regulations.[6]

Ford's decision might be criticized for putting the "wrong" monetary value on life. But the deeper flaw lay in a methodology that undervalued the rights, interests, and expectations of the parties affected by its decision. A generic value-of-life calculation has little to do with most customers' product safety expectations. Typically, these are shaped by customers' experiences, their hopes and fears, and the socially defined rights and responsibilities implicit in the producer-consumer relationship. While customers' actual expectations are not always economically rational, managers cannot ignore these expectations when deciding on and promoting reasonable safety standards.[7]

A stronger orientation to its stakeholders would have focused Ford's attention on its customers and their perspectives on safety and cost-safety tradeoffs. This way of thinking might have opened up a richer array of options for addressing the Pinto problems and certainly would have given Ford a more accurate basis for predicting the consequences of its chosen response. Arguably, a decision process that incorporated customer perspectives would also have made Ford less vulnerable to "irrational" punitive damage awards. In one California lawsuit involving a Pinto fire, for example, the jury awarded the plaintiff $125 million in punitive damages. (The award was later reduced to $3.5 million.) To the extent that such awards seek to punish corporate decision makers for insensitivity to the human consequences of their choices, a decision process that takes those consequences seriously should go some way toward addressing the punitive damages problem and the distrust behind it. Of course, punitive damages are unlikely to disappear entirely, given the persistence of legitimate disagreements about reasonable safety levels, as well as cynicism about corporate motives. And some people who serve on juries will continue to expect risk-free products, not understanding the economics of safety and the prohibitive price of a perfectly safe world—assuming such a state to be attainable.

Ford's Pinto experience and the other examples discussed above illustrate why managers need to think clearly about the people affected by their decisions. These parties have rights, interests, and expectations that deserve to be considered, and in some cases fully respected, in their own right. They may also have the ability to impede or to advance corporate

---

[6] Lost revenues could be conservatively estimated at $100 million, assuming a 5% drop in Pinto sales over the three-year period after the controversy became public. The costs of the eventual recall and the settlement of pending lawsuits were probably in the range of $60–$75 million, assuming 50 lawsuits at roughly $1 million each and adding the estimated $20 million cost of the recall.

[7] Though people may disagree about what levels of safety are reasonable, reasonable safety is not the same as perfect safety or zero-risk.

objectives in ways that managers do not fully appreciate without a thorough analysis of the different parties' perspectives. Understanding who is affected and how the affected parties' rights, interests, and expectations are implicated should be integral to the management decision process.

As the examples show, managers face many complicated and controversial issues of fact and value in making decisions. Given the system of government, law, and morality within which business operates, managers can expect their decisions to be scrutinized from a variety of angles. To chart a responsible path through this complexity, managers themselves need cognitive skills to help them see their choices from multiple perspectives. They need frames of reference for understanding the ethical and social, as well as the strategic, context in which they act. The decision process outlined below highlights these three frames of analysis. For ease of reference, they may be called the frames of *Purpose, Principle,* and *People.*

Modes of Practical Reasoning

Each of these categories—*Purpose, Principle, People*—is associated with a distinctive mode of reasoning and choice, and a tradition of thought about decision making. All are modes of *practical* reasoning: they are directed toward action rather than knowledge. Their aim is ultimately to help people decide what to *do* rather than what to *think*. Although each has its own characteristic internal problems and difficulties, the focus here is on the central features of each tradition.

Purpose

Reasoning from purposes or goals is perhaps the most familiar mode of practical thinking. This type of thinking has many names: strategic, pragmatic, purposive, results-oriented, instrumental, means-end reasoning. All these terms suggest the clarification of objectives and the selection of effective methods for achieving them. Often associated with Machiavelli and with the doctrine that the "end justifies the means," pragmatic thinking also has roots in the American philosophical tradition linked with William James. James characterized the pragmatic mentality succinctly when he described pragmatism as an attitude oriented to "last things, fruits, consequences," as opposed to "first things, principles, 'categories.' "[8]

---

[8]William James, "What Pragmatism Means," in *Essays in Pragmatism* (New York, 1948), p. 146.

Although instrumental thinking is often linked with short-term objectives or self-interested ends, the purposes that drive instrumental thinking need not have these qualities. Purposes may be abstract and public-spirited, or they may be concrete and selfish. Social justice, for example, may be a goal, just as personal advancement may be a goal. Indeed, instrumental thinking, which is concerned with selecting methods and strategies for moving forward, is essential for achieving one's goals, whatever they may be.

Much of the business school curriculum is a refinement of different forms of purposive or pragmatic thinking. With purposive thinking, which has a forward-looking quality, the central question is whether a course of action will achieve the desired objectives. Within this frame of reference, an action is justified insofar as it contributes toward a desired result.

Principle

Principled thinking, a second mode of practical reasoning, involves the interpretation and application of values, standards, ideals, and norms. Sometimes called *formalism* or more negatively, *rigorism*, principled reasoning is most readily seen in the thinking of judges and others charged with interpreting laws or standards specifying the rights and duties of the members of a community. Many ethicists see their role as interpreting and applying principles of right or justice as found in a tradition of moral thought or a conception of community.

The tradition of moral deontology, an approach that treats ethics as the science of duty, relies heavily on principled reasoning. The 18th-century German philosopher Immanuel Kant is perhaps the best known spokesperson for a deontological theory of morality. In Kant's view, behavior is right when it accords with the moral law, irrespective of its immediate consequences for the people affected. The moral law itself follows from a conception of human reason. Within Kant's theory, principled thinking is essential to determine both what the moral law is and how it applies in specific situations.

Principled reasoning may be highly general and abstract, beginning with ideals of individuality, community, justice, or human excellence. Or it may be relatively specific and concrete as in the case of legal rules prohibiting fraud or requiring equal treatment. With principled thinking, the central question is whether a given action is compatible with the principles or values at issue. Only actions that exemplify the relevant principles are justifiable, while actions that violate them are to be avoided.

People

A third tradition of practical reasoning focuses on social consequences: how an action or policy is likely to affect people's well-being. Consequentialist reasoning is often associated with utilitarianism, a tradition of ethical theory that justifies actions and policies by their tendency to serve the interests of the parties affected. In its best-known formulation, utilitarianism seeks the "greatest good for the greatest number." Frequently attributed to 19th-century British philosophers and political reformers Jeremy Bentham and John Stuart Mill, utilitarianism continues to be embraced by many public policy analysts. It has also been favored as a general decision method, though whether it is properly applied to specific acts or only to the selection of general rules is a matter of much debate.

A more personal form of consequentialism can be seen in the relationship-driven morality favored by contemporary advocates of an "ethic of care."[9] These thinkers have focused on the role of concern for others in morally sound decision making. While there are important differences between these theories, both consequentialist and relational thinking are concerned with social impact: who is affected and how. One approach seeks the preservation of positive relationships, and the other is oriented toward aggregate individual outcomes. But both favor actions that enhance well-being and minimize harmful consequences. Within a people-oriented frame of reference, the central question is whether a course of action enhances the welfare of those it affects. Actions are justifiable when they are better than the available alternatives for the affected parties.

These three modes of thought appear to be loosely linked to the fundamental drivers of human behavior that many thinkers have emphasized. The 18th-century philosopher David Hume, for example, believed that humans tended to form groups on one of three bases: shared interests, shared principles, or shared affections.[10] Contemporary economist Amartya Sen criticizes the model of economic rationality based on self-interest for overemphasizing one of these dimensions in relation to the other two. Sen argues that commitment and sympathy, as well as personal interest, are critical for explaining and motivating human behavior.[11] Something akin to these three clusters—purposes and interests, principles and commitments, people and relationships—has appeared in the work of many philosophers and social theorists.[12] Though sometimes undifferentiated under the general rubric of "values," each

---

[9]For an introduction, see Mary Jane Larrabee, ed., *An Ethic of Care* (New York: Routledge, 1993).

[10]David Hume, "Of Parties in General," discussed in "The Secret History of Self-Interest," by Stephen Holmes in *Beyond Self-Interest*, edited by Jane J. Mansbridge (Chicago: University of Chicago Press, 1990), pp. 272–273.

[11]Amartya K. Sen, "Rational Fools: A Critique of the Behavioral Foundations of Economic Theory," in *Beyond Self-Interest*, pp. 25–43.

[12]See, for example, the works collected in Jane J. Mansbridge, editor, *Beyond Self-Interest*; and Mary Zey, editor, *Decision Making* (Newbury Park, CA: Sage Publications, 1992). See also Richard E. Walton, "Legal-Justice, Power Bargaining, and Social Science Intervention: Mechanisms for Settling Disputes," Paper No. 194, Institute for Research in the Behavioral, Economic and Management Sciences, Herman C. Krannert Graduate School of Industrial Administration, Purdue University, 1968.

cluster reflects a distinctive set of considerations that contribute to a worthwhile and satisfying life.

Most people use all of these different ways of thinking from time to time. All three generate good reasons for acting: "It will achieve my goal." "It would be right." "It will be best for us all." Some problems clearly invite one approach rather than another. A question like "How can I land the kind of job I want?" suggests instrumental thinking. Getting clear on objectives and developing a search strategy are needed. However, "Is it okay to continue in the recruiting process after accepting a job offer?" calls for principled thinking, a consideration of rights and obligations in view of the rules and standards of the recruiting process. And "Which job would be best for the family?" requires thinking about the people involved, their interests, and how they will be affected by the alternative choices.

Although some choices are approached most naturally through one of these ways of thinking, many may be seen and evaluated from all three perspectives, each highlighting different dimensions. As illustrated above, the ability to appreciate and address the issues raised by the different perspectives can help managers make better decisions and reduce the risks of dangerous pitfalls.

Much has been written about these three modes of reasoning (by philosophers, economists, sociologists, and legal theorists) as if they were mutually exclusive ways of thinking. They are, without doubt, quite distinct in form. Yet, in practice, they are often interdependent, and all are of practical importance for the manager. As a result of considering these differing perspectives, it may be necessary to redefine purposes, to clarify or modify principles, or to alleviate harmful effects on others. While each perspective may be characteristic of particular institutions and social roles, and while certain people may be more inclined toward one or the other, sound decision making requires skill at all three and attention to the factors characteristically associated with each.

A Decision Framework

These different modes of practical reasoning suggest three distinct approaches to evaluating decisions:

- Their effectiveness in achieving the decision maker's purposes.
- Their compatibility with relevant principles.
- Their impact on the well-being of the people affected.

Each of these approaches may be thought of as a *lens* that helps decision makers *see* their possible actions from a distinctive perspective. Taken together, these lenses constitute a powerful framework for identifying critical aspects of a situation, for generating action options, and for evaluating possible choices. Each lens suggests a cluster of questions that should be considered in a specific problem or decision context. The clusters may be examined in any order. In most situations, they should be examined several times as new options emerge and accommodations are made to satisfy the various decision criteria.

Lens One: *Purpose*

Identification

- What are my overarching aims?
- What are my objectives in this situation—long and short term?

Evaluation

- Which actions will contribute most to achieving those objectives and overarching aims?
- Are there more effective and efficient ways to accomplish these objectives?

Lens Two: *Principle*

Identification

- What normative principles are relevant to this situation, including those arising from ethical principles, laws, policies, and agreements?
- What are my rights, duties, and ideals in this situation?

Evaluation

- Which actions are within my rights in this situation?
- Which are compatible with my obligations?
- Which exemplify relevant ideals and aspirations?

Lens Three: *People*

Identification

- Who will be affected by this decision?
- What are the rights, interests, and legitimate expectations of the affected parties?

Evaluation

- Which actions respect the rights and legitimate expectations of those affected?
- Among those actions respecting rights and legitimate expectations, which will do the most good, considering the interests of the affected parties?

By using the three dimensions of this framework, decision makers will naturally and routinely build ethical considerations into their decision process. Although no single lens is designated as the "ethical" lens, the ethical point of view is implicit throughout. The categories of *principle* and *people* are perhaps most closely allied with the ethical point of view. As defined above, principled thinking involves reasoning from ethical ideals and standards, and the *people* perspective concerns the benefits and harms for the affected stakeholders. These ways of thinking reflect important traditions of ethical theory. While sometimes regarded as the two leading modes of ethical thought, they can also be regarded as two levels of a single theory.[13]

The strategic perspective focused on *purpose* is frequently set in contrast to an ethical perspective. But this contrast is misleading if it means that achieving organizational goals is unrelated to responsible business conduct. To the extent that businesses have a responsibility to provide goods and services in an efficient and effective manner, a strategic perspective is critical to responsible practice. In this sense, a strategic perspective is rooted in an ethical point of view even though it is not directly concerned with issues generally regarded as ethical in nature.

Each of these lenses brings a critical perspective to bear on management choices. A thorough decision process will incorporate all three, though the order of use is relatively unimportant. In fact, it may be necessary to revisit each perspective several times in the process of working toward a satisfactory proposal. Satisfying the decision criteria associated with all three perspectives will rarely be straightforward. By definition, difficult decisions are those for which the answers are not obvious, even on reflection. Sometimes competing considerations cannot be reconciled, and trade-offs are necessary. In other cases, the governing objectives, principles, or stakeholders may be undefined or controversial.

For example, managers may be unsure whether a claim of moral right should be respected. Such situations call for a higher level of thinking, requiring managers to assess the general claim before considering its particular application. At this higher level, too, the three lenses provide useful touchstones for evaluation. By considering the purposes to be served by the claimed right, the consequences for the affected parties, and the principles at issue, managers can develop a reasoned response to the claim.

---

[13]See R. M. Hare, *Moral Thinking: Its Levels, Method, and Point* (Oxford: Clarendon Press, 1981).

Using the Framework

This framework is useful for eliciting a set of important decision considerations and testing possibilities against differing criteria. However, it does not provide a decision rule or algorithm for responsible action. Nor does it provide guidance on how to reconcile conflicts within or across the three types of thinking. As noted earlier, it presupposes a set of substantive ideas about the relevant *purposes, principles,* and *people* to be respected—what was called an ethical framework in Part II.

These substantive ideas are no less important than the thought processes used to arrive at a sound decision. Managers with differing conceptions of corporate purpose will, in many situations, make different decisions because of this difference, even when using the same modes of reasoning. For instance, managers who regard their central purpose as shareholder wealth maximization and those who regard it as corporate wealth maximization will act differently in an important range of cases.[14]

Differences in guiding principles or relevant stakeholders are equally critical. The manager who looks to the law to identify rights and duties will sometimes act differently from the manager who looks to norms of fundamental fairness. Similarly, the manager who considers the impact of corporate action on third parties will act differently from the manager who thinks only of its impact on the corporation or on stakeholders with whom the company has a contractual relationship.

The framework's value lies in its capacity to order complexity, focus attention, test possibilities, and stimulate thought. Applying the three lenses helps to elicit critical issues to be addressed and highlight important differences among actors in a situation. It may point the decision maker to ambiguities that need clarification or to standards that need to be developed. It may also be useful for identifying sources of disagreement among different parties to a dispute.

The framework is a reminder that the best decisions will meet all three criteria: they serve the actor's purposes, they respect relevant principles, and they promote the well-being of the parties affected. When it is not possible to satisfy all three dimensions, managers must seek creative solutions and responsible trade-offs. In each situation, however, the goal is to arrive at a responsible decision—one that is ethically informed and for which the decision maker is literally "able to answer." In the final analysis, such decisions are the fundamental building blocks of organizational integrity.

---

[14]Conceptions of corporate purpose are discussed in the concluding section of this book.

Overview of Cases in Part III

The cases in Part III present difficult high-stakes decisions involving conflicting and ambiguous responsibilities. Each features a different group of stakeholders. Together, the cases provide an opportunity to apply the decision process sketched above and to consider a variety of issues important for business leaders of the future: data privacy, organizational restructuring, risk disclosure, product safety, environmental responsibility, employment practices, and human rights. These issues are likely to remain both important and controversial well into the future, given the pace of technological development, the intensity of global competition, and the diversity of conditions around the world.

The first case, "Lotus MarketPlace:Households," recounts the situation faced by executives of Lotus Development Corporation and Equifax, Inc., when their new jointly developed compact disk database and software product was attacked as a threat to consumer privacy. In late 1990, several months before the product's planned release, Lotus received more than 30,000 messages from individuals concerned about the spread of personal information on the 80 million U.S. households included in the database. In the face of criticism from privacy advocates, media figures, and lawmakers, executives from the two companies, a software maker and a consumer credit bureau, must decide how to respond.

The second case concerns a proposal to split Marriott Corporation, the premier hotel developer, owner, and manager, into two separate companies. One of the new companies would hold most of Marriott's profitable management operations, while the other would retain ownership of its hotel properties as well as almost all of its long-term debt. The proposed spin-off will most certainly enhance shareholder wealth, but at some cost to bondholders. A central issue is the extent of management's responsibilities to bondholders and other constituencies in this situation. Marriott's chairman and CEO must decide whether to recommend the split to the company's board of directors.

"Manville Corporation Fiber Glass Group" presents a situation that arose in 1988 when leading scientists suggested that fiberglass, the source of 75 percent of the company's profits, might be carcinogenic. At the time Manville was just emerging from bankruptcy, the result of enormous legal liabilities arising from its mismanagement of hazards related to asbestos, the company's leading product up through the 1970s. According to Manville's medical director, the asbestos crisis was "the worst occupational health disaster ever known to any company in the free world." Manville executives must decide how to respond to the emergence of evidence that their new core product might be carcinogenic.

"Dow Corning: Product Stewardship" centers on an escalating controversy over the safety of silicone breast implants that Dow Corning has manufactured since the 1960s. The case is set in early 1992 just after a federal court jury has returned a $7.5 million verdict against the company in a suit by an implant user alleging injury to her autoimmune system. Complaints about implants have led the U.S. Food and Drug Administration to ask implant makers and surgeons to suspend sales and insertions, pending further study. In the wake of these developments, Dow Corning's newly appointed CEO must decide what to do about the implant product line and how to handle the legal, regulatory, and public relations challenges facing the company.

The fifth case, "AT&T Consumer Products," poses a plant location decision. Facing stiff competition in its telephone answering machine business, AT&T is evaluating alternative sites for a new manufacturing facility that will be part of its global manufacturing network. A leading possibility is Mexico, where labor costs are low and environmental enforcement less stringent than in the United States. Moreover, a Mexican plant located near the U.S. border would be classified as a *maquiladora*, making goods produced there eligible for duty preferences. The vice president of manufacturing for AT&T's Consumer Products Division must decide on a site for the new plant. He must also determine what policies the plant will adopt concerning wage levels, working conditions, environmental controls, gender and age preferences, and gifts and payments.

The final case, "Levi Strauss & Co.: Global Sourcing," focuses on a question the world's largest brand-name apparel maker faced in 1993 soon after adopting a comprehensive set of global sourcing guidelines: should the company continue its involvement in China given human rights and other problems in the country? At the time, Levi's marketing presence in China was minuscule; sourcing costs there were about $50 million. But the company's Chinese contractors were excellent suppliers. With a population of 1.2 billion and one of the world's fastest growing economies, China could potentially become a major market for Levis®. A senior-level cross-functional group has been chartered by the CEO to make a recommendation to the Executive Committee, the company's most senior decision-making group.

Study Questions for Part III

A first step in preparing each case is to view the situation through the decision lenses sketched above: *Purpose, Principle,* and *People.* This exercise will point to important ethical issues that must be resolved in reaching a recommendation. After analyzing these issues, an action recommendation should be developed and supported with reasoning from each perspective. The following study questions provide a guide to preparing each case:

CASE 1: Lotus MarketPlace:Households

1. Why is Lotus MarketPlace:Households an attractive product for Lotus and Equifax?
2. As an executive of each company—Lotus and Equifax—what would be your primary concerns in November 1990?
3. What is your assessment of the ethical issues in the case? How serious is the threat to privacy? Are privacy advocates right to favor a legally enforceable right to data privacy?
4. What would you advise Lotus and Equifax executives to do in November 1990?
5. How did two companies committed to responsible information practices get into this mess?

CASE 2: Marriott Corporation (A)

1. Why is Marriott's chief financial officer proposing Project Chariot?
2. Is the proposed restructuring consistent with management's responsibilities?
3. The case describes two conceptions of managers' fiduciary duty: the shareholder conception and the corporate conception. Which do you favor? Does your stance make a difference in this case?
4. Should Mr. Marriott recommend the proposed restructuring to the board?

CASE 3: Manville Fiber Glass Group (A)

1. Why have Dr. Doll's comments precipitated a crisis?
2. Does Manville have another asbestos on its hands? In your judgment, who or what was responsible for the asbestos disaster?
3. What should Manville's top executives do in view of Anderson's news? Be sure to consider the following:
   a. Should they communicate with anyone? Who? What? How? When?
   b. Should they scale back or exit the fiberglass business?
   c. Should they modify the fiberglass MSDS label? How?
   d. Whom should they consult in their talks?
   e. Should they tailor their response to different markets such as the United States, Europe, and Asia?
4. Outline a plan to implement your recommendations.

CASE 4: Dow Corning: Product Stewardship

1. What are the origins of the breast implant controversy? How might the present crisis have been avoided?

2. In your judgment, who should bear any risks associated with the use of breast implants? Why?
3. What should McKennon do about the breast implant line?
4. How should he handle the pending legal, regulatory, and public relations issues?

CASE 5: *AT&T Consumer Products*

1. Should AT&T build its telephone answering machine plant in Mexico?
2. What obligations, if any, do AT&T managers have to their U.S. employees and to the United States?
3. If Stevens decides on the Mexican site, what policies should he adopt on the following issues: wage levels, gender preferences, environmental standards, working conditions, and the payment of bribes?

CASE 6: *Levi Strauss & Co.: Global Sourcing (A)*

1. How attractive is China as a business opportunity?
2. What is your assessment of the global sourcing guidelines? Would you have voted for the guidelines as written?
3. How vulnerable is Levi Strauss & Co. to the charge of "moral imperialism"? How concerned should company executives be about this issue?
4. As a member of the China Policy Group, what would you recommend on (1) continued sourcing and (2) possible direct investment in manufacturing or marketing ventures in China?

Case 1
Lotus MarketPlace:Households

If you market this product, it is my sincere hope that you are sued by every person for whom your data is false, with the eventual result that your company goes bankrupt.

—Electronic mail message to Jim Manzi[1]

This message was among the 30,000 that Lotus Development Corporation had received in the nine months since its April 9, 1990, new product announcement of Lotus MarketPlace:Households, a compact disk database of 80 million U.S. households for use on the Apple Macintosh personal computer. Designed as part of a family of tools to make it easy for businesses to target customers, MarketPlace:Households paralleled MarketPlace:Businesses, a database of information on 9 million businesses.

Lotus developed the household database in an unusual alliance with the consumer credit bureau and information services company, Equifax, Inc. Lotus provided software and technical expertise, along with a distribution system, while Equifax supplied information and expertise on information collection and analysis. The union brought together two very different companies and industries. Lotus, like the software industry, was young and fast-paced, while Equifax was older and more conservative. But both companies saw themselves as technology leaders committed to responsible information practices and principles.

Priced at $695, the proposed household database and software package would allow small businesses to do desktop market and sales analyses and to generate targeted mailing lists for direct mail marketing.[2] The initial purchase price included access to 5,000 names and records. The data fields on the MarketPlace:Households disk included name, address, age, gender, marital status, estimated household income, lifestyle (one of 50 categories including "inner-city singles," "mobile home families," "accumulated wealth," etc.), and buying propensity for more than 100 specific products (including cloth diapers, luxury cars, frozen dinners, etc.). Although lists of names and addresses could be defined and generated using any of these criteria, users could obtain only names and addresses from the product.

Unlike Lotus, Equifax had not received extensive electronic mail. However, several organizations, including the American Civil Liberties Union, had earlier, when contacted by Equifax, expressed concerns that the proposed product represented an invasion of personal privacy. In the fourth quarter of 1990, with

---

[1]Mary J. Culnan, "The Lessons of the Lotus MarketPlace: Implications for Consumer Privacy in the 1990s," paper presented at the Conference on Computers, Freedom, and Privacy, March 1991.
[2]*Direct marketing* was defined as "selling via a promotion delivered directly to the consumer." Jane Imber and Betsy-Ann Toffler, *Dictionary of Advertising and Direct Mail Terms,* Barron's Educational Series, Inc., 1987, p. 144.

MarketPlace scheduled for shipment in the spring of 1991, Lotus and Equifax managers undertook an intensive reevaluation of the privacy issue. In a number of strategic sessions they considered how to respond to the privacy concerns.

Background

Lotus Development Corporation

Lotus Development Corporation, the software company developing Market-Place, was headquartered in Cambridge, Massachusetts. It had become a dominant player in the business applications segment of the personal computer software market in January 1983 with the introduction of its first product, Lotus 1-2-3, a spreadsheet software package. Like most software companies, Lotus was founded by a "techie" entrepreneur, Mitchell Kapor, a coauthor of 1-2-3. However, in 1990, it was being run by marketing executive Jim Manzi, a former consultant with McKinsey who joined Lotus in 1983 as a marketing director and quickly rose to president in 1984. Kapor's involvement in Lotus ended in 1986 when Manzi became CEO and chairman.

As Lotus entered 1990, most of its revenues of $556 million derived from sales of its spreadsheet product, 1-2-3, although the company also sold business graphics and database management products (see **Exhibit 1**). The company's product strategy was to further develop these three core software business applications. MarketPlace came under a fourth area, CD-ROM (compact disk read-only memory) products, a smaller business but one expected to provide added value.[3]

Lotus had been one of the first companies in the CD-ROM market, and its Lotus One Source had the largest share of PC-based business financial information products. Three international versions of One Source were introduced in February 1990, and Lotus planned to continue expanding the number of databases it offered on CD-ROM.[4] Although the market for CD-ROM products had looked promising for several years, sales were still limited as few companies had yet invested in optical read-only disk drives. (Total unit shipments in 1989 were 140,000 versus the 20 million PCs sold.)[5] Lotus manufactured its CD-ROM products at its manufacturing facility in Cambridge. Although most Lotus products were sold directly to resellers or to distributors selling to resellers, One Source was sold directly to customers by specialized sales forces.[6]

In March 1990, as a first step toward its product strategy, Lotus reorganized its 2,800 employees into four operating units: the software business group, the international business group, the software consulting business, and the information services group (whose responsibilities included CD-ROM products). By

---

[3]Lotus Development Corporation, Annual Report for the fiscal year ending December 31, 1989.

[4]Lotus Development Corporation, Form 10-K for the fiscal year ended December 31, 1989.

[5]Karen Juliussen and Egil Juliussen, *The Computer Industry Almanac 1991* (New York: Simon and Schuster, Inc., 1990), pp. 10.13, 10.26.

[6]Ibid.

EXHIBIT 1   Lotus Development Corporation Consolidated Statements of Operations

(In thousands, except per share data) Year Ended December 31	1989	1988	1987
Net sales	$556,033	$468,547	$395,595
Cost of sales	104,949	90,825	68,676
Gross margin	451,084	377,722	326,919
Operating expenses:			
Research and development	94,343	83,837	58,420
Sales and marketing	221,745	170,750	126,848
General and administrative	61,078	54,124	46,546
Total operating expenses	$377,166	$308,711	$231,814
Operating income	$73,918	$69,011	$95,105
Interest income, net	$5,644	$9,568	$3,960
Other income, net	5,389	1,295	3,853
Income before provision for income taxes	$84,951	$79,874	$102,918
Provision for income taxes	16,990	20,949	30,875
Net income	$67,961	$58,925	$72,043
Net income per share	$1.61	$1.29	$1.58
Weighted average common and common equivalent shares outstanding	$42,301	$45,551	$45,720

Source: Lotus Development Corporation Annual Report, 1989.

mid-year, Lotus had expanded its spreadsheet franchise with introductions of 1-2-3 for non-PC markets. In addition, the company was looking at expanding into network operating system software through a merger with Novell, Inc., manufacturer of NetWare. In May, however, the proposed merger fell through, and instead of becoming the world's largest personal computer software company, Lotus was back to relying on 1-2-3.

Personal Computer (PC) Software Industry
During its first six years, Lotus had dominated the personal computer software industry with its virtual ownership of the spreadsheet category. However, by 1990, other U.S. companies had gained share at Lotus's expense. Microsoft, Lotus's main competitor, had surpassed Lotus as the market leader in PC software in 1988. In 1990 Microsoft was not only far larger but better positioned with a wide range of products beyond applications software.

Worldwide sales of PC software had reached $6.8 billion in 1990. Still quite young and dominated by U.S. companies, the industry was highly fragmented and experiencing fast growth. Applications software, Lotus's product focus, comprised a little over half the market with systems software and entertainment software the next largest segments.[7] Within the applications software segment, word processing commanded the largest share with spreadsheets a close second. However, the spreadsheet category was fairly mature and growing at a slower pace than newer segments like graphics and other productivity tools.[8]

---

[7]Karen Juliussen and Egil Juliussen, *The Computer Industry Almanac 1991,* p. 10.28.
[8]Ibid.

EXHIBIT 2   **Financial Highlights—Equifax Inc.**

(In thousands, except per share data)

Year Ended December 31	1989	1988	1987
Operating revenue	$840,283	$743,078	$670,007
Income from continuing operations before income taxes			
Before gain	58,711	58,046	56,378
Gain on sale of businesses	1,384	—	—
	$60,095	$58,046	$56,378
Provision for income taxes	24,432	24,090	25,822
Income from continuing operations before cumulative effect of the change in accounting for income taxes	35,663	33,956	30,556
Income before cumulative effect of the change in accounting for income taxes	$35,663	$33,956	$30,556
Cumulative prior years' effect of the change in accounting for income taxes	—	5,400	—
Net income	$35,663	$39,356	$30,556
Net income per common share	.73	.85	.71
Number of shareholders of record	5,369	5,217	5,035
Number of employees	12,714	12,275	10,767

Note: All share and per share data have been restated to reflect a two-for-one common stock split effective December 18, 1989.

Source: Equifax, Inc. Annual Report, 1989.

Equifax

Equifax, Lotus's partner in developing MarketPlace:Households, was the leader of the $900 million industry in providing personal credit information.[9] The company was founded in 1899 in Atlanta, Georgia, as the Retail Credit Company. C. B. Rogers, Jr., president and CEO, had joined the company in October 1987 after 33 years at IBM, where he had spent many years in the Information Systems Group. In Rogers's two years at Equifax he had seen it grow 25% to $840 million in sales (see **Exhibit 2**).[10] Equifax's annual return to investors had averaged 30.9% throughout the 1980s, ranking it first among the 100 diversified service companies on *Fortune's* Service 500.[11]

Much of Equifax's recent growth had come through the acquisition of regional credit bureaus. The company's 12,700 employees worked in 45 company-owned and 200 affiliated credit bureaus as well as several hundred offices that provided information services to insurance companies.[12] These facilities were spread across the United States and Canada. Equifax's U.S. credit reporting network provided credit histories on an estimated 150 million Americans for the

---

[9]Company and analyst reports for TRW, Trans Union, and Equifax.
[10]Equifax, Annual Report for the fiscal year ending December 31, 1989.
[11]Laurie Kretchmar, "How to Shine in a Sullied Industry," *Fortune,* February 24, 1992.
[12]Ibid.

company's two operating units, Credit and Marketing Services, and Insurance and Special Services. These units, in turn, provided information services to credit grantors and insurance companies.

Marketing Decision Systems at Equifax, the provider of information and data collection expertise for the proposed Lotus MarketPlace:Households, helped companies identify and market their products to targeted consumer groups. In addition to providing traditional market research, such as focus-group interviews and mall-intercept surveys, Marketing Decision Systems used its massive consumer information database to generate customized mailing lists, to predict product purchase interest through statistical modeling techniques, and to generate specialized mailing lists focusing on groups such as "Super Seniors," "Credit Seekers," and "Hispanic Power Buyers."[13]

The Equifax Consumer Marketing Database (ECMD) comprised both actual and inferred information on 150 million individual U.S. consumers and 89 million households. As explained in Equifax marketing materials, "Over 400 elements go into the construction of a single record in the ECMD, and the data is cleaned, screened, unified and updated from sources that are updated more than 65 million times a day."[14] The ECMD included indicators of the recency and frequency of a consumer's financial activity based on data (not available on ECMD) on the consumer's purchase and payment history acquired from banks and other credit grantors, as well as other information drawn from a variety of public, private, and in-house proprietary sources (see **Exhibit 3**).

Credit Bureau Industry

Equifax competed in both the credit bureau industry and the mailing list industry. In 1990, it was one of three large companies providing consumer credit reports. TRW Credit Data, and Trans Union Corp., like Equifax, owned databases on virtually every U.S. household. These three companies issued a combined annual total of approximately 450 million reports based on public records of financial items such as bankruptcies and foreclosures, combined with customer information from banks, stores, and other credit grantors.[15]

The credit bureaus' collection and use of information about consumers was regulated by a number of state laws and by the 1970 Fair Credit Reporting Act (FCRA), which required

> . . . consumer reporting agencies [to] adopt reasonable procedures for meeting the needs of commerce for consumer credit, personnel, insurance, and other information in a manner which is fair and equitable to the consumer, with regard to the confidentiality, accuracy, relevancy, and proper utilization of such information in accordance with the requirements of this title.[16]

Enforced by the Federal Trade Commission (FTC), the FCRA allowed credit bureaus to share consumer information only with those who had "legitimate business need for the information in connection with a business transaction

---

[13]*Power Lists* (Equifax marketing materials).
[14]*Power Data Overlays from Equifax* (Equifax brochure).
[15]Associated Credit Bureaus' 1989 data.
[16]Fair Credit Reporting Act, 15 U.S.C.S. §1681(b) (199).

EXHIBIT 3 *Equifax Consumer Marketing Database*

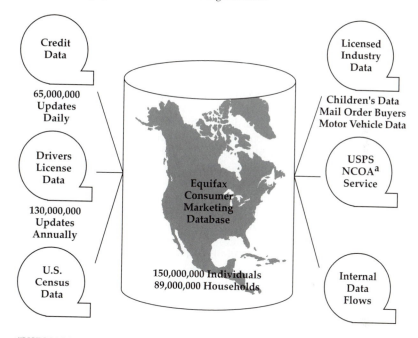

- Credit Data
- 65,000,000 Updates Daily
- Drivers License Data
- 130,000,000 Updates Annually
- U.S. Census Data
- Licensed Industry Data
- Children's Data / Mail Order Buyers / Motor Vehicle Data
- USPS NCOA[a] Service
- Internal Data Flows

Equifax Consumer Marketing Database

150,000,000 Individuals
89,000,000 Households

[a]"USPS NCOA" refers to "United States Postal Service National Change of Address."

Source: Company marketing documents.

involving the consumer."[17] Otherwise, the consumer's written authorization was required. Under the FTC's 1990 interpretation of this provision, credit bureaus could use their data to develop lists of consumers for purposes of making them offers of credit (a practice called "prescreening"), but not for merely inviting them to apply for credit.[18]

Since the fall of 1989, several bills had been introduced in the U.S. Congress to amend the FCRA. In hearings, witnesses testified that consumers knew little about the sources of credit report information and expressed concern about insufficient controls on access to credit data. Witnesses also questioned the use of credit data for transactions not initiated by the consumer and argued for "opt-out" mechanisms to allow consumers to remove their names from mailing lists generated from credit data.

Heightened concern about credit bureau and direct marketing practices was not confined to the United States. In 1990, the International Credit Association sponsored an industry forum on privacy. The European Community was considering legislation that would give data subjects control over sensitive personal information.

---

[17]15 U.S.C.S. §1681(b)(3)(E).
[18]55 Fed. Reg. 18804 (May 4, 1990).

Mailing List and Direct Marketing Industries

By 1990, all three major credit bureaus had been in the mailing list business for three years. (They had provided prescreening services since before 1970.) Analysts estimated that profit margins were as high as 40% on incremental businesses such as prescreened mailing lists, compared to 20% on credit reporting activities.[19] The list industry, like the credit bureau industry, was dominated by three large companies with electronic databases on nearly every U.S. household. R.L. Polk, Donnelly Marketing, and R.R. Donnelly & Sons each generated annual sales between $150 million and $250 million from selling households' addresses and selected data such as phone numbers and estimated income.[20] In addition, hundreds of small companies provided specialized lists (new parents, birthday club members, pet owners, etc.). For 1989, the total U.S. industry was estimated at $1.23 billion annually in list sales and rentals, with consumer lists accounting for about 60%, and business lists, the rest.[21]

Equifax operated as both a list owner and a list manager. A company doing a direct marketing campaign could either contact Equifax directly to rent a list or go through a list broker.[22] List brokers rarely rented lists of fewer than 5,000 names. In order to protect against objectionable or illegal offers and to monitor compliance with the list usage agreement, list owners usually reviewed a sample of the proposed mailing and seeded names and addresses in the list. Lists were generally rented on a one-time-usage basis, and a renter could do repeat mailings only to consumers responding to its initial mailing. In the case of MarketPlace, buyers would own all the names purchased and could use them as frequently as desired.

The average cost to rent a mailing list of consumers in 1990 was about $78 per 1,000 names.[23] The more detailed a list's category selectors, the higher the rental price. At the very high end of the market, several companies offered detailed databases in conjunction with software packages for modeling the data. For $35,000 to $70,000 per year, Donnelly Marketing Information Services (a subsidiary of Dun & Bradstreet) offered "Conquest," a database and software package used by more than 300 packaged goods marketers, media companies, and advertising agencies to identify the most suitable market segments and geographical areas for a given product.[24] Data stored on the compact disk included U.S. household demographics, Nielsen scanner data on product purchases, economic and lifestyle data, Arbitron data on media viewership, Simmons data on product usage, census data, business data, and Donnelly's Market Potential Database (total and per household expenditures on 250 product groups).[25]

---

[19]Peter Maloney, "Credit Bureaus—An Oligopoly Raking in the Dollars," *United States Banker,* October 1989, p. 22.

[20]Michael W. Miller, "Hot Lists: Data Mills Delve Deep to Find Information About U.S. Consumers," *Wall Street Journal,* March 14, 1991, p. A1.

[21]"List Industry Overview," *Direct Marketing Magazine,* August 1990, p. 75. (Breakdown between business and consumer lists estimated by case writer.)

[22]Since there were numerous companies offering many different kinds of lists, list brokers helped marketing companies identify the appropriate list and then arranged its rental.

[23]"Worldwide List Price Index," *Direct Marketing Magazine,* August 1991, p. 14.

[24]Wally Wood, "Tools of the Trade," *Marketing and Media Decisions,* January 1990, p. 152.

[25]Wally Wood, "Tools of the Trade," *Marketing and Media Decisions,* June 1988, p. 148.

Although Equifax's Marketing Decisions Systems offered fewer databases than Conquest, Equifax customers received the most up-to-date data available and were offered a wide range of list selection options with highly specific targeting capability. The targeting choices included household income, credit card activity, demographics, special selects (telephone numbers, children in the household, etc.), shopping psychographics (nine distinct types), and purchasing power indices. Marketers were also offered MicroVision®, a micro-geographical consumer targeting system at the Zip + 4 level of geography which could identify the profile, purchase behavior, and lifestyles of customers based on individual and census data. MicroVision® could accurately target as few as 10 households.[26] The Direct Marketing Association reported that advertising expenditures for direct mail were $21.9 billion in 1989.[27]

Regulation of Direct Marketing

Unlike credit bureaus, direct marketers were self-regulated. In 1974, a commission created under the U.S. Privacy Act had advised against government regulation, favoring self-monitoring by businesses dealing with personal information.[28] The commission pointed to the need for a mechanism to allow consumers to remove their names from direct marketing lists. In response, the Direct Marketing Association (DMA), the trade group representing mailing list companies and users of mailing lists, had established guidelines for ethical business practice, and created a service to assist in removing names from national lists. By joining the DMA, members agreed to abide by the guidelines, and all DMA member companies developed name removal options. Articles 32 and 33 in the DMA's ethics handbook stated:

> *Article #32* Customers who provide data that may be rented, sold or exchanged for direct marketing purposes periodically should be informed of the potential for the rental, sale or exchange of such data. Marketers should offer an opportunity to have a consumer's name deleted or suppressed upon request. . . .
>
> *Article #33* . . . Information and selection criteria that may be considered to be personal and intimate in nature by all reasonable standards should not provide the basis for lists made available for rental, sale or exchange when there is a reasonable expectation by the consumer that the information will be kept confidential.[29]

The credit bureaus' entry into the mailing list business had caused some industry concern since the credit bureaus' lists were generated, in part, from consumer credit information. In a May 1989, *Direct Marketing Magazine* article, Roy Schwedelson, CEO of a leading list management and list brokerage firm, stated his concern:

> When a consumer goes to a bank to file a credit application, they give information of the highest sensitive matter to the banker. . . . The consumer has an implied confidentiality pact with their banker . . . not to use this information for any other purpose but credit checking. Consumers should be allowed to have a negative option clearly available to them—the consumer's right to prohibit disclosure. Unfortunately, TRW

---

[26]*Equifax Marketing Decision Systems* (Equifax brochure).
[27]Direct Marketing Association, *1993–94 Statistical Fact Book*, p. 10.
[28]Privacy Act, Public Law 93–579, December 31, 1974 (88 Stat. 1896).
[29]Direct Marketing Association, *Guidelines for Ethical Business Practice*, p. 13.

cannot offer this negative option in an open and clear form. They can't do this because the banks would balk and most consumers would balk. It flies in the face of TRW's primary business. And that's why this data is not an informational list medium. It's not usable data, regardless of its potential value.[30]

The credit bureaus maintained that they were acting within the bounds of the FCRA because they didn't give out specific financial data but only used it to sort consumers into groups. A company buying a list from a credit bureau never knew the details behind the list. The bureaus argued that their use of credit information to create lists came under the FCRA definition of a "legitimate business need." One commentator, writing in *Direct Marketing Magazine,* claimed that the provision of lists by credit bureaus was protected by the right to free speech.[31]

Lotus MarketPlace:Households

Development   The plan for a desktop marketing product for small businesses had emerged from initial discussions between Lotus and Equifax in the second half of 1988. The original emphasis on marketing analysis had evolved into a focus on direct marketing.[32] By December 1990, about 40 people were working on the project, and significant out-of-pocket costs had been incurred. Since MarketPlace was a revolutionary product, it was hard to predict a payback timetable, but everyone involved was optimistic about its ultimate success. Lotus estimated that all businesses in 1990 were spending $400 million annually on electronic sources of information.[33] A U.S. Small Business Administration official put the number of small businesses—companies with fewer than 500 employees—at 5.2 million for 1990.[34] For 1989, the Internal Revenue Service reported roughly 1.04 million tax-exempt organizations, including some 460,000 religious and charitable organizations, as well as labor organizations, clubs, and fraternal societies.[35] Approximately 115,000 nonprofit charitable organizations filed returns showing revenues in excess of $25,000, including 77,000 with revenues over $100,000.[36]

[30]Roy Schwedelson, "Privacy vs. Free Speech," *Direct Marketing Magazine,* May 1989, p. 44.

[31]Robert J. Posch, Jr., "Privacy vs. Free Speech," *Direct Marketing Magazine,* May 1989, p. 42.

[32]"Lotus MarketPlace:Households—A Case Study in Corporate Social Responsibility," Attachment B to Statement of John Baker, *Hearing on Public and Corporate Attitudes on Privacy,* House Subcommittee on Government Information, Justice, and Agriculture (April 10, 1991).

[33]Jim Manzi statement, Lotus MarketPlace News Conference, January 23, 1991.

[34]Telephone interview with SBA official, September 1994.

[35]Internal Revenue Service, Statistics of Income Division, "Charities and Other Tax Exempt Organizations, 1989," Table 1.

[36]Internal Revenue Service, *Annual Report 1990,* Table 25.

EXHIBIT 4   *Sample Screen for MarketPlace:Households*

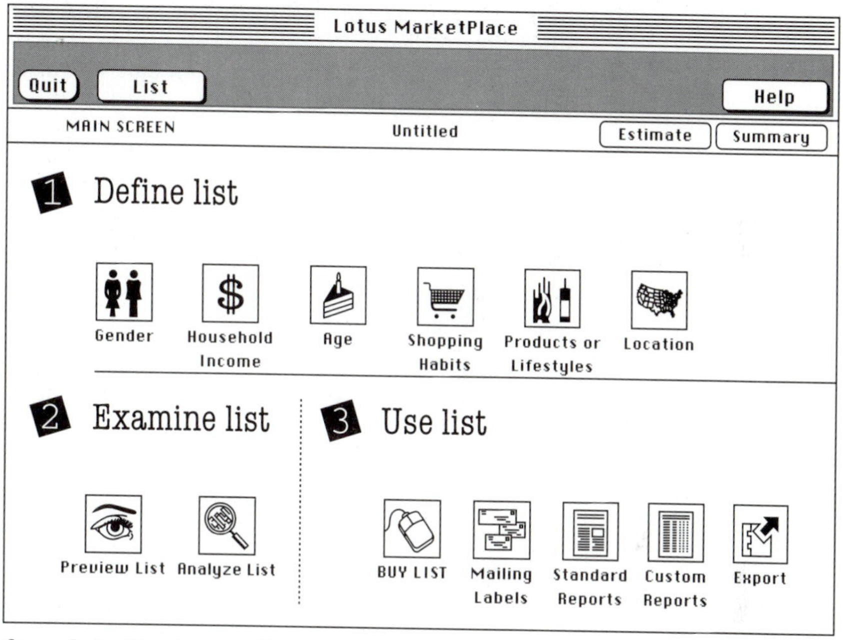

Source: Lotus Development Corporation.

The Product   Intended primarily for smaller organizations, both MarketPlace: Households and MarketPlace:Businesses would give small companies and non-profit organizations up-to-date data and the ability (already available to large companies through products like Conquest) to quickly and easily identify prospective customers. Instead of going through a list broker, MarketPlace users would be able to generate, explore, and refine potential customer lists from their desktops. Users would also have the ability to analyze lists and sales territories, print labels, and export mailing lists and certain types of aggregate data into other software packages such as word processing, presentations, and database management software (see **Exhibit 4**).[37] According to the manual with the demonstration model of MarketPlace:Households, "Before Lotus MarketPlace:Households, only large businesses with an abundance of resources could participate in direct marketing. It was cost prohibitive for small businesses to utilize direct marketing."

The data actually on the MarketPlace:Households disk fell into a few categories: name, address (including Standard Metropolitan Statistical Area and dwelling type), age, gender, marital status, estimated household income, lifestyle, and buying propensities for certain products. Originally included, but later dropped, were shopping psychographics—consumers' inferred preferences for certain types of stores (prestige, value-conscious, etc.).

[37]Lotus MarketPlace, *The Lotus Desktop Marketing Advantage* (1990), pp. 1–2, 33–34.

Data Sources   Names and addresses on the disk were to be taken from Equifax's credit report database, while the other information included in each record was derived from the Equifax Consumer Marketing Database (ECMD), including MicroVision®. Professors Mary J. Culnan and H. Jeff Smith, specialists on information privacy, traced the main data flows behind the information on the Marketplace disk as follows:[38]

Names and Addresses: from credit grantors and U.S. Postal Service National Change of Address Service.

Geographic Information: Zip and Metropolitan Statistical Area from U.S. Postal Service.

Age: from voter registration records and, in some states, drivers' license records.

Gender: inferred from Equifax name table.

Marital Status: inferred from reports received from credit grantors. If reports showed only individual accounts, the individual was listed as "single."

Estimated Household Income: modeled by computer based on self-reported incomes from consumer surveys and extrapolated across the population within the same zip + 4 area.

Lifestyle: inferred from census data using proprietary Equifax modeling product, which assigned every address in the country to one of 50 categories such as "Lap of Luxury," "White Picket Fence," etc.

Buying Propensities: inferred from purchase histories derived from credit grantors and licensed data purchased from companies such as direct mail companies, mail order retailers, etc.

Pricing   The proposed list price for MarketPlace:Households was $695, which included the first 5,000 names and records. Buyers would have the flexibility to view (names only), edit, and customize a list before their initial purchase (see **Exhibit 5**). Once satisfied, customers would buy the list by clicking a button icon on the computer screen. A metering system counted the records purchased. Additional records beyond the first 5,000 could be secured by calling Lotus for a meter refill at a cost of $400 per 5,000 names. Lotus would give the customer a code to type into the computer, permitting access to the additional records and allowing the names and addresses to be printed out. Payment for the additional records would be arranged separately. As with the initial purchase, customers could view, edit, and customize the data before their purchase. MarketPlace buyers were to be offered a quarterly data update subscription for $200 per year.

---

[38]Information about data sources is taken from Mary J. Culnan and H. Jeff Smith, *Lotus MarketPlace:Households, Managing Information Privacy Concerns (A)*, Georgetown University School of Business Administration Case No. 192–193 (1991), p. 4.

EXHIBIT 5   **Lotus MarketPlace:Households Prospect Profile Example**

Washington, D.C. Art Gallery Owner

A Washington, D.C. art gallery owner is looking to expand her base of customers. Art is not a product selection in MarketPlace, so she must find other criteria to target potential customers.

List Definition:

- •Location. The gallery owner combs her current customer file to find out that most live in Prince George's County, Maryland, which contains several suburbs of Washington, D.C.

- •Household income. Her current customers have a household income of at least $100,000.

- •Product selection. Art isn't listed as a choice, but other luxury items are: champagne, for instance, or luxury cars. She selects all lifestyles with a strong likelihood to buy these items.

Source: Lotus MarketPlace, "The Lotus Desktop Marketing Advantage," 1990, pp. 13, 14.

Privacy Protection Mechanisms   Planners had focused on privacy and other social impacts of the product early in the development process. The political environment and the ongoing debate about credit bureau mailing lists had made social considerations even more important than usual. Dr. Alan Westin,[39] a national authority and Equifax's regular adviser on privacy matters, provided input on privacy protection during the development of MarketPlace:Households.

Like most companies considering a new product introduction, Lotus and Equifax tested the concept for MarketPlace with several consumer focus groups. In addition to input on specific performance features, they were interested in consumers' attitudes on privacy.

> The focus groups . . . initially expressed reservations about having information they considered to be personal made available to any legitimate small business with a computer. However, . . . they were comfortable with the idea once they understood that no actual detailed personal financial information appears in Lotus MarketPlace, and that they could opt out of MarketPlace. . . .[40]

Upon announcing MarketPlace in April 1990, Lotus and Equifax brought representatives of the DMA, including the director of its Ethics and Consumer Affairs committee, to Boston to review the product. These industry experts identified three problems with MarketPlace. First, they were concerned that consumers did not have enough ability to opt out. Second, they favored a strict policy for screening buyers. Presumably, most mailing list managers and brokers provided

---

[39]Dr. Alan Westin had helped draft the federal Privacy Act of 1974 as well as portions of the 1970 Fair Credit Reporting Act.

[40]"Consumer Privacy Protection, Lotus MarketPlace:Households," Attachment C to Statement of John Baker. See note 32 above.

this function by reviewing a sample mailing piece before supplying a list. Since MarketPlace buyers owned their list, the DMA felt it was critical to confirm that all buyers were legitimate and reputable businesses. Their third issue focused on marketing: How would consumers perceive MarketPlace and how did Lotus and Equifax plan to educate them?[41]

In response to the DMA's concerns, Lotus and Equifax changed some features and built in more privacy controls as they finalized MarketPlace. Working with Dr. Westin, they developed 12 privacy controls in total. The five areas addressed by these controls included:

1. **Access to the data:** Lotus and Equifax planned to screen purchasers to limit access to the data only to legitimate companies (no individuals), who would purchase the discs directly from Lotus and sign a form agreeing to use the data only as spelled out by Lotus. For example, the agreement prohibited use of the data to generate mailings for lotteries, speculative real estate investments, misleading offers, pornographic materials, or computer-driven telephone solicitations.

2. **Excluded data:** No actual detailed purchase history, telephone numbers, or personal financial data (such as income or credit data) would be included on the discs.

3. **Controls built into the product:** All included data would be encrypted to ensure the physical security of the data[42] and users would not be able to look up a specific name or see street addresses or individual data on the screen. In order to print out, a minimum number of names would need to be selected and no selection criteria (financial, demographic, or lifestyle) would print, only names and addresses. Like most mailing lists, Market-Place would have decoy names seeded throughout the database to monitor for adherence to the terms of the software license agreement and for ethical use of lists.

4. **Ability to opt out:** Consumers could choose to exclude their names by contacting the DMA, Equifax, or Lotus and supplying their Social Security number.

5. **Enforcement:** Consumers could address questions, concerns, and complaints to the Equifax Office of Consumer Affairs, which reported to the president. Lotus and Equifax would take legal action against anyone disobeying the rules for proper use.

Materials distributed with the product explicitly mentioned Lotus's and Equifax's commitment to enforcing legal and ethical use of the software and data and included the Direct Marketing Association's guidelines for ethical business practice.[43]

---

[41]Lorna Christie (director of the Direct Marketing Association Ethics and Consumer Affairs Committee), telephone interview with the author, April 1991.

[42]Encryption is a process that scrambles and condenses the data into a series of coded numbers to enhance security.

[43]Lotus MarketPlace, "The Lotus Desktop Marketing Advantage," 1990, pp. 45–55.

Exhibit 6 Information Policies

Equifax provides a wide range of consumer and business information services for decision makers. As the corporate name implies, the company realizes and accepts its responsibilities for equity and fairness in its handling of factual data; first, to the person applying for the benefit; secondly, to the evaluator or risk taker; and finally, to the public at large.

The company's commitment to integrity in the information industry must take primacy. Therefore, Equifax believes:

- every person has a right to be considered for credit, insurance, employment and other benefits on his/her own merits;

- every person who seeks to qualify for a transaction should be treated with respect and fairness;

- every person has a right to know what information has been reported on him/her so that its accuracy can be assured, corrected or explained as needed in fairness to all involved;

- every person has a right to personal privacy consistent with the demands and requests he or she makes of business; and

- every person is entitled to have this privacy safeguarded through the secure storage and careful transmittal of information.

March 1989

J.V. White
Chairman of the Board

Source: The Equifax Report on Consumers in the Information Age, 1990. Reprinted with permission of Equifax, Inc., 1600 Peachtree Street, Atlanta, Georgia 30302.

Information Standards at Equifax

At the same time MarketPlace was being developed, Equifax was taking a broader look at its relationship with consumers. In March 1989 Equifax published a statement of its Fair Information Practices (see **Exhibit 6**). A statement from Equifax's management summarized the company's view:

> As we looked at the ways information technology has developed and is making possible more extensive and sophisticated uses of consumer information, it became clear to us that information integrity and confidentiality is our company's most important asset. Accordingly, we launched a number of initiatives . . . to ensure that our corporate policies, practices, and systems fully support the singular objective of preserving effective information standards.[44]

---

[44]*The Equifax Report on Consumers in the Information Age,* (hereafter, *The Equifax Report*). A national opinion research survey conducted for Equifax by Louis Harris & Associates and Dr. Alan F. Westin, 1990, p. ii.

In order to have accurate, well-documented information on consumer attitudes, Equifax sponsored a national survey of consumer attitudes on privacy. In 1990 Louis Harris & Associates (Harris) and Dr. Alan Westin interviewed a cross section of the public and a sample of leaders in privacy intensive industries (insurance, credit grantors, banks, and direct marketers). Harris compared the 1990 responses with results of a 1978 survey.[45]

In 1990, Harris found that significantly more Americans had a general concern about threats to personal privacy than they did in 1978 (79% versus 64%) and a majority felt that Americans had lost control over how personal information was circulated and used by companies.[46] When asked about the use by direct marketers of mailing lists based on consumer characteristics, 69% of respondents felt it was a bad thing and 86% were somewhat to very concerned about it.[47] Hypothesizing that the public didn't fully understand the direct marketing industry, Harris developed a new series of questions that "balanced the benefits gained by direct marketers and credit card issuers with the benefits gained by consumers."[48] More than 65% of the respondents found direct marketing/mailing list practices acceptable when questioned this way (see **Exhibit 7**).

The survey results were released in June 1990. Dr. Westin commented:

> The compilation by list brokers and marketing companies of names, addresses, and consumer characteristics (type of car owned, neighborhood lived in, charge card used, publications subscribed to, etc.) troubles many consumers. . . . However, a very large public majority would consider it acceptable for original information collectors to furnish names and addresses of persons who meet criteria as prospects for direct marketers to use in making offers to consumers if three conditions are met:
>
> 1. Only broad categories of consumers are identified to marketers (e.g., ranges of income, not detailed financial status);
> 2. Consumers can opt out of having their names furnished by the original collector or can have their names removed from mailing list databases; and
> 3. Such lists will not be used to screen out or deny consumers a benefit or opportunity they apply for.[49]

In reporting on the year-long project, Equifax's CEO told shareholders at the 1990 annual meeting that the company's ". . . goals of market leadership and technological innovation must be balanced with a commitment to protecting our most important asset—the confidentiality of information."

Industry and Consumer Response to MarketPlace:Households

When Lotus and Equifax announced MarketPlace in April 1990, it was in an environment of renewed interest in privacy. In addition to governmental attention to privacy, "there were unmistakable signs of public nervousness that some technologically enhanced consumer information services might be crossing the line

---

[45]"The Dimensions of Privacy," A National Opinion Research Survey of Attitudes Toward Privacy. A Louis Harris & Associates, Inc., survey for Sentry Insurance, 1978.

[46]*The Equifax Report*, p. v.

[47]Ibid., p. vi.

[48]Ibid., p. 71.

[49]Ibid., p. xxiv.

EXHIBIT 7   The Equifax Report on Consumers in the Information Age

First Series of Questions

Whether Lists of Consumer Characteristics Should Be Sold: Public

Businesses marketing goods and services directly to consumers are now able to buy from mailing list–making companies information about your consumer characteristics—such as your income level, residential area, and credit card use—and use such information to offer goods and services to you. Do you feel this is a good or bad thing?

	Total Public %
	Base: 2,254
Good thing	28%
Bad thing	69
Not sure	3

Level of Concern with Selling Lists of Consumer Characteristics: Public

How concerned are you about this—are you very concerned, somewhat concerned, not very concerned, or not at all concerned?

	Total Public %
	Base: 2,254
Very concerned	40%
Somewhat concerned	46
Not very concerned	10
Not at all concerned	4
Not sure	a

[a]Less than 0.5%

Whether Use of Consumer Information by Direct Marketers Is Acceptable: Public and Direct Marketing

Some companies want to identify consumers with a certain income and a good credit history, to send them an offer for a premium credit card or a product. They ask credit reporting bureaus to screen their computerized files for those who meet the requirements and then supply just the consumer's name and address. However, they do not get the consumer's advance permission. Do you feel this practice is acceptable or is not acceptable?

	Total Public %	*Direct Marketing %*
	Base: 2,254	150
Is acceptable	23%	75%
Is not acceptable	76	21
Not sure	1	3

Exhibit 7   Continued

Second Series of Questions

Whether Use of Names and Addresses by Direct Marketers Is Acceptable: Public
Increasingly, companies are marketing goods and services directly to people by
mail. Some reasons for this trend are that many people have less time to shop or
they prefer to make shopping decisions at home. Also, companies are trying to
reduce their costs of advertising and selling in stores, and they find direct marketing can reduce their expenses and their product prices.

Companies try to learn which individuals and households would be the most
likely buyers of their products or service. They buy names and addresses of people in certain age groups, estimated income groups, and residential areas with
certain shopping patterns so they can mail information to the people they think
will be most interested in what they are selling. Do you find this practice acceptable or unacceptable?

	Base	Acceptable %	Unacceptable %	Not Sure %
Total Public	2,253	67%	31%	2%
Sex				
Male	1,018	67	30	2
Female	1,235	67	31	2
Age				
8–29 years	505	79	20	1
30–49 years	990	70	28	2
50 years and over	734	54	42	4
Education				
Less than high school	264	62	35	3
High school graduate	794	69	30	2
Some college	570	67	31	3
College graduate	357	75	24	1
Postgraduate	253	64	34	2
Race				
White	1,934	66	31	2
Black	186	70	27	3
Hispanic	133	69	29	2
Household Member				
Bought/responded to credit offer by mail	883	76	23	1
Hasn't bought/responded to credit offer by mail	1,345	61	36	3

Exhibit 7 Continued

Whether Use of Names and Addresses by Direct Marketers Is Acceptable with Protective Measures: Public

If (*read each item*) people not wanting to receive these offers by mail could have their names excluded, would this use of names and addresses be acceptable or unacceptable to you?

	Total Public %
People not wanting to receive these offers by mail could have their names excluded	
Acceptable	88%
Unacceptable	10
Not sure	1
You could be sure that no personal financial information was provided to the company	
Acceptable	75%
Unacceptable	22
Not sure	3

Source: The Equifax Report on Consumers in the Information Age.

---

into unacceptable intrusions on personal privacy."[50] Feature news articles and network television alerted consumers to the use of personal information by direct marketing companies, prompting some commentators to argue that individuals should have a legal right to control the use of consumer and personal data. Congressman Bob Wise, a Democrat from West Virginia, proposed the creation of a federal Data Protection Board comparable to those in many European countries.

In the summer of 1990, privacy advocates began a coordinated effort opposing MarketPlace, testifying at congressional hearings and commenting in the press.[51] They objected to the database because it entailed secondary use of personal information without the data subject's consent and provided no mechanism for opting out. Many privacy advocates considered the principle of "no secondary use without consent" to be the cornerstone of an adequate privacy protection system. Opponents also found the use of desktop technology threatening. MarketPlace lacked the controls of a centralized mailing list database. Hence, the risks of unauthorized use and misuse were thought to be greater.

In response to mounting opposition, the MarketPlace project manager (also a lawyer) set up informational meetings with various privacy advocates in the summer of 1990. On August 31, Equifax and Lotus representatives met with Janlori Goldman, director of the ACLU Project on Privacy and Technology. The meeting only heightened Goldman's concerns.[52] Similar meetings with other privacy advocates had the same results. Several meetings followed in the fall as

---

[50]*The Equifax Report*, p. xix.

[51]Robert E. Smith, editor, *Privacy Journal*, telephone interview with the author, April 1991. The effort was headed up by Smith and by Marc Rotenberg, director of the Washington, D.C., office of Computer Professionals for Corporate Responsibility.

[52]Janlori Goldman, telephone interview with the author, April 1991.

EXHIBIT 8   Privacy Principles

An integral part of Lotus MarketPlace:Households' development was a set of Privacy Principles written and incorporated into the initial product plans. It constitutes the basis of the product.

1. Equifax and Lotus believe that organizations in the information industry have a responsibility to protect the privacy rights of consumers.
2. At the same time, consumers want opportunities to learn about new products and services, and to exercise their options to buy or not to buy those offerings.
3. Some consumers may be concerned when their names and addresses are forwarded to mailing list compilers and brokers. Providing a well-publicized and practical procedure for meeting these concerns is a privacy protection obligation of responsible companies, and Equifax and Lotus accept this obligation.
4. Direct marketing involves the use of information from many sources. It is our objective to increase levels of consumer participation, including the consumer's ability to express the desire not to receive information generated by Lotus MarketPlace or other direct marketing products.
5. Information companies have a responsibility to guard against misuse of mailing lists they compile, sell, or use for purposes that will be offensive, distasteful or misleading to many consumers. They also, however, have a duty not to become censors of what are acceptable or unacceptable messages for responsible business advertisers, publications, or non-profit organizations to put forward in our society—except in clear and well-defined instances, including fraudulent or misrepresented offers.

Source: Company document.

Equifax and Lotus attempted to address the privacy issue by building further controls into MarketPlace, including a list of privacy principles to accompany demo copies of the product (see **Exhibit 8**). In late 1990, Goldman's objection to MarketPlace had not gone away. She did not consider the MarketPlace opt-out mechanism sufficient to satisfy the FCRA since the name of a consumer requesting removal would remain on all discs sold prior to the request and up until an updated version was released.[53]

Meanwhile, opposition by consumers was mobilized on the "Net"—public computer networks, bulletin boards, and conferences. The number of people wishing to remove their names was increasing. (Each removal cost the company about $1.) A November article on MarketPlace in the *Wall Street Journal* got posted on the electronic bulletin boards at computer companies as an industry newsclip. As the article was forwarded through the system, comments were appended urging readers to write letters of protest. This campaign resulted in 30,000 letters, calls, and e-mail messages. Although 30,000 consumers represented only .025% of the population included in MarketPlace's files, the letters

[53]Ibid.

threatening a boycott came from Lotus's customer base. In response to the electronic debate, Lotus issued a statement defending the product on the Computers and Society public conference bulletin board.

As Lotus and Equifax managers considered their next steps in November and December 1990, they reflected on the privacy issues surrounding Market-Place:Households. Although Dr. Westin considered "the critics' objections . . . off-base,"[54] perhaps the intensity of the public's privacy concerns had been underestimated. In any event, it seemed clear that many consumers and critics did not understand the technology, the privacy safeguards, or the benefits of the product.

---

[54]John R. Wilke, "Lotus Product Spurs Fears About Privacy," *Wall Street Journal*, November 13, 1990, p. B1.

Case 2
Marriott Corporation (A)

*Over the next few years we will place special emphasis on enhancing our strong customer pref-
erence, increasing operating cash flow and reducing debt.*

—Chairman's letter to shareholders,
Marriott Corporation
1990 Annual Report, p. 3

*Priorities for the next few years: Reduce our long-term debt to about $2 billion by the end of
1994, by maximizing cash flow and selling assets.*

—Chairman's letter to shareholders,
Marriott Corporation
1991 Annual Report, p. 5
(Third in a list of four priorities.)

J. W. Marriott, Jr., chairman of the board and president of Marriott Corporation
(MC), had weathered difficult times in the last few years. The company his father
had founded in 1927 had grown explosively during the 1980s, developing hotel
properties around the world and selling them to outside investors while retaining lucrative long-term management contracts. However, the economic slow-
down in the late 1980s and the 1990 real estate market crash left MC owning
many newly developed properties for which there were no buyers, together with
a massive burden of debt. As Marriott had promised in successive annual reports
over the last few years, the company was working to sell properties and reduce
that burden, but progress was slow. Looking ahead to the end of 1992, three
months away, financial results promised to be only slightly better than for 1991,
although still a significant improvement over the low point reached in 1990. For
the foreseeable future, MC's ability to raise funds in the capital markets would be
severely limited.

But Marriott now faced a decision that had the potential to change this situation completely. He was considering a radical restructuring of the company proposed by Stephen Bollenbach, the new chief financial officer, under which the
bulk of MC's service businesses would be split off from its property holdings—
and debt. A new company would be created for the service businesses, with existing shareowners of MC receiving a share of stock in the new company to
match each share they owned in the old one. The new company would have the
financial strength to raise capital to take advantage of investment opportunities.
The old one, valued for the chance of appreciation in its property holdings when
the real estate market recovered, and not on the basis of earnings, would be
under less pressure to sell properties at depressed prices.

This case was prepared by Charles A. Nichols, III under the supervision of Lynn Sharp Paine. Copyright
© 1993 by the President and Fellows of Harvard College. Harvard Business School case 394–085.

Bollenbach had served as treasurer of MC in the early 1980s at the beginning of its period of rapid growth. After leaving in the middle of the decade he had built a reputation for creating innovative financial structures in the hotel industry with the 1987 recapitalization of Holiday Corporation (later named Promus Companies, Inc.), and then with his rescue of Donald Trump's heavily indebted real estate holdings. Bollenbach returned to MC as CFO in February 1992. His proposed restructuring, called "Project Chariot," reflected the imaginative and innovative thinking characteristic of the financial advisors who had contributed so much to MC's growth in the 1980s.

Project Chariot seemed like the perfect solution to the company's problems. Was it the right step to take now? MC's board of directors would be meeting soon, and Marriott needed to decide what to recommend.

Company and Industry Background[1]

Founding and Early Years   With 202,000 employees at the end of 1991, MC was ranked as the twelfth largest employer in the United States.[2] The company traced its beginnings to 1927, when J. W. Marriott, Sr., opened a small root beer stand in Washington, D.C. The business soon began to sell food, and was renamed the Hot Shoppe restaurant. Working with his wife Alice, Marriott, Sr., saw the business grow throughout the 1930s and 1940s to a family-owned chain of 45 restaurants in nine states. The Marriotts also acquired contracts to run cafeterias and company kitchens, as well as to supply food to the airline industry. Growth and success were based upon a policy of careful attention to details and centralized and standardized operating procedures.

Initial Public Offering   MC went public in 1953, selling one-third of its shares. Although the company continued to sell stock to the public over the years, in 1992 the Marriott family still owned 25% of the company. In the first five years after the initial stock offering, it had doubled in size. In 1956 it opened its first hotel, in Washington, and in the next eight years had grown to 120 Hot Shoppes and 12 hotels. J. W. Marriott, Sr., resigned the position of president in 1964, passing it to his son J. W. Marriott, Jr., then only 32. Under the son's leadership MC abandoned the father's conservative financial policies. It turned to major borrowing to finance expansion that would maintain its historical 20% annual revenue growth rate. In the 1970s MC began to use bank credit and unsecured debt instead of mortgages to finance development. According to new financial thinking developing in the company, borrowing was acceptable so long as cash flow was maintained at a sufficient multiple of interest charges. The company acquired restaurant chains and entered new businesses, such as theme park development and operation.

---

[1] Much of the material in this section is based upon Keith F. Girard, "What the Hell Happened to Marriott?" *Regardie's,* April/May 1991, pp. 71–91.
[2] *Dun's Business Rankings,* 1993.

Joint Ventures   In 1978 MC embarked upon its first joint venture, constructing a group of hotels and then selling them to the Equitable Life Assurance Society, a major insurance company. Thus began a powerful growth strategy in which the company would plan and develop hotels, sell the properties to investors, and retain long-term management contracts. By 1980, following a five-year period of 30% annual growth, 70% of MC's hotel rooms were owned by outside investors. MC possessed an enviable reputation for quality and reliability in service, and together with careful site selection procedures and hotel sizing, this reputation translated into occupancy rates 4%-6% above industry averages. This gap had widened to more than 10% by 1992; when the industry average was only around 65%, MC's rate was 76%–80%.[3]

The Economic Recovery Tax Act of 1981 created new incentives for the ownership of real estate, which further fueled MC's hotel-developing activities. Its first real estate limited partnership, offered in that year, gave investors $9 in tax writeoffs for every $1 invested. Beginning in 1983, MC also branched out into the midprice lodging market with "Courtyard" hotels, which were bundled into groups of 50 or more for limited partnership offerings. In 1985, scaled-down but full-service "compact hotels" for smaller city markets, as well as all-suite hotels and longer-term residence inns were introduced; MC entered the budget hotel market with "Fairfield Inns" in 1987. MC also continued to acquire restaurant chains, including Gino's in 1982 and Howard Johnson's in 1985, although its success in establishing a national business in this area was limited. In 1984 the company discontinued its theme park operations.

End of the Boom   In 1986, the Tax Reform Act ended most of the tax incentives for real estate investment, but MC, relying on the strong economy and its own reputation, continued its high-paced development activities. However, the market for its limited partnerships was drying up, and in 1989 the company experienced a sharp drop in income. It froze capital expenditures, which had increased threefold over the previous six years, sold off its airline in-flight catering business, and discontinued its restaurant operations. In 1990 the real estate market collapsed. MC's income plummeted and its year-end stock price fell by more than two-thirds, a drop of over $2 billion in market capitalization. For the first time, investor-owned Marriott hotels went bankrupt.

MC was saddled with large interest payments on properties it was unable to sell. Industry excess capacity led to low occupancy rates and deep discounting on room rates, resulting in large losses for many of MC's competitors and even bankruptcies in some cases. In 1991 MC intensified its focus on contract and management opportunities that required less capital outlay. These included captive food service markets such as hospitals, office buildings, and turnpike service plazas, as well as management of golf courses. The development and management of "life-care" community facilities for senior citizens was also a high-

---

[3] Joseph J. Doyle, CFA, *Marriott Corporation*, Smith Barney Research Report (released December 18, 1992).

Exhibit 1   Market Statistics on Marriott Corporation (September 1992)

Recent market price	$16.00
Estimated earnings per share	.75
Stock Beta	1.30
Price/earnings ratios	
Marriott Corporation	21.30
S&P 500 Industrials (close of 3Q1992)	26.00
S&P Hotel/Motel (close of 3Q1992)	22.70

Sources: Value Line reports (September 4, 1992), MC Annual Statement, S&P Analysts' Handbook.

---

growth market that MC had entered, but capital constraints forced it to cut back on planned new construction.

Thus, the MC of September 1992 was a far cry from the real estate development engine of the 1980s. Capital spending had been reduced to an annual level of $350 million, only the amount necessary to maintain and refurbish the existing properties. While the company had improved its position from the low point in 1990, investors still regarded it at best as a company beset by the problems of a severely depressed industry, with several years of slow recovery ahead before it could begin to grow again. (See **Exhibit 1** for market statistics on MC.)

Corporate Culture   However, MC remained a company with many strengths, not least of which was a unique corporate culture built around the personality and values of the Marriott family, and especially of J. W. Marriott, Sr., the founder. In every Marriott hotel lobby hung a painting of the two J. W. Marriotts; every Marriott hotel room contained a Gideon Bible, the Book of Mormon, and an authorized biography of J. W. Marriott, Sr., a book commissioned and written in the 1970s and published in 1977.[4] The biography detailed the life of the founder, beginning with his roots in the Mormon frontier communities in Utah, his childhood and early struggles in difficult economic circumstances, and his work for several years as a missionary for his church. It described the source of his life-long aversion to borrowing: the burden of debt on his family's sheep farm in Utah and the resulting foreclosure during the depression following World War I. The book closed with the picture of a wealthy and respected man, a leader in his church and active in politics and philanthropy.

In describing the growth of MC, the book stressed the themes of careful attention to detail and organization, and above all of service to customers. But the organization itself was focused on the employees. On his retirement in 1964, in a letter to his son and successor, J. W. Marriott, Sr., listed a number of "guideposts" in his management philosophy, including the principle that "People are No. 1—their development, loyalty, interest, team spirit."[5] And nine years later, in

---

[4]Robert O'Brien, *Marriott: The J. Willard Marriott Story*, (Salt Lake City: Desert Book Company, 1977).
[5]Ibid., p. 266.

introducing J. W. Marriott, Sr., as a speaker to the employees at the opening of the Los Angeles Marriott, a company senior executive remarked, "Marriott believes that the customer is great, but you come first. Mr. Marriott knows that if he takes care of his employees, they'll take care of the customers."[6]

Project Chariot[7]

Under Project Chariot, MC would become two separate companies. The division would be effected by a special stock dividend, giving stockholders of MC a share of stock in the new company to match each share they held of MC. The new company, to be called Marriott International, Incorporated (MII), would comprise MC's lodging, food and facilities management businesses, as well as the management of its life-care facilities. Food management had become a major segment of MC's business. With nearly 3,000 accounts, it included as clients some of the largest corporations and educational institutions in the United States. The existing company, to be renamed Host Marriott Corporation (HMC), would retain MC's real estate holdings and its concessions on toll roads and in airports (see **Exhibit 2** for details). The transaction would be conditioned upon a ruling from the Internal Revenue Service that the special dividend would be tax-free to shareholders, and upon ratification by a majority of MC stockholders. The plan called for the distribution of the dividend by mid-1993.

Under the plan, MII and HMC would have separate management teams. J. W. Marriott, Jr., would be chairman, president, and chief executive officer of MII, while his brother Richard Marriott (currently vice chairman of MC) would be chairman of HMC and Stephen Bollenbach (the current MC chief financial officer) would be HMC's president and chief executive officer. The two companies would also have separate boards of directors, except that the two brothers would each serve on both boards. MII would have an ongoing contractual relationship with HMC similar to the current relationship between MC and owners of hotel properties managed by MC. Such contracts typically involved the payment by the property owners of an annual management fee of 2%–3% of revenues. Similarly, MII would have the right to lease and operate the senior living facilities owned by HMC.

Under the spin-off, MII would have the right to purchase up to 20% of HMC's voting stock at market value in the event of a change in control of HMC. MII would also have right of first refusal if HMC offered its toll road and airport concessions for sale.

In the past several years MC had reduced its work force significantly in response to its difficult economic situation. It was not expected that Project Chariot would lead to further cuts in the work force. After the division, MII would have 182,000 employees, and in 1992 on a projected pro forma basis, would have had $7.9 billion in sales and operating cash flow before corporate expenses, interest expense, and taxes of $408 million. HMC would have 23,000 employees, and 1992

---

[6]Ibid., p. 8.

[7]Much of the material in this section is taken from a Marriott Corporation Press Release, October 5, 1992, and from Mitch Hara, James Kirby, and Renee Noto, "Analysis of the Marriott Restructuring," a paper dated May 5, 1993, and written for the Harvard Business School class on Corporate Restructuring.

Exhibit 2 **Project Chariot: Division of Marriott Corporation into Marriott International, Inc. and Host Marriott Corporation (amounts are projected and are in millions of dollars)**

	1992 Year-End Long-term Debt	*1992 EBIT*[a]	*1992 Interest Expense*	*1992 Cashflow from Ops*[b]
MARRIOTT INTERNATIONAL, INC. Marriott trademarks, trade names, Reservation and franchise systems	21	250	22	408
Lodging Group: Management and Franchise Contracts Marriott Hotels, Resorts and Suites (246 hotels) Courtyard (202 hotels) Residence Inn (178 inns) Fairfield Inn (114 inns) Marriott Golf (17 golf facilities) Marriott Ownership Resorts 20 timesharing resorts				255
Service Group: Marriott Management Services (food and facilities management) 2,927 accounts Marriott Senior Living Services (manages 18 retirement communities) Marriott Distribution Services (food and related supplies) 5 distribution centers				153
HOST MARRIOTT CORPORATION Owned Properties (managed by Marriott International) 27 Marriott hotels 55 Courtyard hotels 29 Residence Inns 30 Fairfield Inns 16 retirement communities Land leased to affiliates	2,870	169	224	363 231
Host/Travel Plazas 68 airports—food, beverage and/or merchandise concessions 14 tollroads—food, beverage and/or merchandise concessions Other operations				123
Partnership interests in affiliates Excess land				(19)

[a]Earnings before interest expense and taxes. (EBIT is net of $16 million and $59 million in corporate expenses for MII and HMC, respectively, not including restructuring expenses.)
[b]Cashflow from operations. (Total for HMC also includes interest income of $28 million.)

Sources: MC press release (data as of September 11, 1992); Smith Barney Research Report (December 19, 1992).

projected pro forma sales of $1.8 billion with operating cash flow before corporate expenses, interest expense, and taxes of $363 million. Under the plan, HMC would retain nearly all of MC's long-term debt of nearly $3 billion, although it would have access through December 1997 to a revolving line of credit of $600 million from MII. However, MII itself would have very little long-term debt (see **Exhibit 2**).

Management Perspectives

Pure Plays   Dividing MC into two companies was consistent with the company's general strategy of separating property ownership from management operations. The theory was that added value came from finding investment opportunities and developing and managing hotels, not from the ownership of real estate. MC management had long felt that the financial markets undervalued the company's stock because of the difficulty investors had in distinguishing and separately valuing property ownership and management. Project Chariot offered investors the opportunity to participate in "pure plays" in the hotel management business and in hotel real estate investment business for longer-term appreciation.

Career Opportunities   In many ways, Project Chariot would offer attractive possibilities to Marriott's management. In the downsizing of the previous few years many executive positions had been lost. MC had also seen the departure of "fast-track" executives who decided that their chances of rapid ascent in the organization and wealth accumulation were not as good as elsewhere. With two separate companies there would now be twice as many top-level positions, and with MII poised for rapid growth, ambitious managers would be more likely to stay. Managers with stock holdings and options would also benefit personally from the expected increase in the value of the company's stock after the Project Chariot restructuring.[8]

Opportunities for HMC and MII   Because HMC would be valued more on the basis of the chance of appreciation in its property holdings than on expected income, the company would be under less pressure from investors to sell off hotels at distress prices. To the extent that HMC operated at a loss, the combined after-tax earnings of the two separate companies would be smaller than that of MC as a single entity, for HMC's losses would no longer offset MII's positive earnings. On the other hand, unburdened by debt, MII would have the ability to

---

[8]According to the MC March 1992 proxy statement, the Marriott family was deemed to control 25.75% (approximately 25.6 million shares) of common stock of MC. The holdings of all other directors, nominees, and executive officers amounted to approximately 300,000 shares. An additional 800,000 shares were set aside for executive officers under a restricted stock plan and deferred stock agreements, as well as approximately 2.8 million stock options (of which 1.1 million were currently exercisable) under a stock option plan.

EXHIBIT 3   **Marriott Corporation Long-Term Debt (in millions of dollars)**

	1991	*1990*	*Moody's*	*S&P*
Secured notes, with an average rate of 8.6% at January 3, 1992, maturing through 2010	527	175	Baa3	BBB
Unsecured debt				
Senior notes, with an average rate of 9.3% at January 3, 1992, maturing through 2001[a]	1,323	1,198	*Baa3	*BBB
Debentures, 9.4%, due 2007	250	250	Baa3	BBB
Revolving loans, with an average rate of 5.3% at January 3, 1992, maturing through 1995[b]	676	1,780		
Other notes, with an average rate of 7.8% at January 3, 1992, maturing through 2015	193	209	Baa3	BBB
Capital lease obligations	62	61		
	3,031	3,673		
Less current portion	(52)	75)		
	2,979	3,598		

[a]Includes approximately $230 million (current valuation) of 8.25% Liquid Yield Option Notes, maturing in June 2006 for the face amount of $675 million and rated Ba1 (Moody's) and not rated by S&P.
[b]By year-end 1992, MC expected to have reduced its revolving loan borrowings by $500 million and its other debt by approximately $150 million.
*On April 29, 1992 MC issued $200 million of 10% 20-year senior notes, and on May 5, 1992, $200 million of 9-1/2% 10-year senior notes. Both issues were rated as Baa3 (Moody's) and BBB (S&P) and sold at yields in line with other Baa3 issues at the date of issue (see **Exhibit A-1** in **Appendix A**).

Sources: MC Annual Statement; Moody's and S&P reports.

raise additional capital to finance growth, perhaps to participate in the consolidation of the hotel industry by purchasing the assets of competitors in financial difficulty. These new acquisitions would strengthen MII from a customer service point of view.

Implications for Bondholders

While Project Chariot would very likely benefit stockholders in MC, the situation was quite different for bondholders. (See **Exhibit 3** for a summary of MC's long-term debt.) Although MC management was confident that HMC would have the financial strength to make all payments of interest and principal on long-term obligations when due, the separation of the two companies would affect the security of MC debt holders. Bond rating agencies such as Moody's Investors Services (Moody's) and Standard and Poor's Corporation (S&P) were likely to lower the ratings on MC's long-term bonds to a level below investment grade. (See **Appendix A** for a discussion of bond ratings.) This development could force some institutional holders of MC debt to sell their holdings, since banks, insurance companies and pension funds often operated under legal restrictions that limited the amount of noninvestment grade securities they could own. Fiduciaries managing such funds were also typically required by law to follow the "prudent person" rule in making investment decisions.

Legal Considerations

Covenants   MC's debt indentures contained the usual provisions, but lacked so-called "event risk" covenants that would have blocked the Project Chariot restructuring or required any measures to protect bondholders from its potentially adverse effects. Event risk covenants had emerged in the 1980s when transactions such as leveraged buy-outs (LBOs) had provided stockholders with large profits from tender offers at premium prices while creating large losses for bondholders in the reduced market value of their newly speculative investments. In response, bondholders began to insist on new covenants to protect them against the risk of the occurrence of such transactions.

These covenants provided that, on the occurrence of certain "triggering events," such as a merger or consolidation, a change in ownership, or a major distribution of cash or securities, the company might be required to redeem immediately all or a specified proportion of the debt, provide collateral, or increase the interest rate to market levels. Research revealed that in 1989 30% of bonds issued included such covenants, with the securities of companies expected to be targets of takeovers more likely to be so protected.[9]

While event risk covenants protected bondholders, they often did so at the cost of lower interest rates. With the collapse of the junk bond market in the early 1990s and the slowing of takeover and LBO activity, the use of such covenants decreased. None of MC's long-term debt indentures contained event risk covenants, including the indentures under which MC issued $400 million of long-term bonds in April and May of 1992 (see **Exhibit 3**). These were now selling at 110, reflecting a general decline in market interest rates during 1992.

Fraudulent Conveyance[10]   Several LBOs that became insolvent were attacked by creditors using the legal theory of "fraudulent conveyance." The doctrine of fraudulent conveyance, which dated to a 16th-century English statute, protected creditors from debtors who tried to shelter their wealth or avoid their debts by conveying their property to others. In some cases of failed LBOs, unsecured creditors attempted to recover funds from those benefiting from the LBO transaction, such as shareholders or advisors to the transaction. Because it was often difficult to prove intentional fraud by these parties, most LBO-related fraudulent conveyance actions were brought under the constructive fraud provisions of statutes

---

[9]Kenneth Lehn and Annette B. Poulsen, "Contractual Resolution of Bondholder-Stockholder Conflicts in Leveraged Buyouts," *Journal of Law and Economics*, Vol. 24, October 1991, pp. 645–673.

[10]Material in this paragraph is taken from Timothy A. Luehrman and Lance L. Hirt, "Highly Leveraged Transactions and Fraudulent Conveyance Law," *The Continental Bank Journal of Applied Corporate Finance*, Vol. 6, No.1,(Spring 1993), pp. 104–105.

such as the Federal Bankruptcy Code, the Uniform Fraudulent Conveyance Act, or the Uniform Fraudulent Transfers Act. According to section 548(a)(2) of the Bankruptcy Code, constructive fraud could be established when the debtor:

1. received less than reasonably equivalent value for the property transferred; *and*
2. *either*
   a. was insolvent or became insolvent as a result of the transfer,
   b. retained unreasonably small capital after the transfer, *or*
   c. made the transfer with the intent or belief that it would incur debts beyond its ability to pay.

In the LBO situation, the tests of solvency and capitalization were the critical factors in determining constructive fraud.[11] Since courts excluded from consideration both intangible value created by a transaction and tangible value received by anyone other than the debtor (the corporation), LBOs failed the "reasonably equivalent value test" by their very nature.

LBO lawsuits were rarely successful. In large cases plaintiffs almost always agreed to settlements averaging less than 10 cents for each dollar of their claims.[12] A review of two dozen decisions found only five with a verdict for the plaintiffs, and federal appeals courts ruled for the defendants in virtually every key case considered between 1986 and 1992. Among the most favored defendants were "public shareholders who received most of the funds, but did not control the deal."[13]

Duties to Bondholders   U.S. courts had held that corporations have no responsibilities to safeguard the interests of bondholders other than those spelled out by the terms of the bond indenture. For example, in 1986, the Delaware Court of Chancery stated in *Katz v. Oak Industries:*

> Arrangements among a corporation, the underwriters of its debt, trustees under its indentures, and sometimes ultimate investors, are typically thoroughly negotiated and massively documented. The rights and obligations of the various parties are, or should be, spelled out in that documentation. The terms of the contractual relationship agreed to, and not broad concepts such as fairness, define the corporation's duty to bondholders.[14]

However, a more recent Delaware Chancery Court decision took the position that the duties of corporate boards of directors toward holders of corporate debt could be more extensive than simply to observe indenture provisions, particularly when the corporation was facing serious economic difficulties or bankruptcy. In such cases very risky courses of action could be beneficial to stock-

---

[11]Ibid., pp. 106–107.

[12]Jack Friedman, "LBO Lawsuits Don't Pick Deep Pockets," *The Wall Street Journal,* January 27, 1993.

[13]Ibid.

[14]Cited in Lehn and Poulsen, p. 646.

holders yet injurious to the interests of debt holders. In *Credit Lyonnais Bank N.V. v. Pathe Communications* (1991 WL 277613), the court imposed a duty on the board to respect "the community of interest that sustained the corporation, to exercise judgment in an informed, good faith effort to maximize the corporation's long-term wealth creating capacity."[15] A commentator noted that this decision altered the traditional approach in which "the board's duties to the company ran primarily to the stockholders, unless the company became insolvent, in which case the board's duty in some sense 'flipped' to creditors." In contrast, the new decision

> . . . recognizes that there is no magic point at which duties should shift from stockholders to creditors. Instead, there is a continuum approaching insolvency in which the board's incentives become increasingly distorted and the creditor-stockholder conflict increases.[16]

The Delaware Chancery Court's decision in the *Credit Lyonnais* case was not based upon completely novel ideas about the legal responsibility of corporate leaders. As far back as 1932, E. Merrick Dodd, Jr., in an article in the *Harvard Law Review* noted that: "Despite many attempts to dissolve the corporation into an aggregate of stockholders, our legal tradition is rather in favor of treating it as an institution directed by persons who are primarily fiduciaries for the institution rather than for its members."[17] However, Professor Dodd's view was far from the orthodox position of most financial economists and lawyers in 1990, who regarded managers as agents for the shareholders with responsibility primarily to protect and promote shareholders' interests.

Social and Economic Climate

As the junk bond market collapsed and many of its high-risk issues headed towards bankruptcy or renegotiation, public opinion regarding the acceptability of massive wealth transfers through financial "engineering" shifted. Although there were still defenders of such transactions, they were viewed with suspicion by large segments of the public who condemned them as "paper" transactions contributing no real value to the economy. Junk bonds and real estate investments had left many financial intermediaries such as commercial banks, pension funds, and life insurance companies in financially shaky positions. Although commercial bank profits were starting to improve, the real estate market continued to languish as financial institutions shed nonperforming real estate loans, and residual fears dampened the enthusiasm of potential investors.

The Decision

Marriott wondered what he should recommend to the board of directors regarding Project Chariot. (See **Exhibits 4–8** for relevant financial data.) He had been assured by legal counsel that the corporation was within its rights as a debtor to restructure itself in this way. Investment advisors had given him an opinion that

---

[15]Richard P. Swanson, Esq., "Directors' Duties to Creditors," p. 16.

[16]Ibid., p. 16.

[17]E. Merrick Dodd, Jr., "For Whom Are Corporate Managers Trustees?" *Harvard Law Review* XLV, No. 7 (May 8, 1932), pp. 1162–3.

the transaction was in the best interests of shareholders. His CFO, Bollenbach, was convinced that cash flows for HMC were more than adequate to cover debt service requirements. And surely, if public reaction were extremely negative, or if other difficulties arose, Project Chariot could be abandoned without significant loss. But with this transaction the company was entering new territory.

The board would be meeting soon, and Marriott needed to decide.

EXHIBIT 4 **Marriott Corporation Consolidated Statements of Income (in millions, except per share amounts)**

	1991	*1990*	*1989*
SALES			
Lodging:			
Rooms	$2,699	$2,374	$2,093
Food and beverage	1,194	1,146	1,082
Other	486	422	371
	4,379	3,942	3,546
Contract services	3,952	3,704	3,990
	8,331	7,646	7,536
OPERATING COSTS AND EXPENSES			
Lodging:			
Departmental direct costs:			
Rooms	628	554	481
Food and beverage	915	870	816
Other, including payments to hotel owners and net restructuring charges of $65 million in 1990 and $194 million in 1989	2,511	2,279	2,117
Contract services, including restructuring charges of $57 million in 1990 and $51 million in 1989	3,799	3,590	3,818
	7,853	7,293	7,232
OPERATING PROFIT			
Lodging	325	239	132
Contract services, including $231 million gain on divestiture of airline catering business in 1989	153	114	403
Operating profits before corporate expenses and taxes	478	353	535
Corporate expenses, including restructuring charges of $31 million in 1990 and $11 million in 1989	(111)	(137)	(107)
Interest expense	(265)	(183)	(185)
Interest income	43	47	55
INTEREST INCOME	43	47	55
INCOME FROM CONTINUING OPERATIONS BEFORE INCOME TAXES	145	80	298
Provision for income taxes	63	33	117
INCOME FROM CONTINUING OPERATIONS	82	47	181
DISCONTINUED OPERATIONS, net of income taxes			
Income from discontinued operations	—	—	35
Provision for loss on disposal	—	—	(39)
	—	—	(4)
NET INCOME	$82	$47	$177
EARNINGS (LOSS) PER COMMON SHARE			
Continuing operations	$ .80	$ .46	$ 1.62
Discontinued operations	—	—	(.04)
	$ .80	$ .46	$ 1.58

Source: MC Annual Report.

EXHIBIT 5   **Marriott Corporation Consolidated Balance Sheets (in millions)**

	1991	1990
ASSETS		
Current Assets:		
Cash and equivalents	$ 36	$ 283
Accounts receivable	524	654
Inventories, at lower of average cost or market	243	261
Other current assets	220	230
	1,023	1,428
Property and equipment	2,485	2,774
Assets held for sale	1,524	1,274
Investments in affiliates	455	462
Intangibles	476	494
Notes receivable and other	437	494
	$6,400	$6,926
LIABILITIES AND SHAREHOLDERS' EQUITY		
Current Liabilities:		
Accounts payable	$ 579	$ 675
Accrued payroll and benefits	313	305
Other payables and accruals	391	582
Notes payable and capital leases	52	75
	1,335	1,637
Long-term debt	2,979	3,598
Other long-term liabilities	351	388
Deferred income	232	312
Deferred income taxes	614	584
Convertible subordinated debt	210	—
Shareholders' Equity:		
Convertible preferred stock	200	—
Common stock, issued 105.0 million shares	105	105
Additional paid-in capital	35	69
Retained earnings	583	528
Treasury stock, 9.5 million and 11.4 million common shares, respectively, at cost	(244)	(295)
Total Shareholders' Equity	679	407
	$6,400	$6,926

Source: MC Annual Report.

Еxнивıт 6   **Marriott Corporation Consolidated Statements of Cash Flows (in millions)**

	1991	*1990*	*1989*
OPERATING ACTIVITIES			
Income from continuing operations	$ 82	$ 47	$ 181
Adjustments to reconcile to cash from operations			
Depreciation and amortization	272	208	186
Income taxes	27	18	41
Net restructuring charges	—	153	256
Proceeds from sale of timeshare notes receivable	83	—	—
Amortization of deferred income	(38)	(50)	(31)
Losses (gains) on sales of assets	3	(1)	(273)
Other	3	50	98
Working capital changes			
Accounts receivable	88	(76)	(100)
Inventories	63	(22)	(39)
Other current assets	13	(5)	(19)
Accounts payable and accruals	(47)	63	123
Cash from continuing operations	549	385	423
Cash from discontinued operations	3	(10)	86
Cash from operations	552	375	509
INVESTING ACTIVITIES			
Proceeds from sales of assets	84	990	1,648
Less noncash proceeds	—	(15)	(258)
Cash received from sales of assets	84	975	1,390
Capital expenditures	(427)	(1,094)	(1,368)
Acquisitions	—	(118)	(242)
Other	(126)	(129)	(223)
Cash used in investing activities	(469)	(366)	(443)
FINANCING ACTIVITIES			
Issuance of convertible preferred stock	195	—	—
Issuances of long-term and convertible subordinated debt	815	1,317	873
Issuances of common stock	3	24	41
Repayments of long-term debt	(1,316)	(846)	(581)
Purchases of treasury stock	—	(294)	(280)
Dividend payments	(27)	(27)	(26)
Cash from (used in) financing activities	(330)	174	27
INCREASE (DECREASE) IN CASH AND EQUIVALENTS	(247)	183	93
CASH AND EQUIVALENTS, beginning of year	283	100	7
CASH AND EQUIVALENTS, end of year	36	283	100

Source: MC Annual Report.

EXHIBIT 7   **Marriott Corporation Ten-Year Financial Summary (dollars in millions, except per share amounts)**

	1991	1990[a]	1989[b]	1988	1987
	(53 weeks)				
SUMMARY OF OPERATIONS[c]					
Sales	$8,331	$7,646	$7,536	$6,624	$5,846
Earnings before interest expense and income taxes	410	263	483	448	425
Interest expense (net)	265	183	185	136	90
Income before income taxes	145	80	298	312	335
Income taxes	63	33	117	123	148
Income from continuing operations	82	47	181	189	187
Net income	82	47	177	232	223
Net income as percent of sales	1.0	0.6	2.3	3.5	3.8
CASH FLOW INFORMATION					
Cash from continuing operations	549	385	423	411	326
Proceeds from asset sales	84	975	1,390	1,016	675
Capital expenditures	427	1,094	1,368	1,359	1,053
Cash dividends and share repurchases	27	321	306	381	446
CAPITALIZATION AND RETURNS					
Total assets[d]	6,400	6,926	6,496	5,981	5,371
Sales/assets	1.30	1.10	1.16	1.11	1.09
Total assets/equity	9.4	17.0	10.3	8.4	6.6
Long-term debt[e]	2,979	3,598	3,050	2,857	2,499
Percent to total capital	58.8%	68.0%	60.0%	60.9%	58.8%
Times interest earned	1.5	1.4	2.6	3.3	4.7
Shareholders' equity	679	407	628	710	811
Return on average common shareholders' equity	18.3%	9.7%	23.8%	30.4%	22.2%
PER COMMON SHARE AND OTHER DATA[f]					
Earnings per common share[g]:					
Continuing operations	.80	.46	1.62	1.59	1.40
Net income	.80	.46	1.58	1.95	1.67
Cash dividends declared	.28	.28	.25	.21	.17
Common shareholders' equity	5.02	4.35	6.11	6.53	6.82
Market price at year-end	16.50	10.50	33.38	31.63	30.00
Common shares outstanding (in millions)	95.5	93.6	102.8	108.7	118.8
Hotel rooms:					
Total	161,379	150,416	134,349	117,789	102,893
Company-operated	132,125	124,622	109,561	94,253	81,244
Employees	202,000	209,000	229,900	229,600	210,900

[a]Operating results in 1990 included pretax restructuring charges and writeoffs, net of certain nonrecurring gains, of $153 million related to continuing operations.
[b]Operating results in 1989 included pretax restructuring charges and writeoffs of $256 million related to continuing operations, a $231 million pretax gain on the transfer of the airline catering divisions, and a $39 million after-tax charge recorded in conjunction with the planned disposal of restaurant operations.
[c]The company's restaurant operations were discontinued in 1989 and the company's theme park operations were discontinued in 1984.
[d]Total assets do not include the assets of Marriott's unconsolidated affiliates.
[e]Excludes convertible subordinated debt of $210 million at January 3, 1992.
[f]All share and per share data reflect a five-for-one common stock split in June 1986.
[g]Computed on a fully diluted basis using the weighted average number of outstanding common and common equivalent shares, plus other potentially dilutive securities.

EXHIBIT 7 Continued	1986	1985	1984	1983	1982
			(53 weeks)		
SUMMARY OF OPERATIONS[a]					
Sales	$4,654	$3,611	$2,875	$2,378	$1,992
Earnings before interest expense and income taxes	357	304	236	196	163
Interest expense (net)	60	76	62	63	72
Income before income taxes	297	228	174	133	91
Income taxes	139	99	74	55	35
Income from continuing operations	158	129	100	78	56
Net income	192	167	140	115	94
Net income as percent of sales	4.1	4.6	4.9	4.8	4.7
CASH FLOW INFORMATION					
Cash from continuing operations	287	257	217	198	158
Proceeds from asset sales	365	302	204	—	184
Capital expenditures	821	911	627	462	433
Cash dividends and share repurchases	78	19	105	11	9
CAPITALIZATION AND RETURNS					
Total assets[b]	4,579	3,664	2,905	2,501	2,063
Sales/assets	1.02	.99	.99	.95	.97
Total assets/equity	4.6	4.3	4.3	4.0	4.0
Long-term debt[c]	1,663	1,192	1,115	1,072	889
Percent to total capital	46.7%	41.7%	47.8%	53.4%	54.4%
Times interest earned	6.0	4.0	3.8	3.1	2.3
Shareholders' equity	991	849	676	628	516
Return on average common shareholders' equity	20.6%	22.1%	22.1%	20.0%	20.0%
PER COMMON SHARE AND OTHER DATA[d]					
Earnings per common share[e]:					
Continuing operations	1.16	.96	.74	.56	.41
Net income	1.40	1.24	1.04	.83	.69
Cash dividends declared	.136	.113	.093	.076	.063
Common shareholders' equity	7.59	6.48	5.25	4.67	3.89
Market price at year-end	29.75	21.58	14.70	14.25	11.70
Common shares outstanding (in millions)	130.6	131.0	128.8	134.4	132.8
Hotel rooms:					
Total	77,730	67,034	60,873	54,986	49,432
Company-operated	64,502	55,920	50,930	45,909	41,126
Employees	194,600	154,600	120,100	109,400	109,200

[a]The company's restaurant operations were discontinued in 1989 and the company's theme park operations were discontinued in 1984.
[b]Total assets do not include the assets of Marriott's unconsolidated affiliates.
[c]Excludes convertible subordinated debt of $210 million at January 3, 1992.
[d]All share and per share data reflect a five-for-one common stock split in June 1986.
[e]Computed on a fully diluted basis using the weighted average number of outstanding common and common equivalent shares, plus other potentially dilutive securities.

Source: MC Annual Report (except times interest earned).

EXHIBIT 8   Unconsolidated Affiliates

Marriott Corporation held ownership positions ranging from 1% to 50% in 267 hotels. This financial interest was reported as a $445 million "Investment in Affiliates," under either the cost or equity method of accounting (depending on the percent ownership). Marriott held management contracts and ground leases on these properties, and provided limited guarantees on the debt of some of the properties in the form of a commitment to advance additional amounts to affiliates, if necessary, to cover certain debt requirements. Such commitments were limited to $349 million. Marriott Corporation's pretax income from affiliates was $97 million in 1991 and included management fees, net of direct costs, $81 million; ground rental income, $18 million; interest income, $19 million; and equity in net losses, ($21 million). Pretax income from affiliates was $47 million in 1986.

In 1991, the Affiliates reported sales of $1,855 million, down slightly from the $1,900 million reported in 1990. Operating expense before interest totalled $2,076 million in 1991 versus $2,082 million in 1990.

Balance Sheets of Affiliates at December 31 (in millions)

Assets	*1986*	*1991*	*Liabilities & Equity*	*1986*	*1991*
Current	$ 194	$ 158	Current liabilities	$154	$445
Noncurrent	2,721	4,842	Long-term debt	2,377	4,233
Total	$2,915	$5,000	Other liabilities	242	565
			Equity	142	(243)
			Total	$2,915	$5,000

APPENDIX A
EXPLANATION OF BOND RATINGS[18]

Since the early 1900s, bonds have been assigned quality ratings that reflect their probability of going into default. The two major rating agencies are Moody's Investors Service (Moody's) and Standard & Poor's Corporation (S&P). These agencies' rating designations are shown in [**Exhibit A-1**]. The triple and double A bonds are extremely safe. Single A and triple B bonds are strong enough to be called *investment grade bonds,* and they are the lowest-rated bonds that many banks and other institutional investors are permitted by law to hold. Double B and lower bonds are speculations, or junk bonds; they have a significant probability of going into default, and many financial institutions are prohibited from buying them.

---

[18]Based on Eugene F. Brigham and Louis C. Gapenski, *Financial Management* (Fifth Edition), (New York: The Dryden Press), pp. 545–547. [Data on bond yields have been added.]

EXHIBIT A–1   Comparison of Bond Ratings

	Moody's	S&P	Yields[a]
High Quality	Aaa	AAA	7.80%
	Aa	AA	8.07
Investment Grade	A	A	8.26
	Baa	BBB	8.72
Junk Bonds			
Substandard	Ba	BB	9.04
	B	B	10.81
Speculative	Caa	CCC	—
	C	D	—

[a]Yields of corporate bonds with ten-year maturities as of September 28, 1992.

Note: Moody's and S&P use "modifiers" for bonds rated below triple A. S&P uses a plus and minus system; thus, A+ designates the strongest A-rated bonds and A– the weakest. Moody's uses a 1, 2, or 3 designation, with 1 denoting the strongest and 3 the weakest; thus, within the double A category, Aa1 is the best, Aa2 is average, and Aa3 is the weakest.

EXHIBIT A–2   Bond Ratings of Industrial Corporations (1987–1989 Medians)

	AAA	AA	A	BBB	BB	B	CCC
Times interest earned	12.0	9.1	5.5	3.6	2.3	1.0	.8
Long-term debt as percent of capital	12%	19%	30%	38%	51%	66%	62%

Bond Rating Criteria

Although the rating assignments are judgmental, they are based on both qualitative and quantitative factors, some of which are listed below:

1. Debt ratio.
2. Times-interest-earned ratio.
3. Fixed charge coverage ratio.
4. Current ratio.
5. Mortgage provisions: Is the bond secured by a mortgage? . . .
6. Subordination provisions: Is the bond subordinated to other debt? . . .
7. Guarantee provisions: Some bonds are guaranteed by other firms. . . .
8. Sinking fund: Does the bond have a sinking fund to insure systematic repayment?
9. Maturity: Other things the same, a bond with a shorter maturity will be judged less risky than a longer-term bond. . . .
10. Stability: Are the issuer's sales and earnings stable?
11. Regulation: Is the issuer regulated, and could an adverse regulatory climate cause the company's economic position to decline?
12. Antitrust and legal: Are any antitrust actions or lawsuits pending against the firm that could erode its position?

13. Overseas operations: What percentage of the firm's sales, assets, and profits are from overseas operations, and what is the political climate in the host countries?

14. Environmental factors: Is the firm likely to face heavy expenditures for pollution control equipment?

15. Pension liabilities: Does the firm have unfunded pension liabilities that could pose a future problem?

16. Labor unrest: Are there potential labor problems on the horizon that could weaken the firm's position? . . .

17. Resource availability: Is the firm likely to face supply shortages that could force it to curtail operations?

18. Accounting policies: . . . conservative accounting policies are a plus factor in bond ratings.

Representatives of the rating agencies have consistently stated that no precise formula is used to set a firm's rating—all the factors listed, plus others, are taken into account, but not in a mathematically precise manner. Statistical studies have borne out this contention, for researchers who have tried to predict bond ratings on the basis of quantitative data have had only limited success, indicating that the agencies do indeed use a good deal of subjective judgment when establishing a firm's rating.

Appendix B
Glossary of Financial Terms[19]

CAPITAL LEASE lease that under Statement 13 of the Financial Accounting Standards Board must be reflected on a company's balance sheet as an asset and corresponding liability. Generally, this applies to leases where the lessee acquires essentially all of the economic benefits and risks of the leased property.

COLLATERAL asset pledged to a lender until a loan is repaid. If the borrower defaults, the lender has the legal right to seize the collateral and sell it to pay off the loan.

COVENANT promise in a trust indenture or other formal debt agreement that certain acts will be performed and others refrained from. Designed to protect the lender's interest. . . .

CURRENT RATIO current liabilities divided by current assets.

DEBENTURE general debt obligation backed only by the integrity of the borrower and documented by an agreement called an indenture. An unsecured bond is a debenture.

DEBT-TO-EQUITY RATIO 1. total liabilities divided by total shareholders' equity. . . . 2. total long-term debt divided by total shareholders' equity. . . . 3. long-term debt and preferred stock divided by common stock equity.

---

[19]From John Downes and Jordan Elliot Goodman, *Dictionary of Finance and Investment Terms (Third Edition)*, (New York: Barron's, 1991). [Except bracketed definitions.]

FIXED CHARGE COVERAGE ratio of profits before payment of interest and income taxes to interest on bonds and other contractual long-term debt. . . .

LEVERAGED BUY-OUT takeover of a company, using borrowed funds. Most often, the target company's assets serve as security for the loans taken out by the acquiring firm, which repays the loans out of cash flow of the acquired company. . . . In almost all leveraged buyouts, public shareholders receive a premium over the current market value for their shares.

[**LIQUID YIELD OPTION NOTES** debt instruments which the debtor issues at a discounted price. No interest is paid but the notes accrue value at a predetermined rate of interest until they are redeemed at maturity for the full face amount. The creditor may require the debtor to purchase the note for the accrued value at certain dates prior to maturity, and subject to conditions the debtor may redeem them for the accrued value at any time. The dates and conditions are specified in the indenture.]

REVOLVING CREDIT

Commercial banking: contractual agreement between a bank and its customer, usually a company, whereby the bank agrees to make loans up to a specified maximum for a specified period, usually a year or more. As the borrower repays a portion of the loan, an amount equal to the repayment can be borrowed again under the terms of the agreement. In addition to interest borne by notes, the bank charges a fee for the commitment to hold the funds available. . . .

SECURED BOND bond backed by the pledge of collateral, a mortgage, or other lien. The exact nature of the security is spelled out in the indenture. . . .

SENIOR DEBT loans or debt securities that have claim prior to junior obligations and equity on a corporation's assets in the event of liquidation. Senior debt commonly includes funds borrowed from banks, insurance companies, or other financial institutions, as well as notes, bonds, or debentures not expressly defined as junior or subordinated.

[**TIMES INTEREST EARNED** earnings before interest expense and income taxes divided by interest expense.]

CASE 3
MANVILLE CORPORATION FIBER GLASS GROUP (A)

Bob Anderson, Manville Corporation's medical director and a physician, was still reeling from Sir Richard Doll's comments when he headed for the telephone. One thing was clear: Manville had cause for concern. Sir Richard, one of the world's leading epidemiologists and an authority on asbestos, had just concluded a major World Health Organization (WHO) symposium by suggesting that fiberglass could be as dangerous as asbestos.

Fiberglass was an $807 million business at Manville in 1986 and accounted for 75% of the company's profits. In its heyday just 10 years before, asbestos had been the company's mainstay, contributing 50% of its profits. But asbestos, "the worst occupational health disaster ever known to any company in the free world" according to Anderson, killed tens of thousands of people and sent Manville into bankruptcy.[1] Now fiberglass, a man-made replacement product for asbestos that shared many of its properties, was implicated as a serious health threat. Was fiberglass a man-made asbestos? Anderson did not think so.

Anderson had not expected the "International Symposium on Man-Made Mineral Fibres in the Working Environment" in Denmark to include anything other than predictable updates on research on fiberglass and other man-made mineral fibers (MMMF).[2] Anderson oversaw Manville's in-house research and followed other studies closely; he even negotiated Manville's partial funding of some of them. In his opinion, there was no significant relationship between fiberglass and cancer.

Just as he boarded his plane for Copenhagen, however, he received a preliminary report on epidemiological research being conducted by Drs. Philip Enterline and Gary Marsh of the University of Pittsburgh. Anderson became concerned as he read it. It reported a small, but statistically significant, excess in cancers at plants producing glass wool, a type of fiberglass. But the research conclusions were tenuous and done with "the most crude of tools."[3] The researchers indicated that further study was necessary to determine the factors associated with the reported increased risk.

The conference organizers had pressured Enterline to present his findings to date. It was obvious as soon as Anderson arrived that many other participants had also read the preliminary report. Anderson was upset; as a funder of the research,

This case was prepared by Sarah B. Gant under the supervision of Lynn Sharp Paine. Copyright © 1993 by the President and Fellows of Harvard College. Harvard Business School case 392–026.

[1]Bob Anderson, interview, May 19, 1993.
[2]Fiberglass, rock and slag (mineral) wools, and refractory ceramic fiber (RCF) make up a family of man-made, noncrystalline, glassy products known as man-made mineral fibers (MMMF), or, more technically correct, man-made vitreous fibers (MMVF). Fiberglass is the largest of the three types of MMVF.
[3]Anderson, interview.

Manville was entitled to see results well before others did. The study, the most important MMVF research on humans ever designed, soon became the center of conference debate even though its conclusions were based on incomplete data.

Anderson's concern deepened when Sir Richard, a voice of reason during debate over asbestos, concluded the conference. At first Sir Richard seemed to put the Enterline research into perspective, but he finished with personal speculation arising from the incomplete data. He said:

> If I now abandon the firm basis of scientific judgment . . . I do so because I know that in the absence of such a conclusion many people may think that the whole symposium has been a waste of time. Let me therefore add . . . accepting that MMMF fibres are not more carcinogenic than asbestos fibres, we can conclude that exposure to fibre levels of the order of 0.2 respirable fibres per milliliter is unlikely to produce a measurable risk even after another 20 years have passed.[4]

The press conference that followed focused on Sir Richard's remarks. The between-the-lines allusion to the safe exposure levels of inhaled asbestos fibers, and the long latency period between exposure and cancer, was not lost on anyone. Sir Richard was saying that any risk associated with fiberglass would not be any worse than that associated with asbestos—a material essentially banned from manufacturing in the United States by the Environmental Protection Agency (EPA). The room was abuzz.

Manville Hears the Alarm

It was early morning on October 29, 1986, when Anderson placed his call and woke Bill Sells, president of Manville's Fiber Glass Products Group, from a sound sleep in Denver. When Sells heard the news, he was jolted awake and into action. He immediately set up rolling meetings that would go on day and night for the next several weeks. Why Sir Richard had spoken as he had was certainly a question he needed to answer, but until then he would manage the immediate crisis on the assumption that "perception is everything."[5]

Tom Stephens, Manville's CEO, along with Dick Von Wald and Bob Batson, Manville's corporate counsel, joined Sells and Anderson to manage what all agreed was a crisis. They brought in experts to help them review the scientific data and to assess the potential economic, legal, and social impacts that the new research would have on the company's leading business division.

In North America, fiberglass was a $3 billion industry; two-thirds of that fiberglass went into insulation in people's homes, offices, and cars. Manville executives expected the press to report Sir Richard's conclusions, creating the perception that fiberglass was a man-made asbestos. They anticipated tremendous concern among Manville's employees, unions, distributors, stockholders, and customers, not to mention government regulators and scientists who would now scrutinize fiberglass with a far more critical eye.

Manville managers took the matter very seriously. The former Johns-Manville Corporation, Manville had filed for bankruptcy four years earlier when faced

---

[4]Sir Richard Doll, transcript of concluding remarks, "International Symposium on Man-Made Fibres in the Working Environment," Copenhagen, October 28, 1986.
[5]Bill Sells, interview, April 28, 1993.

with $2 billion in expected legal claims related to the company's production, distribution, and sales of cancer-causing asbestos products. Senior managers vividly recalled this episode in the company's history as they confronted critical decisions about how—and whether—to proceed with the manufacture, distribution, and sale of fiberglass products.

Accounting for History: Company Background

Denver-based Manville Corporation traced its origins to patents issued in 1858 to Henry Ward Johns, an inventor of roofing and insulations, and to the Manville Covering Company established in 1886. In 1901, Johns and Manville together established the Johns-Manville Corporation. In 1981 the company simplified its name to Manville Corporation. From the 1920s through the early 1970s, Johns-Manville was the foremost manufacturer of asbestos products and supplier of raw asbestos in the United States. In its prime, the company produced more than 500 asbestos products at 33 plants and mines in the United States and Canada.

Until asbestos sales declined in the late 1970s, Johns-Manville enjoyed operating-profit margins of over 15%. In 1976, 12% of Johns-Manville's sales and 50% of its profits derived from asbestos. The remainder came from its growing fiberglass business and a diverse line of specialty products ranging from lighting fixtures to filter aids, pipe, roofing products, and perlite and diatomite mines.

Asbestos Uses and Risks

Asbestos was a strong, flexible, acid- and fire-resistant fibrous mineral. During World War II the U.S. government classified it as a strategic material, and until the 1950s it was known colloquially as "the miracle mineral." An 1897 account described it as "a physical paradox, a mineralogical vegetable, both fibrous and crystalline, elastic and brittle: a floating stone as capable of being carded, spun, and woven as wool, flax, or silk."[6] Archaeologists found asbestos in textiles dating from 2500 BC. The Greeks used it for wicks in oil lamps. They also reported its adverse effects on the lungs of slaves who wove it into textiles.

Modern asbestos use began in the 1860s. Manufacturers promoted its sound absorption and insulation qualities. Because of its fire-retardant characteristics, it was widely used as floor coverings, wall boards, ceiling tiles, and curtains. Asbestos-bonded cement was used in products ranging from cosmetics to asphalt-surfaced roads. Between 1934 and 1964, the world's annual use of raw asbestos climbed from 500,000 tons to 2,500,000 tons.[7] Manufacturers understood asbestos health hazards early on, long before they were generally known to workers and consumers.[8] Scientific journals began to publish the first modern studies of asbestos-related morbidity and mortality in the 1930s.

In 1932, the Department of Labor recommended the exclusion of minors from asbestos industries. In 1943 the Navy required workers to wear respirators when

---

[6]Amended memorandum, order and final judgment in *Findley v. Blinken* (U.S. Bankruptcy Court, Southern District of New York, June 27, 1991), pp. 20–21, quoting Jones, *Asbestos and Asbestic* (1897). The history of asbestos manufacture and use, as well as Manville's litigation history, comes largely from this document.

[7]Amended memorandum, p. 24.

[8]Amended memorandum, p. 27.

using asbestos. Yet, asbestos manufacturers and the U.S. government, preoccupied with wartime asbestos applications on Navy ships, suppressed most information concerning asbestos-related hazards.[9] In 1978 the Department of Health, Education and Welfare estimated that employers had exposed between 8 million and 11 million workers to asbestos since World War II.[10] In 1982, as studies began to link asbestos-related disease to nonoccupational exposures, exposure estimates climbed to 21 million.[11] Scientists predicted 500,000 asbestos deaths and millions of asbestos-related illnesses. Due to a 40-year latency period, asbestos deaths were expected to peak in the year 2000.[12]

Litigation

In 1933, Johns-Manville settled its first lawsuit over asbestos-related health injuries, a suit involving 11 plaintiffs. It would take 30 years for science to definitively link asbestos to cancers, and 40 years before the frequency of litigation became significant. Most claimants relied on a "failure to warn" theory of liability. They argued that the company had known about the hazards associated with asbestos, but had failed to disclose them, failed to disclose them adequately, or taken deliberate steps to conceal them.

"I knew from the day I went to work for the company [in 1951] that asbestos could cause disease," said John A. McKinney, Johns-Manville's patrician chairman and CEO until 1986.[13] Yet, the company began to put warning labels on its asbestos products only in 1964. It took more than seven years to get every Manville product containing asbestos labeled. By then, laws mandated specific language that a company "deviated from at its peril," according to Stan Levy, a plaintiff's attorney who later joined Manville's board.[14]

Johns-Manville faced its first major asbestos suit in 1974 when 448 World War II shipyard workers sued the U.S. government and asbestos manufacturers for impaired health. Other suits followed. Initially Manville won 50% of the cases brought against it, and insurers settled the rest for $7,000 on average.[15] However, juries became more hostile as evidence from the 1930s mounted, showing that Manville actively suppressed information linking asbestos to cancer. McKinney strove to limit liability by spreading responsibility to the government. He slowed the pace of litigation and insurance settlements. His tactics backfired when juries cast Manville as greedy and wholly unconcerned about worker health. As the number of claims began to balloon in the late 1970s, the company lost more frequently and juries began to award ever greater punitive damages. As settlements climbed to as much as $40,000 per case, insurance carriers balked. Johns-Manville sued them.

Prior to 1982, the courts either settled or litigated to judgment (only 1%) more than 3,570 asbestos-related claims against Johns-Manville. The average disposi-

---

[9]Amended memorandum, p. 32.

[10]Amended memorandum, p. 39.

[11]Amended memorandum, p. 25.

[12]Amended memorandum, p. 26.

[13]Stephen W. Quickel, "Triumph of Wile," *Business Month,* November 1988, p. 30.

[14]Stan Levy, telephone interview, June 28, 1993.

[15]Quickel, p. 30.

tion cost was $20,000.[16] In 1982 plaintiffs filed 425 claims each month, and 17,000 claims were pending. Consultants hired by the company conservatively estimated that another 50,000 claims were forthcoming and that the average settlement would be $40,000. Manville's projected asbestos liability exceeded $2 billion.[17]

Bankruptcy and Restructuring

On August 26, 1982, Manville Corporation shocked the business world by becoming the largest U.S. industrial corporation ever to file for Chapter 11 bankruptcy protection. The company had assets valued at $2.25 billion, and a net worth of $830 million. If Manville had not declared bankruptcy, mounting liabilities would have led to insolvency. The accounting rules established by the Financial Accounting Standards Board, for example, would have required the establishment of a $2 billion reserve account to cover potential liabilities—wiping out the company's assets and forcing default on $428 million in unsecured long-term debt.

Even to the combative McKinney, it was clear Manville needed to get out of asbestos—a divestment not completed until 1985—and to focus on other products such as fiberglass and forest products. Manville had entered the fiberglass business in 1959 by acquiring LOF Glass Fibers, and in the 1970s purchased a German firm, Glaswerk Schuller, specializing in fiberglass mat products. In 1979, Manville had also acquired Olinkraft, a paper company and major player in forest products. McKinney began to grow the fiberglass and forest products divisions and to build up Manville's specialty products.

Pre-recession downturns and the recessions of 1980–1982 added to Manville's woes. Losses of $88 million in 1982 compared unfavorably with earnings of $122 million in 1978. Over the same period, revenues fell to $1.8 billion from $2.3 billion. McKinney resolved to trim salaried overhead by 20%. Manville offered managers over the age of 55 full pension and the equivalent of full Social Security benefits while waiving early retirement penalties. More than 30% of those eligible, including seasoned managers and foremen, jumped at the offer. With layoffs, Manville reduced its staff to 20,000 from 25,000.

Manville filed a reorganization plan in November 1983. For the next five years its 12 bank lenders, hundreds of commercial creditors, thousands of stockholders, and tens of thousands of asbestos plaintiffs—along with their legal counsel—appealed. Negotiations frequently sputtered to a halt as Manville, still under McKinney's stewardship, attempted to wear down constituencies. By 1986, after share values tumbled to a low of $4 compared with $30 at the time of bankruptcy, the broad outlines of a final plan were clear (see **Appendix A,** "Manville Reorganization Plan").[18]

The court would enjoin future asbestos claimants from legal actions against Manville and direct them to two trusts substantially funded by the company's current assets and future earnings. The trusts would become 80% owners of the company, and some of their trustees would sit on Manville's board. Obligations to creditors would be met in full, but shareholders would see their holdings vastly diluted.

---

[16]Amended memorandum, p. 68.

[17]Quickel, p. 30.

[18]The court executed a final reorganization plan on November 28, 1988.

Management Changes

Under pressure, McKinney retired on September 1, 1986, his 35th anniversary with Manville. He received a final volley of criticism for accepting a $1.3 million "golden handshake" while creditors and claimants remained unpaid. The board replaced him with Tom Stephens, 43, a relative newcomer to the company. McKinney had groomed Josh Hulce, an attorney who joined Manville in 1972, to succeed him. But when the court would not see McKinney's protégé rise further, Hulce quit and cleared the way for Stephens.

Stephens, who considered himself a country boy, was born in Crosett, Arkansas. Crosett was a company town. Most of its inhabitants worked at the local paper mill, but Stephens's father raised livestock, grew vegetables, ran a welding shop, and had a pulpwood business. One of a multitude of fifth-generation Stephenses in Crosett, Stephens hunted with his dogs and enjoyed the exuberance of an extended family during his youth.

Despite the recommendation of his high school guidance counselor to pursue a trade, Stephens went to the University of Arkansas to study engineering. To pay his way he did odd jobs at a mill in West Monroe, Louisiana, 60 miles south of Crosett and headquarters of Olinkraft, Olin Corporation's forest products subsidiary. Olinkraft hired Stephens after he earned a B.S. in 1965 and an M.S. in 1966. He quickly took to the computer room. In 1974 Olin spun off Olinkraft and Stephens became its treasurer. When Johns-Manville acquired the company in 1979, McKinney invited Stephens to be his assistant for a year.

Back in West Monroe in 1980, Stephens was named head of the wood products division, and soon became president of the forest products subsidiary. After Manville filed for bankruptcy in 1982, Stephens managed downsizing and reorganization in his operation with aplomb. He held small meetings with employees to listen and get feedback on management decisions. He learned about communicating. He invited workers to feel responsible for results, and in two years net income doubled. Headquarters liked Stephens's performance. He was brought back to Denver in 1985 as executive vice president for finance and administration and soon became CFO. He immersed himself in the bankruptcy; his arrival at the negotiating table corresponded with the emergence of a workable reorganization plan.

Manville Corporation in 1986

In 1986, Manville owned or operated 63 facilities, 730,000 acres of timberland, and four mines in the United States and 10 other countries. The company employed 19,400 people worldwide; 8,437 employees were union members and 2,144 were covered by labor agreements that would expire in 1987. These assets and employees supported three business groups: Fiber Glass Products, Forest Products, and Specialty Products (see **Exhibit 1**). When Stephens became CEO, Manville was working to retire $500 million in high-interest debt and invest in its core businesses.

Leaving oversight of the legal issues to others, Stephens dedicated himself to making the core businesses lean and efficient. His goal was to increase earnings by 15% a year. He put Manville's 750,000-square-foot corporate headquarters in the mountains southwest of Denver up for sale and looked for utilitarian space downtown. He sold or idled several money-losing plants. To meet the financial

Eᴄʜɪʙɪᴛ 1

Financial Information

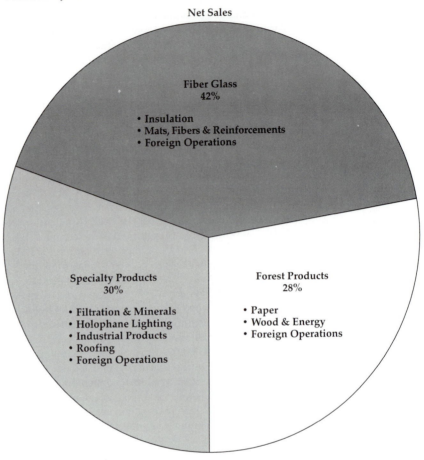

Net Sales

Fiber Glass
42%

• **Insulation**
• **Mats, Fibers & Reinforcements**
• **Foreign Operations**

Specialty Products
30%

• **Filtration & Minerals**
• **Holophane Lighting**
• **Industrial Products**
• **Roofing**
• **Foreign Operations**

Forest Products
28%

• **Paper**
• **Wood & Energy**
• **Foreign Operations**

Five-Year History (thousands of dollars except per share amounts)

Years Ended December 31	*1986*	*1985*	*1984*	*1983*	*1982*
Net sales[1]	$1,920,262	$1,880,048	$1,814,184	$1,729,465	$1,684,588
Net earnings (loss)[1]	81,228	(45,067)	77,227	60,126	(20,953)
Long-term debt and redeemable					
preferred stock[2]	380,933	392,530	384,367	304,860	312,749
Total assets	2,513,343	2,393,247	2,339,134	2,253,262	2,236,104
Per common share data:					
Net earnings (loss)[1]	2.34	(2.92)	2.18	1.47	(1.93)
Dividends	—	—	—	—	.68

[1]The results of discontinued operations have been segregated from the net sales and earnings information for 1983 and 1982.
[2]Long-term debt does not include obligations of the corporation then in Chapter 11

Source: Manville Corporation 1986 Annual Report and Form 10-K.

demands of restructuring, Stephens had to find a radically different way to do business. Manville, he said, had "a very hierarchical structure with a lot of layers, a very centralist approach."[19] He decentralized. He delegated authority to his operating divisions and gained a reputation for strict follow-up.

According to Stephens, the rapid changes created "a lot of smoke and sparks and gnashing of teeth and pain."[20] But retirement buyouts left him leading Manville's most committed, younger managers. They had risen quickly to fill the shoes of the old guard, and many were as eager to change Manville's corporate culture and public image as was Stephens.

Stephens had serious people issues to address. He had to reinvigorate the 20,000 employees who remained at Manville and rebuild alliances with investors, customers, and the media. Once a perennial on *Fortune's* list of most admired companies, Manville had become the magazine's least admired company by 1984. Stephens practiced what brought him success in West Monroe. He opened up his organization by talking and listening; in his first six weeks as president he visited 20% of the company's plants and offices.

The company's majority shareholder also needed attention. The prolonged reorganization and appeals process gave the trust time to commit to hundreds of settlements long before it was free to disburse funds.[21] The trust would exhaust its initial capitalization and be under pressure to sell stock. Technically, the cash flow problems belonged to the trust.

Stephens understood his responsibility to the trust to be the same as every CEO's obligation to any shareholder—to increase value. "[The trustees] are pretty visible and they don't go away, but the trust doesn't try to run the company and we don't try to run the trust," he said. Nevertheless, as an 80% shareholder (which Stephens has referred to as "the 300-pound gorilla"), the trust and Manville "have a stake in each other's success."[22] In effect, problems at the trust remained a major concern.

Stephens pledged that by the time the trusts could vote their shares in 1992, they would be convinced they were working with the best management team in America. The pledge was known throughout the company. John Gebert, a fiberglass plant manager, understood Manville's ownership structure to mean: "We have a hefty mortgage to pay . . . We have a responsibility to earn more at a higher rate than the typical industry because of that. . . . Our philosophy is if we run a good business, some owner is going to be delighted to have us."[23]

The Fiberglass Division

The Fiberglass Division, headed by Bill Sells, had $807 million in sales in 1986. The division generated about two-thirds of the company's operating income (**Exhibit 2**) and 75% of its profits in that year. Manville shipped its fiberglass products to Europe, Japan, Canada, Mexico, Argentina, and Brazil, as well as within the United States. Domestic sales represented about 85% of the division's total.

---

[19]Tom Stephens, interview, May 19, 1993.

[20]Stephens, interview.

[21]Spurred by generous settlement terms, the number of claims filed monthly soared from 425 in 1982 to 2,000 in 1987. Quickel, pp. 30 and 35.

[22]Stephens, interview.

[23]John Gebert, interview, May 18, 1993.

EXHIBIT 2 **Sales and Operating Income by Segment (thousands of dollars)**

Years Ended December 31	1986	1985	1984
Fiber Glass Products			
Net sales	$ 806,792	$ 800,101	$ 778,388
Costs and expenses	675,709	696,613	666,380
Restructuring charges	12,979	37,047	
Other income	1,946	2,709	2,928
Income from operations	$ 120,050	$ 69,150	$ 114,936
Forest Products			
Net sales	$ 539,948	$ 444,900	$ 435,498
Costs and expenses	472,791	415,488	387,635
Restructuring charges	6,625	9,471	
Other income	1,251	13,637	17,010
Income from operations	$ 61,783	$ 33,578	$ 64,873
Specialty Products			
Net sales	$ 606,676	$ 671,327	$ 642,287
Costs and expenses	564,791	640,995	616,880
Restructuring charges	12,325	70,843	1,300
Other income	4,298	2,504	2,851
Income from operations	$ (33,858)	$ (38,007)	$ (26,958)
Corporate and Eliminations			
Net Sales[a]	$ (33,154)	$ (36,280)	$ (41,989)
Costs and expenses	12,270	1,016	2,510
Restructuring charges	15,046	35,555	1,073
Other income	31,310	44,582	38,608
Income from operations	$ (29,160)	$ (28,269)	$ (6,964)
Consolidated Total Company			
Net sales	$1,920,262	$1,880,048	$1,814,184
Costs and expenses	1,725,561	1,754,112	1,673,405
Restructuring charges[b]	46,975	152,916	2,373
Other income	38,805	63,432	61,397
Income from operations[c]	$ 186,531	$ 36,452	$ 199,803
Depreciation and Depletion			
Fiber glass products	$ 28,632	$ 26,678	$ 24,959
Forest products	42,804	36,570	34,755
Specialty products	14,645	17,085	15,917
Corporate	3,595	3,973	3,741
	$ 89,676	$ 84,306	$ 79,372
Addition to Property, Plant and Equipment			
Fiber glass products	$ 44,388	$ 51,607	$ 49,090
Forest products	52,513	73,304	46,600
Specialty products	31,176	26,754	26,056
Corporate	(2,500)	1,471	23
	$125,577	$153,136	$121,769
Assets[b]			
Fiber glass products	$ 640,793	$ 623,700	$593,135
Forest products	890,737	870,399	843,468
Specialty products	420,452	457,707	479,215
Corporate[e]	652,211	544,593	538,034
Eliminations and adjustments[d]	(90,850)	(103,152)	(114,718)
	$2,513,343	$2,393,247	$2,339,134

[a]Net sales included in Corporate and Eliminations relate to the elimination of intersegment or intergeographic sales (at prices approximating market). Intersegment sales principally relate to sales from the Fiber Glass Products segment to the Specialty Products segment. Intergeographic sales principally relate to U.S. sales to the Company's foreign segment.
[b]Restructuring charges are included as operating expenses of the related industry segments and geographic areas. Certain reclassifications and restatements of prior years' data by industry segment and geographic area have been made.
[c]In 1986, the Company adopted Statement of Financial Accounting Standards No. 87, "Employers' Accounting for Pensions." Income from operations by business segment and geographic area was affected as follows (see Note 12):

Fiber Glass Products	$11,390	U.S.	$25,596
Forest Products	6,229	Foreign	5,229
Specialty Products	13,206		
	$30,825		$30,825

[d]Includes the elimination of intersegment and intergeographic inventory profits and the adjustment of business segment and geographic inventories, which are carried at standard costs, to the historical bases used in consolidation.
[e]Corporate assets are principally cash, marketable securities, prepaid income taxes, investments, long-term receivables, and a portion of property, plant and equipment.

Source: Manville Corporation 1986 Annual Report and Form 10-K.

The company had 15 fiberglass manufacturing plants (five in Ohio, two in California, two in Texas, and one each in Georgia, Indiana, Kansas, New Jersey, Tennessee, and West Virginia) and three support facilities in the United States, one plant in Canada, and two in West Germany. The fiberglass division employed 5,000 people, 3,000 of whom were union members.

By 1986 Manville had a highly diversified line of fiberglass products made from glass wool fibers and continuous strand textile fibers. The two forms of fiberglass resulted from separate production processes (see **Appendix B,** "Fiberglass Manufacture"). Glass wool was used primarily for insulation. Continuous strand fibers were used mainly as reinforcements for materials such as roofing, vinyl flooring, and draperies. Manville's products included a wide range of thermal and acoustical insulations for aerospace, automotive, appliances, and other commercial as well as residential uses; fiberglass specialty and roofing mats; glass fiber reinforcements; and filtration media. Fiberglass was also used in clean rooms in the medical and computer chip industries.

Fiberglass was sold to both direct users and distributors—with contractors and retailers each making 50% of total purchases. Customers ranged from small contractors to commercial accounts and large retail chains. Demand for some products, particularly residential insulation, tended to be seasonal, resulting in inventory increases in the winter and spring, with decreases during construction season.

Residential building insulation alone accounted for nearly 30% of Manville's total 1986 fiberglass sales. All commercial product sales (roofing mat, specialty fiber, specialty mat, etc.) accounted for 40% of total sales, and industrial product sales (aerospace insulation, auto headliners, hoodliners, molded parts, etc.) accounted for the remaining 30%.

Fiberglass products, especially insulations, were a boon to the company during the twin recessions of the early 1980s. As energy costs rose, more insulation went into new construction, and owners looked to save on their bills by reinsulating older homes. In California alone, there were 314,000 housing starts in 1986, compared with 172,600 in 1983.[24] All these buildings were stuffed with insulation, about 99% of which was fiberglass. In the mid-1980s the insulation market was "red hot," according to Joe McGinty, Manville's fiberglass sales manager for the area.[25] Fiberglass was about the only building material shielded from the downturn.

Fiberglass Industry

In the mid-1980s, North American manufacturers produced 1.8 million tons, or $3 billion worth, of fiberglass annually. In 1986 Manville was the world's largest producer of nonwoven fiberglass mat, the second-largest producer of fiberglass insulation, and third-largest producer of continuous-strand fiberglass. Owens-Corning Fiberglass Corporation was the largest—and Certain-Teed Corporation the third-largest—producer of insulation. Owens-Corning was the largest—and PPG Industries, Inc., the second-largest—producer of continuous-strand fiberglass.

Mineral wool and wood-based cellulose competed with fiberglass insulation products. Mineral wool was widely used in Europe, but little used in the United States in 1986. Cellulose, with less than 5% of the U.S. market for insulation products, was produced and distributed largely through small "mom-and-pop" businesses, and rarely used union labor. Though cellulose was not a significant threat to fiberglass, it began to be promoted in the early 1980s as "God's natural insulation" by a man named Richard Munson, a founder of National Consumer Products Marketing, Inc., a cellulose trade association. Munson was also president of Thermolite Corporation, a cellulose manufacturer. Munson's zealous promotion of cellulose prompted *The Wall Street Journal* to call him the "rebel without a pause."[26]

A few other products competed with Manville's fiberglass. Corrugated board was sometimes used as an automotive insulation; foam was used both in auto and appliance insulation; and other synthetic fibers were sometimes used for air filtration and mat products.

Fiberglass Regulation

Fiberglass was not specifically regulated in the United States or anywhere else in 1986. However, the spirit, if not the letter, of several U.S. regulations affected fiberglass producers. To protect workers from eye and respiratory tract irritations, in 1977 the National Institute for Occupational Safety and Health (NIOSH) recommended a workplace exposure limit of three fibers per cubic centimeter of air. The Occupational Safety and Health Administration (OSHA) did not specifically regulate fiberglass exposure, but classified it as a "nuisance dust" with corresponding exposure guidelines. Fiberglass producers were also well aware of the 1976 Toxic Substances Control Act (TSCA) which required manufacturers to notify the Environmental Protection Agency (EPA) within 15 working days of acquiring new and previously unknown information about a potential hazard to worker health.[27]

---

[24]Internal Correspondence from J. E. McGinty to R. Mathewson, May 7, 1993.

[25]Joe McGinty, interview, May 20, 1993.

[26]Rick Wartzman, "A Foe to Fiberglass Tells All Who Listen It's Dangerous Stuff," *The*

[27]Following scientific practice, Manville used the term *hazard* to refer to potential harms; and the term *risk,* to refer to the probability that harm would occur. Risk was a function of exposure: a carcinogen to which no one was exposed carried no risk.

Since 1976, Manville fiberglass products had carried a voluntary "itch-scratch" label stating that temporary skin and upper respiratory tract irritations might result from exposure. Following industry custom dating from the early 1970s, Manville also provided customers with Material Safety Data Sheets (MSDSs) containing this information. Together with labels which were usually printed on packaging, MSDSs were the principal means to communicate health and safety messages to customers and workers. MSDSs were included with bills for initial shipments of fiberglass and were available to employees during work shifts.

Beginning in 1985 OSHA's Hazard Communication Standard (HAZCOM) and various state "workers' right-to-know" laws required MSDSs and product labels for all substances and operations that potentially exposed workers to hazardous materials. These laws gave manufacturers the responsibility for identifying potential hazards and communicating hazard information downstream. It was thus incumbent on manufacturers to review available scientific evidence concerning hazards of materials they used or produced and to keep information current. Under HAZCOM, notification on the MSDS was required whenever a single statistically significant study done in accordance with scientific principles indicated the presence of a hazard. OSHA's compliance standard under HAZCOM required that any International Agency for Research on Cancer (IARC) classification as a "possible carcinogen" be disclosed on MSDSs but not on labels. Classification as a "probable carcinogen" had to be disclosed on both MSDSs and labels. To date, OSHA had not given high priority to enforcement of this aspect of the compliance standard.

Though HAZCOM required that certain categories of information be included on MSDSs and on labels, the law did not mandate specific language. Manville's MSDSs identified products and their ingredients, listed physical data and fire and explosion data, summarized health hazards, risks, symptoms, and first-aid procedures, and provided reactivity data, spill or leak procedures, along with special precautionary information. (See **Exhibit 3** for the "Health Hazards" section of Manville's MSDS for fiberglass.)

Manville also published a variety of fiberglass health and safety documents for customers and workers. These publications detailed the hazards of exposure, recommended safe handling practices, and noted resources for more information. Internal training programs emphasized fiberglass safety procedures, and Manville monitored worker health. Since the 1950s Manville had assessed ambient fiberglass levels in all its manufacturing facilities, and had striven to have state-of-the-art filtration systems. All of this was voluntary.

Fiberglass Research

In 1986 fiberglass was the most widely studied industrial material known. Since 1942, manufacturers, unions, scientists, and regulators had published 400 reports on it. Tens of thousands of workers had participated in its manufacture and use; there was considerable interest in its health effects. Manville was especially eager to ensure sound research. Independently, and through the Thermal Insulation Manufacturers Association (TIMA), Manville funded several fiberglass studies. "Our future was fiberglass," said Anderson, "our past was asbestos."[28]

---

[28]Anderson, interview.

Exhibit 3   **Material Safety Data Sheet for Manville Fiber Glass Insulation, Section V.A. Health Hazards Summary/Risks**

| V. HEALTH HAZARDS | A. Summary/Risks |

Summary: CURRENT ANIMAL AND EPIDEMIOLOGICAL STUDIES INDICATE THAT GLASS FIBERS AND DUST DO NOT REPRESENT A HAZARD TO HEALTH.

THIS PRODUCT IS NOT CONSIDERED A CARCINOGEN BY NTP, IARC, AND OSHA.

Medical conditions which may be aggravated: PRE-EXISTING UPPER RESPIRATORY AND LUNG DISEASES SUCH AS, BUT NOT LIMITED TO, BRONCHITIS, EMPHYSEMA, AND ASTHMA.
Target Organ(s): LUNGS and SKIN.
Acute Health Effects: IRRITATION TO SKIN AND UPPER RESPIRATORY SYSTEM.

Chronic Health Effects: NO LONG-TERM EFFECTS HAVE BEEN IDENTIFIED.

Primary Entry Route(s): INHALATION, SKIN CONTACT.

Source: Manville Corporation.

The Enterline study discussed in Copenhagen was one of two epidemiological studies begun in the early 1980s that followed the health of fiberglass workers more fully than any previously undertaken. The Enterline U.S. study followed 16,661 MMVF workers in 17 plants (14,800 fiberglass workers in 11 plants). The second, a European study conducted by IARC, a WHO agency, followed 23,609 workers in 13 European MMVF plants (11,852 fiberglass workers in six plants).

The European study, reported in 1984 and updated in 1986, found no excess mortality among fiberglass workers from lung cancer. It did, however, report excess cancers among slag and rock wool workers—particularly among those employed before the use of modern dust control technologies. Too little information existed to assess workers in the continuous filament industry. In each of these MMVF industries, some workers were smokers or had exposure histories with asbestos or other known carcinogens.

Besides the U.S. and European studies, animal studies were also being conducted—both inhalation experiments in which scientists exposed laboratory animals to high concentrations of breathable fibers, and implantation studies in which scientists inserted fiberglass directly into animal bodies. Inhalation studies showed no increased risk of lung scarring or cancers, though reversible irritations occurred. Results of some of the animal implantation studies, however, suggested that fiberglass particles smaller than 1.5 microns in diameter produced scarring and cancers.

Critics of these studies, including their lead investigators, noted that inhalation doses exceeded any possible workplace exposure, and implantation bypassed normal respiratory tract defense mechanisms. According to Anderson, "Almost any foreign body can cause cancer if you implant it in the right place."[29]

---

[29]Anderson, interview.

Because the results of the implantation studies were less applicable to humans than epidemiological studies, NIOSH stated in 1977 that scientists should not use them to assess potential workplace hazards. Nevertheless, all the studies were reviewed by international bodies such as IARC, the International Programme on Chemical Safety (IPCS), and the International Labour Organization (ILO); U.S. regulatory agencies such as EPA, OSHA, and NIOSH; as well as labor organizations and consumer groups.

The Role of IARC

Many in the international scientific and regulatory community considered IARC the preeminent authority on carcinogen review and classification. IARC sponsored research, and since 1971 had evaluated carcinogenic risks to humans in the workplace. Primarily to aid in identifying issues for further study, IARC had developed a classification system which grouped substances under review in one of five categories:

Group 1	carcinogenic to humans
Group 2A	probably carcinogenic to humans
Group 2B	possibly carcinogenic to humans
Group 3	not classifiable as to human carcinogenicity
Group 4	probably not carcinogenic to humans

IARC's rules of evidence for classifying substances were very liberal. For example, IARC required one of the three cancer classifications when data demonstrated carcinogenicity in animals even if the route of exposure was artificial, did not duplicate human dose levels or durations of exposure, or existing human data was insufficient for such a classification. Once IARC classified a material it took a year or two to publish the findings in a monograph, making them official. IARC specified that its classifications were not intended for regulatory purposes. However, EPA, OSHA, and other regulatory bodies, especially in the United States, but also in Europe, followed IARC rulings closely.

Despite IARC's recommendations, cancer classification did trigger product labeling requirements in a few states. For example, such classification created a statutory obligation to label under California's Safe Drinking Water and Toxic Enforcement Act of 1986 ("Proposition 65"). If IARC were eventually to classify fiberglass as a carcinogen, Manville would not have to meet this statutory obligation until some time after the classification became public, however, and the California law did not mandate specific label language.

Taking It Personally

As Anderson placed his call to Bill Sells, he reviewed the recent pace of change at Manville and his own history. His medical school and public health training, along with his experience at Manville and elsewhere—five years as chief of aeromedical services in the U.S. Air Force and senior medical positions at Trans World Airlines and Air Canada—pointed to the seriousness of the situation.

Anderson had joined Manville in 1982 just as the company filed for bankruptcy. Within a month, his name was on creditors' lists because Manville had not paid his moving expenses. He knew Manville's circumstances when he signed on, but, like other senior managers, he was surprised to learn the extent to which bankruptcy impacted his professional and, less expectedly, his personal life. Even Tom Stephens got caught. Soon after bankruptcy, Stephens was entertaining at a restaurant. When he went to pay, he was embarrassed to be told that the restaurant could not honor his company credit card.

There could never have been a good time to get Anderson's news. But Sells, head of the Fiberglass Division since 1981, wondered if there could have been a worse time. Within the previous 18 months, Manville had lost its chairman, CEO, and president. Tom Stephens, a young outsider to headquarters, was now in the corner office. Downsizing had undermined company morale, and early retirements had replaced a number of seasoned managers with less experienced ones. As bankruptcy court headed for a confirmed reorganization plan, the media and public called for retribution for Manville's past mistakes. Creditors argued that the company was worth more liquidated than operating. Appeals dragged on. Even in this negative climate Manville was on Wall Street looking for credit. And now Sir Richard Doll had just suggested the company's largest business could be the next asbestos.

Sells knew about asbestos. He worked with it for 20 years before moving into fiberglass. Sells grew up near Manville, New Jersey; parents of friends worked for Johns-Manville. When he graduated from Gettysburg College in 1956 he joined the Marines, but after four years he resigned his commission to spend more time with his family. He wanted to be an architect but the economics of a growing family forced him to look for something more concrete. Manville was the logical place to send his resume. Sells returned from an overseas post on a Thursday in 1960, interviewed with Manville on Friday, and went to work on Monday. He started in sales, rose to staff engineer, and then product manager. By 1966 he was plant manager at the asbestos facility in Waukegan, Illinois. It was, according to Sells, "the most powerful experience" of his life.[30]

By 1986, without a single exception, every person who had been on his staff in Waukegan was dead of an asbestos-related cancer. He had sat by the bedsides of co-workers and friends as they succumbed to terminal cancers caused by workplace exposures. He had sat with widows listening to understand what he, personally, could do for them. "No one, till the day I die," Sells said, "can take out of me the belief I have in industry's need for product stewardship . . . that it avoids personal and business pain is so clear."[31] All of the managers involved in the fiberglass decision had personal experience from Manville's asbestos years. "Most of the people around the [decision-making] table had been deposed *ad nauseam* about these issues," according to Anderson.[32]

Managing the Crisis—Making Decisions

What did Anderson's news mean? How should Manville respond? Should the company relabel fiberglass products with a cancer-hazard label? What would a label say? Could the fiberglass business—and Manville—survive the likely

---

[30]Bill Sells, telephone interview, June 7, 1993.

[31]Sells, telephone interview.

[32]Anderson, interview.

panic? What if IARC reviews of Enterline's research and other epidemiological and animal studies led to a Group 2A, "probably carcinogenic to humans," classification—as seemed likely? According to Von Wald, senior managers "met forever" analyzing every aspect of every possible decision. "We considered everything from doing nothing to shutting the [fiberglass] business down."[33]

If anyone mentioned a lawyer, scientist, or business advisor who might offer a unique perspective on the fiberglass crisis, Stephens "hauled them into Denver." Asbestos was not far from anyone's mind. "For those of us who were around that table, this looked just like the asbestos history,"[34] said Von Wald. To Sells, "the parallels were frightening."[35]

Several of Manville's decision makers, like Anderson, were convinced that there was no cancer risk associated with fiberglass and that a review and updates of studies would bear them out. Anderson briefed everyone on the Copenhagen studies and emphasized that the Enterline data was preliminary. "We knew the truth lay in the data," he said, "we just needed to get the study done."[36] It was now clear that 1987 was going to be the "year of MMVF evaluation." An IARC classification conference was scheduled for Lyon, France, in June, and a conference of WHO's International Programme on Chemical Safety (IPCS) was slated for London in September. Anderson pushed to get the Enterline study done.

In this environment, Stephens, Sells, Anderson, and Manville lawyers weighed the possibilities and considered the implications of various options. Brainstorming meetings also focused on the response of organized labor, investors, and all those plaintiffs' attorneys looking for post-asbestos work.

APPENDIX A
MANVILLE REORGANIZATION PLAN

On December 22, 1986, bankruptcy court confirmed a reorganization plan for Manville Corporation and opened the courts to a final two-year stretch of appeals. Critics still argued that Manville was worth more to creditors and asbestos claimants dead and liquidated, than alive. Ultimately, claimants realized that if they fought to liquidate Manville, creditors would deplete the resultant accounts long before they would see any money. And, Manville's 20,000 employees would lose their jobs. The confirmation order became final on October 28, 1988, and the 554-page plan was executed and delivered on November 28, 1988.

In a precedent-setting agreement, the court granted Manville an injunction against all future asbestos-related claims. The plan also established two trusts to administer the claims: the Manville Personal Injury Settlement Trust and the Manville Property Damage Trust. Manville would fund the trusts for at least the next 25 years.

---

[33]Dick Von Wald, interview, May 20, 1993.
[34]Von Wald, interview.
[35]Sells, interview, May 20, 1993.
[36]Anderson, interview.

The Manville Personal Injury Settlement Trust (the "health trust") was seeded with $615 million in insurance proceeds, $150 million in cash, and $50 million in notes from Manville. Two bonds with an aggregate face value of $1.8 billion were also executed by Manville in favor of the trust, payable in annual $75-million installments beginning August 1991 and continuing through November 2015. Beyond these assets, beginning in 1992 Manville would make additional payments to the trust of up to 20% of its annual profits if necessary—anticipating an extended life for the trust, and closely linking its financing to the health of the reorganized company.

The trust was also given up to 80% of the stock of the reorganized Manville Corporation—24 million shares of common stock (50% of common outstanding at the time) plus 7.2 million shares of new Series A preferred stock convertible under certain circumstances to an additional 72 million common shares (constituting an additional 30% interest). The stock was hedged with restrictions to prevent the trust from interfering with management's control for some years. Negotiators designed the long payment period to ensure the viability of Manville.

The second trust, the Manville Property Damage Trust, was begun with $125 million ($100 million from Manville and $25 million from the health trust). It was also granted a right to any unused funds from the health trust after all its claims were fully met, as well as entitlement to 20% of Manville's annual profits for as long as necessary to pay claimants after health trust claims were met. Estimates put the cost of removing asbestos from properties and refitting them with replacement products at more than $85 billion, far more than the health claims.

Manville would also pay $250,000 per year for the duration of the trusts to defray administrative overhead. Altogether, Manville agreed to pay approximately $2.5 billion into the trusts over 25 years.

Manville would make its banks and other unsecured creditors whole with $247.5 million in immediate cash, and the rest through payments of $67.5 million per year for the first three and one-half years after bankruptcy. Commercial creditors, negotiating for interest on accounts payable that were frozen when Manville filed for bankruptcy, were satisfied with debt, stocks, and warrants.

Preferred-stock holders received new $2.70 Series B cumulative-preference stock for each of their old $5.40 shares. They were also entitled to 2.16 shares of new diluted common stock. They would end up with only 6.3% of Manville's common shares, 3 million out of 48 million outstanding. They would see their common equity shrink to 2.2% if the health trust converted its preferred holdings.

APPENDIX B
FIBERGLASS MANUFACTURE

Fiberglass is produced in two primary forms: fiberglass wool and textile fibers. Fiberglass wool is made by pouring molten glass onto a rapidly spinning disk with thousands of fine holes in its rim. Centrifugal force propels the molten glass through the holes. The resultant fibers are coated with a binder, oven-cured, then formed into insulation batts or blankets, or chopped into loose fill for insulation and acoustical control products. Wool fibers generally vary from two to nine microns in diameter and can be several centimeters long. These larger fibers are used in thermal and acoustical applications. About 1% of all U.S. fiberglass wool is special-purpose, fine-fiberglass wool with diameters of less than one micron.

Rather than being blown or spun, fiberglass textile fibers are produced by extruding molten glass through holes in a platinum container. The resultant fibers are typically 8 to 25 microns in diameter and are used to reinforce other materials, especially plastics. They are used in draperies, roofing felts, and shingles.

Fibers greater than five microns in diameter are most likely to cause skin and respiratory tract irritations. Generally, only fibers and particles smaller than three microns in diameter can enter the lungs. There is an industry trend toward production of smaller diameter fibers because of their greater insulation qualities.

An important difference between fiberglass and asbestos is that when fiberglass fibers break, they do so across their long axis, resulting in shorter fibers of the same diameter. Asbestos breaks along its long axis, resulting in fibers of the same length but smaller diameters. Fiberglass is also less durable in body fluids than is asbestos. High dissolubility lessens the likelihood of adverse effects from fibers imbedded in the body.

CASE 4
DOW CORNING CORPORATION: PRODUCT STEWARDSHIP

In December 1991, a federal court jury in California awarded Mariann Hopkins $7.3 million in her suit against Dow Corning Corporation for injuries to her autoimmune system allegedly resulting from breast implants manufactured by the company.[1] Hopkins was just one of thousands of women who had undergone breast implant surgery for reconstructive or cosmetic purposes during the previous 25 years, and one of many who had begun to question the safety of implants in the 1980s. The federal court judgment was seen as a landmark victory by the plaintiff's lawyers. Dow Corning and other breast implant manufacturers now were facing the possibility of substantial litigation from others claiming to be harmed by silicone gel implants. With perhaps as many as two million breast implant operations completed, the potential existed for thousands of lawsuits to be filed against the manufacturers.[2]

As Dow Corning entered 1992, problems with silicone gel implants loomed large, even though implants represented less than 1% of total 1991 revenues.[3] On January 6 the U.S. Food and Drug Administration (FDA) requested that breast implant producers and medical practitioners halt the sale and use of silicone gel breast implants pending further review of their safety and effectiveness.[4] As a precautionary measure, Dow Corning retained former U.S. Attorney General Griffin Bell on January 10 to conduct a complete investigation of the company's development, production, and marketing of silicone gel breast implants. On February 3 the company took a pretax charge of $25 million against 1991 earnings to cover expenses associated with frozen inventories, dedicated equipment, and other related costs.[5]

On February 10, in light of the implant controversy, Dow Corning's board appointed Keith R. McKennon chairman and CEO, replacing chairman John Ludington, who was forced to retire, and CEO Larry Reed, who was demoted. McKennon, a career Dow Chemical employee, had previously served as president of Dow Chemical USA, and for six years had been a member of Dow Corning's

This is a revised version of "Dow Corning Corporation: Marketing Breast Implant Devices," which is forthcoming in *Business Case Journal* (Nacogdoches, TX: Society for Case Research) and which was prepared from public sources by Andrew D. Dyer and Todd E. Himstead of Georgetown University School of Business, under the direction of N. Craig Smith. Some material also was drawn from a report compiled by Georgetown MBA students Kirsten D. Marlatt, Daniel Rabbit and Michael Vechery. Charles A. Nichols, III, research associate at Harvard Business School, prepared the case revisions. Copyright © 1995 by Andrew D. Dyer, Todd E. Himstead, and N. Craig Smith.

[1]Josephine Marcotty, "Implant Lawsuits: Floods of Litigation Possible Because of Health Problems with Silicone Gel," *Star Tribune*, January 30, 1992, p. D1.

[2]Gail Appleson, "Court Orders Kept Breast Implant Data Secret for Years," Reuters, AM cycle, January 30, 1992.

[3]Marcotty, "Implant Lawsuits."

[4]Boyce Ressberger, "Silicone Gel Data Faked, Firm Says," *Houston Chronicle*, November 3, 1992, p. A7.

[5]Dow Corning Corporation, Form 10–K, December 31, 1991.

board of directors. Having managed two previous product crises for Dow Chemical (including one related to Dow's manufacture and distribution of the 'Agent Orange' pesticide) now he was now charged with deciding what to do with the silicone gel implant product line and how to manage the legal, regulatory, and public relations challenges facing Dow Corning.

Dow Corning

Dow Corning Corporation was founded in 1943 with a mission to develop the potential of silicones, which were then new materials based on silicon, an element refined from quartz rock. The resulting chemical compounds were the basis for an infinite range of versatile, flexible materials that ranged from fluids thinner than water to rigid plastics. The company was established as a 50/50 joint venture of Dow Chemical Company of Midland, Michigan, and Corning Glass Works (now Corning Inc.) of Corning, New York. Corning provided the joint venture with basic silicone technology while Dow Chemical supplied chemical processing and manufacturing know-how. Both companies provided initial key employees and maintained their ownership of Dow Corning from the outset.

The Dow Corning venture became successful in developing, manufacturing, and marketing silicone-based products. As one of the fastest growing firms in the chemical industry after World War II, it grew steadily in revenues, profits, and employees. By 1991 it generated revenues of $1.85 billion and income of $152.9 million, and employed some 8,300 people.[6] In 1991, it was ranked 241 in the *Fortune* 500.[7] (For a five-year summary of Dow Corning's financial statements, see **Exhibit 1.**) In addition to developing silicone products, Dow Corning had expanded into related specialty chemical materials, poly-crystalline silicon and specialty health care products. With 5,000 products, Dow Corning served a wide range of industries including aerospace, automotive, petrochemicals, construction, electronics, medical products, pharmaceuticals, plastics, and textiles. It had become a global enterprise with 33 manufacturing locations worldwide, R&D facilities in the United States, Japan, France, Germany, Belgium and the United Kingdom, and over 45,000 customers in countries including the United States, Canada, Japan, Australia, Taiwan, and Korea, as well as in Europe and Latin America.

Organizational Innovations

Dow Corning was an innovator not only in research and development but also in organizational design. In 1967 the company introduced a then-novel global matrix form of organization to replace its conventional divisional structure. Under the new structure the company carried on its business through profit centers, each of which had its own manager and business board. Each profit center contained cross-functional product management groups (PMGs) responsible for product families. The new structure emphasized teamwork and communication, as well as an open and informal culture.[8]

---

[6]Dow Corning Corporation, Form 10–K.

[7]"Largest U.S. Industrial Corporations," *Fortune*, April 20, 1992, pp. 220f.

[8]Anne T. Lawrence, "Dow Corning and the Silicone Breast Implant Controversy," *Case Research Journal*, 1993, p. 239.

EXHIBIT 1   **Dow Corning Corporation: Five-Year Summary of Selected Financial Data**

Consolidated Balance Sheets (in millions of dollars)

Year Ended December 31	1991	1990	1989	1988	1987
ASSETS					
Current Assets					
Cash and cash equivalents	$ 7.9	$ 9.1	$ 4.1	$ 36.9	$ 10.8
Short-term investments	0.4	1.9	3.3	5.1	3.0
Accounts and notes receivable	334.1	336.3	293.4	289.6	258.8
Inventories	358.7	381.2	251.8	242.2	242.1
Other current assets	110.0	84.7	64.5	53.5	57.2
Total current assets	811.1	713.6	617.1	627.3	571.9
Property, plant, equipment					
Land and land improvements	107.4	95.8	92.5	88.6	80.1
Buildings	391.3	354.3	276.1	241.0	214.6
Machinery and equipment	1,533.9	1,272.3	1,109.7	1,066.3	1,000.5
Construction-in-progress	179.4	235.9	242.6	140.3	56.7
	2,212.0	1,958.3	1,720.9	1,536.2	1,351.0
Less accumulated depreciation	(1,000.1)	(846.6)	(740.3)	(705.2)	(630.2)
	1,211.9	1,111.7	980.6	831.0	721.7
Other assets	96.9	97.5	80.4	70.5	67.6
	$2,119.9	$1,922.4	$1,678.1	$1,528.8	$1,361.2
LIABILITIES & SHAREHOLDERS' EQUITY					
Current Liabilities					
Commercial paper payable	—	—	—	—	$39.7
Notes payable	$59.3	$104.0	$23.6	$13.0	7.3
Current portion of long-term debt	4.0	13.2	0.5	5.4	30.9
Trade accounts payable	135.3	121.0	107.3	114.2	90.3
Income taxes payable	28.2	26.0	36.8	29.2	42.7
Accrued payrolls and employee benefits	52.4	43.3	31.2	33.2	30.9
Accrued taxes, other than income taxes	15.8	16.3	18.9	19.7	12.3
Other current liabilities	113.6	70.3	68.2	79.4	71.5
	450.0	394.1	286.5	294.1	325.6
Long-term debt	286.8	267.7	274.3	200.4	95.7
Other liabilities	198.5	196.9	190.4	183.9	183.7
Minority interest in consolidated subsidiaries	77.1	65.3	54.8	54.1	48.7
Stockholders' equity					
Common stock, $5 par value—2,500,000 shares authorized and outstanding	12.5	12.5	12.5	12.5	12.5
Retained earnings	1,028.8	953.4	853.8	758.0	668.5
Cumulative translation adjustment	66.2	32.5	5.8	25.8	26.5
Stockholders' equity	1,107.5	998.4	872.1	796.3	707.5
	$2,119.9	$1,922.4	$1,678.1	$1,528.8	$1,361.2

Exhibit 1   Continued

Consolidated Statements of Operations and Retained Earnings (in millions of dollars except per share amounts)

Year Ended December 31	1991	1990	1989	1988	1987
Net Sales	$1,845.4	$1,718.3	$1,574.5	$1,476.8	$1,303.0
Operating costs and expenses:					
Manufacturing cost of sales	1,195.5	1,105.2	1,000.8	954.4	842.1
Marketing and administrative expenses	397.3	351.6	314.2	293.3	263.8
Implant costs	25.0	—	—	—	—
Special items	29.0	—	—	—	—
	1,646.8	1,456.8	1,315.0	1,247.7	1,105.9
Operating Income	198.6	261.5	259.5	299.1	197.1
Other income (expense)	10.4	(0.5)	6.9	5.8	15.4
Income before income taxes	209.0	261.0	266.6	234.9	212.5
Income taxes	58.3	80.1	94.6	75.3	74.1
Minority interests' share in income	14.1	9.8	9.2	9.1	3.4
Net income	152.9	171.1	162.8	150.5	135.0
Retained earnings at beginning of year	953.4	853.8	758.0	668.5	587.5
Cash dividends	(77.5)	(71.5)	(67.0)	(61.0)	(54.0)
Retained earnings at end of year	$1,028.8	$953.4	$853.8	$758.0	$668.5
Net income per share	$61.16	$68.44	$65.12	$60.20	$54.00

Source: Dow Corning 10K Filings.

In the 1970s Dow Corning was a pioneer in emphasizing corporate ethics.[9] Under the leadership of a board-level Audit and Social Responsibility Committee established in 1976, the company created a six-member Business Conduct Committee, developed its first code of conduct, and set up a detailed system of annual audits to evaluate code compliance. The initial code focused heavily on issues around general integrity, responsibilities to employees, and relationships with host countries, particularly the avoidance of improper payments. Every year, some 20 one-day audits were conducted at various sites around the world, each involving 5 to 15 people at the area management level and just below. In preparation for an audit, managers at the audit site were sent a worksheet with a detailed set of questions designed to elicit issues and assess compliance. Worksheet questions covered issues such as relationships with customers, distributors, competitors, and host country governments, as well as protection of proprietary information. Results of the audit were submitted annually to the board of directors and presented to the company's global management. Videotapes of the annual audit report were used to keep employees informed about the code and

---

[9]Material on Dow Corning's corporate ethics program is based on David Whiteside and Kenneth E. Goodpaster, "Dow Corning Corporation: Business Conduct and Global Values (A)," HBS case 385–018.

about ethics issues. Certain employee training programs included modules on the code, and business conduct updates were sometimes included in management reports.

Dow Corning revised its code in 1981, adding provisions on customer and distributor issues such as:

> We will continually strive to assure that our products and services are safe, efficacious and accurately represented in our literature, advertising, and package identification.
>
> Product characteristics, including toxicity and potential hazards, will be made known to those who produce, package, transport, use and dispose of Dow Corning products.[10]

Throughout the 1980s, the company regularly reviewed and updated its code and conducted ethics audits. The 1990 audit of the plant that manufactured breast implants turned up no concerns about product safety. As a member of the Business Conduct Committee pointed out, product safety issues usually were handled through the relevant business board, not the ethics review process.[11]

Dow Corning in 1991 was divided into two primary line organizations, Area Operations and Business Organization (see organizational chart in **Exhibit 2**). Area Operations were responsible for sales and service of Dow Corning products around the world and were grouped into the U.S., Inter-America (Canada and Latin America), Europe and Asia. The Business Organization was responsible for the development and manufacturing of Dow Corning's products and was organized on a product line-of-business approach.

Dow Corning's product line in 1991 included gasket sealants and windshields for the aerospace industry; silicone rubbers for the automotive industry; adhesives and sealants for the building trades and for consumer home improvement; and fluids, emulsions, and transdermal patches for the pharmaceutical industry; as well as a variety of medical products, such as tubing, adhesives, and surgical implants.

Dow Corning Wright

In 1991, silicone gel breast implants were being manufactured and sold for Dow Corning by Dow Corning Wright Corporation, a wholly owned subsidiary that also manufactured and marketed metal orthopedic implants. Headquartered in Arlington, Tennessee, Dow Corning Wright was headed by chairman Bob Rylee and president and CEO Dan M. Hayes, Jr., who reported to Dow Corning's Business Organization. Considered a stand-alone line of business, Dow Corning Wright was established in 1978 when Dow Corning acquired Wright Medical, a small manufacturer of artificial hips and knees. Dow Corning then transferred all of its medical devices manufacturing and sales, including breast implants, to this new subsidiary. (Note: As Dow Corning Wright was 100% owned by Dow Corn-

---

[10]Whiteside and Goodpaster, "Dow Corning Corporation," p. 13.
[11]Lawrence, "Dow Corning," p. 254.

Exhibit 2

Dow Corning Corporation Organizational Chart, February 10, 1992

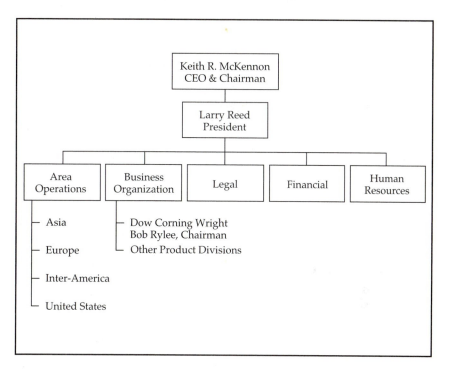

ing Inc., it is referred to hereafter as "Dow Corning," unless specific reference to Dow Corning Wright is required.) Dow Corning Wright 1991 revenues were approximately $80 million.[12]

Breast Implant Devices

Efforts to achieve breast augmentation dated to the 16th century. Materials such as ivory, glass and paraffin had been used for contour enhancement (by applying these materials to the breast externally). The first augmentation mammoplasty was accomplished in the late 19th century. Following this operation, a variety of nonsilicone materials were injected or implanted to cosmetically alter or reconstruct breasts. The most successful implant device, developed during the 1950s, was a product with an outer sack made of polyurethane foam or silicone, and filled with saline.

---

[12]*Ward's Business Directory of U.S. Private and Public Companies* (New York: Gale Research Inc., 1992).

The next breakthrough came in 1962, when Dow Corning was approached by two plastic surgeons who wanted help in further developing breast implants for mastectomy patients, who typically had suffered from cancer, as well as for victims of congenital deformity. The surgeons had designed an implant and had begun limited production, but looked to Dow Corning for silicone gel and manufacturing expertise. In 1964, as a result of this request, Dow Corning developed a product based on an envelope of silicone elastomer (a rubber-like elastic substance) filled with silicone gel. The product was touted to be superior in terms of its look and feel for the recipients, and compared with saline fluid-filled implants, was less likely to migrate through body tissue that surrounded the breast. Silicone gel breast implants became the market leader from that time on.

The advantage of silicone gel implants was that the silicone could hold its shape. This was particularly important for reconstructive patients, where there was little or no foundation to build on. Saline implants (made with salt water contained in a silicone envelope) were "water-like" and held no shape by themselves. As a result, they were much less effective in providing either an enhanced figure or a complete reconstruction.

Although safety testing was not legally required during the 1960s when silicone gel implants were being developed, Dow Corning conducted its own safety tests, following good manufacturing practice of the time. Through independent laboratory contractors hired to study the safety of silicones, Dow Corning learned that injection of silicone fluids into animals could cause persistent, chronic inflammation and scarring, and that the fluid could migrate widely within the body. However, the company firmly believed silicones to be biologically inert and safe for internal use.[13]

From 1965, when Dow Corning launched the first silicone gel breast implants, demand for the product was consistently high. Other manufacturers entered the market and the company became one of seven manufacturers in the United States producing the silicone gel product. Dow Corning introduced new models over time, with improvements in gel texture and envelope characteristics, and in a variety of sizes and contours.

For example, in 1975, when Dow Corning was facing serious competitive pressures from other breast implant products, the company set up a cross-functional team of 20 men to develop a new generation of implants that would be softer and more pliable. The team moved quickly to develop the new version—doing no additional medical testing since the new product was based on materials substantially similar to those used in its predecessors.[14] Although questions surfaced about the new implant's propensity to "bleed" through its envelope into surrounding tissue, laboratory tests indicated, albeit inconclusively, that the new product was no more likely to bleed than the standard one. Bleeding problems that emerged in early product demonstrations were attributed to improper handling. The new implant was marketed aggressively, despite early production problems. In 1976, an engineer who had served on the new product task force resigned, citing the company's decisions to market a product of unproven safety. The company dismissed his charges, noting that he was a disgruntled employee.[15]

---

[13]Lawrence, "Dow Corning," p. 240.
[14]Lawrence, "Dow Corning," p. 241.
[15]Lawrence, "Dow Corning," p. 244.

From 1965 to 1992, Dow Corning sold approximately 600,000 implants, 45% of them outside the United States.[16] The company's share of the market for breast implants never exceeded 25% once the industry became established. In 1991, chairman Bob Rylee admitted that the breast implant line had sustained five consecutive years of financial losses. The company continued to sell implants and to supply silicone to other implant manufacturers, however, because millions of women were "counting on them."[17] During the 1980s, Dow Corning's focus on medical devices moved to knee implants; breast implants were not viewed as a strategic product. In 1991, the company's market share of breast implant sales was approximately 18%, placing it third behind McGhan Medical and Mentor.

Sales Agents

Dow Corning Wright's medical devices were sold by independent agents who had contracts to sell the products in specified geographic areas and who were paid a commission on sales and reimbursed for expenses. In 1991, Dow Corning had some 70 medical device agents across the United States. They were managed by a Dow Corning national sales manager and supported by two marketing staff members. Some of the more senior agents also coordinated or supervised other agents regionally.

Some independent agents also sold non-Dow Corning products, though typically these products did not compete with Dow Corning's line. The agents relied on their strong relationships with surgeons to make sales, maintaining those relationships by providing quality products and good service. Of the 70 independent agents operating in 1991, two relied heavily on Dow Corning's breast implants, with some 50% of their sales derived from them. For the remaining agents, their primary focus was hip and knee implants, with between 5% and 25% (an average of 10%) of their sales coming from breast implants.[18]

Geography was the major contributor to variations in volume, with certain regions having a higher demand for implants than others. The Pacific region was the site of the most (approximately 25%) breast augmentation procedures in the early 1990s, followed by the South Atlantic region with 21%, according to the American Society of Plastic and Reconstructive Surgeons (ASPRS). New England had the fewest procedures, with only 1.5%. California represented 19% of the total, Florida 12%, Texas 10%, and New York 4%.[19]

[16]Scott McMurray and Thomas M. Burton, "Dow Corning . . . ," *Wall Street Journal,* March 19, 1992, p. A3.

[17] Thomas M. Burton, Bruce Ingersoll, and Joan E. Rigdon, "Dow Corning Makes Changes in Top Posts," *Wall Street Journal,* February 11, 1992, p. A3.

[18]Gary E. Anderson, Executive Vice President, Dow Corning Corporation, interview, January 7, 1994.

[19]American Society of Plastic and Reconstructive Surgeons (ASPRS), *1992 Statistics,* Arlington Heights, IL, 1992.

The Medical Devices Industry

Breast implant products were considered part of the medical devices industry, an industry that was generally fragmented, with 97% of manufacturers employing 500 employees or less and 70% of manufacturers employing 50 employees or less.[20] Medical devices (also known as surgical appliances and supplies) included crutches, wheelchairs, orthopedic devices and materials, surgical implants, bandages, hearing aids, and protective clothing. In 1991, the United States manufactured and shipped some $10.7 billion worth of medical devices, up 6.4% from 1990. The industry employed an estimated 89,500 people in 1991, up 3% from 1990, 58,300 of whom were production workers. U.S. exports of medical devices also grew in 1991 by 18% to $1.4 billion, the fourth consecutive year of double digit growth.[21] The principal export items included respiratory products, orthopedic equipment and supplies, and artificial joints and internal fixation devices.

The principal manufacturers of breast implants in 1991 were Baxter Healthcare Corporation (Deerfield, IL), Bioplasty Inc. (St. Paul, MN), Cox-Uphoff (Carpinteria, CA), Dow Corning Corporation (Midland, MI), McGhan Medical Inc. (Santa Barbara, CA), Mentor (Santa Barbara, CA), Porex Technologies (Fairburn, GA), and Surgitek (Racine, WI).

Regulation

When Dow Corning first sold implants in 1965, the medical devices industry was not subject to specific U.S. government regulation. In May 1976, the FDA was given the responsibility to regulate all medical devices and device establishments, following the medical device amendments to the Federal Food, Drug and Cosmetics Act of 1938. The goal of the amendments was to ensure that the medical devices used by the public were safe and effective, by regulating the industry, by analyzing product samples, and by researching the risks and benefits of those products. The 1976 amendments directed the FDA to issue regulations to set up an approval process for new devices and classify existing ones into Class I, II, or III, depending on the degree of testing necessary to provide reasonable assurance of their safety and effectiveness.

In 1977, an FDA advisory panel dominated by plastic surgeons recommended that existing breast implant models receive the less restrictive Class II designation, which allowed them to remain on the market without additional testing. This recommendation was based on a lack of conclusive studies and the panel members' own positive experience with breast implants. FDA staff scientists disagreed, and in 1982, based on information from doctors who claimed that implants could break or leak, a new advisory panel proposed a Class III rating requiring the existing devices to meet the same standards of safety and effectiveness as new ones. But the lack of consumer complaints lowered the priority on implants, as the FDA screened its huge backlog of other devices, and the agency took no action on implants through 1988. John Vilforth, the FDA's med-

---

[20]According to the U.S. Food and Drug Administration.
[21]U.S. Department of Commerce, *U.S. Industrial Outlook 1993* (Lanham, MD: Bernan Press, 1993).

ical devices division manager during the 1980s, commented during a later interview that few of the million or more women with implants had complained to the FDA and that the longer term effects allegedly occurring in 1991 had not been observed in the previous decade.

In January 1989, the FDA reclassified breast implants as Class III, and on April 10, 1991, required all manufacturers (including Dow Corning) to submit, within 90 days, implant safety and effectiveness data in premarket approval applications (PMAAs) for the FDA's evaluation. According to its 10-K filing, on July 8, 1991, Dow Corning submitted 30,000 pages of documentation along with its PMAA, detailing silicone gel breast implant manufacturing processes, product design and labeling, and 30 years of safety studies. On September 25, after previewing the PMAAs, the FDA ordered manufacturers to provide more implant risk data to the physicians who inserted them, while the FDA continued its review. In November 1991, after hearing testimony, the FDA's advisory panel recommended keeping implants on the market, noting that the psychological benefits outweighed the health risks. It was up to FDA Commissioner David Kessler to make the final decision, however, and on January 6, 1992 Kessler requested that producers and physicians halt the sale and use of breast implants for 45 days. Dow Corning voluntarily suspended shipments on that day.

Plastic Surgery

The plastic surgeons who inserted breast implants were specialists in surgery to reconstruct human deformity or enhance or modify human features. In 1992, there were over 5,000 certified plastic surgeons in the United States. In the early 1990s, these plastic surgeons performed over 1.5 million procedures a year, with fees ranging from $100 to over $6,000 per procedure.[22]

The two main categories of plastic surgery were general reconstructive and cosmetic. Reconstructive procedures were performed to improve a patient's function, but also to approximate a normal appearance. Two types of patients sought reconstructive surgery: those with congenital deformities and those with developmental deformities resulting from an accident, infection, disease, or aging. Tumor removal was the leading cause for reconstructive surgery, accounting for almost half of all reconstructive procedures, and breast reconstruction was one of the top 10 plastic surgery procedures. Cosmetic surgery was performed to reshape normal structures of the body to improve the patient's appearance and self esteem. Breast augmentation was the leading cosmetic plastic surgery procedure. See **Exhibit 3** for a comparison of statistics on reconstructive and cosmetic breast implant surgery.

ASPRS estimated that its members billed $330 million a year for breast implant procedures in the early 1990s.[23] Plastic surgeons performing breast implant

---

[22]ASPRS, *How To Choose a Qualified Plastic Surgeon* (Arlington Heights, IL: ASPRS, 1992).
[23]Carol Lachnit, "Controversy That Won't Go Away," *Los Angeles Times*, October 7, 1993, p. E1.

EXHIBIT 3   Comparison of Reconstructive and Cosmetic Breast Implant Surgery

	Reconstructive	Cosmetic
1965–1991 procedures	20%	80%
1990 procedures	30,000	120,000
Age of patient		
Under 19	1%	3%
19–34	11%	60%
35–50	54%	34%
51–64	29%	3%
Over 64	5%	0%
Average surgeon's fee (1992)	$2,340	$2,754

Source: ASPRS, *1992 Statistics.*

surgery typically became specialized in that procedure, and would average one implant operation per week. These procedures provided between 20% and 40% of their income.[24]

Surgeon Selection of Medical Devices

In buying medical devices such as breast implants, plastic surgeons looked primarily at four criteria in making their selection:

Quality. The quality of the products had to be uniform and consistent. The surgeon could only inspect the product at the time of the operation, when the product was removed from its packaging. A faulty product would cause the operation to be delayed or postponed while backup supplies were sought.

Service. Product availability was mandatory at the time of surgery, and had to meet the schedule of the surgeon. Successful suppliers therefore had to ensure very high service levels and were subject to high inventory carrying costs as a result.

Price. Price, while not the primary factor in the purchase decision, needed to be competitive with alternatives so that the procedure would be affordable for the patient.

Relationship. The relationship between the sales agent and the surgeon was critical. The surgeon relied on and trusted the agent to provide the best and latest products together with quality service. Without such a relationship, it was unlikely that a medical device manufacturer could sell its products to a surgeon regardless of how well it scored in the other three criteria above.

Dow Corning felt that its strengths were the production of quality products and its relationships with surgeons. Dow Corning generally had very strong credibility with plastic surgeons, based on its leadership and innovation in products. Dow Corning's scientists and physicians were highly regarded by the plas-

---

[24]Betsy Pisik, "Dangerous Curves: For Many Women, Rewards of Breast Implants Worth Risks," *Washington Times,* January 29, 1992, p. E1.

tic surgeons and were researching and publishing constantly on key areas of interest. The independent agents were well connected to the plastic surgeons and provided an effective channel for sales of Dow Corning's products.

Patient Selection of a Plastic Surgeon

Patients requiring or requesting plastic surgery either were referred by their physician to a plastic surgeon or selected their plastic surgeon directly. The latter was especially the case for cosmetic surgery, where the costs were not covered by health insurance. Patients used a number of steps to decide which plastic surgeon would be best:

- Gathering names of plastic surgeons from friends, family doctor, nurses, hospitals, advertisements, and directories (e.g., the Plastic Surgery Information Service, or state and city directories of certified plastic surgeons).
- Checking credentials such as their training, board certification (i.e., certified by the American Board of Plastic Surgery), hospital privileges (i.e., approved to perform the specific procedure at an accredited hospital), experience and membership in professional societies (e.g., ASPRS, which required certification by the American Board of Plastic Surgery together with peer review, adherence to a strict code of ethics, and continuing education to maintain membership).
- Consulting and interviewing the surgeon to compare personalities and obtain opinions on the type of surgery and approach. Typically, the interview also included discussion of the surgeon's fees and an assessment of the way the surgeon answered questions and described the risks involved. Generally, patients would pay a fee for this consultation and thus would have narrowed down the list of potential surgeons to two or three by this stage.

According to a pamphlet prepared by the ASPRS and distributed in plastic surgeons' offices, a good plastic surgeon should exhibit some or all of the following qualities:[25]

- Has been recommended by a friend who has had a similar procedure.
- Has been recommended by a family doctor or operating room nurse.
- Is listed by the American Society of Plastic and Reconstructive Surgeons.
- Is board-certified by the American Board of Plastic Surgery.
- Has completed a residency in a specialty related to (your) procedure.
- Has answered all (your) questions thoroughly.
- Has asked about the patient's motivations and expectations of the surgery.
- Has offered alternatives, where appropriate.
- Has welcomed questions about professional qualifications, experience, cost, and payment policies.
- Has clarified the risks of surgery and the variations in outcome.
- Has made sure that the final decision to undergo surgery is the patient's decision.

---

[25]ASPRS, *How to Choose a Qualified Plastic Surgeon.*

Consumer Need for Implants

Reconstructive breast surgery patients usually had contracted a form of breast cancer, but also could be accident victims, or women with a congenital deformity. The most common reconstructive surgery took place after a patient had undergone a mastectomy (surgical removal of one or both breasts). Augmentation surgery patients desired an increase in breast size to enhance their appearance (known as augmentation mammoplasty).

Reconstructive Surgery

Without plastic surgery, patients desiring reconstructive surgery faced spending the rest of their lives with one or both breasts removed. The silicone gel breast implant operation provided them with a means to regain their original physical appearance. Hence, the availability of breast implants was a major breakthrough for women suffering from breast cancer. In the early 1990s, about one woman in nine developed breast cancer in the United States. It was the most commonly occurring cancer in women, accounting for more deaths than cancer of any other part of the body except the lungs. It was the leading cause of death among U.S. women aged 40–55.[26]

Before implants were available, some women refused to undergo a mastectomy, opting for lumpectomy (surgical removal of the breast tumor), radiation, or no action at all. While a lumpectomy or radiation abated the cancer's growth, neither treatment necessarily eliminated the breast cancer and, if unsuccessful, the patient could face a painful and premature death. Women refusing mastectomies were either afraid of the operation or were concerned with the permanent disfiguration and their perceived inability to be accepted back into society.

But with breast implants available, women were more accepting of the mastectomy operation. During the February 1992 FDA Advisory Panel hearing on breast implant safety, breast implant recipient Elaine Sansom testified:

> My mother's fear of losing her breast kept her from an early diagnosis, which allowed her cancer to spread before her mastectomy. She lived horribly from that point on, going through the rounds of chemo [therapy] and radiation; having a tumor eat through her first vertebra, ending up in a halo vest with bolts in her head.
> Being diagnosed with breast cancer [myself] was devastating. . . . The choice to have implants was life-saving for me. Because I'm a diabetic, I wasn't a candidate for other types of reconstruction. If silicone gel breast implants had not been available at that time, my decision would have been a different one.[27]

In a letter to the *Washington Times* on January 31, 1992, another silicone breast implant recipient wrote:

> Since the FDA's moratorium on silicone breast implants has occurred, I would like you to hear the other side (the majority)—from satisfied recipients. I am one of nearly 2 million.

---

[26]U.S. Department of Commerce, *Statistical Abstract of the United States*, 113th ed. Washington, (D.C.: Bureau of the Census, 1993).

[27]Elaine Sansom, National Organization for Women with Implants, FDA Panel Hearing, February 1992.

These lifelike implants have helped the majority of women to recover faster physically and psychologically by restoring their femininity. I would rather die than be denied the option of having to go through life horribly disfigured. The alternative saline implants are a poor substitute, and they, too, are surrounded by silicone.

Just give us the facts—we will decide, along with our doctors. Don't legislate my life anymore.[28]

Breast Augmentation Surgery

Breast augmentation surgery consumers were women who wished to enlarge their breasts for reasons of appearance. The images portrayed by some fashion models and "sex symbols" had created certain perceptions regarding the size of women's breasts. As a result, clothing sizes and designs, as well as male expectations, centered on the "appropriate" size for a woman's breasts. However, normal variations in humans resulted in a wide variation in breast sizes. Breast augmentation surgery offered a way for women with smaller breasts to artificially enlarge their breasts permanently.

Given the breast implant controversy, many examples were reported of women who had undergone augmentation surgery and their rationales. Carol Lachnit, journalist with the *Los Angeles Times*, wrote:

> Back in 1991, Patricia Fodor was a newlywed with "a cute little figure" and the belief that silicone gel breast implants would enhance it. It was "a self-esteem issue," she said. Because she worked in a doctor's office, Fodor even got a discount on the procedure.
>
> . . . Catherine, a 64-year-old Orange County woman . . . [received] her implants in 1987, when she was 58. "I was one of those women who didn't get everything some women have," she said. "I have poor hair, fine, thin hair. I can't do much about my hair, but for my bust, I thought this would be great. I was so thrilled." Catherine immersed herself in the world of ballroom dancing. She had gowns made to show off her new figure. She made friends and "everyone commented on how good I looked," she said.[29]

Other comments from breast augmentation surgery patients were included in an article in the *Washington Times*, January 29, 1992:

> "I just wanted to be average," sighs Janet, 34, of Alexandria, Virginia. Having her breasts enlarged from a "boyish" 32 A to a "beautiful" 36 C has improved Janet's self-image and outlook. She says she can shop in half the time, buy clingy clothing on sale and doesn't feel at all self-conscious. "You wouldn't look at me on the street and say, 'There goes a busty woman,' " says the 5-foot-4-inch, full-time mother. "I look just right."
>
> "Look, there's a pressure on women for physical beauty," says Janet, who does aerobics regularly. "Models can get three times their salary when they get implants, and if that doesn't tell you something about our society . . . ." She calls it an "unfair, idealized image of beauty," but Janet subscribes to it.
>
> . . . And Jacki Buckler, 26, credits her new 36 C breasts—"very round, very full"—with giving her the confidence to go back to the University of Maryland to finish her degree in oceanography. "I'm pushing myself now," the part-time Giant

---

[28]*Washington Times*, "FDA Chief David Kessler Joins the Hysteria Over Silicone," January 31, 1992, p. F2.
[29]Lachnit, "Controversy That Won't Go Away."

[Supermarket] cashier and waitress says. . . . "I did this [the surgery] for myself, for no one else," Miss Buckler says. She paid for the $3,500 procedure in monthly $600 installments and says she hasn't regretted the expense or the pain of surgery for a minute.[30]

Consumer Problems with the Product

By 1985, some 1.3 million implant operations had been completed.[31] Already, though, complaints were being received by the manufacturers and the FDA from customers citing painful hardening lumps and seepage of the silicone gel into the body after the implant bag had ruptured. Concerns began to arise about the potential of implants to rupture, the tightening of scar tissue that often formed around implants, causing the breast to harden, and the possible seepage of silicone which was alleged to generate a host of immune-system disorders that were painful, debilitating, and untreatable. Over the next seven years, consumer activists in Washington, DC, began to challenge the product's safety, while plastic surgeons and some women's groups lobbied in defense of implants.

Documents released by Dow Corning and other manufacturers revealed that medical studies performed as early as the 1970s had warned of possible problems with implants.[32] Consumer activists criticized the manufacturers for "hiding" the information, the plastic surgeons for not questioning the safety of the implants, and the government for being negligent and not acting earlier on the studies. Leading the charge was Public Citizen's Health Research Group (Public Citizen), an organization founded by Ralph Nader and Dr. Sidney Wolfe to represent consumer interests in health related matters. Public Citizen became actively involved in the implant controversy in 1988 after it obtained internal Dow Corning and FDA documents that suggested silicone gel implants were not safe for human use. It continued to lobby Congress and the FDA and also provided information packets to consumers and acted as a clearinghouse for plaintiff attorneys.

With growing legal activity and media attention, implants eventually assumed a higher priority on the FDA's agenda. At the end of the 1980s, the agency forced several implant products off the market after it was discovered that the foam covering the silicone slowly disintegrated at body temperature. This disintegration allowed a chemical known as TDA to be released, which in very high doses developed cancer in rats. By 1991, using data from the FDA's request that manufacturers provide evidence of research on the safety of implants, Public Citizen had begun selling $750 kits of evidence to trial lawyers interested in filing suits on behalf of implant patients. The Command Trust Network, a nationwide educational network of 8,000 "implant victims," raised $30,000 and gave interviews to hundreds of reporters.[33]

---

[30]Pisik, "Dangerous Curves."

[31]Christopher Drew and Michael Tackett, "Access Equals Clout: The Blitzing of FDA," *Chicago Tribune*, December 8, 1992, p. C1.

[32]John A. Byrne, "The Best Laid Ethics Programs," *BusinessWeek*, March 9, 1992, p. 69.

[33]Bruce Ingersoll, "Industry Mounts Big Lobbying Drive Supporting Implants," *Wall Street Journal*, February 14, 1992, p. A5.

The ASPRS, meanwhile, dedicated $1.3 million to lobby for the continued use of implants. In October 1991 it orchestrated a "fly in," paying the expenses of 400 women to travel to Washington, DC, to lobby Congress to keep implants on the market. Simultaneously, it placed newspaper ads and organized a letter writing campaign which generated 20,000 letters in favor of implants to the FDA.[34] In November 1991, an FDA Advisory Panel concluded that the psychological importance of the implants outweighed the medical risks.

In December 1991 the verdict in the case of *Mariann Hopkins vs. Dow Corning* was announced.[35] The company immediately moved to have the legal records in the case sealed. Following the court's decision, Mariann Hopkins's lawyer, Dan C. Bolton, wrote to FDA Commissioner Dr. David A. Kessler about concerns with silicone breast implants. (An extract from this letter appears as **Exhibit 4.**)

The verdict was followed by the FDA moratorium on the sale of all silicone gel breast implant devices until such time as the agency received evidence to allay fears of any links to disease. Canada followed the United States by instituting a similar ban; however, the United Kingdom and France allowed implants to remain on the market. The moratorium, which prevented the sale of silicone gel implants unless their insertion was supervised as part of a clinical study sponsored by the manufacturer and the FDA, sparked strong reaction from plastic surgeons and women's groups. The plastic surgeons stood by the product and their surgical procedures, while the women's groups claimed that women were being deprived of the right to make their own medical decisions.

A lawsuit filed after this moratorium by an augmentation surgery patient was reported in the *San Diego Union-Tribune,* January 30, 1992:

> A woman who was given Dow Corning Corp.'s silicone gel breast implants to improve her figure has sued the company, claiming they made her ill and accusing the company of ignoring safety warnings about the devices, her attorney said.
>
> Stanley Rosenblatt said yesterday the Dade County woman, identified only as "Jane Doe," is in her 30s and received the breast implants in 1985 to enhance her figure. She is seeking $100 million in damages. The lawsuit, filed in Dade County Circuit Court, claims the woman was in perfect health before the operation but has since suffered "recurrent flu, recurrent strep throat, infections, excessive hair loss, constant fatigue, excruciating joint pain, rashes across her face and a constant low-grade fever." The woman has been bedridden "for months at a time" because of systemic lupus erythematosus, a disorder of the immune system, the suit claims.
>
> Dow Corning ignored warnings from its own employees about implant defects and concealed the information from doctors, patients and federal regulators, the lawsuit alleges. "Plaintiff is a victim of an incredible 'con' perpetrated upon the public at large and women in particular," the lawsuit said. It accused Dow Chemical of constructing a "vast experiment" on 2 million women that should have been performed on laboratory animals instead.
>
> The surgeon is not being sued because Dow Corning convinced him the implants were safe, Rosenblatt said. The woman still has the implants but is deciding whether to have them removed, he said. The lawsuit alleges an internal company memo shows

---

[34]Drew and Tackett, "Access Equals Clout."
[35]Clair Cooper, "Thousands Await Decision as Implant Suit Hits Appeals Court," *Sacramento Bee,* June 19, 1993, p. A6.

EXHIBIT 4   **Excerpt of Letter from Mariann Hopkins's Attorney Dan C. Bolton to FDA Commissioner David Kessler, December 30, 1991**

I am writing to express my serious concerns relating to the dangers of silicone breast implants and the conduct of a principal manufacturer of breast implants, Dow Corning Corporation, in engaging in a consistent pattern of corporate deceit and dishonesty relating to the safety of implants. . . .

Mariann Hopkins . . . underwent breast reconstruction with silicone gel filled breast implants manufactured by Dow following a bilateral mastectomy for fibrocystic disease in 1976. A bilateral rupture of the implants was discovered in February 1986. Mrs. Hopkins suffers from mixed connective tissue disease, an immune disorder, caused by her exposure to silicone gel.

On December 13, 1991, the jury unanimously rendered a verdict in the amount of $840,000 for compensatory damages, and $6,500,000 for punitive damages. . . . [T]he jury found that Dow's silicone breast implants were defectively designed and manufactured, that Dow had failed to warn of risks associated with implants, that Dow had breached implied and expressed warranties relating to its product and that Dow had committed fraud. The jury also found by "clear and convincing evidence" that Dow's fraud, in addition to its "malice" and "oppression" warranted the imposition of punitive damages. Under Californian law, "malice" means conduct that is "intended by the defendant to cause injury to the plaintiff or despicable conduct which is carried on by the defendant with a willful and conscious disregard of the rights and safety of others." "Oppression" requires a finding by the jury that the defendant has engaged in "despicable conduct that subjects a person to cruel and unjust hardship in conscious disregard of that person's rights."

Considerable evidence was presented at trial that Dow was aware of the risks of silicone as early as the 1960s, and continued to market a medical device intended for long term use despite the absence of any studies demonstrating the long term safety of silicone in the human body. Dow's conduct is especially unconscionable in light of the fact that Dow's own product literature represented that breast implants were safe for long term use by women.

. . . [T]he time has come to hold implant manufacturers, such as Dow, accountable for the safety of their product. I urge you to take appropriate steps to ensure that women do not continue to be victimized by irresponsible companies that are more concerned with their financial well-being than the health and safety of consumers. . . . Dow's corporate response to the increasing numbers of women injured by its dangerous and defective implants was to issue a warranty program in the mid-1980s. This program provides partial reimbursement for the medical expenses incurred in removing implants because of rupture or immune sensitization so long as the physician extracts a release from the patient extinguishing all of her legal rights against Dow. This conduct is not only legally questionable but morally indefensible.

Dow Corning salespeople misled surgeons by washing "the often greasy gel implants before showing them to physicians, with full knowledge that the product was dangerous to women."[36]

Another complainant, Pamela Johnson, filed a lawsuit against another implant manufacturer. As described in the *Houston Chronicle*:

Johnson's first set of breast implants, manufactured by MEC, [were] surgically implanted in 1976. O'Quinn [her attorney] said the company led Johnson's doctor to

---

[36]United Press International, "Dow Sued Over Breast Implants," *San Diego Union-Tribune*, January 30, 1992, p. A9.

believe the implants had been tested and engineered so that the outer shell would contain the silicone gel, that the gel was cohesive and would not run if the shell ruptured, and that, if the gel did escape the shell, it would not harm human tissue. The doctor was told [that] the product would last a lifetime, O'Quinn said.

In 1989, Johnson's implants ruptured. Her doctor, believing the product's problems had been solved, then inserted a new set of silicone gel implants. . . . The second set was removed that same year, and another implant done, with a product made by a different manufacturer. Those implants were removed [in early 1992].[37]

In response to these suits, Dow Corning defended its product. Bob Rylee, Dow Corning Wright's chairman, stated that the true risk with implants was less than 1 percent.[38] He cited the cumulative body of scientific evidence showing implants to be safe and effective.[39] Nevertheless, when FDA Commissioner Kessler called for a moratorium on breast implant sales and insertions, Dow Corning halted implant production, placing its workers on temporary layoff with full pay and benefits.

On January 20, Kessler asked Dow Corning to release any remaining documents on breast implants to allow women and their doctors to review the risks and benefits for themselves. On January 22, the company released a group of scientific studies, but retained "nonscientific" documents relating to its handling of the scientific evidence.

Ongoing Investigations

The FDA Advisory Panel was scheduled to reconvene on February 18, 1992, to reconsider implant PMAAs. In addition to the FDA studies, another probe into Dow Corning's breast implants was launched on January 30 by the Los Angeles County district attorney's office, under its Corporate Criminal Liability Act.[40] The investigation aimed to determine whether Dow Corning sold the breast implants without fully disclosing health risk information required by law. District attorney Ira Reiner had requested that Dow Corning provide substantial information about the product, including laboratory data, internal memoranda, and copies of informational and promotional material about the implants. (**Exhibit 5** outlines Dow Corning's implant package insert.) LA County's Corporate Criminal Liability Act makes it a felony for corporate managers to fail to provide regulatory agencies with written notification of a "serious concealed danger" associated with a product, and penalties included up to three years, imprisonment and fines up to $1 million.

At the same time, Griffin Bell came on board to investigate Dow Corning's development and marketing of implants. Well known for such independent counsel assignments, Bell had been retained to investigate crises such as E. F. Hutton's check kiting scandal and the oil spill from the Exxon *Valdez* tanker. Bell planned to select independent scientific and medical experts to assist his investigation, and was given free access to all of Dow Corning's records, resources, and

---

[37]Ruth Piller, "Trial Starts in Lawsuit Against Maker of Silicone Gel Implants," *Houston Chronicle,* December 11, 1992, p. A33.

[38]Marcotty, "Implant Lawsuits."

[39]Lawrence, "Dow Corning," p. 254.

[40]Robert Steinbrook and Henry Weinstein, "County Will Investigate Maker of Breast Implants," *Los Angeles Times,* January 31, 1992, p. B1.

EXHIBIT 5   **Outline of Package Insert for Dow Corning's 1985 SILASTIC II Brand Mammary Implant H.P. Package Insert (with excerpts)**

Description

Specific Advantages
- "Envelopes have greater tear propagation resistance."
- "A special silicone layer within the envelope provides a barrier to significantly reduce gel bleed."
- "Generally recognized as having acceptable level of reactivity."

Indications
- "Criteria for patient selection must be the responsibility of the surgeon."

Contraindications
- "A mammary implant may not be well tolerated in any patient who exhibits certain types of psychological instability e.g., does not want implants, displays a lack of understanding, or inappropriate motivation or attitude."
- "These are general, relative contraindications and each individual patient must be evaluated by her surgeon to determine the specific risk/benefit ratio."

Precautions and Warnings
- "SILASTIC brand medical-grade silicone elastomers made exclusively by Dow Corning are among the most non-reactive implant materials available."

Possible Adverse Reactions and Complications
- "Thousands of women per year have had cosmetic or reconstructive surgery with implantation of mammary prostheses. A number of patients are reported to have significant complications or adverse reactions. Typically, a patient undergoing a surgical procedure is subject to unforeseen intra-operative and post-operative complications. Each patient's tolerance to surgery, medication, and implantation of a foreign object may be different. Possible risks, adverse reactions and complications associated with surgery and the use of the mammary prosthesis should be discussed with and understood by the patient prior to surgery. The adverse reactions and complications most likely to occur with the use of this product are listed below. IT IS THE RESPONSIBILITY OF THE SURGEON TO PROVIDE THE PATIENT WITH APPROPRIATE INFORMATION PRIOR TO SURGERY."

1. Capsule Formation and Contracture
2. Sensitization
- "There have been reports of suspected immunological sensitization or hyperimmune system response to silicone mammary implants. Symptoms claimed by the patients included localized inflammation and irritation at the implant area, fluid accumulation, rash, general malaise, severe joint pain, swelling of joints, weight loss, arthralgia, lymphadenopathy, alopecia, and rejection of the mammary prosthesis. Such claims suggest there may be a relationship between the silicone mammary implant and the reported symptoms.
  "Materials from which this prosthesis is fabricated have been shown in animal laboratory tests to have minimal sensitization potential. However, claims from clinical use of the silicone prosthesis in humans suggest that immunological responses or sensitization to a mammary prosthesis can occur. If sensitization is suspected and the response persists, removal of the prosthesis is recommended along with removal of the surrounding capsule tissue. This procedure is recommended to minimize the amount of residual silicone that may be left at the implant site."

3. Implant Rupture Gel Extravasation
- "Dow Corning is not responsible for the integrity of the implant should such techniques as closed capsulotomies (manual compression) be used."

- "As reported in the literature, when an implant ruptures gel may be released from the implant envelope despite the cohesive properties of the gel. If left in place, complications such as enlarged lymph nodes, scar formation, inflammation, silicone granulomas and nodule formation may result."
- "These potential consequences should be understood by the surgeon and explained to the patient prior to implantation."
- "In the event of a rupture, Dow Corning recommends prompt removal of the envelope and gel. The long term physiological effects of uncontained silicone gel are currently unknown."
- "The patient should be informed that the life expectancy of any implant is unpredictable."

4. *Infection*
5. *Hematoma*
6. *Serous Fluid Accumulation*
7. *Interruption in Wound Healing*
8. *Skin Sloughing/Necrosis*
9. *Incorrect Size, Inappropriate Location of Scars, and Misplacement or Migration of Implants, etc.*
10. *Palpability of Implant*
11. *Asymmetry*
12. *Ptotic (Drooping) Breast*
    - "It is important that this possibility be discussed with the patient."
13. *Nipple Sensation*
    - "This should be discussed in detail with the patient."
14. *Microwave Diathermy*
15. *Implant Gel Bleed*
16. *X-ray Pre-Operative & Post-Operative*
    - "Post—Some physicians state an implant may pose difficulties in detecting tumors in certain locations in the breast via xeromammography."
17. *Calcification*
18. *Absorption of Biologicals By Implants*
References to Carcinogenesis
    - "During the past twenty years of clinical use, the medical literature indicates that the silicone mammary prosthesis is not carcinogenic."

Instructions for Use

1. *The surgeon should discuss possible risks, consequences, complications, and adverse reactions associated with the surgical procedure and implantation of the mammary prosthesis with the patient prior to surgery.*
2. *Surgical Procedures*
    - "Prior to use, the prosthesis should be carefully examined for structural integrity."
3. *Packaging*
4. *Recommended Procedure for Opening Package—Sterile Product*
5. *To Clean and (Re)Sterilize Mammary Implants*

References

Warranty

- "Dow Corning warrants that reasonable care in selection of materials and methods of manufacture were used in fabrication of this product. Dow Corning shall not be liable for an incidental or consequential loss, damage, or expense, directly or indirectly arising from the use of this product."

  "Dow Corning neither assumes nor authorizes any other person to assume for it any other or additional liability or responsibility in connection with this product. Dow Corning intends that this mammary implant product should be used only by physicians having received appropriate training in plastic surgery techniques."

employees. Bell's final recommendations would be made available to the FDA and the public. Dow also announced on January 29, 1992, that it would make public internal memoranda and other information by the week of February 10.

Lawyers and Public Citizen criticized the delays in releasing these documents, claiming that they had been locked up for years and that, if the FDA had been given earlier access to the information, breast implants would have been off the market a long time ago.[41] Dow Corning disputed this view, stating that the FDA had possession of the relevant documents for many years. Dow Corning also claimed to have performed some 900 studies into the safety of the implants, none of which concluded that implants would cause harm to a recipient.[42] Plaintiff lawyers, keen to obtain any new information surrounding implants, estimated that there were as many as 1,000 suits filed or about to be filed alleging that the implants had caused cancer, immune system disorders, or connective tissue disease.[43]

The seriousness of the implant issue escalated quickly. On February 10, 1992—the same day Keith McKennon was appointed chairman and CEO—Dow Corning released nearly 100 potentially embarrassing documents that had come to light in the Hopkins trial and more recently had been leaked to the press. Among these documents, what appeared to be the most potentially damaging items were two internal company memoranda:

- The 1980 "Pinto" memo, in which a Dow Corning salesman had reported indignant complaints from a plastic surgeon about gel bleed from breast implant envelopes. The salesman wrote: "To put a questionable lot of mammaries on the market is inexcusable. . . . It has to rank right up there with the Pinto gas tank."
- A memo from a marketing manager which stated that in speaking with a group of doctors he had "assured them, with crossed fingers, that Dow Corning had an active study [of safety issues] under way." The manager later claimed that he had meant the term *crossed fingers* in a *hopeful* rather than a *lying* sense.[44]

New Approach Required

McKennon had been asked by the board to personally assemble Dow Corning's strategy and action plan to resolve conclusively the implant situation. With many stakeholders to satisfy and ethical issues to deal with, the problem was going to be complex to solve. McKennon's first step was to understand what caused the implant controversy in the first place and to decide whether Dow Corning should continue to market the product. It was unclear what future steps the FDA advisory panel might take, but many in the company believed that the huge Hopkins settlement would be reduced greatly on appeal, and that the $250

---

[41]Appleson, "Court Orders."
[42]Anderson, interview.
[43]Appleson, "Court Orders."
[44]Lawrence, "Dow Corning," pp. 255, 252–3.

million the company carried in product liability insurance would be sufficient to cover any losses.[45] McKennon had to assess the validity of the customer complaints, estimate the financial and legal exposure from future customer litigation, respond to the FDA's moratorium announcement, and determine the potential damage to Dow Corning's brand name and reputation.

---

[45]Lawrence, "Dow Corning," p. 256.

Case 5
AT&T Consumer Products

In the fall of 1988, Nick Stevens, the vice president of manufacturing at AT&T Consumer Products, had to select a site for a new answering systems manufacturing facility. He was inclined to choose Mexico, but he had not ruled out Malaysia or the United States.

As Stevens pondered the many factors which would affect his decision, he could not help but reflect on the profound changes which had occurred at AT&T in recent years. AT&T in 1988 was vastly different from the company he had joined 22 years earlier. Some changes were clearly reflected on the organizational chart, others involved new policies, but the most challenging ones related to AT&T's role in society, and Stevens had to consider all these factors in making his decision.

History

Like Singer with its sewing machines and Gillette with its razors, American Telegraph and Telephone was an American icon. Long known as Ma Bell, AT&T had been the world's largest corporation. In the early 1980s, it had more than $150 billion in assets and its annual revenues of $70 billion represented almost 2% of the U.S. Gross National Product. Until January 1984, AT&T employed one million people and had over three million shareholders. (See **Exhibit 1**.)

Alexander Graham Bell, who patented the telephone in 1876, founded the Bell Telephone Company in 1877. While Bell was credited with inventing the telephone, it was Theodore Vail who created the Bell System. Vail, one of the first managers hired by the founders of what would become AT&T, stated as early as 1879 that AT&T's goal was "one system, one policy, universal service."[1] Since Vail's time and until the 1984 divestiture, AT&T's annual reports consistently reiterated a commitment to furnishing "the best possible service at the lowest possible cost."[2]

Vail devised an organizational structure that lasted for a century without fundamental change. Local telephone companies, known as Bell Operating Companies, were organized as nominally independent subsidiaries. They provided local telephone service and access to the long-distance network. (See **Exhibit 2**.) They also billed customers for long-distance and international service provided by the AT&T Long Lines Department.

This case was prepared by Wilda White under the supervision of Joseph Badaracco. Harvard Business School case 392–108. Copyright © 1992 by the President and Fellows of Harvard College.

[1] Robert W. Garnet, *The Telephone Enterprise: The Evolution of the Bell System's Horizontal Structure, 1878–1909* (Baltimore: Johns Hopkins University Press, 1985), p. 173.
[2] Garnet, *The Telephone Enterprise.*

Exhibit 1 Seven-Year Summary of Selected AT&T Financial Data (dollars in millions; except per share amounts)

	1982	1983	1/1/84	1984	1985	1986[a]	1987	1988[a]
Results of Operations								
Total revenues	$70,022	$72,357		$33,187	$34,496	$34,213	$33,773	$35,218
Total costs and expenses	50,678	57,338		$30,892	31,476	33,847	30,252	38,276
Net income (loss)	7,279	249		1,370	1,557	139	2,044	(1,669)
Dividends on preferred shares	142	127		112	110	86	23	1
Income (loss) applicable to common shares	7,137	122		1,258	1,447	53	2,021	(1,670)
Earnings (loss) per common share	$8.06	$6.00		$1.25	$1.37	$0.05	$1.88	($1.55)
Dividends declared per common share	$5.81	$6.10		$1.20	$1.20	$1.20	$1.20	$1.20
Assets and Capital								
Property, plant and equipment–net			$20,569	$21,343	$22,262	$21,101	$20,808	$15,280
Total assets	$150,004	$140,229	35,545	39,773	40,688	39,534	39,473	35,152
Long-term debt including capital leases			9,137	8,718	7,794	7,660	7,919	8,128
Common shareowners' equity			12,368	13,763	14,633	13,550	14,455	11,465
Other Information (data at year end except 1/84)								
Market price per share	$62.86	$63.02	$17.88	$19.50	$25.00	$25.00	$27.00	$28.75
Employees	1,000,000		373,000	365,200	337,600	316,900	303,000	304,700

[a]1988 data significantly affected by a charge for accelerated digitization program costs. 1986 data were significantly affected by major charges for business restructuring, and accounting changes and other charges.

Exhibit 2
Predivestiture AT&T

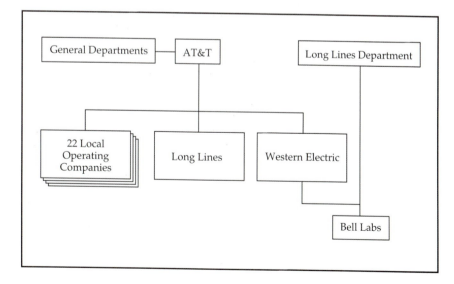

Western Electric Manufacturing Company was founded in Cleveland in 1869 as an electric-equipment shop. In the 1870s, it became a mecca for inventors. In 1881, Bell Telephone bought an interest in Western Electric, and the following year it formally became the manufacturer of Bell telephones and equipment.

In addition to producing or procuring practically all Bell System telephone equipment, Western Electric developed the high vacuum electronic amplifying tube that made possible coast to coast telephone calls and cleared the way for radio broadcasting, sound motion pictures, and television; it produced the first air-to-ground radio telephones; made and installed one of the pioneer commercial radio broadcasting systems, WEAF in New York; developed the first motion-picture sound system; built all of the radar used by the U.S. armed forces in World War II; and in the space age, built the Nike missile systems, the DEW line radar defense system, the Sentinel and Safeguard antiballistic missile systems, and much of the communications and control equipment for the U.S. space program.

Western Electric was the largest component of the Bell System. Had it not been wholly owned by AT&T, Western Electric would have been the twelfth largest industrial company in the United States. At its height, Western Electric operated 23 major plants scattered around the United States from Atlanta, Georgia to Phoenix, Arizona to North Andover, Massachusetts.

Bell Telephone Laboratories was formed out of the Western Electric engineering research department in 1925. It was equally owned by Western Electric and AT&T. Bell Labs developed and designed the equipment that Western Electric manufactured and the Bell System used. Originally a small organization, Bell Labs grew into a giant as a result of World War II military hardware requirements. Before divestiture, it had 25,000 employees and an annual budget of $2 billion, and employed 20,000 Ph.Ds. It maintained 17 locations in 9 states. Its inventions included the electrical digital computer (1937), transistors (1947), lasers (1958), the communications satellite, Telstar (1962), radar, semiconductors, fiber optics, and electronic switching equipment.

Regulatory History

In 1934, the United States Congress created the Federal Communications Commission (FCC) to regulate the telephone industry. Its mission was "to make available, so far as possible, to all the people of the United States a rapid, efficient, nationwide and worldwide wire and radio communications service with adequate facilities at reasonable charges." Under FCC regulation, each Bell Operating Company was guaranteed an area of operation without competition and assured a certain maximum profit margin. Local operating companies were required to serve anyone within their operating area who requested telephone service. Charges for local telephone service were subject to state or local government approval.

As of the late 1960s, all telephone sets, private branch exchanges, and other standard equipment used in residences or by businesses were owned by the telephone company and leased to users. Nearly all telephone equipment (referred to as customer premises equipment [CPE] by the telephone industry) was manufactured by Western Electric and sold to the operating companies.

Carterfone. In 1968, the FCC issued its *Carterfone* decision. This case arose when AT&T refused to permit the *Carterfone,* a non-Bell device that linked mobile car radios with the national telephone network, to be connected to the Bell System. AT&T threatened service termination to anyone connecting the device to the network, arguing that non-Bell equipment could harm the system. When Tom Carter appealed to the FCC, the commission ruled in his favor and ordered AT&T to allow customers to connect their own telephone equipment to the Bell System. However, customers were required to lease a protective device from AT&T to link the non-Bell device and the Bell System telephone line.

Many consumers and competitive telephone equipment manufacturers complained that the protective devices constituted a barrier to competition, intended to protect AT&T's monopoly. In 1972, the FCC reexamined its *Carterfone* ruling and held that any equipment could be connected to the network without a protective device, if it had been certified as safe for use on the network. This decision became effective in 1980.

1982 Modified Final Judgment Decree. In January 1982, AT&T and the U.S. Department of Justice announced that they had reached a settlement of the government's longstanding antitrust case against the company. The 1974 lawsuit had charged AT&T with monopolizing the market for telephone equipment and long-distance service. The government maintained that as long as AT&T controlled the local circuits that provided the only access to most consumers, competition could not exist in long-distance service, data services, private branch exchanges, key telephone systems, large telephone switching machines, or other telephone equipment and services.

The settlement, which became known as the Modified Final Judgment, called for the divestiture of the Bell Operating Companies by AT&T on January 1, 1984. The 22 BOCs would be regrouped under 7 separate and independent Regional Bell Operating Companies and would be restricted to providing local telephone service. They could not offer long-distance services and would be barred from manufacturing telephone equipment. They could, however, sell telephone equipment manufactured by others.

Under the terms of the settlement, AT&T would retain part of Bell Labs, all of Western Electric, and its long-distance and customer premises equipment operations. The settlement forbade AT&T's use of the "Bell" name, except for Bell Laboratories. It permitted AT&T to enter other electronics businesses, including computers. Many observers expected the settlement to initiate a great commercial contest between IBM and AT&T in the telecommunications and computing fields.

The New AT&T

Organizational Structure. In anticipation of divestiture, AT&T's vertically integrated, functional organizational structure was replaced by an organizational structure built around the lines of business in which the company would now be engaged. Each line of business would be responsible for its own profitability and its contribution to AT&T's revenues.

EXHIBIT 3
Postdivestiture AT&T

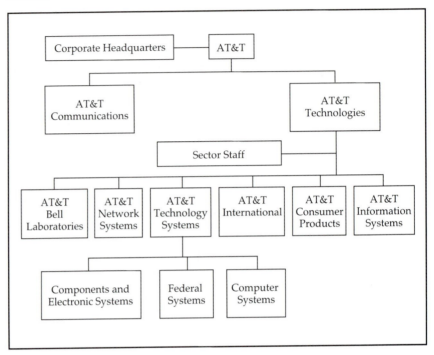

Two sectors were created and given responsibility for the overall management of resources to support the lines of business. AT&T Communications would handle the long-distance service, and AT&T Technologies encompassed the unregulated parts of the business and included AT&T Consumer Products. (See **Exhibit 3.**)

Regulation. After 1984, only telephone equipment was fully deregulated. All telephone services remained under federal and state regulation. For example, AT&T's prices for long-distance services still had to be approved by the FCC.

Labor. Before divestiture, three unions represented over two-thirds of the Bell System's one million workers. The Communications Workers of America (CWA) represented 675,000 AT&T workers, the International Brotherhood of Electrical Workers (IBEW) represented 100,000 AT&T workers, and the Telecommunications International Union (TIU) represented 50,000 AT&T workers.

On August 7, 1983, after the antitrust settlement was announced but before it became effective, a nationwide strike against the Bell System began after the unions representing Bell System employees rejected the Bell Systems' wage package. The strike was the first since a six-day walkout in 1971. Beyond the wage dispute, the pending January 1984 divestiture of AT&T's 22 operating companies had cast a shadow across the bargaining table. The unions pushed for an "employment security" package that would provide training and retraining for members and that would protect jobs after divestiture. AT&T, faced with nonunion competition in a deregulated environment, was trying to control costs and maintain maximum flexibility in the way it utilized its work force.

After 22 days, AT&T and the unions reached an accord. In addition to wage increases for each of the three years of the contract, AT&T agreed to increases in retirement pay, better pension protection for workers transferred to lower-paying jobs, and additional training, transfer rights, and retraining for laid-off workers.

After divestiture, the unionized workers were spread throughout AT&T and the divested Bell Operating Companies. Of AT&T's 375,000 workers remaining after divestiture, 63.6% were members of a union.

Range of Businesses. After divestiture, AT&T described its primary business as "moving and managing information." It provided consumers with basic long-distance service, special calling plans, and other miscellaneous services. AT&T also sold and leased telephones and answering systems to consumers. To businesses, the company offered communications and networked computer systems and telemarketing services. It also provided communications services and products and computer systems to all levels of government in the United States and abroad.

Dealings with the U.S. Government. AT&T's largest customer was the U.S. government. It sold its full range of customized and standard products to such agencies as the U.S. Army, Navy, and Air Force, and the Federal Aviation Administration. AT&T also managed Sandia National Laboratories as a service to the U.S. government on a nonprofit, no-fee basis. Sandia was one of the United States's largest research and development engineering facilities, with projects in areas such as the safety, security and control of weapons systems, and the development of new energy sources.

International Activities, Joint Ventures and Alliances. AT&T did business in more than 40 countries and had approximately 21,000 employees outside the United States. It was involved in numerous joint ventures and alliances, both in the United States and abroad. For example, it had agreements and alliances with British Telecom, France Telecom, and Kokusai Denshin Denwa of Japan. It also had an agreement to share technology with Mitsubishi and to make and market worldwide a static random access memory chip. AT&T was also cooperating with NEC in Japan on a wide range of semiconductor products and technologies. AT&T also had an agreement with Zenith to co-develop an all-digital, high-definition television system using AT&T's microchips and video compression research and Zenith's television technology.

AT&T Consumer Products

Although consumers were permitted as early as 1980 to connect non-Bell telephone equipment to the Bell System, the market for residential telephones did not take off until 1983, when leasing charges were listed separately from service charges on consumers' bills. The unbundling of leasing charges alerted consumers to the economic benefits of owning their own telephones. In 1983, retail telephone sales jumped 230% to about $1.1 billion.[3] In the first nine months of 1983, imports of telephones from Taiwan, Hong Kong, Japan, and Korea increased 568% over the same period in 1982 to 25.7 million telephones.[4]

The imported telephones were unlike the old U.S.-manufactured electromechanical telephones which were built to operate over a 30-year depreciation period. Some were one-piece models selling for as little as $20. Japanese companies, led by Matsushita under the Panasonic label, introduced feature-laden electronic telephones with integrated chips that made possible the inclusion of a variety of features at a reasonable cost.

The onslaught of new competition spelled trouble for AT&T Consumer Products (CP). This unit, formed after the telephone equipment market was deregulated, had never sold as much as a telephone cord before 1983. Moreover, AT&T's telephones were never designed to be marketable. In many ways, AT&T's attitudes toward its customers had been "we make it, you take it." Its telephones had cost $20 to make, while a repair call cost $60, so AT&T's goal had been to make highly reliable telephones, even if they were somewhat overengineered. As Jim Bercaw, a 35-year AT&T veteran described it: "We would bring pellets and metal in the back door, and send telephones out of the front door. We even made our own screws."

In the face of daunting competition, declining revenues, and unacceptable profit levels, CP consolidated its residential telephone production in AT&T's Shreveport, Louisiana facility and spent tens of millions of dollars to upgrade and automate the facility. After the expense of integrating new technology and methods, CP discovered that its labor costs were still too high. A McKinsey & Company competitive analog study revealed that CP was out of line with its competitors on all points and scores, including such critical areas as cost of goods sold and SG&A expenses. In fact, the cost of goods sold was 90% of revenues, and CP executives reasoned that it had to be at 65% in order to be competitive. In late 1984, AT&T corporate told CP management to "fix the business or exit the business."

CP soon began making changes. In recalling their impact on its people, Ken Bertaccini, a 25-year veteran of AT&T and president of CP since 1985, said:

> On January 1, 1984, our people went from a world of guaranteed customers, guaranteed profits and guaranteed jobs—to the much less certain world of a fiercely competitive consumer electronics world—with the only guarantee of success coming from excellent and sustained performance.

Employee surveys revealed massive trauma within the work force; morale was low and employees were angry and frustrated.

CP's Competitors

In the mid-1980s, there were three types of competitors in the telephone equipment market: (1) telephone companies; (2) consumer electronics companies; and

---

[3]"The Big and Bruising Business of Selling Telephones," *Business Week,* March 12, 1984, p. 103.
[4]"The Big and Bruising Business of Selling Telephones."

(3) housewares companies. The telephone companies included AT&T, other traditional providers of service and equipment, such as GTE and ITT, and some of the divested Bell Operating Companies. As providers of telephone services, these companies had a strategic interest in the telephone equipment market. But like AT&T, these companies were, for the most part, unfamiliar with the world of competitive consumer marketing.

The consumer electronics companies ranged from sophisticated Japanese manufacturers like Matsushita and Sony, which offered full lines of consumer products, to smaller, specialized companies like Code-A-Phone, Unisonic, and PhoneMate. The consumer electronic companies were market-driven competitors with well-developed distribution networks and considerable expertise in designing products for the consumer market.

Consumer electronics companies' interest in the market was based on long-term possibilities and not just short-term profit and loss. As homes became more and more automated, telephones seemed likely to take on more the role of a home computer terminal. Therefore, the consumer electronics companies wanted the telephone terminal business as a platform for new generations of higher value-added products.

The housewares companies were primarily represented in the telephone equipment market by General Electric. It had a good reputation for reliability and quality and significant experience designing, marketing, and distributing consumer products.

Matsushita, a $40 billion Japanese company which manufactured under the Panasonic label, was CP's most formidable competitor. Panasonic was the predominant residential telephone vendor in Japan. Its strategy had been to offer products that competed with the market leader, but offered marginally more functions for the price. Matsushita manufactured its telephone products entirely in Japan. It used a highly automated manufacturing process and did not subcontract any of its production. Because of the volume of business it did and the wide range of associated products it manufactured, Matsushita was able to operate its manufacturing operations at full capacity year round.

CP's Survival Period: 1985–1986

Establishing a Foundation and Culture for CP. CP's management realized that it had to be transformed from a regulated monopoly to a highly flexible organization which not only accepted change, but embraced it. "Business Passion" and "Shared Values" were established as the new foundation of CP. They were created to provide the basis and guidelines for all CP decisions and actions. Said Nick Stevens, CP's vice president of Manufacturing: "The passion is truly part of the decision process and there is seldom a decision not made in its frame of reference."

"Business Passion," depicted in **Exhibit 4,** signified CP's commitment to "Be the Best" for its owners, customers, and people. CP referred to its workers as "people." Executives strongly discouraged the use of the term "employees," and they incurred a fine for using what they called the "E-word." Management believed that to achieve long-term success it had to weigh equally the effect of each business decision on all three stakeholder groups. The pyramid in the background of the "Business Passion" graphically represented the relationship between the "Business Passion" and "Shared Values."

Exhibit 4

AT&T Consumer Product Business Foundation: Business Passion and Share Values

Business Passion

Shared Values

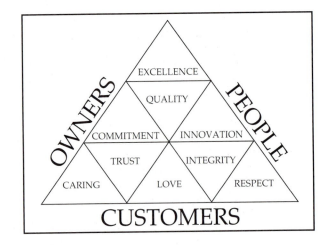

CP's "Shared Values" described what the business was and aspired to be. On an individual level, the business wanted to create an environment of caring, trust, love,[5] integrity, and respect. On a business level, CP wanted to create an environment that valued commitment, quality, and innovations, and achieved excellence in everything it did. CP managers placed a significant part of their compensation "at risk," making it dependent upon the unit's performance.

CP also made what its executives called a "huge" investment in its people. It developed education programs as well as honor and recognition programs. Everyone had the opportunity for two weeks of business education each year. There were also several recognition events each year. Spouses or guests were invited to an annual event honoring CP's top performers.

Creating an Organizational Structure. CP's organizational structure was redesigned to promote flexibility and market focus. The nine product lines were formed into Strategic Business Units (SBUs).[6] Product managers and representatives from all relevant functional areas (e.g., sales, finance, etc.) formed an SBU. These SBUs operated as profit centers.

Between 1985 and 1988, the number of executive-level managers was reduced from 40 to 16. The work force was reduced by almost half. In 1985, CP had as many as six layers of supervision between its operational levels and its president. In 1988, CP had as few as three. A comprehensive measurement system was also developed and implemented. The system focused on assessing owner, customer, and people satisfaction on a regular basis by looking at profits, needs, and attitudes, respectively.

Developing a Business Strategy. In late 1984, Jim Bercaw, who was vice president of Manufacturing at the time, was told to develop a "global manufacturing plan." To that end, he traveled to the Far East. His trip revealed that all of CP's competitors were manufacturing in Asia. He later said: "I have a second-fastest-gun-in-the-West philosophy. If you can't be the fastest gun in the West, it is better to travel in crowds."

With all its competitors in Asia, CP decided that it also had to move its manufacturing operation there. At the same time, it also decided to contract out the remainder of its manufacturing requirements to Asian original equipment manufacturers (OEMs). After 1986, CP no longer had any U.S. production of residential telephone equipment. (See **Exhibit 5.**)

---

[5]"Love" had not always been a part of CP's "Shared Values." After extensive discussion, it was included in 1989 in order to deepen, in the words of one manager, "CP's commitment to live up to its personal values of caring, trust and respect." This decision was reinforced by the outpouring of support for a CP executive who successfully battled cancer during the mid-1980s.

[6]CP's product lines included: (1) leased telephones, (2) corded telephones, (3) cordless telephones, (4) answering systems, (5) special needs systems (communications products for people with hearing, speech, motion, and vision impairments), (6) telephone accessories, (7) home security systems, and (8) public pay telephones.

EXHIBIT 5   **U.S. Manufacturers' Shipments, Exports, and Imports of Telephone Sets, Selected Years, 1978–1988 (millions of dollars)**

	1978	1982	1988
Shipments	$824	$1,065	$359
Exports	10	24	56
Imports	42	149	1,400
Apparent consumption	856	1,190	1,703

Source: United States Bureau of Census, "Selected Electronic and Associated Products, 1979, 1983," series MA36N, and "Communications Equipment, 1988," series MA36P.

The Decision to Move Off-Shore

Choosing a Location.   CP chose Singapore as the site of its first off-shore manufacturing operation. The facility would first manufacture corded and then cordless telephones. Singapore, an island nation in Southeast Asia, was founded as an *entrepôt* because of its strategic position and excellent natural harbor. In 1988, however, manufacturing employed almost a third of the labor force, and the Singaporean government played a major role in managing the economy.

CP management chose Singapore in part because it was an English-speaking country and its Economic Development Board provided a kind of one-stop shopping for foreign companies that wanted to do business there. Corruption was not a problem: "the place was squeaky clean," recalled a CP manager. In addition, an existing building was available immediately for lease. According to Jim Bercaw, Singapore was not the lowest cost option, but it was considerably cheaper than the United States. Jim Bercaw described the decision this way:

> It was a jiffy quick decision. In January 1985, we began to negotiate, in March 1985, we received budgetary and financial approval. In May 1985, we buttonholed a lease in an existing factory. By January 1986, we shipped our first product.
>
> Logically, the decision to go to Singapore and sacrifice 500 jobs to save 10,000 jobs was a "no-brainer." However, culturally the decision created a struggle around taking jobs from our own facility out of America.[7]
>
> We also had to decide what kind of facility we wanted Singapore to be. We knew we wanted to attract the right kind of people there. We wanted to treat our people well. The labor rate was not crucial because the gap was so large. We wanted the facility to be world-class. And we had a notion that at some point we wanted the factory to be solely operated by Singaporeans. We did not want to create an American factory in Singapore.

The move to Singapore reduced CP's labor costs 90% and its overhead costs 40%. Overall, CP saved 30% of its manufacturing costs by moving to Singapore, even after accounting for tariffs and transportation costs.

---

[7]Approximately 10,000 people worked throughout CP. According to CP management, these jobs were at risk if CP did not make competitively priced telephones.

Impact on Labor. In 1985, the Shreveport Western Electric plant employed between 6,000 and 7,000 workers and was the largest employer in northwestern Louisiana. Some 750 workers at the plant were involved in the production of telephones. These workers were represented by the International Brotherhood of Electrical Workers (IBEW).

In July 1985, AT&T laid off 875 workers at the plant, 100 of whom made residential telephones. The remaining 650 residential telephone workers were phased out through later layoffs, transfers, or attrition. At the time of the July 1985 layoffs, AT&T announced that it was shifting the manufacture of residential telephones from the Shreveport facility to a new leased building in Singapore to cut costs and remain competitive.

The Singapore announcement came in the second year of the union's three-year contract. Under the union contract, union workers were not permitted to strike while the contract was in force. The local union officials in Shreveport characterized the union as extremely vocal and unified in its opposition to the move to Singapore. According to the union local, AT&T did not attempt to discuss or negotiate alternatives to moving off-shore with the union.

In recalling this period, Ken Bertaccini said:

> The decision to downsize was very difficult but clear. It cost American jobs and sacrificed the livelihoods of people who were part of the AT&T family. It meant moving jobs to parts of the world without any associations or relationships with AT&T. Patriotic emotions were involved, as well as the pain of looking great people in the eye and telling them that they would no longer have jobs.

Laid-off workers received Trade Readjustment Payments, as well as the benefits outlined in the union contract. These included severance pay based on years of service as well as extended medical benefits.

During the 1986 contract talks, the union negotiated retraining programs for its membership to help prepare them for life after AT&T. An Enhanced Training Opportunity Program was adopted which provided educational opportunities for workers, including computer training and classes at community colleges.

Excellence Period—1987–1988

When Nick Stevens joined CP in November 1987, he noticed that the Singapore facility had strayed from its original manufacturing strategy. Stevens decided CP needed another manufacturing location. The new facility would focus exclusively on manufacturing corded telephones.

According to Nick Stevens, the new location had to be able to sustain a world-class facility. Geographic proximity to Singapore, the cost and availability of labor, government incentive packages, and infrastructure were all among the criteria considered by Stevens. Ultimately, he decided on Bangkok, Thailand.

Thailand, known early as Siam, was one of the world's largest producers of rubber. Thai was spoken by approximately 97% of the population and was the official language, although English was used in government and commerce. Manufacturing accounted for about one-fifth of the country's gross national product and employed about 11% of the work force. In the late 1980s, the country had one of the highest rates of economic growth in the world.

In February 1988, Stevens presented his Bangkok proposal to the AT&T Board and received approval. By June 1988, the facility was announced in Bangkok.

EXHIBIT 6   **Growth of U.S. Telephone Equipment Markets, 1984–1988 (millions of current dollars (1990)**

Type of Market	1984	1985	1986	1987	1988
Telephone sets—corded	$1,200	$1,585	$1,685	$1,750	$1,825
Telephone sets—cordless	410	305	410	438	474
Answering systems	298	371	535	557	634

Source: North American Telecommunications Association, *Telecommunications Market Review and Forecast,* 1990 Edition, pp. 12, 144, 154, 162, and 178.

Answering System Market.   In 1987, CP adopted a five-year plan to make CP's answering systems the market share leader by 1992. As early as 1985, industry experts predicted a robust market for telephone answering systems. Unit sales in 1986 exceeded four million. (See **Exhibit 6.**)

The answering systems market had two segments: adjuncts and integrated. Adjunct answering systems did not include a telephone, while integrated systems did. In both segments, the strongest competitors were Panasonic, Phone-Mate, and GE/Thompson. The market set the price for answering systems and there were no real differences in the margins between the segments. In both segments, however, low-end products (those with less features) commanded smaller margins. In general, the market for answering systems was in affluent countries. In 1987, the largest market by far was the United States. Europe, especially Germany, was expected to develop in future years.

CP's goal for answering systems required it to look for another site for an answering systems manufacturing facility. Stevens' goal for 1988 was to explore the opportunities in Mexico and Europe. In June 1988, he saw an item in *The Wall Street Journal* advertising a seminar in Tucson, Arizona on Mexican *maquiladoras.*[8] The seminar included a side trip into Nogales and Hermosillo, Mexico to tour various *maquiladora* operations. (See **Exhibit 7.**)

Mexico

Mexico was the third largest country in Latin America, after Brazil and Argentina. In 1988, approximately 83,528,000 people lived in Mexico, making it the eleventh most populous country in the world. Officially known as the United States of Mexico, it was organized into 31 states and a *distrito federal.* It shared a 2,000-mile border with the United States of America.

Although Mexico secured its independence from Spain in 1821, it was the Mexican Revolution in 1910 that initiated a period of dramatic social change. A new Constitution was adopted in 1917 which restricted foreign economic control

---

[8]A *maquiladora* is a plant which assembles components that are usually imported into the home country of the *maquiladora* duty free. The assembled components are then re-exported. On re-export, a duty is paid only on the value of the labor which assembled the components and the value of any other home country inputs.

Exhibit 7

Map of Mexico

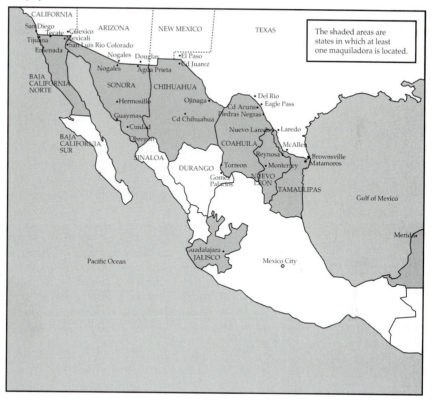

The shaded areas are states in which at least one maquiladora is located.

Population Estimates			
Mexico City	14,000,000	to	18,000,000
Guadalajara	3,000,000	to	5,000,000
Monterrey	2,700,000		
Ciudad Juarez	1,120,000		
Puebla de Zaragoza	1,100,000		
Leon	1,000,000		
Tijuana	600,000		
Acapulco	500,000		
Chihuahua	400,000		
Mexicali	350,000		

and gave workers new protections. In 1929, the *Partido Revolucionario Institucional* (PRI) was formed. Since its founding, it never lost an election. Rapid industrial growth after 1940 improved living standards for much of Mexico. Import substitution, which entailed manufacturing locally what had been previously imported, and aggressive promotion of Mexican products for Mexican consumption were adopted as the country's strategy for development.

Unrest in the late 1960s spurred increased government investment in the infrastructure as well as increased spending on social programs. Despite these aggressive policies, the six-year term (1970–1976) of President Luis Echeverría Alvarez was marked by 30% annual inflation, budget deficits, and political unrest.

In the late 1970s, major new oil fields were discovered in Mexico which gave it easy access to foreign credit at low interest rates. Public debt nearly doubled between 1979 and 1981 from US$40 billion to US$78 billion. Despite the growth in government expenditures, by the end of the 1970s, about 50% of all Mexican households lacked running water and sewage services, 25% lacked electricity, and 22% had neither running water, sewer services, nor electricity. Twenty percent of the population suffered from malnutrition and 45% of the population did not receive adequate health care.[9]

The decline of world oil prices in the early 1980s, as well as a sharp rise in world interest rates, plunged Mexico into economic crisis. In August 1982, Mexico announced that it could not meet the interest payments on its foreign debt of US$88 billion. In September, banks were nationalized and new currency controls were put in place.

In December 1982, foreign debt exceeded US$91 billion. Mexico turned to the International Monetary Fund (IMF) for assistance. The government budget was slashed, food subsidies were eliminated, and the peso was sharply devalued. The combination of inflation and the peso devaluation substantially reduced the real wages of workers. (See **Exhibit 8.**) In 1986, in exchange for new foreign loan agreements with the IMF, the World Bank, and its commercial bank creditors, Mexico agreed to major reforms of its economic policies, including liberalization of foreign investment, reductions in public spending, tax reform, and divestiture of state-owned enterprises.

In July 1988, Carlos Salinas de Gortari, the PRI's candidate, won the presidency with 50.4% of the vote,[10] amid widespread charges of irregularities in the polling. Cuauhtémoc Cárdenas, the son of the Mexican president who had nationalized the oil companies in 1938, had mounted a strong campaign against the PRI. Cárdenas was critical of the PRI for abandoning Mexico's history of national self-determination. According to the PRI, Cárdenas won 31.1% of the vote in the election, including four states and the *distrito federal*. However, many Mexicans believe that Cárdenas actually won the election. As president, Salinas renegotiated the foreign debt, continued the austerity plan, and continued privatizing government-owned businesses.

Maquiladoras

In 1965, the government of Mexico initiated the Border Industrialization Program (BIP). The program permitted foreign corporations to establish wholly owned

---

[9]Helen Shapiro, *Mexico: Escaping from the Debt Crisis?* Harvard Business School case 390–174, 1991, p. 6.

[10]In comparison, de la Madrid received 71.6% of the vote in 1982 and López Portillo received 95% of the vote in 1976. M. Delal Baer, "Electoral Trends," in *Prospects for Mexico*, ed. George W. Grayson (Washington, D.C.: Center for the Study of Foreign Affairs, Foreign Service Institute, Department of State, 1988), p. 43.

EXHIBIT 8   Hourly Compensation of Production Workers in Manufacturing

Country	Wages (US$ per hour worked)								
	1980	*1981*	*1982*	*1983*	*1984*	*1985*	*1986*	*1987*	*1988*
United States	$9.84	$10.84	$11.64	$12.10	$12.51	$12.96	$13.21	$13.40	$13.85
Japan	5.61	6.18	5.70	6.13	6.34	6.43	9.31	10.83	12.80
Singapore	1.49	1.79	1.96	2.21	2.46	2.47	2.23	2.31	2.67
Hong Kong	1.51	1.55	1.67	1.52	1.58	1.73	1.88	2.09	2.40
Taiwan	1.00	1.18	1.22	1.27	1.42	1.50	1.73	2.26	2.82
Thailand	NA	NA	NA	NA	NA	NA	NA	NA	1.40
Brazil	1.38	1.64	1.86	1.26	1.07	1.12	1.47	1.38	1.46
Mexico	NA	3.71	2.54	1.85	2.04	1.60	1.09	1.06	1.32
Malaysia	NA	NA	NA	NA	NA	NA	NA	NA	1.60

Note: Hourly compensation is defined as (1) all payments made directly to the worker—pay for time worked, pay for time not worked, all bonuses and other special payments, and the costs of payments in kind, and (2) employer contributions to legally required insurance programs and contractual and private benefit plans.

Source: Except Malaysia and Thailand, 1980, 1984–1988, United States Department of Labor, Bureau of Labor Statistics, May 1991, Report 803; 1981–1983, unpublished data from United States Department of Labor Bureau of Labor Statistics, Office of Productivity and Technology; Malaysia and Thailand, 1988, Swiss Bank Corporation.

subsidiary operations in Mexico. Under the program, the subsidiary could import into Mexico duty free machinery, raw materials, and component parts to be used in processing or assembling goods in Mexico.[11] As long as the end product was exported, Mexican duties were not levied on the imported components. Under the laws of the United States and most industrialized countries, when the imported components are exported back to their country of origin in the form of finished products, only the value added in Mexico—labor, overhead, raw materials—and not the value of the imported raw materials or components was subject to duty.[12] Operations established under this program were commonly known as *maquiladoras, maquilas,* or in-bond assembly operations.[13]

Maquiladora or *maquila* is derived from the Spanish verb *maquilar*, which means to measure or take payment for grinding corn. In colonial times, the *maquila* was the portion of flour that the miller kept as payment for grinding the

[11]Without the provisions of the Border Industrialization Program, products could not be imported into Mexico without an import license. After Mexico joined the General Agreement on Tariffs and Trade (GATT) in 1986, tariffs at an initial level of 50% were substituted for import licenses. At the end of 1987, the tariff ceiling for most items was lowered to 20%. Import licenses are still required for electronic and computer equipment and automotive imports. Sidney Weintraub, *Transforming the Mexico Economy: The Salinas Sexenio* (Washington, D.C.: National Planning Association, 1990), p. 5.
[12]In the United States, Tariff Schedules of the United States (TSUS) items 806.30 and 807.00 permit the portion of the product made of U.S. components to re-enter the United States duty free.
[13]All maquiladora facilities which export the assembled products are part of the "In-Bond Industry." The in-bond feature of the BIP requires that an importing maquiladora plant guarantee the payment of duties on imported materials which would otherwise be due. The guarantee usually consists of a surety bond. After processing, if the assembled products are exported, the bond is canceled.

corn. In the 1980s, *maquiladora* or *maquila* referred to the system under which foreign companies provide the corn (e.g., electronic components), Mexico keeps its portion for assembling or processing (e.g., foreign currency changed into pesos for wages and production costs), and the assembled goods return to their country of origin with a duty paid only on the value added in Mexico.

Twin plant is another term often associated with *maquilas.* Originally, the BIP envisioned the establishment of complementary plants across the border from one another. The Mexican twin was intended to provide labor-intensive assembly of components fabricated in the United States. The assembled components would then be shipped to the twin in the United States where they would be finished, inspected, distributed, and sold. However, in most cases, the complementary U.S. plant was not located along the border but elsewhere within the United States at preexisting facilities. In 1987, fewer than 10% of all Mexican *maquilas* had a U.S. twin.[14]

The BIP was adopted to provide permanent employment for Mexico's rapidly growing population along the U.S.-Mexico border. The program sought to create jobs by attracting foreign manufacturing facilities that would not compete directly with domestic Mexican producers. The program also attempted to absorb migrant agricultural workers displaced by the expiration of the U.S. Bracero Program.[15] To address the problems resulting from the end of the Bracero Program, the law initially required that all foreign owned assembly operations be located within a 20-kilometer strip along the U.S.-Mexican border. New regulations were adopted in 1977 that permitted *maquilas* to locate in the economically depressed interior regions of Mexico. In 1983, the Mexican government extended the program to all regions of Mexico. However, by 1986, over 88% of all *maquila* operations were still concentrated along the border. *Maquiladoras* located near the border accounted for approximately 87% of the total *maquiladora* work force.[16]

The number of *maquiladoras* grew from 12 in 1965 to over 1,450 in 1988.[17] Over the same period, the number of *maquiladora* workers grew from 3,000 to over 361,800. (See **Exhibit 9.**) The type of *maquila* production had also changed. In 1965 and 1966, the vast majority of *maquiladoras* were textile firms. In 1988, *maquiladora* production included automobiles and auto parts, electronics, telecommunications equipment, and scientific instruments.

---

[14]U.S. International Trade Commission (USITC), *The Use and Economic Impact of TSUS Items 806.30 and 807,* Publication No. 2053 (Washington, D.C.: U.S. International Trade Commission, January 1988), p. 8–2.

[15]The Bracero, or Mexican Labor Program, allowed migrant Mexican workers to enter the United States on a temporary (seasonal) basis from 1942 through 1964. It was initiated to alleviate labor shortages in the U.S. agricultural and railroad industries during World War II. The Bracero Program attracted to the border unemployed workers from the Mexican interior who were seeking the guaranteed U.S. minimum wage. The railroad portion of the program ended in 1946. The agricultural program expired in 1964. A large segment of the border population became dependent on income earned by Braceros in the United States.

[16] USITC, *The Use and Economic Impact of TSUS Items 806.30 and 807,* p. 8–4.

[17]Khosrow Fatemi (ed.), *The Maquiladora Industry: Economic Solution or Problem?* (New York: Praeger Publishers, 1990), pp. 4, 28.

Beginning in the early 1980s, a substantial number of major U.S. multinationals, including many *Fortune 500* companies, established *maquiladoras*. Several European and Japanese firms also established *maquiladoras* or employed subcontractors to perform their assembly in Mexico. In 1987, there were 20 Japanese *maquiladoras* in Mexico. The most prominent Japanese manufacturers operating *maquiladora* facilities were Sanyo, Sony, Toshiba, Hitachi, Matsushita, and TDK.[18]

Maquiladoras for Mexico

Impact on the Economy   Mexico earned foreign exchange on the value added to products assembled or processed in Mexico and then exported. (See **Exhibits 9** and **10.**) In less than 25 years, the *maquiladora* industry had become Mexico's second largest industry after oil and oil-related production. In 1987, the *maquiladora* industry accounted for approximately 44% of Mexican exports to the United States. That year, *maquiladoras* contributed approximately US$1.6 billion in foreign exchange earnings. Between 1982 and 1987, the industry created 178,000 new jobs out of a total of 408,000 jobs created over this period.[19]

Impact on the Environment   It was estimated that *maquiladoras* generated over 20 million tons of hazardous waste annually. Such wastes include corrosive acids and bases, sludge from electroplating processes, cyanide solutions, paint sludge and thinners, and heavy metals such as cadmium, chromium, lead, mercury, and silver.[20] Under the Mexican law which had regulated *maquiladoras* since 1983, hazardous wastes had to be returned to their country of origin.[21] American-owned *maquiladoras* had to comply with both Mexican and U.S. laws regulating hazardous waste disposal. U.S. law required would-be generators of hazardous waste to obtain an EPA identification number. In addition, *maquiladoras* which planned to transport hazardous waste for off-site treatment, storage, or disposal within the United States had to prepare a manifest. Each time the waste changed hands, the manifest had to be signed. Biennial reports were required to be submitted to the EPA by all companies shipping hazardous waste to the United States.

EPA records showed that in 1987 only 20 out of more than 1,000 U.S. *maquiladoras* returned their hazardous waste to the United States.[22] A study by the Texas Center for Policy Studies found that in a two and one-half year period only 33 of the approximately 600 *maquiladoras* in the Texas-Mexico border area had filed the required notices for return of their hazardous wastes to the United

---

[18]USITC, *The Use and Economic Impact of TSUS Items 806.30 and 807*, p. 8–12.

[19]Instituto Nacional de Estadística, Geografía e Informática (INEGI), National Income and Product Accounts, 1988.

[20]Douglas Alexander and L. Roberto Fernandez, "Environmental Regulation of Business in Mexico," *Doing Business in Mexico* (New York: Matthew Bender, 1990), pp. 79–29 and 79–30.

[21]1982 Decree for Promotion of the Maquiladora Industry (Diario Oficial, August 15, 1983), Art. 26.

[22]"Transfrontier Health and Environmental Risks," *Natural Resources Journal*, Winter 1990, p. 177.

EXHIBIT 9   **Selected Data on the Maquiladoras**

	1980	1981	1982	1983	1984	1985	1986	1987	1988
Number of firms	620	605	585	600	672	760	891	1,125	1,450
Average annual employment (000)	119.5	131	127	151	200	212	250	305	362
Imported materials (million US$)	$1,750	$2,227	$1,979	$2,823	$3,749	$3,825	$4,351	$5,507	$ 7,808
Exported material (million US$)	2,523	3,202	2,830	3,641	4,904	5,092	5,646	7,105	10,146
Value added (million US$)	773	975	851	818	1,155	1,267	1,295	1,598	2,337
Wages, salaries, loans	458	596	463	385	595	660	586	739	1,141
Domestic raw materials and packaging	30	29	26	37	51	36	54	86	132
Utilities and other expenses	129	153	174	183	206	238	295	314	388
Miscellaneous expenses	155	197	189	213	303	334	360	458	676

Note: Figures may not add due to rounding.

Source: Banco de Mexico, "La Industria Maquiladora de Exportación, 1980–1986," mimeo. Mexico, 1987; 1987 and 1988, INEGI, "Advances de Informacion Economica—Industria *Maquiladora* de Exportación," November 1988 and November 1989.

EXHIBIT 10   **Selected Data on Mexico's Balance of Payments**

	1980	1981	1982	1983	1984	1985	1986	1987	1988
Merchandise exports	16,070	19,940	21,230	22,312	24,196	21,663	16,031	20,655	20,566
Merchandise imports	(18,900)	(24,040)	(14,435)	(8,550)	(11,255)	(13,212)	(11,432)	(12,222)	(18,898)
Trade balance	(2,830)	(4,100)	6,795	13,762	12,941	8,451	4,599	8,433	1,668
Foreign direct investment	2,090	2,540	1,655	461	390	491	1,160	1,796	635
Current account balance	(8,160)	(1,390)	(6,307)	5,403	4,194	1,130	(1,673)	3,968	(2,443)

Trade Balance, also known as Balance of Trade, is a country's exports of goods minus its imports of goods.

Foreign Direct Investment is the acquisition of physical assets outside the home country with substantial management control (usually defined as 10% or more of the ownership of a company) held by the parent corporation of the home country.

Current Account Balance is the net of the country's imports, exports, services and government unilateral transfers (sums sent outside the home country by the government for foreign aid, emergency relief, etc.).

Balance of Payments is the record of the goods and services an economy has received from and provided to the rest of the world and of the changes in the economy's claims on and liabilities to the rest of the world. Michael G. Rukstad (ed.), *Macroeconomic Decision Making in the World Economy: Text and Cases* (Florida: Holt, Rinehart and Winston, Inc., 1989), p. 485.

Source: Balance of Payments Statistics, Vol. 41 Yearbook, Part 1 (IMF: 1990).

States.[23] A November 1990 study by the Secretaria de Desarrollo Urbano y Ecología (the Ministry of Urban Development and Ecology or SEDUE), the Mexican Government's equivalent of the U.S. Environmental Protection Agency, revealed that only 19% of the plants using toxic materials could show that they had disposed of wastes properly.[24] Other studies had revealed that primary sources

---

[23]Remarks of Mary E. Kelly, Executive Director, Texas Center for Policy Studies, before the Senate Finance Committee, February 20, 1991, p. 3.

[24]"Border Industry's Nasty Byproduct Imperils Trade," *The New York Times*, March 31, 1991, p. 16, col. 3.

of drinking water in the border area had been contaminated with industrial solvents and other chemicals.[25]

Historically, Mexico had less stringent environmental standards than the United States and lax enforcement of its standards.[26] In a 1988 survey of *maquiladoras* in Mexicali, a Mexican city near the California border, by El Colegio de la Frontera Norte, 10% of the 100 *maquiladoras* surveyed freely admitted that "environmental legislation" in Mexico was one of the main factors in their decision to leave the United States and relocate in Mexico. Seventeen percent of those surveyed considered it a factor of importance.[27]

In 1988, Mexico enacted the General Law on Ecological Balance and Environmental Protection. The administrator of the U.S. Environmental Protection Agency said about the law:

> . . . what we know about Mexico's 1988 comprehensive environmental law indicates that it may be sufficiently stringent to rebut the "pollution haven" argument. Properly enforced, the law should result in greatly improved environmental protection.[28]

SEDUE was the federal Mexican agency charged with enforcing the 1988 environmental law. Its annual budget for pollution control was approximately US$3.1 million. In contrast, in the same year, Texas' annual budget for pollution control was US$50 million. In Ciudad Juarez, a Mexican city near El Paso, Texas, there was one Mexican federal inspector for over 300 *maquiladora* plants and all Mexican domestic industry.[29]

Most of the *maquiladoras* were clustered around Tijuana–San Diego in California and Ciudad Juarez–El Paso in Texas. The resulting population growth in these cities severely strained the water supply and infrastructure. A 1981 University of Mexico study on border resources found that the aquifer under El Paso–Ciudad Juarez was being depleted faster than it was being replenished. In the lower Rio Grande Valley, closer to the Gulf of Mexico, municipal and industrial needs were expected to reduce drastically the water available for crop irrigation by the year 2000.[30]

Wages and Working Conditions The Mexican Constitution and federal Mexican labor law set forth the minimum rights and benefits to which Mexican workers were entitled. The law regulated employment conditions such as work schedules, overtime, vacation periods, legal holidays, payment of salaries, employ-

---

[25]"Border Industry's Nasty Byproduct," p. 4.

[26]"The Texas Border: Whose Dirt?" *The Economist*, August 18, 1990, pp. 24–25.

[27]"Transfrontier Health and Environmental Risks," *Natural Resources Journal,* Winter 1990, p. 177.

[28]William K. Reilly, "Mexico's Environment Will Improve With Free Trade," *The Wall Street Journal*, April 19, 1991, p. A15, col. 2.

[29]Remarks of Mary E. Kelly, pp. 6–7.

[30]"The Texas Border: Whose Dirt?" p. 24–25.

EXHIBIT 11   **Average Hourly Compensation Cost for *Maquiladora* Workers**

Year	Compensation
1980	$1.42
1981	1.67
1982	1.23
1983	0.91
1984	1.06
1985	1.07
1986	0.80
1987	0.75
1988	0.80

Source: 1980–1986, (USITC), *The Use and Economic Impact of TSUS Items 806.30 and 807,* p. 8–9; 1987 and 1988, Leslie Sklair, *Assembling for Development* (Boston: Unwin Hyman, Inc., 1989), p. 72.

ment of women and minors, occupational risks, and minimum wages. Article Three of Mexico's federal labor law provided:

> Work is a social right and social obligation. It is not an article of commerce; it requires respect for the freedom and dignity of the person performing it and it shall be carried out under conditions protecting the life, the health, and a decent standard of living for the worker and his family.[31]

Mexican workers also had the right to unionize. In major Mexican cities, nearly all workers were members of a union. Under Mexican law, the union had the right to approve or disapprove an employer's hiring decisions.

A survey conducted by the International Trade Commission found that U.S. companies viewed the Mexican minimum wage as the major attraction of foreign investment in Mexico.[32] (See **Exhibit 11.**) Minimum wages in Mexico were set by commissions comprised of members of the government, organized labor, and private industry. The commissions set minimum wages for 86 different unskilled and skilled occupational classifications in 11 different economic zones in Mexico. The highest minimum wages had traditionally been along the northern border.[33]

Base *maquiladora* wages averaged about $3.50 to $4.00 per day for production workers.[34] (See **Exhibit 11.**) According to the American Friends Service Committee, comparable Mexican manufacturers in major cities paid two to three times *maquiladora* wages.[35] Common fringe benefits, such as attendance bonuses and

---

[31]Commercial, Business and Trade Laws, Mexico, F. Labor Law (Title first to ninth) (United States of America: Oceana Publications, Inc., 1983), p. 3.

[32](USITC), *The Use and Economic Impact of TSUS Items 806.30 and 807,* p. xxx.

[33]Barbara Chrispin, "Manpower Development in the Maquiladora Industry: Reaching Maturity." In Khosrow Fatemi (ed.), *The Maquiladora Industry: Economic Solution or Problem?* p. 75.

[34]Chrispin, "Manpower Development in the Maquiladora Industry," p. 76.

[35]*Background and Perspectives on the U.S.-Mexico-Canada Free Trade Talks* (Philadelphia, PA: American Friends Service Committee, April 10, 1991), p. 6.

transportation subsidies, could raise the wage to $7 to $9 per day. Attendance bonuses were in response to a 10% to 35% turnover rate which came to characterize *maquiladoras*. The average hourly wages paid to *maquiladora* workers placed strict limits on their purchasing power. In the town of Matamoros, for example the average worker had to work an hour and a half to buy a half gallon of milk, three hours to buy a box of cereal, five and a half hours to buy two pounds of beef, and 17 hours to buy a toddler-size dress.[36]

Limited studies of *maquiladora* working conditions indicated that employees had experienced many work-related health and safety problems. Eye disease and the weakening of the optic nerve were prevalent among electronics workers. Among textile workers, inadequate seating had been associated with the development of lumbago.[37]

In a Tijuana, Mexico *maquiladora* of one of CP's Asian competitors, the casewriter observed an assembly line of workers, 98% of whom were women, hunched over a moving conveyor belt that carried printed circuit boards (PCBs) in various stages of completion. The plant made cable boxes and tuners. The women workers sat on nonergonomic stools while placing capacitors or other minute components on PCBs. Some workers used magnifying glasses to place components on the printed circuit boards. Some women soldered or tested PCBs. Testing was done by manually manipulating a component on a PCB or by staring at a computer screen as the PCB was tested by a machine.

The *maquiladora* employed a handful of male workers. These workers attended the automated processes in the plant, though there seemed to be little for them to do. No women were assigned to the machines. All employees worked a nine and one-half hour day, from 8:00 A.M. to 6:00 P.M., with a half hour break for lunch. A trailer outside the plant indicated that it was for the storage of hazardous waste.

Half of Mexico's population was below the age of 18. Although it was illegal in Mexico to hire children under 14, the Mexico City Assembly estimated that between 5 million to 10 million children were employed illegally, often in hazardous jobs.[38] *The Wall Street Journal* profiled Vicente Guerrero, a 12-year-old Mexican boy who had been compelled to leave the sixth grade to work in a shoe factory.

> . . . Vicente spends most of his time . . . smearing glue onto the soles of shoes with his hands. The glue he dips his fingers into is marked "toxic substances . . . prolonged or repeated inhalation causes grave health damage; do not leave in the reach of minors." All [the boys who work in the factory] ignore the warning.
>
> Impossible to ignore is the sharp, sickening odor of the glue. The only ventilation in the factory is from slits in the wall where bricks were removed from a window near Vicente that opens only halfway. Just a matter of weeks after he started working, Vicente was home in bed with a cough, burning eyes, and nausea.

---

[36]Simon Billenness and Kate Simpson, *Franklin's Insight: The Advisory Letter for Concerned Investors*, Franklin Research and Development Corporation, Boston, MA, September 1992, p. 8.

[37]Judith Ann Warner, "The Sociological Impact of the Maquiladoras." In Khosrow Fatemi (ed.), *The Maquiladora Industry: Economic Solution or Problem?* (New York: Prager, 1990), p. 193. Lumbago is pain in the lower back (lumbar region) often caused by muscle strain.

[38]Matt Moffett, "Working Children: Underage Laborers Fill Mexican Factories, Stir U.S. Trade Debate," *The Wall Street Journal*, April 8, 1991, p. 1, col. 1.

> When a teacher came by the factory to chide school dropouts [the plant superintendent's 13-year-old son] rebuked her. "I'm earning 180,000 pesos a week," he said. "What do you make?" The teacher, whose weekly salary is 120,000 could say nothing.[39]

Estimates placed the savings, compared to average *maquiladora* wages, from hiring younger (ages 14–18) and less skilled workers at 30%–40%.

Some critics charged that *maquiladoras* had disrupted the social and family structure of Mexican society by discriminating against Mexican males, the traditional breadwinners, and hiring predominantly women. The critics also contended that women were preferred over men because they were more docile, politically unaware, inexperienced, and less demanding. In the 1970s, women comprised 23% of the Mexican labor force overall but 72.3% of the *maquila* industry.[40] (See **Exhibit 12.**)

Living Conditions   In the Mexican border towns, many *maquiladora* workers lived in dwellings fashioned from cardboard and scraps of wood taken from *maquiladora* trash bins. Some of the cardboard had once contained polyvinyl chloride; written on the cardboard walls were warnings that the former contents could release hazardous fumes. The workers' water supply was stored in 55-gallon drums also found in *maquiladora* trash bins. The drums contained labels indicating that their former contents were fluorocarbon solvents whose vapors were harmful if inhaled.

Maquiladoras and the United States

Impact on the Economy   Advocates argued that *maquiladoras* help keep U.S. manufacturing internationally competitive, saving jobs that would otherwise be lost if U.S. manufacturers went to the Far East, since *maquiladoras* primarily use components made in the United States. According to a U.S. Department of Commerce report, nearly 75,000 U.S. workers were employed during 1986 to produce and ship $2.9 billion of components and raw materials used annually by *maquiladoras*.[41]

Organized labor in the United States contended that *maquiladoras* take jobs out of the United States—some of which could be held by the estimated 27 million workers and unemployed people in the United States who were functional illiterates. The Communications Workers of America (CWA) estimated that had there been no increase in foreign production by U.S. companies, over 20,000 of the 120,000 jobs lost in the telecommunications industry since 1981 would have been

---

[39]Moffett, "Working Children," p. A14, col. 1.

[40]Leslie Sklair, *Assembling for Development: The Maquila Industry in Mexico and the United States* (Boston: Unwin Hyman, 1989), pp. 165–166.

[41]USITC, *The Use and Economic Impact of TSUS Items 806.30 and 807*, p. 8–15.

EXHIBIT 12   Distribution of Men and Women in the Maquila
Work Force in 1986

Various Manufacturing Activities	Men	Women
Electrical and electronic machinery and equipment	9,610	29,001
Furniture and fixtures	5,803	1,910
Nonelectrical equipment and parts	1,857	897
Footwear and leather products	1,776	2,052
Transportation equipment and accessories	17,850	23,144
Total industry	64,812	139,076

Source: USITC, *The Use and Economic Impact of TSUS Items 806.30 and 807,*pp. 8–11.

saved.[42] In 1988, the jobless rate in the U.S. electronics industry was 86% higher than it was in 1979. In the five years between January 1979 and January 1984, employment for production workers manufacturing telephone and telegraph equipment declined in the United States by 23.4%.[43]

Maquiladora workers tended to shop in U.S. border towns, thereby returning a portion of their *maquila* wages to the United States. Studies have suggested that *maquila* workers spent more than half of their wages in the United States, mainly in the stores and shopping malls of the U.S. border towns.[44]

Impact on the Environment   The *maquiladoras* brought rapid development on the U.S. side of the border. The pace of development outstripped the ability of the region to absorb it. Mexican officials have complained that growing development on the U.S. side of the border threatened surface-water supplies promised to Mexico under a 1944 treaty. A legal advisor to the Mexican Foreign Ministry believed that by the mid-1990s the United States would be unable to deliver the volume of water promised Mexico.[45] The primary source of drinking water on the Texas border was the Rio Grande, which was consistently drunk dry.[46]

Not only was there a shortage of water, but the water that was available was frequently contaminated. Most Mexican border towns did not have sewage treatment plants. Ciudad Juarez dumped all of its raw sewage into a canal that paralleled the Rio Grande. A study in San Elizario, Texas, showed that everyone there had been exposed to hepatitis at least once by the time he or she was 20 years old.[47] More than 20 million gallons of untreated sewage and chemicals ran into

---

[42]John Cavanagh, Lance Compa, et al., *Trade's Hidden Costs: Worker Rights in a Changing World Economy* (Washington, D.C.: International Labor Rights Education & Research Fund, 1988), p. 21.

[43]Full Employment Action Council, "Economic Dislocation and Structural Unemployment: The Plight of America's Basic Industries," September 6, 1985.

[44]Leslie Sklair, "Mexico's Maquiladora Programme," in George Philip (ed.), *The Mexican Economy* (London, Routledge, 1988), p. 299.

[45]"The Natural Limits to Growth," *The Economist*, April 20, 1991, p. 24.

[46]"The Natural Limits to Growth."

[47]"Border Industry's Nasty Byproduct," p. 16, col. 3.

the Tijuana River each day. Some ended up on the Imperial Beach on the California coast which had been closed for ten years.[48] Recreational use of the Rio Grande below Laredo, Texas, has long been considered unsafe because its sister city in Mexico, Nuevo Laredo, dump about 25 million gallons of untreated sewage into the river every day.[49]

The air quality along the border had also been affected. On the Mexican side of the border across from El Paso, Texas, firewood was the chief cooking and heating fuel for most of the 1.2 million residents of Ciudad Juarez, Mexico. Rubber tires were burned in kilns that made decorative tiles. Along with pollution from motor vehicles and industry, the smoke from these fires produced an acrid cloud over both cities under certain weather conditions.[50]

Considerations on Plant Location

In late 1988, Stevens enrolled in the seminar advertised in *The Wall Street Journal* and toured the *maquiladora* operations situated around the U.S.-Mexico border. Stevens described his reactions to the tour:

> I did not like what I saw. I saw exploitation in the form of sweat shops, I saw wage inflation, horrible environmental conditions, and huge work force turnover.

CP management had also heard that bribery and corruption were a way of life in Mexico.

Stevens was considering other sites in Mexico including Monterrey, Hermosillo, Chihuahua, and Guadalajara. He was also considering locations outside Mexico: Malaysia, a U.S. greenfield operation in Texas, and a U.S.-AT&T "factory-within-a-factory" operation. A plant outside the United States would employ approximately 1,800 people at full capacity of 3.5 million units per year. The work week would average 45 hours.

Projections indicated that a *maquiladora* plant in the border region was the lowest cost option. (See **Exhibit 13**.) Wages elsewhere in Mexico were likely to be higher—by 15%–20%, for example, in Guadalajara. Expenditures on pollution controls were another cost issue. Complying with U.S. "good citizen" standards with on-site facilities would add $2–$3 million to the estimates in **Exhibit 13** during the first few years. However, a number of companies avoided those expenditures by paying local firms relatively small amounts to dispose of waste—though some of these disposal firms did not actually comply with Mexican laws and regulations.

Malaysia offered several advantages. AT&T had significant experience in Asia, as well as infrastructure and support systems in the area, and the Malaysian Industrial Development Authority offered, like Singapore, a central, one-stop shopping opportunity for foreign companies. On the negative side, Stevens was concerned about putting too many eggs in one basket in Asia and feared that Malaysian wages and salaries would rise as more companies moved there.

---

[48]"The Texas Border: Whose Dirt?" p. 24.
[49]"Border Industry's Nasty Byproduct."
[50]"Border Industry's Nasty Byproduct."

EXHIBIT 13   **Initial Estimates of Average Cost per Unit at Alternative Sites (labor costed at average *maquiladora* rates)**

		Existing AT&T Factory			
	Greenfield	*Full*	*Incremental*	*Malaysia*	*Mexico*
Landed cost[a]	$47.33	$52.33	$51.89	$41.48	$39.94
Additional cost[b]	.72	.66	.65	3.40	2.96
Total cost	$48.04	$52.99	$52.54	$44.89	$42.89
Incremental carrying costs	—	—	—	0.49	—
Total cost including carrying costs	$48.04	$52.99	$52.54	$45.37	$42.89

[a]Landed cost includes material, labor, and overhead.
[b]Additional cost includes transportation fees, duties, asset tax, and a charge for AT&T's internal hurdle rate.

Data have been disguised. The essential relationships have, however, been preserved.

At the time Stevens was considering where to locate CP's new manufacturing facility, AT&T's senior management was reviewing its capital budgeting process. It seemed it would be more difficult to get approval for the current project than for the Singapore and Thailand operations.

Wherever the plant was located, the plant would be devoted to manufacturing answering systems. Electronic components, printed circuit boards, power adapters, pellets and cardboard boxes would be brought into the plant. The plant would make the body of the answering systems in-house using plastic injection molding. Completed answering systems would leave the plant boxed and ready to ship.

Even if the project were approved, Stevens and CP management still had to reach decisions on wages and benefits, sourcing of components, and the profile of its work force in terms of gender, age, and educational background, as well as a host of other issues.

CASE 6
LEVI STRAUSS & CO.: GLOBAL SOURCING (A)

Levi Strauss & Co. has a heritage of conducting business in a manner that reflects its values. As we expand our sourcing base to more diverse cultures and countries, we must take special care in selecting business partners and countries whose practices are not incompatible with our values. Otherwise, our sourcing decisions have the potential of undermining this heritage, damaging the image of our brands and threatening our commercial success.

—Levi Strauss & Co.Business Partner Terms of Engagement and Guidelines for Country Selection

"If we really are an aspirational company, shouldn't we be in there trying to make a difference?" asked one member of the China Policy Group at Levi Strauss & Co. (LS&CO.), the world's largest brand-name apparel manufacturer. Another responded, "We've got to be careful not to get into the wrong bed—we don't want to wake up with the fleas. There are some things we just can't be associated with—and still maintain our reputation."

The China Policy Group (CPG) had been chartered in late 1992 by CEO Robert D. Haas and Vice President of Global Sourcing Peter A. Jacobi specifically to consider whether LS&CO. should continue sourcing and purchasing fabric in China and whether it should make direct investments in marketing and manufacturing ventures there. The CPG had been asked to use the "principled reasoning approach" to make a recommendation based on the company's ethical values and global sourcing guidelines. Announced in March 1992, these guidelines were part of a comprehensive set of sourcing standards widely acknowledged to be among the most far-reaching of any adopted by a U.S. company.[1] (See **Exhibits 1** and **2.**) The CPG would report its recommendation to the nine-member Executive Management Committee, LS&CO.'s most senior decision-making group, early in 1993.

The CPG's leaders—Pete Jacobi; Lindsay Webbe, president of the Asia–Pacific Division; and Robert Dunn, vice president of Corporate Affairs—had carefully identified and recruited nine others to join the group. They sought individuals with relevant knowledge and a range of perspectives informed by differences in experience, functional area, race, and gender.[2] Elissa Sheridan, a specialist on loan from Corporate Affairs, prepared voluminous background reports to aid the discussion. Once formed, the CPG reviewed its membership, studied the background materials, and identified additional information needed for its work. The group also decided to try for a consensus recommendation while reserving to anyone who disagreed the right to submit a minority opinion.

This case was prepared by Jane Palley Katz under the supervision of Lynn Sharp Paine. Harvard Business School case 395–127. Copyright © by the President and Fellows of Harvard College.

[1]For example, see "A Stitch in Time," *The Economist*, June 6, 1992, p. 27 ff.
[2]Members were drawn from Human Resources, Levi Strauss International, Legal, Global Sourcing, the Asia Pacific Division, and Corporate Affairs.

EXHIBIT 1 **Levi Strauss & Co., Global Sourcing Guidelines, Business Partner Terms of Engagement**

Business Partner Terms of Engagement

Our concerns include the practices of individual business partners as well as the political and social issues in those countries where we might consider sourcing.

This defines Terms of Engagement which addresses issues that are substantially controllable by our individual business partners.

We have defined business partners as contractors and suppliers who provide labor and/or material (including fabric, sundries, chemicals and/or stones) utilized in the manufacture and finishing of our products.

1. **Environmental Requirements**

   We will only do business with partners who share our commitment to the environment. (Note: We intend this standard to be consistent with the approved language of Levi Strauss & Co.'s Environmental Action Group.)

2. **Ethical Standards**

   We will seek to identify and utilize business partners who aspire as individuals and in the conduct of their business to a set of ethical standards not incompatible with our own.

3. **Health and Safety**

   We will seek to identify and utilize business partners who provide workers with a safe and healthy work environment. Business partners who provide residential facilities for their workers must provide safe and healthy facilities.

4. **Legal Requirements**

   We expect our business partners to be law abiding as individuals and to comply with legal requirements relevant to the conduct of their business.

5. **Employment Standards**

   We will only do business with partners whose workers are in all cases present voluntarily, not put at risk of physical harm, fairly compensated, allowed the right of free association and not exploited in any way. In addition, the following specific guidelines will be followed.

   - **Wages and Benefits**

     We will only do business with partners who provide wages and benefits that comply with any applicable law or match the prevailing local manufacturing or finishing industry practices. We will also favor business partners who share our commitment to contribute to the betterment of community conditions.

   - **Working Hours**

     While permitting flexibility in scheduling, we will identify prevailing local work hours and seek business partners who do not exceed them except for appropriately compensated overtime. While we favor partners who utilize less than sixty-hour work weeks, we will not use contractors who, on a regularly scheduled basis, require in excess of a sixty-hour week. Employees should be allowed one day off in seven days.

EXHIBIT 1   CONTINUED

- **Child Labor**

  Use of child labor is not permissible. "Child" is defined as less than 14 years of age or younger than the compulsory age to be in school. We will not utilize partners who use child labor in any of their facilities. We support the development of legitimate workplace apprenticeship programs for the educational benefit of younger people.

- **Prison Labor/Forced Labor**

  We will not knowingly utilize prison or forced labor in contracting or subcontracting relationships in the manufacture of our products. We will not knowingly utilize or purchase materials from a business partner utilizing prison or forced labor.

- **Discrimination**

  While we recognize and respect cultural differences, we believe that workers should be employed on the basis of their ability to do the job, rather than on the basis of personal characteristics or beliefs. We will favor business partners who share this value.

- **Disciplinary Practices**

  We will not utilize business partners who use corporal punishment or other forms of mental or physical coercion.

Source: Company document.

EXHIBIT 2   Levi Strauss & Co., Global Sourcing Guidelines, Guidelines for Country Selection

---

Guidelines for Country Selection

The following country selection criteria address issues which we believe are beyond the ability of individual business partners to control.

1. **Brand Image**
   We will not initiate or renew contractual relationships in countries where sourcing would have an adverse effect on our global brand image.
2. **Health and Safety**
   We will not initiate or renew contractual relationships in locations where there is evidence that Company employees or representatives would be exposed to unreasonable risk.
3. **Human Rights**
   We should not initiate or renew contractual relationships in countries where there are pervasive violations of basic human rights.
4. **Legal Requirements**
   We will not initiate or renew contractual relationships in countries where the legal environment creates unreasonable risk to our trademarks or to other important commercial interests or seriously impedes our ability to implement these guidelines.
5. **Political or Social Stability**
   We will not initiate or renew contractual relationships in countries where political or social turmoil unreasonably threatens our commercial interests.

Source: Company document.

Company Background

LS&CO. traced its roots to the 1850s, when a Bavarian-born immigrant, Levi Strauss, came to San Francisco from New York and joined his brother-in-law's dry goods business. The company achieved early success producing and selling sturdy canvas trousers, the first jeans, to the many miners who arrived during the gold rush. In 1873, Strauss adopted the idea, from a Nevada tailor, to rivet the pockets for added strength. The double-arcuate pattern sewn on the hip pockets, the oldest apparel trademark in the United States, was added the same year. By the last half of the 20th century, "Levi's®" had become synonymous with "jeans," while the spread of American popular culture—movies, television, and music—made the company's clothes a symbol of American values, sought after across the globe. Explained the vice president for Corporate Marketing, Levi's® jeans epitomized "freedom, originality, youthfulness and the spirit of America" in markets worldwide.[3] They were even included in the permanent collection of the Smithsonian Institute, a museum of U.S. history and culture located in Washington, D.C.

For the first 100 years of its history, LS&CO. was a private company. Family members owned nearly all of its stock, with employees holding most of the remaining shares. In 1971, needing funds for expansion, the company went public, although the Haas family retained a significant amount of the stock, with some of its members opposing the move.[4]

During the early 1980s, in response to a decline in the U.S. jeans market and a larger decline globally, LS&CO. closed 58 plants and laid off more than a third of its work force. In 1984, Robert D. Haas, the great-great-grandnephew of founder Levi Strauss, became president and chief executive officer, following in the footsteps of both his uncle, Peter Haas, and his father, Walter Haas, Jr., who had previously served as president and chairman of the board, respectively, and were board members in 1993. In 1985, under Robert Haas's leadership, certain descendants of Levi Strauss's family repurchased publicly held shares for $50 a share—a 42% premium over the market price—or a total cost of $1.6 billion, at that time the biggest leveraged buyout in history.[5] In 1993, 95% of the company's stock was held by descendants of Levi Strauss and by certain nonfamily members of management. The remainder was held by the company's employee investment plans.

As the apparel industry became more competitive, with faster style changes and fewer, though larger, retail customers, LS&CO. reconceived itself from a manufacturer to a marketer. The company reorganized at the end of 1988, reducing layers of management and consolidating personnel, finance, and operations to advance its strategy of providing better and faster service to retail customers. Robert Haas became chairman of the board in 1989.

---

[3]Michael Janofsky, "Whether It's Bluejeans or Mini-Motors or Power Plants. . . .: Levi Strauss, American Symbol with a Cause," *The New York Times,* January 3, 1994, p. C4 ff.
[4]"Levi Strauss & Co. and the AIDS Crisis," HBS case 391–189, p. 5.
[5]"Levi Strauss & Co. and the AIDS Crisis," p. 5.

EXHIBIT 3   **Levi Strauss Associates Inc. and Subsidiaries, Consolidated Statements of Income, 1990–1992 (dollars in thousands, except per-share data)**

Year Ended	November 29, 1992[a]	November 24, 1991[a]	November 25, 1990[a]
Net sales	$ 5,570,290	$ 4,902,882	$ 4,247,150
Cost of goods sold	3,431,469	3,024,330	2,651,338
Gross profit	2,138,821	1,878,552	1,595,812
Marketing, general and administrative expenses	1,322,079	1,148,129	985,361
Stock option charge	157,964	—	—
Operating income	658,778	730,423	610,451
Interest expense	53,303	71,384	82,956
Other income, net	28,646	32,314	26,173
Income before taxes and extraordinary loss	634,121	691,353	553,668
Provision for taxes	271,673	324,812	288,753
Income before extraordinary loss	362,448	366,541	264,915
Extraordinary loss: Loss from early extinguishment of debt, net of applicable income tax benefits[b]	(1,611)	(9,875)	(13,746)
Net income	360,837	356,666	251,169
Dividends on preferred stock	1,895	11,570	7,899
Net income available for common stockholders	$ 358,942	$ 345,096	$ 243,270
Income per common share:			
Income before extraordinary loss	$ 6.94	$ 6.44	$ 4.28
Extraordinary loss	(.03)	(.18)	(.23)
Net income	$ 6.91	$ 6.26	$ 4.05
Average common shares outstanding	51,928,655	55,136,212	60,129,546

[a]Fiscal year 1992 contained 53 weeks. Fiscal years 1991 and 1990 each contained 52 weeks. (See Note a on **Exhibit 4.**)
[b]Applicable income tax benefits for fiscal years 1992, 1991, and 1990 are $947, $5,799, and $8,073, respectively.

Source: Levi Strauss Associates Inc., Form 10-K/A Amendment No. 1, July 30, 1993.

The Business in 1993

For 1992, LS&CO. recorded net earnings of $360 million on revenues of $5.6 billion, marking the sixth consecutive year of increased sales and earnings. (See **Exhibits 3** and **4** for selected data on financial performance.) The company marketed products with the Levi's® brand name in more than 60 countries, using a variety of arrangements, including wholly owned and operated businesses, joint ventures, licensees, and distributors. Production and distribution facilities were located in more than 20 countries. LS&CO. employed 25,000 people in the United States and 9,000 people overseas. About half of its hourly work force was represented by the Amalgamated Clothing and Textile Workers Union (ACTWU) and the International Ladies Garment Workers Union (ILGWU).[6]

---

[6]Frank Swoboda, "Levi Strauss to Drop Suppliers Violating Its Worker Rights Rules," *The Washington Post*, March 13, 1992, p. D1 ff.

EXHIBIT 4   Levi Strauss Associates Inc., Selected Balance Sheet Data, 1988–1992 (dollars in millions, except per-share data)

The Company Fiscal Year[a]	1992	1991	1990	1989	1988
Total assets	$2,880.7	$2,633.4	$2,389.9	$2,020.0	$1,933.4
Long-term debt and capital lease obligations	262.0	432.7	158.7	406.8	528.0
Redeemable Series A preferred stock	—	82.0	81.9	81.9	92.4
Employee Stock Purchase and Award Plan common stock	16.4	—	—	—	—
Stockholders' equity	768.2	558.3	641.3	394.5	339.3

[a]Fiscal year 1992 contained 53 weeks and ended on November 29, 1992. Fiscal years 1991, 1990, 1989 and 1988 each contained 52 weeks and ended on November 24, 1991, November 25, 1990, November 26, 1989, and November 27, 1988, respectively.

Source: Levi Strauss Associates Inc., Form 10-K/A Amendment No. 1, July 30, 1993.

One estimate put the value of LS&CO., if publicly traded, at $5.5 billion.[7] When asked about the possibility of going public again, Tom Tusher, president and chief operating officer, replied, "We have no reason to go public. Being private helps us focus on long-term strategies. We don't have to worry about quarter-to-quarter results all the time. And we can take more risks."[8]

LS&CO. officials attributed the company's success of the late 1980s and early 1990s, in part, "to sales of jeans and related products outside the United States, principally in Europe and the Asia-Pacific region."[9] International sales had become a significant element of the business, accounting, in 1992, for 37% of total revenues and 53% of pretax profits. (See **Exhibit 5** for data on worldwide operations.) The company credited higher foreign profit margins to foreign consumers' willingness to pay for the perceived high quality of Levi's® clothing.[10] Overseas, a pair of jeans sold for up to $60 to $100—more than twice the average price in the United States. In some areas, a legal "grey market" surfaced in which jeans were bought in bulk off the shelves of U.S. retail stores, shipped to foreign countries, and sold in unauthorized outlets at cut-rate prices. The company estimated that the grey market cost it millions of dollars in sales each year and damaged the image of its product. Noted a spokesperson for LS&CO., "Our jeans are a

---

[7]Kenneth How, "The Finance Lowdown on 25 Big Private Firms," *The San Francisco Chronicle,* September 23, 1993, p. D2 ff.

[8]Gavin Power, "Levi's Plan to Sew up Europe Growth Aided by Rise of 42% in Yearly Profits," *The San Francisco Chronicle,* February 20, 1992, p. B1 ff.

[9]"Apparel Business Unwrinkled by Retailing Slump," *San Francisco Business Times,* May 22, 1992, p. 5 ff.

[10]John Eckhouse, "Record Profit as Levi's Sales Top $5 Billion," *The San Francisco Chronicle,* March 2, 1993, p. D2.

EXHIBIT 5   **Levi Strauss Associates Inc., U.S. and Non-U.S. Operations, 1990–1992 (dollars in thousands)**

The following table presents information concerning U.S. and non-U.S. operations (all in the apparel industry).

	1992	*1991*	*1990*
Net sales to unaffiliated customers:			
United States	$3,482,927	$2,997,144	$2,560,662
Europe	1,367,783	1,209,428	1,032,404
Other non-U.S.	719,580	696,310	654,084
	$5,570,290	$4,902,882	$4,247,150
Sales between operations:			
United States	$ 139,652	$ 111,742	$ 121,134
Europe	28	67	383
Other non-U.S.	34,467	9,842	7,238
	$ 174,147	$ 121,651	$ 128,755
Total sales:			
United States	$3,622,579	$3,108,886	$2,681,796
Europe	1,367,811	1,209,495	1,032,787
Other non-U.S.	754,047	706,152	661,322
Eliminations	(174,147)	(121,651)	(128,755)
	$5,570,290	$4,902,882	$4,247,150
Contribution to income before other charges:			
United States	$ 460,218	$ 390,468	$ 312,697
Europe	362,174	334,220	295,954
Other non-U.S.	151,644	137,359	136,468
	$ 974,036	$ 862,047	$ 745,119
Other charges:			
Corporate expenses, net	$ 128,648	$ 99,310	$ 108,495
Interest expense	53,303	71,384	82,956
Stock option charge	157,964	—	—
Income before taxes and extraordinary loss:	$ 634,121	$ 691,353	$ 553,668
Assets:			
United States	$1,480,527	$1,346,033	$1,251,537
Europe	491,491	400,197	376,780
Other non-U.S.	273,355	317,284	272,549
Corporate	635,328	569,870	488,991
	$2,880,701	$2,633,384	$2,389,857

Gains or losses resulting from certain foreign-currency hedge transactions are included in other expense, net, and amounted to losses of $10.2 million, $19.7 million, and $18.3 million for 1992, 1991, and 1990, respectively.

Source: Levi Strauss Associates Inc., Form 10-K/A Amendment No. 1, July 30, 1993.

premium product—and this damages their reputation and consumer confidence."[11]

To protect its brand name, the company registered its trademark, Levi's®, in more than 150 countries, calling it "the most recognized apparel brand and one

---

[11]Ros Davidson, "Levi Strauss Sees Red Over Jeans Grey Market," *Reuters,* September 10, 1993. LS&CO. also feared that U.S. retailers, in clearing their shelves to grey-market buyers, might be unable to offer the full selection to regular customers. As a result, it raised U.S. prices to "narrow the gap" and asked U.S. retailers to limit the number of jeans sold to each shopper.

of the most famous consumer brand names in the world."[12] One study valued the Levi's® brand at $4.811 billion, the top apparel brand measured.[13] Levi's® was the market leader in every country where the company sold jeans.

In general, LS&CO. manufactured goods in the countries or regions where they would be sold.[14] Throughout much of its history, almost all manufacturing occurred in its own facilities or through a small number of contractors in the United States. However, like most U.S. apparel manufacturers, LS&CO. had moved an increased portion of its production to contract manufacturers, many of them offshore, to cut costs. (See **Exhibit 6** for a comparison of labor costs and hours in selected countries.) By 1993, contractor sourcing around the world accounted for about half the company's global production. Company officials estimated that 45% of the LS&CO. apparel sold in the United States was made overseas, with 40% coming from contractors in Asia, and 60% from Central America, South America, and Mexico. Efforts were under way to consolidate and secure relationships with long-term contractors worldwide.

The loss of domestic jobs in the apparel industry was an ongoing concern for both labor unions and the consuming and voting public. An official from the ILGWU estimated that, in 1992, the apparel industry employed 816,000 production workers, down from 1,079,000 in 1980 and substantially lower than the industry's largest work force of 1,257,400, in 1973. The unemployment rate in the industry hovered around 11%, about twice as high as for the nation as a whole.[15]

When in early 1990 LS&CO. closed a 1,115-employee plant in San Antonio, Texas, and moved production to contractors in Costa Rica, it gave 90 days' notice, continued employee medical insurance, contributed $100,000 to local agencies, and gave $340,000 to the city of San Antonio to fund additional services and retraining programs for laid-off workers.[16] Instead of praise for its handling of the situation, LS&CO. faced harsh public criticism, a class-action lawsuit, a boycott of its products, substantial bad publicity, and even a small demonstration in front of its San Francisco offices. Judy Belk, vice president of Community Affairs, remarked on the San Antonio experience, "We were honest about what we were doing—work was going to be taken offshore—and we exceeded all the legal requirements in terms of severance. But the employees who were impacted did not think we were ethical in our attempts to make them whole."

In 1993, achieving preeminent customer service was a top priority at LS&CO. Management knew that continuing success would require ongoing development of new products and improved processes for getting goods into retail outlets.

---

[12]Levi Strauss & Co. "Fact Sheet," company document, May 1993.

[13]The study also valued the Lee brand (jeans) at $.758 billion. See "Brands," *Financial World,* September 1, 1993, p. 41.

[14]Levi Strauss & Co., "Fact Sheet".

[15]Dr. Herman Starobin, research director, International Ladies Garment Workers Union, AFL-CIO, statement before the U.S. House of Representatives Ways and Means Committee, September 15, 1993.

[16]Robert Levering and Milton Moskowitz, *The 100 Best Companies to Work for in America* (New York: Doubleday, 1993), pp. 501–502.

EXHIBIT 6   Labor Costs and Operator Hours, Production Workers in the Textile and Apparel Industries—Selected Countries, 1993

Country	Hourly Labor Cost Textile (in US$)	Hourly Labor Cost Apparel (in US$)	Normal Equivalent Days Worked Textile (per operator per year)
North America			
United States	11.61	8.13	241
Canada	13.44	9.14	237
Mexico	2.93	1.08	286
European Community			
Denmark	21.32	17.29	226
France	16.49	14.84	233
East Germany[a]	14.17	11.90	231
West Germany[a]	20.50	17.22	232
Greece	7.13	5.85	231
Holland	20.82	15.41	207
Ireland	9.18	7.44	243
Portugal	3.70	3.03	246
United Kingdom	10.27	8.42	234
Other European Countries			
Austria	18.81	14.30	231
Czech Republic	1.43	1.29	223
Finland	11.86	9.25	236
Hungary	1.80	1.62	233
Slovakia	1.29	1.14	230
Switzerland	22.32	18.08	227
Near East			
Israel	7.20	5.54	244
Syria	1.12	0.84	275
Turkey	4.44	3.29	300
Africa			
Egypt	0.57	0.43	288
Mauritius	1.42	1.04	285
South Africa	1.64	1.12	302
Tanzania	0.22	0.18	239
Tunisia	2.97	1.54	232
Zambia	0.32	0.24	249
Zimbabwe	0.47	0.35	278
South America			
Argentina	2.47	1.85	268
Brazil	1.46	0.73	274
Peru	1.43	1.00	276
Uruguay	3.09	2.35	288
Venezuela	1.90	1.48	245
Asia and Pacific			
Australia	10.84	8.67	229
Bangladesh	0.23	0.16	250
Peoples Republic of China	0.36	0.25	306
Hong Kong	3.85	3.85	294
India	0.56	0.27	289
Indonesia	0.43	0.28	297
Japan	23.65	10.64	261
South Korea	3.66	2.71	312
Malaysia	1.18	0.77	261
Pakistan	0.44	0.27	310
Philippines	0.78	0.53	288
Singapore	3.56	3.06	284
Taiwan	5.76	4.61	291
Thailand	1.04	0.71	341
Vietnam	0.37	0.26	287

[a]Designations "East" and "West" are used for economic purposes only.

Source: Compiled by casewriter based on data from Werner International Management Consultants, New York, New York.

Based on intensive research begun in 1991, the company was reengineering the entire customer service supply chain, from the generation of new product ideas to the moment of purchase.

Company Philosophy

LS&CO. was known for its long-standing commitment to employees and the communities where they lived and worked. The company's founder had served as a board member of the California School for the Deaf and established 28 scholarships at the University of California; after his death, the tradition of corporate citizenship continued. Following the great San Francisco earthquake and fire of 1906, LS&CO. continued to pay its employees, even though there was no work for some of them for six months. During the Great Depression, it kept its workers on the payroll to install hardwood floors. The company desegregated its plants in the southern United States "before law or practice compelled them to do so."[17] In the 1970s, it set up the Community Affairs Department, which staffed the Levi Strauss Foundation and granted millions of dollars in its focus areas of AIDS, economic development, and social justice to institutions and groups in the communities it served.[18]

As LS&CO. contracted out more of its manufacturing, it also expanded its community affairs activities, recognizing that the new production arrangements did not extinguish its social responsibilities. In 1993, for example, it donated $127,000 toward maternal and child health care in Bangladesh, a valuable source of contract labor. The company received praise from the Amalgamated Clothing and Textile Workers Union, which represented its workers: "In an industry noted for sweatshops and abuses of workers' rights, LS&CO. has earned a reputation as a good employer in the United States. Its labor relations are among 'the best in the country.' "[19]

Until the late 1980s, LS&CO. managers had viewed the company's community and employee responsibilities "as something separate from how we ran the business." Noted Robert Haas, "We always talked about the 'hard stuff' and the 'soft stuff.' The soft stuff was the company's commitment to our work force. And the hard stuff was what really mattered: getting the pants out the door."[20] That view changed as the business environment of the 1980s changed. Increasing competition, new technology, corporate restructurings, the globalization of enterprises, greater consumer choice, and a new generation entering the work force led Haas and other LS&CO. managers to conclude that the "hard stuff and the soft stuff [were] becoming increasingly intertwined."[21] Haas saw values as the link.[22] He explained:

> In a more volatile and dynamic business environment, the controls have to be conceptual. They can't be human anymore: Bob Haas telling people what to do. It's the *ideas* of a business that are controlling, not some manager with authority. Values provide a common language for aligning a company's leadership and its people.[23]

---

[17]"Levi Strauss & Co. and the AIDS Crisis," p. 7.

[18]"Levi Strauss & Co. and the AIDS Crisis," p. 6.

[19]Louise Kehoe, "Bold Fashion Statement, " *Financial Times,* May 8, 1993, p. 9 ff.

[20]Robert Howard, "Values Make the Company," *Harvard Business Review,* September-October 1990, p. 134.

[21]Robert Howard, p. 134.

[22]Robert Howard, p. 138.

[23]Robert Howard, p. 134.

LS&CO.'s top managers were convinced that values-based companies that honored their social responsibilities would ultimately achieve greater competitive success. Believing that a company's reputation had become increasingly important to customers, investors, employees, regulators, and other stakeholders, management reasoned that there was "not generally a conflict in the long term [between] doing good versus doing well."[24] Noted Toni Wilson, manager of the company's ethics initiative, "LS&CO. invites the whole person to the job. . . . Doing the right thing may cost in the short run, but in the long run it brings intangible benefits: trust, creativity, innovation. You can't buy trust, you have to earn it."

In 1987, under Haas's leadership, LS&CO. adopted a Mission and Aspirations Statement to communicate "where we wanted to go . . . [and] how we wanted to behave."[25] (See **Exhibit 7.**) Senior management defined the company's mission as "responsible commercial success," which was operationalized as "consistently meeting or exceeding the legal, ethical, commercial, and other expectations that society has of business."[26] In 1991, LS&CO. introduced a values-driven, principled approach to ethics, replacing its code of ethics (described by one manager as "very proscriptive—rules and regulations in a big binder") with a more open-ended statement of core principles (**Exhibit 8**). The company also articulated its environmental philosophy and principles (**Exhibit 9**).

Though LS&CO.'s Executive Management Committee saw a strong link between good ethics and good business over the long run, they recognized that particular decisions could pose difficult dilemmas. Senior management made it clear that ethics was to be a ground rule, not just a factor in decision making, and that ethical values would take precedence over nonethical values. Moreover, conflicts between and among ethical principles were to be resolved through an ethical process. As the paradigm for all of its decision making, the company adopted the "principled reasoning approach" (PRA), a thorough and explicit procedure that involved six discrete steps: (1) defining the problem, (2) agreeing on the principles to be satisfied, (3) identifying both high-impact and high-influence stakeholders and assessing their claims, (4) brainstorming possible solutions, (5) testing the consequences of chosen solutions, and (6) developing an ethical process for implementing the solution.

LS&CO. managers agreed that this process could be extremely exacting and time consuming, and some favored a more streamlined approach, especially for routine and medium-impact decisions. Yet most were convinced that understanding and applying the PRA was worth the effort. Bob Dunn explained,

> If there is anyone with a moral claim on the outcome [of a decision], their views have to be clear and present. The principled reasoning approach insists that we identify the ethical issues, the people who are affected, the possible solutions, and the ways to minimize harm. At the beginning, people are frustrated with the process, but at the end they feel it serves us well. It prevents the pressure of the moment, of personal involvement from getting in the way. Over time, people do it more naturally.

---

[24]Levi Strauss & Co., "Going Global," company document, January 31, 1994, p. 11.
[25]David Sheff, "Mr. Blue Jeans," *San Francisco Focus*, October 1993, p. 128.
[26]The LS&CO. definition of "responsible commercial success" was adapted from the work of Professor Archie B. Carroll, a management professor specializing in corporate responsibility at the University of Georgia.

EXHIBIT 7   Mission Statement and Aspiration Statement

Mission Statement

The mission of Levi Strauss & Co. is to sustain responsible commercial success as a global marketing company of branded casual apparel. We must balance goals of superior profitability and return on investment, leadership market positions, and superior products and service. We will conduct our business ethically and demonstrate leadership in satisfying our responsibilities to our communities and to society. Our work environment will be safe and productive and characterized by fair treatment, teamwork, open communication, personal accountability and opportunities for growth and development.

Aspiration Statement

We all want a company that our people are proud of and committed to, where all employees have an opportunity to contribute, learn, grow, and advance based on merit, not politics or background.

We want our people to feel respected, treated fairly, listened to, and involved. Above all, we want satisfaction from accomplishments and friendships, balanced personal and professional lives, and to have fun in our endeavors.

When we describe the kind of LS&CO. we want in the future, what we are talking about is building on the foundation we have inherited: affirming the best of our Company's traditions, closing gaps that may exist between principles and practices, and updating some of our values to reflect contemporary circumstances.

What type of leadership is necessary to make our Aspirations a Reality?

New Behaviors

Leadership that exemplifies directness, openness to influence, commitment to the success of others, willingness to acknowledge our own contributions to problems, personal accountability, teamwork, and trust. Not only must we model these behaviors but we must coach others to adopt them.

Diversity

Leadership that values a diverse work force (age, sex, ethnic group, etc.) at all levels of the organization, diversity in experience, and diversity in perspectives. We have committed to taking full advantage of the rich backgrounds and abilities of all our people and to promote a greater diversity in positions of influence. Differing points of view will be sought; diversity will be valued and honesty rewarded, not suppressed.

Recognition

Leadership that provides greater recognition—both financial and psychic—for individuals and teams that contribute to our success. Recognition must be given to all who contribute; those who create and innovate and also those who continually support the day-to-day business requirements.

EXHIBIT 7   Continued

Ethical Management Practices

Leadership that epitomizes the stated standards of ethical behavior. We must provide clarity about our expectations and must enforce these standards through the corporation.

Communications

Leadership that is clear about company, unit, and individual goals and performance. People must know what is expected of them and receive timely, honest feedback on their performance and career aspirations.

Empowerment

Leadership that increases the authority and responsibility of those closest to our products and customers. By actively pushing responsibility, trust, and recognition into the organization, we can harness and release the capabilities of all our people.

Source: Company document.

EXHIBIT 8   Levi Strauss & Co., Code of Ethics and Ethical Principles
---

Code of Ethics

Levi Strauss & Co. has a long and distinguished history of ethical conduct and community involvement. Essentially, these are a reflection of the mutually shared values of the founding families and of our employees.

Our ethical values are based on the following elements:

- A commitment to commercial success in terms broader than merely financial measures.
- A respect for our employees, suppliers, customers, consumers and stockholders.
- A commitment to conduct which is not only legal, but fair, and morally correct in a fundamental sense.
- Avoidance of not only real, but the appearance of conflict of interest.

From time to time the Company will publish specific guidelines, policies and procedures. However, the best test whether something is ethically correct is whether you would be prepared to present it to our senior management and board of directors as being consistent with our ethical traditions. If you have any uneasiness about an action you are about to take or which you see, you should discuss the action with your supervisor or management.

Exhibit 8   Continued

Ethical Principles

Our ethical principles are the values that set the ground rules for all that we do as employees of Levi Strauss & Co. As we seek to achieve responsible commercial success, we will be challenged to balance these principles against each other, always mindful of our promise to shareholders that we will achieve responsible commercial success.

The ethical principles are:

Honesty: We will not say things that are false. We will never deliberately mislead. We will be as candid as possible, openly and freely sharing information, as appropriate to the relationship.

Promise-Keeping: We will go to great lengths to keep our commitments. We will not make promises that can't be kept and we will not make promises on behalf of the Company unless we have the authority to do so.

Fairness: We will create and follow a process and achieve outcomes that a reasonable person would call just, even-handed and nonarbitrary.

Respect for Others: We will be open and direct in our communication and receptive to influence. We will honor and value the abilities and contributions of others, embracing the responsibility and accountability for our actions in this regard.

Compassion: We will maintain an awareness of the needs of others and act to meet those needs whenever possible. We will also minimize harm whenever possible. We will act in ways that are consistent with our commitment to social responsibility.

Integrity: We will live up to LS&CO.'s ethical principles; even when confronted by personal, professional and social risks, as well as economic pressures.

Source: Company document.

Exhibit 9   Levi Strauss & Co., Environmental Philosophy and Guiding Principles

---

Environmental Philosophy

Consistent with Levi Strauss & Co.'s Mission and Aspirations, the Company will protect the environment wherever it is engaged in doing business. We will set high standards for responsible environmental stewardship and encourage our business partners to do the same. We will meet or exceed local practices, laws and Levi Strauss & Co. standards worldwide. In addition to our owned and operated facilities, we will also require our licensees, contractors and others who produce Levi Strauss & Co. products on our behalf to adhere to these standards. We will work diligently to safeguard the environment.

Exhibit 9   Continued

Guiding Principles

Reduce, Reuse and Recycle: We will reduce and eliminate wastes from our business operations and ensure responsible disposal by supporting the "Three Rs: reduce, reuse and recycle."

Preservation of Non-Renewable Resources: We will reduce our dependence on non-renewable natural resources through the use of more effective technologies and recovery techniques.

Environmental Hazard Reduction: We will exercise high standards of care in the transportation, storage, use and disposal of chemicals. We will seek safe alternatives to hazardous chemicals to reduce their use and the potential for environmental harm.

Communications: We will communicate our environmental policies, programs and actions to our employees, suppliers, customers, stockholders and the public.

Environmental Policy Assessment: We will continually assess and revise our policies, programs and actions to ensure industry leadership as responsible environmental stewards.

Environmental Relationships: We will establish environmentally responsible relationships with licensees, contractors and others who produce Levi Strauss & Co. products on our behalf. We will also seek to influence our major suppliers who provide raw materials for our products to be responsible environmental stewards and to demonstrate a commitment as strong as our own.

Compliance Reviews: We will conduct ongoing reviews of our owned and operated facilities, licensees, contractors and others who produce Levi Strauss & Co. products on our behalf. We will use the results of these reviews to help us prioritize our environmental efforts and will report no less than annually on the status of these efforts.

Planning and Decision Making: We will consider our individual and corporate duties as responsible environmental stewards through the capital allocation process and in other business decisions. We will address both current environmental issues as well as anticipate future issues.

Printed on 100% reclaimed Levi's® denim.

Source: Company document.

To support the new thinking and increase the organization's ability to do the right thing, LS&CO. managers developed a three-part core curriculum with a week of leadership training, four days of diversity training, and three days of ethics training, which introduced participants to the PRA. Management modified the criteria for performance evaluations, which were linked to compensation, basing a significant portion of the evaluation on adherence to aspirations and the rest on meeting business goals.

Global Sourcing Guidelines

In September 1991, after several managers expressed misgivings about the business practices employed by some of LS&CO.'s overseas contractors, top management set up a 12-person Sourcing Guidelines Working Group (SGWG) to determine what standards the company should expect of its contractors worldwide. Dunn explained, "As we expanded our operations to more diverse cultures and countries, we felt that we needed to set standards to ensure that our products were being made in a manner consistent with our values, that would not be damaging to our brand image."[27] In looking at both internal and external stakeholders, this senior-level, cross-functional working group would consider the full range of sourcing issues that could affect the company's assets, people, or products. As Dunn noted, they would in many cases be developing a vocabulary for issues previously left to individual discretion.

LS&CO.'s actions coincided with a rising public focus on the issue of supplier standards.

> Scrutiny by labor unions, activists and socially conscious investors is forcing importers to monitor not just their foreign subsidiaries but their far-flung networks of independent suppliers—and their suppliers' suppliers as well. . . . Socially conscious investors and mainstream religious groups promote the positive message that companies should extend their own high standards to all their business partners. Environmentalists and other activists tend toward the more direct pressure that comes from naming names. Union officials are taking a more investigative approach to locate human rights and other violations, including schemes in which foreign manufacturers, especially in China, circumvent U.S. textile quotas by misidentifying the country in which their goods were made.[28]

Some U.S. companies benefiting from questionable labor practices abroad had been targeted on television shows, such as NBC's news magazine *Dateline*. At the same time, marketers were beginning to pay more attention to consumers who based their purchasing decisions, at least in part, on ethical concerns. Termed "vigilante consumers" by one British consultant, such consumers were interested not only in the products or services they bought but also "in the behavior of the company behind the brand and the way the product or service is developed."[29] Dunn agreed that consumers were increasingly "sensitive to goods being made under conditions that are not consistent with U.S. values and fairness."[30]

The Saipan Incident

LS&CO.'s sourcing initiative proved timely. The SGWG approved a set of guidelines in December 1991. In February 1992, before the guidelines were ratified by

---

[27]Louise Kehoe, p. 9 ff.

[28]John McCormack and Marc Levinson, "The Supply Police," *Newsweek*, February 15, 1993, p. 48 ff.

[29]Nicole Dickenson, "Consumers Get Ethical With Choices," *South China Morning Post*, May 29, 1993, supplement.

[30]Brian Dumaine, "Exporting Jobs and Ethics," *Fortune*, October 5, 1992, p. 10 ff.

management, the media turned a spotlight on a company supplier in Saipan, a U.S. territory in the western Pacific, accused of paying workers substandard wages and forcing them to work long hours in fenced and guarded factories. In a suit filed four months earlier in October 1991, the U.S. Department of Labor charged that five garment manufacturers owned and operated by the Tan family recruited workers from China—mostly non-English-speaking women in their late teens and early twenties—and then seized their passports and kept them in padlocked and guarded barracks and factories for the duration of their employment contract. The government's investigation, which had begun in 1990, found that Tan employees worked up to 11 hours a day, seven days a week, for as little as $1.65 an hour, well below Saipan's minimum wage of $2.15.[31] The companies were cited also for deducting between $270 and $365 a month from workers' pay for room and board, "management fees," and other expenses.[32]

Saipan manufacturers, such as the Tans, were allowed to ship their goods to the United States, labeled "Made in the U.S.A.," without quota limits or duty. They were exempt from the U.S. minimum wage, but were legally required to comply with all other U.S. labor laws. According to government estimates, the Tan operations manufactured garments worth $100 million to be sold by U.S. clothing companies in the United States under brand names such as Perry Ellis, Eddie Bauer, Chaps Sportswear, Christian Dior, and Van Heusen, as well as private labels.[33]

When queried by LS&CO. managers in San Francisco in late 1991, Tan officials denied the charges and downplayed their seriousness. The media stories prompted LS&CO. to take a closer look. Within 48 hours of the February broadcast, LS&CO. suspended new business with the Tans and sent a team to investigate. As a result of the investigation, LS&CO. canceled its contract with the Tan family, incurring several hundred thousand dollars in contract penalties. Although LS&CO. investigators found the media's allegations of "slave labor" to be unwarranted, the Tans' practices did not conform to the company's new guidelines.

Later in May 1992, as part of a consent decree with the Labor Department, the five Tan companies agreed to pay $9 million in back pay and damages to contract employees who had worked for them from 1988 to 1992. Under the decree, in which the companies neither admitted nor denied breaking the law, they agreed to be monitored for four years.[34] According to Dunn, LS&CO.'s soon-to-be-ratified sourcing guidelines were "the best insurance policy we could have" to deal with the situation. Noted another manager, "If anyone doubted the need for guidelines, this convinced them."

---

[31]"A Stitch in Time," p. 27 ff.

[32]"U.S. Alleges Illegal Treatment of Garment Workers in Saipan," *Reuters*, October 1, 1991.

[33]Frank Swoboda, p. D1 ff.

[34]"Five Saipan Garment Manufacturers to Pay $9 Million to Settle FLSA Suit," *BNA International Business Daily*, May 26, 1992.

Guidelines Announced

In March 1992, LS&CO. publicly announced its new global sourcing guidelines, which established standards in the areas of worker health and safety, employment practices, ethics, the environment, and human rights. Recognizing that some matters were under the control of individual contractors, whereas others were not, the SGWG had developed the guidelines in two parts: the Business Partner Terms of Engagement (see **Exhibit 1**) and the Guidelines for Country Selection (see **Exhibit 2**).

LS&CO. officials expected the standards, which were intended to be visionary and strategic, as well as practical, to result in higher production costs in 1993, affecting both 1993 net income and gross profit.[35] Noted Dunn, "Sourcing decisions that emphasize cost to the exclusion of all other factors will not best serve our long-term business interest. . . . Sometimes it costs a little more in the short term, but it really is possible to have your cake and eat it too."[36]

LS&CO. began an intensive communications program to inform employees and contractors worldwide about the guidelines. According to Sabrina Johnson, a corporate communications manager, the company took care to explain the reasoning behind the guidelines and to convey its willingness to cooperate with contractors in meeting them. Merchandisers, who were responsible for negotiating with and selecting contractors, received special briefings. Senior management indicated the possibility of "margin relief" for merchandisers whose bonuses might suffer if sourcing cost increases were necessary to meet the guidelines.

Business Partner Terms of Engagement

To implement the Business Partner Terms of Engagement, management sent audit teams to inspect the facilities of all the company's contractors. Training for these teams became a top priority. Richard Woo, at the time Community Affairs manager for the Asia Pacific region, was involved in designing and delivering the first training program, which was held in Singapore for employees from 13 Asian nations. Recalling that some managers wondered whether LS&CO. was imposing Western values on the rest of the world, Woo noted the challenge of "calibrating what was happening on the factory floor with the written standards," especially in differing cultural contexts. After refinement, the training program and audit instruments were introduced around the world.

Inspection teams visited more than 700 facilities in 60 countries. LS&CO. managers focused initially on sewing and finishing contractors and planned later to look at suppliers of fabric, sundries (e.g., buttons, thread), and chemicals. The auditors found 70% of the contractors to be in compliance. Another 25%, found lacking, made significant improvements in bathrooms, emergency exits, ventilation, and wastewater treatment equipment as a result of LS&CO.'s review. About 5% were dropped because of poor personnel practices, child labor, health and safety conditions, and trademark or other violations.

---

[35]Levi Strauss Associates Inc., *Form 10-K/A Amendment No. 1,* July 30, 1993, p. 3.
[36]"Apparel Makers Can Do Well By Doing the Right Thing," *Apparel Industry Magazine,* September 1993, pp. 108–110.

The sourcing guidelines introduced new factors into the process for selecting contractors, who had previously been chosen on the basis of price, quality, and delivery time from the pool of firms with available quota.[37] With adoption of the guidelines, LS&CO. began to require that potential contractors satisfy the Business Partner Terms of Engagement and the company's environmental principles, in addition to meeting the traditional selection criteria. LS&CO. sought long-term relationships and offered contractors large-volume orders and technical advice. Many contractors liked to have LS&CO. as a customer and took pride in their ability to meet the company's demanding quality standards. Having LS&CO. on a contractor's "resume" could help attract new business. At the same time, contractors resisted becoming too dependent on LS&CO. and claimed they could not make as much money on LS&CO. contracts as on some others.

Recognizing that certain improvements, particularly environmental ones, could be costly, LS&CO. sometimes accepted higher prices or offered contractors generous timetables, loans, and volume guarantees. However, contractors slow to upgrade their practices were reminded that LS&CO. would have to discontinue the relationship if changes were not made by the agreed-on deadline. In some instances, LS&CO. took extra steps to help contractors meet the guidelines. In Bangladesh, for example, two contractors employing underage workers agreed to send them to school—with pay—after LS&CO. offered to cover the cost of their books, tuition, and uniforms. The contractors agreed to rehire the children wishing to return when they turned 14. In both instances, the children represented less than 2% of the contractor's 200-person workforce.

Though a few contractors balked at making improvements, most were quite receptive. According to Y. S. Chan, manager of the Hong Kong branch of LS&CO.'s Asian sourcing organization,

> Most contractors don't mind spending money to make the improvements we recommend, since we try to be fair and reasonable, and we make it clear that we would like to work together. . . . We don't force things. . . . There are different ways to establish mutual understanding.

---

[37]The United States limited apparel and textile imports through quotas permitted by the MultiFiber Arrangement (MFA) under the auspices of the General Agreement on Tariffs and Trade (GATT). The MFA allowed the United States to set quotas, either by imposing them unilaterally or, more commonly, by negotiating bilateral agreements with other nations. Most Asian countries, including China, had an agreement with the United States which established that country's quota by product type and fiber content—men's cotton pants, men's noncotton pants, and so on. These agreements had some flexibility: there were usually provisions for category shifting, for borrowing against next year's quota, and for increasing the quota each year. Each government had the right to administer and divide that country's quota among local contractors on whatever basis they desired. Most countries distributed quota based on past shipping record; those contractors who had shipped large quantities in the past were most likely to get assigned large quota again, so as to minimize the risk of not shipping all allowable quota. Under serious consideration in 1993 was a proposal to phase out all textile and apparel quotas for GATT signatories over a 10-year period.

One approach was to show contractors video clips from television documentaries exposing shoddy conditions. A manager involved in training LS&CO. inspection teams around the world found that "regardless of whether they agreed with the media coverage or not, they understood [the relationship between the guidelines and the brand]."

Iain Lyon, vice president of Offshore Sourcing and, later, a member of the CPG, recalled his apprehension at the guidelines initiative. "This was America interfering with another country's business," he remembered thinking. But Lyon, English by birth, changed his mind after seeing the specifics of the company's approach and "how quickly contractors see the point and want to do the right thing." He added, "It's hard for anyone to say it's wrong to open up the fire exits, stop polluting, or give children an education." A relative newcomer to the company, Lyon found LS&CO.'s approach refreshing. He noted, "The vast majority [of sourcing managers outside LS&CO.] don't give a damn. . . . Taking maximum advantage of contractors seems okay because they are foreigners. Getting away from that has been a great relief to me."

Guidelines for Country Selection

Administering the LS&CO. Guidelines for Country Selection required an assessment of every country in which LS&CO. did business. The first evaluations concentrated on countries suspected of being in violation. In mid-1992, LS&CO. decided to withdraw its business from Burma, canceling contracts to buy 850,000 trousers and shirts annually, because, "under current circumstances, it is not possible to do business without directly supporting the military government and its pervasive human-rights violations."[38] Run by a military junta that had taken power in 1962, Burma was ranked by the human-rights watchdog Freedom House as one of the 12 most repressive regimes in the world.[39] The military continued to rule in defiance of a 1990 election that gave 60% of the vote and 82% of the parliamentary seats to the National League for Democracy (NLD) party of Daw Aung San Suu Kyi, the recipient of the 1991 Nobel Peace Prize, who had been held under house arrest since July 1989. In its 1992 report, the U.S. State Department called the human rights situation in Burma "deplorable," noting:

> Arbitrary detentions and compulsory labor persisted, as did harsh treatment and torture of detainees. Freedom of speech, the press, assembly and association remained nonexistent. . . . Over 25% of the NLD winners [in 1990] had either resigned under pressure, fled into exile, been disqualified after conviction on political charges, or died.[40]

---

[38]Simon Billenness, "Burma: A New Issue for Social Investors," *Franklin's Insight: Investing for a Better World,* Franklin Research and Development Corporation, October 15, 1993.

[39]John N. Maclean, "Abuses in Burma Stir Questions of Conscience," *The Chicago Tribune,* October 25, 1993, Business, p. 3. ff.

[40]*Country Reports on Human Rights Practices for 1992,* Report Submitted to the Committee on Foreign Relations, U.S. Senate, and the Committee on Foreign Affairs, U.S. House of Representatives, by the Department of State, 103rd Congress, 1st Session, February 1993, p. 523.

Human rights groups reported the systematic rape, torture, and murder of Burmese and minority peoples, forcing 300,000 refugees into Bangladesh and 80,000 into Thailand.[41] The military was charged with "selling off natural resources at a rapid rate with little concern for the environmental impact, including destruction of rain forests."[42]

The decision to withdraw from Burma was fairly uncontroversial within LS&CO., though some managers, such as Lyon, felt mixed emotions. Said Lyon, "I have no sympathy for the Burmese government at all. . . . [but] it was a shame because of the impact on the people . . . . The operators in Burma were university graduates—we were the best job in town. When we left, I felt badly for them."

The China Situation

When the China Policy Group began its work in late 1992, LS&CO.'s presence in China was small. Though the company had been sourcing in China since 1986, sales remained "minuscule" since Levi's® clothing was not mass marketed there. In early 1991, LS&CO. managers had decided in the "11th hour" of negotiations to forgo a China joint venture to produce clothes for sale in local markets after discovering that the venture would be responsible for enforcing China's one-child-per-family policy. In many parts of China, the work group was still the central organizing fact of life—where citizens received medical care and women registered their chosen form of birth control. Employers could be required to fine or dock the pay of workers who had second children. Some worker groups, it was reported, used physical force to "encourage" abortions and sterilization, even though such tactics were unlawful. Although support for the government's birth control policy was widespread in China, many LS&CO. managers found it abhorrent to risk involvement in family planning at this level. Operational concerns added to the troublesome nature of the venture.

Senior management put the China issue on hold, waiting until the company fully implemented its new principled reasoning approach (PRA) and global sourcing strategy. At that point, wrote the president of LS&CO.'s Asia-Pacific division, the company would be better prepared "to address the human rights issues in a full, responsible, [and] effective way." Meanwhile, LS&CO. made no direct investment in China, although Asia managers continued to investigate and hoped to enter the market at some time in the future. By 1993, some of LS&CO.'s low-priced jeans competitors were beginning to become popular in China.

As for sourcing in China, LS&CO. purchased, either directly or indirectly through contractors, a large quantity of sundries (buttons, thread, and labels) and about eight million yards of fabric in China, which was increasingly popular as a site for fabric mills relocating from other parts of Asia.[43] The company also sourced about five million items of clothing (called "units"), totalling about $50

---

[41]"From South Africa to Burma," *The Boston Globe*, October 18, 1993, p. 12.
[42]Ken Bertsch, "Coalition for Withdrawal from Burma Intensifies Shareholder Campaign," *IRRC News for Investors*, Social Issues Service, November 1993, p. 5.
[43]Levi did not contract directly with fabric mills for fabric purchases. Instead, the mill generally contracted with the sewing firm, which in turn, contracted with Levi.

million, from Chinese sewing and laundry contractors.[44] More than half the units sourced in China were finished in Hong Kong and shipped to the United States with a "Made in Hong Kong" label as part of Hong Kong's legal quota.[45]

Any change in LS&CO.'s China stance would be felt most directly by employees in the Hong Kong branch of the company's Asian sourcing organization. Responsible for all Hong Kong and China sourcing, the 120-person office arranged for a total of 20 million to 22 million units from about 20 contractors in 1992. The Hong Kong branch was confident there would be no problem finding satisfactory contractors if LS&CO. expanded its China presence. In fact, the company's Chinese contractors were doing well under the Business Partner Terms of Engagement—better even than contractors in some other parts of Asia with whom LS&CO. had very successful relationships.

However, withdrawing from China was another matter. Even though China represented only about 10% of LS&CO.'s total Asian contracting (and 2% of worldwide contracting), it would not be easy to find alternative contractors with available quota at reasonable prices. In most Asian countries, the largest part of the quota was held by a few large contractors, with the remainder spread among many small ones. Moving production would mean increasing the number of contractors, sacrificing scale economies, and increasing auditing costs. Also, shifting production to other locations would add to the cost and complexity of transportation. (Items sourced in China could be transported relatively easily to Hong Kong, the preferred port for shipping to the United States.) Employment opportunities in the Hong Kong office would very likely diminish. It was estimated that moving production to other parts of Asia over a three-year period would raise costs between 4% and 10%, depending on the country.

Business Conditions

In contrast to LS&CO., many companies were rushing to establish an early foothold in China. Economic liberalization of the Chinese economy and a shift toward free markets which had begun in the late 1970s ushered in a period of rapid growth, estimated at more than 10% a year.[46] With retail sales rising an average of 15% per year since 1979[47] and a potential market of more than one billion customers, a U.S. Treasury Department official predicted that "China will soon have the world's second-biggest economy."[48]

---

[44]Jim Carlton, "Ties With China Will Be Curbed by Levi Strauss," *The Wall Street Journal*, May 4, 1993, p. A3 ff.

[45]This system of "outward processing," which was entirely legal, permitted apparel companies to take advantage of Hong Kong's large quota, while substantially bypassing its expensive wage rates.

[46]"Cracking the China Market," *The Wall Street Journal*, December 10, 1993, p. R1.

[47]Sally D. Goll and Yukimo Ono, "Consuming Passions," *The Wall Street Journal*, December 10, 1993, p. R15.

[48]Joyce Barnathan, Lynn Curry, Owen Ullmann, "Behind the Great Wall," *Business Week*, October 25, 1993, p. 43.

Procter & Gamble, Johnson & Johnson, and H. J. Heinz were among the firms adding production facilities in 1993. Coca-Cola Co. Chairman Roberto C. Goizueta announced a deal to add 10 bottling plants to increase the total to 22, noting that the Chinese market had "virtually limitless long-term potential."[49] Total U.S. investment was expected to increase to $5 billion in 1993, up from less than $0.5 billion in 1990; U.S. exports rose from $5 billion to $9 billion during the same period.[50] In 1992, U.S. imports from China totaled $26 billion, mostly consumer goods such as clothing, shoes, and toys.[51] One commentator noted,

> If you don't take the dive into China, you may be missing the biggest sales opportunity of your generation. It could take years for your investment to bear fruit, but right now—while the market's still immature—may well be the time to make the jump. China may pitch into convulsions tomorrow, but that will always be a risk. And remember, that's also what people were saying about Japan in the 1950s.[52]

John B. Wing, the chairman of Wing-Merrill, a U.S. energy company with a $2 billion contract to build a power plant in Henan province, agreed: "China is going to be a big global player, and if Americans aren't part of it, we are fools."[53]

The apparel and textile industry was particularly active in China. With shipments totaling $7.3 billion a year, China was the largest supplier of textiles and apparel to the United States, accounting for 20% to 25% of U.S. textile and apparel sales.[54] The removal of trade quotas for Chinese-made apparel (likely to occur if China were admitted to GATT), would most certainly boost China's share even more.

Challenges

Nevertheless, China still posed difficulties for business. Outmoded infrastructure and tariffs meant it was difficult and expensive to transport goods across its vast distances. Though large, the China market was hardly unified; tastes and buying power varied greatly by region, and distribution systems were chaotic or nonexistent. Furthermore, economic growth had been accompanied by inflation and sharp rises in stock prices and property values, adding to the cost of doing business and the expense of stationing American workers in major Chinese cities. Restrictions on imports and currency convertibility created other problems. And, the threat of political instability was always present.[55] China experts consulted by the CPG advised that the death of Deng Xiao Ping, China's then 88-year-old

[49]Pete Engardio, Lynn Curry, Joyce Barnathan, "China Fever Strikes Again," *Business Week,* March 29, 1993, p. 46 ff.

[50]Joyce Barnathan, Lynn Curry, and Owen Ullman, p. 43.

[51]Daniel Southerland, "China Purchases Nearly $1 Billion in U.S. Goods; Recent Buying Spree Turned a Bid to Preserve Trade Status," *The Washington Post,* April 13, 1993, p. A23 ff.

[52]"Cracking the China Market," p. R1.

[53]Pete Engardio, Lynn Curry, Joyce Barnathan, p. 46 ff.

[54]David Skidmore, "U.S. Penalizes China Over Illegal Trade," *The Boston Globe,* January 7, 1994, p. 59.

[55]China Supplement, *The Wall Street Journal,* December 10, 1993, p. R1 ff.

leader, could be followed by a period of chaos, probably with increased repression, social unrest, and antiforeign sentiment. A coup or another "Cultural Revolution" could not be ruled out.

The CPG learned that foreign companies operating in China were under increasing pressure to accept government-backed Communist party representation on their boards and faced intensified levels of government inspections and audits. Though government-supported party organizing in the workplace was common, union organizing was illegal. Since 1989, companies' authority to hire, fire, and compensate employees as they wished had become more limited. The wages payable by joint ventures were capped at 150% of the amount paid by state-owned enterprises. To secure greater control over the workplace, some companies had chosen to establish wholly owned enterprises rather than joint ventures. Companies taking the joint venture route favored partnerships with private companies, collectively owned companies, or local government entities rather than national or provincial government entities.

The Chinese legal system remained a concern. Business laws and their enforcement lagged behind economic development, and the country still ran on power politics and personal relationships. Corruption was a problem, and public officials sometimes accepted bribes.[56] Laws and rules were vague and arbitrarily enforced. In the apparel industry, manufacturers were allowed to use false country-of-origin labels to avoid U.S. quotas.[57] If caught by U.S. Customs, these mislabeled goods were deducted from China's quota, reducing the quota amount that remained and potentially jeopardizing U.S. companies' ability to take delivery on contracted items. The Chinese government lacked clear policies on foreign investment, though officials eagerly courted foreign capital and technology. Withdrawal from joint ventures posed particular problems for foreign firms because dissolution required the Chinese partner's consent. Unable to secure such consent, some Western companies had been forced to abandon the assets of their ventures.

Protection of intellectual property, nonexistent under Communist ideology, was a particular worry for many American businesses. Copyright and patent protection had existed on paper since 1979, but, according to the U.S. Embassy, "procedures for enforcement were still unclear." Legislation implementing trademark laws was not passed until 1987. The U.S. government called China "the single largest pirator of U.S. copyrights" and estimated the cost to American companies at $400 million in 1991.[58] In 1992, U.S. customs made 104 seizures of counterfeit merchandise worth $4.56 million in China, second only to its seizures of $5.85 million in goods from South Korea.[59] In January 1992, under pressure

---

[56]China Supplement, p. R1 ff.

[57]John Maggs, "Levi's Gets the Blues After Explosion of Fakes Hits the Market," *Journal of Commerce,* December 29, 1991, p. B8 ff.

[58]Stuart Auerbach, "China, U.S. Reach Trade Accord; Beijing Agrees to Curb Piracy of Products, Safeguarded Material," *The Washington Post,* January 17, 1992, p. A24 ff.

[59]Louise Lucas, "U.S. Brings War Against Copiers from H.K.," *South China Morning Post,* January 6, 1993, p. 3 ff. Officials believed that merchandise seized at customs represented only a fraction of all counterfeit goods because only a small portion of all imports were examined. As in the instances of mislabeled goods, the amounts seized were deducted from China's quota.

from the U.S. government, China agreed to improve protection of intellectual property by extending patent protection on chemicals and pharmaceuticals to 20 years, joining international copyright conventions, and agreeing to protect all existing copyrights on computers, software, books, and recordings. However, later that year, some companies still complained about a lack of "follow up."[60] LS&CO.'s legal department could find no reports of successful actions for trademark infringement in China.

As of May 1992, LS&CO. had seized nearly two million pairs of counterfeit "501" jeans produced in China with "Made in the U.S.A." labels. Most were destined for Europe, where they would fetch high prices. According to David Saenz, LS&CO.'s director of Corporate Security, few consumers could detect that the blue jeans did not meet Levi's® standards. He noted also that the Chinese authorities had been cooperative in investigating reports of false labeling.[61] However, the authorities' effectiveness was limited by China's size and the fragmentation of political power. In 1993, the problem of counterfeit jeans from China persisted; it remained unclear how aggressive U.S. and Chinese officials would be in trying to shut down factories making such goods.[62]

Human Rights

The CPG learned that leading human rights organizations considered China's human rights record among the worst in the world. Using the 1948 Universal Declaration of Human Rights as a benchmark, organization such as the United Nations, Human Rights Watch, and Amnesty International, found human rights violations in China to be severe and persistent (see **Exhibit 10**).[63] Freedom House, for example, included China among the countries where political rights and civil liberties were absent or virtually nonexistent in 1992.[64] Since the Tiananmen Square attack on pro-democracy students in June 1989, the Chinese Communist Party had continued its harsh practices with the backing of its military and other security forces. According to the U.S. State Department, China's human rights practices fell "far short of internationally accepted norms."[65]

---

[60]Nancy Dunne, "Patent Pirates 'Still Dodging the Rules': U.S. Complaints Over Enforcement of Anti-Counterfeiting Measures," *Financial Times*, December 3, 1992, p. 6 ff.

[61]John Maggs, p. B8 ff.

[62]Jim Doyle, "U.S. Crackdown on Bogus Levi's; Smuggling Ring Accused of Plot to Import Jeans Made in China," *The San Francisco Chronicle*, November 13, 1993, p. A17 ff.

[63]For 1992, China appeared on the "worst country" lists prepared by Freedom House, the World Human Rights Guide, and the United Nations Commission on Human Rights.

[64]Other countries on the list were Afghanistan, Burma, Cuba, Equatorial Guinea, Haiti, Iraq, North Korea, Libya, Somalia, Sudan, Syria, and Vietnam.

[65]For a catalog of human rights practices in China, see, for example, *Country Reports on Human Rights Practices for 1992*, pp. 540–554.

EXHIBIT 10 Universal Declaration of Human Rights (adopted by the United Nations General Assembly, December 10, 1948)

. . . the **General Assembly** *proclaims* this **Universal Declaration of Human Rights** as a common standard of achievement for all people and all nations, to the end that every individual and every organ of society, keeping this Declaration constantly in mind, shall strive by teaching and education to promote respect for these rights and freedoms and by progressive measures, national and international, to secure their universal and effective recognition and observance, ...

Article 1. All human beings are born free and equal in dignity and rights. They are endowed with reason and conscience and should act towards one another in a spirit of brotherhood.

Article 2. Everyone is entitled to all the rights and freedoms set forth in this Declaration, without distinction of any kind, such as race, colour, sex, language, religion, political or other opinion, national or social origin, property, birth or other status.

Article 3. Everyone has the right to life, liberty and security of person.

Article 4. No one shall be held in slavery or servitude; . . . .

Article 5. No one shall be subjected to torture or to cruel, inhuman or degrading treatment or punishment.

Article 6. Everyone has the right to recognition everywhere as a person before the law.

Article 7. All are equal before the law and are entitled without any discrimination to equal protection of the law. . . .

Article 8. Everyone has the right to an effective remedy by the competent national tribunals for acts violating the fundamental rights granted him by the Constitution or by law.

Article 9. No one shall be subjected to arbitrary arrest, detention or exile.

Article 10. Everyone is entitled in full equality to a fair and public hearing by an independent and impartial tribunal, ...

Article 11. Everyone charged with a penal offence has the right to be presumed innocent until proved guilty according to law in a public trial at which he has had all the guarantees necessary for his defence. . . .

Article 12. No one shall be subjected to arbitrary interference with his privacy, family, home or correspondence, ...

Article 13. (1) Everyone has the right to freedom of movement and residence within the borders of each State. (2) Everyone has the right to leave any country, including his own, and to return to his country.

Article 14. (1) Everyone has the right to seek and enjoy in other countries asylum from persecution. . . .

Article 15. (1) Everyone has the right to a nationality. . . .

Exhibit 10   Continued

Article 16.   (1) Men and women of full age, without any limitation due to race, nationality or religion, have the right to marry and to found a family. . . .

Article 17.   (1) Everyone has the right to own property alone as well as in association with others. (2) No one shall be arbitrarily deprived of his property.

Article 18.   Everyone has the right to freedom of thought, conscience and religion; . . . .

Article 19.   Everyone has the right to freedom of opinion and expression; . . . .

Article 20.   (1) Everyone has the right to freedom of peaceful assembly and association. . . .

Article 21.   (1) Everyone has the right to take part in the government of his country, directly or through freely chosen representatives.

Article 22.   Everyone, as a member of society, has the right to social security and is entitled to realization, ... of the economic, social and cultural rights indispensable for his dignity. . . .

Article 23.   (1) Everyone has the right to work, to free choice of employment, to just and favourable conditions of work and to protection against unemployment. (2) Everyone, without any discrimination, has the right to dual pay for dual work. (3) Everyone has the right to just and favourable remuneration ensuring for himself and his family an existence worthy of human dignity. . . . (4) Everyone has the right to form and to join trade unions. . . .

Article 24.   Everyone has the right to rest and leisure, including reasonable limitation of working hours and periodic holidays with pay.

Article 25.   (1) Everyone has the right to a standard of living adequate for the health and well-being of himself and of his family, ...

Article 26.   (1) Everyone has the right to education. . . .

Article 27.   (1) Everyone has the right to freely participate in the cultural life of the community, ...

Article 28.   Everyone is entitled to a social and international order in which the rights and freedoms set forth in this Declaration can be fully realized.

Article 29.   (1) Everyone has duties to the community. . . .

Article 30.   Nothing in this Declaration may be interpreted as implying for any State, group or person any right to engage in any activity or to perform any act aimed at the destruction of any of the rights and freedoms set forth herein.

Adopted by the United Nations General Assembly, December 10, 1948.

Legal Process   The State Department did note some "modest progress" in resolving a few individual human rights cases and reported that "rigid ideological controls reimposed after June 1989 were beginning to ease."[66] However, there had never been a comprehensive public accounting of those detained after the Tiananmen demonstrations, and trials of dissidents, religious figures, and other political offenders continued. These trials often violated China's own legal principles, as well as international standards of due process and fair-trial procedures: trials were conducted rapidly, often in secret by judges, police, and prosecution working together; defendants had limited access to legal counsel; and many were threatened with a harsher sentence if they did not "show the right attitude" and confess. The country's security apparatus was responsible for numerous instances of arbitrary arrest, detention without formal legal proceedings, maltreatment, and torture. Furthermore, there were no independent Chinese organizations that publicly monitored human rights conditions, and authorities made it clear that they would not allow the existence of such groups.

Expression and Association   Although guaranteed by the Chinese Constitution, freedom of expression and association were severely restricted. Some well-known dissidents were not permitted to travel abroad. The press and academic institutions were tightly controlled, and the authorities extensively monitored personal and family life. Freedom of religion, also constitutionally guaranteed, became increasingly difficult in the 1990s, with government crackdowns on Christian, Buddhist, and Muslim religious groups that refused to practice their faith through government-supervised bodies—particularly in Tibet and Mongolia, where cultural and religious groups were intertwined with forces for independence. Though laws existed to protect minorities and women, in practice, discrimination based on sex, religion, and ethnicity continued in the areas of housing, jobs, and education.

Prison Labor   Although China had mostly ended its traditional use of massive forced labor to build public facilities, there was still some reliance on "mobilized" workers for security forces and public works. Moreover, imprisonment usually involved forced labor in prison or in the *laogai*,[67] a network of government "reeducation" camps where political and other offenders were compelled to work for little or no pay in tiring and often dangerous conditions. It was difficult to estimate accurately the extent of forced-labor production. A news article reported that one such prison facility consisted of 850 textile looms capable of producing sweaters worth "hundreds of millions of dollars" annually, all for export.[68] Chinese authorities valued prison labor production at about $500 million in 1990, not including output from the *laogai*. In 1991, the U.S. State Department found "substantial evidence" that China was exporting products produced with

---

[66]*Country Reports on Human Rights Practices for 1992*, p. 540.

[67]The term *laogai*, pronounced lau-guy, means "reform through labor."

[68]Joyce Barnathan, "It's Time to Put Screws to China's Gulag," *Business Week,* December 30, 1991/January 6, 1992, p. 52 ff.

forced labor.[69] Since imports of products made by convict labor were prohibited under the Hawley-Smoot Tariff Act of 1930, the U.S. government responded by barring specific Chinese products known to be produced with prison labor from entry into the country.

In August 1992, the U.S. State Department and China's Ministry of Foreign Affairs signed an agreement prohibiting forced-labor exports and permitting the United States to inspect certain facilities to ensure compliance with the agreement.[70] Nonetheless, press accounts indicated that neither the suppliers in question nor the Chinese authorities could always be relied on to monitor abuses. Peter Yeo, an aide to the U.S. House of Representatives Subcommittee on Trade and the Environment, cautioned, "Don't trust your suppliers to tell the truth."[71] Harry Wu, a research fellow at the Hoover Institute, Stanford University, claimed, "You can get a guarantee from the Chinese government. No trouble at all. But these people lie."[72] And, in 1993, the U.S. Customs Department reported that the Chinese government had denied members of the U.S. Embassy access to all or parts of five factories, in violation of the earlier agreement. Monitoring difficulties were compounded because forced-labor exports were "often falsely labeled, mixed with other products and sold through intermediaries," according to the Customs Department's memorandum.[73]

The Concept of Human Rights   The Chinese government rejected reports made by the U.S. State Department, Amnesty International, and Asia Watch on its human rights violations.

> Despite the [Chinese] Government's adherence to the United Nations Charter, which mandates respect for and promotion of human rights, Chinese officials do not accept the principle that human rights are universal. They argue that each nation has its own concept of human rights, grounded in its political, economic, and social system and its historical, religious, and cultural background. Officials no longer dismiss all discussion of human rights as interference in the country's internal affairs, but remain reluctant to accept criticism of China's human rights situation by other nations or international organizations.[74]

However, Chinese officials had begun to promote academic study and discussion of concepts of human rights. Chinese research institutes organized centers and symposia on the subject and sent a group to France, Sweden, and the United Kingdom to study human rights practices there. The U.S. State Department be-

---

[69]Daniel Southerland, "China Said to Still Use Forced Labor," *The Washington Post*, May 19, 1993, p. F3 ff.

[70]Daniel Southerland, "China Said to Still Use Forced Labor," p. F3 ff.

[71]Mark Veverka, "China Syndrome: Firms Struggle on Rights Issue," *Crain's Chicago Business*, July 5, 1993, p. 3 ff.

[72]Mark Veverka, "China Syndrome," p. 3 ff.

[73]Daniel Southerland, "China Said to Still Use Forced Labor," p. F3 ff.

[74]*Country Reports on Human Rights Practices for 1992*, p. 549.

lieved that these activities were motivated by the Chinese government's desire to improve its image abroad and strengthen its ability to respond to criticism of its human rights record.

Engage or Withdraw   Thus, China presented a thorny problem; many considered it "the proverbial test case."[75] It was a country both "marred by systematic violations of fundamental rights, and at the same time. . . . in massive need of support in reaching its development and modernization goals."[76] Human rights activists were divided as to whether socially responsible corporations should "remain and act as a progressive force or divest and withdraw."[77] Those advocating divestment argued that "economic growth and trade will merely finance a corrupt Communist elite"[78] and that the Chinese government would use the presence of reputable companies "to boost its image and maintain its grip on power." Concerned that economic liberalization would not necessarily lead to political liberation, they argued that development and growth in Southern China's special economic zones had not been accompanied by human rights advances. Advocates for a presence in China believed that foreign corporations that were "actively engaged" with the Chinese economy were "helping to create power structures outside the government and state industries."[79] They stressed the dangers of isolating China, arguing that constructive engagement could contribute to human rights improvements. In South China, they said, people had become free to start their own businesses, to change jobs at will, and to talk and travel.

Code-of-Conduct Bill   Several human rights groups favored a federal "code-of-conduct bill" under discussion in Washington. The bill asked companies with a significant presence in China to "adhere to a basic set of human rights principles, on a 'best efforts' basis."[80] Under the proposal, U.S. businesses would extend the same minimum rights protection to foreign employees that they provided to their U.S. workers, such as protection against discrimination based on religious or political beliefs, gender, or ethnic background. They would not allow their premises to be used for human rights violations in, for example, compulsory indoctrination programs. And they would try to use their influence to end human rights abuses—for example, in raising before Chinese public officials cases of individuals detained because of their political views. Compliance would be volun-

---

[75]Diane F. Orentlicher and Timothy A. Gelatt, "Public Law, Private Actors: The Impact of Human Rights on Business Investors in China," *Northwestern Journal of International Law and Business* (Fall 1993), p. 98.

[76]Diane F. Orentlicher and Timothy A. Gelatt, p. 69.

[77]Simon Billenness and Kate Simpson, "Thinking Globally: Study of International Corporate Responsibility," *Franklin's Insight: The Advisory Letter for Concerned Investors,* Franklin Research and Development Corporation, September 1992, p. 11.

[78]Simon Billenness and Kate Simpson, p. 12.

[79]Simon Billenness and Kate Simpson, p. 12.

[80]In 1991, then-Congressman John Miller (R-Washington) introduced code-of-conduct legislation, which was never enacted. See Diane F. Orentlicher and Timothy A. Gelatt, pp. 82–83.

[81]Diane F. Orentlicher and Timothy A. Gelatt, p. 110.

tary.[81] The only requirements would be that the U.S. parents (1) register with the Secretary of State and indicate whether they would implement the principles; and (2) report annually on their China operation's adherence to the code.

MFN Debate   As LS&CO.'s CPG conducted its deliberations, China watchers were beginning to speculate on whether the United States would renew China's most-favored-nation (MFN) trade status when it expired, in June 1993. MFN status, which entitled China to the same tariff treatment accorded normal U.S. trading partners (the lowest available), had been conferred yearly on China since the 1970s. But, in 1993, the debate on Capitol Hill was expected to be fractious, with the substantial U.S. trade deficit with China—$18.2 billion in 1992—affected by the outcome.

The Clinton administration was thought to favor continuing China's MFN status, but with conditions attached, such as changes in China's coercive family-planning program and its alleged missile sales to Pakistan, as well as overall progress in human rights. The Democrats in Congress planned to move for legislation that would apply lowest tariffs only to products produced by private firms—which accounted for about half of U.S. imports from China—while imposing higher tariffs on those made in state ventures. Some business research groups opposed attaching any conditions to MFN status, fearing Chinese retaliation could jeopardize up to 171,000 American jobs.[82] Michael Bonsignore, chairman and chief executive of Honeywell, believed there were better ways to encourage human rights in China, noting: "The Chinese do not respond terribly well to ultimatums."[83]

Company Experience   Despite conditions in China, none of the U.S. companies consulted by the CPG had taken steps to become informed about or to address human rights issues related to their business activities.

The Decision

CPG members had met five times for a total of 19 days between November 1992 and February 1993. They had heard directly from a wide range of internal and external stakeholders, along with outside sources knowledgeable about the China situation. They included a former prisoner in China, a former head of the U.S.–China Business Council, and several China experts, as well as representatives of human rights organizations, the U.S. government, Chinese pro-democracy groups, U.S. labor unions, and other companies doing business in China. With the information and insights gained from these sources, the CPG was reviewing the company's global sourcing guidelines and working through the steps of the principled reasoning approach (PRA). Soon the group would have to settle on its recommendation to LS&CO.'s Executive Management Committee.

---

[82]Nancy Dunne, "Clinton's $7 Billion Dilemma on China: Linking Human Rights to Trade Could Backfire," *Financial Times*, May 20, 1993, p. 5 ff.
[83]John J. Osland, "High Stakes in China," *Star Tribune*, May 21, 1993, p. 1D ff.

LEADING FOR INTEGRITY
Corporate Purpose and Responsibility

The cases and essays in this book have focused on understanding, building, and maintaining organizational integrity. As the materials have demonstrated, organizational integrity is not simply, as is sometimes assumed, the natural result of management's good will and benign intentions.[1] It depends on a broad range of skills and knowledge. Equally critical, if not more so, are active leaders who build supportive organizational systems and decision processes and who foster commitment to the organization's values through their own conduct.

Success in building integrity requires leaders with a clear conception of their organization's purpose and responsibilities. This conception is central to the ethical framework that anchors a company's value system and guides its strategy, structure, and decision making. Without such a conception, the effort to build integrity is unlikely to advance very far because it will lack substance and direction. While every company has a distinctive purpose and set of responsibilities reflecting its specific circumstances, each is inevitably shaped by broad social ideas about the role of the modern business corporation.

This concluding section outlines several conceptions of corporate purpose and responsibility that emerged in the 1970s, 1980s, and 1990s. The excerpts below give readers an opportunity to explore these conceptions and to consider their own views in light of the earlier cases and their own experiences. Readers who aspire to lead high-integrity companies will want to examine these conceptions carefully as they work toward an ethical framework to guide their organizations.

[1]This point is underscored by the title of Laura Nash's book on management ethics, *Good Intentions Aside* (Boston: Harvard Business School Press, 1990).

Recent Debate

Although discussion of corporate purpose and responsibility is as old as the corporate form of organization, the debate has been particularly vigorous in recent decades. In the 1970s, for example, corporate responsibility became an important topic of public discussion in the United States after a series of scandals resulted in a dramatic decline in the public's trust in business. One commentator estimated that business lost roughly 80% of its public good will during this period.[2] According to one study, 70% of the public thought business tried to strike a fair balance between profits and the public interest in 1968. By 1976, only 15% answered positively.[3] In 1979, the percentage stood at 19%.[4]

Leading the list of corporate misdeeds that captured public attention in the seventies were illegal campaign contributions and the bribery of foreign government officials. But critics pointed to a host of other management failings: environmental pollution, racial and gender discrimination, disregard for worker and consumer safety, mismanagement, fraud, conflicts of interest, and inattention to shareholders. While liberals focused on certain corporate shortcomings, and conservatives on others, the underlying issue—the scope and nature of management's responsibility—cried out for attention. Corporate critics and defenders alike turned to these more fundamental questions: To whom and for what are corporate managers responsible? What is the purpose of the business corporation?

In the 1990s, similar questions are being raised on a worldwide scale. Globalization of the economy and the adoption of market systems in Asia, Eastern Europe, and Latin America have prompted business and government leaders in many parts of the world to reexamine the corporation's goals and responsibilities. Far from an idle philosophical exercise, the effort to achieve a shared understanding of the central elements of corporate purpose and accountability is essential to the ongoing legitimacy of these systems. Without a moral compass calibrated to society's expectations, business leaders risk forfeiture of their broad authority to act as creators of wealth and managers of society's resources. Without a compelling concept of purpose, they are likely to face great difficulty in mobilizing their organizations for outstanding performance into the future.

---

[2]Fred D. Baldwin, *Conflicting Interests*, D.C. Heath and Company (1984), p. 85.
[3]Id. at p. 75.
[4]Id. at p. 84.

A Little History

These questions of corporate purpose and responsibility are, of course, not new. They have been raised and discussed at various periods during the nineteenth and twentieth centuries. In a celebrated exchange between law professors E. Merrick Dodd and A. A. Berle, Jr., during the Depression, some of the basic positions were being staked out. In that period, too, the place of business in society was being widely debated.

Berle argued in 1931 that "All powers granted to a corporation or to the management of a corporation . . . are necessarily and at all times exercisable only for the . . . benefit of all the shareholders as their interest appears."[5] Berle's position followed from his view that corporate law was a branch of the law of trusts. Accordingly, he argued, managers should view themselves as trustees for the shareholders and act with single-minded devotion to their interests.

Berle's view was also consistent with legal orthodoxy. In the well-known case of *Dodge v. Ford Motor Company*, the Michigan Supreme Court had clearly stated in 1919: "A business corporation is organized and carried on primarily for the profit of the stockholders. The powers of the directors are to be employed for that end."[6]

The year following publication of Berle's article, Dodd responded. He acknowledged that Berle's position was consistent with the traditional view and agreed that shareholders needed protection from self-seeking managers. Dodd nevertheless argued that public opinion was coming to expect managers to recognize and voluntarily fulfill obligations to the community, to workers, and to consumers. He noted that "business is permitted and encouraged by the law primarily because it is of service to the community rather than because it is a source of profit to its owners."[7]

Dodd cited Owen D. Young, then CEO of General Electric, as an example of the new enlightened and professional manager. Young had taken the position that managers were no longer the attorneys or agents of the shareholders alone; they were instead trustees of the corporate institution. Said Young,

. . . it makes a great deal of difference in my attitude toward my job as an executive officer of the General Electric Company whether I am a trustee of the institution or an attorney for the investor. If I am a trustee, who are the beneficiaries of the trust? To whom do I owe my obligations?

---

[5]A. A. Berle, Jr., "Corporate Powers as Powers in Trust," 44 *Harvard Law Review* (1931), p. 1049. Quoted in Baldwin.

[6]*Dodge v. Ford Motor Co.*, 204 Mich. 459 (1919).

[7]E. Merrick Dodd, Jr., "For Whom Are Corporate Managers Trustees?" 45 *Harvard Law Review* (1932), p. 1149.

My conception is this: That there are three groups of people who have an interest in that institution. One is the group of fifty-odd thousand people who have put their capital in the company, namely, its stockholders. Another is a group of well toward one hundred thousand people who are putting their labor and their lives into the business of the company. The third group is of customers and the general public. . . .[8]

Corporate Responsibility Today and Tomorrow

Echoes of the exchange between Berle and Dodd can be heard in discussions today. Below, you will find a selection of the conceptions of corporate purpose and responsibility articulated by groups such as The Business Roundtable, the American Law Institute, the U.S. Catholic Bishops Conference, and the U.K.'s Royal Society for the encouragement of Arts, Manufactures & Commerce (RSA). The views of individuals such as economist Milton Friedman, lawyer Christopher Stone, and Japanese executive Yotaro Kobayashi, are also included. The selections are presented in rough chronological order, dating from 1970 through 1995.

As you review each conception, consider the following questions:

- What are the key ideas embedded in the conception?
- What can be said for and against it?
- What are its implications for corporate governance and organizational design?
- What are its implications for managerial decision making?
- How do the authors' professional training and role influence their conceptions?

Considering the various conceptions as a group, ask yourself:

- How different are they?
- Which is most useful for today's business leader?
- Which are you inclined to favor as a guiding framework?
- Which view is likely to be dominant in the future?

---

[8]Quoted in Dodd, p. 1154.

Selected Readings

Excerpt from Milton Friedman, "The Social Responsibility of Business Is to Increase Its Profits" (1970)[9]

In a free-enterprise, private-property system, a corporate executive is an employee of the owners of the business. He has direct responsibility to his employers. That responsibility is to conduct the business in accordance with their desires, which generally will be to make as much money as possible while conforming to the basic rules of the society, both those embodied in law and those embodied in ethical custom. . . .

. . . [T]he key point is that, in his capacity as a corporate executive, the manager is the agent of the individuals who own the corporation . . . and his primary responsibility is to them. . . .

Of course, the corporate executive is also a person in his own right. As a person, he may have many other responsibilities that he recognizes or assumes voluntarily—to his family, his conscience, his feelings of charity, his church, his clubs, his city, his country. . . . If we wish, we may refer to some of these responsibilities as "social responsibilities." But in these respects he is acting as a principal, not an agent; he is spending his own money or time or energy, not the money of his employers or the time or energy he has contracted to devote to their purposes. If these are "social responsibilities," they are the social responsibilities of individuals, not of business. . . .

. . . [T]he doctrine of "social responsibility" [is] . . . a "fundamentally subversive doctrine" in a free society, and [I] have said that in such a society "there is one and only one social responsibility of business—to use its resources and engage in activities designed to increase its profits so long as it stays within the rules of the game, which is to say, engages in open and free competition without deception or fraud."

---

[9]Professor Friedman's article appeared in the *New York Times Magazine* on September 13, 1970.

Excerpt from The Business Roundtable's *Statement on Corporate Responsibility* (1981)[10]

Public Expectations

Many people believe that corporations are generally concerned only about profits and not about the impact their operations may have on society. At the same time, it is clear that a large percentage of the public now measures corporations by a yardstick beyond strictly economic objectives.

People are concerned about how the actions of corporations and managers affect them not only as employees and customers but also as members of the society in which corporations operate. While the range of these concerns is broad, some of the most prominent relate to:

- product pricing, quality and advertising
- fair treatment of employees
- health and safety in the workplace
- plant openings and closings
- effects on the environment
- role in the community
- philanthropy

At a time when the Federal Government has set a policy of less rather than more regulation and aims to reduce the rates of increase in government spending, public expectations of corporate performance in these areas of concern are even higher. As a result, the responsibility problem for corporations is even greater. More than ever, managers of corporations are expected to serve the public interest as well as private profit. While the business sector must deal with this new challenge, it should not be expected to substitute corporate dollars for a large proportion of the Federal funds that are being reduced or eliminated.

As the corporate community addresses growing public expectations with regard to corporate performance, there must be recognition of the fundamental importance of profits and their contributions to the long-term economic viability of the enterprise. If a corporation is not profitable in the long run, there is no way that it can fulfill any responsibilities to society. If the bottom line is a minus, there is no plus for society. Thus corporate long-term viability and corporate responsibility to society are interrelated.

---

[10]The Business Roundtable includes 200 of the largest U.S. corporations.

The Expectations of Constituencies

Corporations operate within a web of complex, often competing relationships which demand the attention of corporate managers. The decision-making process requires an understanding of the corporation's many constituencies and their various expectations. Key among these are the following:

Customers

Customers have a primary claim for corporate attention. Without them, the enterprise will fail. They expect reliable products and services, fair value, good service and accurate advertising. If customer expectations are not satisfied, the corporation suffers long-term as well as short-term damage. The public attitude toward business is substantially conditioned by the marketplace.

Employees

Management's relationship with employees once was expressed simply as a fair day's pay for a fair day's work. Now the relationship is more complicated. Employees expect not only fair pay but also such conditions as equal opportunity, workplaces that protect health and safety, financial security, personal privacy, freedom of expression, and concern for their quality of life.

Experience has shown that employees will perform well for corporations which have earned their loyalty, rewarded their performance, and involved them in the decision-making process. At the same time, corporations need to weigh employee benefits in the light of competition around the world and the fundamental necessity to produce profits to support the continuing existence of the enterprise.

Communities

While much of the public discussion about the impact of corporations on the lives of people is cast in general terms, corporations most closely touch people's lives in the individual communities where they operate. Here they are expected to be concerned with local needs and problems—schools, traffic, pollution, health, recreation—and to explain their activities to the people of the community.

Society at large

Operating in national and multinational spheres, corporations affect the lives of people around the world. Their performance is subject to scrutiny by a diverse public which includes academia, government, and the media. They are expected to respond to concerns and issues of national and international significance. At the same time, the corporation's first responsibility to society is to maintain its economic viability as a producer of goods and services, as an employer, and as a creator of jobs.

Suppliers

Most suppliers to corporations are smaller businesses, which expect and need fair purchasing practices and prompt payment. The relationship between the large corporations and the supplier is a vital element in the economic system, for the very existence of many suppliers is dependent on fair treatment by corporations.

Shareholders

Shareholders have a special relationship to the corporation. As providers of risk capital, shareholders make the corporation possible. They supply funds for corporate birth, development, and growth. Any approach to corporate responsibility must begin with the practical recognition that the corporation must be profitable enough to provide shareholders a return that will encourage continuation of investment. The interest of shareholders must be considered in all important activities of the corporation.

At one time most shareholders were long-term, personally involved individual investors. Now a high proportion of them is made up of institutionally grouped and often unidentified shorter-term buyers most interested in near-term gain. This has affected their role among business constituencies. The expectation of near-term gain can exert pressure to subordinate long-range objectives to more immediate profit considerations. Despite such expectations, management needs to maintain long-range perspective.

Balancing the Interests of Constituencies

Carefully weighing the impacts of decisions and balancing different constituent interests—in the context of both near-term and long-term effects—must be an integral part of the corporation's decision-making and management process.

Resolving the differences involves compromises and trade-offs. It is important that all sides be heard but impossible to assure that all will be satisfied because competing claims may be mutually exclusive.

A classic example of the varying interests of constituencies arises when management must consider whether to establish, expand, or close a plant. For shareholders, customers, and society at large, closing a plant could bring positive results by paving the way for production of better products more economically in a new plant at a new location. It may be only in that way that the company is able to meet domestic and foreign competition. Employees and the community, however, may object to the plant closing because of the impact on jobs and other local economic factors. Sensitive community issues also arise in connection with decisions on the location of new plants and expansion of existing ones.

Balancing the shareholder's expectations of maximum return against other priorities is one of the fundamental problems confronting corporate management. The shareholder must receive a good return but the legitimate concerns of other constituencies also must have the appropriate attention.

Striving to reach the appropriate balance, some leading managers have come to believe that the primary role of corporations is to help meet society's legitimate need for goods and services and to earn a reasonable return for the shareholders in the process. They are aware that this must be done in a socially acceptable manner. They believe that by giving enlightened consideration to balancing the legitimate claims of all its constituents, a corporation will best serve the interest of its shareholders.

Excerpt from the American Law Institute's *Principles of Corporate Governance* (1979–1993)[11]

§2.01. The Objective and Conduct of the Corporation

(a) [A] corporation . . . should have as its objective the conduct of business activities with a view to enhancing corporate profit and shareholder gain.

(b) Even if corporate profit and shareholder gain are not thereby enhanced, the corporation, in the conduct of its business:

    (1) Is obliged, to the same extent as a natural person, to act within the boundaries set by law;

    (2) May take into account ethical considerations that are reasonably regarded as appropriate to the responsible conduct of business; and

    (3) May devote a reasonable amount of resources to public welfare, humanitarian, educational, and philanthropic purposes.

Excerpt from Christopher D. Stone, "Corporate Social Responsibility: What It Might Mean, If It Were Really to Matter," (1986)[12]

Personal Responsibility as a Model

It has always seemed to me that the best way to supply some hard content to the notion of corporate social responsibility is to go back and examine the general issue, what "being responsible" entails when our subject is not corporations, but ordinary flesh and blood mortals. What are we driving at when we enjoin an ordinary person to be responsible? By getting a clearer understanding of how and why notions of responsibility are enlisted in evaluating and steering ordinary conduct, and "modeling" responsibility in its familiar usage, we establish a firmer and fuller notion to transport into the corporate arena.

The first aspect of "being responsible" is fairly obvious; whatever else responsibility involves, it involves a prima facie obligation to obey the laws. But being responsible entails more than being law-abiding. The concept has a cognitive aspect as well. When we speak of people being responsible or irresponsible, we are inviting attention to how they define and reflect upon a moral dilemma.

An analysis of responsibility in its cognitive aspect best begins on a negative note—with what the responsible person does *not* do. The responsible person does not translate her impulses into immediate gratification; if enraged, she does not just start swinging at the closest person at hand. In Freudian terms, responsibility involves repression, a suspension of action—of muscular response—until there has been time for the tempering influence of reflection.

Viewed positively, the cognitive aspect of responsibility begins with perception. A person who is responsible takes in morally salient features of her environment that the irresponsible person does not seem to see or hear, such as the pains and projects of others. And to be responsible the perception must be morally imaginative. The easiest way for a park visitor to dispose of a bottle is to toss it into the bushes; the person with moral imagination visualizes *litter*.

Moreover, a responsible person makes an honest accounting of her freedom. She rejects the often tempting belief that she has no choice in the matter at hand and that the outcome is predetermined by forces beyond her control. Hence, to be responsible in the sense I am examining entails projecting consequences and weighing alternatives. That much, of course, is implied in reflection. But it is not just any reflection. It is a

---

[12]Christopher D. Stone, "Corporate Social Responsibility: What It Might Mean, If It Were Really to Matter," 71 *Iowa L. Rev.* 557 (1986) (reprinted with permission).

reflection structured by reference to a moral vocabulary; a reflection oriented to "rights" and "obligations" and to rendering judgments in terms of "good," "bad," "just," and "moral worth."

While reflection in moral terms is a necessary condition of responsibility, it is not a sufficient condition. One must have, in addition to a moral vocabulary, a moral inclination—a desire, as much internalized as conscious, to do the right thing, and if called upon, to be prepared to give good reasons to justify one's actions.

Obviously, if I were to carry forward a general examination of responsibility, there would be much more to say. But, for present purposes, considering that the proposed use of the model is essentially analogical and suggestive, the sketch I have offered will do. The general features of the sort of person we would praise as responsible, then, are as follows: someone not only law-abiding, but morally reflective in the manner outlined. Using this outline as a guide, the question of corporate social responsibility acquires, at least, an orientation. In what manner and in what circumstances is it possible and appropriate to translate the properties of human responsible conduct, familiar to us in terms of human properties, into the properties of corporate conduct. . . .

Excerpts from the U.S. Bishops' Economy Pastoral, *Economic Justice for All: Catholic Social Teaching and the U.S. Economy* (1986)[13]

2. Owners

110. The economy's success in fulfilling the demands of justice will depend on how its vast resources and wealth are managed. Property owners, managers, and investors of financial capital must all contribute to creating a more just society. Securing economic justice depends heavily on the leadership of men and women in business and on wise investment by private enterprises. Pope John Paul II has pointed out, "The degree of well-being which society today enjoys would be unthinkable without the dynamic figure of the businessperson, whose function consists of organizing human labor and the means of production so as to give rise to the goods and services necessary for the prosperity and progress of the community." The freedom of entrepreneurship, business and finance should be protected, but the accountability of this freedom to the common good and the norms of justice must be assured.

---

111. Persons in management face many hard choices each day, choices on which the well-being of many others depends. Commitment to the public good and not simply the private good of their firms is at the heart of what it means to call their work a vocation and not simply a career or a job. We believe that the norms and priorities discussed in this letter can be of help as they pursue their important tasks. The duties of individuals in the business world, however, do not exhaust the ethical dimensions of business and finance. The size of a firm or bank in many cases is an indicator of relative power. Large corporations and large financial institutions have considerable power to help shape economic institutions within the United States and throughout the world. With this power goes responsibility and the need for those who manage it to be held to moral and institutional accountability.

112. Business and finance have the duty to be faithful trustees of the resources at their disposal. No one can ever own capital resources absolutely or control their use without regard for others and society as a whole. This applies first of all to land and natural resources. Short-term profits reaped at the cost of depletion of natural resources or the pollution of the environment violate this trust.

113. Resources created by human industry are also held in trust. Owners and managers have not created this capital on their own. They have benefited from the work of many others and from the local communities that support their endeavors. They are accountable to these workers and communities when making decisions. For example, reinvestment in technological innovation is often crucial for the long-term viability of a firm. The use of financial resources solely in pursuit of short-term profits can stunt the production of needed goods and services; a broader vision of managerial responsibility is needed.

* * *

115. The common good may sometimes demand that the right to own be limited by public involvement in the planning or ownership of certain sectors of the economy. Support of private ownership does not mean that anyone has the right to unlimited accumulation of wealth. "Private property does not constitute for anyone an absolute or unconditioned right. No one is justified in keeping for his exclusive use what he does not need, when others lack necessities." Pope John Paul II has referred to limits placed on ownership by the duty to serve the common good as a "social mortgage" on private property. For example, these limits are the basis of society's exercise of eminent domain over privately owned land needed for roads or other essential public goods. The church's teaching opposes collectivist and statist economic approaches. But it also rejects the notion that a free market automatically produces justice. Therefore,

as Pope John Paul II has argued, "One cannot exclude the socialization, in suitable conditions, of certain means of production." The determination of when such conditions exist must be made on a case-by-case basis in light of the demands of the common good.

116. U.S. business and financial enterprises can also help determine the justice or injustice of the world economy. They are not all-powerful, but their real power is unquestionable. Transnational corporations and financial institutions can make positive contributions to development and global solidarity. Pope John Paul II has pointed out, however, that the desire to maximize profits and reduce the cost of natural resources and labor has often tempted these transnational enterprises to behavior that increases inequality and decreases the stability of the international order. By collaborating with those national governments that serve their citizens justly and with intergovernmental agencies, these corporations can contribute to overcoming the desperate plight of many persons throughout the world.

117. Businesspeople, managers, investors and financiers follow a vital Christian vocation when they act responsibly and seek the common good. We encourage and support a renewed sense of vocation in the business community. We also recognize that the way businesspeople serve society is governed and limited by the incentives which flow from tax policies, the availability of credit and other public policies. These should be reshaped to encourage the goals outlined here.

* * *

A. Cooperation Within Firms and Industries

298. A new experiment in bringing democratic ideals to economic life calls for serious exploration of ways to develop new patterns of partnership among those working in individual firms and industries. Every business, from the smallest to the largest, including farms and ranches, depends on many different persons and groups for its success: workers, managers, owners or shareholders, suppliers, customers, creditors, the local community and the wider society. Each makes a contribution to the enterprise, and each has a stake in its growth or decline. Present structures of accountability, however, do not acknowledge all these contributions or protect these stakes. A major challenge in today's economy is the development of new institutional mechanisms for accountability that also preserve the flexibility needed to respond quickly to a rapidly changing business environment.

299. New forms of partnership between workers and managers are one means for developing greater participation and accountability within firms. Recent experience has shown that both labor and management suffer when the adversarial relationship between them becomes ex-

treme. As Pope Leo XIII stated, "Each needs the other completely: Capital cannot do without labor nor labor without capital." The organization of firms should reflect and enhance this mutual partnership. In particular, the development of work patterns for men and women that are more supportive of family life will benefit both employees and the enterprises they work for.

300. Workers in firms and on farms are especially in need of stronger institutional protection, for their jobs and livelihood are particularly vulnerable to the decisions of others in today's highly competitive labor market. Several arrangements are gaining increasing support in the United States: profit sharing by the workers in a firm; enabling employees to become company stockholders; granting employees greater participation in determining the conditions of work; cooperative ownership of the firm by all who work within it; and programs for enabling a much larger number of Americans, regardless of their employment status, to become shareholders in successful corporations. Initiatives of this sort can enhance productivity, increase the profitability of firms, provide greater job security and work satisfaction for employees, and reduce adversarial relations. In our 1919 Program of Social Reconstruction we observed "the full possibilities of increased production will not be realized so long as the majority of workers remain mere wage earners. The majority must somehow become owners, at least in part, of the instruments of production." We believe this judgment remains generally valid today.

* * *

305. The parts played by managers and shareholders in U.S. corporations also need careful examination. In U.S. law, the primary responsibility of managers is to exercise prudent business judgment in the interest of a profitable return to investors. But morally this legal responsibility may be exercised only within the bounds of justice to employees, customers, suppliers and the local community. Corporate mergers and hostile takeovers may bring greater benefits to shareholders, but they often lead to decreased concern for the well-being of local communities and make towns and cities more vulnerable to decisions made from afar.

306. Most shareholders today exercise relatively little power in corporate governance. Although shareholders can and should vote on the selection of corporate directors and on investment questions and other policy matters, it appears that return on investment is the governing criterion in the relation between them and management. We do not believe this is an adequate rationale for shareholder decisions. The question of how to relate the rights and responsibilities of shareholders to those of the other people and communities affected by corporate decisions is complex and insufficiently understood. We therefore urge serious, long-

term research and experimentation in this area. More effective ways of dealing with these questions are essential to enable firms to serve the common good.

Excerpt from Yotaro Kobayashi, "A Message to American Managers" (1989)[14]

I have been requested to deliver some words of advice to American managers. The fact that a Japanese manager would be asked for such a message is at once a testament to how far the Japan-U.S. relationship has progressed and a sign of how far it still has to go. In looking at the progress thus far, I feel it is noteworthy that not so long ago I myself was a student in the United States, where I studied American management. That I have been given an opportunity to offer a message back to those under whom I once studied is indicative of the shifting balance of world relations. It demonstrates how the one-directional transfer of leadership and managerial ideas that once characterized the bilateral relationship has changed to a give-and-take flow of information, products, and services. . . .

Who are American managers? In preparing to write, this was the first question I wrestled with. In the past a clear image of these managers quickly sprang to mind. They are people with a pioneering spirit who rise to meet any challenge. Unafraid of taking risks, they seek rational means to reduce the dangers to the minimum. Imbued with Protestant values, they are ethical, socially responsible, and humanitarian. That, at least, is how I saw it.

There used to be many Americans who conformed to this model. . . . Today, however, many Japanese hold a different image of American managers. It is one of people who love to plot takeover bids and play the mergers and acquisitions game, who have their minds on only short-term profits, and who readily lay off workers while rewarding themselves with fat bonuses. These managers are seen as being particularly prevalent in big business; by industry they are most closely associated with high technology as well as investment banking and other financial services.

Actually, there are too many approaches to management in the United States nowadays to identify just one as quintessentially American. If I were to claim that this or that was a "typically American" way of business—that is, a way not often found in Japan or Europe—I might find myself describing only a small part of the private sector in the United States. Yet while bearing this pitfall in mind, I wish to address my com-

---

[14]Mr. Kobayashi was president of Fuji Xerox when he gave this speech. It appeared originally in *Gaiko Forum* (November 1989).

ments—and point out problem areas as I see them—to the American companies and managers who, for better or for worse, have come to represent the American business community in the eyes of the world. I do this because these business leaders, together with those of Japan, Europe, and the newly industrialized countries, will have a decisive impact on the developments in the globalized economy. . . .

Profits—An End or a Means?

. . . Turning now to American managers, I would ask that they think hard once again about fundamental corporate goals and responsibilities.

Today, as in the past, two schools of corporate philosophy exist. One says that the ultimate goal is profits. The other counters that profits are but a means—albeit an indispensable means—to a broader end, which includes the creation and provision of valuable goods and services and the promotion of respect for human beings through the employment opportunities offered.

I myself endorse the latter goal, but it is not my intention here to argue the merits and demerits of either school. I bring up the debate only because it seems to me that recently too many American managers have been placing undue emphasis on the former goal—and indeed that some have been pursuing profits with little regard for the means employed. . . .

Profits are, of course, important, and no stock company can exist without shareholders. Frankly, however, I doubt that a company focused narrowly on making money for shareholders can be turned into a "going concern," one that contributes to society and encourages the establishment of other socially valuable businesses. I would not claim that there is never a reasonable cause for laying workers off. But I would say that when managers pay inadequate attention to recruitment, brushing off a long-term commitment to the work force, and then lay their employees off to make short-term profits and safeguard management's fringe benefits, they are acting contrary to the ideals of fairness and respect for human dignity.

In the East and West alike, a company's performance ultimately depends on the quality and talent of its human resources and on management's success at channeling workers' concerted efforts toward short- and long-term goals.

Whatever business the company is in, the capacity to manufacture and market a continuing supply of competitive products depends on the creativity and enthusiasm of the personnel in all departments, from planning and development to production, sales, and after-sale services.

A dedicated work force is especially important to firms in the manufacturing sector. Unfortunately, America's manufacturing competitiveness seems to be in decline. An excessive emphasis on short-term profits, a lack of interest in the production side of business among today's managers, and bottlenecks in labor productivity are probably all contributing factors, but the underlying factor is, I suspect, inefficient handling of workers. . . .

Perhaps I will make myself clearer if I ask, to whom does the company belong? Or said another way, for whose purpose does it exist? In broadest terms the company is, of course, an institution belonging to and serving society. But for the company to fulfill this role effectively, we must adopt a microeconomic perspective and ask whether the primary owners are shareholders, managers, employees, customers, or the community. . . .

In a nutshell, my message to American managers is that they might benefit by asking once again who the company is for and by giving more attention to their employees and customers. Is it too old-fashioned—or perhaps too Japanese—to believe that this will, in the long run, benefit not only the shareholders with long-term goals, but also the United States as a whole?

Excerpt from the RSA Inquiry's *Interim Report—Tomorrow's Company: The Role of Business in a Changing World* (1993–1995)[15]

This Report challenges business leaders to change their approach.

It represents the thinking to date of a group brought together by the RSA from leading U.K. businesses, with the objective of developing a shared vision of tomorrow's company.

The Inquiry's central concern is how to attain sustainable business success in the face of continuing and substantial changes in the nature and intensity of global competition.

We believe that to achieve sustainable success tomorrow's company must take an inclusive approach.

In an inclusive approach success is not defined in terms of a single bottom line, nor is purpose confined to the needs of a single stakeholder. Each company makes its own unique choice of purpose and values, and has its own model of critical business processes from which it derives its range of success measures. But tomorrow's company will understand and measure the value which it derives from all its key relationships, and thereby be able to make informed decisions when it has to balance

---

[15]The *Tomorrow's Company* project was led by 25 of the United Kingdom's top businesses under the sponsorship of the Royal Society for the encouragement of Arts, Manufactures & Commerce (RSA). This excerpt used with permission. RSA Inquiry. *Tomorrow's Company: The Role of Business in a Changing World.* Interim Report 1994. *Inquiry Findings* (Final Report), June 1995. RSA, 8 John Adam St., London WC2N 6EZ.

and trade off the conflicting claims of customers, suppliers, employees, investors and the communities in which it operates.

The Inquiry has reached this conclusion on the basis of the following considerations.

- Businesses of all sizes are competing in a global marketplace, either directly or through the customers they serve, and must perform as well as the world's best to succeed.
- The level of performance of the world's best is constantly being raised as a result of innovation in communications, technology and learning. Rapid improvement based on continuous learning, or in some cases a step-change in performance, has become a critical success factor for individuals, companies and economies.
- Only successful businesses will fund the standard of living and quality of life to which society aspires.
- Competitive pressures are complicated by the following:
  - Rising population and consumption, putting pressure on finite resources.
  - Rapid changes in technology, leading to changes in employment patterns.
  - Changes in individual aspirations.
  - The rise of pressure groups.
  - Reduction in public confidence in governments and other institutions.
- The nature of competition is changing as the interdependence increases between companies and the community. In order to be internationally competitive the company requires a supportive operating environment. The responsibility for maintaining this is shared between business, government, and other partners who therefore need to develop a shared vision and common agenda. Failure to do so will have a serious effect on the competitiveness of companies.
- Businesses are increasingly competing for the attention and approval of individuals, whether as customers, suppliers, employees, investors or members of the communities in which they operate. Internationally competitive companies will be those which maintain their "license to operate" by securing high levels of support from all those with whom they interact, directly or indirectly.
- If it is to achieve sustainable success in the demanding world marketplace, tomorrow's company must be able to learn fast and change fast. To do this, a winning company must inspire its people to new levels of skill, efficiency and creativity, supported by a sense of shared destiny with customers, suppliers and investors.

- The conventional wisdom in the United Kingdom is to define the purpose of business in terms that stress the importance of immediate financial performance and returns to shareholders, and treat other participants merely as means to this end. Of course, a Board must continually attend to its company's financial performance and level of shareholder return, but an exclusive concentration on any one stakeholder will not lead to sustainable competitive performance. It is therefore not necessarily in the best interests of shareholders themselves to be singled out in this way.

We believe that sustainable success is available from the inclusive approach in which the company includes all its relationships in its definitions and measures of success.

Tomorrow's company will:

- Be clear about its own distinctive purpose and values.
- Give a lead in all its relationships by defining both in a consistent manner.
- See itself as part of a wider system.
- Recognize that all its relationships are reciprocal.
- Recognize the potential need to make trade-offs between stakeholders.
- Recognize the need to measure and communicate its performance in all its relationships.

This will lead to a process in which it:

- Identifies key relationships.
- Understands the demands of these relationships.
- Defines measures of success.
- Sets appropriate performance targets.
- Evaluates performance against these targets.
- Reports on all its stakeholder relationships.

We believe that unless United Kingdom companies adopt this inclusive approach, both individually and as part of the wider economic system, they will fall behind, no longer able to compete internationally, or to support current living standards.